CULINARY COLONIALISM,
CARIBBEAN COOKBOOKS,
AND RECIPES FOR NATIONAL
INDEPENDENCE

CRITICAL CARIBBEAN STUDIES

SERIES EDITORS:
Yolanda Martínez-San Miguel, Carter Mathes, and Kathleen López

EDITORIAL BOARD:
Carlos U. Decena, Rutgers University; Alex Dupuy, Wesleyan University; Aisha Khan, New York University; April J. Mayes, Pomona College; Patricia Mohammed, University of West Indies; Martin Munro, Florida State University; F. Nick Nesbitt, Princeton University; Michelle Stephens, Rutgers University; Deborah Thomas, University of Pennsylvania; and Lanny Thompson, University of Puerto Rico

Focused particularly in the twentieth and twenty-first centuries, although attentive to the context of earlier eras, this series encourages interdisciplinary approaches and methods and is open to scholarship in a variety of areas, including anthropology, cultural studies, diaspora and transnational studies, environmental studies, gender and sexuality studies, history, and sociology. The series pays particular attention to the four main research clusters of Critical Caribbean Studies at Rutgers University, where the coeditors serve as members of the executive board: Caribbean Critical Studies Theory and the Disciplines; Archipelagic Studies and Creolization; Caribbean Aesthetics, Poetics, and Politics; and Caribbean Colonialities.

For a list of all the titles in the series, please see the last page of the book.

Culinary Colonialism, Caribbean Cookbooks, and Recipes for National Independence

KEJA L. VALENS

RUTGERS UNIVERSITY PRESS
New Brunswick, Camden, and Newark, New Jersey
London and Oxford

Rutgers University Press is a department of Rutgers, The State University of New Jersey, one of the leading public research universities in the nation. By publishing worldwide, it furthers the University's mission of dedication to excellence in teaching, scholarship, research, and clinical care.

Library of Congress Cataloging-in-Publication Data
Names: Valens, Keja, 1972– author.
Title: Culinary colonialism, Caribbean cookbooks, and recipes for national independence / Keja L. Valens.
Description: New Brunswick: Rutgers University Press, [2024] | Series: Critical caribbean studies | Includes bibliographical references and index.
Identifiers: LCCN 2023014647 | ISBN 9781978829541 (paperback) | ISBN 9781978829558 (cloth) | ISBN 9781978829565 (epub) | ISBN 9781978829572 (pdf)
Subjects: LCSH: Food writing—Political aspects—Caribbean Area—History. | Cookbooks—Caribbean Area—History. | Cooking—Political aspects—Caribbean Area—History. | Caribbean Area—History—Autonomy and independence movements.
Classification: LCC TX644 .V35 2024 | DDC 808.06/6641—dc23/eng/20230414
LC record available at https://lccn.loc.gov/2023014647

A British Cataloging-in-Publication record for this book is available from the British Library.

Copyright © 2024 by Keja L. Valens

All rights reserved

No part of this book may be reproduced or utilized in any form or by any means, electronic or mechanical, or by any information storage and retrieval system, without written permission from the publisher. Please contact Rutgers University Press, 106 Somerset Street, New Brunswick, NJ 08901. The only exception to this prohibition is "fair use" as defined by U.S. copyright law.

References to internet websites (URLs) were accurate at the time of writing. Neither the author nor Rutgers University Press is responsible for URLs that may have expired or changed since the manuscript was prepared.

∞ The paper used in this publication meets the requirements of the American National Standard for Information Sciences—Permanence of Paper for Printed Library Materials, ANSI Z39.48-1992.

rutgersuniversitypress.org

Contents

PREFACE: WHOSE CARIBBEAN COOKBOOKS?   ix

Introduction: Reading Caribbean Cookbooks   1

1
Nineteenth-Century Cocineros of Cuba and Puerto Rico   33

2
Domestic Control in West Indian Women's Cookbooks at the Turn of the Twentieth Century   71

3
Colonial and Neocolonial Fortification in the French Antilles, Puerto Rico, and the U.S. Virgin Islands   121

4
Cuban Independence, to Taste   181

5
Dominican and Haitian (Re)Emergence   239

6
National Culture Cook-Up and Food Independence
in Jamaica and Barbados 301

Conclusion 357

ACKNOWLEDGMENTS 379

NOTES 381

WORKS CITED 423

INDEX 459

Preface

Whose Caribbean Cookbooks?

One of the things that people—from the Caribbean themselves and not—often ask when I describe this book to them is whether the cookbooks I am studying are by "native" Caribbeans. I could just answer yes, the great majority are written by people who were born or lived a great part of their lives in the Caribbean, because I excluded from consideration cookbooks written from the Caribbean diaspora across the world and those written by non-Caribbean tourists and travelers. But the questions of what exactly is, or how exactly something gets to be, a "native" Caribbean person or food or recipe, that is, who "owns" or has agency over what is Caribbean, who authors what is Caribbean, how something is made Caribbean, are precisely among the central questions or concerns that emerge in the cookbooks I study and, in particular, in this study of them.

As those familiar with Caribbean studies know, these are indeed among the central questions of the discipline. Even the answers formulated by Kamau Brathwaite, Édouard Glissant, Fernado Ortiz, and many more—that the Caribbean is the creole—are only points of entry establishing that what is Caribbean is what is made or raised in the Caribbean. The question of how what is made or raised in the Caribbean got to be that way remains open. This both justifies my shorthand "yes" and emphasizes that my discomfort with my answer is not just about history (it is native Caribbean now, but when, how, and from where did it arrive in the Caribbean?), it is also about epistemology (what is meant when someone says "native Caribbean"?). Is "native" a question of the birth of the individual? Is it a question of ancestry, and if so how far back does one need to trace ancestors born in the Caribbean to be "native"? Is "native Caribbean" a euphemism for race? Does asking the question imply that there is one "native race" of the Caribbean? What race would that be?

These questions, as I discovered, mirror a certain trajectory of Caribbean cookbooks: for the first ones, written from colonialist and White Creole settler perspectives between the mid-nineteenth and mid-twentieth centuries, a central task was to show how Europeans and their direct descendants could and should rightly reside and rule in the Caribbean. It was possible, they demonstrated, for European-derived knowledge, skills, and imported and naturalized goods to be applied to Indigenous and African-derived raw materials and labor in such a civilizing way that good profits, good manners, and good tastes would result. These cookbooks refer to Afro-Indigenous people and products as "the natives" and base their authority to do so on their own status as "of and for" the Caribbean. Their culinary colonialism worked to appropriate Afro-Indigenous foods that they also constructed as insufficient. Colonial-era cookbooks described the "native" Caribbean cooking as needing European order and products (like white flour) even as they demonstrated the reliance of European tastes on colonial products like sugar and of colonial homes on the preparation, consumption, and enjoyment of the "native" ingredients and dishes that marked these cookbooks as different from their European counterparts.

By the early to mid-twentieth century, at the same time as culinary colonialism persisted, claims of "native" authorship were also shifting. In nationalist cookbooks, more and more authors claimed their own native status, one that was sometimes directly racialized (Black, Mulatto, Mestizo, or White). Even more often, however, this status was asserted through a claim to being Creole, a reference that increasingly gestured toward being of mixed ancestry rather than toward any specific race in a way that, with all of the ambiguity of José Vasconcelos's "cosmic race [*raza cósmica*]," is both not exactly White and exactly not not-White. Thus, while more and more authors who claimed to write "native" Caribbean cookbooks also claimed to be "native" Caribbean people, they only sort of became more representative of the majority population, especially the majority of cooks, on the island of their nativity. It was not until the mid- to late twentieth century that large numbers of cookbooks were written by women, and a few men, who directly claimed to be—and sometimes to come from generations of—"native" cooks with deep and explicit connections to the Afro-Indigenous as well as the European heritages of their foods; in other words, as attached in their persons as in their preparations to the processes and outcomes of creolization.

Worth noting, of course, is that cookbook authors write not so much about themselves as about the foods on whose preparation they instruct. Cookbooks rarely come with "author blurbs" and rather sporadically include introductions or other narrative parts that provide biographical information. Plus, women who write cookbooks often author only a single cookbook in their lifetime. Like the very cookbooks I study that foreground recipes even when they include narrative notes about history and culture and rich paratextual material in prefaces and glossaries, I foreground analyses of the cookbooks with much of the genealogical and historico-contextual research that shores up this study compacted into brief summaries and relegated to the notes of this book. While I am certainly interested in who the authors are, I remain primarily focused on the question of how something is made Caribbean: how do the authors of Caribbean cookbooks, through the selection of recipes, the naming of ingredients, and the narratives that sometimes accompany them, claim, construct, and position themselves in relation to Caribbean, Cuban, Puerto Rican, Jamaican, Barbadian, Antillean, Virgin Islands, Dominican, or Haitian cuisines?

CULINARY COLONIALISM, CARIBBEAN COOKBOOKS, AND RECIPES FOR NATIONAL INDEPENDENCE

Introduction

Reading Caribbean Cookbooks

TO WRITE ABOUT FOOD in the Caribbean is to write about identity. In *Caribbean Discourse*, Édouard Glissant invokes the association when he describes the Caribbean as belonging to "civilizations of maize, manioc, sweet potato, [and] pepper" (115). Cookbooks are food writing par excellence, and women across the Caribbean have been writing, reading, and exchanging cookbooks since at least the turn of the nineteenth century. Yet, in his 1999 "culinary memoir" *Pig Tails 'n Breadfruit*, Austin Clarke claims that "in every self-respecting Barbadian household the woman (who does most of the cooking, whether she is wife, daughter, or maid) would not be caught dead with a cookbook. To read a cookbook would suggest that she had not retained what her mother taught her" (3–4). Clarke's two assumptions—(a) cookbooks are for cooking; and (b) real Caribbean women do not read or need cookbooks—reiterate the stereotype of women's bodies as living repositories of a natural and traditional knowledge no book could capture. By casting the *absence* of cookbooks as evidence for the living tradition and authenticity of Caribbean cuisine, Clarke elides and mistakes the role cookbooks play in Caribbean culture. As *Culinary Colonialism, Caribbean Cookbooks, and Recipes for National Independence* shows, Caribbean cookbook production is vast, varied, and a vital mode of women's expression and instruction. At the same time, as Clarke alludes, the great majority of cooking in the Caribbean, especially through the mid-twentieth century, has been done by women with extensive oral and practical training in food preparation and often limited literacy. These women rarely needed or even used cookbooks for the cooking instruction whose delivery could seem to be their sole function. What, then, do Caribbean cookbooks do other than instruct in making the dishes that they list?

This book offers the most extensive study of Caribbean cookbooks and Caribbean food writing to date. It opens the lid on how women (and a few men) have used cookbooks, across the Caribbean and since the mid-nineteenth century, to shape, embed, and contest colonial and domestic orders, as well as to delineate the contours of independent national cultures and to transform tastes for independence into flavors of domestic autonomy.

Cookbooks transmit and play out the tensions between colonial dependence and decolonial national projects through their manifest content (accounts of the history and nutritional value of foods, directions for preparation and consumption), their generic form (language, writing, mode of instruction), and through the activities they denote and promote (creating, nurturing, sustaining families and communities, communicating shared practices). *Culinary Colonialism* examines how Caribbean cookbooks contend with the layered and uneven pasts of settler colonialism, genocide, slavery, and forced and voluntary migration that indelibly mark and shape culinary practices and render impossible the often singular or straightforwardly ancestral claims to Caribbean tradition endemic to early articulations of Caribbean culture. While scholars have largely imagined Caribbean nations as *public* productions of male voices in politics, theory, and culture, *Culinary Colonialism*'s focus on cookbooks (written predominantly by women) locates Caribbean culture and its concoction in domestic spaces that are gendered female and that negotiate race, language, and class in particularly domestic ways. Cookbooks, this book shows, are packed with rich interfaces of colonial and decolonial order; of women of different races, ages, and classes; of the forces of tradition and the requirements of creation. Reading Caribbean cookbooks, this book explores how they instruct and engage their readers in the intimate processes of nourishing families and friends, of cooking and eating together, and of forming and transmitting family ties, at the same time as they codify, inscribe, and publish orders for colonial control and independent national culture.

Inspired by the burgeoning study of cookbooks as literary genre and material culture, my point of departure in *Culinary Colonialism* is a crossroads of Caribbean food studies—pioneered by Sidney Mintz and elaborated by Cruz Miguel Ortiz Cuadra, Sarah Lawson Welsh, and Hannah Garth, among others—and Caribbean food history as proffered by scholars like Berta Cabanillas and B. W. Higman. Theoretically, I pare Frantz Fanon's argument for the centrality of national culture in colonial domination and decolonization with Glissant's studies of creolization to chart the emergence of national culinary cultures from what Fanon calls "native culture" reawakened after being squashed by colonial domination and to account for how the multiple traditions and practices that have met in the Caribbean under varying degrees of duress came to be incorporated into so many stewy ajiacos, pepperpots, sancochos, and callaloos. Glissant's rhizomatic poetics of Relation models how to trace these connections, extensions, and emplacements throughout Caribbean cookbooks. His analytic insistence on the interplay of word- and world-making furnishes a vital ingredient for my view of cookbooks that write, make, and nourish Caribbean tastes bearing the weight of history, responding to the need for nutrition, and grounded in the domestic praxes of Caribbean women. Along its entangled path, this book meets up with scholars of U.S. cookbooks who have shown how cookbooks encode and challenge gender, racial, and class positions,[1] participate in nation-building,[2] and shape American cuisine and the lives of Black women;[3] it engages Hilary Beckles and Verene Shepherd on Caribbean Women's history, Evelyn O'Callaghan on White Creoles, Alison Donnell on Caribbean archives, and Elizabeth DeLoughry on the Caribbean environment; takes up with Benedict Anderson on imagined communities and with Arjun Appadurai on cookbooks and nationalisms; and encounters the few scholars who have begun, before and with me, to look at Caribbean cookbooks.[4] At these rich meeting points,

Culinary Colonialism, Caribbean Cookbooks, and Recipes for National Independence savors what so many Caribbean cooks bring to the page.

This book rests on two paradoxes: colonialism both destroyed and created the Caribbean as we know it; independent nationhood created the "native" cultures whose autonomy it putatively restored. Through the examination of how these paradoxes play out in cookbooks, I dig into the forces of destruction, creation, and restoration that are cause and effect of colonialism and national independence in the Caribbean and that are inscribed in the foods, peoples, cultures, and sociopolitical formations served up by Caribbean cookbooks.

Colonialism in the Caribbean started in the fifteenth century when Columbus claimed Caribbean islands for the Queen of Spain; the appropriation and expropriation of land, labor, and material from the Caribbean for European and now U.S. profit continues today. In fullest force and at greatest extent from the seventeenth through nineteenth centuries, colonialism in the Caribbean was settler colonialism. Europeans not only took over positions of power and control as emissaries of their governments but also literally moved in as residents, adding as much as they took away. Settler colonialism vastly and irrevocably transformed the Caribbean. Colonizers decimated Indigenous populations. They forcibly relocated Africans to the Caribbean and held generations of their descendants as nativized slave labor. As slavery ended, they coerced Indians and Chinese into indentured labor. And that is a sketch of only the human level.

Independent nationhood in the Caribbean ended colonial rule, but decolonization in the Caribbean could not throw out all or even most of what arrived with colonialism. Those who fought for independent nationhood in the Caribbean were often themselves the descendants of colonizers. Independent nationhood wrested political and economic control from the centers of empire and created a diverse array of national cultures that variously implanted the descendants of European, African, Indigenous, Asian, and Levantine people as the native and rightful autarchs. The independence period in the Caribbean started with the Haitian revolution of 1804 and lasted through the 1980s.

The paradoxes of colonial rule and independent nationhood in the Caribbean both operate through creolization. As I explain in more detail in the section on process and terminology, I use the noun *creole* in the senses in which the word first emerged: in the early colonial period, *creole* referred to people (now often capitalized), plants, foods, music, dance, and so on from elsewhere born in the Caribbean and thus become Caribbean; in the later colonial period and through today, the term refers to a mixture of Indigenous, African, European, and sometimes also Asian and Levantine, that is born in the Caribbean. Creolization is the collection of processes that form these creoles. Creolization is the action of making the creole; it is an action that continues, as the creole is not made once to become stable and static but is always being remade. The paradoxes of colonialism and national independence in the Caribbean operate through creolization because colonialism and national independence in the Caribbean creolize. They are among the processes that make the creole. Creolization also makes Caribbean colonialism and national independence. The particular ways that people, plants, animals, and customs came together and then reconfigured in the Caribbean is what constitutes the particular character of colonialism and national independence in the Caribbean. This book takes cookbooks as settings for creolization in its culinary, racial, cultural, and sociopolitical manifestations that reflect and produce the processes of colonialism and independent nationhood.

A focus on cookbooks highlights women and race in the domestic concoction of colonialism and national independence in the Caribbean. Caribbean cookbooks are most often written by and for women and openly draw on and manifest women's knowledge and practice. Even when Caribbean cookbooks are written by men, they explicitly draw on and comment on women's knowledge and practice (whether it is to give praise, offer guidance, or both). Through cookbooks, women's domestic work enters the public sphere. Race is one of the primary dividing social and political lines that is created or at least relied on by colonialism. In the colonial period, Black and Indigenous women, and increasingly Afro-Indigenous women, bore the non-European food knowledge and did the great majority of the cooking. Cookbooks were not, however, openly written by Afro-Indigenous or non-White women until the independence period.[5] The ways in which cookbooks acknowledge the Indigenous and African origins of Caribbean foods and they ways in which they address Afro-Indigenous women work to maintain, break down, or reformulate racial divisions and hierarchies.

Theoretically, Fanon and Glissant guide the work of this book. *Culinary Colonialism, Caribbean Cookbooks, and Recipes for National Independence* follows Fanon's analysis of colonial domination and national independence especially in its attention to national culture. It follows Glissant's theorization of creolization, linked to Kamau Brathwaite's work also on creolization and to Fernando Ortiz's work on the sister concept of transculturation. Fanon charts how colonial domination dislocates culture such that "one cannot divorce the combat for culture from the people's struggle for liberation" (168). I study how cookbooks participate in what Fanon identifies as the key stages in colonial destruction, starting with colonial attempts to establish "the objective nonexistence of the conquered nation and culture," and how cookbooks are part of the "mutual foundations for national culture and liberation struggles" that culminate in the revival of "a cultural dynamism" (170–171). Glissant helps me to look at how the messy processes of creolization run across those stages and mess up any neat chronological ordering of Caribbean development from colonial domination to national independence and any neat moral ordering of development from bad colonizers dominating good natives to good natives throwing off bad colonizers. "Creolization," Glissant writes, is "one of the ways of forming a complex mix," focusing on creolizations as a processes that "bring into Relation" "the cultures of people in the turbulent confluence whose globality organizes our *chaos-monde* [chaos-world]" (*Caribbean Discourse* 89, 94). This concept of creolization as generalizable without being universal and as part of a chaos that "is neither fusion nor confusion" guides my analysis of the processes and products of Caribbean identification in and through culinary processes and cookbook productions (*Caribbean Discourse*, 94). Similarly, Glissant's observation that

Introduction 7

"those who meet up *here* always come from an 'over there,' from the expanse of the world, and here they are, determined to bring to this 'here' the fragile knowledge they have taken from over there" grounds my analysis of the plays of native and transplant, insider and outsider, owner and usurper, deterritorialization and reterritorialization that I find in Caribbean cookbooks (*Treatise*, 9). Finally, Glissant's analytic insistence on the interplay of word- and world-making furnishes a vital ingredient for my view of cookbooks that write, make, and nourish Caribbean tastes bearing the weight of history, responding to the need for nutrition, and grounded in the domestic praxes of Caribbean women. Extending Fanon's work on national culture and independence into the realm of culinary culture, this book illuminates how women joined and created forces of colonialism and national independence through cookbooks. Drawing Glissant's work on creolization into the reading of cookbooks, this book shows how women have molded the particular traces and tropes that meet in the Caribbean into distinct local and national delicacies and identity relations.

To look at colonialism and independence in the Caribbean through the lens of cookbooks, and vice versa, I deploy the two titular culinary metaphors: culinary colonialism and recipes for national independence. Culinary colonialism conveys the ways that colonial projects operated through culinary processes. Culinary colonialism refers to the transformations that result from imports and exports across the colonial world and speaks specifically to the work of colonizers to assert the superiority of European food cultures even as they praised the exotic bounty of Caribbean food products. In the colonial period, Whiteness dominates. Europeans and White Creoles hold the great majority of political, economic, and social power, and all things associated with Europe are, in the public sphere and in elite semi-public domestic spaces like cookbooks, held in the highest regard. Traces of Blackness and Indigeneity appear in cookbooks, signals of the vast knowledge, skill, and taste of African and Indigenous culinary cultures and cooks, but they are rarely if ever acknowledged as such. Recipes for national independence plays on the slippage between a first meaning of "recipe" as, according to the

Oxford English Dictionary, "a statement of the ingredients and procedure required for making something, especially (now) a dish in cookery," and an extended meaning as "a means, procedure, or plan for attaining or effecting some end." It also plays on the multiple meanings of "for." A recipe "for accra" is a set of instructions that tell you how to make accra. A recipe "for your mother" is a recipe to give to your mother, for her benefit. What I hope to underline with this phrase is that there is a slippage between recipes that tell you how to make specific dishes and recipes that help national independence. This slippage centers on the concept of national culture, whose importance for national independence is a focus of Fanon's, and on the idea that food is a central component of national culture. During the independence era, recipes for independent national culture come to the fore. Literally, cookbooks with titles like *Recipes for Independent Jamaica* were published. Cookbooks include direct political statements of national aspiration or affiliation along with assertions of the value of local foods, "national dishes," and food independence. In this period Blackness and Indigeneity were revalued as African and Indigenous culinary cultures were retraced, acknowledged, and held up. What origins, what inheritances, what mixtures, what dominant flavors cookbooks of the independence period highlight, how they are titled, and how they name ingredients, recipes, and sections, demonstrate their political, cultural, and racial identifications. While most of these embrace independence, their instructions and tastes for that independence—democratic or autocratic, White-affiliated or Afrocentric, for example—are quite different across islands and over time.

While the concept-metaphors of culinary colonialism and recipes for national independence show the culinary division of the colonial period from the independence era, they also are marked by the messiness of that division. The colonial period did not quite end everywhere all at once, or ever, and culinary colonialism exceeds the colonial period, even if it is centered in it. Cookbooks and recipes with titles that include island names that would become nation names were already present in the first colonial cookbooks. Caribbean cookbooks with direct and indirect attachments to independence movements were written by the descendants of colonizers as much as by the descendants of African and Indigenous peoples (and often, of course, cookbook authors, like so many other people of the Caribbean, descended from all three and more). These entanglements began as soon as Europeans arrived in the Caribbean, when the paradoxes of colonialism and national independence and the processes of creolization were anticipated in the tropes of danger and scarcity, edibleness and abundance that were embedded in the colonial process of collecting, transplanting, claiming, and naming.

Scarcity and Danger, Abundance and Edibleness: Enduring Tropes from the Prehistory of Caribbean Cookbooks

The first writing about Caribbean foods and food practices, in the letters and chronicles of men like Christopher Columbus, Gonzalo Fernández de Oviedo y Valdés (Oviedo), and Père Labat, established the tropes of scarcity and danger, abundance and edibleness that persist into twentieth-century Caribbean cookbooks. The weight of these colonial tropes on Caribbean cuisine led me to start this book with the record of culinary colonialism and to finish with recipes for independence. Cookbooks of the colonial period and the independence era repeat, rework, and reject colonial figures and figurations of the Caribbean. Much as Caribbean cookbooks also draw on, trace, and recover Indigenous, African, and Asian foodways that colonial tropes misunderstood or just missed, the tropes that explorers and colonizers used in the first writings on Caribbean foods make an inaugural stamp on Caribbean cookbooks with which they all contend in some way.

In order to claim "terra nullius," that the land they "discovered" belonged to no one and could thus be unilaterally claimed, European explorers could find no established civilization, no homes, and no hearths. People and food had to be scarce, or so barbaric that they hardly qualified as human. It is not surprising, then, that human flesh was high on the list of foods that Columbus recorded in his letters.[6] Diego Alvarez Chanca, the physician to the King and Queen of Spain who was appointed to accompany Columbus on the second voyage, describes cannibalism as the first significant discovery they made upon landing on Guadeloupe:

> The captain put into land on a boat and seeing some houses, leapt on shore and went up to them, the inhabitants fleeing at sight of our men; he then went into the houses and there found various household articles that had been left unremoved. . . . He found a great quantity of cotton, both spun and prepared for spinning, and articles of food, of all of which he brought away a portion; besides these, he also brought away four or five bones of human arms and legs. On seeing these we suspected that we were amongst the Caribee islands, whose inhabitants eat human flesh. (286–287)

Chanca goes on to recount that their guides, Taíno Indians already in conflict with the Caribs, explained that "women also say that the Caribbees use them with such cruelty as would scarcely be believed; and that they eat the children which they bear to them. . . . Such of their male enemies as they can take alive, they bring to their houses to slaughter them, and those who are killed they devour at once. They say that man's flesh is so good, that there is nothing like it in the world" (290). As other Europeans built on the work of Columbus and Chanca, they quickly repeated and developed the accounts of Caribbean people as cannibals defined by their consumption of other humans.

Later explorers and chroniclers kept lack and danger at the center of descriptions of Caribbean food by detailing the absence of what was for them the greatest staple—bread—and the dangers of the main Caribbean starch, yuca (aka manioc or cassava).[7] Even colonial descriptions that mention the processing of yuca into flour and cakes describe them as a poor substitute for bread and highlight the danger of the deadly poison that yuca can contain rather than the techniques that turn the yuca root into a flour, a starch (tapioca), a hunting and fishing resource (the raw extracted poison), and a preservative and flavoring (the extracted poison in cooked form) through the streamlined procedure of grating, pressing, drying, and cooking. Time and again, the Europeans' tendency to find all things "Indian" dangerous and their limited view of what even counts as food and culinary technique relegated Caribbean culinary culture to savagery and facilitated its destruction, as when the pigs that the Spaniards released, out of what they saw as nutritional necessity, ruined Indigenous canucos (plots of yuca).

At the same time, and especially after they established possession-by-discovery, explorers and chroniclers waxed poetic about the natural bounty of Caribbean fruits, fish, and fowl just waiting to be plucked and devoured. Chanca describes the island that they called Marie Galante as holding "such varieties of trees, unknown to anyone, as was astonishing" (24). But even their bounty was lacking—unordered, uncultivated, and uncertain. The abundance of produce, meat, and starches was attributed to the fertility of the ripe soil open for European seed. Chanca writes that "great quantities of vegetables have been planted which certainly attain a more luxuriant growth here in eight days than they would in Spain in twenty (308). Peter Martyr repeats with added detail how "the Admiral took on board [for the second voyage] ... vegetables, grain, barley, and similar seeds, not only for provisions but also for sowing; vines and young plants such as were wanting in that country were carefully taken.... The Spaniards declare that there is not in the whole universe a more fertile region" (Book I).

The combination of taking and adding that marks the early explorers' interactions with Caribbean plants and animals—edible and not—fully transformed the flora, fauna, and foodways of the Americas, Europe, and Africa. Alfred Crosby names "Columbian Exchange" the series of interactions that "accomplished what was probably the greatest biological revolution in the Americas since the Pleistocene era" (66), most obviously through the introduction of vast numbers of new animal and plant species from cows and pigs to sugar cane and breadfruit.[8]

The colonial/modern food and plant system emerged out of the Columbian Exchange and the efforts of Europeans to codify their vast new "findings" in a universal classificatory system, the most successful and enduring of which is Linnaean taxonomy (186).[9] Antiguan writer and gardener Jamaica Kincaid summarizes and satirizes the project of Carolus Linnaeus's 1751 *Philosophia Botanica*: "In the beginning, the vegetable kingdom was chaos, people everywhere called the same things by a name that made sense to them, not by a name arrived at by an objective standard" (*My (Garden) Book*, 166). Implementing the Enlightenment/colonial mandate to categorize, to identify/discriminate and systematically organize, to collect and enclose, to divide and conquer that underlies the naturalization of colonial demarcations in the Caribbean environment, Linnaeus created a new taxonomy.[10]

While naturalists used Linnaean taxonomy to systematize botanical knowledge, agriculturalists and planters across the Caribbean turned to its commercial and administrative applications. Men from Hans Sloane, physician to the governor of Jamaica in the 1680s, to Stanislas Foäche, French plantation owner in Haiti in the late eighteenth century, catalogued the botanical, agricultural, and culinary practices and advice they gathered from the growing African, Afro-Indigenous, Afro-Caribbean, White colonial, and planter populations. Scattered amid Sloane's observations about botany and Foäche's instructions on how to manage subsistence farming that fed slaves who produced sugar for export and livestock for colonial tables are notes about culinary practices that increasingly combined Indigenous, African, and European elements. For example, Sloane's recipe for "Perino"—"Take a Cake of bad Cassada Bread, about a Foot over, and half an Inch thick, burnt black on one side, break it to pieces, and put it to steep in two Gallons of water, let it stand open in a Tub twelve hours, then add to it the froth of an Egg, and three Gallons more water, and one pound of Sugar, let it work twelve hours, and Bottle it; it will keep good for a week" (xxix)—uses fermentation, a process developed independently in Africa, the Caribbean, and Europe,[11] to combine the Indigenous cassava bread, by then widely made by Afro-Caribbeans, with the plantation product par excellence, sugar.

Puerto Rican food historian Berta Cabanillas has demonstrated that we can read early colonial writing not only for records of prejudice, destruction, and appropriation but also to see what these men noticed, and so to pick up on the traces of other voices and other views (199). As Glissant writes, "For some people, over there, so far so near, right here, on the hidden face of the earth, the trace was lived as one of those places of survival" (*Treatise* 9). Cookbooks emerge from the tradition of colonial writing about Caribbean food and inscribe the long oral-practical continuation of cooking that persists in kitchens and yards. Accordingly, we can read colonial cookbooks for the traces of the sources that are not named, the voices that are not authorized, and the contributors who are not authors. At the same time, as domestic objects, cookbooks serve as loci where those voices take on authorship, where initially White colonial and then an increasingly racially diverse range of women wrote the oral and practical culinary histories they held, their versions of colonial inscriptions, and their own recipes for independence.

As Kit Candlin and Cassandra Prybus have documented, White women and women of color in the Caribbean have been writing and collecting receipts—culinary and commercial—since at least the eighteenth century. In the nineteenth century, women's travel writing recorded the culinary scene with a domestic focus and told the stories of those making and observing the making of Caribbean food. Lady Nugent's journal (1801–1805) and Mrs. Carmichael's *Domestic Manners and Social Condition of the White, Coloured and Negro Population of the West Indies* (1833) detail the preparation and consumption of plants and animals with some confusion and much concern about what they saw as a lack of order endemic to the kitchens and dining rooms of established colonial families in the Caribbean. At the same time, they, along with Mary Prince's *The History of Mary Prince, a West Indian Slave, Written by Herself* (1831) and Mary Seacole's *The Wonderful Adventures of Mrs. Seacole in Many Lands* (1857), point to the ways that slave cuisine—developed on provision grounds, in slave quarters, and in "big houses"—engendered creole cuisine and reveal the vital culinary roles of free Blacks and Mulattoes,[12] especially women, in running establishments that undertook, among other things, food preparation and service. As much as these texts reflect the shift in Caribbean food writing from the exclusive domain of European men to a space where European and Caribbean women and men—White, Black, and mixed race—interact, the tropes of danger and scarcity, abundance and edibleness persist in their worldviews and extend through the twenty-first century.

Cookbooks as and in the Archives

A cookbook is an archive (a repository, a rulebook) of recipes, of household management. As collections of "receipts" (from whence "recipe"), cookbooks preserve selected culinary documents for consultation and posterity. Cookbooks are also stored in archives. However, national archives, those under the watch of the archon, tend to ignore cookbooks. They are collected instead in libraries, homes, the archives curated by the demos. Of course, the first Caribbean cookbook writers and collectors belonged to the social and political elite, and their libraries were not accessible to the general population that was often both illiterate and denied entry to the front doors of elite homes and establishments. The status of cookbooks as esoteric objects prized by women in the ruling classes resonates with Clarke's objection to cookbooks as disconnected from the practical transmission of culinary knowledge in many Caribbean homes. However, as the grande dame of Martinican letters, Maryse Condé, points out, the "ruling classes" "are but the other face of the same society" (90). Furthermore, if the archive is the record kept by the elite of the society as they (over)see it, it is also a site of revolutionary contest, where new rulers assert new orders. Indeed, as instruction manuals, tools of everyday practice, mechanisms of living transmission and interaction—sometimes even read to illiterate or semi-literate cooks and used in rural education programs, and part of the increasing literacy of women who used them alongside their orally and practically acquired culinary knowledge—cookbooks bridge the esoteric and the living archive.

The archives where cookbooks are most common are also the most ephemeral. Even libraries have often ignored cookbooks as either too domestic or too commercial to collect. The idea that revolt, revolution, and nation-building come from the public products of men's labor reinforces, and is reinforced by, this archival prejudice. Even after Fanon's compelling argument that national culture demands, as much it is demanded by, decolonization, cookbooks remain scarce in studies of decolonial nation-building. My own circuitous journeys to find Caribbean cookbooks illustrate their scarcity in the archives and attest to the exacerbating forces of the slow colonial violence of the global distribution of patrimony, and the ongoing commercial exploitation of Caribbean products by local and international players.

Planning to follow up on Efraín Barradas's determination of the relationship between the first Cuban and Puerto Rican cookbooks with close readings of each, I searched for copies of the two nineteenth-century—1856 and 1857—editions of Eugenio de Coloma y Garcés's *Manual del cocinero cubano*. The only 1856 editions were in the Biblioteca de la Agencia Española de Cooperación Internacional para el Desarrollo in Madrid and in the British Library, where a catalog entry notes the volume was destroyed when the library was bombed in World War II. The Biblioteca Nacional José Martí holds the only extant copy of the 1857 edition, which the Cuban historian Olga García Yero and Cuba's Editorial Oriente reissued in 2017. But rather than resulting in no one knowing the contents of the book between the mid-nineteenth century and 2017, the inaccessibility of the original is accompanied by a relative wealth of variously edited, selected, and attributed versions of the *Manual del cocinero cubano*. In 2016, when I began my search and the only way to see the 1857 original was to go to Cuba, I quickly found Argentine chef Norberto Petryk's blog that claims to provide digital access to a copy of the 1857 edition that, he writes, "was sent to me a few years ago from Havana, Cuba, on a CD, in a pdf format that does not allow for the copying of parts."[13] The link to the profile was—and at the time of this writing remains—broken, and the link that Petryk provides to the Google Books open-access e-copy of the text instead directs to

J. P. Legran's 1864 *Nuevo manual del cocinero cubano*, which is indeed in free digital circulation. Petryk's blog features transcription of two recipes from the 1857 manuscript of the *Manual del cocinero cubano*. The combination of a promise of full access, accompanied by the purveyor's tale of the restrictions and lacks overcome and an at-best partial and curiously identified text turned out to be the norm for nineteenth-century Caribbean cookbooks.[14] The tropes of a Caribbean marked by scarcity and abundance, and thus in need of regulatory control, established in colonial narratives and repeated in colonial cookbooks, manifest again in archival preservation and recovery. As this book outlines the corpus of Caribbean cookbooks, it attests to the ongoing, intersecting, and divergent commercial and national interests Caribbean cookbooks from the nineteenth century through the present elicit. Following the traces of foodways in recipes, of recipes in cookbooks, and of cookbooks in archives, I argue that we can examine how political machinations and innovations feed and are fed by those who, by choice and by force, do and record the cooking. Women, slaves, first peoples, and indentured servants emerge, thus, not only as the invisible downtrodden—or supports—of colonization and creolization, but among their authors. What that authorship looks like, and how it shapes colonial practice and decolonial imaginations, is the focus of the first three chapters of this book.

Caribbean cookbooks published in the second half of the twentieth century are often easier to locate than their predecessors. Collectors like Lafcadio Hearn and libraries like the University of the West Indies at Cave Hill, Barbados, and Saint Augustine, Trinidad and Tobago, the University of Miami, and Harvard's Schlessinger Library have made special efforts to collect cookbooks, often in connection with decolonial and feminist projects. That the balance of holdings remains heavily weighted toward libraries outside of the Caribbean, and that those in the Caribbean struggle to secure the funding needed for such things as maintaining archival conditions, digitizing documents, and expanding these collections, underlines the long reach of colonial disparities. Of course, mid-to-late twentieth-century cookbooks also circulate on the market, are held in private mini-collections on kitchen shelves, pass among family and friends, and take on new archives of hand-scribbled notes and drips of fat. These holdings and passages are often hard to trace. One has only to mention cookbooks to a Puerto Rican or a Cuban to hear about the popularity of Carmen Aboy Valldejuli's *Cocina criolla* or Nitza Villapol's *Cocina al minuto*, both of which continue to be used, bought, and gifted throughout the islands and the diaspora. Discussing food in Barbados brings up the name Carmeta Fraser, whose recipes—published in advertisements and spread on packaging—are widely used, even if her cookbooks are not. Cookbooks like Amanda Ornes Perelló's *Cocina criolla* that served as a textbook for home economics programs remain the treasured possessions, and inheritance, of many who studied and taught them—Ornes Perelló's book, though it has been out of print since the 1993 edition, has a Facebook page dedicated to it.[15] Nevertheless, many cookbooks that were widely sold and used in the 1940s, 1950s, 1960s, 1970s, and even 1980s and 1990s are out of print. Furthermore, while deeply influential among a powerful few around the time of their publication, some cookbooks, like the first Haitian cookbook, Herzulie Magloire-Prophète's 1955 *Cuisine sélectionnée*, have nearly fallen off the public radar while others—like Leila Brandon's 1963 *A Merry-Go-Round of Recipes from Independent Jamaica*—widely circulated and released in new editions for several decades, eventually went out of print without making the kind of mark on families that leads them to be preserved for generations in large quantities. Even works like Fraser's *National Recipe Directory* or Mildred V. Anduze's *Virgin Islands Native Recipes* are accessible only through personal connection, the used-book circuit, libraries, and archives. Pinterest boards, Facebook pages, blog logs, and personal conversations register the interest of today's generations of reader-cooks in the books they remember from their mothers' and grandmothers' kitchens, so perhaps reissues and new editions will follow.

The traces of Indigenous, and then Afro-Indigenous, foodways recorded and appropriated by explorers and early colonizers, continued and modified by cooks across the Caribbean, represent the grounds of Caribbean cooking. The persistent tropes, of danger and scarcity, abundance and edibleness, resurface in instructions for preservation, substitution, denial, and enjoyment and are put to the service of arguments for both colonial control and independence. Much of the work of nineteenth- and twentieth-century Caribbean cookbooks involves establishing Caribbean native, national culinary cultures at the confluence of a particular combination of people, plants, and practices that combine these traces with imports and implantations, primarily but not exclusively from or via Europe. These cookbooks work for a coincidence of the domestic and the national even as they offer divergent depictions of the state of the home and the home of the state. They become, in turn, the grounds for the formation of independent national cuisines. It is the argument of this book that by examining Caribbean cookbooks we can see how women participated in both colonial and decolonial nation-building through the curation of national tastes and also how those tastes emerge out of and merge into creole cuisines marked by shared histories, distinguished by local conditions, and embroiled in racial tensions.

Process and Terminology

When I started this project, I thought that I would be doing a lot of "distant reading," counting how many cookbooks were published in what places at what times, counting title terms, comparing page lengths. But the cookbooks drew me in, led me to their authors, to the specifics of colonial rule, independence movements, and the nation-building projects they were and are a part of. They begged close readings of the introductions, the organization of sections, the categorization of dishes and foods, and the titling of recipes, not to mention the naming of ingredients and the detailing of instructions.

Like the chronicler, the naturalist, and the archon, the cookbook author or compiler exercises the privilege of gathering, unifying, identifying, and classifying, and in so doing reveals the ordering principle of their rule.[16] My analysis looks at the ordered relation between four central components of cookbooks: foods (edible plants and animals), dishes (the prepared versions of those foods), recipes (the titled description of how to make those foods), and ingredients and instructions (the components of the recipes). Foods and dishes—as they are named, defined, and ordered in sections, often by their place in meal order—reflect categorization. Recipes—as they are titled and grouped into sections, often by dish—demonstrate identification, the process of naming that holds up a specific set of affiliations and associations. Ingredients and instructions reveal foodways—how flora and fauna, encountered wild, cultivated, or canned in different places, come together in pots and racks—and tastes—what is considered savory or sweet, delicacy or everyday fare, healthy or harmful. The terms used for ingredients, amounts, techniques, the ones that get elevated into titles, reflect the writer's familiarity with the food, their cultural geographies, and the languages that they speak and value.

Although I wish I could include every quote in the original language, the work of translating all of the material that was not written originally in English has led me to be especially aware of the many different ways of designating foods.[17] Many names of dishes and foods, of course, are the same in Spanish or French as they are in English—as, for example, ajiaco, accra, or chayote. This is especially often the case with words that originate from Indigenous or African languages, encountered with relative simultaneity by Europeans from various locations. Often, multiple terms exist for a food or dish within as well as between languages, as with the root called yuca in Spanish, manioc in French, manyòk in Kreyòl (Haitian Creole), and in English either yuca or cassava, the latter of which is also the English term for the flour form (itself casabe or caçabi in Spanish, cassave in French, and farin manyòk in Kreyòl). I use brackets and explanations to make these as explicit as I can. Drawing from the example of Daniel Jurafsky's *The Language of Food*, I follow the etymologies of food words to trace their histories. Where spellings vary, I leave them—as for example fufu, foofoo, fufú, foufou. I have chosen to use untranslated a small number of commonly used words that I find to be tied to not just a language but a specific place and history of use and whose repetition in the original I take to be part of the formation of the national cuisine itself, notably what are often called "provisions" (or ground provisions, but also hard food or just food) in English: viandas in Cuba and Puerto Rico; víveres in the Dominican Republic; viv or vivres in Haiti, Guadeloupe, and Martinique. While "provisions" derives from the name for the provision grounds allotted to slaves to grow their own food (so that masters could give them smaller rations), reflecting their central role in slave diets, "viandas" and "vivres" come from the Spanish and French for "victuals" and the Dominican víveres from the use of "vivres" in Haiti, marking the proximity of the cuisines and their respective nations.

Although this book is the most extensive study of Caribbean cookbooks and Caribbean food writing to date, it is far from comprehensive. The archive is vast, if often difficult to locate. Every time I search in a new way in a library catalog or wander through the stacks, read an old publisher's catalog, ask a new friend about the books they have, or step into one more little shop, I find more books. This book therefore examines—out of necessity—a fraction of the cookbooks that I have found, or found out about, in a set of detailed studies that delve into colonial, proto-nationalist, and nationalist cookbooks in Cuba, Puerto Rico, Jamaica, Barbados, Guadeloupe, Martinique, the U.S. Virgin Islands, the Dominican Republic, and Haiti, with dips into works from Guyana, Grenada, and Trinidad and Tobago as part of the "Eastern Caribbean." It accounts for islands larger (the Greater Antilles of Cuba, Puerto Rico, Jamaica, Hispaniola) and smaller (the Lesser Antilles of Barbados, Guadeloupe, Martinique, U.S. Virgin Islands); leeward (U.S. Virgin Islands, Guadeloupe) and windward (Martinique, Barbados); Spanish, French, English, and Danish colonization; independence achieved in the nineteenth (Haiti) to twentieth centuries (Jamaica, Barbados), and continued colonial status (Puerto Rico, U.S. Virgin Islands, Guadeloupe, and Martinique). It uses both island-specific and subregional demarcations. It leaves out Curaçao, Aruba, Bonaire, Saint Lucia, Antigua, Saint Martin, and much more, thus skirting the

Dutch- and Papiamentou-speaking Caribbean. It does not examine deeply the places of Indo- and Chinese-Caribbean cuisines, primarily because it does not examine Trinidad and Tobago, Guyana, or Grenada—where Indo- and Chinese-Caribbean populations are concentrated—after the colonial period. These exclusions arise not from any paucity of cookbooks in those regions but from the constraints of my own trajectories of scholarship and travel, the fact that I do not read Papiamentou or Dutch, the time and length limitations associated with publishing this book, and, most of all, that this book makes no claim to be comprehensive or even to be representative of every aspect of the Caribbean. This book studies a cross-section of exemplary, but not defining, sets of cookbooks and offers a framework for examining cookbooks as political and literary interventions over time and across the Caribbean, illuminates the places and times that it does delve deeply into, and, I hope, can launch further study, especially of what it leaves out.

Focusing on national cuisines in a regional context, referring to that region as the Caribbean, opens up yet more questions of terminology as well as of conceptualization. To even call it "the Caribbean" privileges an Anglophone perspective, for the region is more often called "les Antilles" in French and alternately "el Caribe" and "las Antillas" in Spanish. While, writing in English, I use Caribbean myself, I translate the French "Antilles" and the Spanish "Antillas" as the English "Antilles" to mark the variation. In *How Food Made History*, Higman refers to the Caribbean as one of several megaregions, "culinary systems identified with large regions made up of multiple national units" (182). However, Higman continues, "What underlies the shared food histories and unity of these megaregions is variable. Even the apparent geographic unity of the Caribbean, for example, is less than certain" (183). Questions of whether the Caribbean includes only the islands in the Caribbean Sea or also the coastal regions of the continent that open to that sea have significant implications for what counts as Caribbean food, especially as food indigenous to the Caribbean, but a clear contemporary palate of regional foods is relatively easy identify, as are the rough contours of its history. Yuca is an indigenous staple, grouped with other starchy vegetables that grow on low-maintenance plants such as indigenous sweet potato and pumpkin, as well as plantain, yam, and breadfruit brought by slaves and colonists from Africa and Polynesia and grown by slaves in provision grounds. Corn, indigenized from Latin America, and rice, brought via colonial trade from Asia, round out the starchy bases of Caribbean diets. Large numbers of tropical fruits and vegetables with similar origin points are a classic marker of Caribbean food, as are fresh fish that abound in local waters. Fresh pork, chicken, and beef—mostly introduced from Europe—and salt fish, beef, and pork, brought through the Triangle Trade primarily to feed to slaves, if at times scarce, are the symbolic centerpieces of many dishes.[18] The Caribbean palate also includes a large number of fruits and vegetables brought from Europe, often originally from North Africa, the Middle East, and Asia. Grain flours imported from Europe and North America may be less symbolically significant but appear throughout Caribbean cooking. And, of course, there is sugar and its by-products, made from grasses initially imported by colonists from Polynesia. A common set of cooking techniques and dishes, conglomerates of Indigenous, African, European, and Asian traditions, are also easy to identify: stews, often served with pounded starches; meats, fowl, and fishes roasted or grilled over an open fire; savory "cakes" made of all kinds of flours and cooked on griddles, and their stuffed cousins, sometimes fried, sometimes wrapped in leaves and steamed; braises served with rice and often accompanied by some kind of fried plantain; and rice prepared with legumes or meats.

As much as these foods constitute a Caribbean or Antillean palate, cookbook writers tend to generalize them with the adjective "creole," probably the most polyvalent term on which I rely. Its significance varies over time and refers at moments simultaneously to quite distinct things, signifies differently when applied to people, language, music, food, and so on. It translates almost homonymically as criollo/a in Spanish, créole in French, and kreyòl in Kreyòl. It is also used in the United States to designate the food of Louisiana, and especially New Orleans, that emerges out of and in conversation with the same histories that mark the Caribbean (some argue that Louisiana belongs to the Greater Caribbean or Circum-Caribbean, along with Florida, Panama, and Columbia; I make multiple connections, throughout this book, across Black diasporic foodways that run throughout the Americas). In Caribbean studies, literary theory, and philosophy since the 1980s, creoleness (créolité) and creolization (créolisation) gained traction when, as Martin Munro summarizes, Patrick Chamoiseau, Jean Bernabé, and Raphaël Confiant's *Éloge de la créolite* launched the noun créolité or creoleness to "replace essentialist racial identities with an ever-evolving *diversalité*" and Glissant's creolization nominalized the verb form to designate "a phenomenon of exchange and transformation that is indispensable to understanding the New World experience . . . posit[ing] contact and chaos, cultural relativity, exchange, and transformation as key tools in a polyvalent, process-driven system of thought" (165).[19] As I come back to the adjective to examine the distinct valences of Caribbean Creole cooks, communities, and cuisine in the following chapters, I develop more of the nuances of those uses. In broad strokes, however, all of the versions of creole in the Caribbean relate, as the etymology indicates, to a place where something is born, and particularly to indicate something that is born in the Caribbean.[20] Its first uses in the sixteenth and seventeenth centuries, applied to people, served to designate place of birth as distinct from place of ancestry, so it could designate equally someone of "pure" European heritage and someone of "pure" African heritage born in the Caribbean. By the late seventeenth century, "creole" also referred to things—including languages and people—born in the Caribbean of the mixing of any combination of African, European, and Indigenous elements. This triple usage both creates confusion and arises out of the suspicion that whatever the heritage—of a person, a language, a food—when it is born in the Caribbean, it is somehow mixed. The multiple meanings also allow the term to be taken up, in the twentieth century, in the construction of diverse national characters and qualities, as for example in the Dominican Republic under Trujillo, where "criollo" was used to include all Dominicans and vacate them of Blackness, regardless of their heritage, or in Haiti after 1946, where "kreyòl" signifies the Blackness of all Haitians, regardless of their skin color.[21]

While I read all the cookbooks here with the background of the Caribbean regional context and its creole people and foods, the articulation of a regional cuisine as such in regional cookbooks must occupy a different study. My interest here is in how, even during the colonial period, various sets of Caribbean cookbooks articulate island-specific, proto-national, and national cuisines, ones that take regional components and terms and present them as or in politically salient terms related to national independence and nationhood. In other words, I am interested in how cocina criolla is Cuban in cookbooks published in Cuba, sauce créole is Haitian in cookbooks published in Haiti, Creole Seasoning is Jamaican in cookbooks published in Jamaica, and so on.

Caribbean Cookbooks: From Culinary Colonialism to Recipes for National Independence

The overlapping concept-metaphors of the title organize the book: the first three chapters focus on culinary colonialism, and the last three on recipes for national independence. If the titular organization of the chapters of this book suggests neat progress *from* culinary colonialism *to* recipes for national independence, a chronological one troubles the progress narrative. Chronologically, the first two chapters lay out the first Caribbean cookbooks written by settler-colonialists who may also be proto-nationalists, and the last four chapters parallel one another, each charting a set of shifts and continuations of and from the colonial period through the twentieth century. These different possibilities for dividing the sections of this book, and thus understanding the relationships among the chapters, convey the multiple possibilities of doubling, enfolding, and dividing that characterize Caribbean (culinary) cultures.

It is tempting, to me at least, to try to neatly line up positions, people, and books in the Caribbean as either colonized or independent, colonialist or decolonial, heteropatriarchal or feminist, capitalist or free, but colonialism is profoundly incoherent, responsible as much for creating as for destroying the Caribbean, and resistance is as much the product as the opposite of colonialism; is often wrapped up in it, coopted by it, or engaged in repeating its moves in conscious and unconscious ways. If—as I consider in the first three chapters—culinary colonialism has destroyed local food cultures through a combination of disdain and appropriation, it has also—as I also examine in those chapters— facilitated acculturation, developed new native tastes, and preserved the traces that decolonial movements can follow to new nationalisms. Culinary colonialism breaks down and mixes up the Caribbean as we know it and is the batter from which new colonial formations and independent nations rise. Culinary colonialism and recipes for national independence together inscribe the togetherness-in-difference, the creolization, that makes up the Caribbean.

Though the grouping and ordering of the chapters in this book is not fixed, taken together in various ways they allow for a view of the togetherness-in-difference that makes up Caribbean food cultures and their inscription into cookbooks, for a sense—though not an exhaustive display—of the common flavors and distinct flares of national and regional cuisines and of recipe collectors and writers. I have arranged the chapters to suggest the tensions between narratives of progress— from colonialism to independence, from culture clash to creolization— and the realities of the unevenness of "development" across the Caribbean and in any given island trajectory.

In the second half of the nineteenth century, the first Caribbean cookbooks domesticated the naturalists' project, gathering Caribbean recipes under a universal (read: European) ordering system. As nineteenth-century Caribbean cookbooks identified, named, codified, and packaged the national cuisines of the nascent nations, they both continued European possession and control of things Caribbean and also claimed self-possession. That the self-possessed writers and readers of nineteenth-century cookbooks were members of colonial administrations, the planter class, and the merchant elite invokes the roles that those groups played in decolonization, and the ways that decolonization can take the form of a transfer of power from Europe to a Creole elite deeply invested in many aspects of European culture. Much of what is at stake in nineteenth-century Caribbean cookbooks is not only the relative value and vibrancy of "native" versus "colonial" but also who and what counts as native, Criollo, West Indian, Creole, Cubano, Puertorriqueño, Jamaican, and so on, and how those identifications do and do not overlap and intersect.

Chapter 1, "Nineteenth-Century Cocineros in Cuba and Puerto Rico," emphasizes the abundance and richness of Cuban and Puerto Rican cuisine at the crossroads of the world and discusses the cocineros' insistence that Cuba and Puerto Rico had become so developed that they no longer needed Spanish rule. At the same time, any independence that they formulated was by White or White-affiliated Criollos. Taíno, Carib, Spanish, and African dishes and culinary customs became "Puerto Rican" or "Cuban," and the "native" was reconfigured to be not "Indigenous" or Afro-Indigenous but Criollo. The men who wrote the nineteenth-century Cuban and Puerto Rican cookbooks reinforce images of Cuba and Puerto Rico as islands rich in native raw material run by powerful Criollo men who maintain domestic control independent of Spanish rule and pass on culinary knowledge to Criolla housewives. At the same time, their cookbooks abound with traces of the work of Indigenous, African-descended, and European-descended women. These traces allow for a reading of the cookbooks for the things that they try to dominate and use. At the turn of the twentieth century, elite White British and Creole women took up cookbook authorship in the British West Indies, exerting, as chapter 2 examines, "Domestic Control in West Indian Women's Cookbooks at the Turn of the Twentieth Century." Caroline Sullivan's *The Jamaica Cookery Book* (1893) codifies a set of recipes and relationships between English, Creole, and "native" women in Jamaica that acknowledges the acumen and work of Black women, inscribes culinary creolization, and asserts the organizing power of Creole women in delicate balances of racial and national interests. In increasing numbers of West Indian cookbooks in the early twentieth century, White English and Creole women negotiated the domestic space as a site where they could exercise control—over their own affiliations and tastes as well as over the people and plants whose independence they feared. They also and unavoidably inscribed traces of the many centuries and the many modes of creolization that the cookbooks of the mid-twentieth century uncover and incorporate into recipes for independence. By the early twentieth century, as the end of colonial rule in the Caribbean had become a reality in some places, the United States was rising as a neocolonial power and France was holding tight to its remaining colonies in Guadeloupe and Martinique. The cookbooks that exemplify "Colonial and Neocolonial Fortification in the French Antilles, Puerto Rico, and the U.S. Virgin Islands" (in chapter 3) vociferously engage in what Fanon calls a colonialist "defense of native style" that serves to delegitimize, stall, and bury emerging native national consciousness. Through distinct French and U.S. conceptions of "bonnes recettes" and good food, the cookbooks discussed in this chapter extend the tropes of the New World land as woman and of the kitchen as the womb of the house. Alongside these imperial family romances, however, both the French- and U.S.-Caribbean cookbooks of the early twentieth century chart the shifting places of women within colonial structures and societies, the resulting new negotiations of relations between women and across racial and ethnic divides, and the simmering of creolizations that re-cognize their Afro-Indigenous elements.

Recipes for national independence emerged throughout the twentieth century as cookbook authors sought to upend the last holds of colonial control and to (re)establish autonomous Caribbean nations and cuisines in Cuba, the Dominican Republic, Haiti, Puerto Rico, Jamaica, Barbados, and beyond. These recipes (re)inscribed native Caribbean and Creole cuisines and persons as born from mixed African, Indigenous, European, and sometimes Asian and Middle Eastern descent, both united and distinguished by their versions of rice and beans, fish, chicken, callaloo and pepperpot, plantains mashed, fried, baked, and boiled. As independence movements grew across the Caribbean, women inscribed national culinary cultures. Their focus on domestic production, local markets, and home-cooked tradition and innovation render them like the storytellers Fanon writes of who "revive [once inert episodes] and introduce increasingly fundamental changes" (174) to achieve "the awakening of national consciousness" (175). Their cookbooks belong to the "new [cultural] forms [that] are linked to the maturing of national consciousness" from which "comes the need for nationhood" (176–177). Unsurprisingly, the establishment of national cuisines is as messy as that of independent nationhood. As Fanon notes, "The liberation struggle does not restore to national culture its former values and configurations; this struggle which aims at a fundamental redistribution of relations between men, cannot leave intact either the form or the substance of the people's culture" (178). And in the Caribbean there is no single original "people's culture"; native cultures and national cultures in the Caribbean were not only reconfigured but also invented by colonial and decolonial movements. Independence-era and nation-building cookbooks elaborate the reproduction and recombination necessary to those processes of creolization, especially as it has been carried out by women in Caribbean homes.

The imprint of the culinary colonialism that I examine in the first half of this book might lead one to suspect that independence-era cookbooks remain "tools of empire" that cannot deliver proper emancipation because they extend the colonial print-economy and fail to deliver the revolutionary authenticity of the colonized's lived experience—the way that women, to return to Clarke, "really" think and learn about food: without cookbooks. Arjun Appadurai's adjacent argument, in "How to Make a National Cuisine," that cookbooks are deeply bound with the class interests of the elite and middle-class women who most often write and read them similarly assumes that "authentic" national culture is not inscribed in cookbooks. These points about the class interests and the potential loss of oral traditions and lived experience that mark independence-era cookbooks are important, but they are only part of the story. While it would be nice to be able to say that by reading independence-era cookbooks we can find how women wrote the instructions for national cultures that ended colonial rule, neither the relationship between cookbooks and independence nor that between the end of colonialism and national sovereignty is so straightforward. The blossoming of independence-era cookbooks grew out of a long process of Caribbean women taking up tools of power and control and modes of public and political representation that has always included, albeit often in tension and often without credit, the work of elite, middle-class, working class, and poor, White Creole, Afro-Indigenous, Afro-Caribbean, Indo-Caribbean, and Chinese Caribbean women. In sum, political actors, especially women, turn to, produce, and use cookbooks as tools of power and prospective control to shape the appetite for independence in ways that do more and less than simply reconfirm the binarisms of class conflict, of colonizer and colonized, print and oral cultures, or even colonial dependence and independent nationhood.

"Cuban Independence, to Taste," chapter 4 of this book, examines how, after Cuba won independence from Spain in 1898, Cuban cookbooks developed the work of their nineteenth-century criollo predecessors in three phases: anticolonial criollismo, modernization and cosmopolitanism, and the Revolutionary turn. Over the course of the twentieth century, Cuban cookbooks dished up changes brought by independence, developed a sweet cosmopolitan elite, and reoriented for perpetual revolution. These recipes for national independence show that independent nationhood with increasing women's participation can maintain the hierarchies of the colonial period and that it can continue to change with further attempts to bring to the table of power the enfolded European, Indigenous, and African flavors that nourish it and the techniques of improvisation and substitution that cooks have always used to serve it up. Although Haiti and the Dominican Republic were the first two Caribbean nations to gain independence, they did not develop cookbook cultures until the early twentieth century, when elite Dominican and Haitian women garnered domestic control under and with tides of increasingly dictatorial regimes that emerged in the wake of U.S. occupation. The Dominican and Haitian cookbooks that are the subject of chapter 5, "Dominican and Haitian (Re)Emergence," reveal how recipes for national independence can turn into dictatorship not just because of "bad actors" but because of so many convergences, co-optations, and complications of postcolonial nation formation. They also remind us that racial affiliation or descent from a previously colonized or dominated group does not determine "good" or "bad," "democratic" or "despotic." In spite of their historical parallels and their shared island, Dominican and Haitian cookbooks of the mid-twentieth century navigated and nourished ruling national tastes in very different ways and for two nearly opposing versions of the creoleness that they both embraced. In contrast to Cuba, the Dominican Republic, and Haiti, in Jamaica and Barbados cookbooks of the twentieth century trace a gentler process of continuity and change. The last chapter, "National Culture Cook-Up and Food Independence in Jamaica and Barbados," traces the culinary movement from White Creole women's community building, self-fashioning, and "defense of native style" to mid-century recipes for independent national culture and then into commitments to food independence that align local food production with local food consumption for economic, political, and nutritional benefit of Jamaicans and Barbadians, respectively, living and storing their profit and their families and their futures in Jamaica and Barbados. These cookbooks show how recipes for national independence can evolve slowly into greater degrees of autonomy and a greater embrace of a native cuisine formed from what is born together on an island in the wake of the colonial period. They instruct in picking up the traces of Blackness strewn across earlier cookbooks for reformulations of national cuisine and national culture as Afro-Caribbean. In significantly different ways in most of the Caribbean nation-states, the national cuisines were built in ways that freed them to be less beholden to the domination of all things European. In the nineteenth century and most of the twentieth century—the periods on which this book focuses—independent nationhood was the horizon of independence from colonial domination. Since the later part of the twentieth century, as the prospect of political independence has receded in places where it was never achieved, a new generation of cookbooks have posited diasporic, post-, and trans-national culinary cultures. It is a delectable array that I hope others will dig into for further study. Cookbooks are like pepperpots; for every serving someone takes out and digests, a new batch of ingredients will be added in and kept cooking.

Reading cookbooks, even reading about them, arouses—at least for me—the desire to use them in the kitchen, follow the recipes, and savor the tastes that they evoke. And the practice of engaging with cookbooks as manuals, performing as they instruct, produces the sensory learning, and enjoyment, that they promise. A recipe, as Ashanté M. Reese writes, can be an invitation to remember how we have been nourished, to feed ourselves and others, to improvise, to reclaim sweetness and pleasure, to share it with ancestors and friends. Thus, rather than just citing exemplary parts of recipes, I include many of them in full with only the formatting standardized. The selection of recipes derives from the analysis, showcasing the various ways the cookbooks instruct in how to make both classics, often designated as national dishes, and some of the more unusual, "traditional" or "innovative," formulas. Some of the recipes are likely to be recognizable and useful to anyone who wants to follow them as cooking instructions. Often, the process of making them allows the experience of some of the confusions and quirks that I analyze—that many of these recipes were not written by or for people who cooked them, and that others were written by and for people who cooked them so regularly that they needed to note only a rough outline or a special tip, that conventions of measurement and naming change, as do tastes, and that Caribbean cookbooks, colonial as much as national, are written primarily for folks cooking in the Caribbean, with access to things like fresh breadfruit and chayote, and seasonings like cassareep and culantro. Luckily, as many of their authors insist, cookbooks are general guides, kept alive by substitution, modification, and re-creation. Enjoy!

1

Nineteenth-Century Cocineros of Cuba and Puerto Rico

THE FIRST COOKBOOKS published in the Caribbean, Don Eugenio Coloma y Garcés's *Manual del cocinero cubano* (1856) and the unattributed *El cocinero puertorriqueño* (1859), imagined Cuban and Puerto Rican national cuisines a decade before leaders like Carlos Manuel Céspedes in Cuba and Ramón Emeterio Betances in Puerto Rico made their first declarations of independence and waged their first battles.[1] The *Manual del cocinero cubano*, *El cocinero puertorriqueño*, and the set of Cuban cookbooks that followed nourished a half-century of struggle that ended Spanish colonial rule, established, however briefly, independent nations, and inscribed the culinary imaginations whose foundational tropes and tastes this chapter explores. The complication at the center of these cookbooks is that they write up independent national cuisines under the control of White Criollo men who they posit as both the inheritors of Spanish power and the authors of Cuban and Puerto Rican sovereign tastes.

Cuban and Puerto Rican cookbooks of the second half of the nineteenth century reinforce colonialist images of Cuba and Puerto Rico as islands rich in native raw material and in need of oversight and control by European or European-descended men. They assert that each island has a distinct culture, different from one another and from the Spanish, and they suggest that Cuba and Puerto Rico have become so developed that they may no longer need Spanish rule. They constitute a

33

confluence of Spanish, Taíno, Carib, and African dishes and culinary customs as "native," asserting that it is not just a mixture of things from elsewhere but that it is local. However, as they overwhelmingly emphasize Spanish ancestry and lineage, they whiten this mixed lineage. They offer, in other words, Puerto Rican and Cuban distinctions that result from the coming together of the Indigenous, African, and European in Caribbean geography and that result in new cultures, perhaps new nations, where European-derived domination remains intact, as if naturally. These cookbooks exemplify that stage of colonialism Franz Fanon describes in which the colonialist and the "native intellectual" agree that colonial culture is superior, but in the settler-colonial situation, that Fanon does not consider, the colonizer is replaced by the White Criollo who sees himself as both native and distributor of a superior culture whose origin elsewhere is supplemented by the benefits from here that it has taken in, ameliorated, and can now redistribute. The cookbooks offer, thus, what Édouard Glissant calls "hybrid cultures" that are not "cultures of hybridity." These cookbooks, written by men, show how very little power anyone other than Spanish and White Criollo men wielded even in the semi-private sphere of cookbook writing. At the same time, they abound with traces of the work of Indigenous, African-descended, and European-descended women. These traces allow us to read the cookbooks for the things that they try to dominate and use. They allow us to read how hard the cookbooks work to maintain Spanish-derived Criollo predominance that is both local and White, belying the naturalness of the order that the cookbooks assert.

By the mid-eighteenth century, Cuba was known as the "jewel of the Caribbean." Massive sugar plantations, run on slave labor, operated across the large island, and Havana's highly developed urban infrastructure supported profitable sugar exports as well as a vibrant urban population. Puerto Rico, Spain's other remaining Caribbean colony, had in contrast a smaller set of sugar plantations worked by a smaller slave population, more economic and agricultural diversity, more small farmers, and more Indigenous communities than Cuba. On both islands, Spain ran the government and the military and profited, primarily via taxes, off the plantations and related industries that were generally run by White Criollos, often from families with generations of local residence. Many from this powerful White Criollo elite sought in various ways to shed, transform, and control colonial structures, working for changes to Spanish rule that generally kept them in power even as they also might end slavery, integrate elite Mulattos[2] into their ranks, and ally with Black Criollos, enslaved and free.[3] The growing independence movements depended on efforts of slaves, free Black Criollos, and Mulattos, both separate from and alongside those White Criollos, as well as on the peasant farmers of a mix of races—siterios in Cuba and jíbaros in Puerto Rico—who literally and figuratively fed the nascent national projects.[4] However, the White Criollo plantation owners, functionaries, and urban elite rarely acknowledged their dependance on anyone else. It is from and for this group of White Criollos that the first cookbooks were written.

Nineteenth-century Cuban and Puerto Rican cookbooks include recipes for vast numbers of Afro-Indigenous dishes alongside Spanish ones, use local names for local ingredients, and inscribe the profoundly creolized and distinctly Caribbean cuisine of the islands. However, as they establish the existence, legitimacy, and distinction of Cuban and Puerto Rican culinary cultures, they present them in the possession and under the control of White Criollo men.[5] They do not mention the Indigenous or African histories of the foods, let alone the slaves, free Blacks, and Mulattos who developed the recipes and probably cooked and served them to the writers. As Efraín Barradas writes, these cookbooks are "the product of a literate society that wants to systemize and control its entire world" (275). The systematization and vision of Cuba, Puerto Rico, and their places in the world in nineteenth-century cookbooks enacts dominant narratives and contains subordinate stories. These are distinctly and proudly Criollo, marked by all the specifications of geography and history that include Indigenous, African, slavery and plantation cultures, albeit unacknowledged. The writers' identities—White and male—underline and reify that power in both colonial and independence-era Cuba and Puerto Rico is White and patriarchal. Their Cuban and Puerto

Rican cuisines enact culinary colonialism as they appropriate and subsume Afro-Indigenous foods and recipes under White Criollo order, but the derivation can itself resist colonial rule and emplace new, and what Fernando Ortiz would later call transculturated, Criollo orders.[6]

This chapter takes the histories of authors, islands, and books as frames for the close reading of narrative sections; of selection, organization, and order of recipes; and of titles, lexicons, and instructions of and in those recipes. It starts with who writes what and for whom and then moves into what is written. Eugenio Coloma y Garcés exemplifies Spanish and White Criollo proto-nationalism in both his biography and his political, cultural, and culinary attachments. The distinctions between his *Manual del cocinero cubano* and *El cocinero puertorriqueño* reveal how even under the single hand of White Criollo control, proto-national differences between Cuba and Puerto Rico are recognized, or put in place. An investigation of authorship and authority after Coloma y Garcés introduces new information about other cookbooks and authors and demonstrates how much they share with one another and with Coloma y Garcés. A turn to audience shifts attention from male authorship to female readership. Finally, an examination of the treatment of "lo criollo" highlights the imbrications of race with gender, authorship, authority, taste, and conceptions of the Cuban and the Puerto Rican in nineteenth-century cookbooks. The inaugural positions and moves of these cookbooks, and my study of them, become the points of comparison for the extension of European and White Criollo control through culinary colonialism and for the stirrings of proto-nationalism and traces of Afro-Indigenous identifications that rise back up in recipes for national independence.

Cuban and Puerto Rican Coincidence: Eugenio Coloma y Garcés

Among Caribbean cookbooks, the *Manual del cocinero cubano* and *El cocinero puertorriqueño* have received relatively significant attention. *El cocinero puertorriqueño* has remained well known to the Puerto Rican cookbook-reading public and is widely acknowledged as the first Puerto Rican cookbook. Complicating the idea of the *Manual del cocinero cubano* and *El cocinero puertorriqueño* as articulating, respectively, Cuban and Puerto Rican national cuisines, is Barradas's 2010 discovery that they are different editions of the same text.[7] Barradas astutely argues that, rather than discrediting the cookbooks as articulations of national culture, their coincidence reveals a shared Cuban and Puerto Rican project of differentiation, and distancing, from the Spanish: "Boricua [Puerto Rican] and Cuban communities of the time relied on Coloma's manual to define their cuisine and thus to define themselves as a community distinct from that of the metropolis, Spain" (277). Nonetheless, the question of the identification of the author of these, or this, cookbook(s), Eugenio Coloma y Garcés, exposes complexities of various forms of culinary colonialism, independence, and nationhood, and complications of authorship, attribution, and acknowledgment that persist in formulations of sovereignty and affiliation and in practices of opaque duplication and reproduction of these and other Caribbean cookbooks from the nineteenth century through the present.

Eugenio Coloma y Garcés was probably born in Cádiz, Spain, around 1812. His parents, the Cantabrian Pedro Coloma Partearroyo and the Portuguese María de la Paz Garcés y Muñoz, both had strong ties to Cuba, and the family moved there when Coloma y Garcés was young. Though little is known about his education and early career, he was raised in Cuba and lived there his entire adult life. He must have worked in the Spanish colonial government in Cuba, for his first publication was the 1853 *Manual de práctica pedánea*, advertised as a governance manual with a focus on bureaucracy: "useful to captains and party leaders, as it has the way to proceed in criminal cases, fill out orders and create dossiers, documents, wills, official correspondence, how to maintain an archive with a form for what can be offered" (cited in José María de la Torre, 181). Coloma y Garcés's position in the colonial government meant he was involved in the complicated end of the slave trade in Cuba. His second publication was an *Indispensable and Necessary Appendix for Rural Governance that contains the ways to act in a complicated case in the disembarcation of African slaves [Apendice necesario e indispensable para la práctica pedánea, que contiene el modo de actuar en una causa complicada en desembarco de negros bozales]*, which probably refers to the famous last slave ship to arrive in Cuba, in 1854, more than thirty years after the official end of the slave trade in the Spanish colonies, but still more than thirty years before the end of slavery in Cuba.

Coloma y Garcés took to writing manuals, publishing at least eight more, on a variety of topics that, like his cookbook(s), instruct in how to carry out specific tasks and how to carry oneself in the execution of those tasks. The first edition of *El Manual del cocinero cubano* appeared in 1856, signed with the author's initials, E. de C. y G; the second edition, published in 1857, bore his full name. No publisher is listed for either edition of the *Manual del cocinero cubano*. *El cocinero puertorriqueño* appeared without naming an author or a publisher in a first edition in 1859, in a second edition of which nothing remains beyond the fact of its existence, and in a third edition published in 1890 by the Puerto Rican publishing house Acosta without listing an author.[8] Neither publishers' records nor Coloma y Garcés's personal papers appear to have survived, and so it is not at all clear what role Coloma y Garcés had in the Puerto Rican editions, or if he even knew of them.[9]

Coloma y Garcés's works paint a picture of a man deeply invested in rural governance, agriculture, and education as well as in domestic life. His focus on rural bureaucracy and management aligns him more with the interests of the pro-independence White Criollos than with those of Spain and the large-scale sugar planters who were most invested in maintaining Spanish rule. He must have spent important amounts of time outside of Havana and had ample opportunity to be in contact with the dishes served not only in elite urban homes and hotels but also on ranches and plantations of various sizes and types. It is not clear if Coloma y Garcés ever married or had children. He dedicated several of his books to "Cuban women," with a typical combination of reverence and paternalism for "the weaker sex" whom he set out to praise and to help. He must have been aware also of the power and influence of some women in nineteenth-century Cuba, for he had a special edition of his home economics manual bound with a dedication to the Condesa de San Antonio (Antonia María Micaela Domínguez Borrell), a well-known political force who was born in Cuba and married to Francisco Serrano Domínguez, who was governor-general of Cuba from 1859 to 1863. Like the Condesa de San Antonio and other politically engaged women of the time, such as the novelist and abolitionist Gertrudis Gómez de Avellaneda, Coloma y Garcés recognized the imbrications of the "private" and the "public," the ways that the life of the home was related to the life of the nation, domestic management and politics being the territory of both.

Coloma y Garcés framed his interest in food as an interest in pleasure, noting in the preface to the *Manual del cocinero cubano* his conviction that "one of the pleasures of this miserable life is gastronomy." Experiencing the joys of gastronomy in a well-ordered home, set up for "the use, custom and temperament of the island of Cuba" or conforming to "the special circumstances of the Puerto Rican climate and customs" was, his titles asserted, the greatest pleasure of all. To his own question, "what greater pleasure is there that presents itself so flatteringly to the imagination as to the taste, than a table on which under a reign of order and cleanliness are found foods that look, smell, and taste delicious?," Coloma y Garcés answers: "I don't think, dear reader, that anything can surpass the sublime pleasure, not of the gastronomes who with their delicate taste know how to appreciate its merit, but even of those who, cruelly tormented and exhausted by a lack of appetite, see the door of their salvation in this charming art" (cited in Cubaencuentero). Criollo society had been characterized since the eighteenth century as one of pleasure and excess, alternatively Edenic and hedonistic. Coloma y Garcés embraces the pleasure principle, but he shows Cuba and Puerto Rico as well-organized spaces able to take care of their own physical and spiritual needs.

Coloma y Garcés's authorship exemplifies the paradoxical culinary colonialism of the nineteenth century in which the Criollo elite both carried and interrupted colonial rule; both represented and mistreated "native" Cuban and Puerto Rican foods and peoples. The close readings of recipe titles, ingredients, and instructions that follow reveal how his cookbooks convey White Criollo patriarchal proto-nationalisms that contain the Afro-Indigenous traces and women's work on which their distinctions—from Spain and from one another—rely. In other words, how as cookbooks serve the White Criollo extension or takeover of colonial orders they also carry other voices, other views.

Puerto Rican Differentiation

The claiming and repackaging of things Caribbean for the benefit of persons European is one of the primary modes of colonialism. Assertion of local identification, of distinct and autonomous culture, is in contrast one of the primary acts and demands of independence. Thus, to consider how these cookbooks represent extensions of colonial control and moves toward independence, we must examine the distinction between *Manual del cocinero cubano* and *El cocinero puertorriqueño*, the degree to which their difference represents claiming by naming, with local titles slapped onto dishes pell-mell, or demonstrates attention to culinary autonomy, local configurations of race and racialization, and regional coincidence.

While *El cocinero puertorriqueño* coincides vastly with the *Manual del cocinero Cubano,* the insular identity of the titular cook is prominently different. Similarly, the recipe titles in each cookbook name Cuba or Puerto Rico and Cuban or Puerto Rican cities, towns, and regions, respectively. But as much as it is clearly a version of the *Manual del cocinero cubano*, *El cocinero puertorriqueño* is not just the same cookbook with "Puerto Rican" in place of "Cuban" throughout. The organization of the recipes is slightly different. The Puerto Rican cookbook does not have every recipe that the Cuban does, and it has some recipes that the Cuban version does not. In those differences we can see assertions of distinct Cuban and Puerto Rican proto-national culinary cultures. In Puerto Rico, *El cocinero puertorriqueño* was the only cookbook published in the nineteenth century; its distinctions from the *Manual del cocinero cubano* represent the only inscription of a national cuisine until after the island gained, and lost, independence. So, while I will delve into the details of the Cuban cuisine of the *Manual del cocinero cubano* alongside those of the several Cuban cookbooks that quickly followed it later in this chapter, I start here with a consideration of how the distinctions of *El cocinero puertorriqueño* establish the distinction of a Puerto Rican proto-national cuisine that is linked to and different from the Cuban. From a detailed accounting of sections, titles, and recipes that are specific to *El cocinero puertorriqueño* emerges a picture of a Puerto Rican culinary culture with deep regional links to Cuba, marked by but only obliquely acknowledging its African Indigenous heritage, under White Criollo control and serving (up) the powerful sugar industry that feeds that control.

One hundred and two recipe titles change between the *Manual del cocinero cubano* and *El cocinero puertorriqueño*, while the recipes themselves remain the same. Of these, eighty-one drop or change a Cuban location from the corresponding recipe title in the *Manual del cocinero cubano*.[10] The majority simply omit location all together in the new title, and most others change a Cuban location for a variation on "country style [del país]," "peasant [campesino]," or "criollo." Cuban food and Puerto Rican food share a regional link to land, people, and the criollo, and at the same time, these changes suggest, to name something specifically Cuban or Puerto Rican matters. The small number of recipe titles in *El cocinero puertorriqueño* that replace a Cuban location with a Puerto Rican location might indicate that whoever made the changes had the idea of Puerto Rican specificity but did not know or care enough to name very many Puerto Rican locations. However, while less frequent, other changes assert knowledge of and attention to Puerto Rican culinary specificity that clarify *El cocinero puertorriqueño*'s work to not simply position Cuba and Puerto Rico as two interchangeable islands or to repackage Cuban cuisine for Puerto Rican cooks, but to lay out a distinct Puerto Rican culinary culture. Fifteen recipe titles in the Puerto Rican cookbook replace a Cuban food word with a Puerto Rican one, and *El cocinero puertorriqueño* adds fourteen new dishes, many of which were particularly popular in Puerto Rico. In the Puerto Rican soup

> ### *Sopa puertorriqueña o puré paradisiaco*
> ### (Puerto Rican Soup, or Paradisiac Puree)
>
> *Lávese perfectamente con limón y agua de sal el plátano verde de mejor calidad. Córtesele en rajaditas tan delgadas como la hoja del cuchillo. Lávense esta del mismo modo que el plátano, y divídaselas en 6 u 8 partes cada una. Hecho esto, se ponen estas partecitas en una cazuela o sartén con manteca muy caliente, y se remueven continuamente hasta que estén bien tostadas, pero sin quemarse. Así calientes se ponen en la sopera, y agregándolas al caldo consumado se sirve en la mesa.*
>
> Perfectly wash with lemon and salted water the best-quality green plantain. Cut it in slices as thin as the blade of the knife. Wash these in the same manner as the plantain and divide them each into 6 or 8 parts. This done, put these parts in a casserole or pan with very hot lard and turn them continuously until they are well toasted but not burnt. Put them in the tureen while hot and adding them to the broth serve them at the table.
>
> —EL COCINERO PUERTORRIQUEÑO, 17

section, for example, in addition to all of the recipes in the Cuban cookbook, albeit in a different order, are a first recipe for "Sopa puertorriqueña o puré paradisiaco" and a last recipe for "Sopa de tortuga o de la Isla de Mona," neither of which is in the Cuban cookbook. Along with adding Puerto Rican place names—Isla de Mona is a smaller island that is part of Puerto Rico—these distinguish Puerto Rico as paradisiacal and as home to a delicacy, sea turtles. Of course, both of these enhance the Edenic stereotype, making use of local ingredients in a way that plays up and plays to culinary colonialism. As much as they served in 1859 to distinguish Puerto Rican from Cuban cuisine, these recipes did so by uplifting Puerto Rico as just as well fit as Cuba to a colonialist Caribbean trope; unsurprisingly, these two soups have not persisted as classic Puerto Rican dishes.

However, in the section on plantains, the additional recipe in the Puerto Rican cookbook is "Mofongo criollo," which remains not only one of the classic dishes of Puerto Rico but also one that represents the

> ### *Mofongo criollo* (Creole Mofongo)
>
> *Se toma una libra de ternera, un cuarterón de gallina, un pedazo de tocineta y otro de jamón. Después de lavado, se pone al fuego. En seguida se limpia el caldo con una espumadera, agregándose el orégano, ajos y ají dulce, todo bien majado. Cuando haya hervido, se la agregan plátanos verdes, lavándolos antes con limón, los cuales se molerán en un mortero. Después de cocidos, se hacen grandes pelotas, a las que se les echará un poco de caldo para que no se peguen.*
>
> Take a pound of veal, a quarter of chicken, a piece of bacon and another of ham. After they are cleaned, put them on the flame. Then clean the broth with a skimmer, adding the oregano, garlic, and sweet pepper, all well mashed. When it has boiled, add green plantains, previously washed with lemon, which will be ground in a mortar. Once cooked, make big balls, to which will be added a little broth so they do not stick.
>
> —EL COCINERO PUERTORRIQUEÑO, 133

African heritage of Puerto Rican cuisine.[11] Both the word and the technique of mofongo are of African origin, and mofongo was widely recognized in the nineteenth century as a product of slave cuisine both because all green plantain dishes retained that association to a certain degree and because the name has recognizably African associations.[12] The recognition of mofongo as a Puerto Rican dish in *El cocinero puertorriqueño* solidifies its place in the national cuisine and the cookbook's place as nationally specific.

If *El cocinero puertorriqueño* marks Puerto Rican cuisine with African traces by including mofongo, it foregrounds, though it does not explicitly name, Indigenous culinary connections with changes from the Cuban cookbook in the opening section. In *Manual del cocinero cubano*, the first section of recipes is titled "First and Essential Part [Parte Primera y Esencial]" and starts with a paragraph on "broths [caldos]" and their function as a basis for both hearty stews and soups for the convalescent. *El cocinero puertorriqueño* titles its first section "Broths [Caldos], Salsas, and Stews [Guisados]" and in it calls up "atoles" first. European cookbook and meal order prescribes soups first, and a common concern of colonial Spain and Criollo planters was how to maintain health and hygiene. At the same time, boiled or braised one-pot meals are a staple of Afro-Indigenous cuisine, so this essential starting point is also one of conjunction, where European, Indigenous, and African traditions overlap. It appears to be "essential" to the *Manual del cocinero cubano* to start with a nod to a shared concern of Spaniards and White Criollos. For *El cocinero puertorriqueño*, those same broths [caldos] are neither essential nor first. The Puerto Rican cookbook starts with a single paragraph on "de los atoles" with suggestions for several different kinds of atole.[13] A Nahuatl word, "atole" draws a connection to Indigenous heritage and to Mexico—where independence from Spain was won in 1821. The atole described in the first paragraph of *El cocinero puertorriqueño*, like that in the recipes that appear later in the *Manual del cocinero cubano*, is a custard or porridge rather than the Mexican drink, marking regional if not national specificity, asserting that Puerto Rican cuisine is very much like Mexican—and thus equally ready for independence—but not the same—and thus ready for its own independence.[14]

By starting with an Indigenous connection between Puerto Rico and Mexico, the Puerto Rican cookbook positions its racial difference from Spain as one that rests on the greater Indigeneity, rather than the greater Blackness, of Puerto Ricans. *El cocinero puertorriqueño* worked not to reflect the population of Puerto Rico, but to establish a distinction from Spain that allied it with the successful former Spanish colonies in Central and South America. That Taíno and Carib culinary connections are not given pride of place—they appear throughout both cookbooks in ingredients and methods but are not recognized as such or brought to the fore in any way—makes clear that *El cocinero puertorriqueño* invests its opening with a general idea of Indigeneity rather than any effort to connect Puerto Rican foods to the first peoples of Puerto Rico or their descendants.[15]

Rounding out the prominent changes to the book's opening, the highest concentration of differences between the *Manual del cocinero cubano*

> ### *Cafiroleta* (Cafiroleta)
>
> *Se raya el coco seco, quitada la película que tiene unida a la almendra. Se echa en almíbar clara y se pone al fuego para darle punto. Luego se agrega bizcocho mojadao en vino seco, en cantidad igual a la que se empleó de coco, y yemas de huevo batidas. Se deja un poco al fuego, revolviéndolo bien. Después se echa en platos y se espolvorea con canela fina.*
>
> Grate the dried coconut, with the film around the kernel taken off. Put it in clear syrup and put it on the flame to reach the point. Then add in biscuit moistened with dry wine, in the same quantity as the coconut, and beaten egg yolks. Leave it a little on the flame, stirring it well. Then put it onto plates and dust with finely ground cinnamon.
>
> —EL COCINERO PUERTORRIQUEÑO, 221;
> MANUAL DEL COCINERO CUBANO, 252

and *El cocinero puertorriqueño* appear in the culminating desserts and sweets sections, with twenty-five recipes in the former that are not included in the latter and twenty-two in the later that are not in the former. Sweets, of course, are linked to the access to sugar and sugar byproducts. What is interesting then, given Cuba's far larger share of sugar production, is that there is not a larger difference, that for nearly every sweet recipe taken out of the Cuban for the Puerto Rican edition, one is added. Here it seems that *El cocinero puertorriqueño* is careful to keep up, to show both equality and difference. The differences are not concentrated in any one type of sweet or dessert. The Puerto Rican classic tembleque, a "jiggly" coconut pudding dusted with cinnamon, now known as the Puerto Rican dessert par excellence, does not appear in *El cocinero puertorriqueño*, though several dishes that resemble tembleque appear in both cookbooks: cafiroleta, generally considered a Cuban specialty,[16] albeit not one of the most well-known, "Pudín del país" (titled "Pudín cubano" in the Cuban), and "Natilla criolla." In contrast, the Cuban classic cusubé, a sweet often said to be of Indigenous origin because of its reliance on yuca (though the second most important ingredient, sugar, and the method, baking, were introduced during the colonial period), appears only in the *Manual del cocinero cubano*. It appears that Cuba, with a longer history of sweets, enshrined its specialties earlier and while Puerto Rican sweets were well enough developed to easily match Cuban sweets in volume, its classics were not yet recognized. Tembleque either had not yet been "invented" or was not yet recognized as a dish worth including in a cookbook,[17] not even one nominally focused on Puerto Rican specialties, but *El cocinero puertorriqueño* could still assert that Puerto Rico had its own sweets and desserts, its own service from and for its own sugar industry that, while smaller than the Cuban, was being steadily developed through the concerted efforts of plantation owners and the milling industry.[18]

My close readings of these cookbooks expose rather than resolve the multiple implications of the differences between the *Manual del cocinero cubano* and *El cocinero puertorriqueño*, for some distinctions, while hard to disentangle, are best considered by closely tracking the words, their associations, and the ways that they are, or are not, prioritized.

What manifests overall is less any pointed distancing from Cuban cuisine—*El cocinero puertorriqueño* does not eliminate recipes for things like the ajiaco that, at least later, symbolizes Cubanness—than an embrace of a set of distinctively Puerto Rican dishes. While the distinction follows from as much as it is recorded by the Puerto Rican cookbook, *El cocinero puertorriqueño*'s consistent use of distinctly Puerto Rican vegetable names—for example, tayote and batata for what is in Cuba chayote and boniato—suggests that the cookbook holds up, inscribes, and renders important distinctions that precede its existence.

El cocinero puertorriqueño begins to articulate the contours of Puerto Rican national culinary culture, tied to Puerto Rican locations, words, icons, and histories. It does this not by resuscitating a precolonial native culture of Puerto Rico, as Fanon calls for in Algeria and West Africa, but by inscribing the particular qualities, characters, and ideas of Puerto

Rican cuisine that have come together under Spanish control over nearly three centuries of settler colonialism. The distinctions I have drawn out from *El cocinero puertorriqueño* show how closely one has to read in order to see the traces of African and Indigenous foodways even when they constitute some of the most significant changes that the book makes from its Cuban predecessor to set up Puerto Rican specificity. *El cocinero puertorriqueño* does not present a Glissantian culture of hybridity that could "save us from the limitations of the intolerances that lie in wait" (*Treatise*, 7), for it is like the *Manual del cocinero cubano* an example of how colonial and White Criollo men work to keep their own control in and over the mixes that they describe. Under colonial and White Criollo control, a hybrid culinary culture is an exotic possession. However, it is also a manifestation of the traces that mark "one of the places of survival" for Indigenous and African heritages through the violence of conquest and slavery (*Treatise*, 9). If, as Glissant says, "the trace goes into the land, which will never again be a territory" (*Treatise*, 10), it readies the ground for further decolonization and creolization. And the traces of food are furthermore the traces of women, of Indigenous, African, and also European descent.

After 1859, in Puerto Rico the characteristics and distinction of *El cocinero puertorriqueño* became reified in subsequent editions and in the absence of any other cookbooks. *El cocinero puertorriqueño*, by the start of the next major push for independence a century later, remained *the* Puerto Rican national cookbook.[19] That Puerto Rican women continued to use *El cocinero puertorriqueño* for the next century indicates how they preserved those traces even as they continued to be largely excluded from publishing not only under Spanish colonial and White Criollo rule but also under the U.S. control that would take over in 1898. In the hands of the women who continue to use it, the cookbook distinguished by traces became itself a trace of a proto-national moment in Puerto Rico. In contrast, in Cuba a relative explosion of cookbooks manifested competing, evolving, and compounding visions of Cuban national culture in the second half of the nineteenth century.

Authorship, Authority, and Authenticity after Coloma y Garcés?

Coloma y Garcés's biography, in combination with the selection of recipes in both the *Manual del cocinero cubano* and *El cocinero puertorriqueño*, leads Barradas to conclude that while his book is "an anthology of typically Cuban recipes" along with "others taken from European cookbooks of the period," it was "others who tried to define the Antillean through more authentic collections of gastronomic traditions, for the Cuban cookbooks published after *Manual del cocinero cubano* are more true to the national reality than the former" (276; 273–274). But those who wrote the cookbooks that followed Coloma y Garcés's were from similar backgrounds as he and recorded quite similar recipes, all privileging European heritage and control while relying on, without acknowledging, Afro-Indigenous knowledge and production. Rather than proving that they too were inauthentic, however, their similarities to Coloma y Garcés and his work beg the inclusion of elite White Criollos in a concept of Cuban authenticity and a reading of their and Coloma y Garcés's work for the traces of multiple voices and views that they contain.

In Cuba, five cookbooks followed *El manual del cocinero cubano* in the nineteenth century: J. P. Legran's 1857(?) *Nuevo manual del cocinero cubano y español*;[20] Juan Cabrisas's 1858 *Nuevo manual de la cocinera catalana y cubana*; the unattributed 1862 *El cocinero de enfermos convalecientes y desganados*;[21] *Cocinera económica de la Señora Winslow o sean instrucciones de la manera de preparar diversos platos al estitulo [sic] español*, published in the 1860s or 1870s in Boston (figure 1.1); and J. F. Noviatur's 1891 *Novísimo manual del cocinero pastelero dulcero y licorista cubano*. To complicate matters, while the *Nuevo manual del cocinero cubano y español* and the *Nuevo manual de la cocinera catalana y cubana* are entirely distinct cookbooks, both from one another and from Coloma y Garcés's, the other three cookbooks are composed nearly entirely of selections from the *Manual del cocinero cubano*. The prologue to *El cocinero de enfermos convalecientes y desganados* resembles so closely that of Coloma y

Garcés's other works, and so clearly draws together his particular combination of concerns about management, good health, and good taste, that it is highly likely that in 1862 that book was readily recognized in Cuba as his own selection from the *Manual del cocinero cubano*. Winslow and Noviatur, on the other hand, claim authorship of Coloma y Garcés's work, though the *Novísimo manual del cocinero pastelero dulcero y licorista cubano* does have a new section on "licores," new recipes for ice creams, and new preservation methods that are Noviatur's own additions.[22] Biographical details for Legran, Cabrisas, and Winslow are even more scarce and far more contradictory than for Coloma y Garcés, but they, along with the more voluminous information on Noviatur, do concur on one thing: these men and woman were, each in their own way, as elite and foreign in Cuba as Coloma y Garcés. Cuban culinary authenticity through the end of the nineteenth century, these cookbooks show, is authored and packaged by European and White Criollo men and an American woman. Europeans, White Criollos, and Americans were working to establish their places as authentic producers of a Cuban proto-national culture. By authoring Cuban cookbooks, they asserted that their commercial and social power, in Cuba or elsewhere, along with their care for the Cuban raw materials to which they applied their skill, entitled them to the leading role in distinguishing, modernizing, and leading Cuba.

Rita De Maeseneer identifies Legran, author of *Nuevo manual del cocinero cubano y español,* as French (29), as does D. Jacomé, who specifies that Legran owned a restaurant in Havana. Jeffrey Pilcher concurs that Legran was "a chef at a Havana restaurant" (27). Jorge Méndez Rodríguez-Arencibia identifies Legran as a Spaniard living in Havana. Christine Folch gives Legran's first name as José (209). The discrepancies point both to the difficulty of finding historical documentation of nineteenth-century Cuba and to the complexity of the question of what it means to "be" Spanish or French or Cuban in Cuba in the mid-nineteenth century. Many from the French colonial elite came to Cuba fleeing the Haitian Revolution at the turn of the nineteenth century, "Spanish-Americans" immigrated to Cuba from the Spanish colonies in Central and South America in large volumes in the early nineteenth century as those colonies were gaining independence, and Spanish- and Cuban-born elite families moved between the island and the peninsula with some regularity.[23] Whatever his background, Legran focuses his *Nuevo manual del cocinero cubano y español* on "Cuban and Spanish" cooking, addressing himself in the subtitle "to all the classes of society, and in particular to gastronomes, mothers, innkeepers, etc." and touting in the preface his "experience and study" in the field.

The front cover of Cabrisas's *Nuevo manual de la cocinera catalana y cubana* offers the only biographical information available about him. It makes one thing clear: he was the "former chef of the Tres Reyes Inn." Presumably, this inn was in Havana and named for the "Castillo de los Tres Reyes del Morro" that guards the entrance of Havana Bay.[24] De Maeseneer and Beatriz Calvo Peña, drawing from Cabrisas's titular reference to Catalan and Cuban cooks, refer to him as a Catalonian. Cabrisas is indeed a Catalonian surname; by the early nineteenth century there were Cabrisases well established among the Criollo community in Cuba, as well as throughout Latin America. In his introduction, Cabrisas writes of his knowledge of European and Cuban tastes, offering instructions to cooks on how to maintain proper cleanliness and etiquette in a kitchen equipped for banquets and fine dining. With biographies and titles tying themselves and Cuba to Europe, Legran and Cabrisas's cookbooks foreground Cuban contributions (wealth and interest) but not Cuban independence from Spain. They represent the European and White Creole men's construction of a Cuba that needs them.

The most curious authorship of a nineteenth-century Cuban cookbook, and one that has not, to date, been noted, is that of Mrs. Charlotte N. Winslow (see figure 1.1). Born Charlotte Newman Noyes on January 17, 1789, after she married she lived in Freedom, Maine, worked as a nurse, and in the late 1840s collaborated with her son-in-law, Jeremiah Curtis, and Benjamin A. Perkins of Bangor, Maine, to market Mrs. Winslow's Soothing Syrup. From the 1860s through the 1870s, Jeremiah Curtis & Sons and John I. Brown & Sons of Boston published

Nineteenth-Century Cocineros of Cuba and Puerto Rico   51

1.1. Advertisement and recipe in *Cocinera económica de la Señora Winslow*. Source: University of California, San Diego Library, Special Collections and Archives.

Mrs. Winslow's domestic receipt book annually. The cover of each reads, "This book will be issued Annually, with entirely New Receipts. By preserving them, and sewing them together, you will have in a few years, the best collection of Receipts in the country." But by whom and why, under the Winslow name and the Rand and Avery publishing house, a selection from the *Manual del cocinero cubano* was published as the *Cocinera económica de la Señora Winslow o sean instrucciones de la manera de preparar diversos platos al estitulo [sic] español* remains unclear. By the 1870s there was an established Cuban exile and immigrant population in New York who actively read and wrote Spanish-language publications, often on behalf of Cuban independence. Did Winslow, Curtis, Perkins, or Rand and Avery figure out that they could constitute a new audience? Did they care about profiting off the repackaged recipes or just about marketing Mrs. Winslow's products, ads for which take up as much of the cookbook as the recipes do? Did Cubans or other Spanish-speakers in Boston or New York buy *Cocinera económica de la Señora Winslow o sean instrucciones de la manera de preparar diversos platos al estitulo español*? No information on the circulation of or reactions to Mrs. Winslow's Cuban cookbook remain.[25]

More information is available for Noviatur, who was actually José Florencio Turbiano y Paula. His day job was as a primary school teacher. Under his given name as well as the anagrammatic pseudonyms Nobiatur and Nobiatur y Laplau, he published a great number of works, many focused on agriculture. Leida Fernández Prieto, in her study of nineteenth-century Cuban agricultural practices, identifies him as a Spaniard and an agricultural reformer (82, 212). His works, including his 1891 cookbook, show him to be deeply concerned about health and hygiene, particularly in response to the persistence of yellow fever in Havana in the nineteenth century.[26] His choice of pseudonym might convey a desire to associate with Frenchness, or an understanding of the Francophilia of Cuban consumers of books and recipes. Together, the works show him to a be a man active in Havana's high society, invested in the modernization of Cuba, and eager to publish voluminously, so much so that he was happy to put only his own name on a selection and expansion of Coloma y Garcés's work.

It would not be until after Cuban independence that a set of cookbooks with definitively Cuban authorship and more targeted focus on local foods would appear, and even those, as I examine in chapter 4, belong to the Criollo elite. To find Cuban and also Puerto Rican cookbooks that explicitly reject colonial influence and openly embrace Afro-Indigenous heritage and practice, readers would have to wait until the mid-twentieth century. Along with their authorship, the content of nineteenth-century Cuban cookbooks offers a proto-nationalism grounded in Europhilic elitist tastes and a strong sense of regional, local independence. Together, the *Manual del cocinero cubano*, the *Nuevo manual del cocinero cubano y español*, the *Nuevo manual de la cocinera catalana y cubana*, *El cocinero de enfermos convalecientes y desganados*, the *Cocinera económica de la Señora Winslow o sean instrucciones de la manera de preparar diversos platos al estitulo [sic] español*, and the *Novísimo manual del cocinero pastelero dulcero y licorista cubano* construct a Cuban cuisine whose distinctness they attribute most explicitly to the climate. They inscribe a Cuban cuisine by and for an elite audience in a way that belies the peasant and slave origins of many dishes. It is presented as the territory of (male) planters, politicians, and doctors but transparently made for them by slaves and servants managed by wives and housekeepers. Together, these allow for the construction of a national cuisine separate from Spanish empire, maintain a social order of White Criollo rule, and betray the power and the complexity of Afro-Indigenous work that rule contains.[27]

Readership and Use: What European and White Criollo Men Give to Women Who (They Expect to) Read and Use Nineteenth-Century Cuban Cookbooks

As they establish the public nature of national cuisine, Coloma y Garcés's cookbooks address men, in the tradition of manuals for government agents and farmers that Coloma y Garcés also wrote. The prologue to *El cocinero puertorriqueño* speaks to an "intellectual reader [lector sesudo]" who "will remember sometimes with pleasure, those moments spent among four friends, at times in the sheltering dining room of an inn, at times under the friendly shade of a laden mango or along the shores of a softly murmuring crystalline stream," a freedom of association and movement and, especially in the inn, set of locations markedly masculine. Legran's *Nuevo manual del cocinero cubano y español* similarly addresses male diners and inn owners, with a nod to mothers sandwiched between the two as it asserts that the book is "indispensable for teaching to cook with the greatest perfection and necessary economy to all classes of society, and in particular gastronomes, mothers, innkeepers, &etc."

Cuban cookbooks written by European and White Criollo men lay out a male and public knowledge that they impart. As they do this, they lay out the places of women: the elite White Criolla women to whom they speak, if primarily to instruct as their weaker helpmeets, and the other women whom they speak of, primarily as the possessions and responsibilities of the Criolla women they speak to. In these instructions and degrees of recognition, we can see how elite Criollo men thought of and treated women of various races, while in their choices and work with the recipes we can see how they constructed and viewed the value and relationship among things of European and other origins in the Caribbean more generally.

Beyond inns and other professional kitchens, most cooking belonged to the domestic sphere of women and their servants, and thus most of the cookbooks to some degree also addressed women and their servants as their readers and users. The subtitle of *El cocinero puertorriqueño* specifies that "this book, which has all that is select from the most popular treatises on the art of cooking, is the first of its kind to be published in this country, and is of the greatest utility to housewives and to all who are interested in preserving their health." On the back of Coloma y Garcés's 1863 *Catecismo de agricultura cubana* an advertisement for the *Manual del cocinero cubano* announces that "this work is recommended to mothers so that they can keep their tables always varied with dishes well-seasoned to the tastes of this country; which they can achieve by reading to the cook how to season the dish that they want." The *Nuevo manual de la cocinera catalana y cubana* feminizes the "cocinera," underlining and distinguishing from the maleness of the cocineros of the other works.

Elite White Criolla women are addressed by these cookbooks in their roles as wives and mothers; other women are addressed through the former as their servants and staff. Cabrisas's *Nuevo manual de la cocinera catalana y cubana* offers an entire section on the selection and management of kitchen staff, from the "qualities that a good cook should have"—"first of all a good cook should be patient and friendly . . . secondly, active and diligent, . . . finally clean and meticulous" (7)—to the rules for "cleanliness of the cook," "cleanliness of the kitchen," and "cleanliness of the kitchen utensils"(8). The authorial assertion of knowledge about and concern for hygiene and order depict the cook as needing instruction in such basics as to put on an apron in order to keep one's clothing clean while cooking, and the reader as needing instruction in instructing the cook about the same (8). Perhaps many portions of the cookbook are intended for the woman of a house to read to her kitchen staff, but the prefatory material offers no direct recognition of such a role and instead bundles mistress and cook into one body in need of instruction from a higher (male) authority. This paternalistic address to women also appears in Legran's remarks on language: "We write for the people and we speak to them in their language." This may be a reclamation of Cuban vernacular, but it is framed as offering simple material to a simple audience, "a composition that is in its essence easy to understand." Whatever uses these cookbooks had in private and in public, their framing mechanisms, from dish titles to prefatory material, construct an image of a rich Cuba run by powerful White men who paternalistically appreciate and care for the "natives" and women who make their tables distinct. *El cocinero de los enfermos*'s "dedication to mothers" addresses women more directly, and constrains women to service, rendering them the "sweet" purveyors of the author's knowledge. The prologue concludes "if all this, seasoned and well condimented, is accompanied by the sweet assistance of a good mother or an adored wife, will not the convalescence of the sick be enjoyable? To mothers, thus, this book is dedicated: receive it with the refined benevolence that distinguishes, and my efforts to please will be recompensed" (viii). The desire to address and please women is wrapped up in the desire for the satisfaction of the (male) author who can expect to be graciously served his own medicine.

The grammar of instruction in these cookbooks further positions the reader as a passive vehicle. Nineteenth-century Spanish-language recipes use the "impersonal *se*" rather than the imperative, so that instead of telling the reader what to do, they describe what is done.[28] This reinforces the codifying force of the cookbooks: they offer instruction less in the form of a teacher addressing a student and more in the form of an explanation of tradition, indeed because the impersonal *se* creates a subjectless sentence, it works not by showing what one should do or even what one does but by making the doing independent of any doer, a tradition so established that subject-intervention does not matter.[29] In as much as an author composes the sentences with the impersonal *se*, he is the authority asserting the action as tradition.[30]

The overwhelming authority and control of the White Spanish and Criollo authors of these cookbooks is, however, undermined by the vagueness, and often the strangeness, of the recipes themselves. These are not recipes that could be followed by someone who does not already know the dishes and if not how to cook them exactly at least how to cook quite well in general. Like most nineteenth-century recipes, the ones in these cookbooks rarely list volumes or times, often refer to "spices" in general, and regularly call for steps to be completed previously or separately that are not detailed anywhere else in the cookbook. Furthermore, many of the Cuban cookbooks include instructions that are at the least unusual and probably incorrect. Legran's *Nuevo manual del cocinero cubano y español* promises that it is "written from experience and intelligible to all," but even it has recipes like the one for "Malanga á la Criolla" that omits instructions to peel a malanga before cooking it or proportions of malanga to egg and spices. This fits with the fact that the motherly audience is likely and expected to oversee and order the cooking more than to complete it herself, and thus in some ways reveals the cookbooks' reliance on the knowledge of cooks (and obliquely affirms that knowledge). However, the introductions that place the author as the holder of knowledge and the reader as the innocent and uninformed vessel do not set up the kind of space for the sharing of information and building of community among elite women and cooks that emerges in the turn-of-the-century cookbooks from Jamaica, Barbados, Grenada, Guyana, and Trinidad and Tobago that I examine in chapter 2.

The strangeness of a number of the recipes might lead any reader who actually tried to follow them to question the authors' knowledge

> ### *Malanga á la Criolla* (Creole Malanga)
>
> *Se toman malangas, que se pondrán primero á asar, machacándolas en seguida en el mortero. Después se les pone manteca, perejil picado y anis con huevos batidos; se revuelven bien y se agrega un poco de canela, poniéndose á freir después de hecho una pasta, dándosele la figura que se quiera.*
>
> Take malangas that are first put to cook, then mashed in a mortar. Then, add lard, chopped parsley and anis with beaten eggs; mix well and add a little cinnamon, putting them to fry after they have been made into a paste, giving them the shape that is desired.
>
> —LEGRAN, *NUEVO MANUAL DEL COCINERO CUBANO Y ESPAÑOL*, 69

and authority. Coloma y Garcés's and Cabrisas's recipes for "Olla cubana" and Legran's recipe for "Olla cubana o ajiaco," for example, expressly instruct not to peel plantain before adding it to the pot and do not mention peeling it later, where nearly every twentieth-century recipe for ajiaco and other soups and stews that call for cooked plantain instructs, often with great detail as to how, to peel the plantain before adding it.[31]

This strangeness also underlines another aspect of the address: these cookbooks are less focused on teaching anyone how to cook or on sharing recipes than they are on establishing the knowledge of the authors and the field of study: Cuban food. They delineate the character and qualities of Cuban cuisine for political as much as for culinary use. That they use the culinary shows a deep understanding of the roles of the domestic in the nation, of the need to have not just political but emotional and cultural engagement, and that they understand Cuban independent culture to have its own tastes. When White Creole women take up cookbook writing in the British West Indies at the turn of the twentieth century, as the next chapter shows, they assert the role of women in this domestic formation of proto-national tastes. As they, too,

> ### *Olla cubana o ajiaco* (Cuban Pot or Ajiaco)
>
> *Póngase agua en una cazuela, la suficiente para contener carne salada, ahuja de puerco, carne de vaca, tocineta y tasajo de vaca; póngase á hervir todo junto con garbanzos puestos á remojar desde el día anterior; añádase después boniato, dos o tres plátanos que empiecen á madurar, sin pelarlos, malanga, yuca chayote, berenjenas, y si se quiere una mazorca de maíz verde, calabaza y unas papas, se deja que hierva como uno hora, tritúrese en el mortero toda clase de especias, sin que falte comino que es muy esencial; deslíese con un poco de caldo del mismo ajiaco, mójese un poco de azafran, el cual, revuelto con un poco de zuma se echará dentro, dejandole hervir por un cuarto de hora. Cualquiera clase de sopas puede hacerse con este caldo, siendo muy gustosa la hecha con sémola.*
>
> Put water in a pot, enough to hold salt meat, pork, beef, bacon, and dried beef; boil it with garbanzos that have been soaking since the previous day; later add boniato, two or three plantains that are beginning to ripen, unpeeled, malanga yuca, chayote, eggplant, and if desired a green cob of corn, calabaza, and some potatoes, let it boil for about an hour, crush in a mortar all kinds of spices, without leaving out cumin which is very essential, loosen with a little broth from the same ajiaco, wet a little saffron, which, mixed with a little peel will be thrown in, leaving it to boil for a quarter of an hour. Any kind of soup can be made with this broth, especially tasty is that made with semolina.
>
> —LEGRAN, *NUEVO MANUAL DEL COCINERO CUBANO Y ESPAÑOL*, 17

write cookbooks they and their readers are not likely to cook from themselves, they also remind that as women claim places in power they often do so in ways that do not change, or that even reify, racial orders.

A lo criollo: Tracing Racialization in Nineteenth-Century Cuban Cookbooks

For nineteenth-century Cubans of European ancestry, Criollo was more important than "White" to assert that ancestry, for "White" legally included people of fully European, Indian, Mestizo (Spanish and

Indian), and some Asian ancestry, as well as Mulattos with a fully White paternal line and at least four generations from their Black maternal line (Sarmiento Ramírez, "Cuba," 115). At the same time, the Europeanness of those Criollos was understood to be attenuated by their birthplace, both because of suspicions about how frequently Europeans had secret sexual encounters with people of other descent in the Caribbean, and because of ideas about how things like climate and food could affect the body. An 1865 editorial in the prominent Cuban agriculturalist newspaper *El Siglo*, for example, argued that the wheat tariffs imposed by Spain were leading to an increased consumption of "viandas" (provisions) that would in turn "blacken" White Cubans (cited in Dawdy, 53).

The concern about how eating "Black" criollo foods might impact White Criollo cultures and bodies operates through a metonymic slippage, from "Criollo" assigned to people to "criollo" assigned to the food those people eat, like the one that underlines Anselme Brillat-Savarin's famous 1825 aphorism "Tell me what you eat and I will tell you what you are" (*Physiologie du goût*, 5). According to Freud, metonymy is a form of displacement. Is this metonymic slippage from people to food, then, a displacement of the complication of human criollismo, with all of the charge of racialism, onto the less charged culinary sphere? Did this allow the association of criollo with racial mixing to increase? While people regularly continued to claim "pure" European or African ancestry along with Cuban birth throughout the nineteenth century, languages, music, and food "born" in Cuba was more clearly syncretic, hybrid, what Ortiz would later call transculturated. Or do the White Spaniards and Criollos who write these books embrace the Criollo in a way that works to erase Black and mixed-race Criollo persons, and their racialized experiences, in the name of a criollismo displaced from racialized humans onto de- or re-racialized foods? In other words, is their criollismo a form of whitewashing, or do they operate a whitewashing of criollismo? The absence of any direct naming or discussion of African or Indigenous origins of the foods, in contrast to the regular naming and discussion of Spanish and other European origins, suggests the latter. On the other hand, the very thing that distinguishes these cookbooks from their

European counterparts are the various dishes named for the Cuban locations, designated as criollo, or recognizably distinct from European preparations in ways that relate directly to their basis in Indigenous, African, slave, and peasant ingredients and methods. The combination itself of recipes titled as European, Cuban, and criollo in single cookbooks operate multiple types of creolization. In one sense, Cuban cookbooks delineate a domain of White Criollos with recipes born in Cuba of European heritage, formed by the Cuban climate and soil on which they gestate and grow. At the same time, the recipes labeled Cuban or criollo and with Indigenous and African food words establish the version of the criollo that Ortiz would later see embodied in ajiaco, a mixed pot ("The Human Factors of Cubanidad").

In her analysis of a selection of late nineteenth- and early twentieth-century Cuban cookbooks, Calvo Peña finds that "dishes considered properly Cuban always appear with the designation 'a lo cubano,' 'a lo criollo,' or 'a lo habanero'" (79) and are characterized by a combination of ingredients and methods that center on "a large quantity of products of American origin (plantain, corn, yuca, malanga, chayotes, yam) and of tropical fruits"; a base of fried onion, tomato, peppers, and garlic; an accompaniment of bananas or plantains; the use of pork lard as the primary fat; the predominance of pork in general; complex elaborations with a large number of spices; the combination of salty and sweet; and the emphasis on colorful presentation (79). Across nineteenth-century Cuban cookbooks, however, dishes titled "criollo" or with a Cuban place name regularly have no ingredients that are specific to Cuba or the Caribbean whereas several dishes whose names invoke European locations and a great many recipes with no identifying markers do have specifically Cuban or Caribbean ingredients. A selection of the lengua (tongue) recipes from the *Manual del cocinero cubano* (see figure 1.2) offers a clear example: "Lengua a la criolla" calls for serving with fried ripe plantains; "Lengua a la habanera" has no distinguishably Caribbean ingredients or techniques; "Lengua asada a la granadina" (referring to the Spanish city of Granada) calls for serving with hot sauce, the recipe for which calls for hot peppers (ajíes dátiles picantes) (58–59; 31). "Criollo," it

1.2. *Manual del cocinero cubano*, 1856, pages 58–59. Source: University of Florida, George A. Smathers Library, Special Collections and Area Studies.

turns out, is used synonymously with "Cuban," and both represent an ideological but not necessarily any material difference from "Spanish."

While early colonial writing, botanical history, and archaeology, as noted in the introduction, can help trace the development of foodways, literary descriptions, newspaper accounts, and cookbooks themselves reveal and inscribe the popular associations and symbolic meanings of foods. "Ropa vieja" becomes Cuban through the inclusion, in the *Manual del cocinero cubano,* of just one recipe for "Ropa vieja andaluza" alongside recipes for both "Ropa vieja cubana" and "Ropa vieja habanera" (45–46).[32] The presence in Legran's cookbook of only "Ropa vieja á la Americana" (25), in Cabrisas's of only "Ropa vieja cubana" (62–63), in *El cocinero de los enfermos* only "Ropa vieja cubana," and in Noviatur's

> ### *Ropa vieja cubana* (Cuban Ropa Vieja)
>
> *Se toma manteca, se deslie con harina y se le echan ajos, peregil, cebolla, tomates y pimientos, todo bien picado, se pone á freir, y se le añade una taza de caldo, otra de vino, unas gotas de limon, se revuelve el todo y se le pone la carne de vaca deshilachada, se deja hervir un poco y se sirve con plátanos maduros fritos.*
>
> Take lard, whisk it with flour, and add garlic, parsley, tomatoes, and peppers, all finely chopped, sauté it, and add a cup of broth, another of wine, a few drops of lemon, mix well and add shredded beef, let boil a little and serve with fried ripe plantains.
>
> —CABRISAS, *NUEVO MANUAL DE LA COCINERA CATALANA Y CUBANA*, 62–63

Novísimo edition only "Ropa vieja habanera" erases the Spanishness of the dish. As it becomes emblematically creole and Cuban, however, "Ropa vieja" inscribes a mixing of European (flour, beef, wine), Indigenous (tomatoes and peppers), and African (plantains) ingredients, doing so under a recognizably Spanish-language title. As much as they declare its independence from Spain, these White Criollo authors claim the dish. "Ropa vieja" serves settlers who occupy, incorporate, and claim as their own the tables and kitchens of Cuba. As they break from the colonial center, the settlement remains.

Some dishes, however, entitle Indigenous and African heritage and racialized affiliation, using words like ají, yuca, and casabe. The designation of these foods as "primitive" in José María de la Torre's popular 1857 history of Havana confirms that they were well recognized as such. The unexplained use of Indigenous and African culinary terms in nineteenth-century Cuban cookbooks shows both their persistence in Cuban culinary vocabulary and their appearance, as such, as undifferentiated from the Spanish language or criollo cuisine. An exception that proves the rule is the *Manual del cocinero cubano*'s recipe for "Manatee or Sea Cow a lo pinero [Manatí o vaca marina a lo pinero]" that starts,

"This fish has a most exquisite flesh whose taste resembles that of pork but is much more tasty" (112). Manatí is indicated as non-Spanish by the accompanying Spanish name, "sea cow [vaca marina]." Its non-European origin (manatee live in tropical waters) is also indicated in the need to describe it via a comparison to a European animal, while a certain failure of comprehension is also revealed in the categorization of the manatee as a fish rather than a mammal.[33]

Perhaps the most iconic Cuban dish with a Taíno-based name is ajiaco. While the nineteenth-century recipes for this dish bear a clear resemblance to the stew described in Coloma y Garcés's publications as a combination of fresh and salted meats, root vegetables, and spices, ironically, ajíes themselves feature in only a small number of the nineteenth-century recipes for ajiaco. Three of the six ajiaco recipes in the *Manual del cocinero cubano* call for "ajiaco broth," for which there is no recipe in the broth section and that may refer simply to the broth made in the first steps of the recipe, where ají does not appear. The other three ajiaco recipes in the *Manual del cocinero cubano* and the two in Cabrisas's *Nuevo manual* do not even call for "ajiaco broth." Legran's *Nuevo manual* offers the only ajiaco recipe that instructs that the dish should be spiced with ají, and it refers to a previous recipe, as if the primary, as a point of reference. Every ajiaco recipe across the cookbooks, on the other hand, does call for some combination of Afro-Indigenous vegetables. Ajiaco transfers thus from a dish based on a specific Indigenous ingredient to one with a vague allusion to Indigeneity. Ají is no longer materially central to the dish, but it is conceptually central to Cuban cuisine. The question remains: what is ají conceptually if it is no longer tied to a material object of Indigeneity? Dishes prominently featuring yuca and ají throughout nineteenth-century Cuban cookbooks inscribe Indigenous contributions to creole and Cuban cuisine. However, without any mention of living Indigenous people or of the paths of transmission through Indigenous, Afro-Indigenous, and Mestizo cooks, the Taíno presence in Cuban and creole cooking appears as the dying gift of a long-gone people to the conquistadors and their rightful Criollo heirs.

Ajíaco de monte (Mountain Ajiaco)

En un puchero regular se llena la mitad de agua y se la pone tres libras de vaca salada, y tres de tasajo de cerdo, procurando desalarlo antes con agua caliente, se le añade, media gallina, una cebolla, cuatro dientes de ajos mojados, se espuma y se deja hervir cosa de una hora. Despues se le añade plátanos verdes, malanga, ñame, boniato, calabaza, yuca, chayote y maiz tierno dejándolo hervir junto otra hora; en un mortero se machacarán culantro, comino, pimiento negra y un poco de azafrán y un pedazo de malanga cocida, despues se deslíe con el caldo del puchero, y se le echa con un poco de zumo de limon; se deja hervir un poco y se sirve.

A regular pot is filled hallway with water and three pounds of salt beef are added, and three of dried pork, having been desalted first in hot water, then are added half a chicken, an onion, four garlic cloves, the foam is removed, and it is left to boil for about an hour. Then are added green plantains, malanga, yam, boniato, calabaza, yuca, chayote, and ripe corn and left to boil together for another hour; in a mortar mash culantro, cumin, black pepper, and a little saffron and a piece of cooked malanga, then it is dissolved into the chicken broth and added in with a little lemon zest; it is left to boil a little and served.

—CABRISAS, *NUEVO MANUAL DE LA COCINERA CATALANA Y CUBANA*, 30–31

Ajiaco de tierra-dentro (Inland Ajiaco)

Se hace de un todo como el anterior, sin echarle carne de vaca, maíz ni ninguna clase de especia; solo sal y ají con ajos fritos con manteca, de donde viene derivado el nombre de ajiaco.

Made like the previous, without adding beef, corn or any spices; just salt and ají fried in lard, for which is derived the name *ajiaco*.

—LEGRAN, *NUEVO MANUAL DEL COCINERO CUBANO Y ESPAÑOL*, 17–18

Recognition of distinctly African elements in the Cuban creole cuisine of these cookbooks is no more prevalent or explicit than that of distinctly Indigenous ones. A few recipes with the most clearly identifiable African technique—the pounding of starchy vegetables to make balls or masses eaten in or with broths—are named with a West African word: "fufú."[34] Versions of the dish designated "fufú criollo" maintain the titular "fufú" while they call for more Indigenous and Spanish ingredients and techniques, a combination that keeps Cuban creole cuisine from being totally whitewashed.[35] The other recognizably African food word used in Cuban recipes is "quimbombó."[36] Like fufú, its West African origins are maintained both by its accenting a last syllable that ends in a vowel, which is rare in Spanish, and its lack of resemblance to any Spanish words, along with its lack of an easily parallel Spanish dish or ingredient.

Fufú de malanga y plátano/
Fufú de malanga ó plátano
(Malanga and Plantain Fufú/
Malanga or Plantain Fufú)

Se toman cuatro malangas grandes, se pelan, quitándoles las raíces, y se parten en cuatro, se toman tres plátanos machos pintones, se les cortan las dos pantas y se le hace una cortada de arriba abajo, que deje abierta la cáscara, para quitársela, partiéndolos en tres ó mas trozos; se ponen en una cazuela á salcochar en agua con sal, luego que ya estén cocidas, se machacan en un mortero, amasándolo perfectamente con manteca y sal así que esté todo bien mezclado se hacen las bolas de un tamaño regular, y se sirve con el caldo de ajonjolí, que se esplicará mas adelante.

Take four big malangas, peel them, taking off the roots, and cut into quarters, take three male pinton plantains, cut both ends and make a long slice from top to bottom that opens the skin, to take it off, dividing then in two or more slices; put into a pot to cook in salted water, once they are cooked, mash them in a mortar, kneading them perfectly with lard and salt and once everything is well mixed, make balls of a regular size and serve with sesame broth, which will be explained later.

—*MANUAL DEL COCINERO CUBANO*, 141–142; *EL COCINERO DE LOS ENFERMOS*, 88–89 (WITH MINOR CHANGES TO THE LAST SENTENCE)

Although the word "plátano" (and plantain) is of Latin etymology, plantains were widely recognized as slave—if not quite distinctly African—food.[37] Plantains, along with yams [ñame], malanga, yuca, boniato, and calabaza,[38] now frequently grouped together as "viandas,"[39] formed the basis of slave and peasant diets across the Caribbean. Their significant presence in titles and ingredients in these cookbooks is a large part of what distinguishes the cookbooks and the recipes as criollo not only in the sense of descended from Spain and born in the Caribbean but also in the senses of descended from Africa and born in the Caribbean and mixed together in the Caribbean. These foods represent both the Indigenous and the African presence in criollo foods via slave cuisine. However, the inability to recognize either Indigenous people or Africans as having cultures equal to that of Europeans—an inability that is foundational to the maintenance of the myth of "discovery" and the institution of slavery—combines with the expansion of viandas into peasant diets across the Caribbean, to render them

---

Sopa de plátanos verdes ó criolla
(Green Plantain or Creole Soup)

Después de quitadas las cáscaras se echan en una cazuela con caldo de carne, se deja hervir hasta que se hallen bien blandos, se sacan y se machacan en un mortero, y luego que este hecho pasta se deslie con el mismo caldo, echándole especias, culantro machacado con un poco de agrio de limon, y después que se ha dado un hervor ya se puede hacer uso de ella. Si se quiere espesar, cuando se machacan las especias se echa un pedazo de pan tostado ó almendras y quedará muy sabrosa.

After removing the skins place in a pot with meat broth, boil until soft, remove and mash in a mortar, then when it has become a paste, dissolve into the same broth, adding spices, culantro crushed with a little lemon juice, and once it has returned to a boil, it can be used. If you want it thicker, when crushing the spices add a piece of toasted bread or almonds and it will come out quite delicious.

—MANUAL DEL COCINERO CUBANO, 17

representative primarily of peasantry and secondarily of the Creole descendants of slaves. The plantain stands out as the accompaniment that most frequently appears in recipes "a la criolla" or "a la Cubana." The recipes in which plantain is a central ingredient—including and exceeding fufú—are distinctly, if not namedly, of African origin and of slave and peasant elaboration.

If, as Cabrisas writes, Cuba is "the land of sugar," the color of sugar is also worth noting. Cruz Miguel Ortíz Cuadra explains that "azúcar moscabado, or very dark, unrefined sugar was synonymous with African or Black cooking" (7). Thus, he reads *El cocinero puertorriqueño*'s recipe for "Manjar blanco criollo" and its specification of "refined sugar rather than moscabada [sic] or melao (a rich syrup from sugarcane) as reflecting not only material and economic distinctions but a more primordial identification as well, an identification with the brightness and luster of the color white, which in the minds of some was viewed as a symbol of prestige" (33). The majority of the sweets recipes in nineteenth-century Cuban cookbooks call simply for "sugar," most likely a medium-processed sugar. A significant minority do specify "white sugar [azúcar blanco]," "refined sugar [azúcar refinado]," or "powdered sugar [azúcar en polvo]," all marked by degrees of refinement that both whiten the color and render the grains smaller or pulverized, and several give recipes for "clarified sugar [azúcar clarificado]" to be made at home from white, "terciado," or "mascobado" sugar. A small but significant number of dessert recipes also call for "azúcar de pilón" or "melado de caña." These include recipes for "Melcocha," "Mala-Rabia," "Palanqueta," "Zambumbia," "Grajea Menuda," and "Alegría de Maní." While each cookbook has some recipes made with these sugars, they are not always the same ones, such that no subset of sweets recipes stands out as particularly marked by the use of darker or lighter sugars, and, at the same time, the darker sugars stand out as less common and tied to recipes that share other connections to Afro-Indigenous tradition (palanqueta is made with yuca flour [casabe], alegría de maní with groundnuts, zambumbia with corn). As much as sugar represents the basis of slavery and of Spanish profit from its

> ### *Palanqueta criolla* (Creole Palanqueta)
>
> *Se hacen con el melado de la caña clarificada con clara de huevo y bien batido con azúcar, revuélvase bien despues con casabe y canela en poca cantidad, téngase siempre al fuego, y estará en su punto cuando se vea que la masa deja de ser pegajosa.*
>
> This is made with cane syrup clarified with egg white and well beaten together with sugar, then mixed well with yuca flour and a little cinnamon, keeping it over the fire the whole time, it will be ready when the paste stops being sticky.
> —LEGRAN, NUEVO MANUAL DEL COCINERO CUBANO Y ESPAÑOL, 145

colonial holdings, Cuban and criollo cuisine can and does draw from all parts of the sugar-making process, including its subjugation to ideals of Whiteness and its reliance on Afro-Indigenous Cubans' ability to create uniquely Cuban and Caribbean delicacies under, alongside, and around that subjugation.

These cookbooks work to separate and equalize the Cuban and the Spanish. They simultaneously include and obscure the Afro-Indigenous. Subsumed into the Cuban and the Criollo, the Afro-Indigenous is rarely recognized as equal in importance to the Spanish. At the same time, constitutive of the Cuban and Criollo difference from the Spanish, the centrality of the Afro-Indigenous persists. Emblematically, Cabrisas's introduction to the *Nuevo manual de la cocinera catalana y cubana* names the "land of good wine [pais del buen vino]" and the "land of sugar [pais del azúcar]" as if the two, and the only two, central points of reference for Cuban cuisine were Europe and the products of European colonialism (5–6). The list of foods from the *pais del azúcar* includes "Ajiaco, Boniato, Corn, Plantains, Creole Mondogo and other New World style stews," erasing Africa and also rendering the precolonial Cuban as the product of colonialism (6, emphasis in the original). In all of these cookbooks, European histories precede, enter, and remain in Cuba via the titles of dishes. Afro-Indigenous ingredients, on the other hand, are claimed as Cuban or criollo. The new "native" that comes into being visibly recognizes the Spanish while erasively incorporating the African and Taíno.

Nineteenth-century Cuban and Puerto Rican cookbooks' unmarked inclusion of traces of Indigenous and African elements enacts the pain and persistence of the wounds of genocide and slavery in ways that render them part of the Cuban and Puerto Rican landscape.[40] These cookbooks allow, if not perform, a whitewashing of the "native" Cuban and Puerto Rican, so that the Cuban and Puerto Rican that is on a par with the Spanish appears to have a distinctness that comes from the island, from the Caribbean, from the "climate," although contemporary readers may have recognized and later Caribbean (food) writers can trace the scars, or even pick at them. This is the work of White Criollo men who, however much they wanted to help women and slaves—to imagine an independent nation without slavery and with happy homes run by women who fed them exquisite Criollo meals, with inns where travelers could enjoy the same—they imagined it as an enhanced version of their own world, not a massive turning over of power and privilege and self-conception like the Haitian revolution (imagined if not delivered) but a subtler shift, from White Criollo rule subjected to Spanish control and taxation to a more "inclusive," modernized version of the same. Inclusion, they show, can maintain and even extend the power of those who already have it. Who controls the including, and whether it leads, through transculturation or creolization to cultures of hybridity or holds (admittedly or not) hybrid cultures in (their) place, is one of the central questions in the development of recipes for national culture.

Domestic Control in West Indian Women's Cookbooks at the Turn of the Twentieth Century

BRITISH COLONIAL RULE persisted in the West Indies well into the twentieth century,[1] first often under systems of "home rule" in which the ruling homes were those of the planter class and then primarily through "Crown Colonies" that combined constitutional forms of government with the absolute power of the British Crown as embodied in the Colonial Office, its governors and officers, in some places—like Jamaica—nominally attenuated by "representative" assemblies. Neither representation nor power was extended beyond the British and predominantly White Creole elite, and any pro-independence collaborations among planters and the emerging Black and mixed-race[2] middle classes were disempowered. It is not surprising, in this context, that the first West Indian cookbooks, published between 1893 and 1912, were from and for the White Creole and British elite and served their tastes. While these cookbooks perpetuate culinary colonialism, they reveal the domestic implications of, and the domestic work in, maintaining British and White supremacy in the West Indies. At the same time, they betray the labor and the power of Afro-Indigenous and Indo-Caribbean cooks and convey the traces of Indigenous, African, and Asian culinary histories that distinguish West Indian cuisines.

In this chapter, I examine how Caroline Sullivan's 1893 *The Jamaica Cookery Book* and a set of West Indian cookbooks published in the first dozen years of the twentieth century fortified communities of White women and obscured everyone else as they managed and inscribed culinary creolization in the West Indies. These cookbooks delivered "native" Jamaican, Barbadian, Grenadian, Trinidadian, and West Indian recipes to English and White Creole women, asserting the possessive and organizational power of White women in delicate balances of racial and national interests and at the same time beginning to acknowledge the acumen and work of Black women. The (scant) biographies of the authors gathered in this chapter reveal their places in the colonial order while my analyses of the organization, attributions, introductions, and narrative sections of the cookbooks show their community-defining work. Close readings of the recipes illuminate their treatment of culinary history and identification. Following the intertwining of gender and race in these cookbooks, this chapter's analyses move between the two, sometimes explicitly and sometimes implicitly.

Like the Cuban and Puerto Rican cookbooks of the nineteenth century examined in chapter 1, late nineteenth and early twentieth-century West Indian cookbooks work to articulate local culinary cultures that are distinct, and that can and should remain under White/Creole/European control, even if perhaps with some degree of independence. They participate in the culinary colonialism that works to articulate Caribbean foods as precious, delicious, part of the raw material that serves British power, and at the same time not capable of existing on their own both because they are incomplete and unorganized—overall unrefined, perhaps dangerous, or just necessarily dependent even if unique and yummy. At the same time, different from the Cuban and Puerto Rican cookbooks, and in increasing measure over time, they show the work of White Creole women who wrote the cookbooks to negotiate a complicated position, under heterocolonial power themselves and over the colonized "natives."

West Indian cookbooks throughout the nineteenth and early twentieth centuries instruct women in how to take their place in the heterocolonial order. Like their British counterparts that Margaret Beetham studies, West Indian cookbooks detail "the responsibility for the preparation and consumption of food [that] placed the mistress of the house in a position of power" and circumscribed that power "in the domestic economy" where "their role in the economy was to manage consumption" in contrast to the public and productive power of men (17). Furthermore, in the British colonial context, as Mills specifies, "British women were only allowed to figure as symbols of home and purity" (1931, 3; cited in O'Callaghan, 63). Thus, as Evelyn O'Callaghan argues, "women participated in colonial ideology and praxis differently from the way that men did," which does not mean that "women as a group would share an awareness of oppression with other marginalized groups" (62). The purity that British colonial women symbolized was racial as well as spiritual. Like their counterparts in colonial India that Susan Zlotnik studies, West Indian cookbooks demonstrate and institute the separation of White womanhood from Black, mixed-race, and Indian womanhood. Feminist scholars such as Francine Masiello demonstrate that women have long "utilized the domestic sphere" to do such things as "develop new codes of learning and enhanced their limited opportunities for public circulation by building intra-domestic networks of dialogue" (527). The women cookbook writers of turn-of-the-century West Indies did so in ways that more closely resemble Amelia Simmons's establishment of a voice of White Northern womanhood in a dominant narrative of rugged American individualism[3] than Black women's work to "break the Jemima Code" and write back against racist tropes of unskilled service.[4]

Who Was Caroline Sullivan?

Caroline Sullivan's 1893 *The Jamaica Cookery Book* is, as far as is known at the time of this writing, the first cookbook written by a Caribbean woman, the first Jamaican cookbook, and the first cookbook from the (British) West Indies. Yet little is known about Caroline Sullivan beyond a few competing claims to her work and biography. A consideration of who she was and how her cookbook has circulated lays the ground for an analysis of how White British and Creole women carved out power for themselves in and through colonialist discourses that limited them

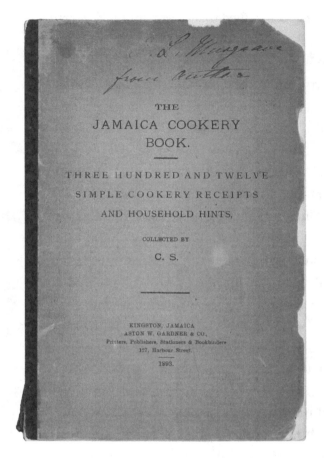

2.1. *The Jamaica Cookery Book*, 1893, title page. Source: Library of Congress, Rare and Special Collections Division.

because of their gender and empowered them because of their race. This analysis complexifies Frantz Fanon's picture of colonial domination by accounting for gender and especially for the place of women who were both dominated and dominating in the colonial context. How Sullivan and women like her got to be living and writing cookbooks in the Caribbean, and had their work circulated and obscured, is the starting point that informs the subsequent close reading of community formation through culinary management in *The Jamaica Cookery Book*.

The Jamaica Cookery Book was first published in Kingston, Jamaica, in 1893, with a preface signed by "C. S., St. Andrew, Jamaica" (see figure 2.1). In the preface, C. S. refers to "*our* ordinary Jamaica cooking" (emphasis mine), introducing right away the questions of grouping, belonging, and possession that run throughout the cookbook even as it aligns her clearly with the Jamaican. A review of *The Jamaica Cookery Book* printed in the "Current Items" section of the Monday, December 18, 1893, *Daily Gleaner* notes that "in spite of the modest disclaimer of the compiler, it is a most exhaustive work and we question if any simple native would [?] claim to the possession of a knowledge of all [?] the varied recipes given here."[5] A second edition of *The Jamaica Cookery Book* appeared in 1897 with "collected by Caroline Sullivan" spelled out on the front cover.[6] A third edition, with no further additions or revisions, appeared in 1908.[7]

The Sullivans first came to Jamaica from Ireland in the second half of the seventeenth century. They were joined over the next two hundred years by many more hailing both from Ireland and England. John Augustus Sullivan, born in England in 1797, served as provost general marshal of Jamaica from 1825 to 1871, living at Highgate House. He married three times and had a great number of children. The Caroline who wrote *The Jamaica Cookery Book* may well have been one of them, or one of their daughters or wives.[8] That she uses a first and last name without marital title indicates that she may not have married, in which case it is likely that she ran a household either for a (male) member of her family or as a housekeeper for another family. While unmarried White women both from Britain and from Creole planter families regularly served as housekeepers in large plantations, if the Caroline Sullivan of *The Jamaica Cookery Book* was a daughter or granddaughter of John Augustus Sullivan, her class status makes work outside of her own family less likely. A handwritten dedication to "J. L. Musgrave from author" on the front cover of the 1893 edition held at the U.S. Library of Congress (see figure 2.1) suggests that Caroline Sullivan was familiar with Lady Jeanne Lucinda Musgrave, wife of former governor of Jamaica Anthony Musgrave and founder of Jamaica's Women's Self Help Society (later renamed the Lady Musgrave Self-Help Society).[9] It is also likely that she is the "Caroline Sullivan of the Parish of Saint Andrew," named in a notice in the *Daily Gleaner*'s legal section as "deceased on about the 14th day of August, 1904," whose "creditors and others having claim against the estate" should send their claims "verified by Charles

Frederick Sullivan and Lillian Hope Page [?], the duly qualified Administrators of the estate of the said deceased to the care of S. R. Cargill, No. 4 [?]oke St., Kingston, Sollicitor." As much as these details fit together and paint a picture of a woman connected to Jamaica's British and White Creole elite who maintained significant wealth and position through the end of her life, they are difficult to confirm, and the absence of any print mention of Caroline Sullivan or *The Jamaica Cookery Book* between 1908 and 1990 sets up the competing claims to her person and the versions of her work that emerged a century after the original.

In 1990, *A Collection of 19th Century Jamaican Cookery and Herbal Recipes* was published, listing Marjorie Pringle Campbell as the author and containing the very same material as the 1897 and 1908 editions of *The Jamaica Cookery Book*. The 1990 book claimed to be an edited copy of a manuscript created by a Pringle family housekeeper in Jamaica in the nineteenth century, kept in the family papers, and "serendipitously" published, according to the publisher's note, at the very same time as

> a small book was found, printed by Aston W. Gardener, Kinston [sic], Jamaica in 1893 with almost the same recipes and the following title, *The Jamaica Cookery Book—Three Hundred and Twelve Simple Cookery Receipts and Household Hints* collected by 'C. S. In searching the newspapers of the time, two advertisements were discovered. . . . The second, from *The Daily Gleaner* of Monday, January 10, 1898, reveals the collector (the mysterious "C. S.") as one Caroline Sullivan in addition to the fact that the book had been printed a second time in 1897 by the same printer.

The publisher's note ends with, "Who was Caroline Sullivan? As we go to press this intriguing question remains unanswered," though the logical conclusion would certainly be either that Sullivan was the Pringle family housekeeper who left a manuscript copy of the 1897 edition that ended up in the family papers or that the Pringle family acquired Caroline Sullivan's manuscript in some other way and the story of the housekeeper is family lore but not historically accurate. Of course, other possibilities include everything from disingenuity on the part of the Pringle family to Caroline Sullivan being the creation of another person or persons who actually wrote or compiled the book.

In 1995, *Classic Jamaica Cooking: Traditional Recipes and Herbal Remedies* was released, listing Caroline Sullivan as author. The first title page explains that "Caroline Sullivan was the mistress of a large Jamaican household at the end of the nineteenth century. She was the author of the first ever book on the island's cooking, *The Jamaican [sic] Cookery Book*, of which this is a lightly revised edition." Cristine MacKie's forward to that edition claims that Sullivan's family was in Jamaica since the 1650s and "lived in the grand colonial style," and Sullivan "came to run the Great House in the nineteenth century" (9). MacKie mentions in her forward that in research for her 1991 *Life and Food in the Caribbean* she "found a mass of journals and diaries from the sixteenth to the nineteenth centuries that described the dining tables of the Great Houses but there was almost nothing published on the subject of food and its historical influences so complete and revealing as Caroline Sullivan's book" (9). Although MacKie lists a number of Caribbean journals, diaries, and letter collections in the bibliography of *Life and Food in the Caribbean*, she does not mention Sullivan in that book.[10]

Few other scholars have written on Sullivan and *The Jamaica Cookery Book* to date. Ilaria Berti refers to Sullivan as "the governess of a sugarcane plantation" (127). B. W. Higman and Sarah Lawson Welsh describe her as "the mistress of a large Jamaican household" (Lawson Welsh, 101). Higman posits that after the 1897 reprint, Sullivan's cookbook "was soon lost to local memory and returned to manuscript form in a reverse progression for oral to written to printed," explaining the Pringle family claim as stemming from their housekeeper having owned one such "manuscript copy of Sullivan's published book" (81). This explanation allows the Pringle family story to be reconciled with MacKie's claim. However, it rests on the hypothesis that "for most of the twentieth century authorship slipped away from Caroline Sullivan" (*Jamaican Food*, 49). The release of the 1908 edition in both Jamaica and London indicates the continued popularity of the book, and that edition's front cover clearly includes "collected by CAROLINE SULLIL-VAN" [sic], suggesting that the book itself, at least to some degree, continued to circulate and to be known as the work of Caroline Sullivan.[11]

The genre of the cookbook, with its prevalence of passive voice and imperative mode, can help to obscure authorial identity. Like Sullivan, cookbook authors often explain their work in a preface and brief narrative sections. Also, like Sullivan, cookbook authors prove their credentials not with personal details but with the recipes themselves. The authorial imperative and its presumed performance by the reader establishes a relationship between the author and the reader and delineates the positions of each. Where information is sparse, where the reader is called on to adjust to preference or taste, the reader appears as a near-equal to the writer, their shared knowledge assumed and also written into the recipes. At the same time, like any instruction manual, the cookbook imparts information that will allow the reader to become more like the author. The cookbook, in other words, creates community among author and reader that reveals a good deal about each.

A close reading of *The Jamaica Cookery Book*'s type and manner of instruction, of the ways that Sullivan asserts her own authority and imparts it to readers, uncovers Sullivan's position in and on Jamaica, revealing who she was through what she knew, did, and wanted and how she both represented and guided a community of White women in Jamaica. In other words, the big issues of colonialism, gender, and race that mark Sullivan's life—and the lives of women like her—in colonial Jamaica can be seen and analyzed in the small details of word choice, grammar, and organization. Analyses of *The Jamaica Cookery Book* both reveal the particularities of Sullivan's work and preview the larger landscape of West Indian women's cookbooks at the turn of the century.

Caroline Sullivan's Communities

Sullivan identifies herself not as the composer but the collector of the recipes in *The Jamaica Cookery Book*, joining a long line of colonial "collectors" who expropriate and appropriate Afro-Indigenous material, labor, and knowledge and then use it to solidify relations among those in power at the expense of the objects of exchange. Since, as Gayle Rubin's analysis of "the traffic in women" demonstrates, women are often the object of exchange among men in power, by occupying the position of collector and redistributor, Sullivan claims power in and of a male-dominated position. [12] At the same time, as a collector, Sullivan aligns racially with the men (and women) who hold power over the objects of exchange that come from and are associate with Afro-Indigenous Jamaicans. She delicately slices this cake by positioning herself as an intermediary between "the people" and her readers and as the owner of "our ordinary Jamaica cooking," a facilitator of exchange who, as she takes possession of "the people" and their culinary history, also acknowledges their contributions. She is like Fanon's "oppressor [who] is no longer content with the objective inexistence of the conquered nation and culture," but rather than simply engaging in "every effort ... to make the colonized confess the inferiority of their culture" she also undertakes the "scattered instances of a bold attempt to revise a cultural dynamism" that Fanon attributes to the colonized intellectual (*Wretched*, 171). Of course, doing so from the position of the colonizer, she enacts the appropriative gesture of settler colonialism. As Sullivan addresses and forms community with her primarily colonialist White female audience and positions the predominantly colonized Black female sources of her recipes, *The Jamaica Cookery Book* participates in colonialism and proto-independence work, colonial heteropatriarchy and proto-feminism, White elitist racism, and creolization in the Glissantian and Brathwaitian sense of hybridity and cultural pluralism (that must include, though unlike *The Jamaica Cookery Book* never privileges, the European).

Sullivan names her primary audience as women recently arrived in Jamaica. "I venture to hope that those [various methods of cooking] here given may be of some little use to newcomers, on whose behalf this work has been undertaken," she writes in the preface to the first edition. At the same time, she addresses "those whose long residence in the island renders them familiar with all the details of our ordinary Jamaican cooking," with whom she expects direct communication beyond the cookbook, for "from them I should be glad to receive notes on any articles which I may have omitted."[13] Reiterating the primary address to women for whom England is home, Sullivan positions herself and her audience as sharing a familiarity with English cookbooks and with cooking in general, delineating a sphere of expertise and knowledge as she explains that she does not include recipes for British staples because "my desire is merely to introduce to newcomers to Jamaica our own native methods of cooking our own products, and by no means to attempt to cope with the many excellent works that at present exist on English or other cookery" (22).[14] Sullivan neither asserts for herself a grand breadth expertise nor for her audience a great innocence or lack. Rather, she offers "some assistance," "help and use" in the form of "simple" and "faulty" receipts from an author for whom "it has been my pleasant occupation to gather together from time to time." In contrast to other British colonial cookbooks like Grace Gardiner and Flora Annie Steel's 1888 *The Complete Indian Housekeeper and Cook*, Sullivan includes only a few paragraphs of information related to managing the domestic budget, purchasing or overseeing the purchase of foods, and preparing or overseeing the preparation of home meals in upper-class households; never mentions directly the qualities of a good housewife or woman; and does not refer to an ultimate goal, of her cookbook or of women, to serve men. To a certain degree, then, Sullivan offers to "newcomers" an idea that in Jamaica it is possible to build communities of women who run households and share knowledge for their own benefit, sidestepping or even refusing Gardiner and Steel's heterocolonial positioning of women and their work. Sullivan claims knowledge of housekeeping, cooking, and multiple cultural affiliations as belonging to "us" women—perhaps even of all races—who live in Jamaica, and posits a Jamaican culture that is distinct from the English and worthy of English attention.

Sullivan recognizes that her English readership has arrived in Jamaica not only as "strangers to our native dishes" (22) but also with certain prejudices—against salt fish and goat mutton, for example.[15] Prejudices against foods like salt fish and mutton are racialized, for these foods are associated with Black Jamaicans (salt fish was a primary staple slave food, and goat, as the "poorer"—tougher, gamier—cousin of lamb, was associated with the poor Black majority). As she addresses the unfamiliarity and prejudice, Sullivan outlines a uniquely Jamaican cuisine, delicately poised between independent identity and service to the British Empire. Sullivan declares the superiority of things English as she affirms that some discomfort on the part of the "new-comer" is reasonable for "sometimes one is disappointed," notably by the way that meat is butchered and sold (22). She assures that goat mutton can be thoroughly enjoyed, but she also concludes her recipes for it with, "All my endeavor is to make the best of an *inferior* thing when one cannot get the *best*" (24, emphasis in the original). A few things, in other words, the English reader will rightly conclude are "the best" in England. These are balanced, however, by others from Jamaica that are "almost better" (26), or "more nourishing" (33), even some worthy of being "put in a parcel and sent to England" (38), and far outweighed by new "delicious" Jamaican "delicacies" Sullivan introduces to her English audience. The prejudices, Sullivan ultimately shows, are misguided and can be cured by an actual encounter with Jamaican cuisine: "I have heard people say over and over again that no matter how disguised 'goat mutton' may be they would never eat it. Yet those very people have enjoyed it in my presence; so much so in fact as to ask for another helping" (23). Proper information and encounter with Jamaican cuisine served with the skills of Sullivan's cooking (or cooks) can remediate English ignorance. By offering English women her insights into Jamaican food, Sullivan not only positions herself and her book as the bridge between English and "native" cultures, raising all of the questions of alliance, translation, and treachery that bridges beg, but also asserts it as a space of community distinct from both the English and "the native."

Sullivan's use of the first-person plural in her preface and commentary represents and embodies a distinct community. She shares "our" recipes, though she only rarely specifies who "we" are. Sullivan's own position, and "ours," match that of the White Creole—born in the

Stewed Kid or Goat Mutton

Meat, beans or peas, thyme, pepper, water, skellion, cloves, parsley, herbs, limejuice.

Put on the mutton in cold water with enough water to cover it, adding five cloves. Let it stew gently for about an hour, then add a little pepper, skellions, tomatoes, some parsley and herbs. If you want sugar beans or broad beans served with it, put in these now; the mutton is excellent, done, either with those or with cockle crease peas or even with very young goongoo peas (the green ones). Turnip and carrot can, of course, be used instead if preferred. When the vegetables are tender, add a little salt, a little lime juice and a thickening of flour to the gravy. The stew will take about two hours; do not let the water dry in the pot or the meat will burn.

—SULLIVAN, *THE JAMAICA COOKERY BOOK*, 25

Caribbean, of "pure" European heritage. Berti finds that "Sullivan's cookbook allows us to understand that the kitchen can be regarded as a site of creolization in which a food-based identity emerges from the encounter of various eating cultures," for "in her codification of local cuisine, Sullivan included butter and the traditional British sauces, Worcester or Harvey, with Jamaican pepper; she used Porto, a common drink of the British colonizers, to prepare patties; and in her 'cool drink' section she suggested squeezing lime, a tropical citrus fruit, instead of lemon, more common in Great Britain" (128). As promised in the introduction, nearly every recipe in *The Jamaica Cookery Book* centers on a Jamaican ingredient or technique that is not common in England. Nearly all the recipes also use English ingredients, such as the recipe for "Cornmeal Duckoonoo" that calls for butter and milk along with corn and plantain. Sullivan's selection of dishes and the recipes themselves demonstrate the long and complex history of culinary crossings that render West Indian cuisine distinct and that lead many to refer to is as creole. Sullivan's recipe for "Ochro Soup," for example, calls for ingredients of African (ochro), European (salt beef, thyme, salt pork), and

Cornmeal Duckoonoo

Cornmeal, butter, sugar, flour, spice.

A cupful of cornmeal boiled thick with some butter, two tablespoonfuls of sugar, a dessertspoonful of flour and a little spice. Let it cool. Then roll up in bits of plantain leaf and bake.

—SULLIVAN, *THE JAMAICA COOKERY BOOK*, 87–88

Ochro Soup

Two dozen ochros
One and a half pound of salt beef
Two quarts of water
Seasoning, tomato and skellion and thyme
Indian kale or callilu
Penny halfpenny worth of salt pork

Put the ochros into the water and boil until the seeds get red: then add the pork and beef and go on boiling, adding the seasoning and other ingredients. Chop fine some kale or callilu and add to the soup, and serve. It can be strained if preferred. A few black crabs boiled and added to the soup make it excellent.

—SULLIVAN, *THE JAMAICA COOKERY BOOK*, 2

Indigenous (Indian kale or callilu, tomato, skellion) origin, with salt beef and pork bearing also the history of their prevalence in slave diets.[16]

These recipes were born in the West Indies out of its unique historical and geographical mixture—creolization in Édouard Glissant's definition of it as a process "which mixes the substance of the world, which joins up and changes the cultures of today's humanities [and] acts to maintain relations between two or more culture 'zones,' brought together in a meeting place" (*Treatise*, 14). However, Sullivan never once uses the word "creole" to describe either people or recipes. Neither the self-defined Creoles whose "engagement with island society and landscape reflect," as O'Callaghan explains, "a sense, however ambivalent, of attachment to the region" (11) nor the white and "brown" middle class that Leah Rosenberg has shown to have emerged as a major site of both nationalism and feminism in turn-of-the-century Jamaica receive any direct attention or even mention in *The Jamaica Cookery Book*. Sullivan managed a delicate balance to avoid the negative connotations of Creole as disordered and decadent, keep "us" as close to the "newcomers" as possible, not a different type but simply in possession of different information, and assert not regional but island, proto-national, culinary culture.

For Sullivan, the groups who matter, and who are distinguished though also at times confused, are the English newcomers, the longtime residents of Jamaica, and "the natives." Though she rarely designates gender, the domestic material as well as her own gender render superfluous any specification that she is writing to and speaking of women. Sullivan's description of "those whose long residence in the island renders them familiar with all the details of our ordinary Jamaican cooking" indicates that like the "newcomers," this community is not "native" to Jamaica, either because they were born elsewhere or because, like Sullivan herself, they understand themselves to have an ancestral origin somewhere else. The expectation that these long-term residents would convey to Sullivan "notes on any articles which I have omitted" denotes upper-class status via literacy while the invitation to communicate with no indication of how to do so implies that this audience is one that travels in the same social circles as Sullivan and knows how to reach her without further instruction.[17] This is a pivotal group for Sullivan's combination of culinary colonialism and proto-nationalism as they are, in her writing, the collectors and organizers of native knowledge that prove them equal to and distinct from the English.

Sullivan writes in the preface to the second edition of *The Jamaica Cookery Book* that "the kind appreciation with which my Jamaica

Cookery Book has been received encourages me to place a second edition of it before the public." However, she makes no mention of having received any recipe "notes" from readers of the first edition. She credits only her own continued work of collection as she explains that "I have been fortunate enough to collect between sixty and seventy additional receipts, which may I trust, prove of some small service to those in need of them, as the others have been."

The few recipes that Sullivan attributes are her recipe, in the second edition, "To Exterminate Ants," "copied from the 'Gleaner,'"[18] and recipes for "Stewed Tree-Tomato" to the *Bulletin of the Botanical Department*.[19] The alignment Sullivan establishes with these two publications affirms the position of *The Jamaica Cookery Book*—and of Sullivan herself—in the British-affiliated White community and helps to show the contours of that community. Sullivan also asserts herself as a reader of newspapers and bulletins primarily written by and for men in charge of commercial, scientific, and political activity. She translates material from them into the domestic realm of the cookbook and the space she was creating for a woman's "longtime resident" community, refusing the necessary Englishness of the good colonial housewife and the necessary maleness of interest in and knowledge of the life of the colony. The *Daily Gleaner* covered White, mixed-race, and Black Jamaican interests, though the majority of its articles and ads focused on the concerns of the predominantly White elite and its frequent reprints of articles from English newspapers solidified its alliance with the White elite; its editors refused to support any specific political position or faction. The *Daily Gleaner* did not have a regular recipe or cooking column until well into the twentieth century, though in the 1890s it occasionally included recipes as part of articles on such things as "Kitchen Management" and "Our Ladies Letter" and in the "How" section, "Agricultural Notes," and "Notes from the Botanical Bulletin."[20] Edited and often written by William Fawcett, born in England and director of the Public Gardens and Plantations in Jamaica from 1887 to 1908, the *Bulletin of the Botanical Department* focused on plantation crops and their cultivation and processing for large-scale markets and on the botanical description of plants, and only rarely included recipes. Although Sullivan's recipe for "Stewed Tree-Tomato No. 2" is directly copied from it, the February 1893 *Bulletin of the Botanical Department* presents the recipe in an entry on "Jamaica Plum or Tree Tomato" that starts, "the Jamaica Plum (*Cyphomandra betacea*) is an excellent fruit and is said to have a beneficial action upon the liver. It can be eaten as a dessert fruit, cutting in two, and using a spoon, or it can be cooked like an ordinary tomato" (Fawcett, 4). Sullivan selected only the second of the two names that the *Bulletin* gave for the fruit and reproduced not the recipe for eating it "as a dessert fruit" but only the one for cooking it "like an ordinary tomato." In so doing, she corrected the bulletin's mistaken conflation of Jamaica plum (in Linnaean taxonomy *Spondias purpura*, jocote in Central America, and related to the pommecythère or June plum) and the tree tomato (which is in the same family as other tomatoes—Linnaean Solanaceae). She also put the recipe not in her section on fruits but rather along with another, unattributed, recipe for "Stewed Tree-Tomato No. 1" and recipes for "Tree-Tomato Dolce" and "Tomato Preserve," in her section on "Puddings and Preserves," which includes recipes using a range of fruits, vegetables, and nuts (nearly all prepared with sugar). Sullivan thus affiliates herself with the *Bulletin of*

Stewed Tree-Tomato No. 1

Ripe tree-tomatoes.
Sugar, water.

Take the ripe tree-tomatoes and scald them with boiling water, and this will allow the skin to be pared off. Then weigh the fruit, and to one pound of fruit allow half a pound of sugar. Make a syrup with a gill of water to half a pound of sugar. Some of the seeds of the tomato should be scooped out. Put the fruit into the syrup which has previously boiled up, and allow it to boil until tender and the syrup is thick.

—SULLIVAN, *THE JAMAICA COOKERY BOOK*, 64

the Botanical Department as someone who can translate and supplement its information with the benefit of local culinary knowledge, in order to offer it back to English newcomers for their domestic use in Jamaica. Her position is that of the domestic partner in the colonial plantation economy. She pivots between public rule and private management and also between White service and Black production.

Organizing the sections of the cookbook according to upper-class English service—Soups, Fish, Meat, Vegetables, Puddings and Preserves, Ices, Fruits, Cakes—followed by categories that accompany and supplement—Pickles, Savouries and Sauces, Drinks, Household Hints—Sullivan establishes English order for "our ordinary Jamaica cooking." The separate section, just after Fish, on Salt Fish exemplifies Sullivan's work to simultaneously fit "our native" cookery into an English order and demonstrate its distinction as a delicious supplement. In Jamaica "Salt fish and Akees" and "Salt Fish Fritters" are breakfast dishes. Although Sullivan keeps them in the Salt Fish section, she also mentions their consumption at breakfast, betraying the tradition of savory and hearty morning meals that resist English ordering.[21]

Salt Fish and Rice

This is a favourite native dish. The saltfish and rice, about half a pound of salt fish to a pint of rice, are boiled together with the usual bit of salt-pork and a little butter.

Salt Fish Fritters No. 1

Some people add an egg or perhaps two to salt-fish and rice, and make fritters of it for breakfast.

—SULLIVAN, *THE JAMAICA COOKERY BOOK*, 17–18

Proudly exhibiting "our own native methods of cooking our own products," Sullivan uses the possessive "our" to designate not only that to which "we" belong but that which "we" possess (22). The advertisements for *The Jamaica Cookery Book* in the *Daily Gleaner* on Tuesday, February 12; Tuesday, March 26; and Wednesday, March 27, 1895, highlight the possessive function of "our." They include an illustration featuring a Black woman in a headscarf in an outbuilding kitchen leaning over a pot while a Black girl stands outside holding up a dish.[22] The words "Our Cook" under the image convey both that the recipes are collected from this cook or others like her and that this cook belongs to C. S., a possession in which her readers share, or can join (see figure 2.2).

At the confluence of gendered and racialized orders, White Creole women suture relations between White men and Black women. Although many of Sullivan's recipes use the imperative that instructs the reader directly, elite and even middle-class women in Jamaica did not generally perform the cooking in their homes. Instead, as O'Callaghan notes, "A major part of [the work of White women] involved the supervision of domestics, who would have been mostly black and female during both the slavery and immediate post-emancipation periods" (42). Sullivan mentions the direct management of domestics only once, to "confess that [. . .] if one has to depend on a cook who is no real cook at all and can only 'roast and boil' (as she thinks, which is again another matter), one may find a tough, stringy, inedible mass served up with a quantity of grease and water as gravy, enough to make paterfamilias enraged and housekeeper in no enviable frame of mind" (23–24). *The Jamaica Cookery Book*, then, can save "one" from being in a position to "depend on a cook," especially one who "is no real cook": "one" wants to feel that one is not dependent on the cook, but that the cook is the dependent who simply executes "one's" instructions.[23] *The Jamaica Cookery Book* informs readers how to enjoy, ask for, and direct the preparation of the foods that those cooks make. This interface between the kitchen and the dining room occurs at the threshold of both racial and gender boundaries.

2.2. Advertisement for *The Jamaica Cookery Book* printed in *The Kingston Daily Gleaner*, February 12, March 26, and March 27, 1895. Source: Newspaperarchive.com.

In her analysis of Juana Manuela Gorriti's 1890 *Cocina ecléctica*, published in postcolonial Argentina, Elisabeth Austin argues that cookbooks written by and for women who do not do their own cooking position the writer and reader as involved in "the keeping of a kitchen [which] involves a much more extensive administration than the simple but arduous task of making food" to ensure not only "the successful presentation of well-known dishes, but also the constant gathering (at times, the appropriation) or recipes for more varied cuisine" (35). However, these powers of administration and collection operate in relation to a patriarchal power structure where men administer colonial rule and organize independent opposition. Thus, Austin notes that often

> an author's attempt at creating a female voice of authority simply mimics the myriad gestures of masculine conquest (whether literal or discursive) that typify the history of Creole Latin America, adding a feminine touch to this most patriarchal gesture. The most common form of masculine mimicry is displayed through narrative that appropriates aspects of indigenous cultures and present them as its own, a gesture of hegemonic appropriation. . . . On these occasions indigenous cultures are ransacked for their culinary gems, which are appropriated by Creole housewives without mention of the indigenous servants who would have had to teach the *señoras* the particular techniques and preparations involved in these foodstuffs. (38)

Striking, then, is the frequency with which Sullivan mentions, if not the cooks and servants who teach and execute the recipes she lists, at least the "natives," "the people," and "the country people." By showing her work of collecting and translating, Sullivan not only highlights the work of the White Creole woman but also indicates that of the "native" informant.

While Sullivan's cookbook articulates a class system where the Europeans order and the "natives" execute, it also betrays the culinary expertise not only of the cooks who are employed by the likes of Sullivan, but also the culinary and economic acumen and practice of "the people"

> ### Hominy for Cake, Pudding, Biscuits, or Pap
>
> It is better to buy this ready-made than to make it at home. The people prepare it from corn-grain by soaking, drying, fanning, sifting, sieving and other tedious processes. It makes excellent pap boiled with milk, or it can be eaten as porridge. It makes a good pudding with the addition of sugar, eggs, and spice.
>
> —SULLIVAN, *THE JAMAICA COOKERY BOOK*, 88

who offer pre-made products for sale, and the tastes of "the people" whose preferences she mentions. While the reason Sullivan gives for recommending that her readers buy "tous-les-mois flour" (33), Bammys (38), and "hominy for cake, pudding, biscuits or pap" (88) is that they are tiring and tedious to make, her brief reference to each process shows them to require not only time and energy but also technical skill. As she reports that "the natives" sell roasted "Pindars" and make a cake with them, Sullivan also mentions cashews and "a bean called wangla" (81), showing the culinary and market savvy of "the natives" that serves English and elite Jamaica buyers as well as their own communities.

Sullivan's work as an intermediary depends on the existence of a body of knowledge, itself created by a group to which she does not belong, ripe for translation. Her power, and that of her peers, depends on "the natives" having much to offer and on the need for her work of collection, translation, and refinement. Sullivan identifies "the natives" as a group when she describes such dishes as "their peas soup," which is distinct from "ours."

A note to the recipe for "Red Peas Soup" that instructs to "press the peas through a cullender" (3) reads: "N.B.—The natives do not strain their peas soup: they eat the whole thing boiled with yam, coco, and dumplings and often with a remarkable concoction called 'foo foo' which consists of yam or coco boiled and beaten and then added to the soup. Needless to say, this makes them decidedly substantial. The

> ### Red Peas Soup
>
> One Pint of Peas.
> Two quarts of water.
> Penny-half-penny worth of salt pork.
>
> Put the peas in cold water and boil three hours till the peas are soft, adding penny-half-penny worth of salt pork about two hours and a half after boiling has begun. At the end of three hours time press the peas through a cullender. Serve with dry toast cut in dice.
>
> —SULLIVAN, *THE JAMAICA COOKERY BOOK*, 3

dumplings are often made with equal parts of flour and cornmeal" (3). Introducing the section on Salt Fish, Sullivan asserts that some "native" preparations improve on the European: "It is surprising to most newcomers, to find that in Jamaica there is hardly a more popular dish among the natives and often among the upper classes than the despised salt fish, eaten at home not from choice, but as a sort of penitential dish. Here, it is the almost daily, and certainly the favourite food of the people generally; and cooked, *as they cook it*, it cannot fail to please the most fastidious" (17, italics in the original). Higman cites this passage as an example of Sullivan's "bringing together high and low cuisines for a middle- and upper-class audience" (81). And it is. At the same time, it exemplifies her distinction between "the natives" and "the upper classes" who can be united in being pleased by the same dishes, when cooked properly, but remain safely separated by the frequency and degree of favor with which those dishes are enjoyed. The separation is important, for "the people"—like or synonymous with "the natives"—soak "mutton with guinea hen weed" (presumably, mutton from an animal that has fed on guinea hen weed) "in vinegar which they fondly hope destroys the detestable taste of the weed," to such little avail that Sullivan instructs her readers to "avoid this altogether" (26). Similarly, "the people put the green plantain and also the green bananas in their soups, or eat them with their salt fish," although Sullivan asserts that "they are less palatable" when green and only when "turned" ("when they are between green and ripe") do they "go excellently well with salt fish or eaten boiled or roasted with butter put inside them" (30). She indicates, in the recipe for "Boiled Pumpkin," that "the natives" use a Creole culinary term, "junks"—set apart in quotation marks—do not use salt and butter, and perhaps most importantly do not prepare the cooked food for presentation (shaping in a dish), marking their lack of refinement (31). Sullivan's descriptions of "the natives'" techniques and tastes hold them up to, expropriate them for, and distance them from European refinement. Much as she names them, Sullivan affirms that her connection to "our native dishes" operates through her possession of, rather than belonging to, "the native."

Boiled Pumpkin

This can be served two ways. The natives prefer it boiled and cut into "junks," with a shake of black pepper over it. The more refined way is to mash it with some butter, salt and pepper, and shape it in the dish.

—SULLIVAN, *THE JAMAICA COOKERY BOOK*, 31

Pumpkin and Rice

One large piece of pumpkin.
Half a pint of rice.
Skellion, tomato, butter.
A penny-half-penny worth of salt pork.

A good sized piece of pumpkin is boiled with rice and well mixed together with a little chopped skellion and tomato, a little pepper, and a dessert spoonful of butter and a penny-half-penny worth of salt pork cut in dice. This is a favourite dish among the natives.

—SULLIVAN, *THE JAMAICA COOKERY BOOK*, 31

Sullivan does not write explicitly about the origins of "the native" foods or techniques but conveys, or allows to pass, traces—in the Glissantian sense of the trace as "a wandering that guides us . . . one of the places of survival" (*Treatise*, 9)—of Afro-Indigenous and slave agricultural and culinary terms and techniques. Her entry on yams, for example—"Yams. They are various. There are the white yam, the guinea yam, the hard yam, the yellow or affoo yam, the negro yam, the Lucea yam, and the Indian yam" (34)—lists six varieties that probably came to Jamaica with slaves from Africa, at least three of which still bear names indicating that origin, and the indigenous "Indian yam," which Sullivan notes is also called a yampee. Sullivan does not explain that salt fish and salt meat were the only proteins that slave owners were required to give their slaves, and she makes no mention of the word "provisions" nor of the provision grounds where slaves grew their own foods—which had to be ones like pumpkin, breadfruit, yuca, and plantains that required little maintenance and did not spoil easily upon ripening, as they were often only allowed to tend to the grounds once a week. Nonetheless, the tastes that Sullivan attributes to "the natives" and "the people" via the dishes that she describes in terms such as their "favourite"—salt fish, pumpkin, breadfruit, cho-cho, cornmeal, and "new sugar"—trace the influence of plantation cooking on Jamaican cuisine that led to the development of a "native" cuisine based on preparations that combine salt fish, salt meat, and "hard food" supplemented with the by-products of sugar processing such as the "new sugar" that Sullivan describes as sugar that is "sold in its unrefined state either as molasses, or, firmer, as pan sugar" (114). Although—or perhaps as—she mentions but does not detail Afro-Indigenous foodways and "country" cuisines that emerged from them to sustain "the native," Sullivan conveys a "native" cooking tradition related to and different from the recipes conveyed in her book.

In Sullivan's domestic construction of proto-national culinary colonialism, the privileged position is gendered female and raced White. *The Jamaica Cookery Book* presents "our ordinary Jamaica cooking" to English and White Creole women in Jamaica, organized for their use and adjusted for their palates. Collecting and managing "native cookery" for English benefit, Sullivan negotiates the social and political structures of nineteenth-century Jamaica, including a position for those whose rightness to run things derives from both their connection to the native and their separation from it. Instead of erasing "native" human sources as nineteenth-century Cuban and Puerto Rican cookbooks did, Sullivan acknowledges and holds them in their place—the "country," the market, the roadside, the kitchen—in service to the "pleasant occupation" of Jamaicans like herself.

Culinary Colonial Investments in Profit and Control

Two recipe pamphlets and one cookbook published by colonial West Indian men in the first decade of the twentieth century display the persistence of a colonial administration and culture dominated by men who were deeply invested in maintaining the status quo, even in the face of a diminished sugar industry and against a backdrop of demands for independence that, while consistently quelled, never disappeared. In contrast to their investments in using West Indian plants for the profit of the planter class and colonial administration and preparing them to serve British tastes, albeit with a tropical flare, Sullivan's attention to local non-White traditions and people stands out. Culinary colonialism comes in gradations, and after Sullivan's relative respect for "the natives" and attention to local consumption, these men's combination of appropriation and expropriation resounds. Their culinary investments are not only more classically colonial, they are also more patriarchal, imagining even colonial women to be in need of their guidance and control. The White West Indian women writing cookbooks alongside and after these men worked around and between patriarchal colonial control and racialized domestic management in the context of shifting landscapes of colonial production and power in the West Indies. In response to the difficulties that plagued the West Indian sugar industry, the Imperial Department of Agriculture for the West Indies was established in 1898, headquartered in Barbados, to supervise agricultural and horticultural research in the West Indies, particularly to revive sugar production but also to diversify the plantation economy (Galloway). Their numerous bulletins, reports, guides, handbooks, manuals, and pamphlets that focused on such things as *Cotton and Onion Industries* and *Notes on Poultry in the West Indies* also included two recipe pamphlets. In these, along with *Cookery in the West Indies Made Easy*, colonial men used the culinary sphere to keep colonial, racial, and gender orders in place while profiting from and highlighting the benefits of "native" products and culinary knowledge for domestic consumption.

The 1901 *Recipes for Cooking Sweet Potatos [sic] from the West Indies* and the 1902 *Recipes for Cooking West Indian Yams* (see figure 2.3) provided marketing support for the Imperial Department of Agriculture's efforts to promote crop diversification and rotation to British and White Creole West Indian planters. As they courted potential English purchasers of sweet potatoes and yams, West Indian planters could give them the pamphlets to pass along to their wives, housekeepers, and cooks and thus have their investment served to them as a delicacy. "The following recipes for cooking and preparing Sweet Potatos," wrote Daniel Morris, commissioner of agriculture for the West Indies, "are issued for distribution in the hopes that, if carefully carried out, those not already acquainted with this nutritious food may ensure that it is presented to them in an attractive and pleasant form."[24]

The pamphlets promoted the continued benefit—to the West Indies as well as to England—of both colonial products and the West Indian colonial project. The introduction to *Recipes for Cooking West Indian Yams*, probably written by John Redman Bovell, who served as Barbados superintendent of agriculture under Morris, suggests that bringing things tropical—plants, people—to the West Indies has allowed them to thrive, for "although grown throughout the tropics, it is in the West Indies that yams are to be found at their best and in the greatest variety and abundance" (1).[25] Furthermore, the introduction depicts a unification, in their enjoyment of yams, of "all classes throughout the West Indies," explaining that yams "are commonly found in 'provision' grounds throughout the West Indies" and are as important for "the

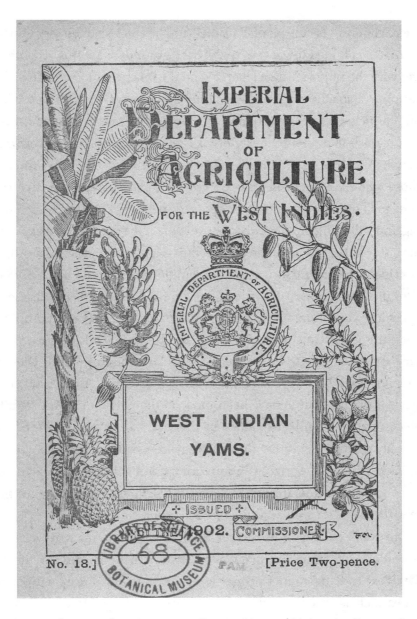

2.3. Cover of *West Indian Yams*, 1902. Source: Harvard University, Economic Botany Library of Oakes Ames.

estate labourer" as "the planter's table" (1). The still recent history of slavery may be alluded to via the "'provision' grounds," but it is smoothed over with the phrase "estate laborer" and the image of food equality. The pamphlet also advertises the West Indies to new waves of British "visitors," anticipating its incarnation as a tropical tourist destination, with the promise that "the majority of visitors to the West Indies become, even in the course of a brief stay, very partial to the yam" (1). For "those who have not visited the tropics," the pamphlet assures that the increasing intercourse and ease of passage between the West Indies and England will bring only an enhanced version of the familiar as it explains that "the general character of the yam plant may perhaps be best described by saying that it closely resembles in habit the black bryony of English hedgerows," for "the plants are near relatives" (2). It is, however, somewhat strange to compare yams to black bryony in a pamphlet marketing their consumption in England because while it is true that yams and black bryony are related in Linnaean taxonomy (family Dioscoreaceae), black bryony roots are known as poisonous. A more apt culinary comparison could have been made to the potato or turnip. While the comparison can be explained by the fact that Bovell and Morrison were horticulturalists rather than cooks, it seems also to betray the Imperial Department of Agriculture's preoccupation with the racial dynamics of yams as it metaphorizes keeping Blackness in its place in the well-trimmed—or well-served—English order.

The small collection of recipes that make up the majority of each pamphlet—fifteen in *Sweet Potatos* and twelve in *Yams*—feature the titular West Indian product primarily in variations on European potato dishes such as French Fried Sweet Potatoes, Escalloped Sweet Potatoes, Roasted Yams, Baked Yams, Boiled Yams, and Yam Chips. While they do include, toward the end of each pamphlet, more West Indian dishes such as Sweet Potato Pie and Sweet Potato Pudding, Yam Fritters, and Yam Pudding, those recipes still resemble more closely their English namesakes than they do Afro-Indigenous dishes such as Sweet Potato Duckanoo or Pone, recipes for which they do not include. The titles "Sweet Potato *Pie*" and "Yam *Pudding*" subsume them under English culinary history and efface the Afro-Indigenous technology and technique that also are integral to the dishes.

The recipes in *Sweet Potatos* are not attributed, but those in *Yams* are introduced as "hints prepared by Mrs. J. R. Bovell."[26] With the nod to the wife of John Redmond Bovell—born Elizabeth Jemmott—these pamphlets hint at the emerging network of British and White Creole women cookbook writers married to men serving in the colonial government and its institutions.[27] However, literally produced by and for the Imperial Department of Agriculture, framed by the men who ran it, and directed to a British audience, the pamphlets offer little room for Mrs. J. R. Bovell to intervene. Indeed, the pamphlets, along with the 1910 *Cookery in the West Indies Made Easy*, offer a contrast against which the subtle intercessions of Caroline Sullivan and the women who published cookbooks in the first dozen years of the twentieth century become more legible, but they also set out the overwhelming participation in the late colonial project of all cookbooks published in the West Indies at the turn of the twentieth century.

Cookery in the West Indies Made Easy presents itself as the work of a "compiler" who is both anonymous—the front cover announces that it is "By 'a Grenadian'"—and male; the preface states "the compiler, in placing this small and unpretentious work before the public, trusts he

---

Yam Pudding

Half a pound yam, two eggs, one lemon, two ounces butter, two ounces sugar.

Pare and boil the yam and rub it through a sieve while hot. Beat the butter and the yam together and allow the whole to cool. Break the eggs and separate the yolks from the whites. Beat the yolks until light, add sugar, juice of lemons, the grated rind and the yam. Whisk the whites to a stiff froth and stir lightly in before baking. Put in a well buttered dish and bake in a brisk oven for twenty minutes.

—*WEST INDIAN YAMS*, 6–7

has succeeded to some extent, in rendering assistance to the West Indian housekeepers." It is the work of a single man for a community to which he does not belong, a cookbook "for" the West Indies and "for" "West Indian housekeepers" but not of them. The preface also ignores the existence of the (admittedly few) other West Indian cookbooks, as it claims that "a practical book of Cookery for the West Indies has been a long felt need." Representing the West Indies as a site of lack, it explains that "owing to the local conditions, and to the fact that most of the principal ingredients cannot be obtained, the majority of the recipes contained in the English cookery books are impracticable in the West Indies." Its remedy is to show how to make European foods out of what little can be had in the West Indies. An elevation of Frenchness blankets the recipes, as the only attributions are to "Maître d'Hôtel," and a great number of the recipe titles are "à la" something, even those identified by other geographic markers such as "Eggs à l'Indienne" or "Fillets of Snapper or Jackfish à la Vénitienne." The sections organized around European meal components and their order of service (soup, fish, meat, vegetable, sweets, drinks), and around single meats, eschew the preponderance in Afro-Indigenous and Creole cuisine of soups, stews, braises, barbecues, and fries that mix meats and vegetables in single service dining. *Cookery in the West Indies Made Easy* includes few Afro-Indigenous or Creole dishes or even ingredients. There are no recipes for oildown, callaloo, or souse, and recipes featuring provisions are nearly nonexistent.[28] When the recipe for "Croûte au Pot" calls for "as many kinds of vegetables as you can," the only suggestions are European staples "such as cabbage, carrots, turnips, cucumbers, celery, parsley, &c." Even the recipes for jackfish—a Grenadian specialty and staple—insert the fish into European recipes, like "Fish à la Zingara," featuring parsley and breading and a Franco-British vinegar and lemon sauce.

Cookery in the West Indies Made Easy does have a relatively important number of Indo-Caribbean recipes (thirteen out of nearly three hundred)—demonstrating the importance of South Asian culinary traditions in West Indian cuisine following the importation of large numbers as indentured servants from India to replace the slave labor that

> ### Fish à la Zingara (Jacks)
>
> Carefully remove the flesh of 2 long fillets on each side of 3 large jackfish. Take off the skin. Brush the insides of the fillets over with a beaten egg. Sprinkle with finely chopped parsley, and *then close each pair together* again, thus re-forming the fish. Let them set for ½ hour and then brush over them with a beaten egg. Roll them in finely sifted panure. Let this coating dry. Repeat it, and fry the jacks one by one in a bath of boiling fat. As soon as they turn a rich golden colour take them out, drain, dry, and serve on a hot napkin.
>
> Make a Sauce Zingara in this way:—Reduce a gill of French vinegar, with a dessert spoonful of minced onion and a small saltspoon of salt and one of pepper till about a dessert spoonful of the liquid remains. Moisten with 2 gills of fish broth. Simmer for 10 minutes, strain, and add 2 tablespoonfuls of lightly fired bread crumbs, and finish with a dessert spoonful of minced parsley and the juice of ½ a lemon.
>
> Serve this with the jack fish.
>
> —COOKERY IN THE WEST INDIES MADE EASY, 27–28

had been outlawed in 1838. However, the recipes for Indo-Caribbean dishes are either filtered through a colonial order that sees them as "devilled" or else Frenchified, like the "Poulet en Piläo" that along with the French title calls for a number of Europeanizing ingredients like a butter-flour thickener and grated cheese.

While the recipes for pilau, kedgeree, chutneys, banana fritters, guava jelly, and a few rum-based cocktails can be identified as distinctively Grenadian, the cookbook does not in any significant way lay out what will later become specifically Grenadian cuisine. *Cookery in the West Indies Made Easy* exemplifies culinary colonialism in which haute cuisine, the domain of French men, can be modified by White West Indian men thanks to whom it is "made easy" for "the West Indian housekeepers." Nonetheless, ispite of the work of men like Morrison, Bovell, and the author of *Cookery in the West Indies Made Easy* to hold

Poulet en Piläo

Set a roomy stewpan on a fire large enough to hold the chicken easily. Pour in enough cold stock, or milk and water (in half and half proportions), to eventually cover the bird when put in. Bring the liquid to the boil, then plunge in the fowl (previously trussed and prepared) keeping up the high temperature for 5 minutes. Then add 4 oz. onion, 2 oz. carrot, 1 oz. celery, 1 oz. parsley, and a bouquet of herbs, with ½ oz. salt a 1 doz. peppercorns. This addition will stop the boiling. After this, ease the heat under the stewpan to a gentle simmering AND ON NO ACCOUNT PERMIT THIS TO BE EXCEEDED. THE TENDERNESS OF THE CHICKEN WILL DEPEND ENTIRELY UPON THE SLOWNESS OF THE COOKING ONE HOUR AND A HALF SHOULD BE SUFFICIENT. Then strain off the broth, wrap the fowl in a hot cloth, and put it back into the hot empty pan, closely covered to keep hot, while you turn a pint of the boilings to a sauce, thickened with 1 oz. butter, 1 oz. flour, bringing it to boil, and passing it through a hair sieve.

BOIL SEPARATELY, during the last half-hour of the simmering of the fowl, 8 oz. best rice. When the rice has been sufficiently cooked (each grain being separate) lift the pan from the fire, empty the contents on a wire sieve, drain off all the water, returning the cooked rice to the hot dry vessel in which it was cooked. Stir in 2 oz. fresh butter, and ½ pint hot tomato sauce. Mix with a fork, and finally shake in 2 oz. grated cheese. Now take a hot dish, and place the chicken in the centre. Mask it as much as possible with the sauce, sending the remainder of the sauce in a boat to the table. Dish the fowl smothered with the rice and garnish as follows:—

A circle of hard-boiled eggs, cut in quarters, all round the bottom of the mould of rice, and a sprinkling of cardamon powder over the rice. Pistachio nuts or almonds slightly fried in butter with an equal quantity of sultana raisins (2 oz. each) should be scattered over the whole. Fry the raisins and nuts in butter over a very low fire, *or they will be hard*. Also add rings round the dish of shallots (3 oz.) sliced finely and tossed in butter till dry.

N.B.—If desired to have a highly spiced dish, the spice must be stirred in with the broth.

All the garnish should be ready before the boiling of the rice, for the dishing should be as quick as possible. A little delay has the effect of making the rice greasy.

—*COOKERY IN THE WEST INDIES MADE EASY*, 81–82

West Indian cookery under the control of White West Indian men, more women followed Sullivan's lead.

White West Indian Women Cookbook Writers, between British Colonial Control and Black Domestic Labor

In the first dozen years of the twentieth century, four women published cookbooks in the West Indies: Mrs. Lickfold, in 1907, *A Handbook of Trinidad Cookery*; Mrs. F. H. Watkins, in 1908, *West India Recipes*; Mrs. H. Graham Yearwood, in 1911, *West Indian and Other Recipes*; and Marie Psaila, in 1912, *The Housekeeper's Guide for British Guiana and the West Indies*. The connections between one another and to the West Indies of Lickfold, Watkins, Yearwood, and Psaila stand out, even as the cookbooks also enact colonialist rhetoric that binds the islands to the British Empire and that buries Afro-Indigenous and Indo-Caribbean cooks under their wing.[29] In these cookbooks, Lickfold, Watkins, Yearwood, and Psaila develop the communities of White English and Creole women that Sullivan wrote for. In the process, they manage their own affiliations and tastes as well as those of their households, exercising and contesting their roles as—as Ann Laura Stoler notes—"white women caring for white men" (2), and performing what Fanon calls a colonialist "defense of native style" that serves to delegitimize, stall, and bury emerging national consciousness. Unlike Sullivan, their work to claim and tame "native" recipes operates through a disappearance of "native" people, contexts, and often even ingredients. Nonetheless, their recipes convey the long history of interactions among Indigenous, European, African, and Asian persons and traditions that form colonial culture for both colonizer and colonized. They show how culinary colonialism, in spite of its work to appropriate and expropriate Caribbean foods for European profit and to impose European order in colonial kitchens and tables, carries traces of the work of Afro-Indigenous and Indo-Caribbean cooks. A consideration of the biographies of Lickfold, Watkins, Yearwood, and Psaila, in conjunction with close readings of their cookbooks, reveals the balancing acts of White Creole women. Lickfold,

Watkins, Yearwood, and Psaila facilitate elite White British and Creole women in the West Indies sharing with one another their recipes for accomplishing domestic and colonial order. In the process, they manifest and at times exploit the intersections of gender discrimination and White power and the liminal position that they occupy between British colonial control and Black domestic labor.

As the predominance of authorial listing by marital title and name indicates, the positions of most White West Indian women in the early twentieth century depended on those of their husbands. Like Mrs. J. R. Bovell, Mrs. Lickfold, Mrs. F. H. Watkins, and Mrs. H. G. Yearwood were married to men who worked for the colonial administration, served in colonial government, and owned plantations. Mrs. Lickfold's husband, John Edmund Lickfold, was an English civil servant and later a cacao planter in Sangre Grande. His generous hosting of the naturalist Frank Chapman at his home in Trinidad is recorded in the 1894 *Journal of the Field Naturalists Club*. Lickfold represented the cacao industry for the Agricultural Society of Trinidad in Tobago in 1923. Mrs. F. H. Watkins's husband, the Honourable Frederick Henry Watkins, was commissioner of Turks and Caicos, at the time a dependency of Jamaica, and later colonial secretary of the Leeward Islands, as well as author of *Daily Thoughts from Horace*, of which a contemporary reviewer remarked, "as befits a servant of the Empire, the anniversaries which Mr. Watkins selects for special commemoration are largely of an imperial nature" ("Daily Thoughts" 11). Mrs. H. Graham Yearwood's husband, Henry Graham Yearwood, was a conservative member of the Barbadian Assembly and owned a sugar mill. It is Henry Graham Yearwood who Brittany Merritt cites in her argument that "more than fear of losing their independence from Britain . . . elite rhetoric reflected a fear of losing the freedom to exploit Barbadian labor and maintain white upper-class political power in the colony" (128). The extant biographical information about the women cookbook writers themselves reveals important aspects of their lives before and around their marriages and contextualizes their work as part of that of women negotiating limited and limiting

Domestic Control in West Indian Women's Cookbooks 105

2.4. Barbara Hilary Hodd Lickfold, center, with her family, Sangre Grande, Trinidad, early twentieth century. Source: Courtesy John Spriggs, grandson of Barbara Hilary Hodd Lickfold.

gender roles as much as that of colonialists trying to stave off the end of empire.

Mrs. Lickfold was born, in England, Barbara Hilary Hodd. In May 1897 she left for Trinidad following her fiancé, John (Jack) Edmund Lickfold, who was working on a cacao estate there.[30] They were married in June 1897 at St. Andrews, Couva, by Reverend Tree, whose wife, after Hilary Lickfold's death, would go on to edit the second, 1911, edition of *A Handbook of Trinidad Cookery*. Shortly after the marriage, Jack Lickfold was released from the cacao estate in Couva and, after a brief stay with the Trees, was hired as estate manager at Sangre Grande, where they stayed for the remainder of Hilary's life (see figure 2.4). Hilary Lickfold raised two children, whom she home-schooled at Sangre Grande along with the children of nearby planters and workers on the estate, was an active member of the Church of England, and was instrumental in the construction of the first Church of England in Sangre Grande.[31]

Mrs. F. H. Watkins may be Edith Haynes Cobbett Watkins, born in London around 1865 and married to Frederick Henry Watkins in London in 1882. However, there is no record that Edith Haynes Cobbett Watkins left England, and it is possible that she and Frederick Henry Watkins divorced or separated shortly after they married. If that is the case, the Mrs. F. H. Watkins who wrote *West Indian Recipes* was probably Mary E. Connel Watkins, born to a minister in Saint Vincent. With her husband, Mrs. F. H. Watkins moved around the British West Indies, living in Jamaica, Turks and Caicos, and Montserrat. They had one daughter, Mary Connel, who married Thomas Robert Robertson in Grand Turk in 1908. By World War I, Mrs. F. H. Watkins had settled in Antigua, where, according to her obituary, "she was best known and is remembered as the great and gracious lady who, with her husband, worked so whole-heartedly for and gave so generously to the Red Cross Society" ("Mrs. Mary E. Watkins," 334).

Mrs. H. Graham Yearwood was born Elizabeth Ann Clarey Manning in 1849 in Barbados. Her father's family, Manning, traces its residence in Barbados to the late seventeenth century; on her mother's side she was a Yearwood. Elizabeth (Bessie) married Henry Graham Yearwood in 1891, following the death of her first husband, Charles Edward Yearwood. She was active in Barbados's elite circles, supporting the Children's Invalid Home, which was later renamed in her honor, and subscribing to *Caribbeana*, the "miscellaneous papers relating to the history, genealogy, topography, and antiquities of the West Indies." She died in 1915.

Marie Psaila stands out for being the only woman of the group not to have married or had children. Psaila was born in Georgetown, Guyana, in 1879, the oldest child of Mary Georgina Walker, herself born in England, and Luigi Psaila. Luigi Psaila had immigrated to Guyana from Malta as a child with his parents, both of whom died of yellow fever before he was ten. It is likely that he knew Mary Georgina Walker's brother Stanislaus, who served in the British Guiana Civil Service. Mary Georgina Walker and Luigi Psaila married in England in 1878 and shortly thereafter settled together in British Guiana, where they would both reside for the rest of their lives. By the time Marie Psaila was a child, her father had become a prominent merchant in Georgetown, owning a store on Water Street.

Lickfold, Watkins, and Yearwood identify themselves as collectors or compilers and name other women—their peers, not their cooks—as contributors, extending a degree of shared authorship. As the names that reappear throughout and across the cookbooks attest and ensure, White West Indian communities in the early twentieth century were closely knit.[32] Their sharing of recipes and advice celebrates the women's connection but also keeps them aligned to the task of maintaining their community intact and unchanged. Psaila's epigraph, from Hannah Moore, "The sober comfort, all the peace which springs/From the large aggregate of little things,/On these small cares of daughter, wife, or friend,/The almost sacred Joys of Home depend," recognizes and celebrates women's traditional roles in the home and also strikes a warning about the necessity of keeping up that work.[33] In the colonial context, White women are under pressure, as Stoler explains, "to counter what was ... increasingly seen as a social problem and a political danger: ... a growing population of mixed-blood children born out of ... 'mixed' unions, of men who had 'gone native' or simply veered off course, of European children too taken with local foods, too versed in local knowledge" (2). That Hannah Moore was herself an evangelical Christian abolitionist and proponent of women's education at the turn of the nineteenth century attests to the complex affiliations of elite women who, advocating for change from positions of power, inhabit as much as they challenge the dominant order.

Fundraising cookbooks offer perhaps the most explicit examples of elite women leveraging their conventional roles as caretakers and guardians of the young and the weak to accomplish public projects and perhaps achieve social change. Lickfold's *Handbook of Trinidadian Cookery* was produced to support the construction of the Church of St. James the Just.[34] Yearwood's *West Indian and Other Recipes* emerged out of a fundraising project for a Barbadian Children's Home.[35] Watkins's *West Indian Recipes* was not only for the benefit of but also published by the Lady Musgrave Self-Help Society.[36] Through fundraising cookbooks,

White women could not only care for their own communities but also provide for Black and mixed-race women and children at a safe distance from their own homes and husbands. Philanthropic as they may be, both the work they funded and the cookbooks themselves promote British culture—from Anglicanism to needlework to tea cake—and preserve the colonial social order in which White women are neatly at the top and poor and non-White women are indebted to them.[37] Thus the openings to a less perfectly White Creole community that Lawson Welsh astutely notices in Yearwood's cookbook serve not to align White Creole housewives with nascent pro-independence creolization but rather to ensure that the emerging "Coloured" middle class is smoothly incorporated into the West Indian elite. Yearwood's cookbook exemplifies how in this group what is exacted is a White Creole organization that pays its respects to England, takes with minimal acknowledgment from the "native" Caribbean, and serves up creoleness. It strives to maintain the precarious balance in which White Creole power persists in the West Indies. In the process, it betrays the ways that White Creoleness is (uncomfortably) aligned with and exists only thanks to (though the thanks are rarely given), Black Creoleness and "native" culture. It also embraces a certain degree of defense of the native that while colonialist also can end up serving decolonization. In other words, Yearwood's cookbook, along with those of her peers, exemplifies the colonial paradox of destruction and creation and its manifestation in reinforcements of settler colonial rule that set up independence that itself paradoxically creates what it recovers.

Colonialist Women's Defense of Native Style

Indulging what Yearwood calls an inherited "mania for collecting," Lickfold, Watkins, Yearwood, and Psaila participate in the long colonial tradition of gathering, classifying, and categorizing Caribbean products for European profit and consumption. Even more than Sullivan, they instruct in the pivotal role of White women in managing the balances between European colonial power and "native" production. As they write about English and Afro-Indigenous foods (whether or not they recognize them as such) and household management, their culinary colonialism manifests in their work to obscure appropriation and creolization while celebrating the results of both. To maintain colonial domestic order, these White women must take from and maintain the absence and expendability of Black women.

Given all of their work maintaining a colonial order in which Whites are separate and superior, it might seem odd that these cookbooks include large numbers of "native" dishes, often right alongside or even crossed with English standards.[38] But while they join Sullivan in inscribing "native" recipes, they surpass her in what Fanon calls the colonialist "rush to the help of the traditions of the indigenous society" (242) that preserves "a hard core of culture which is becoming more and more shriveled up, inert, and empty" (*Wretched*, 238). Lickfold, Watkins, Yearwood, and Psaila manage to include "native" dishes with little if any discussion of native food traditions or practices and often without mention of the Black, mixed-race, and Indian women who must be not only the source of the recipes but also the daily preparers of them in these colonial homes. Indeed, these cookbooks create a culinary terra nullius, rendering dishes free for the taking, belonging to no tradition or preparation, no history of service or consumption.

The erasure of African and Indigenous histories is part of the racist work and justification of colonialism. Eurocentric organization of cookbooks whose material relies on those histories performs this erasure. Lawson Welsh's analysis of Yearwood's organization and categorization of recipes applies equally to those of Lickfold, Watkins, and Psaila: "overwhelmingly Eurocentric rather than based on the traditional cooking or pairing of ingredients in a West Indian context and she makes no attempt to give histories of particular dishes. Indeed, the most striking thing about her cookbook is its almost total disregard for pairing dishes traditionally cooked and eaten together or for distinguishing the cuisines associated with different ethnicities" (447). The results are organizations that do such things as group together peppercorns and peppers (Linnaean: capsicum, Taíno: ají) to preserve the idea of West

Indian food as "spicy" but lose the nutritional and culinary knowledge of ají. They also erase both local knowledge and the history of slavery and colonial trade by confusing corn and sorghum; they leave out or minimize plantains and offer only sweet banana recipes alongside puddings and desserts.[39]

Whereas Sullivan never wrote "creole" in her recipe titles, Lickfold, Watkins, Yearwood, and Psaila all use "creole" in theirs. However, as Higman notes of *A Handbook of Trinidad Cookery*, none makes any "attempt to define creole cuisine" (81). "Creole" does not function as a tag for dishes that incorporate Indigenous, European, and Afro-Caribbean elements; instead, it signals those dishes that have been taken over by White Creoles, de-historicized and de-contextualized or even, like with Yearwood's "Creole Soup" (4) and Lickfold's "Creole Savoury (Melangene),"[40] evacuated of their Afro-Indigenous ingredients.

Recipes that do not include the word "creole" but are nevertheless recognizable—often by their titles—as common to the cuisine that emerged out of the mixing of culinary histories that the term designates, similarly lack local context and even ingredients. Few if any island-specific distinctions mark any of the cookbooks. For example, Psaila's pilau recipes show not the rich mixing of the Indian rice preparation with meats, peas (beans), and Afro-Indigenous spices that characterize the West Indian classic; rather, they present a dish with strangely separated rice and chicken, devoid of either Indian or Afro-Indigenous spices, supplemented only by bacon.

Creole Savoury (Melangene)
(MRS ROSS)

Boil the melangène in salt and water. When done, cut in halves, scoop out the halves and mix with some finely chopped onions, browned in butter, and a little grated cheese. Put the mixture back into the skins, dip in butter and fry.

—LICKFOLD, *A HANDBOOK OF TRINIDAD COOKERY*, 45

> ### Pilau (1)
>
> 1 fowl
> A few slices of bacon
> Rice
> 2 eggs
> Tomato and parsley
>
> Boil a fowl, take it from the water and cut in pieces, then fry some bacon with it. Boil some rice in a little of the water the fowl was boiled in and take the rest of the water and make a nice gravy. Boil two eggs hard. Bank the rice in the middle of a dish, then put alternately pieces of fowl and bacon. Garnish with slices of hard-boiled egg, tomato and sprigs of parsley.
>
> —PSAILA, *HOUSEKEEPER'S GUIDE FOR BRITISH GUIANA AND THE WEST INDIES*, 35

Caroline Sullivan acknowledged White women's proximity to Black women as she showed herself to be a White Creole "compiler" who worked around Afro-Indigenous cooks. Lickfold, Watkins, Yearwood, and Psaila present as White Creole collectors who gather the contributions of their White Creole friends. By not referring to even the management of cooks, they efface not only the labor or their cooks but also their own places—and those of their contributors—both as dominators of and proximate to Afro-Indigenous women. And just as there are no Afro-Indigenous women (seen) in the kitchen, there is no more (evidence of) Afro-Indigenous culinary innovation. Afro-Indigenous women's culinary work may be barely visible in the "old West Indian recipes, many of which were being forgotten in the rush for new things" (I), but the future belongs to the Creoles, whose work preserving the Afro-Indigenous past is part of their rendering Afro-Indigenous women obsolete as active participants in the forging of West Indian culture. The mentions, in Watkins of "Mrs. B's Cook" and in Yearwood of Cook Harris as the contributors of the recipes for pepperpot, pumpkin soup, and

> ### Pumpkin Soup
> (MRS. B'S COOK)
>
> To 2 quarts water add as much pumpkin as needed, a penny half-penny worth of salt pork or beef. Seasonings and a small bit of yam or coco.
>
> —WATKINS, *WEST INDIAN RECIPES*, 56

Swiss toast (Watkins, 55, 56, 84) and turtle soup (Yearwood, 7), are the exceptions that prove the rule.

Of course, race in the West Indies is not only Black and White. As they erase Afro-Indigenous West Indians, a few of the cookbooks incorporate Indo-Caribbeans, marking the influx of indentured laborers from India in the wake of slavery. Lickfold includes a full recipe for curry powder, rather than just calling for it as an ingredient, and she lists the contributor as Banni Singh; similarly, she attributes a recipe for "Mangoes Pickled in Mustard Oil (Anchar)" to "Bhupsingh." While these manifest the incorporation of Indo-Caribbean dishes and also recognition of contact with Indo-Caribbean people, they are again exceptions. Lickfold is the only author to name Indo-Caribbean contributors, and even this recognition afforded to Indo-Caribbeans is minimal, for she attributes only to Mrs. Rankin the recipe for Bobotee (Lickfold, 23).

In spite of Lickfold, Watkins, Yearwood, and Psaila's work to maintain English order and to appropriate and preserve native culture in desiccated form, recipes for dishes developed by slaves, peasants, and indentured laborers from a combination of Indigenous, African, and Indian techniques and ingredients, common slave rations, and provisions appear so frequently across the cookbooks that their status as "native" staples becomes clear. These include callaloo, pumpkin, peas, okra, and turtle soups; pepperpot and other stews featuring salt meats often to be accompanied by foofoo, coucou, or boiled provisions; pilaus, kedgerees, and curries; dozens of salt-fish–based preparations; fritters, cakes, custards, and pones made from cassava, yam, and sweet potato; chutneys, jams, sweets, and desserts made not only from tropical fruits and sugar but also barks and roots. The ways that White Creole women included recipes for these foods in their cookbooks obscure their connections to Afro-Indigenous and Indo-Caribbean recipes, and yet the fact of their inclusion makes the creolization of these cookbooks one that includes Afro-Indigenous and Indo-Caribbean elements.

Pepper-Pot
(R. BRATHWAITE)

To begin a pepper-pot, chose pork, duck, or game in preference to beef or mutton. Cut in pieces and fry till well browned. Boil 3 pints of water in a canaree or other earthenware pot, and add when boiling—2 onions, herbs, sive, mice, cloves, 2 red peppers tied all together in a muslin bag. Add also salt to taste, the browned meat, and 3 dessertspoonfuls of cassareep. Boil rapidly for 2 minutes, then draw aside and simmer till tender. Serve in the same pot, with a wooden spoon. Warm up every day, adding cooked meat, cassareep, and water in the proportion of 1 dessertspoonful of cassareep to 1 pint of water.

—LICKFOLD, *A HANDBOOK OF TRINIDAD COOKERY*, 84

Pepper-Pot
(MRS. E. L. BOVELL)

Take 3 lbs. pig's jowl; boil well, as for souse, in salted water. Cut in large dice. Take also an old fowl or duck, cut it up and fry till brown. Fill a small bag with red peppers cut in slices. Put it in an earthenware pot or canaree with all the meat, and water to cover. Add cassareep to cover. Simmer till the meat is quite soft. Bring to the boil every day, adding any cold cooked meat, and water and cassareep to cover. Never use anything that has been thickened with flour before first washing it.

—LICKFOLD, *A HANDBOOK OF TRINIDAD COOKERY*, 85

Interracial contact is forced by gendered separation; the proximity of women across race in domestic spaces results in culinary creolization that manifests interracial collaboration. Evident in these cookbooks is that women of all races in the West Indies, knowingly or not, supported one another's places at the center of domestic production of protonational culture. To publish these cookbooks, the White women compilers relied on and documented the work of the primarily Black and mixed-race women who cooked for them. At the same time, in the tradition of the "women of color" who, as Kathleen Wilson shows, "also exploited available networks of social power to secure positions of property and influence within Caribbean societies" (21–22), Black and mixed-race women who secured positions as cooks in elite homes and who sold pre-made foods at markets and stands, nourished White women and occupied positions of, albeit limited and unacknowledged, power and influence in their homes and diets. The result are West Indian cookbooks controlled and managed by White women that maintain heterocolonial structures of power and also the mutual influences of British, Afro-Indigenous, and Indo-Caribbean women.

The recipes for pepperpot that appear in Lickfold, Watkins, Yearwood, and Psaila's cookbooks exemplify the traces of Afro-Indigenous cuisine, agriculture, and technology that survive in, and through, White West Indian women's culinary colonialism. These traces, as Glissant writes, convey the "fragile knowledge" that slaves and other dominated people transported and tended "as one of the places of survival" (*Treatise*, 9). Pepperpot originates from Indigenous stews made with cassaripe—a preservative and flavoring made during the processing of yuca for its many uses—and kept cooking indefinitely, in African stews thickened with okra, and in plantation and peasant stews made with salt meats included in slave rations and the parts of animals most often left to them such as jowls, tails, and bones.[41] The absence of any acknowledgment, in the recipes, of pepperpot's origins and development exemplifies the appropriative gesture of the colonialist defense of native style. Nonetheless, each recipe attests to some of the Afro-Indigenous techniques and tastes at the base of any pepperpot recipe.

Pepper Pot
(MRS. B'S COOK)

A penny half-penny worth each of okra, kale, callalu, (spinach), beef and salt pork; a few tomatoes, 1 white coco, 1 country pepper, thyme, skellions, and onion to taste; fresh meat bones.

Put all on with 2 quarts of water, having tied the callalu and kale together. When they are boiled tender rub them through a colander and return to the pot. Strain before serving. Shrimps and black crabs may be boiled with this.

—WATKINS, *WEST INDIAN RECIPES*, 55

Pepper Pot

An ox tail (or calves head), 3 lbs of fresh pork. Cut up all this into pieces about ½ inches square, and put them in a large conaree, fully cover it with water and put it on to boil. When half done, add 4 bonnet peppers tied up in a muslin bag, a large bunch of thyme, 1 lb of sliced onions, 2 large tablespoonfuls of brown sugar (or more to taste) 3 gills of cassaripe, the sauce should be fairly thick after the first two days. It should be warmed every day or it will go sour. Any cold meat can be put into it, provided it is not seasoned meat, as this also will turn it acid.

—YEARWOOD, *WEST INDIAN AND OTHER RECIPES*, 107

The recipes for such things as "Pone" and "Conkies" also bear evidence of European ingredients entering West Indian dishes through Black cooks' work in British and White Creole kitchens during and after slavery. Pone and conkies' Indigenous history is evident in their basis in cassava or corn. Conkies also hark to early Afro-Indigenous innovations that used Indigenous corn and cassava flours with the African preparation of wrapped dumplings.[42] At the same time, the recipes for pone and conkies call for butter and occasionally milk, ingredients that

> ### Cassava Pone
>
> 3 sticks of sweet cassava
> 1 coconut (grated)
> 4 tablespoonfuls of sugar
> 1 tablespoonful of lard
> 1 tablespoonful of butter
> Blackpepper
> 1 small red pepper
> Nutmeg
> Powdered cinnamon
> 10 tablespoonfuls of currents
>
> Grate about 3 sticks of raw sweet cassava, add the grated coconut, then the sugar, melted lard, melted butter, a little blackpepper, a small bruised red pepper, a little grated nutmeg and powdered cinnamon, and the currents washed and picked. Well grease a pan, pack the mixture in and bake.
>
> —PSAILA, *HOUSEKEEPERS GUIDE TO BRITISH GUIANA AND THE WEST INDIES*, 106

entered Afro-Indigenous diets through the cooking of middle-class and elite Black and Creole kitchens and through the work of Black women using it in plantation and inn kitchens where they served, and were often supplied by, White owners and clients. The recipe for "Cassava Conkies" in Yearwood's cookbook also calls for rose water, which entered West Indian cuisine from India (72).[43] These mutual influences and the deeply mixed—creolized—nature of West Indian cuisine blur the distinctions between Indigenous, African, European, and Indian culinary histories.

Creolization does blur distinctions, as does all mixing. If we consider only the amalgam, only the idea of being mixed, without also noting and examining the very different places and paths from and through which the elements have arrived, then the creole becomes at best vacuous and at worst a tool to erase specificity, difference, and the histories

> ### Cassava Conkies
> (MRS. E. T. COX)
>
> Beat ½ lb. of sugar and ½ lb. butter together, add 5 eggs, ¼ of a wineglass of rose water, ½ table-spoonful of beaten spice, and lastly ½ lb. of cassava flour. Wrap a large spoonful at a time in chilled plantain leaves, and steam them (be careful not to let the water get into the leaves) or steam in a pudding mould, and serve with sweet sauce. If steamed in a mould, they will take 2 or 3 hours to cook.
>
> —YEARWOOD, *WEST INDIAN AND OTHER RECIPES*, 72

of the subsumed. But creolization can be that which, as Glissant writes, "puts all of us, wherever we come from, in Relation" (*Treatise*, 9) such that both differentiation and conjoining persist and "being changes while remaining" (*Treatise*, 14). As cookbooks operate this kind of creolization in action, they reveal how terms like "native" and "Creole," as they name that which "belongs" neither to a pre-colonial Caribbean nor to Europe, Africa, or Asia, can indicate recipes for independence that later emerged across Creole communities. They also underline the stakes of control by culinary colonialism in the early twentieth century: the collection and inscription of recipes as property, the containment of nativeness and authenticity, the naming of Creole as one's own, determined who ruled West Indian culinary culture.

In the early twentieth century, Lickfold, Watkins, Yearwood, and Psaila succeeded in building new degrees of separation between White men and Black women and children, but they did so through their own active engagement in domestic management that, whether they say so or not, absolutely includes the management of Afro-Indigenous domestics. The issue of *that* proximity is not ever more mixed children but ever more mixed cuisines. And as they insert "native" practices of preserving and transmitting recipes into the British tradition of cookbook writing, they also give print legitimacy to "native" cuisine and archive the "native" recipes being enjoyed by elite women in ways that will facilitate their recovery and reworking into and by future generations. While Lickfold, Watkins, Yearwood, and Psaila's selection and placement of Afro-Indigenous and Indo-Caribbean dishes, along with the details of the recipes, the attributions, and the narrative portions of the cookbooks, erase "native" contexts and people, maintain colonial order, and assert White women's power within that order, they inscribe traces of the many centuries and the many modes of creolization that will be uncovered and reincorporated into recipes for independence in the cookbooks of the mid-twentieth century.

Who does the work of culinary colonialism and composing recipes for national independence, who writes these cookbooks, along with what they write, inform conceptions of what Caribbean culture is, who contributes to it, and who it belongs to. The biographical information I have found about turn-of-the-century West Indian Women cookbook writers shows the terrain that British and White Creole women tread to get into those positions of power, and how little recognition they continue to receive, both for their pioneering as women and for their participation as colonialists. Locating, gathering, and collating cookbooks and also piecing together the scant biographical information first about Sullivan and then about Lickfold, Watkins, Yearwood, and Psaila from their prefaces, newspaper articles, and family trees, along with searching out the cookbooks that make up thus study, I have engaged in my own collecting. The assemblage that I offer, of the lives and works of Caribbean cookbook authors, exemplifies how, as much as it may try to center the material, the building of an archive, the collecting of materials to form a cookbook, a study of cookbooks, or a section on a set of cookbook authors always relies on and belies the position of the collector. The collector's ideas about what is worthy of collection, the range of their access, as much as "what there is," determines the content of an archive. At the same time, most archives exceed the goals of the collector, can be re-searched and re-read for things that the collector ignored or devalued but included anyway. Thus, the work of collecting and reading colonial and independence-era cookbooks is the work of reading recipe collections for how to make dishes and how to understand constructions and instructions for the management of gender and race in colonial and independence-era Caribbean.

Whereas the first West Indian Cookbooks were published by British and White Creole women wielding (if also under) colonial control and White Creole power, the Afro-Indigenous and Indo-Caribbean cuisines and cooks whose traces they contained not only endured but continued to develop what would be the basis of an Afrocentric national culinary discourse. This discourse would elevate the information codified in the cookbooks, blended with that maintained in kitchens, into "the pulse of a fresh stimulus" that Fanon says both carries and is carried by the movement beyond "the context of colonial domination" (*Wretched*, 176–177). For while the defense of "native style" works to delegitimize and stall emerging native national consciousness, what Fanon terms "unusual forms of expression, original themes no longer imbued with the power of invocation but the power to rally and mobilize" do develop (*Wretched*, 176). And they develop in domestic spaces where White and Black women work as much as in the public squares and workshops occupied by the Algerian storytellers and artisans that Fanon celebrates. When Afrocentric and "native" Creole Caribbean cookbooks start to appear after World War II, as I will examine in chapters 4–6, they take up much of what was captured in the cookbooks of the turn of the twentieth century, both as a tradition they own and as a base from which new creations depart. But the history of Caribbean cookbooks is not one of slow if steady building from culinary colonialism to recipes for national independence and from White patriarchal domination to Black womanist liberation. In the national culinary cultures concocted in Cuba, the Dominican Republic, Haiti, Jamaica, and Barbados over the second half of the twentieth century, race, gender, and independent rule appear in a great variety of formulations. And in the French Antilles, Puerto Rico, and the U.S. Virgin Islands, as I will explore in chapter 3, culinary colonialism continues, and any gathering of the traces of Afro-Indigenous histories occurs under the long arm of colonial and neocolonial extension.

3

Colonial and Neocolonial Fortification in the French Antilles, Puerto Rico, and the U.S. Virgin Islands

THE COOKBOOKS that exemplify colonial and neocolonial fortification in the French Antilles,[1] Puerto Rico, and the U.S. Virgin Islands engage in what Frantz Fanon calls a colonialist "defense of native style" that serves to delegitimize, stall, and bury emerging native national consciousness whose traces nonetheless remain and occasionally gather strength. French Antilles, Puerto Rican, and U.S. Virgin Islands cookbooks of the early and mid-twentieth century solidify local and regional cuisines into quaint artifacts to be protected by colonial hegemony. French colonial cookbooks of the 1930s held in place the French colonial model of inviting its colonial subjects to become perfect little Frenchmen while insisting on the exotic nature of the Other, by blending the local cuisines of distinct colonies into an amalgam of tropical delectables fused with the bodies of exotic women, appositely under French control. For all the differences in the colonial legacies of the two island groupings, in both Puerto Rico and the U.S. Virgin Islands, U.S. home economics and agricultural extension programs from the early to mid-twentieth century produced cookbooks and instructional materials that extended U.S. views and practices in the schools and homes and bellies of girls and women: neocolonialism's hold was secured and contested as much through defining good food as through steering flows of capital.

In spite of the divergent French and U.S. conceptions of *bonnes recettes* and good food, the cookbooks discussed in this chapter share versions of an imperial family romance. Combining the tropes of the New World land as woman and of the kitchen as the womb of the house, the cookbooks use heterocolonial culinary formulations in which a colonial (French) fatherland sows its seed in local fields and kitchens that in turn lend local color to his table or a new (American) patriarch injects modern fertilizer into languishing plots and pots that can then thrive in his backyard. Unlike Glissantian creolization, these combinations hold colonial tropes and hierarchies in place. Alongside their paternalistic narrative, however, both the French- and U.S.-Caribbean cookbooks of the early twentieth century chart the shifting places of women within colonial structures and societies, new negotiations of racial and ethnic divides, and the simmering of creolizations that re-cognize their Afro-Indigenous elements.

Chronologically, these cookbooks are published in the independence era—Haiti, the Dominican Republic, Cuba, and nearly all of the former British colonies were or were becoming independent by the mid-twentieth century. Conceptually, these cookbooks practice culinary colonialism, and they were published in islands where independence was never achieved or was achieved only fleetingly. France never fully withdrew from Guadeloupe, Martinique, French Guiana, and Saint Martin. And in the late nineteenth century, the United States emerged as a neocolonial power in the Caribbean, taking possession of Puerto Rico in 1898—less than a year after it won independence from Spain—and of the U.S. Virgin Islands in 1916. Puerto Rico remains a "commonwealth," the U.S. Virgin Islands an "unincorporated and organized territory" of the United States. Given their contexts of colonial and neocolonial rule, it is not surprising that even when they address "locals," these cookbooks are almost always written by and for the people who ensure and benefit from that rule.

The cookbooks of the French Antilles, Puerto Rico, and the U.S. Virgin Islands represent both the holdout and the extension of culinary colonialism well into the twentieth century and the great variations of political and cultural development across the Caribbean throughout the independence era. The generally chronological ordering of both *Culinary Colonialism, Caribbean Cookbooks, and Recipes for National Independence* as a whole and my treatment of the cookbooks in each chapter or section, as well as the few breaks in that ordering, underscore the moments of coincidence and of non-coincidence of historical trends and culinary developments, of political movements and cookbook publications. By considering in this third chapter these three island groupings that variously complicate the story, I also show the progress from culinary colonialism to recipes for national independence. Cookbooks are sites of colonial regulation and decolonial nation-formation in the multiple ways that I show here and also in others to which I only gesture. Even in Puerto Rico, the French Antilles, and the U.S. Virgin Islands, in the years that follow the chronological end of this chapter, cookbooks have reached for national independence and marked conceptions of independent cultures without independent nationhood.[2] Other cookbooks from across the Caribbean that are also beyond the scope of this book offer more variations both on how to make nations and how to deal with their absence, and I hope that others will join me in examining things like national cuisines without nation-states, regional cuisines, and diasporic constructions of home cooking.[3]

The distinct colonial histories and the different populations, cuisines, and industries of the French Antilles, Puerto Rico, and the U.S. Virgin Islands led to divergent manifestations of colonialist defenses of native culinary style in early to mid-twentieth century cookbooks. And so this chapter is divided into three sections. The first section argues that French Antilles cookbooks from the 1930s through the 1970s present things Antillean, managed and mediated by French colonialists, as entirely desirable to spice up French pleasure. Thus, French Antilles cookbooks play up the exotic appeal of Antillean products and admit shifting roles for women and Afro-Caribbeans that nonetheless uphold the supremacy of French taste and hold the colonial order in place. In the second section, I turn to Puerto Rican cookbooks, arguing that following the United States takeover of Puerto Rico, U.S.-born and -trained women toiled to capture local culinary knowledge and to reconstitute it as the gift of U.S. intervention. Installing English as the language of good nutrition, these women alternately ignored, exoticized, and relegated to a dark past the Spanish-language food writing and culinary traditions that nonetheless persisted, perhaps strengthened by the status of the Spanish language as target and springboard. In the final section of this chapter, I argue that the U.S. extension service cookbooks produced in the Virgin Islands facilitated the work of the colonial education and agricultural extension programs to identify local culinary practice as a site of lack that "rehabilitation and development" programs could correct. The collaboration of Virgin Islands women with U.S. educational and development programs led more to the subsumption of Virgin Islands women into the U.S. programs than to shifting the programs at their hands. Together, these three sections show that while late culinary colonialism continues to work to assert the inferiority of Caribbean cooking in spite of the value of its ingredients, it operates less on appropriation than assimilation, recognizing "the natives" not only as producers of the goods from which colonial control continues to benefit but also as consumers who can be taught colonial culinary values and thus rendered better colonial subjects. These three sections together also show colonial patriarchy's resistance to change even as women gained increasingly public positions in which they worked in increasingly collaborative ways across dividing lines of identification.

Consuming Exotic Objects in the French Antilles

The incorporation of Martinique, Guadeloupe, and French Guiana, in 1946, as "départements d'outre mer"—literally "departments of the far seas"—exemplifies the paradoxical gestures of incorporation and exclusion that characterize French colonialism. While departmentalization supposedly rendered each island equal to any other French department, "outre" conveys great distance, excess, and supplementarity,[4] and thus names the actual place of the Caribbean departments in the French nation. On the culinary front, by the nineteenth century,

French cuisine was well established across Europe and especially in its former and ongoing colonies as, in Zilkia Janer's words, "the highest point of culinary development for the rest of the world to follow" (393). French chefs, maîtres de cuisine, and cookbook writers succeeded in ensuring Marie-Antoine Carême's pronouncement in *L'art de la cuisine française au dix-neuvième siècle* (1828) that "nineteenth-century French cuisine will remain the model of the beautiful in culinary art" (cited in Parkhurst Ferguson, 40)[5] in France and in the colonies as well. Nineteenth- and twentieth-century European, U.S., Latin American, and Caribbean cookbooks consistently name French cooks and French cookbooks as the best source of culinary knowledge. Built on the primacy of the French terroir, French cuisine stood in not only for Frenchness but for hexagonal France—referring to the shape of borders of the nation in Europe—so that throughout the nineteenth century, even as ingredients from the colonies were increasingly called for, no French colonial cookbook was published.

It was not until thirty years after the turn of the century, on the occasion of the 1931 Colonial Exposition in Paris,[6] that the first three French colonial cookbooks appeared: Anne Querillac's *Cuisine coloniale: Les bonnes recettes de Chloé Mondésir*, Raphaël de Noter's *La bonne cuisine aux colonies: Asie-Afrique-Amérique*, and Charlotte Rabette's *La cuisine exotique chez soi*.[7] Building on the use of food to, in Lauren James's words, "demonstrate how the colonies provided and could provide goods to France" (130) and joining what Régine Goutalier describes as "the hymn to the empire so vigorously launched at the Exposition" (285), all three of these 1931 cookbooks are decidedly imperial: they present "exotic," "colonial" cuisine as an enticing addition to overwhelmingly superior French traditions. *Cuisine coloniale* stands out among the three for its Guadeloupean focus and also for its embodiment of the French amalgamation of Antillean food and women. It also highlights how the tropes of edibility and danger, abundance (fruitfulness) and scarcity (infertility)—applied to both the Caribbean and to women—are also the stuff of cookbooks, especially colonial ones. Thus, colonial French Antillean cookbooks instruct in the convergence of gendered and colonial tropes and orders whose preservation and transformation they simultaneously contain. The double meanings of "instruct" and "contain" are in full force, as cookbooks show and teach, hold and transport.

Querillac, de Noter, and Rabette locate their authority in their position as French interpreters of the colonies rather than through any special connection to a particular colonial locale.[8] For Rabette, the colonies are only a general exotic elsewhere. De Noter includes Guadeloupe, Martinique, and French Guiana as relatively indistinct parts of the French colonial empire.[9] Querillac, a journalist, had written previously on both women's work and the French colonies generally. Her *Cuisine coloniale* includes ingredients and dishes from the lotus, loved by "Les Extrême-Orientaux" (18), to pistachios (indigenous to Madagascar and Mauritius), to Matambala (from West Africa) and erases local specificity with such comments as "if game is abundant in the colonies, there is not, properly speaking, any particularly special way to prepare it" (129). In spite of her pan-colonial experience and the title and scope of her cookbook, however, Querillac does detail her own experiences as a traveler in the Antilles in particular and anchors *Cuisine coloniale: Les bonnes recettes de Chloé Mondésir* in Guadeloupe through the figure of Chloé Mondésir, her ostensible cook, whose existence vouchsafes for the authenticity of the recipes. Querillac's *Cuisine coloniale* exemplifies how all of these 1931 French colonial cookbooks, like colonial cookbooks generally, are not written for Caribbean cooks with Caribbean backgrounds. They are addressed to colonialists, both those who live in the Caribbean and those who are average French citizens. That, more than the fact that they are written under persistent colonial rule, makes me characterize them as part of culinary colonialism rather than recipes for independent national culture: they serve French colonialism to French colonialists.

In the food tents at the 1931 Colonial Exposition, James explains, "being served Guadeloupian food and drink products by beautiful Caribbean women in colorful local costume fused the popular images of blacks as domestic servants and entertainers into a multisensory experience" (149). Much of the appeal was erotic, and Querillac's introduction of Chloé Mondésir capitalizes on this trope. Querillac adds to the fusion the image of the Black witch and emphasizes the bewitching sex appeal of Antillean food and women. Claiming to document "the simple and honest food that let us know and appreciate Chloé Mondésir, an adorable câpresse with golden sapodilla skin,[10] sparkling finery, and precious jewelry," Querillac at the same time warns that "every coin has a tail; Chloé, jealous, is vindictive. 'Padon pas ka guéri bosse' she says (the pardon does not erase the wound). And so you can see her sometimes on moonlit nights leaning over a black cauldron where strange brews boil. Her brow furrowed, her eyes sparkling, she murmurs the mysterious incantations thanks to which the perfect philter will know how to prevent or to cure the infidelity of her lover" (xii). By turns innocent savage, prostitute, and witch, offering natural bounty, charms, or poison, Chloé mediates between Caribbean and European audiences while Querillac manages her threat to the French order.

However much she is based on a real person, Chloé's embodiment of colonial tropes renders her a character in the French colonial fiction. A close reading of Querillac's Chloé shows how the cookbook works as part of a corpus of colonial literature and how, through the stories of Chloé, Querillac ensures the colonialist preservation of "native style" in her recipes. The genre of the Caribbean cookbook based on the expertise of one near-mythical cook was only just emerging in the period in which Querillac wrote,[11] but the figure of the devoted Afro-Caribbean servant-cook was already a fixture of colonial Caribbean literature and food advertising, much like the African American mammy.[12] *Cuisine coloniale*'s authorial attribution, "collected by A. Querillac," gestures to the origin of recipes but stops far short of attributing them to Chloé. The recipes reveal to a certain degree the culinary work of Chloé and Afro-Caribbean women like her and the proto-national cuisines that they were cooking up. Querillac's work, therefore, was not only to gather and re-present recipes but also, as close readings can demonstrate, to enshrine the Afro-Caribbean woman and the foods she prepared as exotic objects for French consumption.

As if she were speaking with Chloé, Querillac starts her preface with a proverb in Creole: "Tooth no heart [Dent pas coeur]." But immediately,

Querillac translates the expression for the "Madame" whom she explicitly addresses in the next paragraph: "teeth are not the heart [les dents ne sont pas le coeur]" (vi). Thus, it is no surprise that although Querillac announces that "to please Chloé, let us measure beans, corn, rice or cassava flour by the 'half pot' (liter) and 'pot' (two liters). And we will let her insist on 'scraping [grager]' coconut and cheese rather than finely 'grating [râper' finement]' them" (ix–x), she indicates only French measurements in most of the recipes. Chloé's pleasure is certainly important to Querillac: the reference to the need to please Chloé keeps in mind the threat that she poses and also keeps Chloé firmly in the realm of sensory pleasure rather than culinary knowledge.[13] Indeed, Querillac conveys not so much details of Chloé's recipes as descriptions of Chloé cooking, narrated by her French colonial employer.

The calalou (callaloo) recipes in *Cuisine coloniale* illustrate how Querillac's cookbook serves an audience curious about the Caribbean—not one ready and able to cook Caribbean dishes that they know and love. If anyone were to actually use the ingredients described, they would not end up with a calalou soup at all, for "the leaves of the aralia" are not taro or calalou leaves but the leaves of an entirely different family of plants, albeit one of great interest to French botanists in Madagascar.[14] And if anyone were to actually follow the instructions Querillac gives, they would find themselves in the strange situation of removing from the okra the main edible substance of the plant, for okra pods are never peeled in preparation for cooking, though they may be cleaned, scraped or rubbed.[15] The productive irony is, of course, that as Querillac contrasts what "we studied" with what Chloé says, she actually reveals Chloé's superior knowledge and the botanical precision of, in Chloé's "patois," "calalou herb [z'herbe à calalou]." Querillac, however, offers Chloé as a savage spectacle. Chloé's innocent but rude bounty, conjured as she "tosses" and "adds," belongs to the untamed appetites for which, as Querillac warned in the introduction, we cannot blame her: "We will not chastise her, either, for having in the disturbing shadows of voluptuous Antillean nights, sometimes welcomed *devil Loulou, Prétérit*, or *Cocodo* 'who come tuh talk uh lub [*qui té vini pale d'amour*]' who came

> ### *Calalou au gras* (Fat Calalou)
>
> *Chloé, sous les voûtes épaisses des arbres qui bordent le torrent aussi bien que dans sa cuisine, prépare simplement ce plat avec les feuilles de cette araliée que nous avons étudiée sous le nom de taro et qu'elle appelle « z'herbe à calalou ».*
>
> *Dans un litre d'eau bouillante, elle jettera environ deux livres de ces feuilles et trois douzaines de jeunes gombos encore verts le tout soigneusement épluché et haché. Elle y ajoutera un morceau de petit salé et cinq ou six crabes coupés en morceaux, épices, sel, poivre, piment, oignons et une gousse d'ail.*
>
> *Le tout devra cuire longtemps, et, la cuisson terminée, le calalou devra présenter l'apparence d'une bouillie épaisse et bien liée.*
>
> Chloé, below the thick arches of the trees that block the torrent as well as if she were in her kitchen, prepares this dish simply with the leaves of the aralia that we studied as taro and that she calls "calalou herb."
>
> In one liter of boiling water, she tosses about two pounds of these leaves and three dozen young okra pods, still green and carefully peeled and chopped. She adds a piece of salt meat and five or six crabs cut into pieces, spices, salt, pepper, peppers, onions, and a clove of garlic.
>
> The whole thing should cook for a long time, and, when it is done, the calalou should look like a thick blended broth.
>
> —QUERILLAC, *CUISINE COLONIALE*, 107

to speak to her of love)" (xi). Such behaviors exclude Chloé from the "we" of French first-person plural who exercise discipline and who become, with the next recipe, "Thin Calalou [Calalou au maigre]" the Universal French subject, "one [on]," who respects the religious calendar. Presentation, elevated aesthetics that involve accompaniments, garnishes, seasoning, and the refinement of a filet with vinegar are the realm of a French Universalism from which Caribbean subjects like Chloé are excluded.

Querillac's sexualized view of Chloé—conveyed not least by Chloé's last name, whose literal translation is "my desire"—begs questions of

> ### *Calalou au maigre* (Thin Calalou)
>
> *Pour les jours d'abstinence, on ne met, dans le calalou, ni petit salé, ni même des crabes. On le prépare nature et on le sert toujours avec du riz, accompagné de beaux filets de morue frits dan l'huile, bien dorés, garnis de rondelles d'oignons également frits, le tout assaisonné d'un filet de vinaigre et surtout de piment rouge bien écrasé dans la sauce.*
>
> On the days of abstinence, one does not put, in the calalou, either salt meat or even crabs. One makes it plain and one serves it always with rice, accompanied with beautiful fried cod filet, well browned, garnished with onion slices, also fried, the whole thing seasoned with a drizzle of vinegar and above all crushed red pepper in the sauce.
>
> —QUERILLAC, *CUISINE COLONIALE*, 107–108

Querillac's position. Perhaps the French gaze on the Antilles is so deeply heteropatriarchal that even a woman writer can only see the Antilles through a lens of erotic possession. The stock stereotypes with which Querillac describes Chloé align her text with heterocolonial patriarchy. Querillac's taking up of the heterocolonial gaze indicates her ability to inhabit that position, either as part of a desire to inhabit maleness or as part of a sexual desire for Chloé.[16] This interpretation finds somewhat curious support in "A story of Dahomey" that Querillac includes in her description of manioc (yuca).[17] After describing the differences between sweet and bitter manioc, methods of preparing bitter manioc for safe consumption, and the uses of tapioca, Querillac reports: "in Dahomey, the quality of manioc is of great concern to husbands, this precious and cursed root having, so they say, the power to change women into men, as proven by the story of Alouba, ex-wife of Dako, told by witch-doctors [féticheurs]" (26), which Querillac then tells: the story of "How Alouba Was Changed into a Man (A Story of Dahomey)."[18] The story recounts how during the reign of King Dako, Medina, a boy of great beauty, was born. The king saw Medina, mistook him for a girl, fell in love, and proposed marriage. Afraid of disappointing the king and thinking of the honor, Medina agreed to the marriage with the condition of being given a separate bathroom and a year's time alone. The king agreed, and soon the new wife was such a favorite that the first wife, Alouba, became jealous, spied enough to figure out the secret, and set up a ceremony in which it would be revealed. Fleeing to avoid discovery, Medina encountered Death, to whom he told his story. Death offered a solution: she changed Medina into a girl, giving her a magic manioc that she was to eat only if she wanted to become a boy again. Medina returned to the palace happy and began to cook the manioc, which she then offered to Alouba, who gobbled it up, turned into a man, was discovered by the king at the ceremony and put to death.[19]

Under the guise of a story about how the dangers of manioc are mythologized, Querillac tells a story about how to avoid the dangers of homosexuality. In the story, the king's desire for Medina is either protected or redirected through the divine intervention that changes a potentially dangerous body part into a potentially dangerous food. Chloé with her bewitching beauty and witchlike ability to work with dangerous foods is like Medina, so that Querillac's desire for Chloé is, like the king's desire for Medina, de-homosexualized through culinary magic. Querillac may repress lesbian or transgender desires, as heterocolonial patriarchy prescribes, but primarily, she demonstrates how women who wield the colonial gaze enter complicatedly sexualized positions in relation to colonized women.

Chloé, as a light-skinned Black cook who serves local food to French colonialists and visitors, reminds readers of *Cuisine coloniale* of the intermediary status of Black cooks. Querillac displaces the problem of uncouth mixing onto Afro-Caribbeans as she describes "Soupe à Congo." That Chloé prepares "Soupe à Congo" for people like Querillac indicates her status as an intermediary between what she calls the "plantation negroes" and the old white families and new colonial tourists.

If Chloé is the intermediary between Black and White, both for her position serving White Creoles and French visitors and for her own racially mixed status, Querillac is the intermediary between Chloé's

Soupe à Congo (Congo Soup)

La « soupe à congo » n'a de potage que le nom. Elle constitue à elle seule, potage, entrée, relevé du menu du « nègre bitation » dont elle est avec la morue, le calalou, la farine de manioc, la base alimentaire.

Pour faire la « soupe à Congo », Chloé met dans un grand « canari » (marmite en terre) des pois savons, des malangas, du giraumon, des concombres, des « bélangères » (aubergines), des gombos, des « pois tendres » (haricots verts) et du lard coupé en morceaux. Elle couvre le tout d'eau et fait bouillir le mélange en le remuant souvent, énergiquement, jusqu'à ce que l'eau étant évaporée et les légumes prêts à se réduire en bouillie, elle estime la cuisson parfaite.

Servir alors dans un plat creux (à la case du noir on sert dans un « coui ») en ajoutant un bon morceau de beurre.

"Congo soup" is a soup in name only. It is, on its own, a soup and an entrée, taken from the menu of the "plantation negro" where it is, with cod, calalou, and manioc flour, a basic food.

To make "Congo soup," Chloé puts in a big "canari" (clay pot) lima beans, malangas, pumpkin, cucumbers, "tender peas" (green beans) and cubed lard. She covers the whole thing with water and boils the mixture, stirring frequently, briskly, until, the water evaporated and the vegetables about to dissolve into broth, she deems the cooking perfect.

Serve in a deep dish (in the black's house, it is served in a "calabash bowl") with a nice slice of butter.

—QUERILLAC, *CUISINE COLONIALE*, 89

Creole language, which she frequently cites and translates, and her readers' French, as well as between Antillean cuisine and the French palate. That not all of the dishes that Querillac describes are presented in a manner that would allow the reader to prepare them reinforces the status of *Cuisine coloniale* as a work of introduction, of intermediation, or creating desire for tastes and people and places as much as for teaching how to cook Chloé's dishes. In the recipe for Féroce de Morue (Ferocious Cod), for example,

Féroce de Morue (Ferocious Cod)

Ainsi que son nom vous le pourrait faire supposer, le « féroce » n'a rien d'un plat sucré!

C'est l'un des mets les plus redoutables aux palais ingénues des apprentis coloniaux qui, devant lui, ne sont pas plus fiers que le « ravet » du proverbe devant la poule, (ravette pas tini raison devant poule, dit Chloé) c'est-à-dire: le cancrelat est victime de la poule.

Mais ce "féroce" bien nommé fait la joie de tout colonial qui se respecte et Chloé met un art particulier à sa préparation.

Avec un soin infini, elle écrase ses tranches d'avocat bien mûr dans la farine de manioc pour en former une pâte homogène. Puis, se pourléchant d'avance, elle frotte la morue prélablement grillée de piment z'oiseau et l'imbibe d'huile.

La morue se place au centre d'un plat; la pâte se dresse autour et l'on mange l'une en la tartinant avec l'autre.

As its name makes you think, the "ferocious" has nothing to do with a sweet dish!

It is one of the most formidable foods for the ingenuous palates of apprentice colonialists who, before it, are no more proud than the cockroach before the hen (roach no right befo hen, says Chloé), in other words, the cockroach is the hen's victim.

But this well-named "ferocious" is the joy of every self-respecting colonialist and Chloé puts a special art into its preparation.

With an infinite care, she crushes her ripe avocado slices in manioc flour to make a smooth paste. Then, licking her lips already, she rubs the previously grilled cod with bird peppers and douses with oil.

The cod is placed in the center of a dish; the paste is arranged around it; the one is eaten spread with the other.

—QUERILLAC, *CUISINE COLONIALE*, 118–119

speaking to a French "you [*vous*]," Querillac positions herself as sharing a perspective from which the recipe name alerts to spiciness but is otherwise unknown, but also as knowing more than her audience: how uninitiated palates fall victim to Antillean "hens," and how Antilleans incorporate proverbs throughout their speech.[20] Querillac, in other words, is a Fanonian "self-respecting colonialist," and her cookbook will help her readers join her in that position. French colonialism and self-respect will be improved by the better knowledge of the colonized, drawn from those like Chloé who serve the colonialists by those like Querillac who translate for her.

After *Cuisine coloniale* and the other cookbooks published for the 1931 Colonial Exposition in Paris, the chronology of French Antilles cookbooks is marked by the interruption of the Second World War. When the next French Antilles colonial cookbooks were published in the 1960s and 1970s, they pick up almost seamlessly from Querillac. André Nègre's *Les Antilles et la Guyane: à travers leur cuisine* (1967) does assert the existence of Antillean gastronomy: "Gastronomy is part of the Art of Living; it is an important element of the aesthetic of life, the Antilles and Guyana, who know this, have thus created their own Gastronomy, made up of elements of the diverse civilizations that have come together here, and from local culinary creations" (14). However, Nègre establishes a cultural hierarchy where "On the base of French cuisine, in other words on almost perfect principles, [Antillian cuisine] has been able to combine Carib memories, the roughness of the buccaneers, the brilliant strength of the Blacks ripped from Africa, the delicacy of Hindu dishes. But above all in this sensual climate, in the vegetal exuberance fed by a strong sap, Antillean gastronomy has known how to use and to marry perfectly the strong tastes and the strongest smells of the most varied spices" (11). Local aesthetics are neatly cut off from any kind of cultural or political independence as references to Afro-Indigenous origins are relegated to the kind of distant and damaged past that Fanon identified as a favorite of colonialist defenders of native style. A little investigation into the food histories that Nègre includes reveals their inaccuracy but does not undermine their impact, for Nègre's readers are unlikely to recognize his mistakes. Much as the gastronomy may be "their own" (like "the accras that resemble beignets or croquettes in which Antilleans include different good things from their country and that they serve to you hot"), it serves a French audience who does not know that "accras" comes from the Nigerian akara and its basis, black-eyed peas, came from West Africa with the slaves (30).

Nègre's intention in *Les Antilles et la Guyane: à travers leur cuisine* to "fix, once and for all, the old local customs in 'black and white' if we do not want them to be completely forgotten a few decades from now" exemplifies his commitment to the cultural hierarchy under which the Antilles can participate in the French Universal. Nègre's colonialist defense of native style secures a fading Antillean history by and for colonial control (17). And just as early colonial captures of Caribbean territory and goods allowed France to sell its products on the European markets, this cultural capture of Antillean gastronomy allows France to sell its food on the emerging markets of international tourism. Nègre even offers translations of "Antillean vernacular names" into Latin binomials so that "the non-Antillean reader can know, from this universal botanical language, what I am talking about" (8) before he advises that "when one goes to a country that one does not know, one must certainly visit its museums, its monuments, admire its landscapes, but also taste its cuisine" (9). Antillian particularity feeds not independence but the universal tourist in the colonial universe who, thanks to Nègre's help, will be able to "taste the whole range of the infinite possibilities of gastronomy, whether it be our insurpassable French cuisine, the remarkable raw fish of Tahiti, crocodile with champagne, or certain particularly relevant dishes of the age-old Chinese cuisine; and it is thus the role of the palate to establish a hierarchy in the gustatory sensations felt in the course of these passionate trials" (9). French culinary order, with French gastronomy at its pinnacle, can appreciate the exotic passion of the colonial possessions to which it holds. And France has held on to Martinique, Guadeloupe, Saint Martin, and French Guiana.[21] With orientalist and colonialist rhetoric, Nègre and the several other

French-born gastronomists who made their homes in Guadeloupe and Martinique and wrote similar cookbooks in the 1970s paved the path that Querillac, de Noter, and Rabette set out for the extension of French colonialism and sealed off any other perspectives that Marie-Thérèse Julien Lung-Fou may, however minimally, suggest.[22]

The first cookbook written by a Martinican, Julien Lung-Fou's 1950 *Les recettes de cuisine martiniquaise de Da Elodie*, interrupts the rule of culinary colonialism in French Antilles cookbooks. Julien Lung-Fou presents the cuisine of a specific island with its own well-established racially mixed populations, to which she belongs, to not only a French but also a Martinican audience, albeit an elite Francophile one, to whom she serves both Martinican culinary savoir-faire and colonial tropes. Julien Lung-Fou was an important member of the Martinican intellectual and artistic elite of the mid-twentieth century, a celebrated sculptor who after the publication of her cookbook would go on to author a play, a poetry collection, several collections of Creole stories, and works on Carnival and Martinican oral literature.[23]

Le recettes martiniquaises de Da Elodie has many kernels that might be the basis of recipes for national independence. Like Querillac, Julien Lung-Fou presents the recipes as collected from her cook, but she does not exoticize or sexualize Da Elodie. Instead, she makes gestures of familiarization, for example describing Da Elodie making a Christmas meal as part of a whole household effort (45). While, like Querillac, Julien Lung-Fou includes a few Creole proverbs that she links to Da Elodie, she does not translate them, conveying linguistic familiarity that she and her audience share with Da Elodie. And Julien Lung-Fou does not attribute the proverbs to Da Elodie, instead saying that Da Elodie proves them true. She makes clear, in other words, that, in the tradition of proverbs, they come not from one mouth but from many, and that she and Da Elodie, and presumably many of her readers, share an understanding of their figurative as well as their literal meaning. Julien Lung-Fou explicitly and positively describes the racial mixing of Martinique, noting that "the inventory of local edibles has been long established for. Taste, shared by all the races, presided over the choice of the best combinations" (93). The great majority of her recipes are focused on local ingredients and Afro-Indigenous practices developed through colonial and slave periods (although, in spite of Julien Lung-Fou's connection to her Chinese-Afro-Martinican family, she does not include any Chinese-Martinican foods).[24] She details the difference between water and land crabs and specifies that the "pâté en pot" for which she includes a recipe "is a specifically Martinican dish" (53). Julien Lung-Fou notes that salt cod [morue] "forms the basis of the food of Creoles in the Antilles," implicitly defining Creoles as the descendants of slaves for whom salt cod was one of the few guaranteed sources of protein, but not explicitly naming that particular part of the salt cod's, or Martinique's, history (37). Her food histories, though minimal, include mentions of Africa as well as of Europe. She refers to the French origin of the coffee maker by naming Desclieux as the person who introduced it to the Antilles (19), and she specifies the Angolan origin of "angola peas [pois d'angole]", writing, "Angola peas are a common legume from Angola" (55). When she refers to the importation of "peas (red, white, split . . .) [pois (rouges, blancs, cassés, etc . . .)]" from Europe that "hold an important place in Antillean food" she renders the origin as much Antillean as French by using not the French word, "haricot" [bean], but rather the Creole *pois* that allows for a reorganization that groups, linguistically as well as culinarily, red, white, and split peas where in French she would have had to divide "beans (red and white) and split peas" for a far less elegant sentence (55). These are the kinds of claims and acknowledgments that I have identified earlier as proto-nationalist and that I will return to in the next chapter as what can sprout into recipes for independent national culture. However, in *Les recettes martiniquaises de Da Elodie* colonialist gestures, or gestures of the colonized intellectual, persist.

Julien Lung-Fou's titular "Da Elodie" names the cook with a Creole term that indicates familiarity replete with connotations of possession and an idealized view of servitude: "Da" is best translated as "Mammy." While Da Elodie is not exoticized and sexualized like Querillac's Chloé, her portrayal conforms to a different stereotype, that of the happily dedicated help. Julien Lung-Fou's identification, in the book's subtitle, as the collector of Da Elodie's Martinican recipes positions her, like Querillac, as the translator mediating between her Martinican possessions and her wider audience. While Julien Lung-Fou includes many Creole culinary terms, when she writes explicitly about a Creole term, she explains it as a deformation of French; for example, "There exists in the islands, in the flowing waters, crayfish [des écrevisses] whose name Creole has deformed and that everyone knows under the name of 'cribiches'" (26). She gives no histories of the translation and transformation of African foods into Caribbean staples. Like salt cod, she identifies the classically Afro-Caribbean okra [gombos] only as "popular in tropical countries" (33). And her praise of Martinique echoes the colonialist paradisiac trope: "enchantress island, blessed in every language, 'the Island of Return' [l'Ile des Revenants], Martinique owes more than her seductiveness to her unparalleled climate, her voluptuous Creoles, her unique flowers" (93). "Creoles," here, as in the description of them as having salt cod as a favorite food, seem not to include Julien Lung-Fou herself, such that her self-identification as Martinican and Antillean separates, rather than joins, her to Creole women like Da Elodie.

Les recettes martiniquaises to Da Elodie mixes together instructions for the elaboration of independent national culinary culture by and for a creole Martinique and representations of Martinique's flavor and taste in French colonialist terms that embrace the position of perfect little Frenchmen into which French colonialism invites the colonialized intellectual. Julien Lung-Fou's many subsequent publications show that for her, the cookbook was a starting point for a turn toward an ever-greater embrace of what would come to be recognized as Chamoiseau's decolonial créolité and Glissant's creolization, but the trajectory of Martinican and Antillean cookbooks did not follow that path.

Cookbooks like Querillac's *Cuisine coloniale* and Nègre's *Les Antilles et la Guyane: à travers leur cuisine* not only offer a record of how colonial control persisted but are one of the tools that rendered its acceptance quotidian in both France and among the Antillean elite. *Les recettes martiniquaises de Da Elodie,* even in its nascent gestures toward establishing a Martinican cookbook by and for Martinicans, remained an exception until the late 1970s. The culinary colonialism of Querillac and Nègre that preceded and followed Julien Lung-Fou ensured the persistence in France and the extension across the French Antilles of the idea of French Antilles cuisine as the France's exotic Other, desired for its fruitful flare and otherwise insufficient and inferior. Never mind that French superiority depended on this exploitation. Of course, colonialism and its extension, independence and its achievement, are never monocausal, but when we examine how they appear in and through cookbooks we can see how they play out in and through the most intimate and banal gestures and how they are fed by and feed literal tastes and recipes, and the often competing and messy ways that happens. And the French Antilles are far from the exception in being stained by colonial extension.

Eating Up Puerto Rico

Although a Puerto Rican independence movement triumphed in 1897, after the United States took the occasion to enter into war with Spain the Spanish-American War ended, in 1898, with the United States in possession of Puerto Rico, and Puerto Rican nationalists were unable to regain independence. For the next half-century, *El cocinero puertorriqueño*, discussed in chapter 1, remained the only Spanish-language Puerto Rican cookbook. However, as the United States encouraged anglophone Americans to take up residence in Puerto Rico, promoted cultural Americanization, and alternately encouraged and required the use of English on the island, English-language cookbooks took up the neocolonial mantle: in 1915, the Ladies Aid Society of the First Methodist Church of San Juan published the *Porto Rican Cookbook*; the same year, Grace Ferguson published *Home Making and Home Keeping: A Textbook for the First Two Years' Work on Home Economics in the Public Schools of Porto Rico*; in the 1920s, Elsie Mae Willsey initiated the publication of a series of recipe pamphlets from the University of Puerto

Department of Home Economics, whose later editions and numbers included Puerto Rican authors; and in 1948 Eliza K. Dooley published her *Puerto Rican Cookbook*.

In this section, I examine two predominant modes of culinary colonialism: work to establish American women in domestic leadership in Puerto Rico, seen in the cookbooks written in English by and for American women living or considering living in Puerto Rico, and work to make Puerto Rican women more American, seen in the educational cookbooks written first in English and then in Spanish. In the former, we can see proto-feminism and colonialism coincide; in the latter we see a colonialist shift from appropriation to assimilation. In spite of the effort to educate by Americanizing, the educational cookbooks address Puerto Rican women, and those women eventually, often awkwardly, shifted from student to colleague. As they took up authorship, Puerto Rican women authors of home economics and agricultural extension cookbooks both mimicked the assimilationist lessons and also reinserted other knowledge, demonstrating the mutual impact of collaboration. Of course, there is no single trajectory. Even as, or we might with Fanon say because, national culinary consciousness begins to be inscribed by Puerto Rican women, a colonialist—Dooley—sweeps in to try to defend native culture (from taking off into independence). Its titular use of the spelling "Porto Rico," imposed by the United States in the 1898 Treaty of Paris, announces 1915's *Porto Rican Cookbook*'s (neo) colonial perspective: it was written by and for U.S. women who were trying to make lives for themselves in Puerto Rico and to "help" Puerto Rican women by doing charitable things "for" them. The First Methodist Church of San Juan, for which the cookbook was a fundraiser, is the product of North American missionary work started in 1900. Protestant women's groups like the Ladies Aid Society that put together *Porto Rican Cookbook* worked closely with both the U.S. colonial administration on the island and the development of U.S.-owned sugar, tobacco, and fruit industry companies and processing plants (Walsh, 89–94).[25] They set the terms of such early "Porto Rican" women's movements as the Woman's Christian Temperance Union and the controversial anti-prostitution campaign of 1918.[26] *Porto Rican Cookbook* furthers the community and culture of the American Methodists in Puerto Rico whose limited engagement with lo Puerto Riqueño manifests in the absence of Puerto Rican women's voices in those social and moral campaigns, and in the failure to mention Puerto Rican women or cooks in *Porto Rican Cookbook*.[27]

In order to appear at all in *Porto Rican Cookbook*, "Porto Rican" culinary culture passed through racist U.S. stereotypes and colonial filters. The title pages, organization, and epigraphs mark the colonialist frame. A sketch of a Black woman wearing a white headscarf, button-up shirt, and apron and holding a steaming roast occupies the bottom left-hand corner of the front cover (see figure 3.1). Much as this suggests a Black woman entering the scene as the source of the food, it also captures her forever in that corner of the front cover and in that stereotypical position of idealized servitude. Furthermore, the dish that she bears has no markers of Puerto Rican cuisine: not only are roasts like the one she carries classically Euro-American,[28] even the garnishes on the platter look more like U.S. classics of mashed potatoes or greens than the Puerto Rican standards of rice or fried plantains. The cover of *Porto Rican Cookbook* echoes the portrayals of African American women in White-authored cookbooks far more than it represents any Puerto Rican culinary culture.[29]

Most sections of *Porto Rican Cookbook* open with English or American quotes. In the epigraph to the first section, Bread, Robert Bulwer-Lytton's (unattributed) "We may live without friends, we may live without books, but civilized man cannot live without cooks" (1) suggests an attention to the work of the women in the back of the kitchen, but it also keeps them there, in service to "civilized man." Overwhelmingly, the quotes proffer lessons less related to cooking—Puerto Rican or other—than to Protestant values. That of the last section, Miscellaneous, makes clear the address of this cookbook from and for U.S. women: "Thanks for the friends who with their splendid courage redeem our negative days" appeared already as an epigram in Isabel Goodhue's 1911 *Good Things and Graces* and in the 1913 Village Improvement Society of

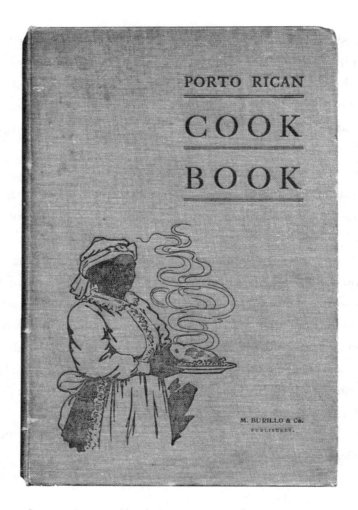

3.1. Cover of *Porto Rican Cookbook*. Source: NYU Libraries.

Barton, Vermont's *The Barton Cookbook* (213). Friendship is extended among U.S. women across wherever they may live.

The "Porto Rican" recipes themselves do not reflect any developed culinary tradition or even a defined subset of the cookbook. All of the recipes in the first three sections of *Porto Rican Cookbook*—Bread, Soups, and Fish—and in the last—Miscellaneous—are Anglo-American.[36] Sandwiched between these Anglo-American frames, the sections on Vegetables, Meats and Luncheon Dishes, Salads, Puddings, Pies, Cakes, Ice Cream, Pickles, Preserves and Jellies, and Candy include a jumble

> ### Pilau of Green Peppers
>
> Cut green peppers length-wise, remove the seeds with care. Fill the halves with boiled rice, into which there has been stirred a tablespoonful of melted butter for a cupful of the boiled rice, and two tablespoons of grated cheese. Salt to taste. Mound the rice smooth and high and after the pilau has cooked ten minutes in a covered pan, brown lightly. Serve hot.
>
> —LADIES AID SOCIETY, *PORTO RICAN COOKBOOK*, 26

of Puerto Rican and Caribbean dishes, some identified explicitly and others implicitly. These include recipes for everything from "Gumbo-West Indian Dish," "Pilau of Green Peppers," and "Mashed Tallotes" to "Guanabana Ice" and "Spanish Panoche." Titles like "West Indian" make an explicit link to the still British-held Caribbean, and "Spanish" to that colonial legacy. "Tallotes" and "Pilau" are recognizably associated on the one hand with Puerto Rico—"tallote" is the specifically Puerto Rico name for a vegetable that has other names across the Caribbean and Latin America—and the West Indies ("pilau" is even more specifically Indo-Caribbean, although the recipe itself much more closely resembles Italian stuffed peppers than any West Indian pilau).[31] The titular "Porto Rican," this reading of the cookbook reveals, is an identification that Anglo-American women use for themselves, their cooking, and the cooking they discover in "Porto Rico" (by hiring cooks, eating in restaurants, and visiting "native" homes). The cookbook instructs in how to render "Porto Rico" a space empty of distinct culture, though also a place where Anglo-American women can find a wealth of raw material to make what they want, and it does provide an exotic range of vegetables and fruits and a kind of tropical exchange.

As the United States established itself as the new colonial power, it engaged in the colonialist work to delegitimize local culture, as Fanon has described, and in the Glissantian atavistic implantation of a single root history—here American—as the legitimate basis that could ensure that Puerto Ricans could be assimilated into it without any recognition of other more creolized histories and presents. The recipes written for and by U.S. women with ameliorative missionary goals to improve Porto Rican culture, like those of the Ladies Aid Society, are part of the larger U.S. colonial project that manifested in the more explicitly governmental work of the U.S. educational project in Puerto Rico. Education was a primary mode of U.S. colonization in Puerto Rico, evident in the requirement that all teachers hold degrees from U.S. or European colleges or universities and perhaps most blatantly in the Department of Education's plan to combine the teaching of the English language with inculcation in "American" values. Assistant commissioner of education José Padín explained in 1916,

> The majority of the people of Porto Rico cannot familiarize themselves with North American ideals at first hand, that is, by actually living in the United States; consequently they must do so through the next best means: through the English language. . . . To catch the spirit that animates the life of a people, to know and absorb their ideals, it is indispensable to master their language, to possess it wholly. Therefore in attempting to give the children of Porto Rico as complete a mastery of the English language as it is feasible to give through the medium of a school education, the department has acted with the fullest realization of the educational interest of the people. (cited in Osuna, 194)

Instruction did continue in Spanish to some degree, and the question of textbooks—how to translate, adapt, or create textbooks in Spanish and English for Puerto Rican schools—concerned the Department of Education. The first textbooks attentive to "insular subject matter" were Bailey K. Ashford's *Hygenie Práctica*[32] and Grace Ferguson's 1915 *Home Making and Home Keeping: A Textbook for the First Two Years' Work on Home Economics in the Public Schools of Porto Rico* (Osuna 197). The idea that hygiene and food both needed to be taught in special ways to "Porto Ricans" by Americans makes explicit the underlying assumptions of both works: that "Porto Rico" was dirty, backwards, uncultured, and thus of course dependent on the United States for betterment.[33]

When we look closely at how the educational project, carried out by women and in culinary terms, played out, we also see how the effort to delegitimize local foods and techniques involved a recognition of them and of the women and girls who were being taught, and how assimilationist projects often have unanticipated multidirectional results. The intimate proximity of women communicating with one another about food, the overlapping moves of U.S. and Puerto Rican women to enter into professional and authorial positions, facilitated exchanges—both colonizing and decolonizing—that inhabit and exceed the broad theoretical and poetic strokes of Fanon and Glissant.

Ferguson's textbook takes for granted "Porto Rican" girls as needing to be taught that "The first essential about a kitchen is that it shall be clean, because dirt or dirty food causes sickness" (17). The introduction to teachers also presents "the Porto Rican girl" as bearing no cooking knowledge or skill of her own, explaining that she "is quick at memory work, slow in practical work at first, but a marvelous imitator who acquires skill rapidly" (3). And while on the one hand we can see a move toward independence in Ferguson's note that "the aim of this work is the training of the girl into a self-reliant, capable woman who is able to cope with her particular home problems in an expert manner" (7), such an aim also establishes not only "Porto Rican" girls but also the education their families might give them as deficient. And Ferguson ignores *El cocinero puertorriqueño* or any of the earlier Cuban or Latin American cookbooks that codify Puerto Rican and criollo cuisine, arguing, "All work should be taught in English, even by those teachers understanding Spanish, because the cookbooks and textbooks which come into the hands of the children are printed in English" (8–9). Ferguson does explain that "Porto Rican recipes have been used largely, including only such American recipes as were necessary to teach cooking processes" because "radical changes in the cooking are not advisable and innovations are introduced only as necessity demands. Unless Home

Economics goes into the home in reality it is not the important factor in education which it should be" (6). Nonetheless, Ferguson's home economics textbook aims at change, specifically change toward U.S. cooking methods that support U.S. industry, for "enough baking lessons have been introduced to show the method and create a demand for ovens" (6). And lest the push to educate girls and women be taken as challenging heteronormativity, Ferguson adds, "The broader results are also brought about by always thinking of the girl not as a student of the seventh or eighth grade, but as a home maker, as the mother of a family, as a woman called upon to manage a home, to do the buying and cooking, to sew for herself and her children" (8). The girl who "learns" (in English) already embodies the maternal role she must bring to fruition.

Ferguson's recipes do include, as promised, a number of "Porto Rican" dishes, but such things as the absence of mofongo and her use of the general Caribbean Spanish term "chayote" rather than the Puerto Rican "tallote" for the first recipe in the book conveys an ignorance of or disregard for local knowledge and skill congruent with the book's perspective (40). Some recipes, however, use Puerto Rican names, including a sweet funche (129) and tostones de plátano (140), made with Afro-Indigenous and "native" ingredients and preparations, often untranslated, from pimentón to yautía to salt beef (see figure 3.2). Ferguson's appeal that home economics teachers get to know the home lives of their students and teach them in ways that are accessible given their economic and cultural backgrounds, along with such observations as that arroz con pollo "is one of the most popular dishes on the island" (157), could enable the recognition of the Puerto Rican sources of the recipes, and thus Puerto Ricans' possession of culinary knowledge before or outside of U.S. instruction. What is strikingly absent, however, is any attribution of recipes or any indication that the food knowledge in the textbook comes from Puerto Ricans.[34] Thus while Ferguson's work serves "Porto Ricans" in ways that what Fanon describes as colonialist "defense of native style" generally does not, it does so in a way that denies Puerto Rican knowledge in order to give it back to "Porto

NOTE TO TEACHERS.—Use the school oven as a model. If a few cans only are available, make this a demonstration lesson, using one can for each class. If several cans have accumulated, let the members of the class work. Boys from the Manual Training department can offer valuable assistance. The making of the ovens will require two class periods.

During the year all cans should be saved. Occasionally have a class come on Saturday morning and make them up into ovens. Give the completed ovens to the students.

FUNCHE.

EQUIPMENT.	INDIVIDUAL RECIPE.	LARGE RECIPE.
saucepan, c.	4 tb. cornmeal.	1 c. cornmeal.
bowl, tb., t.	1 t. flour.	1 tb. flour.
knife, fork.	1/16 t. salt.	½ t. salt.
wooden spoon.	1½ tb. sugar.	¼ c. sugar.
strainer.	¼ c. cold cocoanut milk.	1 c. cold water.
sauce dish.	¾ c. hot cocoanut milk.	3 c. hot water.
	1 piece stick cinnamon.	stick cinnamon.

DIRECTIONS.

1. Measure the cornmeal into the bowl.
2. Sift into it the flour, salt, and sugar, and mix together well.
3. Add the one-fourth cup of cold water and stir until the mixture is smooth.
4. Heat the three-fourths cup of water in the saucepan until it comes to a boil.
5. Pour the boiling water over the mixture in the bowl, stirring constantly to prevent lumping.
6. Place the mixture in the saucepan. Add the cinnamon and cook until the cornmeal tastes done and the mush is thick.
7. Pour into the sauce dish, cool, and serve. More sugar may be added during the cooking if desired.

This may be poured into a mold, cooled, and sliced for serving.

3.2. Funche recipe, *Home Making and Home Keeping: A Textbook for the First Two Years' Work on Home Economics in the Public Schools of Porto Rico*, 1915. Source: University of Illinois Library.

Ricans" through and combined with Americanization. Ferguson teaches "Porto Ricans" to see "Porto Rican" foods as raw materials best processed by and through U.S. methods or as old ideas modernized thanks to U.S. ingenuity.

In 1919, Elsie Mae Willsey took over from Ferguson as the head of home economics in the public schools and then in 1926 became chair of home economics at the University of Porto Rico, where she further developed Ferguson's attention to local ingredients and dishes first with a revised home economics textbook and then with a series of bulletins on a variety of "tropical foods."[35] While Willsey's work does, like Ferguson's, suggest that it is initiating rather than picking up on local knowledge about local foods, her shift to publishing in both English and Spanish and her collaborations with Puerto Rican teachers and cooks mark a significant departure from Ferguson's one-way (educational) model and toward the recognition of Puerto Rican self-sufficiency.

Willsey's work in home economics through the public education system must be seen in the context of governmental and nongovernmental efforts to address Puerto Rico's poverty and hunger in the first half of the twentieth century. In *Reproducing Empire*, Laura Briggs argues that the Puerto Rican family has long been identified as the source of Puerto Rico's economic struggles (6) and that by the 1920s reproduction had been determined to be the central problem of the Puerto Rican family such that "by 1926 the annual report of the Bureau of Vital Statistics had begun routinely to comment on the island's overpopulation. . . . That year's report—distributed widely through the newly founded Porto Rico Health Review—devoted its first pages to commentary on population density and the excessive birth rate, and noted, 'Industrially undeveloped and still backward agriculturally, Porto Rico has been, however, steadily increasing its population at an astounding rate'" (84). Correspondingly, for not only the U.S.-sponsored eugenics movement but also Albízu's independentista party and the left and feminist nationalist movements, controlling population growth was a central focus (though, of course, these different movements had quite different ideas about how that should be done). Willsey, with the Home

Economics Department recipe pamphlets, in comparison, focused on reforming how "Porto Rican" women consumed, prepared, and grew family meals. Whether or not this was a pointed rejection of other tactics, it offered a distinctly different positioning of women: not as the targets of control but as the agents of improvement.

The first of Willsey's tropical food bulletins, *Tropical Foods Bulletin No. 1—Vegetables* (1925), lays out the "aims and methods of this series of bulletins":

AIMS:

1. To standardize the traditional recipes of Porto Rico, and
2. To introduce new ways of serving tropical vegetables, thereby,
3. To improve the teaching of tropical vegetables in the home-economics classes, and
4. To encourage the use of more tropical vegetables in the Porto Rican menus.

METHODS:

1. To collect data from home-economics instructors, housewives, cooks and others concerning the traditional recipes of Porto Rico;
2. By comparisons and eliminations to formulate tentative recipes;
3. To experiment with these tentative recipes until accepted recipes are obtained, and
4. To submit these accepted recipes to instructors of home economics, housewives, cooks and others for their criticisms. (5)

The methods explicitly identify women as the sources and evaluators of information, while the aims implicitly position women as the addressees through the understanding that it is women who take home economics classes and cook and serve "Porto Rican" recipes and menus in "Porto Rican" homes. Just as the writing and reading of cookbooks was for previous generations a space of literacy and public authorship acceptable for women, home economics was a vehicle for women to enter education, including higher education, to assert the academic and scientific nature of their work, and to build networks of women outside of heteropatriarchal families.[36] This worked, of course, because home economics was a course of study that in many ways promised to keep girls in their place in a heteropatriarchal structure, nourishing and serving their fathers, husbands, and children. Willsey's "aims and methods" negotiate the fine line, common to what Josefina Ludmer calls "the tricks of the weak" wherein women use their "weakness" to exercise power, between redefining and reifying women's subservient positions in heteropatriarchy.

The iterative method of collecting, submitting for criticism, and then presumably revising and repeating laid out in Willsey's "aims and methods" inscribes the work in the scientific method and also acknowledges "Porto Rican" women from a variety of social positions as sources of original knowledge and as reviewers of the work. Nonetheless, the aim to standardize, innovate, and encourage the use of tropical vegetables embraces the classic colonial operation by which native knowledge is taken from the natives, reconfigured by the colonialists, and then returned to the natives as the innovation of the colonizers in ways that delegitimize native knowledge and often destroy it via the processing. The idea that "Porto Ricans" needed to be encouraged by Americans to use more tropical vegetables fits with a critique, by U.S. scholars in the 1920s and 1930s, of how U.S.-owned large-scale export monoculture had just destroyed Puerto Rico's small- and medium-scale farms that produced subsistence crops for local use along with tobacco, sugar, and coffee.[37] Willsey's work also reveals the persistence of paternalistic colonialist views among even scholars who purported to "help" "Porto Ricans." Like the proposals of U.S. scholars for reforms to monoculture to assist Puerto Rican subsistence farmers, Willsey's reconsideration of culinary guidelines for home economics fails to recognize Puerto Rican self-sufficiency or relegates it to a gift of nature lost with the fall of a pre-colonial Eden.

The aim of standardization, in "Porto Rico" and elsewhere in the colonized Caribbean, presupposes a disorganized and disorderly native culture in need of colonial order that will supposedly innovate, improve, and encourage. Colonial order thus works to prevent the fertile mixing of Glissantian creolization by putting each part in its proper place and proportion. Willsey's *Tropical Foods* opens with a section on measuring that explains: "Without absolutely correct measuring, good results cannot be expected. Only standard measures should be used. The standard cup is ½ pint and is divided into quarters and thirds" (7). The colonial educational system, of which the home economics bulletins were a part, promoted standardization according to U.S. standards of measurement. That U.S. standards were supported by, and supported, U.S. markets is made clear when the section on measuring continues: "Tea and tablespoons vary greatly. Sets of standard spoons for measuring may be purchased at any house-furnishing store" (7). This aim repeats in a standard disclaimer, reinforced in the later Spanish-language publications that each include an introductory comment like that in *La yuca*: "To ensure success in the confection of these recipes, the following points must be observed: if the measurements are not exact it will not be possible to obtain satisfactory results. Only *standard* measures should be used" (7, emphasis in the original). That "standard" is the only word in emphasis and in English assures that the standard is that of the United States.

The standardization that the bulletins tout in their introductions, however, is not nearly as assiduously practiced throughout the body of the bulletins as it is asserted. In *Tropical Foods*, most, but not all, dishes are given with an English name first, followed by a Spanish name in parentheses.[38] In one dish, "Chayote Stew (*chayote guisado*)," a few ingredients have Spanish translations after them, though when these same ingredients are listed in other recipes, no translations are offered. A few ingredients are listed with slightly different names in different recipes: "wild marjoram (*orégano*)" in "Chayote Stew," "marjoram leaves" in "Plantain Bullion." The recipe for "Yautia Custard" uses a different abbreviation for teaspoon than that listed in the table of abbreviations. That the rhetoric of standardization turns out to be merely rhetoric might suggest a kind of undermining—purposeful or not—on the part the authors and editors who understand and practice "Porto Rican" cuisine as mobile and who know that they and their pupils possess enough knowledge to create and follow recipes that are as much reminders and suggestions as strict rule books. It might also, however, show that what is at stake is not whether the recipes or their execution are actually standardized but whether they ensure that teachers and students and anyone else who reads them accepts the idea of U.S. standards as the best order—and of order itself as best.

As fits with the title and project of the bulletin, Willsey's *Tropical Foods* is divided into sections by vegetable: Chayote, Yautia, Plantain, and Banana. The limited introductory material for each vegetable covers minimal agricultural, market, and nutritional information. While the recipes begin with standard U.S. preparations (boiled chayote, steamed chayote, baked chayote, sauteed chayote), they do also include Puerto Rican dishes like guisados, mofongo, alcapurrias, piononos, and guanime. The only "new ways of serving tropical vegetables" consist of using them in U.S. dishes—like "Sweet Pickled Chayote" (15) or "Scalloped Yautia" (18)—such that if the bulletins "encourage the use of more tropical vegetables in Porto Rican menus," it is through encouraging the use of more U.S. dishes (5).[39]

In spite of its work toward standardization and Americanization, Willsey's 1925 publication begins to blur some distinctions between colonizer and colonized with the plans and acknowledgments that follow the aims and methods. Its announcement that "these bulletins will appear in Spanish in the near future" (5) accepts Spanish not only as a home language but also as a language of instruction, even at the university level. And as "acknowledgement is made to the experimental cooking class of 1924 of the University of Porto Rico, composed of Providencia Urgell, Luz María Ramos, Pura Pastrana, María Adela Valentín and Irene Menéndez, for the valuable services rendered in collecting and testing the recipes included" (5), we see "Porto Rican" women not only as the sources of the recipes but as part of the university structure that is systematizing them. Willsey's actual naming of "Porto Rican" women contributors, even just as testers, grants them a degree of authorship. Perhaps this is a feature of the particular form of colonialism that the United States has practiced in "Porto Rico," where "Porto Ricans" are supposed to be taught to be ready for citizenship, albeit second class—"tropical American citizens" in Ashford's words (80). However, combined with the planned use of Spanish in the context of Puerto Rican language politics, the naming of the Puerto Rican women contributors seems to reveal an alignment on the part of Willsey, and the Home Economics Department at the University of Porto Rico, with the more decolonial elements of the "left and feminist nationalisms." If this partnership leads to exchanges and mixtures in which U.S. domination is not guaranteed, then it enters into the territory of Glissantian creolization—for this creolization, like Ortiz's transculturation, rests not a decolonizing elimination of the "foreign" European element but on the recognition that "those who meet up here always come from an 'over there'" (*Treatise*, 9). Unlike appropriation or assimilation that lead to subsumption, in creolization or transculturation the coming together "here" leads to incorporations in all directions.

The English-to-Spanish translation Willsey planned in 1925 took some time to complete, but in 1931—the same year that the U.S. government officially agreed to give up on "Porto Rico" and call the island Puerto Rico—the University of Puerto Rico Department of Home Economics bulletins began to publish translated and expanded versions of the sections of *Tropical Foods*, each co-authored by Willsey and a Puerto Rican woman.[40] Then, in the mid-to-late 1930s, the University of Puerto Rico Agricultural Extension Service published a series of recipes-based Spanish-language circulars, bulletins, and booklets that continued the translation and extension of *Tropical Foods* (sometimes by adding translations of Ferguson's recipes), most of them with dual authorship by Willsey and Puerto Rican women.[41] Starting with circular no. 10, *Harina de maíz: modos de prepararla para la mesa,* a Puerto Rican woman, María T. Orcasitas, is listed as sole author.[42] Willsey reappears in the last in the series, no. 17, *El conejo, modos de preparar la carne para la mesa*, when Orcasitas notes in the introduction: "The recipes compiled here were prepared by Miss Elsie Mae Willsey, Associate Faculty of Home

Economics, in a different era of the University of Puerto Rico" (4). The era when U.S.-born women collaborated with Puerto Rican women but retained authorship and published in English, as Willsey did in *Tropical Foods* and Ferguson and the Ladies Aid Society before her, appears to be gone. While the work of Willsey, Orcasitas, and others to publish culinary instruction circulars in Spanish rejects the U.S. determination to impose English through Puerto Rican education systems,[43] their circulars also demonstrate the same inability, or unwillingness, to valorize Puerto Rican food history and culinary tradition that marks Willsey's 1925 *Tropical Foods*.

The first Spanish-language home economics extension circular, *La yuca*, co-authored by Willsey and Estrella Moll Schwartzkopf, opens with the Eurocentric claim that "among the products of the vegetable kingdom that are used as food, grains are undoubtedly the most important, tubers occupying second place" (1).[44] Even as they acknowledge that "cassava, generally known as yuca," was used in the Americas before Columbus and that "yuca is a native product of Puerto Rico" (1), Willsey and Schwartzkopf award first place to the European staple, grains. And lest native products of Puerto Rico appear the mark of precolonial civilization, let alone national cuisine, the description of yuca concludes, "and it is used as food for fowl and livestock as well as for the extraction of starch" (1). Before the arrival of the Spaniards, the suggestion goes, the Indigenous people of the island were like animals; their position as second-class citizens follows naturally. Indeed, these Spanish-language circulars help to position Puerto Rico in a trajectory from Spain to the United States. The introduction to circular no. 2, *El plátano*, by Willsey and Angelina Mercador, includes a history of the plantain and banana that refers to plantains being brought to the Americas "by the Spanish discoverers" (3) from "Africa or India," burying the history of slavery and of the plantain's entry to Puerto Rican cuisine through slave diets while holding up the discoveries and contributions of the Spanish. In circular no. 6, *La berenjena*, Willsey and Angela Pastrana, after listing the types, sizes, and costs of locally grown eggplants, add: "The [U.S.] American varieties, which are larger in size, are preferred here for use at the table" (4). Any return to natural bounty will occur in and through the United States.

The later Spanish-language circulars, authored by Orcasitas alone, give more Indigenous histories of Puerto Rican foods, but they do so by emphasizing the connection with "America." *Harina de maíz: modos de prepararla para la mesa*, for example, refers to corn as "the grain most associated with America, since it was in this continent that it was first cultivated as a food." It does not mention the African origins of the word *funche*, though it does offer three funche recipes (a direct translation from Ferguson's funche recipe minus the instructions about molding plus recipes for "funche de coco" and "funche frito" that do not appear in previous home economics cookbooks or circulars). Similarly, it makes no mention of okra's African origins although it features the African-derived Puerto Rican word "quimbombó" in the recipe for "Quimbombó con bolas de maiz."

If Orcasitas does represent Puerto Rican women taking authorship, she also shows them doing so by white-washing Puerto Rican culinary history. Perhaps the very educational processes that they went through to get to the position of teaching in and running the home economics program at the University of Puerto Rico in the 1930s ensures that they know and tell that particular story, or perhaps, Puerto Rican women like Orcasitas use the authorship to bring themselves, via their cooking, closer to a White American ideal. In the canning circulars written by Mary E. Keown and Orcasitas, it becomes clear that Puerto Rican women who accessed culinary control through the economic extension program in the 1930s and 1940s did so by embracing or getting caught in a system that preserved United States interests in Puerto Rico as much as it preserved Puerto Rican culinary culture. The project of food independence was first mentioned as a benefit of canning at home in Keown's *La conservación de frutas y vegetales en Puerto Rico* as "the people will become accustomed to the preferential use of native products" (5). But, it turns out, the instructions for canning require the purchase of U.S.-made equipment. For *La conservación de frutas y vegetales en Puerto Rico*: a stove with at least three burners (8), a thermometer (9), glass

Funche de Coco (Coconut Funche)

½ taza harina de maíz
½ taza azúcar
⅛ cucharadita sal
2 tazas leche de coco (1 coco)
2 pedacitos canela en rajas

1. Mezcle la leche de coco, harina de maíz y azúcar.
2. Póngalo en la parte de arriba de un baño de maría, cocínelo sobre fuego lento hasta que empiece a espesar.
3. Coloque la olla sobre agua caliente y cocínelo por 20 minutos meneándolo de vez en cuando.
4. Sírvalo en platillos individuales.
5. Polvoréelo con canela molida y déjelo enfriar antes de servirlo en la mesa. Sirve cinco personas.

½ cup corn flour
½ cup sugar
⅛ teaspoon salt
2 cups coconut milk (1 coconut)
2 pieces grated cinnamon

1. Mix the coconut milk, corn flour, and sugar.
2. Put it in the top part of a double boiler, cook it over low heat until it starts to thicken.
3. Put the pot on the hot water and cook it for 20 minutes, stirring it occasionally.
4. Serve it in individual plates.
5. Powder it with ground cinnamon and let it cool before serving it at the table. Serves five people.

—ORCASITAS, *HARINA DE MAÍZ*, 6

jars (10), the rubber seals for glass jars, which need to be bought new for each use (11), and the most specific and also "necessary," an "autoclave" and/or "a sealing machine" (13). In Orcasitas's *Conservación de carnes en el hogar*, the same equipment is required in multiples.

Willsey, her co-authors, and Orcasitas are imperfect mouthpieces of a neocolonial project. Orcasitas confirms the double valence of the circulars when she explains in the introduction to *El conejo* that "this circular is part of a series of publications whose purpose is to regularize the typical foods of Puerto Rico" (4). This project "to regularize the typical foods of Puerto Rico" makes them conform to U.S. standards.[45] At the same time, it encodes and inscribes them as Puerto Rican for regular Puerto Ricans for whom Spanish is the language of culinary literacy and independence.[46] The two interpretations of "regularization" are incompatible, yet they both pertain. This double valence rests on and represents the inconsistencies and incoherencies that appear throughout the circulars: they denigrate and uphold Puerto Rican cuisine; they erase and preserve the Indigenous, African, and slave histories of Puerto Rican foods; they start their introductions with the colonialist line and then also include information or practice that contradicts it; they suggest that U.S. instruction is needed for Puerto Ricans to eat well; and they assert that Puerto Rican women can best pass along to one another their own long history of culinary practice. The work of Berta Cabanillas et al., who took over the Department of Home Economics in the 1950s, suggests that Willsey and Orcasitas may have trained the next generation of women to complete the independence work that they could not.[47] But at the same time, the power of the colonial rhetoric among the powerful Americans living in Puerto Rico continued.

Like in the French Antilles, the chronological arc of Puerto Rican cookbooks did not progress smoothly from culinary colonialism toward recipes for independence. Even after the extension pamphlets opened revaluations of Puerto Rican food by Puerto Rican women, Eliza K. Dooley's 1948 *Puerto Rican Cookbook* was published in English. It addressed, like the Ladies Aid Society's *Porto Rican Cookbook* in 1915, an audience of U.S.-born women residing in, visiting, or considering moving to Puerto Rico. Dooley obliquely refers to Puerto Rican women like Orcasitas when she cites "government bulletins" and "Home Economics Department, University of Puerto Rico" among her sources. However, Dooley's prefatory material offers no other bridges to increasingly autonomous or international Puerto Rican women. Instead, it works with U.S. neocolonialism to promote travel, settlement, and exploitation.

The wife of Brooklyn-born merchant and politician Henry W. Dooley,[48] Eliza Dooley is a model case of the benevolent imperialist stance that undergirds the (neo)colonialist defense of native style. Eliza Dooley lived in Puerto Rico for forty years, learned Spanish well, worked for the U.S. government in Puerto Rico, researched enormously, and included much information and a great variety of recipes in her *Puerto Rican Cookbook*. Dooley even recognized the wide credit due to others for the recipes she included, writing "It would be impossible to give adequate credit to the sources of these recipes. They have been gathered together over a period of forty years' housekeeping in Puerto Rico. . . . The actual recipes have been collected from housewifely friends, from government bulletins, from the Home Economics Department, University of Puerto Rico, and from neighboring islands. Those of northern kitchens have been modified to substitute things grown in this island. Mostly, they are from the hand of Isabel," her cook (4–5).

Dooley's dedication to "Isabel"—a four-page section that prefaces the cookbook—succeeds, even as it credits her, in encasing Isabel and by extension Afro-Caribbean women solidly between the stereotype of the West Indian servant and the mammy (between Querillac's Chloé and Julien Lung-Fou's Da Elodie). The dedication reads like a compendium of stereotypes of African American and Afro-Caribbean women, from the physical description of Isabel—"The whites of her eyes and her strong white teeth shone smilingly out of her velvety black face. Clad in light percales, enveloped in a full starched apron, her delight in dress and color found its vent in the care and attention she gave her head handkerchiefs"—to the characterization of her speech always marked by "Yes, Missis" (vii, viii), her incapacity for "innovations"—"I quickly gave up the idea of making innovations. Once having been given a breadmixer, she gazed fascinated as it stirred the sponge. 'Knowledge is increasin'!' was her comment. But a few weeks later her strong right hand was mixing the sponge. A rosebush was planted in the mixer" (viii)—and her joy in servitude: "She took such pride in the house, in cooking and in all she did, that the veriest drudgery took on a holiness and became a beautiful thing by the love she put in the merest detail" (viii). The descriptions of Isabel do acknowledge the importance of cooks in upper-class households in Puerto Rico and the relationship between housewives and cooks, albeit in profoundly stereotypical ways: "For more than twenty-eight years Isabel reigned in my kitchen. We can think of her as a town institution, she found servants for my friends, she comforted their children. Others of my friends have their Isabels, not only in the art of cookery but in the art of faithful service; Amanda, Augusta, Catherine, Louise, remain of the old days and of the old school but their steps are faltering, their ranks are thinning" (ix).[49] Dooley's cookbook is nostalgic for an earlier colonial period where "life went on at a more leisurely tempo" (vii) and "a pickaninny was always around to fan the flame" (viii), that might be less what she herself found in Puerto Rico in the early 1900s when she arrived than what she read of in the accounts—perhaps even the cookbooks—of earlier colonial eras.

Dooley's mid-twentieth-century Puerto Rico was one of transplanted American women writers who made Puerto Rico their homes and the subject of their work. These include the friends Dooley mentions in the dedication and those whose work she includes: Grace Spencer Phillips, whose poems, from *Seven Sonnets on Puerto Rico*, appear throughout *Puerto Rican Cookbook*,[50] and Muna Lee, who wrote the introduction. Lee's introduction praises Puerto Rico as a place that hosts "immigrants" well, blithely linking European invasion, the importation of African slaves, and early twentieth century United States "immigration" through the metaphor of plants like "the now ubiquitous hibiscus [that] is a foreigner who decided to stay" (1). Thus, she can assert, "Mrs. Dooley's cookbook, then, is truly representative of Puerto Rico not merely because of the native Puerto Rican dishes which she gives us an opportunity to savor, but because of the many dishes which she has set down that are suitable to the Puerto Rican table and welcomed there, yet cooked after recipes from far distant regions" (1). Dooley's own account of Puerto Rican plant and food history, given in her section on "Plants for Puerto Rico," compliments Lee's, detailing how Europeans, primarily, brought their cooking techniques to Puerto Rico and used them to build the native ingredients into a cuisine. First, of course, "Columbus discovered Puerto Rico on his second voyage," then Ponce de León's wife appears as the first teacher of cooking to Indigenous women: "Doña Inés, was the first white woman, and their three children the first white children in Puerto Rico so that they established the first Christian home. . . . Doña Inés planted her garden, watching its growing and teaching her Indian women new ways of cookery, so strange to them, and experimenting with produce of the country, so new to her" (3). In Dooley's story of Puerto Rico, cooking appears as a technology that the colonizers bring to the pre-technological "natives"; Puerto Rican food history is that of the "development" that colonialism brings to it. While the formulations and language of Dooley and her friends may be particularly racist and chauvinistic, they offer a logical next layer on the foundation set by Ferguson and left uncontested by Willsey, Ruíz, Janer Vilá, Schwartzkopf, Mercador, Ordoñez, Pastrana, Keown, and Orcasitas.

Dooley's version of the history of Caribbean food appears throughout many Caribbean cookbooks of the twentieth and twenty-first centuries, with slight differences in order and emphasis marking and shaping different understandings of racial and gender relations, of colonialism, slavery, and independence, of national culture and its relationship to nation-states. Her rich narrative framing of dishes and ingredients directs understanding and action in particularly clear terms:

> It is said that Americans are, as a rule, loathe to depart from old habits of eating, because we are not entirely free from sectional prejudice, perhaps, but there is no doubt that exploring the use of native products gives one a more varied and interesting diet. Those who seem to have learned early the secret of maintaining the best of their

traditions by adapting themselves to and utilizing the resources of the country, keep their health in the tropics and sub-tropics. If this collection benefits a newcomer, feeling new to the country and new to housekeeping under strange conditions, as I did myself, I shall be rewarded for the labor of compiling it. (5)

The benefit for the newcomer is that the colony is always theirs to discover, while the reward of the colonizer is to be able to package the fruits of their discovery for those from home. The colonialist defender of native style maintains this by working to ensure that even as every effort is made to bring the colony under the norms of the colonizer, colonial difference is preserved.[51]

Cabanillas and other women educated through and then teaching in the University of Puerto Rico since the Department of Home Economics changed hands (first from Ferguson and then from Willsey) in the 1950s have continued to make efforts to author their own differentiation, and to retrace through the Spanish language the Afro-Indigenous culinary legacies buried in *El cocinero puertorriqueño*. However, the cycle in which cookbooks articulated a national culture that supported national independence that supported cookbooks authoring national culture never took hold in Puerto Rico. The narrative of a Puerto Rico dependent on the United States for even its own food has been reinforced by an ongoing combination of U.S. policies and programs that both limit Puerto Rico's ability to produce and manufacture for itself and supply Puerto Rico with products. Puerto Rican cookbook authors like Carmen Aboy Valldejuli have offered recipes for middle- and upper-class Puerto Rican women to make the best of their position to use those products for their own benefit, as I examine elsewhere in my reading of her 1954 *Cocina criolla*, and Puerto Rican cookbooks written and published in the "mainland" inscribe nations of the mind rather than of the island, as I argue elsewhere in my reading of Aida Lugo McAllister's 2013 *Aida's Kitchen a lo Boricua* and Jacinia Perez's 2019 *Puerto Rican Vegan Cookbook*.[52] The U.S. colonial blend of settlement, education, assimilation, and re-education has been effective to keep both of its Caribbean territories, although not to eliminate local cuisines or the efforts of women to write cookbooks that keep them alive.

U.S. Virgin Islands: Extending (U.S.) National Culture

U.S. Virgin Islands Extension Service cookbooks operated far longer than those in Puerto Rico. They also operated as part of an even more concerted federally funded and planned "education and development" program designed to produce Virgin Islanders as subjects, families, and citizens of the United States who would then become consumers of American products and thus proper members of an extended American "Good Neighborhood."[53] In this section, I examine how the U.S. Department of Education established a program of development that constructs Virgin Islanders as in need of U.S. intervention that has been effectively carried out through the Extension Service cookbooks. Those cookbooks claim to have achieved their goal: Virgin Islanders are, the introduction to *The Heart of the Pumpkin* asserts, "like most Americans." This approximation, of course, minimizes among other things the discussion of racial difference between the largely White U.S.-born settlers and educators and majority Black Virgin Islands population.[54] In these cookbooks maternalism, with its rhetoric of care, obscures racism and Black women share authorship of assimilationism as they either accept the betterment narrative or hone their skills with what Audre Lorde calls "the master's tools."

After being occupied in the seventeenth and early eighteenth centuries by Holland, England, and France, in 1754, St. Croix, St. John, St. Thomas, and the surrounding small islands were united under Danish control which lasted until 1916 when the United States purchased them from Denmark. The islands became a territory of the United States, which they remain to this day. In 1936 the Organic Act established local legislative power in the Virgin Islands, retaining the executive power for the governor, who was appointed by the president of the United States.[55] It was not until 1970, following the 1968 "Virgin Islands Elective Governor Act" amendment to the Organic Act, that U.S.

Virgin Islanders elected a governor. In spite of multiple attempts, a territorial constitution has not been established and the U.S. Virgin Islands are still governed by the Organic Act.[56]

Setting the stage for the Organic Act, the 1934 pamphlet *Public Education in the Virgin Islands*, issued by the U.S. Department of the Interior, Office of Education and written by the chief of the Division of Special Problems, asserts the need for "rehabilitation and development" programs and "the agricultural experiment station" in the territory (13). *Public Education in the Virgin Islands* identified "the chaotic and disorganized condition of family life" in the U.S. Virgin Islands as "one of the most serious problems" facing the education and welfare departments (13). Detailing that "marital relations are so irregular, illegitimacy so common, that for most of the humbler people no family life exists" (13), it concludes: "A surprisingly high percentage of the children of the Virgin Islands lack the protection and care ordinarily provided by wholesome family life, and taken for granted under normal conditions" (13). This project in the Virgin Islands is continuous with education and development efforts undertaken in the United States in African American and Native American communities that Cathy J. Cohen and Mark Rifkin study. The precedents of settler colonialism turned independent nationhood and slave-based economy turned supposedly equal and practically striated society offer here a key supplement to a Fanonian analysis that would focus simply on efforts to denigrate "native culture" or to make "native intellectuals" buy into the superiority of colonial norms. In these U.S. Virgin Islands projects, and in the cookbooks that purvey them, we see how domestication and incorporation can institute a "development" narrative more insidious than the domination one of earlier colonial projects. As Cohen has found in "development" discourse targeting African American communities, *Public Education in the Virgin Islands* identifies "'nonnormative' procreation patterns and family structures" and establishes them as reasons "to regulate and exclude" Black communities from the nation (82). But in the context of the Virgin Islands, whose recently acquired potential citizens are both deemed outside of national and natural law and sought as part of the nation, "public education" offers a retraining option for which "Indian education" provides a notable precedent. As Rifkin has shown, in Native American communities, "Indian education" targeted "the abandonment of indigenous kinship networks, patterns of residence, and forms of communal identification . . . as a self-evidently desirable exchange of 'degraded' traditional society for the marital bliss and private homeownership portrayed as constitutive of civilized life" (335). If a goal of "Indian education" was to make way for private land ownership that would in turn allow the sale of formerly tribal land for marketable development, in the Virgin Islands, the education policy focused on reshaping the remnants of the plantation system so that the Virgin Islands might "be worth much more than their cost as a defensive investment alone," full of new markets, and of course the right kinds of subjects and families to populate them (viii).

Public Education in the Virgin Islands proposes "Policies of Rehabilitation and Development" designed to "work with the islanders in plans that will eventually improve their economic condition, make the island government self-supporting and at the same time achieve desirable goals in human development" (13). It touts the first successes: "Cooperatives for the sale of farm produce are successfully operating, and vegetables heretofore practically unknown on the islands are being produced for sale and to vary the native diet" (14). The pamphlet recognizes already the opportunity to reorder the "chaotic and disorganized family life" by reconstituting not only what but also how food culture operated in the Virgin Islands. This project would be fully developed in the Extension Service cookbooks, but *Public Education in the Virgin Islands* proposed a first step: school lunches.

> [The] generous provisions [of the school health programs] . . . have apparently inspired teachers with some appreciation of the importance of health instruction. . . . Among evidences of this attitude observed were school gardens, school lunches served in a large number of schools, and considerable efforts to realize a closer coordination with the homes. . . . Luncheons are prepared and served by the

Colonial and Neocolonial Fortification 165

teachers and pupils under direction of the supervisor of home economics. Recipes and instructions for serving the school luncheon are mimeographed and on file in each school. The luncheon consists of a one-dish meal supplemented by bread.... Generally a group of the older girls is responsible ... giving [them] experience in helping in the preparation and serving of the meal. The children have been provided with enamel bowls, spoons, and plates. Besides preparing nutritious foods, much attention is given to an attractively served luncheon. (27)

By insisting on the nutritional benefits of the lunches, the pamphlet links malnutrition to a lack of the tools and practices of "civilized eating": enameled tableware and attractive service. The prescribed "nutritious foods" in these luncheons disregards the Virgin Islands' nutritious ground provisions, greens, fish, and more:[57] "Potato soup made of several vegetables, seasoned with a piece of boiling beef, other vegetable soups, beef stew with several vegetables, [and] hot cocoa are among the foods which constitute the main dish in suggested menus, supplemented with bread" (27). Excluding local food and plant names to conceive of "home economics" in Euro-American terms, these soups and stews became part of a coordinated and coordinating project that displaced native health, nutrition, and family practices to make way for properly Americanized subjects.

This is not the only story of Virgin Islands cuisine in the first decades of the twentieth century, though those other stories were only published much later. Laura Moorehead, recalling her own "childhood fifty years ago," in the introduction to her 1977 cookbook *Kruzan Nynyam from Mampoo Kitchen*, notes that she was not encouraged or even allowed to cook as a girl since "cooking was something that the lower class women in the V.I. did" (x). Moorehead might assert a steady path of progress from emancipation to Americanization when she recounts how "the days of the Big House ended, ... young girls no longer entered domestic service, ... Americanization occurred, family life shifted, a girl grew up" (xi). However, she instead posits a trajectory of loss: "Cooking as an art or skill continued to recede to the point where it isn't unusual to find few young parents in the V.I. who have either the interest, the knowhow, or the knowledge of native cooking themselves, much less to be able to pass it on to their children" (xi). Moorehead reminisces that "in former days, nobody could complain of not being satisfied, as there was always a soup tureen with a delicious smell emanating from it" for "soup contained meat, vegetables, potatoes, dumplings, plantains. The vegetables usually were pumpkin, tomato, and potatoes," (1) she recalls, writing that "carrots were added in the 1950s with the introduction of a nutritionist in the Health Department. Before that, soups consisted of mainly starches and little protein" (1). Rather than a contradiction, she lays out a jump between the late 1920s, before "Americanization" was fully in place, and the 1950s, when U.S. government policies had successfully created a void that they needed to fill. Indeed, Moorehead notes that after "Americanization occurred," Virgin Islands families less frequently provided for themselves as "fast lunch eateries appeared, and the persons staffing them were usually from other Caribbean islands" (xi).

Nen Flo, born Florence Connor in St. Thomas in 1897, offers a counternarrative to both *Public Education in the Virgin Islands* and Moorehead, suggesting a different story of school lunch and a different story of Virgin Islands cooking, one in which Caribbean and Virgin Islands cooks were always present, and indeed stepped into the space between the decimation of local foods and the imposition of American ones. Featured in a *Virgin Islands Daily News* article in 1980, Nen Flo "explained how she attended school at Bethany, Coral Bay and East End (St. John). 'We had no school lunch in those days. I had to carry food. Some children were plenty poor. They had no food. Whoever had food would share with the rest' ("Centennial," A11). In Nen Flo's account, Virgin Islanders themselves addressed the problem of school lunches at the start of the twentieth century. She describes the children providing for one another and also offers a very different account of early school lunch programs than does the 1934 pamphlet. Nen Flo says, "I start cooking first down by Dorcas' house for the nursery school children. Aunt Elaine (Elaine Ione

Sprauve) was nursery school teacher then" ("Centennial," A11). Whether or not this was part of any government program, Nen Flo's account suggests that the impetus as well as the work to provide school lunches came from Virgin Islands women who did not need any instruction from governmental organizations to know how to prepare a good meal. Doris Jadan, in another *Daily News* column, recounts how Nen Flo and Mrs. Mildred Thomas "working with real food in a real St. John coal pot, produced great meals. Food in the school lunch at Bethany never lacked for local seasonings.... At Bethany I watched and sniffed and envied the ease with which Mrs. Thomas and Nen Flo prepared nourishing and tasty meals with what seemed like so little. I don't know if the government provided the pig snout and pigtails. I do know the cooks themselves provided the seasonings with assistance from the P.T.A., the oldest P.T.A. in the Virgin Islands, founded by Mr. Leopold Jacobs, in 1934" ("Centennial," A11).[58] These stories of Nen Flo's school lunches indicate that whatever the authors of *Public Education in the Virgin Islands* thought about how the poverty of Virgin Islanders must necessarily be attached to a lack of culinary and nutritional knowledge was incorrect; in fact, if the school lunch program worked, it was because the cooks had all the knowledge they needed and also the support of other Virgin Islanders who could supplement the meager governmental supplies so they could serve not U.S.-style potato soup with bread but Virgin Islands specialties like pea soup cooked in a coal pot. This is not Fanonian development of national culture that reemerges with its full vitality, for Nen Flo's food remains at the level of subsistence and supplement. But it is a demonstration of how Caribbean women preserved knowledge and sustained communities when nothing else was possible not only by keeping their heads down and holding tight to the last bits that they have, as Fanon's craftspeople, but also by recognizing the ongoing need for their work, even when it could not reemerge in the ways that Fanon dreams of.

The first U.S. Virgin Islands cookbooks, the Women's League of St. Thomas's *Virgin Islands Native Recipes* (1954), Doris and Ivan Jadan's *St. John Cookpot Calypso* (195?) and *A Virgin Island Cookpot Calypso*

(1965), and Erva Boulon's *My Island Kitchen* (circa 1960), launch the competing and conjoining culinary interests of Euro- and Afro-descendant native Virgin Islanders, migrants from the United States, and those capitalizing on the growth of U.S. tourism in the Virgin Islands. These cookbooks assert a vibrant culinary culture that picks up more on Nen Flo's offering than on that of the 1934 pamphlet. However, the fact that Mrs. Mildred V. Anduze, who contributed most of the recipes in *Virgin Islands Native Recipes* and appears as the author in later editions, and Doris Jadan both worked in the Virgin Islands schools underlines their collaboration with the system that produced the Extension Service cookbooks and the limited power of other culinary narratives in the face of the investments of the U.S. educational and agricultural administrations in a particular narrative of development. The first Virgin Islands Extension Service cookbook, the 1969 *Virgin Islands Fruits and Vegetables: Recipes*,[59] brings together the work of these early cookbooks with the triumvirate of education, development, and health established in *Public Education in the Virgin Islands*. Slowly but consistently, it was followed up in subsequent Extension Service cookbooks: *Native Recipes* in 1978,[60] *Breads* in 1985, *Virgin Islands Holiday Cooking* in 1987, *The Heart of the Pumpkin* in 1989, *Mango: Bits and Bites* in 1999, and *The World Food Day Cookbook* in 2000.[61] Because home economics, and the culinary side of cooperative extension, are associated with and dominated by women, like the other cookbooks I discuss in this chapter, these cookbooks share an assumption that they are overwhelmingly written by and for women. Female gender becomes the unmarked and assumed gender of both writer and reader. Home economics and agricultural extension programs are one of the first places where the semi-public space of cookbooks are authorized by public support. No longer needing to assert their right to public authority, women authors now write less explicitly about gender while still implicitly from and of gendered positions and spaces. These cookbooks, then, reveal how women participate in and push against colonial and neocolonial orders when they are not also directly pushing against the gendered orders that exceed and inhabit colonial ones.

The first pages of *Virgin Islands Fruits and Vegetables* appear to counter the project of domestic assimilation laid out thirty-five years earlier in the 1934 pamphlet. The opening note that "these recipes are not the only ways by which these foods may be prepared" acknowledges the role of local knowledge and creativity and casts the cookbook not as a manual for cooking instruction but rather as a collection of suggestions, offerings, and options for those who already know how to prepare their own versions of the same foods. The dedication page identifies the recipes as being contributed by "all the homemakers and food and nutrition workers" who participated in the "food in every yard" project—a project whose title refers to the very Caribbean public/private space of the yard that, as Omise'ke Natasha Tinsley writes, "acted as crossroads of networks formed and contested, where neighbors crossed from individual dwellings into communal spaces to cook, gossip, tell stories, fight, sing, and hold religious ceremonies" (34).[62] But in *Virgin Islands Fruits and Vegetables*' recipes and narrative sections, yards are only obliquely mentioned once, in reference to the poverty that reduces locals to cooking in coal pots rather than ovens. The revolutionary seeds that, as I examine in the last three chapters of this book, other cookbooks not only sow but also reap, do not thrive in the yards of *Virgin Islands Fruits and Vegetables*, fallen victim perhaps to the inconsistencies of extending U.S. national culture while nurturing Virgin Islands independence. These inconsistencies are legible in the variety of fonts, organizing principles, and layouts, as well as in the different tones and messages that make *Virgin Islands Fruits and Vegetables* more a collection of cookbook parts than a single cookbook. In what might be Glissantian creolizing chaos, this collage seems to signal a breakdown of the assimilation project in the face of a reassertion of Virgin Islands Creole culture but, as my following close reading suggests, actually harbors an early and messy version of neocolonial culinary control.

Virgin Islands Fruits and Vegetables is organized into approximately sixteen sections of grouped recipes focusing on roughly nine fruits, five vegetables, and two types of food. Most consist of a full-page sketch of a fruit or vegetable followed by a selection of recipes featuring that fruit or vegetable. Some sketches, however, are followed by sets of recipes totally unrelated to them—the sketch of a pumpkin, for example, is followed by a set of recipes involving guava; no pumpkin recipes appear in the cookbook. Some of the sections include a narrative about the history, botany, or nutritional properties of the fruit or vegetable. Some pages name an individual or group author—for example: the page titled "Virgin Islands Native Recipes" (followed by "Try these delicious 'Seasons Drinks'" and featuring three drink recipes) has at the bottom the line "Contributed by: Mrs. Margaret Carter"; the page with the history and botany of the mamey apple has "Virgin Islands Extension Service College of the Virgin Islands" typed across the top. Many of the sections refer to or draw on work from Puerto Rico, underlining the shared project, infrastructure, and even workforce of the departments of education and agricultural extension in Puerto Rico and the U.S. Virgin Islands. The section on "West Indian Cherry" that opens *Virgin Islands Fruits and Vegetables* foregrounds a distinctly West Indian fruit whose name also marks the colonial hybridity of West Indian food as we know it. The first page of the section gives two other names for the same fruit: acerola, the name used by the USDA,[63] and Barbados cherry. That the recipes simply refer to the local term, "cherry," might indicate a departure from the colonial implantation of Euro-American nomenclature. However, the complete absence of the Virgin Islands term "pear" for the fruit featured in the next section, labeled and referred to only as avocado, makes clear that such a move is in no way a consistent feature. The proliferation of voices, languages, and orders is so run through with U.S.-based views that rather than nurturing local culinary knowledge, *Virgin Islands Fruits and Vegetables* seems to infiltrate and contain it.

The third section of *Virgin Islands Fruits and Vegetables* is also the first to carry a description and history of its featured fruits, "Banana and Plantain," that seems to have been composed in and for an Anglophone Puerto Rican audience. It gives a surprisingly antiquarian European history to the banana, described as "probably as old as human records, evolved in the infancy of the race" but recently traced to "the gypsum deposits of the Tertiary Age in Southern France," which "disclose the

> ### Cherry Jam
>
> 2 cups water
> 3-¾ cups sugar
> 3-¾ cups cherries
>
> Wash cherries and remove stems and blossom ends. Combine the sugar and water and bring to the boiling point. Add cherries. Cook slowly for 20–25 minutes or until the juice thickens slightly, but not until it gives the jelly test (sheets off the spoon in large drops). Pour into hot sterile jars and seal with parrafin.
>
> —VIRGIN ISLANDS EXTENSION SERVICE, *VIRGIN ISLANDS FRUITS AND VEGETABLES*, 3.

banana to be a most primitive plant and similar to those found in Abyssinia" but somehow still discount the folkloric notion whereby "in Puerto Rico the tradition exists that they were introduced from the Dark Continent" (8). This attempt to distance the banana from its associations with Africa fits with the promotion of the banana, by the United Fruit Company and others, as an exotic tropical commodity (and a cash crop). However, after noting that "Puerto Rico does not ship many bananas," the narrative moves away from this white-washing of the history of the banana. "People who live in the tropics," it notes next, consume "an immense quantity" of bananas since "nothing is more conveniently and easily prepared, considering the fact that the poor have no ovens, the cooking being done on charcoal braziers" (8). If in *Virgin Islands Fruits and Vegetable*, bananas function not as an attractive commodity but rather as food for the poor, then the cookbook counters the neocolonial effort with a focus on the long history of local sustenance that might even support new forms of independence. Instead, the recipes mark a pivot to new forms of extract profit for U.S. business from Caribbean bananas. That six of the nineteen banana and plantain recipes that follow are *baked* clarifies that a purpose of this cookbook is to move island

Banana Cake with Cream Cheese Icing

½ cup butter or corn oil margarine
1½ cups sugar
2 large eggs
3 large, ripe bananas
1 tsp. vanilla extract
2 cups sifted flour
½ tsp. baking powder
½ tsp. salt
½ tsp. baking soda
½ cup buttermilk

Cream butter. Add sugar gradually, beating until mixture is light and fluffy. Add eggs one at a time, beating well after each addition. Peel bananas and mash fine with a silver or stainless steel fork. Add to butter and sugar. Sift flour, baking powder and salt together. Dissolve soda in buttermilk. Add flour and buttermilk alternately to banana mixture beginning with flour. Beat batter lightly and pour into a buttered and floured loaf pan. Bake in 350 degrees oven until done (about 50 minutes). Let rest in pan or rack for five minutes. Turn out onto rack, cool and cover top with Cream Cheese Icing.

Cream Cheese Icing

2 ounces cream cheese
1 egg white
1½ cup confectioners' sugar
½ tsp. vanilla or lemon extract
1 tsp. grated orange rind (if lemon extract is used)

Beat cheese until soft and fluffy. Beat egg white slightly and add to cheese with rest of ingredients. Beat thoroughly. Spread over cake. This icing freezes well.

FROM THE SAN JUAN STAR COLUMN "THE ISLAND KITCHEN"

—VIRGIN ISLANDS EXTENSION SERVICE,
VIRGIN ISLANDS FRUITS AND VEGETABLES, 15

cooks from yards with charcoal braziers to enclosed single-family kitchens where electric ovens can be regulated to bake "banana cake" while the cook prepares "cream cheese icing" (15). This education aims at progress from poverty in the yard to plenty in the kitchen, from fried plantains and platanutri made with nothing but plantains, water, oil, salt, and sugar to soufflé and muffins baked with additions like (U.S.-produced) flour, margarine, and cream cheese in—don't forget— designated soufflé dishes and muffin pans.

Comparisons to Euro-American culinary norms—as in descriptions of plantain as "delicious and nourishing when eaten like bread" (8)— run throughout the cookbook.[64] Even as the nutritional value of produce like the plantain (8), the yam (54), and the guava (17) is calculated and extolled, the produce itself is rendered but an acceptable substitute for the ideal bread, potato, and stone fruit. It is also probably no coincidence that the foods most remarked upon, the banana and the guava, are ones targeted for export to the "mainland" United States while the much higher nutritional values of other fruits such as the West Indian cherry are not noted.[65] Nutritional value, an ostensibly central concern, turns to be more tied to commodity value on the U.S. market than to vitamin and mineral content, and Virgin Islanders were being produced not as consumers of their own best fruits and vegetables but of that American diet to which they could contribute.

The second Extension Service cookbook, *Native Recipes*, published nearly ten years later,[66] remains ambivalent toward the Virgin Islands and its inhabitants. The forward, authored by Darshan S. Padda, Extension director, alternately treats Virgin Islanders as "them," "us," and "you" (3). Olivia H. Henry, program director of home economics for the Extension Service, is credited with the authorship of *Native Recipes*, though in her brief forward she refers to herself as part of a group of compilers.[67] Henry was born around 1925 in Frederiksted, at least a fourth-generation Virgin Islander with an ancestry tracing back to, among others, Peter Sewer, who was freed from slavery in 1809 at age four in St. John, then the Danish West Indies. Even as Henry centers a great volume of Virgin Islands recipes, *Native Recipes* reiterates the formula: education + development = progress toward a particular kind of U.S. subject-citizen. This twist on Fanon's argument about the native intellectual who embraces and promotes colonial culture, where it is not the "native" men who strive for the power and place they might achieve among the ranks of the colonists but rather the "native" women whose place is far more tied to the domestic center that they continue to inhabit even as they attain colonial rank, is that her promotion of colonial values moves not only outward, away from "native culture," but travels both ways. These cookbooks are to be read at school and bought at bookstores, but also to be taken home, followed to reconfigure domestic practice and feed families. They reveal how susceptible even a Glissantian creolization that accepts and combines elements from the colonized, the enslaved, and the colonizers is to being stripped of intimate connection to Afro-Indigenous traces.

Native Recipes opens with a section on "How to Achieve Success with our Recipes" that establishes its addressees as lacking in any prior culinary knowledge or ability: "2. Do exactly what the recipe tells you. 3. Do not substitute ingredients nor alter key ingredients unless it is absolutely necessary. It is possible to vary seasonings and spices, but never alter the amounts of ingredients. 4. Always measure carefully and use standard measuring utensils when possible. Sloppy measuring insures [sic] failure" (5). The standard is also linguistic, as the subsequent glossary of basic Anglo-American culinary terms confirms. *Native Recipes* does recognize local culinary terminology but works to replace it with U.S. standards. Here, however, the translations reflect a certain confusion of audience and project. While the glossary entry for "yellow plum" is followed by a parenthetical Latin, "(Spondias)," suggesting an informational and corrective mode whereby those familiar with local terms can use the glossary to learn the "scientific" names, on the same page the entry for "prickly pear" is followed by a parenthetical narrative description, "(this is the red fruit from the cactus plant)," suggesting a non–Virgin-Islander audience who by reading the glossary will be able to connect local terms with the things that they designate.

Native Recipes documents the fits and starts that might be part of a Fanonian revitalization of local crafts and inscribes the processes of mixing and folding that might lead to a Glissantian creolization. It exemplifies how cookbooks contain the lists of ingredients and the step-by-step instructions that guide toward dishes, homes, and islands that do and do not emerge from colonial domination, how cookbooks are rich sites for the examination of how colonial and decolonial processes play out on intimate scale, and how women from the domestic center process private desires and public passions. As *Native Recipes* proceeds, in a kind of narrative development that the ordering of recipes in a cookbook asserts even when it may be consulted for a single recipe, it offers more local terms and fewer explanations of any sort, so that by the section on Jams, Jellies, and Preserves, recipes almost turn away from the U.S.-based audience. To simply call for "2 pounds sorrel" (29) or "5 pounds cherries" (29) with no attention to the fact that sorrel in the Virgin Islands is a flower but in most of the United States is a leafy green and West Indian cherries, as noted above, are entirely different from what is referred to as a cherry in most of the United States, is to write only for a cook who is fluent in Virgin Islands plant names. Perhaps, following an initial show of neocolonial power in *Virgin Islands Fruits and Vegetables*, *Native Recipes* supports the reassertion of Virgin Islands culture. In addition to local fruit and vegetable names, Virgin Islands creole appears in the title of "Fried Raise Johnny Cakes" (see figure 3.3).[68] The sheer number of recipes for various types of Johnny cakes (see figure 3.3), Gundys, and fritters, not to mention dishes with yam, plantain, peas, and conch, reveals a vibrant local food knowledge and culture.

Tellingly, however, *Native Recipes* is the last Virgin Islands Extension cookbook to include Virgin Islands traditional staples such as kallaloo, fungi (a cornmeal dish), and Johnny cake. It is as if by adding these to the American melting pot, the Extension Service eliminated the need for Virgin Islands local culinary knowledge and practice so that "Native" took on a value as the extinct origin, extinguished by the very

VIII.

BREADS

BAKED JOHNNY CAKES

1½ cups sifted flour
2 teablespoons crisco or other shortening
1 tablespoon margarine
½ tablespoon salt
2 teaspoons baking powder
½ cup milk or water
2 tablespoons sugar

Sift together flour, salt, sugar, and baking powder. Add shortening and work in gently with fingertips.

Add water gradually until a soft, pliable dough that does not stick to the bowl is formed, Knead for 5 minutes. Roll into small balls, flatten and bake on a greased cookie sheet, until golden brown.

BAKED-COCONUT JOHNNY CAKES

2½ cups sifted flour
½ cup shredded coconut
2 tablespoons shortening (crisco)
1 tablespoon margarine
½ teaspoon salt
2 teaspoons baking powder
Milk from coconut or
¾ cup milk
2 tablespoons sugar

Sift together flour, salt and baking powder. Add shortening and work gently with fingertips. Add coconut. Add coconut-milk or whole milk until a soft pliable dough that does not stick to the bowl is formed. Knead gently. Roll into balls flatten on lightly floured board and bake on greased sheet.

FRIED JOHNNY CAKES

2 cups sifted flour
2 tablespoons shortening or crisco
1 teaspoon baking powder
½ cup water
*Oil for frying
½ teaspoon salt
1 tablespoon sugar (optional)

Sift together flour, salt, and baking powder. Add shortening and work in gently with fingertips. Add water gradually until a soft, pliable dough is formed. Knead gently for a few minutes until dough is smooth. Shape into small balls, flatten and fry in hot cooking oil that half covers the dough. When first side is lightly browned, turn over and brown other side. Drain on paper towels.

Johnny cakes are best served hot, but can be enjoyed cold. They are usually served with fried fish.

FRIED RAISE JOHNNY CAKES

1 pkg. dry yeast
4½ cups flour
2 tablespoons sugar
2 tablespoons dry milk
2 tablespoons softened margarine or crisco
1¼ cups warm water
1 teaspoon salt
Oil for frying

In large bowl, combine dry yeast, 2 cups of flour, sugar, dry milk and salt. Add softened shortening to dry mixture. Pour in warm water and beat for a few minutes. Add balance of flour to form dough which does not stick to sides of bowl. Turn on lightly floured board and knead for about 5 minutes. Grease bowl, put dough in bowl and turn to other side. Cover and let rise for about ¾ hour or until near double in bulk. Punch down. Shape Johnny cakes by forming balls and pressing down into 3" rounds. Set flattened rounds aside to rise for about 2 minutes.

Fry in shallow oil. Brown one side then turn and brown other side. Remove from fat and drain.

3.3. Johnny cakes recipes, *Native Recipes*, 1978. Source: University of the Virgin Islands Library and Digital Library of the Caribbean (DLoC).

policies that valued it in retrospect. Olivia Henry herself worked to maintain not only the historical but also the enduring value of Virgin Islands cooking, writing, for example, in the 1979 *9th Annual Agricultural and Food Fair of the Virgin Islands* pamphlet of Virgin Islands of "bush teas" as "nothing less than herb teas" so touted among the new health foods (22). Asking, "Why not use what we have?," Henry directs Virgin Islands cooks away from U.S. imports, but the subsequent Virgin Islands Extension cookbooks do not do the same.[69]

Virgin Islands Extension cookbooks of the 1980s and 1990s, most of which were reissued in revised editions in the early 2000s, serve up the final courses of cooptation and assimilation that render the Virgin Islands a site of culinary lack. The 1987 *Virgin Islands Holiday Cooking* starts with the claim that "this multi-purpose publication continues to fill a community need for nutritious recipes utilizing local foods." However, the subsequent explanation that "this is especially important here in the Virgin Islands where we often have fewer choices and less variety than on the mainland" relegates the Virgin Islands to the status of a poor satellite dependent on the strong and rich "mainland" and erases such staple Virgin Islands choices as kallaloo, fungi, or any main fish dishes, by failing to even mention them. The Main Dishes section starts with "Christmas Meatballs" featuring a can of beef bouillon, a cup of bread crumbs, and a can of mushroom soup. "Local foods" are tellingly absent.

By 1989 the introduction to *The Heart of the Pumpkin* reads: "Virgin Islanders, like most Americans, consume too much fat, sodium, and sugar and not enough complex carbohydrates" (v). The Extension cookbooks, it appears, achieved their goal: Virgin Islanders are Americans "like most." *The Heart of the Pumpkin*'s focus on legumes like "pink bean, lentil, chickpea and soybean" effects an erasure of native Virgin Islands complex carbohydrates such as plantain, yuca, and even pigeon peas. In spite of the front-cover claim of "healthy cooking with Caribbean fruits and vegetables," Caribbean vegetables are relatively few. Only two recipes feature the titular pumpkin, and the great majority of the "Caribbean" produce is relegated to "side dishes and salads." *The Heart of the Pumpkin* completes the commodification of Virgin Islands cooking by calling extensively for imported canned goods and dried beans.[70] The titular "Caribbean proverb," vacated of its local value, now serves the right kinds of citizens, who no longer wander off to forage in open fields for vitamin- and iron-rich greens or sow sickle-cell fighting yams that they gather to cook in every yard but rather are "organized" in families that circulate around kitchen appliances, a "developed" market for both U.S. dried and canned goods and the standardized U.S. nutritional policies that focus on reducing the processed sugars and simple carbohydrates that Virgin Islands Extension cookbooks taught Virgin Islanders to buy and use.

Like in the French Antilles and Puerto Rico, while culinary colonialism and neocolonial assimilationist practices carried the day, the cookbooks tell the story with all of its spills and stains. These are the messy details that Fanon does not get into and that Glissant considers only as potentials to watch out for. They are also the side notes and yard-sale finds that tell the stories not followed, that hold the recipes perhaps still waiting for a new try. As much as their positioning in and through school and government gave the Extension Service cookbooks great reach, they were not alone. In the 1970s another set of Virgin Islands cookbooks articulated Virgin Islands culinary culture in local terms: Marva Sprauve Browne's 1973 *A Catta Full of West Indian Dishes* and Laura Moorehead's aforementioned 1977 *Kruzan Nynyam from Mampoo Kitchen*, though Amy Mackay's 1980 *"Let Us Cook" = Le Awe Cook: A Collection of Authentic Cruzan Recipes* is the last cookbook to use Virgin Islands Creole in the title.[71] The Jadans also continued to publish cookbooks through the 1970s, joined by other migrants from the United States like Dea Murray and Angela Spenceley, and as the tourist industry grew, so did tourism cookbooks. Just as it is hard to classify the Extension Service cookbooks as simply neocolonial and proto-national, any division between Virgin Islands "native" and "migrant" authors or between a "native" and "foreign" audience in the late twentieth century is fraught. Creolization has happened, blurring neat lines back to African or Indigenous or European origins and neat distinctions between assimilator and assimilated. What is clear, however, is that the tension as well as the collaboration persist between U.S. government programs and local cooks of various positions.

Tension and collaboration—between colonizers and colonized, between mistresses and slaves, between revolutionaries and reformers, between elites and peasants, between White and Black, between the proponents of departmentalization/statehood and those of independence, between "natives" and "newcomers"—characterize Caribbean culinary and political history. While I can list the "betweens" as if they were binary structures, the poles are not two and the options are not either/or. Furthermore, while sometimes one predominates and the balances of power certainly shift, the tension and collaboration rarely resolve. Revolutions and reforms occur, slaves become Maroons and servants and leaders, departmentalization is achieved, and women from different social positions, backgrounds, and political affiliations continue to support and challenge and resist one another in the gathering of food and recipes, the elaboration of tastes and dishes, and the composition of cookbooks and home economics programs. Who is trying to coerce whom to do what and with what power structures behind them, who is resisting and how, who is agreeing to what and why, are the stuff that distinguish the colonial period from the independence era, culinary colonialism from recipes for independent culture. It is not paradoxical to have both tension and collaboration, but the tensions and collaborations among farmers, cooks, mistresses, government employees, cookbook writers, and cookbook readers persist through the paradox of colonialism that destroys and creates the Caribbean as we know it and the paradox of national independence that creates the native Caribbean that it restores.

In the twentieth century, even as neocolonial culinary control were extended, multiple voices and multiple courses found room. The culinary control that France maintains in Guadeloupe, Martinique, and French Guiana and that the United States extends in Puerto Rico and the U.S. Virgin Islands does correspond to the failure, or abandonment, of independence movements. But it does not quash native food culture. The recipes for national culture that I will explore in the second half of this book emerge out of and are often awkwardly continuous with culinary colonialism, and in some cases, perhaps culinary culture can feed national identity without, beyond, or around the nation-state.

4

Cuban Independence, to Taste

IN THE FIRST HALF of the twentieth century, following Cuban independence from Spain in 1898, Cuban cookbooks built on the work of their nineteenth-century criollo predecessors to develop anticolonial criollismo, shift into modernization and cosmopolitanism, and take a revolutionary turn. The first cookbook of independent Cuba celebrated Cuba's new status, rejected U.S. neocolonialism, and—in a continuation from the colonial period—held up White, landowning, elite cubanidad. When, in the 1920s, women took over Cuban cookbook writing and helped to reformulate Cuba as a modern, cosmopolitan update of the colonial state, their cookbooks ushered the plantations of the colonial period into the industries that fed Cuba's ascendance to peerdom with the United States and Europe. They elevated domestic space; encoded Cuban specificity in language, organization, and taste; and transposed the dynamics of race and class characteristic of both the colonial period and criollo independence onto discourses of modernization and cosmopolitanism. By 1950 a new revolution was brewing, and Nitza Villapol was its culinary voice. Villapol embraced a transformation that promised to feed the majority of Cubans still hungry for the fruits of independence and adopted Fernando Ortiz's vision of cubanidad as, like Édouard Glissant's créolité, "a heterogeneous conglomerate of diverse races and cultures, of many meats and crops, that stir up, mix with each other, and disintegrate into one single social bubbling" ("Human Factors" 462). Thus, over the course of the twentieth century, Cuban cookbooks dished up changes brought by independence, developed a sweet cosmopolitan elite, and reoriented for perpetual revolution. These recipes for national independence show that independent nationhood with increasing women's participation can maintain colonial hierarchies of race and class. They also show that independent national culture can continue to change, with new attempts to bring to the table of power the creolized—transculturated, Euro-Afro-Indigenous—flavors that nourish it and the techniques of improvisation and substitution that cooks have always used to serve it up.

The three phases of cookbooks that I examine in this chapter reflect and inform a reading of Cuban history. Cuba's independence from Spain was achieved, like Puerto Rico's, at the end of a war in which the United States intervened and "won." Cuba retained more independence than Puerto Rico but remained under U.S. "protection" that gave the United States, among other things, the right to intervene in Cuba's internal affairs. During the first two decades of Cuban independence, its first presidents sought to establish liberal elitist rule, contending with opposition from within and two occupations by U.S. troops. In the early 1920s, Gerardo Machado, a hero of the war of independence, rose to political power. As Cuba's fifth president, Machado oversaw massive infrastructure development, became increasingly involved with U.S. politicians and banks, and won a second term under which protests against him grew, as did state violence and suppression of detractors. The United States intervened to broker an end to Machado's government and help establish a brief interim presidency that lasted until 1933, when Fulgencio Batista took power. Batista's rise involved popular, intellectual, and military support and was marked by the end, in 1934, of the U.S. right to intervene in Cuba's internal affairs. Batista controlled Cuba through a string of presidents and was himself elected to the presidency in 1940. He retired in 1944, and democratic civilian rule lasted until 1952, when Batista returned to power and established a new brutal dictatorship. It was against this dictatorship that Fidel Castro led a revolt that grew into a triumphant revolution in 1959.

As I examine each phase of cookbooks in this chapter, I consider how articulations of independent cuisine establish the histories on which they are grounded. To assert the newness and the authenticity of their project, they retroject some roots and retrace others. In the first phase, the formulation of national independence draws from the past with which it breaks and forges complex alliances of old and new. In the second phase, increasing attention to women's roles and rights and, in some cases, to what Ortiz terms Afrocubanidad appear as occupations of the elite. While these occupations respond to the reinforcement of the foundational structures established in the first phase, they also end up reinforcing many of them, resulting in relatively minimal, although still significant, change in the content and presentation of cookbooks through the early 1950s. A significant linguistic shift appears in these cookbooks: "criollo" stops indicating primarily European heritage even as it continues to indicate birth and belonging in the Caribbean that is not necessarily non-White. Criollo, in other words, becomes racially unmarked in these cookbooks, which means that it is aligned with the racially unmarked but still White and White-aligned elite and "ideal" Cuban.[1] Ortiz's Afrocubanidad responds to the whitewashing of Cubanness but does not directly address the Whiteness of "criollo." Although the third phase of cookbooks would seem to make a radical break with the previous two, Villapol must like the others both retain and reconfigure Cubanness. Her work secures the social continuity on which the revolution relied for its authenticity as a movement of the people. Nonetheless, as Villapol keeps redoing recipes and cookbooks in ways that are the same but not quite, it becomes clear that an accumulation of minor changes makes for drastic shifts.

José E. Triay: Pivoting into the Cuisine of an Independent Nation

José E. Triay, author of the first cookbook published after Cuban independence, was a Spaniard, albeit one who came to Cuba at age eight. Despite the 1903 publication date of the *Nuevo manual del cocinero criollo,* five years after Cuba gained independence from Spain, scholars have tended to group Triay's *Nuevo manual* among the nineteenth-century Cuban cookbooks that I study in chapter 1, citing the title, the authorship, and the coloniality of its scope.[2] In fact, the *Nuevo manual* feeds off and feeds the changes wrought by independence. While the continuities between the *Nuevo manual* and works of the nineteenth-century cocineros reveal what persisted, the breaks signal how independence changed the criollismo of White Cuban men.

Triay follows, and perhaps exacerbates, the use of women, the construction of criollo as White, the treatment of Indigeneity and Blackness as inferior, and the extensive use of Afro-Indigenous foodstuff from earlier Cuban cookbooks. In this way, he validates the connection of his independent nationalism to the articulation of, and fight for, independence, even as he ignores the racial integration rhetoric and work of figures like José Martí and Máximo Gómez. Triay's parallels between Cuban and Spanish food, then, are legible as assertions of postcolonial affiliation between Cuba and Spain—a claim of parity that is also implicitly racist—in the face of U.S. incursion.

The front cover of the *Nuevo manual del cocinero criollo* abounds with markers of Cuban independence (see figure 4.1). The blue, white, and red of the Cuban flag, designed in 1849 and officially adopted in 1902, predominate, with "manual" in large blue, white, and red striped letters over a woman wearing blue, white, and red. This White Cuban woman, leaning forward to expose the pale cleavage peeking out of her low-cut dress and flanked by Cuban fruits that also open on the table in front of her just at the level of the upper thigh, is one of dishes of fertile and abundant independent Cuba. If, as Christine Folch points out, "she faces the reader, directly meeting her gaze," the gaze also invites a female readership to join her in accepting the larger patriarchal structure (216). Triay's dedication to Sr. D. Enrique Aldabó, "famous liquorist and select gourmet," evokes the spaces where men invent recipes and enjoy meals together as they make deals that assure the success of independent Cuba and suggests that the woman of the cover is less muse or even object of desire than object of exchange for the solidification of

Cuban Independence, to Taste 185

4.1. Cover, *Nuevo manual del cocinero criollo*, 1903. Source: University of Miami, Cuban Heritage Collection.

alliances between men (4). In his "few words," Triay paints a world where women might be entirely obsolete. Alluding to José Martí's "Yo soy un hombre sincero," Triay adds that "I can say, imitating the words of the poet although twisting the phrase, I also am a cook [también soy cocinero]," so that Martí's sincere, revolutionary man occupies the kitchens of the new nation. Triay's men can also take over reproduction, for "they say that experience is the mother of science and nothing is more true. My MANUAL DEL COCINERO CRIOLLO is the son of my experience in culinary art" (30). In Triay's hands, independence changed the face of Cuba, and the men who conceived it remain staunchly, solely, in charge.

The preface to the *Nuevo manual del cocinero criollo*, written by Dr. Gonzalo Aróstegui y Castillo,[3] presents Cuba as a space of such rapid culinary progress that the "luxury and property [propiedad] in meals . . . already achieved in Cuba, was the work of centuries in other countries" (8). Cuban culinary culture, new as the nation may be, is already an equal to the Europeans it joins at the table. The preface notes Triay's attachment to both Spain and Cuba and his long residence in Cuba as the manifestation of a Cuban nation taking its place alongside the Spanish (7). Aróstegui's preface casts Triay's *Nuevo manual* as the successor to Don Eugenio Coloma y Garcés's *Manual del cocinero cubano* (8), many of whose recipes Triay's text closely copies.[4] The continuity between the *Nuevo manual del cocinero criollo* and nineteenth-century Cuban cookbooks affirms the earlier cookbooks as paving the path for independence—what they set out as cubanidad is indeed what becomes the centerpiece of independent Cuban culture in the first decades of independence. As the "criollo" in his title and recipes indicates, Triay does not imagine in Cuban independence the radical break that Martí described where "the government is no more than the equilibrium among the country's natural elements. The natural man has triumphed over the imported book in America; natural men have triumphed over an artificial intelligentsia. The native mestizo has triumphed over the exotic criollo" ("Our America").[5] For Triay, criollo does represent a certain degree of mixing, as in "mojo criollo" with Spanish citrus and garlic poured onto pork but also indigenous turkey and yuca or Afro-Indigenous ñame (55). But he is not able to offer a recipe for following Martí's exhortation that "Our America" "make wine from plantains. It may be sour, but it is our wine!"—Triay does not include any drinks, but he also includes few recipes for dishes that, like plantain wine, are Afro-Indigenous with little or no European component.

Triay's introductory "few words" situate his recipes as representatives of a heterogeneous Cuban landscape and society united in the excellency of their tastes: "I have travelled the most varied tables, from those of princes and magnates, potentates and notorieties in all the branches of human knowledge, to the most modest table of the artisan and the humble one of the peasant [guajiro], I have been able to taste innumerable delicacies served by this range of classes and appreciate their excellencies" (30). In contrast to the social extremes of colonial Cuba, Triay lays out an independent democracy where the citizens can and do eat the same foods, asserting, "I do not write a treatise on haute cuisine but rather one on popular, *creole* cuisine, modest like our tastes and as healthy and comfortable as the best" (36, emphasis in the original). Nonetheless, his audience is of the class that will have full staff ready in the kitchen to wash the dishes immediately "once the delicacies presented in them have been served and the leftovers distributed to the servants" (34). Triay's culinary democracy is one where all Cubans eat the same foods, but not at the same table. He does not mention the difficulty accessing basic nutrition that persisted into the early twentieth century for a great majority of the Cuban poor, rural as well as urban (Forster and Handelman).

Triay's subtitular "a thousand recipes for all the dishes of creole cuisine and of Spanish, French, Italian, German and English dishes that are served at Cuban tables complemented by a treatment of pastry and sweets" maintains Cuba at the crossroads of Europe and the Americas. Triay, however, makes clear that rather than a colonial port of passage through which world cuisines come and go, "our cuisine" has become a site "in which have been introduced dishes from other cuisines that now have a citizenship among us that we must not repudiate" (37). Indeed, Triay lays the groundwork for a notion of Cuban exceptionalism stemming from its near-miraculous ability to meld the best of Old World tradition with the best of New World innovation with his description of Cuban cuisine as combining "products from European cuisine that ... we can say are the aristocracy of European cuisine, mixed with the democracy of the creole, and now indispensable in our gifted table. Because–let it be said in honor and glory of CREOLE CUISINE— today one eats in Cuba as well as where one eats best, and in certain dishes no one can take from us the glory of surpassing the most exquisite in the world" (39–40).

Triay's maintenance of Cuba's association with Europe is both an assertion of equality with the former colonial powers and an act of resistance to the neocolonial force of the United States. His description of the two lard options for Cuban cooks makes this manifest: "the American, that comes in barrels, wedges and cans, and that, depending on brands, is more or less good, and that of back fat, that is made in one's own house, and although it is more expensive, is more exquisite and offers the security that it is not mixed with sebaceous matter nor beaten with water which increases its weight" (38). European cuisine might still have an aristocratic edge that cannot be home-grown in Cuba, but the United States has only volume. Cuba, in other words, can show its equality on the world stage by appreciating European refinement and resisting North American brute force.

Triay's introduction, organization, and recipe selection raises the profile of staples of slave cuisine while the recipes and interstitial narrative sections extend the nineteenth-century Cuban cookbook practices of rendering creolization native in ways that both implant and obscure the Indigenous and the African as well as the painful history of their encounter with European colonialism. Tasajo and bacalao, foundational to slave and peasant diets, each have their own sections. The dish that Ortiz will identify as the national dish of Cuba and the representative of its racial mixing, ajiaco, Triay gives an unprecedented five named recipes and pride of place in the section Ajiacos, Stews, and Potages (77). Each ajiaco recipe is associated with a different Cuban locale—"Ajiaco de Puerto Príncipe," "Ajiaco de monte," "Ajiaco campestre," "Ajiaco Bayamés," "Ajiaco Cardenense"—asserting both its presence across Cuba and the distinction not only of Cuban cuisine but also of regional cuisines within Cuba (79–81). Triay also includes the later standards ropa vieja and arroz con pollo, the latter of which first appears here with the name written as such (130–131).

While throughout the cookbook Triay deploys a specifically Cuban culinary vocabulary that embraces the Cuban, he also insists on its European heritage and proximity with such explanations as "know that in the category of salsas is included the *mojo cubano* with which is served suckling pig, roasted turkey, cooked yam and yuca, stewed fish [pescado en blanco], etc., etc., *mojo cubano* and *salsa española ó francesa* mean the

> ### *Ajiaco de Puerto Principe*
> (Puerto Principe ajiaco)
>
> *En una cazuela mediada de agua se echan varios trozos de tasajo salcochado y tasajo de puerco, media gallina ó un pollo cortado en pedazos, aguja de puerco picada, cebolla partida y dientes de ajo machacado, y después de hervir y de espumar el caldo, se añaden en la cazuela plátanos verdes y maduros en pedazos, sin quitarles la cáscara, un par de mazorcas de maíz tierno partidas en tres ó cuatro pedazos cada una, yuca tierna, boniato, ñame, malanga, chayote y calabaza; y cuando ha hervido bien, en un majado de pimienta, comino, culantro y azafrán, se echan en el mortero unos trozos de malanga y se machaca con las especias; desliéndolo bien y sazonándolo todo, se echa en la cazuela á fin de que espese el caldo, para lo cual se deja hervir una media hora más.*
>
> In a pot with water, add several pieces of reconstituted dried smoked beef and dried smoked pork, half a hen or a chicken cut in pieces, chopped pork neck bone, halved onion and smashed garlic cloves, and then after boiling and defoaming the broth, add to the pot green and ripe plantains cut into pieces, without removing the skin, a few ears of tender corn each divided into three or four pieces, tender yuca, sweet potato, yam, malanga, chayote, and calabaza; and when it is well boiled, in a mash of pepper, cumin, culantro, and saffron, add to the mortar a few pieces of malanga and mash with the spices; incorporating it well and seasoning the whole thing, put it in the pot to thicken the broth by letting it boil another half hour.
>
> —TRIAY, *NUEVO MANUAL DEL COCINERO CRIOLLO*, 79–80

same thing" (41, emphasis in the original). The claim of sameness is not one of non-difference but one of equality, as evidenced in the distinctions between the actual recipes for mojo criollo (there is no recipe titled mojo cubano) and salsa española, the former being a raw sauce of garlic, lard, and bitter orange juice (55) and the latter a cooked sauce of rich pork broth thickened with flour and cut with vinegar or white wine (43). Triay further articulates a specifically Cuban "own [propio]" that is not European when he argues for a Cuban specialization in "stewed dishes [guisos]" with a "considerable number of dishes, some our own,

> ### Gallina encebollada a la matancera
> ### (Onion Chicken a la Matancera)
>
> *Cocida la gallina, se echa en una cacerola, partida en trozos, y se añaden zanahoria, cebollas, laurel, tomillo, malanga y un plátano maduro; añádesele una gelatina de cebollas y manteca, con una cucharada de azúcar, se echa en una cazuela aparte, y cuando se han rehogado en esa salsa, se le agrega un poco de caldo y se aparta así que ha hervido y están blandas las verdura y viandas.*
>
> Once the hen is cooked, put it in a pot, divided into pieces, and add carrots, onions, bay leaves, thyme, malanga, and a ripe plantain; add an onion and lard jelly, with a spoon of sugar, put into a separate pot, and when it has sautéed in this sauce, add a little broth and set aside once it has boiled and the vegetables and meat are tender.
>
> —TRIAY, *NUEVO MANUAL DEL COCINERO CRIOLLO*, 204

some imported from Spanish, English, and Italian cuisine" (203). With dishes like "Gallina encebollada a la matancera," whose titular sourcing in Matanzas makes it one of "ours," "ours" includes elements that originated in the Caribbean (fowl, onion, malanga) as well as ones brought there from Europe (carrots, thyme, bay laurel), Africa (plantain), and Asia (sugar cane); that they are now claimed "ours" by Cubans preserves and buries their histories.

If Afro-Indigenous ingredients and preparation names in recipe titles signal recognition of those aspects of Cuban history and culture, the scarcity—fewer than in previous Cuban cookbooks—of recipe titles with "plantain" and "yuca" might reveal Triay bleaching an already White-washed Cuban cuisine. However, Triay's subtitle for "Sopa Criolla"— "(in other words, plantain soup [sopa de plátanos])"—suggests that rather than a decline in the naming of Afro-Indigenous foods in titles, Triay may demonstrate a shift in the dominant meaning of "criollo," from Island-born of Spanish origin to Island-born of mixed Spanish, Indigenous, and African heritage (66). As in earlier cookbooks, the dishes labeled "criollo" often feature Afro-Indigenous ingredients such as plantains, yams, casava (yuca), and ají, and Triay's remark suggests that such features may be increasingly accepted as coloring the label "criollo." Furthermore, Triay includes three fufú recipes (86), alongside a quimbombó soup recipe and a remark that the two are to be eaten together (85–86), as well as two other quimbombó recipes. As described in chapter 1, fufú and quimbombó are the Cuban food words that are most directly and recognizably tied to their African origins.

By 1903 the racial dynamics of Cuba were discussed as much via references to the various classes in Cuba as via references to Africa or the Taíno. Many of the foods Triay highlights—ajiaco, tasajo, bacalao—have clear class associations. In the tasajo section, for example, Triay notes its historical status of food of the poor (135). However, he prioritizes bacalao for its erasure of class difference: "if tasajo . . . is the meat of the poor in Cuba, bacalao is a food universal consumption. . . . Bacalao is served equally at the table of the rich as at that of the poor" (137). By focusing on bacalao's class status, Triay avoids naming its history as a slave food associated with the Afro-Cuban; the blanchification involved in its class mobility and universalization, then, passes wholly unremarked. The rise of the poor Cuban (food) in the newly independent

---

Bacalao a la cubana (Cuban Salt Cod)

Después de salcochar el bacalao, se tira el agua y se le quitan las espinas, y en un mojo de zumo de tomate, con cebolla y perejil picado y un ají dulce, se sofríe, echándole agua y un polvo de canela y medio vaso de Jerez ó aguardiente de Islas, dejándolo cocer hasta que quede solo la salsa.

After desalting the bacalao, toss the water and remove the bones, and in a sauce of tomato juice, with minced onion and parsley and a sweet pepper, sauté it, adding water and powdered cinnamon and a half glass of Jerez or Island liquor, letting it cook until only the sauce remains.

—TRIAY, *NUEVO MANUAL DEL COCINERO CRIOLLO*, 138

nation is figured as the rise of the peasant (food) to the (food of the) universal man, such that race is at once allegorized in and hidden by class.

Triay's touting of "automatic tropical kitchens" reveals that universalizing peasant foods goes hand-in-hand with transforming them into consumer-friendly goods for the growing middle class rather than transforming the racialized class disparities that persist in Cuba or celebrating its Afro-Indigenous heritage in any explicit way. If "Popular-Style Roast Pig [Lechón asado al gusto general]" represented in the *Manual del cocinero cubano* the popular taste [gusto general] collected by and marked off from the high taste of Spanish and White Creoles, the shadow presence of lechón asado in the *Nuevo manual del cocinero criollo*, never actually detailed but repeated as a point of reference in the "modern," electrified recipe for "Lechón relleno," epitomizes Triay's work to move Afro-Indigenous Cuban classics simultaneously into and out of the politically and technologically modern criollo cuisine of independent Cuba. The recipe for "Lechón relleno" is in the section on roasts, in whose introduction Triay plugs *Automatic Tropical Kitchens* [*Cocinas automáticas tropicales*] and praises their "excellent use and great economy" for making a food that all agree is digested better than any other (185–186, emphasis in the original). His subsequent comment emphasizes the health benefits of electric oven cooking as he notes that "among us, there has not been a complete renunciation of the wood fire for roasting. It is used in the countryside for roasting pig, and truly no other process is better; although for that one needs the guava leaf that is mixed with the wood or embers in which is roasted the most tasty and at the same time most indigestible of meats. Also used is the open fire pit for roasting birds, slices of meat, etc., in *barbecue* [*barbacoa*]. The grill [parilla] is the continuation, perfected, of the old fire pit [asador]" (185–186, emphasis in the original).[6] The italics obliquely gesture to barbecue's indigenous history—the word "barbacoa" comes from an Arawakan term for scaffolding, including one used over a fire for cooking[7]—while the statement ties it to the "open pit" of "the countryside," burying any recognition of indigeneity in the broader reference to peasantry and overshadowing any praise of open-pit barbecuing with a claim of its indigestibility.

Lechon relleno (Stuffed Suckling Pig)

Se prepara un lechoncito como para asarlo y se deshuesa completamente, excepto la cabeza y las patas, que han de permanecer enteras. Se confecciona un relleno picando hígado de ternera con sal, pimienta, un ramito de salvia y un poco de nuez moscada molida. Se embute el interior del lechón con este relleno y se cose la abertura. Méchense con tiras gruesas de tocino los perniles magros, cúbranse con lonchas de tocino las espadillas, y envuélvase la pieza en una tela blanca, atándola bien para que no se deforme. Una vez dispuesto de este modo, se cuece durante cuatro horas en una tartera, con la cantidad necesaria de vino blanco y caldo desengrasado, por partes iguales.

Terminada la cocción, déjese enfriar el lechón en la misma tartera, sáquese del lienzo en que ha cocido, restréguese la superficie con mitades de limón y sírvase frío.

Prepare a little suckling pig as to roast it and debone it completely, except the head and the feet, that should remain intact. Make a stuffing by mincing beef liver with salt, pepper, a salvia branch and a little grated nutmeg. Fill the inside of the pig with this stuffing and sew the opening. Grease the lean parts of the legs with bacon, cover the back with strips of bacon and wrap in a piece of white cloth, tying it well so it holds its shape. Once it is set up in this manner, cook it for four hours in a covered pot, with the necessary amount of white wine and degreased broth, in equal parts.

When the cooking is done, let the pig cool in the pot, remove it from the cloth in which it cooked, rub the surface with lemon halves and serve cold.

—TRIAY, *NUEVO MANUAL DEL COCINERO CRIOLLO*, 199–200

Barbecue, and the (predominantly Afro-Indigenous) peasants who hold on to it, belong to backward elements of Cuba that have yet to be abandoned for the modern grill and electric oven. In the introduction to the section on pastries, Triay follows up: "Not many homes have in the kitchen a good oven, which is the main element in the confection of pastries. The importation to Cuba of automatic tropical kitchens, that is the work of my friend D. Gerardo Villanueva, its only agent, has arrived to obviate the difficulty" (269).[8] The difficulty of lack, which characterizes "old" peasant Cuba, can be obviated by Triay and his (male) friends who usher in a new era of goodness and modern ease where technological progress speeds a class mobility that incorporates the Afro-Indigenous almost to the point of invisibility.

Cuban Domestic Modernization: Sweets, Cocktails, and Cosmopolitanism

In the early 1920s, as the Cuban economy boomed thanks to rising sugar prices and its ability to "modernize" sugar production as well as to a massive tourist industry, female literacy expanded and Cuban women took pen to kitchen.[9] The new Cuban culture inscribed in cookbooks from the 1920s through the 1940s combined domestic modernization and changing places for Cuban women with a cosmopolitan turn to the United States and a continuation, under new names, of the economic and social stratification that marked the colonial period, relegating the traces of Afro-Indigenous Caribbean culinary histories to ancient history and country holdouts.

At least seventeen cookbooks were published in Cuba between 1920 and 1950, at least fourteen of them by women. The dessert cookbook *La sagüera* was probably the first, appearing in what seems to be a second edition in 1923.[10] Maria Antonieta Reyes Gavilán y Moenck's *Delicias de la mesa* was published in 1923; Berta Crespo y Setien's *El arte de bien guisar o La cocina practica en Cuba* in 1926; the Compañía Cubana de Electricidad's *El arte de cocinar eléctricamente en las cocinas eléctricas* in 1929; Blanche Zacharie de Baralt's *Cuban Cookery: Gastronomic Secrets of the Tropics* in 1931; Blanca Prieto Dávila's *Folleto de recetas de cocina y repostería cubana*, Blanca R. Nodal's *Cocina internacional*, and Ernestina Varona de Mora's *Manual de la cocina moderna* in 1932; Ambrosio González del Valle's *La comida diaria* in 1933; Dolores Alfonso y Rodriguez's *La cocina y el hogar* and La Sociedad de Dependientes de Restaurantes, Hoteles y Fondas de la Provincia de La Habana's *Auxiliar gastronómico pro turismo* in 1937;[11] Marquesa de Sevigne's *El arte de la buena mesa* in 1939; Carmen González Pérez's *Encanto del hogar: manual de la buena mesa* in 1940; the bilingual British Ladies Committee in Aid of War Relief's *Cookery Book* in 1941; Aurora López Lay's *El moderno cocinero criollo* in 1943; Blanca Díaz de Mujica's 1945 *Manual de cocina y directorio doméstico*; and Alicia Platt Stockelberg's *Mrs Platt's Recipes Cakes and Confections* in 1947.[12]

The explosion of women's food writing carried over into other popular genres. The first regular food column in a Cuban publication, Adriana Laredo's "El Menú de la Semana" in the popular weekly magazine *Bohemia*, ran from 1946 through January 1959. Laredo also had a radio cooking program, "Hágalo así," sponsored by Frigidaire, in the late 1940s and early 1950s, and as I will detail later in this chapter, televised cooking shows launched in the late 1940s as well. Women food writers were largely elite and professional, writing for a local and international audience. Taken together, their cookbooks present a carefully curated, if voluminous, Cuban modernity in a "common" Cuban kitchen language that married the new and the modern.

In *Delicias de la mesa*, the first Cuban cookbook with a woman author's name printed on the cover, Reyes Gavilán explains: "I put a special effort into using only common words so that a cook who hardly knows how to read can make any dish whose recipe is found in this Kitchen Manual. Furthermore, I have used terms that may appear ambiguous, for example: the word jar [jarro] as a measure, because there are jars of many sizes, but our cooks know perfectly well the jar to which I refer and that is found in all the kitchens of Cuba and that holds approximately three quarters of a liter" (5). Similarly, Crespo explains in her "few words" prefacing *El arte de bien guisar or la cocina practica en Cuba* that "in order to better facilitate the cooking of the dishes, I have included in this book a table of measurements with their approximate equivalencies, in what we might call home measures that, although the equivalencies are not exact, will give good results. I have worked to describe the manner of making the different delicacies in the most simple way, so that they can be easily understood and executed, even by those who are not very well versed in the rudiments of culinary art" (n.p.). And Marquesa de Sevigne writes in the introduction to her *El arte de la buena mesa*, "The text that the work contains is a clear and easy language, amen that the 'measures' of weight it uses are those commonly used in our homes and not those that predominate in other countries [al extranjero], which is a significant advantage for the success of the preparation of each dish" (n.p.) while the inside front cover of her book summarizes its exemplary compilation of "the modern rules for table service, its presentation, etc.,—New information on the gastronomic advances, with an ample recipe selection."

The allusions that these women make to unnamed cookbooks that use inscrutable language and foreign measures gestures less to specific culinary models than to the idea of an old-school European elaborateness (though the pseudonym Marquesa de Sevigne reveals that some such attachments persist).[13] Their simplicity and specificity represent a modern age that is both less recherché and less dominated by "foreign" models. Their claims for domestic language and measures, like similar ones about using ingredients available in Cuba, present what otherwise might be deigned incapacity or limitation as the assertion of modernity and the reach for inclusion. Crespo, for example, insists on positive formulations like, "I have gathered in this book the most varied and in my judgment the best recipes for the preparation of the tastiest dishes, endeavoring to only list those whose execution is possible, here, given that the ingredients that compose them are easy to obtain in this country" (n.p.). That the recipes across the cookbooks actually measure as much by liters, pounds, and cups as by jars and use U.S. and Spanish terms and ingredients as often as Cuban ones only underlines the importance for these authors of the rhetoric of specificity. By asserting the use of their own language, these cookbooks set internal measures, even if they do not always use them. By announcing recipes that are simple and accessible, they set the standard for the modern Cuban woman whose interests in good food do not require endless preparation, even if the recipes often are lengthy and complex.

Changing Places for Cuban Women

The Cuban cookbooks of the 1920s through the 1940s address Cuban women who run home kitchens as well as those who participate in the culinary economy, and even sometimes the cooks they employ. They were written during a period of significant change for Cuban women. Women had participated in the independence movement in the previous century and organized suffragist and feminist groups and parties and women's clubs.[14] Women's suffrage was legalized in 1933. The constitution of 1940 prohibited discrimination on the basis of sex and called for pay equity (though women comprised only 10 percent of the workforce throughout the 1940s). The move of women into cookbook publishing is of a piece with the women's organizing in Cuba in the early twentieth century.[15] Kathryn Lynn Stoner explains that the majority of Cuban feminists and organizers of the time demanded legal rights for women but stopped short of calling for massive economic, political, or social change; they were "privileged women, comfortable with their social and political advantages," who "used their femininity in pursuit of their goals, the most important of which was general recognition that motherhood was women's divine right and that it justified their exercising political authority in nationalist Cuba" (10). Similarly, women cookbook authors of the period present women's homemaking as nation-building by emphasizing the work in national culture accomplished by elite and—to an extent—also middle-class women in the traditional roles of household management and in domestic kitchens. None of the cookbooks mention the concentration of Cuban farmland, the expansion of monoculture, and the significant reduction in nutritional levels in rural Cuba.[16] Elite Cuban women cookbook authors, in other others words, instruct in how elite women contribute to and benefit from the new dominant order in Cuba, and close readings of their texts and contexts reveal how much of the colonial orders of class and race remain as the basis of that new order.

Biographical details about most of the women who authored cookbooks in Cuba between 1920 and 1950 remain scarce. As far as I can ascertain, they were all White,[17] a reminder not only of the continued coincidence of racial and class divisions in Cuba but also of the ways that, as Alison Fraunhar writes, "much of Cuban culture and identity in the 1920s and 1930s relied upon Cuba's African heritage, but Afro-Cubans were largely written out of the discourse of nation building" (88). Details about what I have and have not been able to find about the authors whose work I focus on in this chapter fill in the picture. In spite of Maria Antonieta Reyes Gavilán y Moenck's cookbook being published in at least thirteen editions, through 1957, and still named by Cuban home cooks and chefs as a classic,[18] I can find no biographical information on her.[19] Dr. Abraham Pérez Miró's preface to the first edition attests that Reyes Gavilán prepared many of the dishes that she lists herself and had personal contact with the makers of many others but does not say anything further about the context (3).[20] I can also find no biographical information on Berta Crespo y Setién.[21] Marquesa de Sevigne used a pseudonym and has yet to be named otherwise. Blanca Zacharie de Baralt, who also went by Blanche, was a socialite and writer who recounted her childhood connection to the authors of Cuban independence during their nineteenth-century exile in New York in her book *El Martí que yo conocí*. Dolores Alfonso y Rodríguez taught at Havana's Home Economics School [Escuela del Hogar de la Habana], a public secondary school that trained Cuba's home economics teachers alongside the normal schools founded in 1915 to train teachers in other subjects;[22] her *La cocina y el hogar* (1937) served as a textbook for the school.

The majority of these cookbooks balance between making space for individuated female authors and holding up a symbolic womanhood that, like the figure on Triay's cover, serves the men who retain authority. On the one hand, the identification of individual authors by their full names ensures that (whether or not they are married) they are not simply the wife of someone. Both Reyes Gavilán and Crespo are identified as "Srta.," attesting to their unmarried status. Reyes Gavilán, Crespo, Alfonso, and Sevigne each sign "The Author [La Autora]," with Alfonso capitalizing the words "THE AUTHOR [LA AUTORA] of this book" to claim the position and, together with Crespo, the status of her work in terms of scientific research. Crespo's note that "the recipes I have collected ... in this book have all been tested by me" asserts the value of her methodology as the "fruit of many years of experience, which I will judge well spent if with them I am able to facilitate for housewives [amas de casa] and aficionados in general the task of selecting or making the most exquisite and varied dishes" (n.p.), while Alfonso claims the status of a "professor of cooking and desserts at the Escuela del Hogar de la Habana" (n.p.).

As domestic leaders and teachers, these women focus far less on service to husbands or children than on an outward-facing presentation to a public. Their responsibility to the domestic center is not to stay in it but to ensure that it is well seen, well represented. Thus, when Crespo, Alfonso, and Sevigne do instruct in such things as the "ways of garnishing fine dishes" or how to follow the "new social rules related to the table," they often focus on serving not a family but a public. Both Alfonso and Sevigne remark on how their cookbooks will help women garner praise beyond that of their husbands: "Each table that is served, and each occasion that is presented to participate in such a service, requires great tact and exquisiteness, which grants an opportunity to each head of house [dueña de casa] to radiate her talents" (Alfonso, 8); "this book, in our own medium, turns out to be a great help to busy modern women, to prepare exquisite menus, so that they can toast to the opportunity to be even more admired by their friends ... and by their husbands" (Sevigne, 11, ellipses in the original).

Given the many references to the busy lives of women, the fact that the books feature recipes that require significant time may seem paradoxical. The recipes for ajiaco, for example, take most of a day to make, if not two (Reyes Gavilán, 246; Crespo, 62–63; Sevigne, 104); only Baralt's recipe suggests leaving out the salt beef and its extra steps (24–25), and recipes regularly suggest making things like cativia (yuca flour) from scratch (Reyes Gavilán, 391; Crespo, 219). But a comparison with earlier Cuban cookbooks puts things into perspective: gone are recipes like those in the *Manual del cocinero cubano* that start with instructions to

> ### *Ropa vieja a la habanera* (Havana Ropa Vieja)
>
> *Se pican ajos, perejil, ajíes dulces con una cebolla, se echa en una freidera que tendrá dos o tres cucharadas de manteca, se pone a sofreír y al poco rato se le añade un poco de sal y una taza de caldo y una cucharada de vinagre. Se saca la carne de la olla cuando está ya cocida, se les deshilacha y se echa en la cazuela con dos cucharadas de pasta de tomate, se revuelve todo y deja cocer hasta consumirse el caldo. Se sirve con tostadas de pan frito y plátanos maduros o verdes también fritos.*
>
> Mince garlic, parsley, sweet peppers with an onion, put it in a frying pan with two or three spoonfuls of lard, sauté, and after a little while add a little salt and a cup of broth and a spoonful of vinegar. Take the meat out of the pot when it is cooked, shred it, and put it in the pan with two spoonfuls of tomato paste, stir the whole thing and let it cook until the broth is evaporated. Serve with slice of fried bread and ripe or green plantains also fried.
>
> —CRESPO, *EL ARTE DE BIEN GUISAR*, 178

"pluck and clean" a chicken;[23] Crespo's recipe for "Ropa vieja" calls for prepared tomato paste (178); Baralt references the "time and labor saving expedient" of bouillon cubes that while not recommended "for a clear soup," can be "conscientiously" substituted for a homemade broth "for a bean purée" (20); and Alfonso's recipe for "Plantain puré" calls for "a packet of LA PASIEGA plantain cream" (168). Perhaps most consistently, although also for other reasons that I explain below, the relatively simple arroz con pollo makes inroads against ajiaco and lechón as the most popular Cuban dish.

The tension between "classic" slow preparations and quick "modern" ones is not necessarily a matter of the time women who read cookbooks plan or do spend in the kitchen. The elite and aspiring elite women who wrote and read these cookbooks may have enjoyed the expedience of ready-made preparations, but they relied on the cooks and kitchen staff in their employ for most of their "free time." If they asked their cooks to make arroz con pollo rather than ajiaco, it was more likely to be related to taste or fashion than to preparation time. Even as these cookbooks expand the Cuban domestic range, they also reinforce the places of *amas de casa* and cooks in the hierarchy of orders.[24] Nonetheless, in a marked departure from their nineteenth-century predecessors, these cookbooks regularly speak of—and even occasionally speak to—the cooks themselves. Reyes Gavilán not only explicitly refers to the culinary terminology employed by cooks but even imagines them among her target audience: "What I have undertaken and hope to have achieved is that the 'housewife [ama de casa]' can give the book to her cook and say: make this dish and that the latter can do so" (6). She believes that her cookbook might both benefit from and further the limited literacy of cooks—even as it is placed in the hands of the cook as part of an order: "make this."

Yet to the extent that these modern women held tight to their ability to order and instruct their cooks, they were also held to their own positions in the heteropatriarchy. Reyes Gavilán and Crespo might cherish their positions as unmarried women, and Sevigne might playfully suggest that the husband can appear as an afterthought, but Sevigne warns that modern women remains, under the danger of losing those husbands altogether, beholden to the "five duties": "A good housewife must always accomplish these duties so that her husband prefers to eat at home rather than in a restaurant: to always set the table nicely; to warm the plates; to serve the food piping hot; to have the delicacies ready; and to be for him in that moment, as in all, welcome company" (19). The recipes for modern womanhood in newly independent Cuba guide adjustments to the domestic order, but they stop short of presenting recipes for radical social change.

Cosmopolitan Turn

The culinary independence Cuban women cookbook writers of the 1920s–1950s set out was not isolationist but rather international. They may have rejected foreign measures, but they blithely incorporated U.S. and European products and dishes, configuring thus a cosmopolitan

Cuba poised between European refinement and U.S. modernity that sought to bring the best of both worlds to the table.

When Reyes Gavilán repeats Triay's assertion that bacalao is a food "of universal consumption" (143), the list of recipes she offers as support refers not only to consumption that crosses classes and regions of Cuba but also one that is transnational, including "Bacalao a la Cubana," a la Italiana, a la Mejicana, a la Francesa, a la Portuguesa, a la Peruana, and much more. However, most of these cookbooks do not rely on European counterparts to provide recipes for European dishes. Instead, they assert their own ability to instruct in the making of everything from soufflés to sandwiches and the usefulness of Cuban ingredients such as ají in the making of dishes like "Bacalao a la Italiana." Baralt takes the fact that "Cuban hotels serve a cosmopolitan table" (6) and that "in the homes of wealthy Cuban families French dishes alternate with national ones, forming a most happy alliance" (7) to explain her own focus on "the typical ones of the country, many of which are well worthy of being known and relished by a wider public" (7). Her work, like that of her peers, asserts that Cuban cuisine is an equal party not only at the cosmopolitan tables of Cuba but also at the tables of other nations.

This vision of equality works against the backdrop of growing U.S. control of the Cuban economy, most significantly in sugar mills where U.S.-owned companies went from accounting for 21 percent of sugar production in 1905 to 63 percent of sugar production in 1926, but also in the massive power of the United Fruit Company. The mills did employ (U.S.-educated) Cuban engineers, lawyers, and agents, along with lower-level workers, and they supported and were supported by Cuban politicians.[25] The Cuban elite had deep motivation to tell the story of the U.S. presence in Cuba as a mutually beneficial and balanced arrangement.

Some Cuban writers, like Sergio la Villa and Luis Felipe Rodríguez, published stories in the 1920s that exposed the revolving doors between U.S.-owned sugar mills and Cuban political power. As the Cuban cookbooks of the period represent the places of U.S. foods, tastes, and tourists at Cuban tables, they teeter between offering recipes that nourish Cuban national culture in the face of U.S. incursion and setting the table for the Cuban elite's enjoyment of the power and influence their complicity with U.S. "investments" grant them. La Villa's caricature, in "Un pueblo del interior," of a local pastor's "possession" by the mill satirizes Cuban adoption of American tastes. He is "Cuban by birth, but educated in a college in South Carolina, he liked avocados because they were 'exotic' and was totally unfamiliar with the multiple ingredients of the Cuban stew (*ajiaco criollo*), to which he preferred *corn flakes*" (8).[26] The politics of culinary representation in the story convey the fear that U.S. companies would not only exploit Cubans but also Americanize them. The double movement in which cookbooks of the era approach the United States and distance from it, on the other hand, might achieve a state where U.S. companies benefit Cubans and Cubanness prevails.

Although Reyes Gavilán praises Cuban quality over American size as in this description of oysters, "those of North America are very big and very fit for all the preparations but to eat them plain, which is how they are most often eaten, the oysters of Sagua, of much smaller size, are much more tasty" (157), she and her peers focus less on praising (Cuban) quality over (U.S.) quantity than on asserting their ownership of Americanness, their ability to put U.S. products to Cuban use, and even to make their own things like "panques [pancakes]" and "sandwichs [sandwiches]." Reyes Gavilán employs the designation "American" to describe both dishes that appear to be from the United States—like the "Sandwich americano" made with soda crackers, butter, mustard, and caviar or foie gras (88)—and ones that seem "creolized"—like the "Pastel americano," a cake filled with "guava paste [dulce de guayaba], or strawberry jelly, or cherry" (422)—affirming the shared identity of the two nations and their cuisines as well as their status as equals in the American neighborhood. The Cubanized spellings of "panque" and "sandwichs"[27] and omission of any history of the foods obscure their U.S. provenance, and the instructions to cook all of the "panques" in the oven, sometimes in a square mold, further remove them from the U.S. preparation and traditions. While "sandwichs" appear in separate sections with special descriptions of the food in Reyes Gavilán, Crespo y Setien, and Sevigne's cookbooks, none of the women

> ### Sándwich con Chutney (Chutney Sandwich)
>
> *Los sándwiches de pollo y Chutney son completamente nuevos. A media libra de pechuga de pollo machacada suavemente en el mortero se añade una cucharada de Chutney y una y media de crema bechamel (véase el índice); se mezcla bien y se extiende sobre el pan por ambos lados.*
>
> The sandwiches of chicken and Chutney are completely new. To half a pound of chicken breast gently mashed in the mortar add a spoonful of Chutney and one and a half of bechamel cream (see index), mix well and spread on the bread on both sides.
>
> —REYES GAVILÁN, *DELICIAS DE LA MESA*, 87

mentions that "sandwichs" and the cocktails with which they are associated came to Cuba via the United States. Thus, when Reyes Gavilán singles out a recipe for a "Sándwich con Chutney" for its newness, she implies that wherever the sandwich came from, its modernization is Cuban (which also conveniently dispenses with the need to mention that chutney comes from the Anglo-Indo-Caribbean). Similarly, Sevigne's Sandwichs, Bocaditos y Canapés section gives a history of bocaditos in which she explains that "the bocaditos served with cocktails are more popular every day. Their origin lies in another era when due to lack of time or hurry, people ate wherever they happened to be, so they were a quick lunch, easy to share. Today, cocktails are served at parties with bocaditos" (33). Rather than gesturing to the rising popularity of sandwiches at American lunch counters in the 1920s, Sevigne's history retrojects the fast lunch as part of Cuban history when time was short and work was pressing and lets the sandwich, bocadito, and canapé emerge as an invention of a Cuban midcentury elite who spend their time drinking and snacking at parties.

The push and pull of American influence on Cuba also manifests in the appearance of English-language cookbooks that, as much as they may try to incorporate U.S. elements into the Cuban mix in a way that upholds or even advances the status of the two nations as peers, invite tourists from the United States to enjoy Cuban hospitality and support the Cuban economy in ways that can all too easily be read as simply giving up Cuba to the United States. Baralt's English-language *Cuban Cookery*, La Sociedad de Dependientes de Restaurantes, Hoteles y Fondas de la Provincia de La Habana's *Auxiliar gastronómico pro turismo*'s opening Spanish-English gastronomic dictionary and thirty lessons in English, and Alfonso's display of awards from Quaker Oats Co. indicate the risks, to Cuban autonomy, of embracing the United States. Baralt writes for visitors to Cuba "who have tasted and would 'like some more' of the good things partaken of during their stay in Cuba" (6) and for "the hostess" to said visitor, for "It will surely be a pleasure for a hostess to give her guests a surprise, presenting them with an exotic dish right from the Caribbean, offering them a culinary novelty, which in these days is a prize—indeed a rare and coveted prize" (7). Though she asserts that "the cuisine of a country is one of its psychological aspects, an accumulation of slow growth, almost a synthesis of its civilization" (8), the Cuban synthesis she presents seems simply the apotheosis of centuries of exoticization and exploitation that make Cuba the "jewel of the Caribbean" and also make that jewel the centerpiece of someone else's crown. The circulation of U.S. people and products asserted the sway of U.S. capital and commerce; consumerism, profit, and independence turn out not always to be easy bedfellows. While the Cuban tourist industry boomed on U.S. dollars, it also spent good portions of that money purchasing goods and products from the United States to serve Americans in Cuba. And U.S. products circulated far beyond hotels and restaurants serving Americans. The 1943 edition of Alfonso's *La cocina y el hogar* proudly displays on its inside title page a "medal awarded to the author of this book by The Quaker Oats Company, in recognition of the creation of distinct recipes with this product." As much as this can be one more moment in which Cuban cuisine bests U.S. talent and renders U.S. oats another raw material for Cuban value added, Alfonso's "very important note" commanding "Do not use products different from those listed in the recipe; as every one of them is duly tested with those ingredients and a little change will make it so your recipe does not come out well" shows how the profit from the use of Quaker Oats will remain solidly in the hands of the U.S. company: deviate from consumerism and risk tasteless outcomes.

American profit rather than Cuban taste seems to be responsible for the emergence of arroz con pollo as "the" Cuban national dish. When in 1939 Ortíz followed up on Triay's recognition of ajiaco's importance to announce it as not only Cuba's national dish but also the metaphor for its racially and ethnically mixed identity, the cookbooks of the 1920s and 1930s were already lowering the dish's profile and raising that of the more tourist-friendly arroz con pollo. Reyes Gavilán includes one recipe for ajiaco and one for "Olla cubana ajiacada" and starts her recipe for ajiaco with a comment on its popularity. She indicates their position in the Cuban menu as a main dish by putting the recipes, along with those for "Olla cubana" and other rich meat stews, in her "meats" section rather than, like most of the other cookbooks, in a section on soups and stews. However, Reyes Gavilán also includes five recipes for various types of arroz con pollo. Baralt's headnote to her ajiaco recipe goes so far as to qualify the national status of ajiaco: "This is the national dish of Cuba, especially in the country. Some of each kind should be served in every plate. It is seldom seen at fashionable restaurants, being a homely concoction, but withal a savory one" (23–24). In contrast to the "country" tastes that may be "national" but not "fashionable," Baralt describes the urbanity and popularity of arroz con pollo, especially with tourists (see recipe). The pattern illustrates the power of U.S. tourism in Cuba to, in the words of Louis Pérez Jr., "modify setting and meaning of ordinary life around North American familiarities" (168). By 1941 Sevigne has only one recipe for "Ajiaco a la criolla," signifying its typical character (it is a "plato típico") and offers four different arroz con pollo recipes (132–133).[28] As the recipes attest, ajiaco takes far longer than arroz con pollo to prepare, and while ajiaco features ingredients from Cuba's Afro-Indigenous culinary history, arroz con pollo almost always depends on canned peas and olives in addition to the staples (rice and chicken).[29] The rise of arroz con pollo symbolizes how the pull of

Arroz con pollo (Rice with Chicken)

This is one of the first dishes offered to foreigners on arriving in Havana and it is invariably relished.

A decade or so ago there was a famous restaurant at the Correra, at the end of Vedado, on the Almendares river, where, in a picturesque setting, in the shadow of the old fort, Rice and Chicken was cooked to perfection. One could go for a row on the river while the rice was being prepared.

The "Madama" who kept the place retired eventually with a round fortune.

Behold the recipe:

1 plump, tender chicken
1 lb. best Valencia rice
4 good sized tomatoes or ½ can
1 green sweet pepper
1 onion, 1 kernel garlic
1 pinch Spanish saffron
Bay leaf, 2 cloves, salt and pepper to taste
1 tablespoonful good lard
2 tablespoonfuls olive oil and wineglassful Sherry
1 small can Spanish pimentos
¼ can extra fine petits pois
¼ can artichoke

Arroz con pollo should be cooked in an earthen vessel called "cazuela," widely open at the top and rather shallow. It is the classical utensil for this dish which is sent to the table right off the fire.

Cut up the chicken and brown it quickly with the lard, then the chopped onion and garlic, keep stirring to prevent burning, add tomatoes, green pepper, saffron, bay leaf, cloves, pepper and salt.

Let simmer for 5 to 10 minutes.

Cover with water and let boil until the chicken is tender.

(continued next page)

> *(continued from previous page)*
>
> Then add the rice, previously washed, cook on a moderate fire until the water has been absorbed, then sprinkle over the top the Sherry and olive oil. Cover and allow to steam on very slow fire until done.
>
> A few minutes before serving, cover the surface of your dish with pimentos, petits pois and artichokes. Allow to heat and send to the table in the receptacle in which it is cooked.
>
> Rice can be prepared in practically the same manner using duck, ham or fresh pork instead of chicken.
>
> —BARALT, *CUBAN COOKERY*, 63–64

modernization and service to tourism maintain an independent Cuba dependent on the hierarchical power and privilege of an urban, Americanized elite over its "typical," country-ish Afro-Indigenous majority.

Afro-Indigenous Roots, Secured and Relegated

While the notion of racial equality articulated by Martí that subtends the national character of ajiaco remained central to the idea of independent Cuba throughout the first half of the twentieth century, its realization was, as Frank Guridy argues, "severely restricted by Cuban racism" (111). The town of Sagua was one of the sites where racial tensions were most obvious in the 1920s as it attracted both White and Black tourists from across the Caribbean and the United States and became one of the centers of the Universal Negro Improvement Association in Cuba and also of Cuban governmental efforts to destroy it (Guridy). Sagua's prominence and popularity rested on its longer history as a hub of sugar production and forced Black labor in sugar plantations and mills. The town's roaring sugar production was central to its ability to attract tourists as a site of domestic fine finished goods and conspicuous consumption. The enormous new hotel that opened there in 1925 attests to the

Panatela Ada (Ada's Sponge Cake)

Cinco huevos, cinco onzas de harina cernida, cinco onzas de azúcar, una cucharadita de baking powder.

Se baten separadamente las yemas y las claras, se va echando en las yemas primero el azúcar y después y de muy batido, las claras, luego la harina poco a poco y en esta el baking poder y en seguida se pone en el horno.

Five eggs, five ounces of sifted flour, five ounces of sugar, a teaspoon of baking powder.

Beat the yolks and whites separately, add to the yolks first the sugar and after beating very well the whites, then the flour little by little and into that the baking powder and immediately put it into the oven.

—LA SAGÜERA, 20

many visitors who came to play at the casino and eat at the many restaurants. The dessert cookbook *La sagüera* first published there in the early 1920s may be the first Cuban cookbook written by a woman. Its title certainly holds up a representative woman from Saguas. With no listed author, *La sagüera* both suggests that this woman is herself its creator and renders her entirely symbolic. The recipes themselves fill *La sagüera* with what Sidney Mintz calls "sweetness and power." With only one recipe that calls for melado, or any other by-products of sugar production associated with Afro-Caribbean cuisine, *La sagüera* effaces Afro-Caribbean labor and taste. Instead, the many recipes for meringues, sponge cakes (panatelas), diminutive treats, and complex combinations evoke a nostalgia for the colonial splendor of what Sevigne describes as "those rich Cuban sweets that were made a half-century ago, and that many people today have surely forgotten" (184).

Nonetheless, among its 101 recipes whose main ingredients are sugar, eggs, white flour, butter, milk, and almonds, *La sagüera* includes nearly two dozen desserts centered on Afro-Indigenous ingredients, including

> ### *Buñuelos de yuca* (Yuca Fritters)
>
> *Tan sabrosos como los otros [buñuelos de catibia] y más fáciles de hacer son estos buñuelos. Se hierve la yuca hasta que esté cocida; pero sin dejarla después en agua. Se escurre y se pasa por la máquina. Se le echan huevos, anís y un poquito de mantequilla o manteca si la yuca es muy seca, si no, suprímase. Se amasa, se fríen los buñuelos en manteca abundante y si es posible se sirven muy caliente; pero con el almíbar fría.*
>
> These fritters are as tasty as the others [yuca flour fritters] and easier to make. Boil the yuca until it is cooked; but without letting it sit in the water after. Drain and run it through the machine. Add eggs, anise and a little butter or lard if the yuca is very dry, if not leave it out. Knead it, fry the fritters in abundant lard and if possible serve very hot; but with the syrup cold.
>
> —LA SAGÜERA, 52

ones like "Crema de boniatos" and "Buñuelos de yuca," whose titles feature Cuban terms of Taíno origin. While no narrative acknowledges those origins, their presence remains to be noticed. *La sagüera* unintentionally passes along Afro-Indigenous traces that later collectors and readers, like us, can pick up.

As *La sagüera* and Reyes Gavilan's cookbooks were being published, Ortiz was raising the profile of Afrocuban food among Cuban intellectuals and the growing Afrocuban movement of which he was a centerpiece, publishing in the *Revista bimestre cubana*, which he edited and that was one of the main venues for publishing work on Afrocubanidad, along with other progressive ideas, a series on "La comida afrocubana" between 1923 and 1925.[30] In the first, 1923, installment, Ortiz notes that Africa "undoubtedly" influenced "Cuban food and culinary arts," "Black slaves having been used in domestic service by their masters, the climate and latitude of Cuba being analogous to those of the African regions of the most intense slave trade, and slaves and later freed Blacks have had in their plots enough freedom to, to a certain degree grow and determine their food according to the tastes and customs brought from their faraway native countries" (404). The traces of that influence, Ortiz argues, can most clearly be found in the language of food. Though the conclusions of his detailed etymologies are not always accurate, his errors downplay the Indigenous roots of Cuban cuisine and hold up the African.[31]

The elite Cuban women who wrote cookbooks between 1920 and 1950 largely ignored the Afrocubanists, and their focus on modernization and cosmopolitanism bypassed progressive movements in Cuba. Reyes Gavilán is, however, a notable exception. Although she does not explicitly detail Afrocuban or Afro-Indigenous culinary histories, and although her cookbook does not draw directly on Ortiz's' work, her book holds up both the Afrocuban and the Indigenous with named sections on Quimbombó, Plantain [Plátano], Malanga, Yam [Ñame], Yuca, Boniato, Calabaza, and Corn, and treats them as equals to European vegetables like Turnips and Carrots. Her organization, furthermore, asserts the companionship of the ground provisions—called "viandas" in Cuba— of African (yam, plantains) and Indigenous (malanga, yuca, boniato, calabaza) origin. The placement of the Quimbombó section near these, along with her inclusion of fufú recipes in both the Quimbombó and the Malanga sections, reiterates an organization based on Afro-Indigenous pairings and meal order and follows Triay in directing readers to carry on the African practice of quimbombó and fufú together (327–328). Reyes Gavilán also has great numbers of recipes for Afro-Indigenous dishes including recipes focused on viandas (including in the titles) beyond the named sections, three recipes for ajiaco, eight tasajo recipes, three ropa vieja recipes, four fufú recipes, and a recipe for calalú (callaloo) as well as recipes for catibía, cusubé, matahambre, and melcocha. The cookbook both highlights and integrates these recipes by gathering some of them in sections named for Afro-Indigenous ingredients and sprinkling others throughout other sections of the cookbook, alongside recipes that feature Indigenous dishes from Central America, like tamales (296), tayuyos (297), and arepas (425–426). Reyes Gavilán's book offers an instruction manual for

Quimbombó guisado (Dressed Okra)

El quimbombó debe ser tierno, se la corta la cabeza y la punta, se parte en ruedas o se deja entero y se tiene en agua hasta el momento de cocinarlo. Se echa en manteca bastante cebolla picada, ajo y unos cuantos tomates, jamón picado y se revuelve hasta que esté bien cocinado se añade el quimbombó, se tiene un rato en este mojo y su cubre con caldo suficiente; se sazona con sal y pimienta y cuando esté cocinado se le echa un poco de ajonjolí tostado y molido. En el momento de servirlo se echan las bolas.

The okra should be tender, cut off the top and the end, cut into rounds or leave whole and keep in water until ready to cook. Put into lard a good amount of minced onion, garlic and a few tomatoes, minced ham and stir until well cooked, add the okra, leave it in the sauce for a while and cover with enough broth; season with salt and pepper and when it is done add a little toasted and ground sesame. Add the balls when ready to serve.

Fufú de malanga y plátano
(Malanga and Plantain Fufú)

Se pelan cuatro malangas grandes, se parten en cuatro, se cortan las puntas de tres plátanos machos y pintones, se parte cada plátano en tres o cuatro trozos y se cocinan en agua junto con las malangas; cuando estén blandos se machacan en el mortero, se amasan juntos, se añade un poco de manteca y se forman bolas de un tamaño regular, se sazonan con sal.

Peel four big malangas, quarter, cut the tips off three ripe plantains, cut each plantain into three or four pieces and cook in water with the malangas; when they are soft, mash them in the mortar, gather together and add a little lard and form into balls of a regular size, season with salt.

—REYES GAVILÁN, *DELICIAS DE LA MESA*, 327

preparing and enjoying the taste of "nuestra América" in our kitchens: cubanidad at the intersections of the African diaspora, the indigenous Caribbean, and Central American mestizaje (that blends the Spanish/European with the Indigenous).

Reyes Gavilán's book came out in new editions every few years, but the cookbooks published by other women from the late 1920s through the late 1940s include fewer recipes with titles or even ingredients that stand out as Afro-Indigenous. Indeed, as Folch notes, "With the passing of time, the breadth of recipes in twentieth-century elite texts reestablishes the island's cuisine as oriented firmly toward Europe, not Africa" (214). Crespo, publishing in 1926, still has two fufú recipes along with a "funche cubano" recipe, and even a recipe for the plantain wine—well, plantain liquor—that Martí called for (27). Baralt connects Cuba to Asian, Mexican, and African ingredients (rice, corn, and okra) but dismisses African dishes. She identifies quimbombó as a side dish and only mentions fufú in passing: "This is generally served with 'fufu' which is nothing but boiled, half ripe plantains crushed while hot and formed into balls. It is added to the quimbombó a moment before serving. This [the quimbombó] is served as a vegetable, accompanied by white rice. If you want it as a soup, add a greater quantity of broth and put a ball of 'fufu' in each plate" (88–89). The quotation marks around "fufu," when with other Cuban and Afro-Indigenous terms she has used italics, work as scare quotes, indicating that the reader consider the word, and the concept, with skepticism. The absence of a full recipe for making the fufú turns readers away from doing so.

Baralt's inclusion of the Afro-Cuban not as an equal contributor to Cuban culinary history and a partner in its contemporary preparation but rather as an artifact to be preserved with skeptical attachment is compounded in Conrado W. Massaguer's sketches of stereotypical "African" figures that appear in *Cuban Cookery* alongside recipes that Baralt identifies as "old time" or "country style" (see figure 4.2). It is as if not only Afrocuban foods but also the Afrocuban human presence in Cuba were a quaint feature of the past preserved still in some country enclaves and now dressed up by Baralt for the kind of nostalgic enjoyment that

MEATS

LECHON ASADO. (Roast suckling pig)

The approved manner of preparing this most Cuban of all Cuban dishes is to roast the baby pig on a spit, over a wood fire, with plenty of guava leaves; but this is only practical in the country. In town we must be satisfied to roast it in the oven, seasoning it with salt,

4.2. *Cuban Cookery*, lechón asado recipe with sketch, 1931 [1946].
Source: Schlesinger Library, Harvard University.

> ### *Sopa de plátano* (Plantain Soup)
>
> *1 libra de falda, 2 plátanos verdes, 6 tomates, 1 cebolla grande, 1 ají grande, 3 dientes de ajo, 1 hoja de laurel, 2 limones, 1 cucharada de sal, 6 granos de pimienta.*
>
> *Se hace un caldo corriente y en él se cocinan los plátanos, los cuales después de pelados se untan de jugo de limón y se cortan en rueditas de dos dedos. Cuando el caldo esté, se cuela y los plátanos se reducen a puré pasándolos por un colador fino. Se sazona de sal y jugo de limón, dejándolo hervir hasta que esté cremoso. Da para 6 personas.*
>
> 1 pound of skirt steak, 2 green plantains, 6 tomatoes, 1 big onion, 1 big pepper, 3 garlic cloves, 1 bay leaf, 2 lemons, 1 tablespoon of salt, 6 peppercorns.
>
> Make a regular broth and in it cook the plantains, which after being peeled are wetted with lemon juice cut into rounds the size of two fingers. When the broth is ready, it is strained and the plantains are reduced to a puree as they are passed through a fine strainer. Season with salt and lemon juice, letting it boil until it is creamy. Serves 6.
>
> —ALFONSO, *LA COCINA Y EL HOGAR*, 18

can be had when the "other" is safely diminished. Less blatant examples of this distancing from the Afro-Indigenous appear in the rise of arroz con pollo and the diminishment of ajiaco across the cookbooks, Sevigne's omission of any recipe for ropa vieja, and Baralt, Sevigne, and Alfonso's redirection of bacalao to Europe with their privileging of "Bacalao a la vizcaina (Typical Spanish recipe)" (Sevigne, 87).

Nonetheless, recipes persist, not only for Afro-Indigenous dishes that are marked—at the time or later—as national foods (ajiaco, ropa vieja, lechón) but also for dishes like sopa de plátano, quimbombó, and tasajo of whose African origins Ortiz had recently published a reminder. Folch notes that viandas diminish in recipe titles (214). But they do not disappear. The place of plantains, calabaza, corn, boniato, yuca, and yam as the staple side or accompaniment served in, under, or around stews, soups, and guisos also diminished but did not disappear. Some viandas appear increasingly in desserts, marking perhaps an association of the "traditional" Cuban with sweets but also indicating a creativity that set off a new Euro-American-Cuban fusion. Similarly, they appear in new ways in savory preparations associated with Europe, as in Sevigne and Alfonso's "Soufflé de boniatos" (142; 146), Sevigne's "Puré de maíz tierno" (54), and Alfonso's "Tortilla de plátanos maduros" (204). We could see in these recipes a miniature of how Cuban cookbooks of the first half of the twentieth century were open to experimentation and the new in ways that, as Fanon writes, mark the vibrancy of a national culture that is evolving on its own terms. However, when we note that at the recipe level the primary "innovation" is to use Cuban ingredients in European preparations in new ways, that the overall trend is to include proportionally more dishes with European and American place names in the titles, and that embracing modernity and urbanity are coupled with an increase in references to Cuban dishes as "classic" and "country" and also that there is no attendant increase in attention to Afro-Indigenous heritage, Afrocuban people, or the culinary creations and needs of the—poor and Afro-Indigenous—majority of the Cuban population, we come to understand how and why calls for a new national culture, in and through a new revolution, were emerging.

As Fanon warns, political independence alone is not sufficient to guarantee a lasting free postcolonial nation. It must be built around, from, and through a revitalized "native" national culture. While "what Fanon said" about colonial domination and the shared work of political, military, and cultural work to end it undergirds my analysis of culinary colonialism, his focus on the Algerian context and on the lead-up to national independence render his work less directly relevant to the construction of and instruction in the independent national cultures in the Caribbean after national independence was won. In the Caribbean, a national culinary culture must shake off culinary colonialism and also inscribe a criollo cuisine born out of the encounters of the Indigenous, African, European, and Asian and evolving in and through their continued interactions in the new nation. Ortiz's transculturation and Glissant's creolization become more relevant in these moments, offering models for understanding the multivalent relations and imbrications that are necessarily in play. And while these sometimes come together smoothly, at others, they clump up or curdle. In Cuba, when the new national narrative continued to be controlled by elite men and women who looked to Europe and the United States for company and inspiration and relegated their own compatriots to the rusty pots of history and the terrains leeched by monoculture, it is not surprising that it fed a Fulgencio Batista dictatorship increasingly indebted to international interests.

In addition to allowing for a rich batch of food metaphors, cookbooks show the domestic interior of colonial domination and the stirring of resistance to it and also the intimate details of how recipes for independent national culture can end up making dishes for new forms of domination. By reading them closely, we can see how elite women worked with and against the forces of revolt, repression, and revolution in their own homes and how they interfaced with the goods and people that and who served them and that and whom they served. The very intermediary status of cookbooks that left them out of scholarly consideration is what makes them so important: they are written from positions between domination and dominated, they are about how materials are transformed from raw or processed goods to finished products, they are domestic objects that serve national interests; and in the Caribbean they detail specific processes of mixing, substituting, and varying.

Stir Continuously: Recipes for Perpetual Revolution

Nitza Villapol appeared on the Cuban culinary scene in 1948 as a modern woman—television personality and all. From the first, her cookbooks address a new audience: working-class women. They set up in the early 1950s the engagement of women in the class-work of revolution. As that revolution continued, Villapol's cookbooks took Ortiz's revaluation of Afrocubanidad into cooking. And they showed how to make a virtue, and a delicious dish, of the economic and cultural impacts of Cuban communism by insisting that it was all about independence all the time.

Born in New York in 1923 to parents exiled from Cuba under the Machado dictatorship, Villapol had experienced the unfulfilled dreams of an independent and free Cuba. After her family returned to Cuba in the early 1930s, she survived polio, studied nutrition—although there are competing claims as to whether that was in Cuba, London, Massachusetts, or all three—and landed a job as the star of a new television cooking show that ran regularly, first daily and then weekly, until 1993 and featured dishes largely developed by her assistant, Margot Bacallao.[32] In the early 1950s, before the Batista dictatorship, Villapol authored recipe pamphlets produced by the firm El Encanto and the first of a vast number of editions of her most famous cookbook. *Cocina al minuto*, of which Villapol and others have produced a palimpsestic morass, is Cuba's most famous cookbook. According to Sisi Colmina González, the widow of Villapol's adopted son and executor Marcos E. López González, Villapol published the first edition of *Cocina al minuto* in 1950 and issued revised editions every two years until 1962. The earliest editions of *Cocina al minuto* that I have been able to locate are from 1954, 1956, 1958, 1959, and 1960, all co-authored with Martha Martínez. After 1959, Villapol served the revolution, and her work thrived in it. *Cocina al minuto* was released in new Cuban editions in 1980, 1981, 1988, and 1991 with Villapol as sole author. From the late 1980s through the late 1990s, the Cuban Científico-Técnico publishing agency also released several other titles under Villapol's name and the Cuban Editorial José Martí released an English translation of Villapol's work, titled *Cuban Flavor*. Villapol and *Cocina al minuto* are also darlings of the Cuban exile community. Between 1950 and 1998 at least four editions of *Cocina al minuto* were published in Miami and at least one in Mexico, where several other cookbooks were also published under Villapol's name between 1970 and 2000, along with editions in Spanish and English reproductions that do not credit Villapol. In the United States, the Miami-based Ediciones Cubamerica published its own "selection of favorite recipes" under the title *Cocina al minuto* in 1968 and in four subsequent editions through

1997. Colmina González warns that many of the Mexican and U.S. editions were produced "without the consent of the author and thus legally are considered pirate editions, with no guarantees of full authenticity because they violate the rights of the author" ("Prólogo," 7). Starting in the early 2000s, Colmina González herself, as part of the Cuban "Ediciones Nitza Villapol" and more recently as president of the Florida-based Nitza Villapol, Inc., compiled at least four new editions, each titled *Cocina al minuto*, based on her own selection from the Cuban editions published during Villapol's lifetime.

While Villapol's embrace of the revolution and the changes it entailed would later distinguish her from her peers, the early editions of *Cocina al minuto* are no more revolutionary than the other Cuban cookbooks from the 1950s, Maria Teresa Cotta de Cal's 1951 *Comidas criollas en ollas de presión* and the Madrinas de las Salas Costales y San Martín's 1956 *¿Gusta usted?*, in which Villapol has two articles and several recipes (584–587). Villapol and Martínez advance early twentieth-century cosmopolitan cubanidad with multiple arroz con pollo recipes, an entire section on cakes, and a section titled Pasteles, Tortas, y Tarteleteas that includes "Pie de manzana" and "Pie de limón," in addition to a vast section on cocktails and party snacks. Advertisements, not only in full-page spreads between sections but also in lines at the bottom of pages, as well as ubiquitous product placement, pack Villapol and Martínez's 1950s editions. Most of the advertised products are from the United States, from Libby's Pure de Tomate to Tide. Villapol's early editions contain fewer Afro-Indigenous dishes than *Comidas criollas en ollas de presión*. They have none of *¿Gusta usted?*'s social and political commentary, that includes a new version of Ortiz's "La cocina afrocubana," or its recipes that explicitly claim the Siboney origin of yuca dishes (344–346), though also none of its Christian reminders or references to the country clubs in Costales and San Martín.[33]

In spite—or because—of its commercial investments, Villapol's early editions address the middle-class women who had been largely ignored by the cookbooks of previous decades and thus bring a new class and gender consciousness to cooking.[34] While the early editions of *Cocina al minuto* open in the space of the family with lines like "food carefully selected and prepared assures a double happiness for the family: that of good tasting meals and of enjoying good health by being well fed" (1956, 7), they conceive the family as a collective body whose nutrition is the primary concern. The analogy offered to illustrate good nutrition compares the body to a machine: "When we buy a car, a sewing machine, or a television we want to know how it works, how to care for it and obtain the best return on our investment" (1956, 7). By extension, the woman is included in the "we" who purchases and fixes machines as much as she is the maintainer of happiness in the home. This extension of the woman's range occurs through not a commodity fetish, but shared ownership. It lays the ground for Cuban communism.

As the 1956 edition of *Cocina al minuto* shifts implicitly away from U.S. capitalism, it breaks explicitly from the U.S. Department of Agriculture (USDA) "daily food guide." In 1954 *Cocina al minuto* included a relatively literal translation of the USDA's "basic seven." In the 1956 edition, Villapol and Martínez write: "All the foods that the body needs have been grouped according to the eating habits, production and importation of foods in each country. Until recently, in Cuba we have followed the classification into seven basic groups used in the United States. . . . Recently a new classification has been made using four basic food groups of which we should daily ingest at least two in each group" (10). While the USDA also made a new classification that whittled the basic seven down to a basic four in 1956 (see figure 4.3), Villapol and Martínez's new "basic foods" is quite different from the USDA's "basic four" (see figure 4.4).

In the new Cuban "basic foods," both the examples within each category and the categories themselves are distinctly Cuban and different from their U.S. counterparts. With all "foods of animal origin" in one group and "legumes and seeds" separated from "cereals, tubers, roots, plantains, sugars, and fats" (12), the Cuban "basic four" gives dairy a smaller role than in the USDA version and recommends that 75 percent of food come from nonanimal sources in comparison to the USDA's recommended 50 percent.[35]

4.3. USDA 1956 Basic Four, illustrated in 1966. Source: USDA, National Agricultural Library Digital Collections.

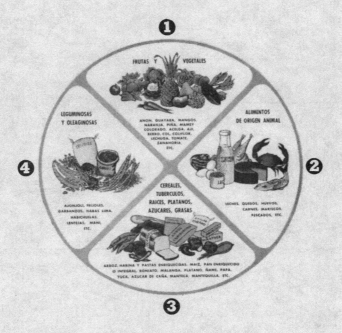

4.4. Cuban basic foods. Source: University of Miami Library, Cuban Heritage Collection.

As they highlight the new independent Cuban nutritional guidelines, Villapol and Martínez also hold up a new class of independent Cuban women. The woman who uses the new guidelines in her cooking and follows Villapol and Martínez's instruction for "how to equip your kitchen," new in the 1956 edition, is "for the first time" ready to "equip her kitchen" (17). She is of variable means but able to purchase at least "the most necessary utensils" (17). She comes from a line of women who do their own cooking and is freed from earlier generations' need for a "wealth of experience" thanks to both modern measures and the cookbook (21). Villapol and Martínez's section on "How to measure the ingredients," also new in the 1956 edition, avoids the regulatory tone of similar entries in other cookbooks by presenting the idea of measuring as a short-cut for the modern woman and with the remark that "for someone with experience, a good recipe tends to be a point of departure from which to follow inspiration and add the personal touch that makes it a work of art" (21). Stories abound about Villapol herself not liking to cook (Antonio José Ponte). However true the stories may be, the *Cocina al minuto* cookbooks are presented by and for middle-class women who do their own cooking, whether they like it or not, by following recipes for ease or changing them for art, and who own their places in the kitchen and outside of it.

The changing places for Cuban women that are written into *Cocina al minuto* from the very first edition are accompanied by some idea of changing economic order, but the 1950s editions do not inscribe changes in Cuba's relationship to Europe or the United States or to its own past or present culinary or demographic connections to Indigenous Cuba or to Africa. Villapol and Martínez's independent women in independent Cuba are not, even in the 1956 edition of *Cocina al minuto*, instructed to turn away from Europe or the United States. There are more recipe titles with allusions to Europe and the United States than to Cuba. Cuban brands, such as Lechera de Cuba and La Dichosa poultry company, are named alongside U.S. products like Ac'cent and Argentine ones like El Cocinero with no indication of preference for the former. The section on sandwiches and bocaditos may insist on calling for

Arroz con pescado a la oriental
(Oriental Rice with Fish)

Ingredientes

1½ lb. de filete de pescado
1 cdta. de sal
¼ cdta. de pimienta
1 cdta. de ajo en polvo
1 cda. De jugo de limón

Relleno

1 lata de bonito
1 huevo de La Dichosa
¼ cdta. de sal
1 cdta. de curri
1 cda. de perejil picadito
1½ taza de arroz Gallo cocinado
1 cda. de vino seco
½ cda. de vinagre
⅛ libra de mantequilla Nela
1 taza de leche Cía. Lechera de Cuba
Encienda el horno a 350° F.

Adobe los filetes de pescado con la sal, pimienta molida, ajo y jugo de limón. Déjelos reposar aproximadamente media hora. Una todos los ingredientes del relleno. Coloque en una pescadera engrasada la mitad de los filetes, cúbralos con el relleno y coloque arriba la otra mitad de los filetes. Echele por encima la leche y coloque la mantequilla en cuadritos sobre los filetes. Hornéelo a 350° F. durante treinta minutos. Da 6 raciones.

"Queso Crema Hacienda" but this appears the result of a product placement deal with Hacienda rather than a snubbing of the U.S. companies that produced most of the cream cheese on the market. Many of the recipes show closer ties to U.S. versions, and spellings, than those of her predecessors, like the recipe for "Pancakes and Hot Cakes," spelled according to English conventions, that instructs to cook in a pan

Ingredients

1½ lb. filet of fish
1 tsp. salt
¼ tsp. pepper
1 tsp. powdered garlic
1 tsp. lemon juice

Filling

1 can of bonito
1 La Dichosa egg
¼ tsp. salt
1 tsp. curry
1 tsp. minced parsley
1½ cups cooked Gallo rice
1 T dry wine
½ tsp. vinegar
⅛ pound Nela butter
1 cup Lechera de Cuba milk
Preheat the oven to 350° F.

Marinate the filets of fish with the salt, ground pepper, garlic, and lemon juice. Let them sit for about a half hour. Mix together all the ingredients for the filling. Put half the filets in a greased fish pan, cover them with the filling and put the other half of the filets on top. Pour the milk over it and put the butter in cubes on the filets. Bake at 350° F for thirty minutes. Serves 6.

—VILLAPOL AND MARTÍNEZ, *COCINA AL MINUTO*, 1956 EDITION

and sets "arepas" as variations on "Pancakes and Hot Cakes," rendering the Cuban food derivative.

In spite of the fact that Martínez was herself Afrocuban, it was only several years after the revolution, and after Martínez was no longer listed as a co-author,[36] that the cookbook began to incorporate Ortiz's vision of a Cuba proud of its African roots and to reflect the reversal of racism that the revolution touted. The 1956 edition of *Cocina al minuto* does have one of the first published recipes for an Asian-Cuban dish "Arroz con pescado a lo oriental." Ajiaco, Ortiz's famous symbol for transculturation, and the noticeably Afrocuban sopa de plátanos do not make it in, and no narrative sections address either the African or Indigenous origins of Cuban foods or the racialized associations between food and people that Ortiz wrote about.

What is revolutionary about Villapol's cookbooks is less how they start than how they keep adjusting, substituting, and reformulating so that the notion of coherent tradition emerges from the very reformulation of White Criollo-based Euro-American-facing bourgeois cosmopolitanism into Afro-Indigenous Criollo-based Caribbean-facing populist internationalism that occurs over the course of the many new editions of *Cocina al minuto*. A year after the triumph of the Cuban Revolution, whereas most if not all of the other living authors of Cuban cookbooks had left for the United States, Villapol published a new edition of *Cocina al minuto* in Havana, where she remained. The 1960 edition displays no drastic change. It still has a "Cockteles" section with seventy-five recipes, and significant numbers of recipes with European and American locations in the titles. There are subtle shifts, however. A few advertisements specify that they are made in Cuba: Libby's is "manufactured by Conservas selectas, S.A., Sancti Spiritus, L.V." (33); "Tide is made in Cuba by Cuban workers" (35). The new recipes in the 1960 edition include "Sopa de plátano," an "Ajiaco criollo," an incredibly complex Matahambre recipe that includes instructions for making catibía from scratch and grinding sugar, and—though without using the word fufú—a recipe for "Okra with chicken and plantain balls [Guiso de quimbombó con pollo y bolas de plátano]." The edition contains more recipes featuring various viandas in their titles as well as their ingredients along with a commentary on the importance of viandas in Cuban cuisine (187), although no mention of their Afro-Indigenous history. The 1960 edition also adds a recipe for "Arroz a la Indiana," whose inclusion of "curri" suggests that it is Indo-Caribbean, as well as two fried-rice recipes and recipes for "Chow Mein" and "Chop Suey." However, the placement of the rice dishes in an Arroces y Pastas (Rices and

Ajiaco criollo (Creole Ajiaco)

Carnes:

½ lb. tasajo
½ gallina de El Liro
1 lb. de falda
1 lb. masa de puerco
1 lb. agujas de puerco
7 litros de agua

Viandas:

2 mazorcas de maíz
½ lb. malanga amarilla
2 plátanos verdes
1 lb. de yuca
1 lb. de boniato
½ lb. malanga blanca
½ lb. de ñame
2 plátanos maduros
2 limones

Sofrito:

2 cdas de manteca
1 cebolla grande
3 dientes de ajo
1 ají grande
1 lata salsa de tomate Libby's
2 cdas. de sal (approx.)

Bollitas de maíz:

1 lb. de maíz tierno molido
1 cdta. de sal
2 cdas. leche Cía. Lechera de Cuba
2 cdas. de manteca
2 dientes de ajo

Corte el tasajo en tres o cuatro pedazos y póngalo a remojar desde la noche anterior. A la mañana siguiente bótele el agua.

En una cacerola grande ponga el tasajo remojado y la media gallina cortada en dos partes. Déjelo hervir aproximadamente una hora. Añádale la falda y la masa de puerco cortada en trozos. Si la masa de puerco tiene mucha grasa, debe aprovechar para sacar la manteca del sofrito y la bolitas de maíz. Añada también las agujas de puerco. Déjelo hervir durante una hora más aproximadamente. Cuando las carnes hayan hervido un rato, debe quitarle un poco de grasa y espuma al caldo.

Mientras se cocinan las carnes haga el sofrito y pele las viandas. Cuando ya las carnes estén blandas, añada las viandas en el mismo orden que aparecen en la receta, cada vez que añada plátanos écheles jugo de limón para que el caldo no se

(continued next page)

(continued from previous page)

oscurezca. Al empezar a echar las viandas eche también el sofrito de modo que todo se vaya cocinando a la vez. Ya cuando vaya a echar los plátanos maduros prepare también las bolitas de maíz para echarlas al final.

Mezcle el maíz molido con la sal, leche y manteca en la que se fríen dos dientes de ajo. Tome esta masa por cucharadas. Ponga las bolitas sobre las viandas en al caldo. Tápele y déjelo cocinar a fuego lento aproximadamente una hora más. No lo revuelva hasta que no se cocinen las bolitas de maíz.

Por espesarlo, aplaste dos o tres pedazos de viandas en un poco de caldo. Da aproximadamente 12 raciones.

Meats:

½ lb. salt beef
½ chicken from El Liro
1 lb. skirt steak

1 lb. pork
1 lb. pork neck bone
7 liters of water

Viandas:

2 ears of corn
½ lb. yellow malanga
2 green plantains
1 lb. yuca
1 lb. boniato

½ lb. white malanga
½ lb. yam
2 ripe plantains
2 lemons

Sofrito:

2 T lard
1 big onion
3 cloves of garlic

1 big pepper
1 can of Libby's tomato sauce
2 T salt (approx.)

Corn Balls:

1 lb. ground fresh corn
1 tsp. salt
2 tsp. Lechera de Cuba milk

2 tsp. lard
2 cloves of garlic

Cut the salt beef in three or four pieces and put it to soak the night before. The next morning, toss the water.

> In a big pot put the soaked salt beef and the half chicken cut into two pieces. Let it boil about an hour. Add the skirt steak and the pork cut into pieces. If the pork is very greasy, use it for the lard for the sofrito and the corn balls. Add the pork neck bones as well. Let it boil for about another hour. When the meats have boiled for a while, remove some of the grease and defoam the broth.
>
> While the meats are cooking make the sofrito and peel the viandas. When the meats are tender, add the viandas in the order that they appear in the recipe, each time that you add the plantains put lemon juice on them so that it does not darken. When you start putting in the viandas put in the sofrito as well so that it all cooks together. And when you are ready to put in the ripe plantains also prepare the corn balls to put in at the end.
>
> Mix the ground corn with the salt, milk, and lard in which the garlic is fried. Take this dough by the tablespoonful. Put the balls on the viandas in the broth. Cover and let cook over a low heat another hour. Do not stir until the corn balls are cooked. To thicken, mash two or three pieces of viandas in a little broth. Makes approximately 12 servings.
>
> —VILLAPOL, *COCINA AL MINUTO*, 1960 EDITION, 36–38

Pastas) section headed with a stereotypical drawing of a Chinese man playing a flute to dancing noodles suggests that any inclusion of Asian-Cuban cuisine represented by this recipe comes not from Asian-Cubans but from cosmopolitanism like that of Cuba's prerevolutionary elites. Overall, the shifts in the treatment of Cuba's relationship to outside and inside populations are minor and do not fundamentally change the character of the cookbook. In part, this is due to the fact that the changes in Cuba generally were gradual, and in part it is because Villapol's success lies in her ability to maintain both an idea of culinary continuity and one of culinary change in which revolution makes Cuba more Cuban.

In the 1970s, Villapol focused on her television show and published articles on Cuban food history. In a 1977 article on "African Food Habits in Latin America," Villapol reflects on Cuba's earliest cookbooks: "Those who knew how to read and write, and thus transmit information in a lasting manner, knew and often enjoyed the work of those who cooked, but rarely were interested in learning and recording how the foods were made" so that most of the cookbooks "respond to the culture—in the case of América—of the colonizers: to the dominant culture" (325). As much as she uses this to explain her own limited knowledge of African contributions to Cuban food, it can also set up the significant changes in her treatment of Afro-Indigenous foods in the later editions of *Cocina al minuto,* in which she builds on the legacy of those colonizers and elite post-independence writers who were interested enough in the making of Cuban foods to capture bits of that information among their colonial and cosmopolitan collections.

Starting in 1980, the next series of Cuban editions of *Cocina al minuto* feature what Villapol is most often recognized for: her embrace of the revolution and her ability to present adaptation to changing availability in ingredients—what many have called scarcity—as opportunity for creative, waste-free refinement. They also enshrine the gender investments she always had and racial investments she has been slowly incorporating. In a new introduction to the 1980 edition, Villapol roots Cuban autochthony in a precolonial ideal of food independence, the ability to formulate new native culinary cultures via transplantation and grafting of Indigenous and African cuisines, and the decolonial struggle against the import-export economy developed under Spanish rule and exacerbated after Cuban independence in the first half of the twentieth century (11). Identifying the 1959 Cuban Revolution as the final resistance to the colonial sugar economy, she fashions a new Cuban cuisine in the sweet spot of preservation and progress, where desserts and drinks make up nearly a third of her recipes, lard is no longer the default grease, and local fish, poultry, and eggs are the majority of the protein.

Villapol's new introduction highlights the advanced food culture of Cuba's Indigenous people:

The first inhabitants of Cuba, like most primitive people, obtained their food from their surroundings and by the time the Spaniards arrived had developed an elevated food culture, not only through the use of fire, clay pots and other cooking utensils, but also through the diversification of their food that in the light of contemporary knowledge seems to have fit their lifestyle. Their recipes, preserved through oral tradition, were transmitted to their conquerors who did not always know how to gauge their full value. (9)

She downplays the culinary contributions of Spain, identifying North Africa as the source of Spanish culinary culture (10). Detailing how Indigenous Cuban cuisine was modified as a result of genocide, she argues that because slavery and indentureship occurred in the context of plantation monoculture and slaves were allowed little time or space to produce their own food, "little by little, Indigenous foods were replaced by different foods that were not produced in the country but imported" (10). In other words, as much as it registers, citing Ortiz, that "Africans undoubtedly influenced Cuban food," Villapol posits that the U.S.-fueled import-export economy obliterated the African contribution to Cuban cuisine.

Villapol's discussion of the plantation period highlights the ills of the import-export economy established under Spanish rule and continued after 1898 to the benefit of the United States thanks to the Platt Amendment and then the Commerce Treaty of 1903 (10–11). Cuba could be food-independent, she suggests, if it could turn to local farming for local consumption. However, Villapol naturalizes the import-reliant national cuisine as she moves from describing "the foods that over centuries had become 'Cuban cuisine'" (12) to decrying "the criminal Yankee blockade" that led to an end of "commerce with the countries where we were used to buying rice, different kinds of beans, lard, milk, salt meat, bacalao, canned meats, preserves, cheeses and innumerable products and condiments that were used in our traditional cuisine" (12). In this account, Spanish and U.S. domination are responsible for the import-export economy, the nutritional weakness of food that is now considered traditionally Cuban, and the difficulty of finding those foods in Cuba after 1960 (12–13). The malnutrition of slaves is the predecessor of the United States "using hunger as a 'weapon of war'" with a pig industry that "knowing the value of pork meat . . . sold to Cuba . . . a large part of the lard that they did not eat" (12) and then with the blockade. Villapol deftly detours around the post-1959 agrarian reforms that, whatever success they may have had, had not managed to render Cuba food independent.[37] Nonetheless, she makes clear that the longer-term project is the admittedly tremendous task of maintaining Cuban culinary culture while modifying the Cuban diet for greater individual and national health. Her critique of imported foods falls away in the face of immediate hunger, and she thanks "the people of the Soviet Union and other countries of the socialist community who in the most difficult moments have extended a friendly hand to us" so that "in no moment have we lacked the wheat to make our bread" (13), but the end point of the 1980 edition is an embrace of ajiaco, "our classic soup" (15).

In spite of its culminating ajiaco section with recipes both for "Traditional Creole Ajiaco" and "Seafood Ajiaco," the recipe selection in the 1980 edition of *Cocina al minuto* manifests the complications of achieving well-rounded national nutrition, embracing local foods grounded in Afro-Indigenous traditions, honoring Asian contributions, and offering recipes that can be made with what is actually available. While the "cocteles" section has been renamed "bebidas" and reduced by two-thirds from the 1960 edition, and while there are more recipes for corn and calabaza, the recipes for quimbombó, ñame, matahambre, "Arroz a la Indiana," "Chop Suey," "Chow Mein," and "Jambalaya" that were included in the 1960 edition are gone. Villapol's beliefs that "cereals" are more nutritious than viandas (37) and that imports of the plantation period are anti-Cuban trumps her interest in Afro-Indigenous foods, explaining the continued preponderance of recipes featuring rice and wheat-based starches and the continued paucity of recipes featuring tasajo and bacalao.[38] In the narrative introduction to "cereals," the description of corn embodies the conjunction of her interests in cereals for their nutritional value and in Afro-Indigenous foods for their social value (38–39). However, this description and the increased volume of corn-based recipes in the 1980 edition also correlate to increased corn imports to Cuba. Villapol, it becomes clear, uses instruction in how to cook with a product imported to make up for agricultural lack to write an elegy to its nutritious Afro-indigeneity. This is one of her great skills: to offer recipes that respond to agro-political needs with innovative modes of return to Cubanness.

Villapol's 1980 introduction avers that her political investments are tantamount even as they are embedded in and with the genre of the cookbook: "To write a cookbook with the pretension of achieving something more than a recipe collection is a very ambitious goal" (15). Villapol's voluminous 1980 edition works as a protest against scarcity and food insecurity as it calls to feed the nation not with more products or more imports or even more local foods, but with more technique, more skill, more knowledge, more understanding, more education, more ability to modify and substitute, to re-create. She is committed to the "vertiginous" changes that will create a fully independent modern Cuba no longer tied to past where "our cuisine was transmitted through practice and oral tradition working alongside someone with a certain degree of experience" at the expense of women's time and mobility. Now, Villapol's readers, applying "the knowledge of science and technique," can achieve a freedom in which they can use a cookbook to learn to "dominate the technique of a few basic recipes" and "succeed no matter what inconvenience comes up" (16). Freed even from being "slave to the book or the recipe," these women work to feed the nation: "We contribute to satisfying one of the needs of our society that increases daily, and we make the tasks that it requires less difficult" (16). Of course, recipes like "Oats to 'Stretch' Meat" and "Pastas a la Alemana," new in the 1980 edition, respond to the scarcity of meat and potatoes. Nonetheless, Villapol's formulation of the meat-and-oat combinations as ways to extend what meat you have and to enjoy "second cuts" of meat frame the situation as an opportunity and the result as an improvement.

> ### Avena para "estirar" la carne
> ### (Oats to "Stretch" Meat)
>
> *Las albóndigas, el picadillo, la pulpeta y la carne fría se pueden hacer con menos cantidad de carne si usted emplea avena. Estas recetas de carne molida, en las cuales podemos emplear la llamada carne "de segunda", resultan más jugosas y suaves cuando se preparan con avena. Por cada libra de carne cruda use ¾ taza de avena cruda mezclada con la carne antes de añadirle los condimentos.*
>
> Meatballs, hash, meatloaf, and cold meats can be made with a smaller quantity of meat if you use oats. These recipes made of ground meat, in which we can use the meat called "seconds," are moister and more tender when they are made with oats. For each pound of raw meat use ¾ cup of raw oats mixed with the meat before adding the condiments.
>
> —VILLAPOL, *COCINA AL MINUTO*, 1980, 57

It is tempting to read the 1980 edition as marking a radical break of a new beginning—a full-scale response to the conditions of post-1959 Cuba. Doing so, however, overlooks the continuity and internal development of Cuban cuisine. Villapol's embrace of variations may be impelled by the need to deal with limited and changing availability of ingredients. As Hanna Garth writes, "Villapol helped household cooks maintain Cuban cuisine, despite a changed food system, through innovative cooking practices with new ingredients" (360). However, variation is not a new feature of Villapol's 1980 edition; rather, this is a development from the 1950s editions where the ability to vary represents the freedom of the middle-class woman. Villapol's embrace of variations neither defends nor recovers a Cuban cuisine from colonial domination and erasure. Instead, it opens a vibrant space of creation from and for a people increasingly certain of their right to exist, their livelihood as a people, and their readiness to grow and transform on their own terms. For Villapol, the perpetual revolution is also a perpetual renovation, not a repeating of the same recipes or the same narrative but an opportunity to continuously experiment. That this set of shifts includes acknowledging and honoring Caribbean cuisine as Afro-Indigenous allows for even a White Criolla woman like Villapol to represent a Cuban criollismo that looks, finally, like the racially and culturally mixed one envisioned by Martí.

In the 1981 edition, again significantly revised, Villapol expands the histories of ingredients and foods begun in the 1980 edition and integrates them in significantly revised and reordered sections. Harking back to nineteenth-century cookbook organization, the 1981 edition opens with Sopas, Arroces, y Guisos, but rather than conforming to a European order in which the soups are light "starters," these soups and stews are the main courses or one-dish meals of Afro-Indigenous cuisine. Villapol explicitly mines nineteenth-century Cuban works for their representation of Afrocuban cuisine, citing the *Manual del cocinero cubano* by name and referring to "Arboleya's description of plantain balls 'shaped by hand and called 'fufú' are eaten with sesame and okra [quimbombó]" (15). And though she still does not use the word "fufú" in relation to the plantain balls that she instructs to be made (in this edition) with "Guiso de quimbombó," she includes multiple recipes with quimbombó in the title and a far greater number of recipes with viandas in the title than in earlier editions. At the same time, Villapol reduces her attention to Indigenous culinary history, and ajiaco disappears. In place of the ajiaco section from the previous edition is one on congrí that, again citing Ortíz, she uses to highlight the Afrocuban.

Villapol's interest in quick, easy, and nutritional food made by busy middle-class women met the revolutionary project of reversing centuries of plantation economy to create a revolutionary cuisine that corrected Cuban national tastes for imported meats and starches and held up Afro-Indigenous foodways. As much as Villapol strove to connect working-class women's interests, good nutrition, food independence, and a truly multiracial Cuba, the distance and difference between them has been part of how the nostalgia for a Cuban cuisine that is both pre-revolutionary and pre-independence has come to characterize the Cuban culinary culture of the exile community. But even as both in

Guiso de quimbombó (Okra Stew)

⅓ taza de aceite
1 pollo
1 cebolla
1 pimiento verde
2 dientes de ajo
2 cucharaditas de sal
¼ cucharadita de pimienta molida
¼ taza de salsa de tomate
1 cucharada de vinagre
1 taza de vino seco
2 tazas de agua
2 limones
1 libra de quimbombó
2 ó 3 plátanos pintones

El quimbombó se debe lavar entero. Al picarlo deben caer directamente las ruedítas en el agua fría con zumo de limón. Si desea un guiso más espeso añada al mismo el quimbombó, escurriéndolo de antemano el agua con zumo de limón.

Caliente el aceite y dore en él el pollo, con la cebolla, el ají y los ajos machacados; añádale sal, pimienta, salsa de tomate, vinagre, caldo y vino seco. Cuando el pollo esté medio cocinado, añádale el quimbombó cortado en ruedítas, con el agua y zumo de limón. Déjelo todo al fuego hasta que el quimbombó esté blando. Añádale los plátanos hervidos, antes reducidos a puré y en forma de bolas. Da para 6 raciones.

Para hacer esta receta con puerco, use alrededor de ½ libra de masa. Si prefiere un guiso con menos sabor a limón, eche el quimbombó (entero o en ruedas) sin mojar, directamente al sofrito, añádale sólo ½ taza de agua y el zumo de 1 limón.

Cuba and in the United States great numbers of new Cuban cookbooks have been published in the decades since Villapol's death, her cookbooks have kept coming out in new editions heralded as a symbol of both revolutionary and exile Cuba. The power of Villapol's national imaginary is that it rests not on political positions—though she

⅓ cup oil
1 chicken
1 onion
1 green pepper
2 garlic cloves
2 teaspoons salt
¼ teaspoon ground pepper
½ cup tomato sauce
1 tablespoon vinegar
1 cup chicken broth
½ cup dry wine
1 cup water
2 lemons
1 pound okra
2 or 3 yellow plantains

The okra should be washed whole. When it is chopped the rounds should go directly into cold water with lemon juice. For a thicker stew add the okra the same way, sprinkling the water first with lemon juice. Heat the oil and brown the chicken with the onion, the pepper and the garlic, smashed; add salt, pepper, tomato sauce, vinegar, broth, and dry wine. When the chicken is half cooked add the okra cut into rounds with the water and lemon juice. Cook until the okra is soft. Add the boiled plantains, previously puréed and formed into balls. Serves 6.

To make this recipe with pork, use about ½ pound of meat. If you prefer a stew with less lemon flavor, put the okra (whole or sliced) without wetting it, directly into the sauteed vegetables and add just ½ cup water and the juice of 1 lemon.

—VILLAPOL, *COCINA AL MINUTO*, 1981, 41–42

certainly took them—but on articulating a national culinary culture both deeply rooted in the details of Cuban history and perpetually open to innumerable modifications.

The paradox of national independence in the Caribbean engenders recipes that render what colonialism destroyed as what is recuperated from colonial domination. Caribbean cookbooks show that the intermediaries of colonial domination—White Criollos and especially White Criolla women—bring about these spiraling changes. In Cuba, White Criollos turned independent Cubans sit at the heads of the tables of power, and elite women pull up chairs without there being significant changes in what is served, how it is produced, and who serves it.

This spiraling structure—whereby what colonialism destroys appears as what Cubans recuperate from (their own) colonial domination—might appear as a circle or a whirligig. But since with each turn of the table a new trace is scraped toward its recuperative center and redistributed around the table, the dishes that appear at the seats of its changing occupants are never the same but reveal small and yet significant layered changes that reflect and—to the practiced reader—reveal the imbrication of grand (national/political) ideals and pragmatic (culinary/domestic) details. The small details of measurement, technique, substitution, and modification that render the same dish or institute minor improvements—as the Cuban cookbooks from 1902 to 1980 attest—highlight how large-scale transformations are wrought from the accumulation of small shifts, how the minutiae of ingredient selection are political, and how gender and race are as much ingredients for the construction of an independent national identity as they are aspects and determinants of the positions of those who write up the recipes and those who carry them out. Case in point, the Dominican and Haitian cookbooks that I turn to in the next chapter result in a strikingly different political seating arrangement despite working with similar ingredients. While Cuban women succeeded in being part of the conversations and conversions that adjusted the taste of national culinary discourses, Dominican and Haitian women were unwilling or unable to maintain the compromises and convictions that might have had a less dictatorial entrenchment, despite their significant successes in regard to women's rights. Nonetheless, and like their Cuban sistren, Dominican and Haitian women secured independent national culinary cultures that continue to define and to serve profoundly creolized cuisines under many different names to this day.

5

Dominican and Haitian (Re)Emergence

THE DOMINICAN REPUBLIC and Haiti share the island of Hispaniola. They were the two first Caribbean nations to gain independence from colonial rule—in 1821 and 1804, respectively, were both occupied by the United States in the early twentieth century, and both suffered long periods of brutal dictatorial rule in the mid-twentieth century. In both countries, cookbooks emerged only as U.S. occupation ended and elite women—White, Mulatto, and Black— reclaimed independence, fostered and sustained dictatorships, and (re)constructed distinct national cultures. In the Dominican Republic, cookbooks supported and were supported by Rafael Leonidas Trujillo's all-encompassing (and whitewashing) nationalist project inaugurated in the early 1930s, shortly after the 1924 U.S. withdrawal. In Haiti, cookbooks thrived in the elite Mulatto and Black circles contesting and cooperating for democratic rule in the two decades between the departure of U.S. troops, in 1934, and François Duvalier's rise to power, in 1957.

Marked by assertions of independence not from former colonial powers—Spain and France, respectively—but from the United States, Dominican and Haitian cookbooks came from communities developed during a century of independent rule in which striations of race and class became well established not only as the remains of colonial economy and power—which they were—but also as the class and caste systems of independent nations. The paradox of independence in the

Caribbean had not been eliminated, but the work to create the "native" cultures whose autonomy independence notionally restored was so well underway that Dominican and Haitian cookbooks could sidestep it by brushing over the period between colonial occupation and independence, albeit in very different ways.

In their mundane elitism and historical amnesia, Dominican and Haitian cookbooks reveal the contradictions and complications of inscribing national culinary cultures in the messy periods between colonial domination, independence, and new forms of domination from powers internal as well as external. They also open the lid on the lives of elite women who worked at once for suffrage and control, liberation and power, who helped to formulate the creoleness that is a predominant pan-Caribbean cultural construct and shaped it into very specific national and racial visions. Though Frantz Fanon's warning about the dangers of revolutionary national independence movements and nationalism as a political doctrine that devolves quickly into dictatorship must haunt any consideration of mid-twentieth century Dominican Republic and Haiti (*Wretched*, 142–143), Édouard Glissant's theoretical tools are most helpful for analyzing the postcolonial questions of creolization that predominate before the ascendancy of the dictatorships and that remain salient even under them. But Glissant, too, skims over the places of women and dismisses the elite as disconnected from "the people" and thus from "collective consciousness" (*Caribbean Discourse*, 205–207). In spite of their distance from the lived experiences of the majority of the population, elite Dominican and Haitian women garnered domestic control under and with waves of increasingly dictatorial regimes as they navigated and nourished ruling national tastes for versions of creoleness, each of which remained internally stable and politically powerful.

Dominican cookbooks formulated a creoleness that is consistent with what is elsewhere called mestizaje, a mixture of European and Indigenous heritage and identification. Although the cookbooks' erasure of the African is more nominal than substantive, it ensures a Dominican culinary vocabulary and imaginary entirely divorced from Haiti's

Blackness or even mulâtrisme (the social and political movement centered on Mulatto or mixed European and African heritage). Haitian cookbooks, on the other hand, present a creoleness born in Haiti in 1804. Writing as if there were no pre-history to Haitian national culture, they embrace French cuisine as if it bore no colonial legacy and Blackness without attention to its passage through slavery. In both cases, albeit in different ways, Dominican and Haitian cookbooks manage to draw on the histories that survived and emerged from the colonial and plantation period while obscuring significant components of the African and slave legacies.

The first part of this chapter focuses on the collaboration between Dominican women and Trujillo's regime that resulted in advances for women, attached to a whitewashed Creole dictatorial elitism. It follows the circular entrapment of elite Dominican women who allied with Trujillo at the beginning of his regime, domesticated a Trujillist "criollo" that is mixed but not with Blackness (even as they included Afro-Dominican foods), and continued to ally with Trujillo through and even beyond the end of his regime. The second part considers the similarities between cookbooks written by elite Mulatto and Black women, supposedly on opposing sides of the racial divide, in early to mid-twentieth-century Haiti. It looks at how these cookbooks charted a Haitian culinary culture with a transversal connection to its tropical neighbors and an 1804 start point that reject external influence from the United States and internal division from the legacies of colonialism, slavery, and U.S. occupation. To inscribe a Haitian national cuisine that is creole without any significant acknowledgment of Indigenous, West African, or slave culinary history, these cookbooks focus on Haiti's place in the tropics and among creole islands, its peasant traditions and language, and its select combination of French and Haitian techniques and tastes, offering a creole cuisine that honors the popular foods from which the cookbooks nonetheless remain distant. Dominican and Haitian cookbooks of the early to mid-twentieth century share an island, a history of early independence and U.S. occupation, a horizon of dictatorship, authorship by elite women invested in their own communities, and an articulation of national creole cuisines, and yet the forms of their nationalism and their cuisine bake in the vast differences that persist between the two countries.

Dictating National Culinary Culture in the Dominican Republic

In the late nineteenth and early twentieth centuries, Dominican agriculture and farming shifted from a combination of elite-serving unenclosed ranching and subsistence agriculture for an autarkic peasantry to increasingly foreign-controlled sugar plantations. Under U.S. occupation from 1916 to 1924, subsistence crops and access routes were destroyed or taken over by military operations while the regulation of private property benefited U.S-owned sugar companies. Dominicans and occupying U.S. forces wrote about Dominican food only to lament its scarcity or to criticize its quality. Trujillo rose to power in 1930 not only thanks to the military training and promotion he received from the U.S. forces but also because he championed the platform of state-controlled small-scale farming laid out by the Nationalist Party, a joint effort of peasants dealing with dispossession and anticolonial intellectuals.[1]

The Trujillo era—the thirty years during which Trujillo ruled the Dominican Republic either as president or in control of others who held the presidency—is famous for its abuses of women, not the least of which were Trujillo's own efforts to literalize, through rape, his position as "father of the new fatherland [padre de la patria nueva]." However, women also engaged in politics in the Dominican Republic with and under Trujillo. In the words of Virginia Mota, the Trujillo era was characterized by "the exploitation and promotion by the right of the political activity of certain women and vice versa" (62).[2] Club Nosotras, which became La Acción Feminista Dominicana, organized in 1931 as a Trujillist group focused on "family values." In response to the movement, and to his understanding that their votes would support him,

Trujillo granted women "trial" vote in 1934 and 1938 and full suffrage in 1940. By 1945, Acción Feminista had solidified its ties to Trujillo, joining the "Sección Femenina" of the Partido Trujillista as it became the "Rama Femenina" of the Partido Dominicano (of which Trujillo was the head).[3] In contrast to the novels of Julia Alvarez and Junot Díaz that showcase the harm Trujillo caused and the Dominicans who resisted him, the cookbooks of the Trujillo era instruct in the mutual sustenance of elite Dominican women, national culinary culture, and Trujillo's rule. Eulalia Cordero Infante's *La cocina dominicana* (193–?)[4] is blatantly Trujillist as it makes a grand appeal to the people that targets key issues like hunger, exalts indigenous heritage, and connects to Latin America at the same time as it ignores and stereotypes the poor, erases the Afrodominican, and promotes the Latin playboy. Amanda Ornes Perelló's 1955 *Cocina criolla* and Ligia de Bornia's 1957 *La cocina dominicana* extend Cordero Infante's construction of a particular kind of Dominican Creole, less explicitly Trujillist but equally consistent with his vision: independent, attached to mythic Indigenous and European heritage, protected by, and protecting elite women's domestic power.[5]

That even after independence and the end of the U.S. occupation, the first Dominican cookbooks were written by and for elite women aligned with a repressive dictator certainly affirms that, as Appadurai wrote of Indian cookbooks, cookbooks articulate a national culture by and for the educated elite. Because cooking is understood as an activity performed mostly, if not exclusively, by lower-class women, the elite nature of early nation cookbooks can certainly lead to questions about authenticity like the ones that Austin Clarke raises and about connection to collective national identity like the ones that Glissant raises. What these cookbooks underline, however, is that national imaginaries are often formed by elite men and a few women in novels and works of political philosophy and also by elite women educated, and educating, in home economics, nutrition, and cooking. These cookbooks reveal the work of those elite women to hold on to power and to manage a populist ideology that authorizes theft and abuse of "peasant" women and men (under a paternalistic guise of care) and whitewashes African foodways under the mantle of celebrating Indigenous foodways, creating a creole that is mixed, but not with Blackness.

In her introduction to *La cocina dominicana*, Cordero Infante sets out a Dominican culinary history and mythology emerging from U.S. domination under Trujillo's wing: "Now, under the protection of this beautiful country, full of sun and tranquility, I have put all of my criollismo in this book; in this happy hour in which the Generalísimo Trujillo is promoting and spotlighting our customs, become nearly unseen in the eagerness to accommodate foreigners" (5). Thanks to this domestic focus, Cordero Infante's dreams could be achieved and shared: "It was always my greatest goal to write a book of Criolla Cooking. And here I am reader [lectora], putting a copy in your hands, so that you can organize your daily meals" (5). The contours of Cordero Infante's "criolla cooking," and the places of elite women ordering it, became the coda for the Dominicanness that she nourished.

Eulalia Cordero Infante herself was born in 1890 in Santiago de los Caballeros into a wealthy White Criollo family established in the Dominican Republic during the colonial period. She does not appear to have married or had children. Her family was generally representative of the majority of the Dominican elite that tacitly tolerated Trujillo, though two of her nephews, Emilio and José Ramón Cordero Michel, were well-known opponents of Trujillo, while Cordero Infante herself appears to have been a vocal supporter. She dedicated *La comida dominicana* to Trujillo and Dominican women—"to you, illustrious leader, inspirer and lover of everything of your country, and to you, Dominican women, owners [dueñas], now and in the future, of your homes" (5). While she accepts Trujillo's dominance and a strictly gendered division of labor, Cordero Infante asserts women's control in the domestic sphere: "In every house there must be a person who governs and directs it; a job [oficio] that should be performed by a woman" (133). Of course, Cordero Infante's governing women are heads of homes replete with "pretty, clean, and unstained tablecloths and napkins, brilliant glassware, crystal, and porcelain" (9). Allowing for class mobility while holding the class system in place, Cordero Infante also instructs anyone who is new to it in the manners of the elite and in the practices of elite women's power: "When you have finished eating, leave the plate where it is, do not take it from its place. When you are done leave the fork with the tines up and the knife with the sharp side in, on the plate. Wait for the servant to clear it" (17). Elite women's power is most directly over the servants who they should ensure do things like "announce to the heads of house [los dueños]: 'the meal is ready' or 'the dinner is ready'" (15). Cordero Infante rarely mentions "the jaunty girl [garrida moza] who makes the sancocho" (19) or other cooks, but she ensures her readers' power over them in the instruction that "the head of house [la dueña de casa] should go to the kitchen every day, for if she does not attend to it, if she neglects the inspection of what is done there, disorder can enter the kitchen" (133).[6]

As she presides over the kitchen and the table, the elite woman occupies an intermediary space between the private and public realms that authorizes and limits her intervention in shaping national culture. Her art of presentation thus takes on a new dimension. In her explanation of sancocho as the symbol of the Dominican people, Cordero Infante writes:

> As the nation has the flag, the shield, the anthem that symbolize it and grant it distinction among the concert of other nations, the people also has its customs, its tastes, its religious rituals that personify it and distinguish it from other people. In the culinary realm, the people also have their symbolic dishes. Thus, like the Spanish people have their stew [cocido] and the Italian their pasta [maccarones], the Dominican people have their sancocho, their classic dish, that is like their flag of good taste and rejoicing at the national table. (18)

The distinction that Cordero Infante makes between "the nation" and "the people" corresponds to a distinction between the public and the private. Cordero Infante respects this distinction, in good Trujillist fashion, and uses it to showcase the work of women in and for the public face of the nation. She keeps women's work preparing sancocho in the private sphere and renders "the national table" the all-important space where public and private, the state and its wards, unite.

As Cordero Infante asserts the domestic power of elite women, she frees men from domestic responsibility. She romanticizes the chaser of good foods who not only "to go off after a sancocho often leaves waiting his beloved, his mother, his friends, and all his cares" but also steals whole pots of sancocho as a joke or retaliation. "They took the sancocho, missa [señore]!," Cordero Infante has the "sancocho girl" say in a peasant vernacular. She continues, "The sancocho girl runs and shouts in stupefaction, and the whole party launches after the knave [bellaco] who played them such a bad turn. Sometimes it's a simple joke and the steaming pot is found behind the kitchen; but sometimes no. . . . Someone who was not invited to the sancocho, or who crashed the party and was kicked out, exacts this terrible vengeance, taking the pot forever" (19). These tales might be cautionary, but overwhelmingly they excuse and celebrate the man who can steal and steal away. Cordero Infante's explanation of the phrase "stolen chicken sancocho [sancocho de gallina robada]," for example, ties it to the excitement that wealthy men get from playing at robber:

> Among street sellers and night owls the classic sancocho is that made with chicken, with the express condition that the chicken be stolen. The excitement of entering another's dark patio with the disagreeable possibility of being surprised by an angry dog, or an angrier owner, adds, like a magic condiment, greater succulence to the sancocho. Some are so attached to this vice of the stolen chicken sancocho, that they go so far as to steal the chicken from their own house, or from the neighbor's, with the premediated good plan of paying for it the following day, even if they have to pay double. (19)

Cordero Infante's conclusion that "thus, sancocho is something that is intimately linked to the popular customs of our people" romanticizes the rich thief as a popular hero and disconnects "stolen chicken sancocho [sancocho de gallina robada]" from any association with slave food where meat, especially fresh meat, was so rare it might have to be stolen (19). Thus, Cordero Infante excuses Trujillo's treatment of women and embraces his appropriation of Afro-Dominican cuisine. Her alignment with Trujillo garners power for women like her not only in domestic leadership but also as citizens with shared interests of class, race, and opposition to the threat of further U.S. intervention.

Cordero Infante's treatment of sancocho emblematizes the Trujillist embrace of and distancing from the peasantry. Sancocho's pride of place, in its own section with twelve recipes at the start of *La cocina dominicana*, situates Dominicanness in and through the embrace of cross-class identification: "Sancocho rubs elbows with every social class and distributes its favors to rich and poor, aristocrat and commoner alike, without ever losing an ounce of its prestige" (19). Under the distinction of sancocho, this touching of classes accords prestige to what has been associated with the peasantry and holds up prestige as belonging neither to the rich nor to the poor but to the symbolic dish around which they unite. At the same time, Cordero Infante is careful to keep the social classes apart through their different places at the party—the theft of the

---

Sancocho (Sancocho)

Ingredientes:—En las recetas de este plato criollo llamamos "Víveres" al surtido de plátanos verdes, amarillos, yuca, papa, auyama, yautía, mapueyes, ñames, rulos, etc. Llamamos "Recado" verde al surtido de hojas le col, perejil, cilantro de España, cilantro ancho (sabanero), distén, ajíes verdes o maduros, dulces o picantes, etc. Y designamos "Sazón" al que se da de ajo, cebolla, pimienta, malagueta, laurel, etc.

Ingredients:—In the recipes for this criollo dish, we call "Víveres" the grouping of green and yellow plantains, yuca, potato, pumpkin [auyama], yautía, mapueyes, yams, rulos, etc. We call "Recado" the grouping of cabbage, parsley, Spanish cilantro, wide-leafed cilantro (culantro), thyme, oregano, green or ripe sweet or spicy peppers, etc. And we designate as "Sazón" that which is made of garlic, onion, pepper, allspice, bay leaf, etc.

—CORDERO INFANTE, *LA COCINA DOMINICANA*, 20

Sancocho de gallina (Chicken Sancocho)

Porción para 6 personas

1 gallina gorda; Víveres, Recado y Sazón

Se sazona la gallina. Se pone a guisar, sin dejarla sofreír. Cuando esté blanda se le pone el recado y 3 granos de malagueta, y un pedacito de auyama para darle color. Cuando se ablande se le desbarata y se cuela todo. Se le agrega agua suficiente y cuando esté hirviendo se le ponen los víveres, teniendo en cuenta poner los plátanos primero y por orden lo demás. Cuidando de poner último la auyama por ser lo que menos tiempo gasta para ablandarse.

Si se desea se le pone un pedacito de jamón. Este hay que ponerlo junto con la auyama pues cuando hierve mucho pierde su sabor. Se retoca de sazón y se deja reposar un rato antes de servirlo.

(Serves 6)

1 fat hen; Víveres, Recado, and Sazón

Season the hen. Start cooking it, without letting it fry. When it is tender add the recado and 3 allspice berries and a piece of pumpkin to give it color. When it is softened break it down and put everything in. Add enough water and when it is boiling add the víveres, being careful to put in the plantains first and everything else in order. Be careful to put the pumpkin in last as it is what takes the least time to soften.

If desired a piece of ham can be added. This should be done with the pumpkin because when it boils for long it loses its flavor. Touch it up with sazón and let it rest a moment before serving.

—CORDERO INFANTE, *LA COCINA DOMINICANA*, 21

---

sancocho pot only happens when "the jaunty girl who makes the sancocho occasionally becomes careless and abandons it in the kitchen to run to the dance floor [bohío] to take advantage of a 'hot' merengue" (19)—and through the language that distinguishes "us" from "the simple peasant who one day says to us:—one uh dese days [un día deto] come tuh my house [vayan poi casa] to eat a little sancocho" (20). "Our" interactions with these peasants show Cordero Infante and her readers to be proud consumers of their products and supporters of their work, though of course the support is paternalistic—"simple" easily reads as infantile, and the peasant's Spanish is markedly "incorrect"— exerting control as much as offering assistance.

If Cordero Infante constructs a Creole that embraces a range of class positions, even if it preserves their ranked order, she is at once less explicit and more restrictive in her definition of its racial boundaries, baking into her national culinary culture the distancing from Blackness that had marked elite and governmental constructions of Dominicanness for the previous century. The period from the Dominican Republic's independence from Spain 1821, through its unification with Haiti under a Black government seated in Port-au-Prince, to the messy separation that started in 1844 and finally ended with Haiti's relinquishment of claims to contested territory in 1855, underlie persistent tensions between the two nations. Haiti's status as the "Black Republic" made it easy to code Blackness as Haitian. As Silvio Torres Saillant explains, since then "the Dominican population's self-awareness as a people of African descent" has coexisted with "the negrophobia contained in prevalent definitions of Dominicanness" (1089). Cordero Infante's *Cocina dominicana* facilitates this seeming paradox by inscribing a Dominican cuisine that fits with what Torres Saillant describes as efforts to "repudiate Blackness" and instill a "negrophobic nationalism" not through "demeaning depictions of Blackness" but instead by incorporating Afro-Caribbean cuisine under the banner of a criollismo that is named consistently and only as having European, Indigenous, and Asian origins—closer to the Latin American "mestizo" than to most twentieth-century definitions of criollo. Although, in accordance with Glissantian creolization, Cordero Infante "demonstrates that henceforth it is no longer valid to glorify 'unique' origins that the race safeguards and prolongs," she also demonstrates how to safeguard and prolong the exclusion of Blackness from the criollo (*Caribbean Discourse*, 140).

Cordero Infante celebrates the first interactions between Spanish and Indigenous as originary of Dominican cuisine: "When Columbus discovered America, he was amazed to find corn being cultivated, which makes it clear that it is something that is ours" (39). Tracing the roots of corn, yuca, avocado, bija (achiote), coconut, and chocolate, she details the nutritional benefits of those foods as superior to nonindigenous parallels and even argues for the superiority of corn over rice, claiming, "There is no doubt that corn will get the attention it deserves and be given its proper place at the Dominican table as a national food and product" (39–40).[7] The Guaraní and Aztec myths and contemporary Colombian poetry relating to corn that she includes tie it both to an Indigenous past and a pan–Latin American present.[8] And though she does not remark on etymologies, in her significant numbers of recipes for Dominican dishes made with local fruits and vegetables, Cordero Infante consistently uses Indigenous and local terms for ingredients and dishes, from the Carib auyama (called calabaza in Spanish)[9] to the Quechua-Dominican locrio (rice with meat).[10]

Cordero Infante's appeal to Spanish heritage appears not only in the figuration of Spanish "discovery" as that which made Dominican

---

Locrio de buen pan (Breadfruit Locrio)

1 libra de arroz; 3 jarros de buen pan; 1 pollo; ajos, cebollas, puerros, vinagre, etc.; salsa de tomates.

Se guisa el pollo y luego se agregan los buen panes que habrán sido salcochados y pelados y partidos en dos. Se deja sofreír un rato. Agréguese el agua, el arroz y la manteca. Tápese y déjese cocer como los anteriores.

1 pound of rice; 3 jars of breadfruit; 1 chicken; garlic; onion, leeks, vinegar, etc.; tomato sauce.

Stew the chicken and then add the breadfruits that have been blanched and peeled and halved. Let it sauté for a while. Add the water, the rice, and the lard. Cover and let cook like the previous ones.

—CORDERO INFANTE, *LA COCINA DOMINICANA*, 35

> ### *Mala rabia* (Mala Rabia)
>
> *Se pone a hervir melado y agua en igual cantidad y se ponen los plátanos partidos en pedazos a lo largo. Cuando hayan cocido un poco los plátanos, se agrega la batata cortada en pedacitos y se les da punto de sirop.*
>
> Boil cane syrup and water in equal quantity and add plantains cut into pieces lengthwise. When the plantains have cooked a little, add the sweet potato cut into cubes and cook until syrupy.
>
> —CORDERO INFANTE, *LA COCINA DOMINICANA*, 82

cuisine visible as such, but also in her comparison of the classic Dominican sancocho to the Spanish cocido and her inclusion of such Spanish colonial delicacies as "Mala rabia" that turned African and Indigenous savory staples—plantain and sweet potato [batata]—into sweet treats through the use of the by-product of sugar production, cane syrup [melado] (which appears vacated of the connections to slave cuisine that it had in Puerto Rico and Cuba in the nineteenth century).

Although secondary to the Indigenous and Spanish, Asian and Arab food origins also belong in Cordero Infante's creole palate. She explains that "rice is a grain of Asian origin" that has become widely loved and cultivated in the Dominican Republic (28), that coffee's "primitive homeland is Moka (Arabia), having been brought and very well acclimatized to Tropical America, so much so that it appears to originate in our regions," (121) and that tea's origins are in China and Japan (127). These brief mentions set up a mode of situating foods as both tied to a foreign place of origin and fully indigenized in Dominican soil and criollo cuisine that renders the absolute absence of any reference to Africa especially glaring. Cordero Infante never mentions Africa as a place of origin for any food. Even when she details plantains as "the true bread of the poor," so nutritional that "with plantains and corn we could live for a long time" (75), Cordero Infante does not mention Africa or slaves and implies that plantain is indigenous to the Dominican Republic when

> ### *Mangú* (Mangu)
>
> *Se hierven los plátanos, se machacan con un plátano partido para el efecto, se les va agregando poco a poco el agua en que han sido hervidos de manera que la masa resulte suave, y se tienen cortados cebollines, que se han puesta en vinagre, se echan en manteca caliente y se echa la masa o plátanos majados y se revuelve bien. Se sirve caliente.*
>
> Boil the plantains, mash with a sliced plantain for effect, add little by little the water in which they boiled so that the dough is soft, and have on hand chives, that have been put in vinegar, put them into hot lard and add the dough or mashed plantains and stir well. Serve hot.
>
> —CORDERO INFANTE, *LA COCINA DOMINICANA*, 75

she writes, "We know a great variety of these vegetables that grow and fruit in our country, to the pleasure of the inhabitants, as it is our everyday bread we cultivate this plant like the best friend of the Dominican" (75). Cordero Infante includes recipes for fourteen plantain preparations, including mangú—whose name has barely changed from the West African mangusi from which it derives—without ever naming their association with Africa or with slaves in the Caribbean. As any and every history Cordero Infante tells turns out to be Indigenous, European, Asian, or Arab, the traces of African origins are obscured without ever being denied.

Cordero Infante's construction of the Dominican Criollo in line with the Latin American Mestizo sets up her figuration, in the history of the cocktail, of the United States as a newcomer trying to claim invention over what has a history that long precedes it and trying to claim as English words whose etymology is in fact Indigenous.

> The origin of the cocktail is rather more ancient than is generally believed and sufficiently fantastic that my readers may believe it or

not as they prefer. Although it appears impossible, it has nothing to do with the cock or his tail.

The chronicles tell that at the beginning of last century, in a semi-savage location, probably some island lost in the ocean, the American troops had to fight endlessly with native tribes. Finally, they requested an audience with the King of the tribe, to take place in the royal pavilion. When they were gathered, the King asked if they would like a drink just as a beautiful woman entered with a cup richly worked and encrusted with gems. There was a moment of silence. Who would drink first, the American general or the King? Noting the general's confusion, the woman smiled at everyone and with a gracious gesture drank the potion she had prepared. Everyone laughed, the ice was broken, and the meeting ended agreeably. "Now, said the general, I would like to know the name of the beautiful young woman who showed such tact," to which the King answered, "She is my daughter, Coctel."

"Well from now on her name will be appropriately honored by my troops," answered the general.

Naturally, the name in English became "Cocktail" and now I believe that this name has been honored, not only by the American troops but by many countries. (113)

By naming the United States as a military power that benefits from Indigenous food knowledge and diplomacy that they end up honoring, Cordero Infante's story diminishes U.S. influence in the Dominican Republic. That she is wrong about the history of the cocktail—although its etymology is not certain, the first recorded description of a cocktail appears to be in a New Hampshire newspaper in 1803 (Wondrich), while the first recorded use of the word is in a British newspaper in 1798 (Regan), neither connected to the supposed Aztec princess—also shows her curation. Rather than delving into the complex debt and burden that the Dominican Republic has to and with such things as slavery and U.S. intervention, Cordero Infante offers a history with no mention of either.

> ### Cocktail "Trujillo" ("Trujillo" Cocktail)
>
> *1 copa de ron "Carta Blanca", 1 copa de Vermouth Cinzano, el jugo de 2 naranjas, y ½ cucharadita de azúcar.*
>
> *Se añade una rebanada de cáscara de limón. Se agita bien con hielo picado y se sirve en un vaso o copa para Cocktail.*
>
> 1 cup of "Carta Blanca" rum, 1 cup of Cinzano Vermouth, the juice of 2 oranges, and ½ teaspoon of sugar.
>
> Add one slice of lemon peel. Shake well with crushed ice and serve in a Cocktail glass or cup.
>
> —CORDERO INFANTE, *LA COCINA DOMINICANA*, 114

The improbable story of a nineteenth-century encounter between American troops and a native king in the Americas is probably based on Fernando de Alva Ixtlilxochitl's seventeenth-century account of the Toltec Xochitl and the alcoholic drink pulque, re-popularized in the mid-nineteenth century by Mexican artist José Obregón's painting of the scene, *El descubrimiento del pulque*. When Cordero Infante puts the recognizably Toltec or Aztec gold-clad princess and Nahuatl-sounding "ctel" not on the mainland but on some semi-savage island, she connects the Caribbean to Indigenous Mexico. Thus, what is criollo and Dominican has a long history of being Indigenous and Latin American. Cordero Infante's version of the history of the cocktail also gives important diplomatic skill and power to the princess that is not common in other versions of the story (where the princess's power is either much less or passes through her seduction of drunk men).[11] Cordero Infante's lengthy selection of cocktails, then, rather than incorporating a U.S. contribution into Dominican national cuisine, secures her place in a line of women who use culinary diplomacy.

Cordero Infante, with Trujillo, transforms criollo from a term that involves the possible mixing of those of European and African ancestry through their shared birth in and around the Caribbean into one that is nearly synonymous with "purely" Indigenous and Spanish Mestizo of Latin America. The African components and histories of Dominican foods could then be hidden, like Trujillo's Mulatto heritage, in plain sight. Elite Dominican women rarely needed to deny their own Blackness for they were primarily White or White-identified, from families whose power had long depended on the appropriation and discrediting of Black labor and history. They could assert their domestic power and independence, maintain the power structures that kept their inherited privileges, articulate a new Dominican national culture that broke from a history of U.S. domination, and support and be supported by Trujillo all at once.

Culinary Education and the Advancement of New Generations of Trujillist Women

As Trujillo's dictatorial control over the Dominican Republic progressed in ever more excessive forms, his commitment to the controlled progress of elite women persisted. And elite women's cookbooks worked to maintain their position and expand their numbers. The two Dominican home economics manual and cookbooks published in the mid-twentieth century continued in Cordero Infante's mode of aligning elite White women with Trujillo and presiding over a Dominican creole cuisine and culture that elevated the mixing of Spanish with Indigenous and to a lesser degree Asian to hold up a creole evacuated of Blackness. Taking on an educational mission, these cookbooks address not only the established elite but also middle-class women aspiring to elitism. The women who wrote these cookbooks, Amanda Ornes Peréllo and Ligia de Bornia, took cooking beyond the home that Cordero Infante uplifted, and into the classroom. Each of these women came to benefit from the increasing access elite Dominican women had to education and took on a teaching role in a distinct way. Nonetheless, their cookbooks offer similar formulas for the next generations of Trujillist women.

A mark of Trujillo's investment in women's education and domestic culture, and of the mutually supportive relationship between Trujillo and the elite women who ran the programs, was the "official program of home economics of the Dominican Republic," for which Amanda Ornes Perelló's four-volume *Manual de economía doméstica* (1938–1940) was the textbook. Born in Puerto Plata in 1897 to a Puerto Rican–born father and a Cuban-born mother, Amanda María Ornes Schewerer studied in Puerto Plata under Mercedes Mota, one of the Dominican Republic's early feminist writers and organizers. She moved to Santiago after completing a teaching degree and married Luis Emelio Perelló Conquet in 1928. In 1934 she was named director of Santiago's Escuela de Economía Domestica. By 1938, when the first volumes of the *Manual de economía doméstica* were published, Trujillo had already renamed the capital city of the Dominican Republic Ciudad Trujillo and overseen the massacre of thousands, perhaps tens of thousands, of Haitians.[12] Ornes Perelló's prologue to the first volume of the *Manual de economía doméstica* starts by honoring "our illustrious president the Generalísimo Dr. Rafael Leonidas Trujillo Molina, benefactor of the nation" (3), and the prefatory material ends with an invocation of Salomé Ureña de Henríquez and her 1887 poem "Ofrenda a la patria" with its impassioned tribute to women's roles in making the domestic space "port and guide [lumbrera y guía]" for "progress and peace and independence [progreso y paz y independencia]" (9–10). By the mid-1950s, when Ornes Perelló published *Cocina criolla* and Ligia de Bornia published her *Cocina dominicana*, Trujillo had become one of the two or three richest men in the world, ordered the assassination of his growing detractors at home and abroad, raped countless women, and made it an act of treason to declare that he had African ancestry (which he did have). At the same time, the Dominican Republic's economy was booming, with a modernized infrastructure and efficient social services. The reasons to support and to resist Trujillo had both increased, as had knowledge of the danger of resistance.[13]

At least a decade younger than Ornes Perelló, Bornia grew up under the U.S. occupation, matured under Trujillo, and outlasted both. Born

Ligia Oneida Vidal Marmolejos in Santiago, Dominican Republic, in the early twentieth century, she married Dr. Manuel Ramón Bornia, with whom she had three children. By 1934 Bornia was a middle school teacher in Santiago. By 1940 she had opened a cooking school in her home, where she taught until 1965. She was also a regular on the cooking shows of Dominican national television. In 1962 she helped to found Santiago's private school of home economics, Escuela Yaque. *La cocina dominicana* is, as of this writing, in its seventeenth edition. Bornia's later cookbooks, the bilingual *Comidas típicas dominicanas/Typical Dominican Meals* (1965), *Cocina Ligia* (1972), *La cocina de Ligia en olla de presión* (1977), and *La cocina Ligia en microondas* (1992) evidence the progression from Ligia de Bornia as the author of Dominican cookbooks to Ligia de Bornia as the emblem of Dominican food. Much as both Ornes Perelló and Bornia's lives and works demonstrate the development of women's education and work, like Cordero Infante, they both clearly delineate women's spaces and contributions as occurring in the domestic sphere. And while Cordero Infante ties women primarily to their homes, Ornes Perelló and Bornia also attach them to husbands and children.

Although they never mention Cordero Infante's *La cocina dominicana*, or one another, Ornes Perelló's *Cocina criolla* and Bornia's *Cocina dominicana* crystalize the synonymy that Cordero Infante established between Dominican and Criollo and her definition of criollo cuisine. Ornes Perelló refers to "cocina criolla" as "our cuisine," which she describes as going "from the most interesting indigenous dishes to the most exotic ones, passing through those that the Spanish brought and others that are typical of the Dominican people" (Ornes Perelló, 1962, 5). Bornia asserts in her introduction that "this book is not a simple collection of recipes of our CRIOLLA COOKING collected haphazardly with the aim of filling a few pages, no, it is a unique and very Dominican work" (n.p.).[14]

Cocina criolla is written like a textbook, and likely served as such, expanding from the few recipes in Ornes Perelló's first textbook, *Manual de economía doméstica*. *Cocina criolla* is distinguished by its extensive didactic material and great number of recipes. Along with criollo

Chop Suey (chino) (Chop Suey [Chinese])

1 lb. masa de cerdo, 1 pedazo jengibre, 1 cucht. salsa china, 2 cuchts. maizena, 1 lb. vainitas, 4 onzas cebollas, 1 onza fideos, ½ cucht. aceite de ajonjolí.

Se corta carne en tiritas finas, se une con jengibre picado en tiritas, salsa china, maizena, y 2 cuchs. manteca derretida; se pica cebolla en tiritas y se prepara salsa cruda con otra cucht. de maizena, pimienta, 1 cuch. vino y 4 onzas agua; se fríen en manteca caliente, fideo, se sacan rápidamente; se sofríe cebolla, vainitas picadas, se mueve hasta que estén transparentes, se añaden 2 cuchs. manteca, se echa carne, se mueve bien; se cocina en fuentes llanas cubiertas con fideos fritos.

1 lb. pork, 1 piece ginger, 1 tsp. Chinese sauce [salsa china], 2 tsp. cornstarch, 1 lb. green beans, 4 ounces onion, 1 ounce noodles, ½ tsp. sesame oil.

Cut meat in thin strips, mix with ginger cut into strips, Chinese sauce, cornstarch, and 2 Tbsp. melted lard; cut onion in strips and prepare sauce with another tsp. of cornstarch, pepper, 1 tsp. wine and 4 ounces water; fry in hot lard, green beans, remove quickly; sauté onion, chopped noodles, stirring until transparent, add 2 Tbsp. lard, add meat, stir well; cook the sauce, covered, for five minutes, add sesame oil; serve in flat plates covered with fried beans.

—ORNES PERELLÓ, *COCINA CRIOLLA*, 185

Dominican staples, it includes a wide variety of international dishes that are absent in both Cordero Infante and Bornia's cookbooks. While many of those are Italian and French, several "American" dishes suggest a reopening to the United States. Already in her 1938 *Manual*, Ornes Perelló included recipes for "Puré de copas de avena (Quaker Oats)," "Crema de trigo (Cream of Wheat)," and "Copas de maíz" (Corn Flakes)" (110). In *Cocina criolla*, she also refers to Asia not only as an ingredient source but also in recipes. Ornes Perelló includes four Chop Suey recipes, "arroz frito chino," a chicken with pineapple recipe that she identifies as "plato chino," "Aro de arroz 'bengalés,'" a pilau recipe, a recipe for chicken with curry sauce, and a recipe for curry sauce that she recommends could be served on "arroz con pollo, fish or hard-boiled eggs" (345).

Given the small numbers of Chinese- and Indo-Dominicans in the 1950s, this inclusion might be more a reflection of Ornes Perelló's cosmopolitanism than a nod to Chinese- and Indo-Dominicans.[15] However, the recipes rest on a culinary integration in which ingredients like "Chinese sauce [salsa china]" need no special explanation and appear to be readily available.[16] And Trujillo encouraged immigration from Asia as part of his efforts to whiten the Dominican population (Chen, 26–27). If Ornes Perelló's Chinese and Indian dishes work, along with her European and "American" ones, toward a cosmopolitan multiethnic Dominican Whiteness, the absence of Chinese and Indian-associated recipes in both Cordero Infante and Bornia's cookbooks shows that they did not hold or acquire any stable place in culinary inscriptions of Dominican Creoleness in the first half of the twentieth century.

Both Ornes Perelló and Bornia repeat and expand Cordero Infante's already significant selection of Dominican dishes, asserting as the core of "our" cuisine a set of recipes recognizable for the predominance of víveres; the richness of soups and stews; the centrality of pork and poultry; a seasoning palate based on onion, peppers, culantro, and citrus; and a culinary vocabulary whose etymology is primarily Spanish but also importantly Arawakan and Cariban.[17] With fewer stories, commentaries, and histories than Cordero Infante, Ornes Perelló and Bornia's focuses on the Indigenous and Spanish heritage of Dominican cuisine are less pronounced, but nonetheless present. Ornes Perelló and Bornia go beyond Cordero Infante in naming and praising Indigenous culinary tools and techniques, such as the macuto and jibe used for preparing cassava flour and the burén used for cooking cassava cakes. Bornia's parenthetical explanations of "jibe" and "burén" suggest that they are not well known to her readers, and that Bornia is introducing or reintroducing them to elite women. That she calls for the macuto, jibe and burén only in the "Catibia" and "Casabe cibaeño" recipes may indicate that few of Bornia's readers will actually prepare those recipes at home. However, by following those recipes with ones for "Panecicos

> ### *Panecicos de catibía* (Catibía Breads)
> *(20 PANECICOS PEQUEÑOS)*
>
> Ingredientes
>
> 2 libras de catibía
> 1 cucharadita de anís
> 2 cucharaditas de sal
> 5 yemas de huevo
> 3 o 5 cucharadas de manteca de cerdo
>
> Preparación
>
> Mezcle la catibía con la sal y anís. Adicione los huevos batidos, mantequilla, 3 cucharadas de manteca y leche.
>
> Haga los panecitos y con el resto de manteca engráselos, envuélvalos en papel encerado y llévelos al horno a 375 grados F por 25 minutos. Sáquelos del horno, suba el calor a 425 grados F. quite el papel a los panecitos y llévelos de nuevo al horno por 12 ó 15 minutos hasta dorarlos.
>
> Nota: Si los prefiere hacer mas grandes deje en el primer tiempo de horneo por 45 minutos.

de catibía" and "Empanadas de catibía" made with ingredients, implements, and processes common throughout the cookbook, Bornia renders all four recipes a seamless part of a living Dominican cuisine in which Indigenous traditions are both preserved and evolving.

The African histories and slave contributions to Dominican foods remain unremarked by both Ornes Perelló and Bornia. Ornes Perelló raises the specter of plantation culture in her entry on "our cane syrup [melado de caña], that our grandparents used with such frequency, as in the confection of sangria, a delicious drink, malarrabia, a typical sweet of the Colonial period and palanqueta" (296). However, she relegates it to a bygone era and describes how to make it almost as if it could be

Ingredients:

2 pounds of catibía
1 teaspoon of anis
2 teaspoons of salt
5 egg yolks
4 egg whites
4 tablespoons of butter
5 tablespoons on lard
3 or 5 tablespoons of milk

Preparation:

Mix the catibía with the salt and anis. Add the beaten eggs, butter, three tablespoons of lard and milk.

Make the breads and with the rest of the lard grease them, wrap in wax paper and put them into a 375 degree F oven for 25 minutes. Remove them from the oven and raise the heat to 425 degrees F. take the paper off the breads and put them back into the oven for 12 to 15 minutes until they are browned.

NOTE: if you prefer to make them larger leave them in the oven the first time for 45 minutes.

—BORNIA, *LA COCINA DOMINICANA*, 193

done in a home kitchen: "The sugar is taken out of the cane; the guarapo or juice is the first thing obtained, which is cooked at a graduation of 9 to 10 degrees so that it passes to the evaporators, where the temperature is raised to 30 degrees, thus obtaining the meladura, which is not yet melado, since the latter is produced later in the cans" (296). Unlike her compatriots, Ornes Perelló mentions that what are generally called "molondrones [okra]" in the Dominican Republic are called "quimbombos" elsewhere, but she does not mention the African origin of quimbombó. She has recipes for Afro-Indigenous dishes developed around plantation culture such as asopado, tasajo, and funche, but the only

> ### Funche
>
> *2 tzs. harina de maiz, 2 cuchs. manteca, 1 onza jamón o tocineta a gusto, sal, 4 tzs. agua.*
>
> *Se sofríe jamón o tocineta, se agrega agua, sal y harina, se cuece a fuego lento, moviendo constantemente hasta que espese, se sirve caliente. Se puede añadir 1 lb. bacalao salcochado y desmenuzado; se hacen bolas echando porciones en una taza engrasada.*
>
> 2 cups corn flour, 2 Tbsp. lard, 1 ounce ham or bacon to taste, salt, 4 cups water.
>
> Sauté the ham or bacon, add water, salt, and flour and cook over low heat, stirring constantly until thickened, serve hot. You can add 1 lb. blanched and shredded salt cod; make balls by putting portions into a greased cup.
>
> —ORNES PERELLÓ, *COCINA CRIOLLA*, 241

indication she gives of their histories is her placement of funche in the section on corn that describes corn as "a food from the age of Discovery" and "a contribution of the Indian to our modern civilization" (240). She never mentions the resonance—in sound and serving—of funche and fufu. Bornia does not expand the range of Afro-Indigenous dishes as does Ornes Perelló. Instead, Bornia generally reasserts the limits of Cordero Infante's African- and slave-origin dishes, ensuring that the creolism of the Dominican cookbooks of the 1950s remains as whitewashed as Cordero Infante's.

Bornia did not need to assert her cookbook's imbrication with Trujillo's vision of Domincanness; the regime did that for her, with prizes and laudatory articles. However, Bornia's prominent featuring of the praise in every edition since 1959 conveys the mutual admiration of a particular version of womanhood shared by elite Dominican women and the Trujillo regime. Bornia's first recipes are in a chapter titled "Feeding the Child [Alimentación del niño]," whose opening lines are

"Mother: you are half Angel, half woman; who have had the privilege of carrying your child inside you.... And you, who are the most important person for your child, who give him the necessary bodily care and education, which must start in the cradle, must concern yourself with feeding him well" (56). Sixto Espinosa Orozco's rave review confirms that Bornia's emphasis on motherhood restricts women's power to the private spaces of kitchen and nursery to which Trujillo's regime, after its initial nominal overtures, progressively reduced them. Described in a 1956 Foreign Service Dispatch as "a specialist in diatribe and part time philosopher imported [to the Dominican Republic] from Spain about a year ago for *El Caribe* and HIT" (Robert Allen), Espinoza Orozco was a darling of Trujillo.[18] His review of Bornia's *Cocina dominicana* urges:

> It is a moral duty to promote the work of a Dominican author who contributes, so judiciously, to the domestic education of young women who need to know how to accomplish their elevated mission on Earth. It is not to be slaves, but rather heads of their homes [dueñas de su hogar], nor to be, exclusively, cooks for their husbands and children, but rather ladies prepared for all of the contingencies of life and knowledgeable in a noble job on which depends, occasionally, the happiness of her people and of herself. For even to order, one has to know what is being ordered. And, in sum, there is not poetry more beautiful, for a man of good means, than which is written in his home, even at the risk of tarnishing her painted nails, by the woman who exercises her apostleship as priestess of the Religion of Christian living, without which every union is unbearable. (9)

While the praise for Bornia's work and the blessing of the Trujillo regime rest more on her ability to teach women to fit Trujillo-approved roles than her ability to promote Dominican culinary pride, the large and lengthy circulation of her cookbook confirms the latter as well.

In the 1997 edition of Bornia's *La cocina dominicana*, along with the prizes from the Trujillo regime and Espinoza Orozco's review, appears an open letter from Lourdes Cruz to Bornia that states, "I believe, Doña Ligia, that you were the mentor of the beautiful butterflies. María Teresa Mirabal, so timid and quiet" (n.p.). The suggestion in this letter is that both its author and Maria Teresa Mirabal were students of Bornia's. The Mirabal sisters, among the most famous detractors from and victims of Trujillo's regime, were born between 1924 and 1935 in the Cibao region, of which Santiago is the largest city. It is certainly plausible that Bornia could have taught one or more of them in some format, but Cruz's claim that Bornia mentored María Teresa Mirabal appears to be supported only by the general desire of many Dominicans in the post-Trujillo era to have some credit for the Mirabal sisters' bravery.

The accolades that preface and surround the many editions of Bornia's work convey the complexities of women's alignments in the Dominican Republic as well as the ways that simple associations—be they with Trujillo or his famous detractors—elide the always more complicated alliances made for personal, social, and political commitments in and out of dictatorial regimes. At the same time, that Bornia's book is used, by her and others, to promote women's interests under the threats of Trujillo and to promote Trujillo under the guises of women's interests shows how deeply political are the articulations of national culinary culture and how ambivalent the politics of cookbooks. Because they intervene in national culture not through political parties but through articulations of the roles of women, the rules of class, the histories and meanings of foods, the shaping of taste, the ideas of where what is "ours" comes from and where it belongs, these cookbooks let us see the messy processes of aligning, inventing, and modifying. They offer, in other words, not works that can be carefully sorted into the already established positions and modes of political and cultural meaning-making, but the work of making, as in the material production of food. Contemporary cookbook writers and authors of new national imaginaries from and for other perspectives must contend with these complex features of twentieth-century Dominican national culture.

Haitian National Culinary Culture between U.S. Occupation and Dictatorship

Haiti was the first country in the Caribbean to gain independence and one of the last to produce its own cookbook, indicating its difficult path of national cultural development. In spite of the triumph of the Haitian Revolution in 1804, and the powerful symbolism of Haiti becoming the first Black republic, where slave rebellion ended colonial domination, the significant class divisions of the colonial period persisted.[19] The French-controlled plantation economy was gone, and the peasant majority that kept up vibrant local food production resisted any return to plantation monoculture, but it had little access to the formal education and economic and political power that the elite enjoyed in the urban centers. In 1915 the United States occupied Haiti, ostensibly to restore order after the violence surrounding the ousting of President Jean Vilbrun Guillaume Sam, and largely as an extension of the Monroe Doctrine under which Latin America and the Caribbean were the "back yard" of the United States. Under U.S. occupation, divisions continued between rural and urban, poor and elite, while those within Haiti's elite between Mulatto and Black were exacerbated by U.S. racism that favored Mulattos. The end of the U.S. occupation, in 1934, set up the success of Mulatto politicians. In 1938 Zora Neale Hurston wrote, "First it was the Haiti of the masters and the slaves. Now it is Haiti of the wealthy and educated mulattoes and the Haiti of the Blacks," underlining how class divisions had become racially coded (73). At the same time, Mark Shuller's analysis of the divisions within Haiti's elite between "northern Black military generals and southern mulatto traders" is typical of the many studies that overlook class unification to focus on racial division. The present study of the contexts and contents of Haiti's first cookbooks exposes the connections among Mulatto and Black elite women's interests and their role in composing a national culinary culture that reached across and maintained Haiti's urban-rural class divide.

Like in the rest of the Caribbean (and much of the world), Haitian women in the early twentieth century were just beginning to acquire things like access to education and the right to vote, and home economics and cookbooks were linked, explicitly and implicitly, to women's literacy and organizing as well as to the struggles for power across the nation and among the elite.[20] In Haiti, the relatively long period of time between the end of U.S. occupation and the establishment of dictatorship made room, however, for the articulation of a national culinary culture that forged class alliances across racial differences even as those differences solidified in the traditional political and military spheres. Haitian cookbooks, and Haitian women, were not able to head off dictatorship. They offered neither radical resistance to what became dictatorial rule nor, as was the case with their Dominican counterparts, strategic acceptance that turned into active support, but a middle ground that did not hold. But especially in a moment, at the writing of this book, when the destructive legacies of colonialism, occupation, and dictatorship are so visible in Haiti, it is important to consider the alternative that Haitian women formulated for themselves. Enmeshed in the political backdrop of Haitian struggle about how to reformulate independent nationhood after U.S. occupation, the cookbooks offer as much contrast as continuity with the historical narrative.

During the decade of independent democratic rule by Mulatto-led governments after 1934, the noiriste movement developed, championed by writers such as Jean Price-Mars who called for a cultural, artistic, and political embrace of Haitian Blackness. During this period, Louise Mayard published *Cuisine des pays chauds* (1940). In 1946 noiristes gained political power and oversaw another decade of independent democratic rule. Niniche Viard Gaillard's *Recettes simples de la cuisine haïtienne* was published in 1950, and Herzulie Magloire-Prophète's *Cuisine sélectionnée* in 1955. The latter year also saw the first Haitian cookbook written by an American, in English: Robel Paris's *Haitian Recipes*. In 1957, with a soon-to-be dictatorial version of noirisme, François Duvalier took over.[21]

Mayard, Gaillard, and Magloire-Prophète's biographies would suggest that their cookbooks trace Haiti's move from mulâtrisme (embrace of

Mulatto-identified culture and power) to noirisme and even through the latter's eventual fall into military dictatorship. Mayard and Gaillard were both from well-established families in Haiti's Mulatto élite. Mayard was born Marie Gaveau in the early 1880s in Port-au-Prince to Louis Gaveau and Emilia Clérié of Jeremi.[22] Mayard's first husband was the Haitian poet, dramatist, and politician Charles Moravia. Charles Moravia also started and wrote for several Haitian newspapers including *Le Temps*; his articles opposed to the American occupation had him jailed by the Vincent government set up under it. Mayard's second husband was Haitian politician, poet, and journalist Constantin Mayard. Constantin Mayard was minister of the interior during the U.S. occupation, which he supported. He ran for president in 1930, losing to Vincent. He then served as a diplomat until his death in 1940.[23] Both Charles Moravia and Constantin Mayard were Black and active in noiriste literary circles. Also born in Port-au-Prince in the late nineteenth century, Marie Anne Rosita Eugénie (Niniche) Viard, too, belonged to a prominent Mulatto family. Her father was a judge, and she was among the first group of women to graduate from Haiti's Ecole Normale des Institutrices. She married Jean Sumner Gaillard, with whom she had six children; President Vincent was the godfather of one of them. Herzulie Magloire was born in 1897 into an elite military and political Black family. She married Marie Emmanuel Léonce Augustin Prophète, with whom she had at least six children. While her brother, Paul Magloire, was president, from 1950 to 1956, Magloire-Prophète served as inspector of domestic arts and a member of the first lady's Madame Magloire charitable foundation. More than a progression from mulâtrisme—of Mayard and Gaillard—to noirisme—of Magloire-Prophète, their three cookbooks show how the shared class interests of Haiti's Mulatto and Black elite brought them together far more than any racial or political differences distinguished them. They instruct not in how Haiti progressed and changed between 1940 and 1955 but in how, in the face of significant changes in both political power and women's rights, the status quo persisted.

In 1940, when Mayard published *Cuisine de pays chauds*, Haitian women, regardless of race, were still excluded from owning property or businesses and from voting. The Haitian feminist movement, which had first organized in 1934 as the Ligue Féminine d'Action Sociale (LFAS), was a primary force in the push for women's rights in Haiti. The LFAS records were mostly lost, but rare copies of their publication, *La voix des femmes*, remain in a box in the Schlessinger Library archives that I stumbled across while looking for Haitian newspapers that might include recipe sections. While the LFAS publications detail the group's instrumental role in the slow fight for women's access to property rights and the vote,[24] they also reveal how, when LFAS addressed the concerns and needs of Haiti's peasant majority, it was generally in the form of patronizing analyses of the plight of peasant women and the establishment of programs that would better train peasant girls for domestic work in the homes and businesses run by elite Haitians.[25]

Directly and indirectly,[26] Mayard, Gaillard, and Magloire-Prophète's elitism and their assertions of women's power, education, and work within the spaces of upper-class Catholic "family values" aligned with the positions of LFAS that contributed to its frequently being discounted by contemporary scholars of Haiti like Patrick Bellegarde-Smith "because it was concerned, really, about the upper class" (Balutansky 446–447).[27] Though Maryse Condé chided, in her 1989 analysis of *Aude et ses fantômes* by Mayard's daughter Adelina Moravia, "We have taken on the habit of despising the ruling classes, of only being interested in the exploited, forgetting the close ties that they maintain with the exploiters who are but the other face of the same society" (90), few studies have addressed the lacuna. Instead, comments like Bellegarde-Smith's fit all to easily into the common twenty-first century "international" story of Haiti as divided between the "authentic" culture of the poor peasant majority, who are however so downtrodden that they cannot survive on their own, and a dictatorial kleptocracy far more interested in personal financial and political control than in the country. This story is explained by and justifies the past century-plus of foreign intervention (via occupation and "aid"). It is told in culinary terms as well, where "authentic" Haitian food is what is served at market stalls, on street corners, and at vodou ceremonies, what cooks prepare for wealthy diners who ask for "local specialties," and what is eaten in peasant homes when they have the benefit of foreign support to help them acquire basic foodstuffs (or the meager provisions they can gather from the island's bounty that while delicious leave them malnourished). But before American and French tourists and aid workers committed that story to paper, Mayard, Gaillard, and Magloire-Prophète inscribed a Haitian cuisine that was elitist, nationalist, Francophile, and grounded in Afro-Indigenous and Creole culinary history.

Examining how noiriste ideology became the Duvalierist populism that took hold in Haiti in 1957, David Nicholls describes Haiti in the mid-twentieth century caught in "a conflict between a noiriste ideology which pictured Haiti as essentially African in its culture and a nationalist which thought in terms of a Créole culture, unique to Haiti, strongly influenced by French as well as African traditions" (7). Mayard, Gaillard, and Magloire-Prophète developed instructions for feeding that nationalist path, understanding Haitian culture as creole and Haiti as a cosmopolitan player on an international stage. That their vision was not followed, at least in the short and medium terms, does not make it any less interesting, and indeed the disaster that ensued with Duvalierism suggests that perhaps rather than dismissing Mayard, Gaillard, and Magloire-Prophète for their elitism, we ought to study them for their innovation.

Creole Tropicalism: Louise Mayard's *Cuisine des pays chauds*

The first cookbook published in Haiti by a Haitian woman addresses a national audience of women cooking in Haiti, knowledgeable about Haitian cuisine in regional and international contexts. The tropicalism inherent in the title, *Cuisine des pays chauds*, may not seem to suggest a strictly national culinary culture. However, in Mayard's treatment, tropicalism works like creolization, geographically grounding Haitianness and connecting it to sister spaces. The nationalism of *Cuisine des pays chauds* works less to show an outside audience the distinctness, vitality, and viability of a national culture that requires an independent nation than to show a local audience the quality and character of a local culture that merits and requires its attention and devotion. This is not, in other words, a performative version of the Fanonian turn to addressing local audiences, but rather a functional one, ironically rendering its investments in national culture less visible to outsiders.

The one review of Mayard's cookbook, published in *La voix des femmes* in 1941, notes:

> *La cuisine des pays chauds* by Mme. Louise Mayard responded certainly to a need. In order to recognize that, we only need to look at the satisfaction with it is received by the young homemakers as also the gentlemen! Nearly 200 well-established recipes for tropical cuisine—recipes sometimes new for us that the author gathered during her travels to France's midi region, Venezuela or Peru, Haitian recipes also that we see with a smile specified in precise measurements (a dash becomes a teaspoon)—mixed with wise advice and lively quotes. (9)

According to this review, what is novel about Mayard's Haitian recipes is their specification in "precise measurements." Mayard's tables and lists confirm that hers is a work of codification and standardization. However, the organizational structure of *Cuisine des pays chauds* is neither top-down nor invested in establishing any singular trajectory of start (origin) to finish. Indeed, Mayard's organization might be best described as Glissantian transversality that enables full creolization as it "relieves us of the linear, hierarchical vision of a single History that would run its unique course" (*Caribbean Discourse*, 66). *Cuisine des pays chauds* starts with introductory material, groups some recipes by type and ingredient, and sometimes uses section titles to demarcate the groupings. Further undermining any notion of hierarchical ordering and standardization, no singular voice of authority emerges in the recipes themselves. While some of Mayard's recipes, as the review notes, specify amounts in spoon sizes, many others do not specify amounts at all, and the recipes also vary significantly in format, tone, voice, and naming of ingredients. "Aubergines à la créole," for example, appears first with the vegetables as eggplants stuffed with an eggplant-meat mix (42) and then in "Cuisine of the Islands" as a casserole of eggplant, tomatoes, and lamb (212). The banana section (which appears to be a subsection under vegetables) includes an essay on "The Nutritional Value of the Banana-Fig" by "Dr. Richard, de la Faculté de Médecine de Paris" that introduces but does not explain the term "banana-fig [figue-banane]," and a note, in the recipe for "Bananes grillées," presumably written by Mayard, that explains the different types of bananas, calling "the banana proper" the one "that is used as a vegetable" but also explaining that "the other variety, more universally known, is the one that results in such great commerce on the international market. . . . In the country of origin, it is called 'banana-fig'" (80).[28] The recipes in the section, however, only one of which is attributed to a separate author, sometimes call simply for "bananas," sometimes distinguish "ripe bananas" and "green bananas" both used as vegetables (83–84), and sometimes call for "ripe green bananes" (87–88) as if "green banana" were contrasted not with "ripe banana" but with "banana-fig." Some of these recipes offer only ingredients, some only instructions, some instructions with embedded ingredients, and some with lists of ingredients first followed by instructions. While this kind of variation marks the subgenre of the recipe collection in which contributors' distinct voices form a polyvocal unit, and the recipes in *Cuisine des pays chauds* make sense as the contributions of many cooks who not only make the same recipes in different ways but also think in diverse ways about how to convey a recipe, Mayard does not announce her book as a collection and attributes only two recipes.[29] Yet she includes them in all of their nonuniformity.

Whatever her sources, Mayard's audience are Haitian women who cook enough (or whose cooks know enough) that while they may be pleased to find standardized measures in some recipes, they do not need them. Indeed, as I have noted across Caribbean cookbooks through this period, many recipes appear more as suggestions than as clear sets of

« Bananes vertes mures » au gratin
("Ripe Green Banana" Gratin)

3 « bananes vertes mûres »

1 tasse de lait;
2 cuillerées à soupe de farine;
1 tasse de chapelure;
2 cuillerées à soupe de beurre;
1 cuilerée à café de sel;
1 pincée de poivre.

1. *Préparer une sauce blanche;*
2. *Laver et peler les bananes;*
3. *Les mettre à l'eau salée pendant quelques minutes;*
4. *Les couper en rondelles;*
5. *Mettre ¼ de la chapelure au fond d'un plat graissé allant au four et couvrir la chapelure de sauce blanche;*
6. *Mettre la moitié des rondelles de bananes;*
7. *Placer ¼ de la sauce blanche; recouvrir d' ¼ de chapelure;*
8. *Ajouter ce qui reste de banane;*
9. *Puis le reste de la sauce blanche recouverte du reste de la chapelure;*
10. *Cuire à four modéré pendant une demi-heure;*
11. *Servir chaud. On ajoute quelquefois du fromage râpé entre chaque couche de chapelure et de sauce blanche.*

instructions for the novice. In *Cuisine des pays chauds*, this is perhaps most clear in the recipe that would also be most familiar to Haitian women, "Haitian national dish [Plat national haïtien]" (51), where some steps in the preparation are mentioned only after they are to have been completed, it is never mentioned that "spices [des épices]" refers to a Haitian blend of bell peppers, scotch bonnet, parsley, thyme, scallions, and sometimes celery, and the instructions end with the beans having been left out after draining, as if they were never added back in. Mayard's readers may well employ cooks, still a common practice among the elite in Haiti, but this recipe exemplifies how a cookbook can write them into

> 3 "ripe green bananas"
>
> 1 cup milk
> 2 soup spoons flour
> 1 cup bread crumbs
> 2 soup spoons butter
> 1 coffee spoon salt
> 1 pinch pepper
>
> 1. Prepare a white sauce;
> 2. Wash the bananas and peel them;
> 3. Put them into salted water for a few minutes;
> 4. Cut them into slices;
> 5. Put ¼ of the bread crumbs in the bottom of a greased baking dish and cover the bread crumbs with white sauce;
> 6. Put on half of the banana slices;
> 7. Add ¼ of the white sauce, cover with ¼ of the bread crumbs;
> 8. Add the remaining banana;
> 9. Then the rest of the white sauce covered with the rest of the bread crumbs;
> 10. Cook in a medium oven for a half hour;
> 11. Serve hot. Sometimes grated cheese is added between each layer of bread crumbs and white sauce.
>
> —MAYARD, *CUISINE DES PAYS CHAUDS*, 87–88

the domestic community, albeit implicitly. Mayard's casual tone, the specificity of some but not all ingredients and amounts, the mention of steps out of strict order, convey not lacunae that indicate the author's own inexperience with preparing the recipes, as in cookbooks compiled by colonial women that I discuss in the first half of this book, but rather the assumption of shared knowledge between herself and her readers, written into many independence-era cookbooks by women who are building communities among independent women.

Even Mayard's apparently international recipes are grounded in Haiti through their ingredients. Indeed, *Cuisine des pays chauds* parallels

Plat national haïtien (Haitian National Dish)

a) 1 tasse de haricots rouges secs.
Mis à tremper depuis la veille.

Cuits à l'eau, jusqu'au point de commencer à éclater (en créole crevés). Passer et laisser égoutter complètement; garder l'eau de cuisson à laquelle on avait ajouté, lorsque les haricots étaient presqu'à point, du sel et des épices et, un peu plus tôt, 125 grammes de lard maigre. Les haricots seront meilleurs si la quantité de sel est suffisant.

Dans cette eau rougie d'une quantité de 2 à 3 tasses, mettre, quand elle est en plein ébullition:

b) 2 tasses de riz bien lavé.
Puis, 2 autres tasses de la même eau rougie. Et lorsque l'eau est sur le point de disparaitre dans le riz, on y répandera une cuillerée à soupe de saindoux très frais porté à l'ébullition. Réduire alors le feu en veilleuse. Couvrir hermétiquement.

Il faut trente minutes pour la seconde opération.

a) 1 cup dry red beans.
Soaked overnight.

Cooked in water just to the point where they start to burst (in Creole, broken). Strain and let drain completely; keep the cooking water into which was added, when the beans were almost ready the salt and the spices and, a little earlier, 125 grams of lean lard. The beans will be better if the amount of salt is sufficient.

In 2 to 3 cups of this reddened water put, when it is at a full boil:

b) 2 cups of well washed rice.
Then, 2 other cups of the same reddened water. And when the water is about to disappear in the rice, sprinkle a soupspoon of very fresh lard brought to a boil. Then lower the heat as low as possible. Cover tightly.
The second part takes thirty minutes.

—MAYARD, *CUISINE DES PAYS CHAUDS*, 51

F. Morisseau Leroy's call, in his 1940 "Letter to the women of Haiti," printed in *La voix des femmes,* for Haitian women to ensure food independence for national security and shift the economic benefit of Haitian elite cuisine from importers to peasant farmers. Mayard gives instructions and incentives for elite Haitian women to buy locally, adapting French and international recipes not only to Haitian climate but to Haitian goods. Mayard, however, gives a reasoning based not on nationalism but on quality—noting, for example, that "the best variety of this excellent vegetable (sweet potato) is the Haitian" (36). Mayard's project is not one of aesthetic sacrifice for political purpose or even aesthetics at the service of politics, but of nationalism because it is the best taste.

Mayard writes a book that brings together Haitian recipes, identified as such in their titles or simply recognizable as local dishes by a local audience, Haitian ways of cooking the dishes of other "hot countries [pays chauds]," and Haitian connections to those "hot countries." In doing so, *Cuisine des pays chauds* establishes a repertoire that positions Haiti in the context of what I call Creole tropicalism. As suggested in the review in *La voix des femmes,* Mayard's tropicalism articulates a regional affiliation. The book's concluding section on "La cuisine des îles" insists on and narrows this connection. The great majority of recipes in "La cuisine des îles" specify creoleness in the title or in a parenthetical "(Creole recipe)" following the title. For Mayard, the "pays chauds," island food, and the Creole overlap in the Americas. Indeed, she seems to use all three designations interchangeably as she includes South and Central American dishes like "Chanfaina" in "La cuisine des îles" with the same "Creole recipe" designation as Caribbean classics like "Hariaco" (her spelling for ajiaco) and "Chutney d'ananas verts." "Pays chauds" also extends around the globe, including the tropical islands in the Indian Ocean that appear in a subsection of "Cuisine des îles," "Cuisine de l'île Bourbon et de la Réunion" as well as throughout the cookbook. While these groupings repeat the colonial tropicalism that saw the "hot countries" needing the "civilizing work" of the colonial enterprise, they also pick up on the uses of tropicalism as a unifying resistance to colonial and neocolonial rule, perhaps most evident in Suzanne and Aimé

Césaire's choice of *Tropiques* as the title for the journal they launched in Martinique in 1941.

Mayard's section on "a colonial dinner," composed of dishes from Latin America, the French holdings in the Indian Ocean and Southeast Asia, and France,[30] combined with her opening odes to French culinary literature, and French recipes from "Spinach [épinards] au gratin" through the various beef daubes, to the almond, walnut, and apricot recipes in the dessert section,[31] might suggest a belated attachment to French colonial rule and the versions of tropicalism in which abundant flora and fauna benefited from European management. However, the temporal distance from French colonial rule in Haiti allows Mayard's Francophilia to function less as nostalgic attachment to France as the "mother country" than as a claim to the inheritance of an haute cuisine that distinguishes Haiti from its more recent occupiers. By excluding recipes from Francophone West Africa and including one from Latin America in her "colonial dinner," rather than mapping her book onto the French empire, Mayard insists on "the hot countries" to which Haiti belongs as a tropical band that extends far from Woodrow Wilson's "neighborhood."

As Mayard traces the origins of Haitian culinary culture to France, Africa, other parts of Europe, Latin America, and also Asia, she both anticipates the attention of Glissantian créolité to the multiple points of origin and intersection for Caribbean people and shows how the embrace of multiplicity can risk diminishing or turning away from specificity.[32] Though her entries on yuca [manioc] and chayote [chayotte ou mirliton] both mention that the plants are native to the Antilles, her history of peppers [les piments] describes them as "very unique to hot countries" but does not mention that they are indigenous to the Caribbean, and none of the entries says anything about yuca, chayote, or peppers being central to Indigenous cooking (30). Her history of "yams [ignams]" extolls the quality of "Chinese yams" but traces their arrival in Haiti not through Chinese Haitians and their foods but through France (37), and her entry for "Oriental rice" makes no historical connection beyond that in the name. Similarly, while she names the

Reunion Islands and Madagascar in the titles of recipes that often have, in their titles or ingredients, Indian elements like curry, she never details how the French colonial enterprise in the Indian Ocean relates to Indo-Haitian foods, and never says anything about whether the several curry dishes and the kedgeree and pilau recipes relate to any other Indo-Haitian culinary history. While relatively frequent and clear, Mayard's mentions of Africa exemplify how, as Condé notes of Moravia's novel, it is possible to hold up an African heritage that "disappears in spite of the incessant references made to it" (90). Like Dominican cookbook authors, Mayard uses "Egypte" as the placeholder for Africa. For example, she lists Egypt as an origin point for okra [gombo], but instead of noting the West African origins of the word "gombo," links it only to the Brazilian "quingombo" (33) without making any connections between Brazil and Haiti. The parallels she elaborates are instead between Egypt and Syria, Greece, and Turkey, thus associating Egypt with the Cradle of Civilization rather than "Black Africa" to claim African history not through Haiti's rural poor and the legacy of slavery but through North African royalty.

All of Mayard's histories and recipes skip over the significant period between origin and 1940: the Columbian Exchange and Triangle Trade; slavery and the plantation period when enslaved cooks developed ways to, in the words of the twenty-first-century Haitian cookbook author Nadege Fleurimond, "bridge the culinary gap between the plate of the white plantation owner and that of the slave" (18). Mayard does not include a recipe for doukounou, the dish that exemplifies the bridging for Fleurimond. She does include recipes in the yuca [manioc] section that call for "Gari," but she only alludes to the fact that gari is the preferred term in Haiti while variations on the indigenous caçabi prevail in the rest of the Caribbean and includes no explanation that "garri" is a West African term for powdered foodstuffs (flours).

Mayard does not try to introduce readers to a more peasant-based, Afro-Indigenous set of recipes or associations than they already have, and she does not use her attention to the "hot countries" to explain how Haitian cuisine links to others through anything besides latitude. What

> ### Galette de Gari (Gari Cake)
>
> *Mettre une quantité de Gari dans un plat creux, un légumier de préférence, bien arroser d'eau, remuer et saler. Se fait dans la poêle, avec un peu de beurre, comme de petites crêpes.*
>
> Put a quantity of Gari in a deep dish, preferably a vegetable dish, sprinkle well with water, stir and salt. To be made in pan, with a little butter, like small crepes.
>
> —MAYARD, *CUISINE DES PAYS CHAUDS*, 50

she does do is to codify how, in 1940, elite Haitian women knew, enjoyed, and expected to have prepared in their kitchens a significant range of dishes from both French and Afro-Indigenous traditions along with others originating from other European, Chinese, Indian, and Latin American cuisines. Mayard implicitly offers a Haitianness that, in the care of elite Haitian women who know what they are doing, inscribes a Haitian Creoleness that embraces multiple origins and intersections—de-specifying Blackness and the specific histories that brought it to Haiti and then divided it between Mulatto and Black—and is localized in a Caribbean nation coming into its own, although explicitly she centers not Haitianness but tropicalism. This is the master sauce that the next generation of Haitian cookbook writers could augment as they brought more women together in the concoction of a more singularly and explicitly Haitian cuisine that continues to resist narratives of racial division and to purvey those of elitism.

Haitian Culinary History Begins in Haiti: Niniche Viard Gaillard's *Recettes simples de cuisine haitienne*

Gaillard never acknowledges building on her predecessor's work, but her 1950 *Recettes simples de cuisine haïtienne* develops, expands, and names the Haitian culinary archive inaugurated by Mayard, where

Francophilic tropicalism and haïtiannité combine in a Haitian national cuisine constructed with minimal historicization. However, Gaillard notably expands both the French- and the African-influenced recipes in the Haitian culinary archive and uses both French and Creole culinary terms, belying even Bellegarde-Smith's nuanced version of the divided Haiti narrative in which, in the first half of the twentieth century, "class antagonisms were reflected in the divisions between French-speaking and Creole-speaking populations, Black and mulatto color distinctions, Roman Catholic and vodou religious groups and African and Western cultural influences" (*Haiti: Citadel Breached*, 95). Gaillard's Haitian cuisine is one of a nation unified in tastes that emanate from elite homes and invite ever more women to enter them.

When *Recettes simples de cuisine haïtienne* was published in 1950, the "Revolution of 1946" had already led to the election of Haiti's first noiriste president, Dumaris Estimé. Estimé had moved, over the course of his presidency, from Black Nationalist rhetoric and deeply progressive labor reforms to anti-communist rhetoric and financial difficulty. Estimé was replaced in 1950 by Paul Magloire, who had risen through the military and represented a more elitist version of noirisme.[33] Both Estimé and Magloire advanced the position of Creole as a language of the elite and the government as well as the language of the peasantry, a project started by Georges Sylvain, father of LFAS-founder Sylvain-Bouchereau. Estimé supported the development of the Faublas-Pressoir orthography, and Magloire officially adopted it, paving the way for the eventual adoption of Creole (now Kreyòl) as an official language of Haiti. Gaillard's expansive vision of elite Haitian women working together, using Creole and French, preparing dishes whose Haitianness does not admit internal divisions, serves up this period not as an ascendancy of noirisme but as a unification under elitist largesse.

Like Mayard's, Gaillard's introductory sections clearly address an upper-class woman who has servants but also takes, or wants to take, a role in planning and overseeing the family meals. Gaillard describes the work of this woman as primarily one of organizing and ordering: "Working in the kitchen, the woman must remember and gently remind her entourage that disorder, dirty things piled up, bring discouragement, fatigue, and botheration" for "it is in the kitchen that one makes known one's good taste and administrative principles" (vii). Gaillard frequently speaks directly to her readers as "my sisters," taking on the role of the eldest, writing, for instance, "The proportions and the ingredients needed to complete my recipes are not listed before the recipes themselves in order to oblige my sisters to study them and to understand them better" (xi). Unsurprisingly, Gaillard does not mention her sisters' ever actually preparing her recipes, and it is unclear what would make them, in the terms of her title, "simple." The imprecision of many recipes—the recipe for the corn drink "acassan," for example, does not give any amounts or volumes—indicates that the persons doing the actual cooking may not be reading the cookbook at all and are likely to be drawing on years of home training and professional experience in the kitchens where they work. *Recettes simples de cuisine haïtienne* demonstrates that the work of Caribbean cookbooks in the first half of the twentieth century was often to bridge the gap between elite housewives and cooks, balancing between authorizing the national cultural value of the knowledge and skills of cooks and helping the "mistress of the house [maîtresse de maison]" direct and order her staff.

Establishing the usefulness of her cookbook, Gaillard suggests that the overtaxed housewife should "give herself a cookbook with simple and easy recipes." Her subsequent question, "Will you ask me which book to choose? Are there so many?" begs the negative answer that confirms the choice of *Recettes simples de cuisine haïtienne*. At the same time, the formulation of the question as rhetorical clarifies that Gaillard is asking not just about an easy cookbook—by 1950 a great number of French cookbooks professed simplicity and facility—but about an easy *Haitian* cookbook. Independent Haitian women need to be able to choose independent Haitian culinary instruction. The questions also demonstrate that Gaillard either did not know of *Cuisine des pays chauds* or did not consider it simple or Haitian.

Simple Haitian recipes, for Gaillard, involve asserting a place for Haitian cuisine in an international order in which race is a subtext of

Acassan (Acassan)

Le préparer depuis l'après-midi ou le soir. Faire bouillir dans un profond faitout aluminium une bonne quantité d'eau. Y jeter la quantité désirée de maïs en grains; et laisser tremper dans cette eau toute la nuit. Le matin, jeter l'eau, laver le maïs à nouveau, le piler au mortier, au moulin ou au mixeur. Mettre le tout dans le faitout, ajouter de l'eau, remuer avec une grande cuillère de bois. Passer cette bouillie dans un fin tamis. Repiler le marc, le jeter à nouveau dans le même liquide déjà passé. Remuer, le repasser. Une 3ème fois repiler et continuer la même opération, plusieurs autres fois jusqu'à ce qu'il ne reste dans le marc que les déchets de paille de maïs dans le tamis. Epicer à la cannelle, à l'anis étoilé, à l'écorce de citron en rubans. Mettre sur bon feu; remuer sans arrêt comme une bouillie, voilà l'acassan prêt à servir.

Prepare starting in the afternoon or the evening. Boil in a deep aluminum pot a good quantity of water. Add the desired quantity of corn kernel; leave it to soak in this water all night. In the morning, toss the water, wash the corn again, put it in the mortar, grinder, or mixer. Put it all into the pot, add water, stir with a big wooden spoon. Strain this boiled mixture through a fine mesh strainer. Gather the grounds, put it into the same water in which it was previously cooked. Stir, strain. A third time gather and continue the same operation, several more times until the only thing left in the grounds is the leftover corn straw in the strainer. Spice with cinnamon, star anis, and ribbons of lemon peel. Put over a good fire, stir constantly like a porridge, voilà the acassan is ready to serve.

—GAILLARD, *RECETTES SIMPLES DE CUISINE HAÏTIENNE*, 37–38

regional and national affiliation and placement. Unlike Mayard, Gaillard maintains a standardized organization and voice. The introductory material in *Recettes simples de cuisine haïtienne* contains instructions in the order of a meal with guests, "a little savoir faire at the table" for setting and seating, sample menus for various occasions, "protocol for serving," "on the washing of the dishes," and "kitchen vocabulary." Gaillard follows the alphabetical organization of the classic French encyclopedic cookbook *Larousse gastronomique*.[34] Along with an order more

French and Francophile than Mayard's, Gaillard includes, and even praises, dishes made with imported products, including a whole section on "preparations with canned fish" that starts, "In addition to our fresh fish, we consume much canned fish that comes to us from the coasts of the United States and from Europe in barrels, in cans, and in cases" (301). Gaillard even at times favors Europeanized ingredients over similar ones associated with Haiti, for example using the Europeanized "potato [pomme de terre]" as the reference point for how to cook Caribbean sweet potatoes [patates] (259). However, Gaillard does not prioritize French techniques or tools—the recipe for acassan equalizes "the mortar, grinder, or mixer"—and she asserts the superiority of some indigenous or indigenized Haitian ingredients and preparations. Gaillard's entry for "coffee," for example, asserts that "Haitian coffee is the best in the entire world and we Haitians, we have the reputation of drinking real, good coffee and knowing how to filter the best coffee," and her entry for "oysters" mentions French oysters but sings the praises of Haitian ones: "The most highly esteemed are those of Cancale or Varennes in France. But I recommend to you the oysters of Haiti, little but fresh and agreeable. The gourmets of the Southern region of Haiti love fried foods and have found for consumers a formula all their own to prepare them specially under the title 'huîtres marinées'" (187). The few recipes for which Gaillard gives taste evaluations are all Haitian: "Croquette de manioc par la cassava" ends with "Exquisite" (223); "it's exquisite" follows the entry for "Bobory" and also the entry for "Rapadou," which is not a recipe for how to make unrefined cane sugar but an explanation of what it is and how to use it (341); in the recipe for "Gombo noir à la viande," Gaillard writes "black okra [le gombo-noir] is absolutely local and very appetizing" (171).

Including even less information than Mayard on the origins of foods or dishes, Gaillard does not recuperate any of the Indigenous, West African, or Latin American legacies that Mayard obscured, and she leaves out entirely any reference to Asia and to Chinese- or Indo-Caribbean dishes. However, with an extensive array of Haitian dishes, she offers a creolist position that what is Haitian or Caribbean is what is implanted

Bobory (Bobory)

Le bobory se fait avec le manioc, il est aussi agréable que la cassave. Il se mange chaud et se garnit comme un sandwich avec une farce très relevée, morue, harengs marinés, grillots, cresson, piment doux.

Le bobory se fait en deux faces séparées l'une de l'autre, et se prépare dans plusieurs petites chaudières à la fois, sur un feu moyen. On met au fond d'une première chaudière une poignée de manioc préparé. Avec la main, donner à ce manioc la forme du fond des chaudières. Puisqu'il faut un minimum de 2 chaudières, pendant qu'une face cuit, on prépare la 2ème face dans la deuxième chaudière. On laisse cuire. Prendre la 1ère face grillée qu'on suppose être déjà cuite, la déposer sur la 2ème face non-grillée dans la 2ème chaudière et l'on recommence à mettre du manioc préparé dans la 1ère chaudière. On sert le bobory sandwich de la 2ème, on y met encore le manioc préparé et ainsi de suite. Encore chaud on le garnit de tout ce qu'on veut, c'est exquis.

Bobory is made with manioc, it is as agreeable as cassava. It is eaten hot and topped like a sandwich with a very strong filling, salt cod, marinated herring, grillots, watercress, sweet peppers.

Bobory is made on two open faces and is prepared in several small pans at once, over medium heat. Put into the bottom of the first pan a handful of prepared manioc. By hand, shape the manioc to the bottom of the pans. Because at least two pans are needed, while one side cooks, prepare the second side in the second pan. Let it cook. Take the first grilled side which should be already cooked, put it on its second un-grilled side in the second pan, and start again putting the prepared manioc in the first pan. Serve the bobory sandwich from the second, put in more prepared manioc, and so on. Top it while it is hot with everything you want, it's exquisite.

—GAILLARD, *RECETTES SIMPLES DE CUISINE HAÏTIENNE*, 64–65

in Haiti from independence forward, regardless of origin. Furthermore, by using a significant amount of Creole culinary language, Gaillard taps into understandings of the Creole as a site of mixing generally and of Creole language in Haiti as a point of political convergence between noirisme and mulâtrisme and of cultural convergence between the elite whose education inclines them to French and the majority of Haitians who speak Creole. Gaillard writes predominantly in French, but a comparison between Mayard's and her use of Creole food words shows a clear shift. Where Mayard referred to the French "champignons noirs," Gaillard writes "diondion"; where Mayard used "giraumon," Gaillard uses "jouroumou."[35] In her opening "kitchen vocabulary," alongside "macerate" and "flambé" Gaillard includes "'Marinades'—Haitian specialty that consists of mixing dough with leftover meat or fish, then deep frying by the spoonful. N.B.—Not to be confused with croquettes and acras" and "'Make the sauce'—It's a local expression that means to emulsify or to thicken after cooking. Generally, sauce is made with red beans, a rich soup, or roasting juices" (xxxv). In her encyclopedic listing of ingredients and dishes, Gaillard includes Creole terms that she refers back to French ones and vice versa in nearly equal measure—"Giraumont" says "(see jouroumou)" and "Haricots""(see pois)"—suggesting that Creole is for her as primary as French.

Along with Creole language, Gaillard includes a Creole tale, the story of Ti-Malice and Bouqui, accompanying the recipe for "Sauce Ti-Malice." She starts, "In our Creole stories, Bouqui is the model for the imbecilic and stupid creature from the backwoods. Ti-Malice, his buddy, the model for the imbecile who is also a cunning trickster," and tells a story of the creation of sauce Ti-Malice. The story is written mostly in French, but the eponymous Ti-Malice is a decidedly Creole name, and the story includes untranslated phrases in Creole (371). Claiming Creole stories, and elsewhere peasants, as "ours," Gaillard asserts their exemplary Haitianness and by using Creole language makes creoleness a shared quality of her readers and her peasants.

Nonetheless, a distance between an elite Haitian "us" and "our" Creole peasantry stands out in the recipe for "Bouillon habitant." The recipe

> ### Sauce Ti-Malice
>
> *Faire macérer échalotes ou oignons émincés dans du vinaigre, jus de citron ou jus d'orange sûre pour les rendre roses. Dans une casserole non chauffée, mettre échalotes ou oignons trempés avec l'acide aussi, un rien d'eau, un rien de graisse de porc ou d'huile; ajouter, pilés ensemble, du sel, de l'ail, du piment zoazo ou du piment bouc. Faire bouillir. Epicer au goût. Ajouter du citron, du persil émincé et un piment vert entier. Servir en saucière.*
>
> Macerate minced shallots or onions in vinegar, lemon juice, or sour orange juice to make them pink. In an unheated pot, put the soaked shallots or onions along with the acid, a tiny bit of water, a tiny bit of pork lard or oil; add, ground together, salt, garlic, birds-eye peppers, and goat peppers. Bring to a boil. Spice to tase. Add lemon, minced parsley, and a whole green pepper. Serve in a sauce boat.
>
> —GAILLARD, *RECETTES SIMPLES DE CUISINE HAÏTIENNE*, 172

describes what "the inhabitant [l'habitant]" does to make it in the third person, ending with: "After a good hour, he passes his spoon all the way around to mix in the flours and also thicken his broth, he enjoys this broth with lemon juice after having drunk his rum [aperitif de clarin] shared with the 'dead,' his old superstitious custom" (73). Gaillard is not aligned with the noiristes who embrace and promote vodou as an Afro-Haitian religion, using the term "superstition" with which the Catholics condemned vodou, though her phrase "his old superstitious custom" is more condescending than it is condemnatory. Like this moment within it, Gaillard's cookbook opens a space where elite Haitian women can embrace not only the food but also some of the language and history of the peasant majority, albeit from above and turned with their backs to Africa. That her book has remained continuously in publication, with new editions every few years, attests to the importance of that space for Haitian women, under, around, and through noirisme's rise and cooptation by dictatorial populism and returns to democracy repeatedly overturned by foreign interests and internal conflicts.

Bananes vertes pesées
(Weighted Green Bananas)

Éplucher les bananes vertes (sans abîmer les peaux que l'on doit conserver) les couper en deux bouts ou en trois. Marquer chaque bout de coups de couteau et les plonger dans la graisse bouillante. Quand elles sont presque cuites, en prendre chaque moitié dans une peau de banane, la presser et la peser entre les deux paumes de la main, pour l'aplatir. La remettre dans la graisse chaude, pour continuer la cuisson et faire ainsi, pour chaque moitié. Chaque bout cuit est immédiatement saupoudré de sel fin.

Peel the green bananas (without damaging the skin which must be saved) cut them into two or three pieces. Mark each piece with a few cuts and then plunge them into boiling grease. When they are almost cooked, take each half in a banana peel and press and weight it between both palms to flatten it. Put it back into the hot grease, to continue to cook, and do the same for each half. Each piece cooks and is immediately powdered with finely ground salt.

—GAILLARD, *RECETTES SIMPLES DE CUISINE HAÏTIENNE*, 56

Grillots (Grillots)

Couper en plusieurs parties la chair du porc pas trop grasse. Epicer au piment, peu de sel et du jus d'orange sûre. Mettre à cuire sur feu moyen à casserole découverte avec peu d'eau. Cuites à point, enlever l'excès de graisse ou saindoux, faire rôtir jusqu'à être « grillée ». Saupoudrer de sel fin. Servir chaud sous une pluie de persil émincé et arroser de jus de citron, accompagner de sauce ti-malice, de bananes pesées, de salade de cresson et d'avocat.

Cut pork skin that is not too fatty into several parts. Spice with pepper, a little salt, and sour orange juice. Cook over medium heat, uncovered, in a pot with a little water. When they are just cooked, take off the excess fat or lard, roast until just "grilled." Powder with finely ground salt. Serve hot sprinkled with minced parsley and lemon juice, accompany with sauce ti-malice, bananes pesées, watercress salad, and avocado.

—GAILLARD, *RECETTES SIMPLES DE CUISINE HAÏTIENNE*, 176

Francophile Noiriste Nationalism: Herzulie Magloire-Prophète

In 1954, a year before she published *Cuisine sélectionnée*, Herzulie Magloire-Prophète wrote the section on "Haitian cuisine" for the *Tricinquantenaire de l'independence d'Haïti*, published by the Haiti Tourist Information Bureau under her brother Paul Magloire's presidency.[36] In its celebration of the Haitian revolution, *Tricinquantenaire* performs what Bellegarde-Smith describes as the historical legend-making of the noiristes to create "a myth of a glorious revolution that had been derailed in the wake of Dessalines' assassination, and then re-ignited with Lescot's overthrow" (38). *Tricinquantenaire* keeps alive the "ideological sympathies with Haiti's revolutionary beginnings [that] served as early inspiration for the noiriste radicals of 1946" that according to Bellegarde-Smith "fast lost prominence once the harshness of Haitian realpolitik set in" (38). In conjunction with *Cuisine sélectionnée*, it also shows how for the Black elite those ideological sympathies were accompanied by praxes of Francophilic nationalism. It is thus on the articulations of national and racial identification that I focus in the analysis of Magloire-Prophète's cookbooks.

In *Tricinquantenaire*, even the celebration of Haitian independence from France affirms the connection between the two countries. Magloire-Prophète uses the phrase "national cuisine" in the context of that for which Haitians in Paris are nostalgic "no matter the social milieu to which they belong," as she knows from their appreciation of her cooking when she was there. Haitians authorize her Haitian cuisine, but she also serves "even the French who only knew Haiti from a few rare images and a few brief writings" but who "made the trip with us through their imaginations as soon as they tasted our dinner." Many of the dishes that Magloire-Prophète names in *Tricinquantenaire* as constituting Haiti's "national cuisine" showcase Haiti's Afro-Indigenous culinary heritage: "Acras au malanga," "Griot de porc," "Bananes pesées," "Riz au djondjon," "traditional 'Peas and Rice' [Pois et riz] that constitutes the Haitian national dish," "Poulet à l'Haïtienne/Poulet en sauce," and "a good

Poulet en sauce (Chicken in Sauce)

Tuer el laisser couler le sang du poulet 5 à 10 min. Laver à l'eau froide, échauder, plumer et plomber le corps du poulet pour enlever soigneusement tout le duvet. Laver à l'orange amère avant de découper.

Découper, bien chercher les articulations, traiter à l'orange amère et au citron avant de laver à une première eau froide.

Un second lavage, toujours à l'orange et au citron à l'eau tiède, puis assaisonner. Toujours commencer par mettre le jus d'orange puis le jus de citron, les épices, sel, poivre, laisser quelques minutes dans la marinade.

Si le poulet est tendre, l'égoutter, le saisir à la graisse chaude, le faire revenir, quand il est bien doré, ajouter oignon en rondelles puis faire une sauce aux tomates.

Si le poulet est dur, le mettre à l'étouffée pendant 30 min. ou plus, puis le faire roussir et finir comme pour le poulet tendre.

Kill the chicken and let the blood drain 5 to 10 min. Wash with cold water, dip in boiling water, pluck and blaze the body of the chicken to carefully removed all the small feathers. Wash with sour orange before cutting.

Cut, looking carefully for the joints, treat with sour orange and lemon before a first wash with cold water.

A second washing, again with orange and lemon and warm water, then season. Always start with the orange juice then the lemon, the spices, salt, pepper, leave for a few minutes in the marinade.

If the chicken is tender, drain, sear in warm grease, sauté, when it is nicely browned, add sliced onion and then make a tomato sauce.

If the chicken is tough, steam it for 30 min. or more, then brown it and finish it as for the tender chicken.

—MAGLOIRE-PROPHÈTE, *TRICINQUANTENAIRE DE L'INDEPENDENCE D'HAÏTI*, N.P.

plate of ground corn, well mixed, sticky, well beaten with all its flour—by hand—augmented by a fish in pepper sauce." Magloire-Prophète use of Creole culinary language—griot, acras, djondjon—and the preponderance of provisions and tropical grains—malanga, banana, corn, rice—mark a focus like Gaillard's. In a return to the food independence of Mayard, Magloire-Prophète's survey of ingredients insists on Haitian production, highlighting the range of zones in Haiti to assure that with only local products, "nothing is lacking for a substantial and healthy menu." She recognizes in particular peasant diets that draw exclusively from local products: "Haitian peasants get the best of these rich foods that nature so graciously puts at their disposition by making meals that cost little but are very rich in nourishment." Magloire-Prophète thus acknowledges the culinary acumen of Haitian peasants, counters the image of dire Haitian poverty requiring foreign intervention, and shows Haitian national cuisine to be based on peasant practice, although she does brush over the struggles of Haitian peasants who in 1954 often did not have enough to eat. Only two recipes accompany Magloire-Prophète's story of Haitian national cuisine in *Tricinquantenaire*, "Poulet en sauce" and "Pois et riz." As she omits amounts, does not specify what goes into épices, and leaves out instructions for portions of the dish (the recipe for "Poulet en sauce" has as an instruction "make a tomato sauce"), Magloire-Prophète addresses a Haitian audience already familiar with the recipes. *Tricinquantenaire* serves Haitians at home or abroad not as instructions for how to cook for themselves, but as a receipt to prove that there is a Haitian national cuisine and they own it.

When, in *Cuisine sélectionnée*, she puts together a full cookbook, Magloire-Prophète establishes herself as a member of both the state apparatus and the intellectual elite working to carry on the revolutionary promise. The prefatory material in *Cuisine sélectionnée* identifies Magloire-Prophète in her governmental post as Inspector of Domestic Arts [Inspectrice des Arts Ménagers]. Magloire-Prophète's dedication, however, elides President Magloire, naming instead their mother, "my older brother Senator Jacques Magloire," Magloire-Prophète's colleagues in Haiti's Rural Education program, and the teachers she studied under in Paris. The preface by Roger Dorsinville, President Magloire's minister of public health and a Black nationalist responsible for some of his most progressive stances, speaks to the genre of the cookbook as "civilizing" and praises Magloire-Prophète for adherence to a long history of women's work that is at once traditional and scientific: "Madame Herzulie Magloire Prophète offers us in her beautiful book a scientific and methodical initiation in the art of eating, such as our mothers have preserved the tradition through the vicissitudes and the avatars of a history too often placed under the signs of combat" (vii). Dorsinville's prefatory signature also asserts an association between Magloire-Prophète's project in *Cuisine sélectionnée* and Dorsinville's literary work. In 1955, Dorsinville's career had primarily been in politics, but he had already published two literary works that heralded his emergence as an Afro-Haitian writer invested in both embracing Haiti's connection to Africa and developing René Depestre's ideal of, in J. Michael Dash's words, "a composite and unstable identity" ("Engagement, Exile and Errance," 751).

Magloire-Prophète's political and intellectual engagements, along with her biographical connections, distinguish her from her predecessors' bridging of mulâtriste and noiriste poles, and *Cuisine sélectionnée* does develop a vision of Haitian national culture that is symbolically more invested in Blackness than Mayard or Gaillard's. Nonetheless, Magloire-Prophète shares with them an attachment to a unified Haiti with a heritage that is at least as French as it is African. The title *Cuisine sélectionée* is devoid of geographic or national reference, but the book's front cover features two Haitian peasants pounding fufu, West African style, in standing mortars with three- to four-foot pestles (see figure 5.1), even though there is no recipe for fufu (or tonmtonm, as it is also called in Haiti) in the cookbook.

Magloire-Prophète offers not an encyclopedic compendium to rival Gaillard's, but a curated exhibit. Elitism becomes the basis of her work, which serves to demonstrate the most select of Haitian cuisine. And this elitism is unapologetically Francophilic. *Cuisine sélectionnée*'s brief introductory material ends with seventeenth-century French writer Paul

5.1. Cover of *Cuisine sélectionnée*, 1955. Source: Schlesinger Library, Harvard University.

Scarron's "Chanson à manger" (4). Magloire-Prophète's bibliography lists three French works and one "Canadian" (ix). The balance of culinary heritage in the selection of dishes and the culinary language in *Cuisine sélectionnée*'s recipes are, like those of Mayard, overwhelmingly French. Magloire-Prophète avoids markedly Creole language in *Cuisine sélectionnée*. She even avoids the use of words like "djondjon" that she used in *Tricinquantenaire*, giving instead a recipe for "riz et champignons." When she does use "peas [pois]" rather than "beans [haricots]" and instructs the reader to "break the peas [faire crever les pois]" in the recipe for "riz national" (119), she does not register her use of Creole language as does Mayard (51). Magloire-Prophète does not praise such things as Haitian fish and fruits as do Mayard and Gaillard, and even describes some Haitian culinary techniques as compensatory rather than gustatory. Her note "Haiti is a hot country where there are many flies. We are obliged to wash meat (rinse it in water after having treated it with sour orange, in order to remove all suffocating odors)" (42), for example, not only positions the Haitian climate as less ideal for cooking than the French, but also disregards the citrus wash's benefits to flavor and tenderness.

Magloire-Prophète's inclusion of Alexis Leger/Saint John-Perse's "Eloge du café" just before the entry for "le café" draws attention to this writer who emblematizes Antillean—and international—Francophilia and the ongoing complications of racialized national identity in the Caribbean. Born in Guadeloupe to a French Creole plantation-owning family, Saint John-Perse was a widely acclaimed poet, claimed as a native son both by France and Guadeloupe. Shortly after the publication of *Cuisine sélectionnée*, he would become the first Nobel Laureate born and raised in the Caribbean. He is one of the figures who demands consideration of White contributions to Caribbean literature and of how White-authored visions of the Caribbean often garner international recognition in ways that others do not. At the same time, Saint John-Perse's poetry regularly elegizes the Francophone Caribbean, and "Éloge au café" heaps praise on this product for which, as Gaillard established, Haiti is especially famous. With Saint John-Perse's "éloge," Magloire-Prophète can assert that French and Caribbean letters, tastes, and cuisines are inextricably intertwined. For as much as she prioritizes French culinary legacies and French orders, Magloire-Prophète also shows Haiti to be a source not only of the raw material but also of the innovation that keeps its own and French cuisine, and perhaps most importantly an evolving elite Creole cuisine, vibrant and delicious.

While the titles of many of Magloire-Prophète's recipes evoke France—soufflés, purées, pâtés—and others Haiti—accra, bananes pesées, tassau de dinde—the absence of geographic identifiers in most

> ### *Pâté de veau à la banane mûre*
> (Veal Pâté with Ripe Banana)
>
> *1 lb. de viande moulue*
> *¼ lb. de jambon ou viande de porc salé*
> *épices*
> *6 belles bananes mûres*
> *2 pains rassis*
>
> *Préparer une farce assez relevée avec la viande moulue, le jambon haché, le pain trempé et les épices. La cuire à la chaudière. D'autre part, faire frire les bananes mûres en belles tranches entières. Faire des tas de la farce su une tôle beurrée, les entourer d'une tranche de banane attachée d'un cure-dents ou d'un fil. Les passer au four 15 minutes.*
>
> 1 lb. ground meat
> ¼ lb. ham or salt pork
> spices
> 6 nice ripe bananas
> 2 dry breads
>
> Prepare a fairly well-spiced stuffing with the ground meat, the minced ham, the soaked bread, and the spices. Cook it in a boiler. Meanwhile, fry the ripe bananas in nice whole slices. Make small piles of the stuffing on a buttered pan, wrap in a banana slice secured with a toothpick or a string. Bake for 15 minutes.
>
> —MAGLOIRE-PROPHÈTE, *CUISINE SÉLECTIONNÉE*, 44

recipe titles along with the minimal narrative descriptions in the recipe sections beyond the instructions for preparation brings together and equalizes such dishes as "Soupe gratinée" and "Tchiaca de pois et maïs" that appear next to one another. Magloire-Prophète also introduces new dishes like "Pâté de veau à la banane mûre" (44) that show an evolving Haitian cuisine whose innovations rest on the ability of its chefs to draw equally on French haute cuisine—veal, boiler—on staples of slave and peasant cooking—salt meats, bananas—and on Haitian specialities like épices, which she calls for throughout the book, without ever detailing.[37]

Magloire-Prophète's *Cuisine sélectionée* is not egalitarian, accessible to all Haitians, or fully reflective of popular eating across the islands. It does not align neatly with the noirisme or the mulâtrisme of 1950s Haiti. It is also not dictatorial. Instead, *Cuisine sélectionée* exemplifies what can come from a state apparatus that enables the selection and innovation from what Haiti and the world has to offer and puts it in the hands of elite women.

There Is a Haitian Cuisine, but Who Owns It?

Together, Mayard, Gaillard, and Magloire-Prophète's cookbooks archive an elite vision of Haitian food that offers the first positive answers to the question that Rolande Valme Thevenin and Paule St. Eloi Alexis probe in their 2006 *L'odyssée de la cuisine haïtienne*: "Is there a Haitian cuisine?" (21). Their cookbooks themselves are part of the answer to Valme Thevenin and St. Eloi Alexis's second question, as well, "Where does it come from?" (21). Haitian cuisine certainly comes, in ways that Mayard, Gaillard, and Magloire-Prophète detail only minimally, from the Indigenous Caribbean, Africa, Europe and Asia, from plantation culture and marronage, from "the people" who make up the majority of the population and who are not included or addressed in cookbooks that circulate among the elite. Nevertheless, it also comes from the cookbooks of the Haitian elite in the first half of the twentieth century. That Valme Thevenin and St. Eloi Alexis do not mention any Haitian cookbooks in their odyssey indicates the difficulty of bringing them home from the dredges of dictatorship, the flinging out of diaspora, and the new forms of occupation that have marked Haiti since the mid-twentieth century. It also points to the tendency of scholars and activists to privilege recovering the work of "the people" and to denigrate or ignore the contributions of the elite.[38] Mayard, Gaillard, and Magloire-Prophète's undeniably elite articulations of Haitian cuisine offer not only the first inscriptions of Haitian cuisine in cookbook form, and windows into the work of elite Haitian women in Haitian national culture after the U.S. occupation, but also alternatives to the narratives that have carried into the twenty-first-century visions of authentic Haitian cuisine as always already in need of rescue from outside.

Published in 1955, Robel Paris's *Haitian Recipes* captures the African and slave legacies of the Haitian peasantry in "typical" (read, nonelite) Haitian cuisine as part of the impoverished beauty of a Haiti desperately in need of once and future foreign rescue. Paris, an American artist who taught at Port-au-Prince's Centre d'Art, published in *Haitian Recipes* a collection of her paintings of Haitian peasants, servants, and plants along with recipes and notes about various dishes (see figure 5.2). Paris glorifies the authentic Haitian peasant and describes their "voudou ceremonies" that somehow seamlessly turn out her favorite dishes and bits of folk wisdom. In the entry on "Lambi (conch shell)" she writes: "During a ceremony in honor of the god Agoué who is the spirit of the sea, a conch shell is used as a wind instrument. It has an eerie sound. To cook, remove the rubbery substance. Some cooks wash it with soap to get rid of the grease. Tenderize by rubbing with a papaya leaf. Pour boiling water over it, rinse. Cut in small pieces or keep it whole. Sauté with 'piment', onion and garlic . . . and a little vinegar . . . and a little water. Tomato sauce can be added . . . parsley. This dish is said to rejuvenate octogenarians!" (11–12). The peasant's struggle is Paris's inspiration, as with the painting "Marchande de Poule (Chicken vendor)," with a chicken in each hand, one under an arm, and three more on her back and shoulders (see figure 5.2) and accompanied by text that reads: "(In the chicken business with no overhead). People don't buy dead chickens in Haiti—unless they are the imported kind. They prefer to pamper them a bit at home with grains of corn to make up for the hard life they have running around the streets looking for something to eat, while their muscles get stronger and stronger" (9). Authentic Haitian people and food, in other words, thrive under adversity to die happy, their pre-death rejuvenation sometimes eerily magical.

5.2. Chicken seller sketch, *Haitian Recipes*, 1955. Source: Schlesinger Library, Harvard University.

In the 1980s, U.S. aid and religious organizations' cookbooks started to tell this same story of Haitian authenticity with more of an eye to the ways that, as Amy Wolff and the 1980 Mountain Maid Self-Help Project's *Best Made Cookbook* puts it, "the newcomer to Haiti" can settle in so as to better help the peasants whose proverbs "show great wisdom in simplicity." Listing the English translation of Mayard's *Cuisine des pays chauds*, *Tropical Cooking*, under the prefatory comment "The following will provide additional recipes and information for cooking in Haiti," *Best Made*'s acknowledgment puts Mayard's book on the side of the foreigners "helping" Haiti and serving one another rather than on the side of the "authentic" Haitians who can serve one another in one of their own languages.[39] In the preface to her 2001 *Goût d'Haïti*, French-born and educated Stéphanie Armand[40] mentions Mayard, along with Gaillard, only to dismiss them in her diagnosis that no "authentically" Haitian cookbook yet exists (and her solution that she herself is offering such a book). In an article on the publication of the English edition of *Goût d'Haïti*, Rosny Ladouceur reports, that because "the 'Niniche Gaillard,' 'Mme Moravia' and other manuals speak more of French than of Creole cuisine," Armand took it upon herself to "conceive *Goût d'Haïti*. Published for the first time in 2000 by the author, thanks to the support of Barbancourt Rum it was re-released in 2004 in English with the title *A taste for Haïti*."[41] Armand appropriates "authentic" Haitianness for the French to express, as part of their touristic attachment to Haiti, and with the generous support of local rum distiller Barbancourt for the exportation of that attachment to the U.S. market.

Haitian Recipes, *Best Made*, and *Goût d'Haïti/A Taste for Haiti* include a relatively small number of recipes that are "authentically" Haitian primarily via their association with the Black peasantry. In *Haitian Recipes* and *Goût d'Haïti/A Taste for Haiti*, this is literally illustrated by the images on at least every other page.[42] All of these cookbooks also make narrative assertions of the dishes as authentically Haitian that are rather curiously connected to the recipes themselves. Armand, for example, gives a recipe for "la marinade à l'haïtienne" that starts, "In Haïti, all meats are washed with a mixture of lemon juice and sour orange juice," followed by some meat recipes that do and some that do not call for doing this and with no mention of the Haitian fried specialty also called "marinade." *Haitian Recipes, Best Made,* and *Goût d'Haïti/A Taste for Haiti* suggest a connection to the home language of Haiti's Black peasantry through their use of Kreyòl culinary terms, but the small number of these renders them purely symbolic. *Haitian Recipes* and *Best Made* also assert the authenticity of the majority of their recipes through their separation from a smaller number of dishes explicitly associated with France or with Haiti's tourist industry. These cookbooks include fewer French dishes than do Mayard, Gaillard, and Magloire-Prophète, but they offer no more Haitian dishes and no more Kreyòl food words than the other three cookbooks. When they include Haitian tales and proverbs, they offer truncations and interpretations that often match Western and Christian views more than the Haitian ones expressed in other versions. Armand, for example, includes the Creole tale of Bouqui and Malice (16), but she leaves out the crucial last twist where Bouqui's attempt to stop Malice from always eating his food by making it extra hot turns out to create the delicious Ti-Malice sauce that Malice loves, so that the trick turns out to be not on Malice, who keeps coming to take Bouqui's food, but on Bouqui, who tries to avoid sharing. *Best Made* translates the Haitian proverb *"Nan mitan diri, ti wòch goute grès"* as "Among the rice the pebble taste grease," inserting a grammatical error ("the pebble taste grease") where there is not one ("ti wòch goute gès") (49). Then, *Best Made* explains the proverb as meaning "Without you, I'd never be where I am. Thanks to you I am sharing this blessing'" (49), when "Nan mitan diri, ti wòch goute grès" can mean that the pebble gets to taste richness when it is among the rich, that the pebble learns richness from being with the rich, or that richness rubs off. Perhaps the cookbook writers are thankful for getting to share the blessing of being in Haiti, for a little Haitianness rubbing off, but the cookbooks offer no critical reflection on the fact that their productions of Haitian authenticity are expressly served to non-Haitians by non-Haitians.

Dominican and Haitian Aporia and Other Options

The Dominican Republic and Haiti are hard to read as independence success stories in terms of democracy or equality of class, race, or gender. Across Hispaniola, in different ways, while vibrant cultures and fantastic food persist, many remain hungry, and more are having to flee. Dominican and Haitian cookbooks allow us to see how elite women participated in or worked around the complications plaguing independence in their respective nations. The cookbooks studied in this chapter make no claims to authentic representation of the masses. Rather, they instruct in the aspirations and ideals of small sets of powerful women at pivotal points in the re-establishment of independence and the acquisition of women's rights in the Dominican Republic and Haiti. These cookbooks reveal alliances and compromises that Dominican and Haitian women make to form and preserve domestic independence: how they uphold many divisions of race and class and cross others, albeit from the heights of privilege; how they accept the ironic independence of dictatorship or prepare less extreme alternatives even if they cannot bring them to the table; how they reconstruct international affiliations that elongate and bend colonial ties. They record how to prepare popular dishes for consumption in upper- and middle-class homes and how to claim and reject the racial and cultural associations of foods and techniques with Africa, the Indigenous Americas, Europe, and the United States for distinct national identifications. They show how many different ways creolization can be spun, and how, as much as understandings of creole have shifted over time, they have not become uniform.

Non-uniformity, the possibility of new spins and remixes, is part of the hopeful promise of creolization. Perhaps, with a companion recuperation of the popular majority and a second revolutionary shift embracing at least the middle classes, like the one in Cuba that I detailed in Cuba in chapter 4, or with education, organizing, and time that brings more of the population together in the national project, which I will examine in Barbados and Jamaica in chapter six, recipes for new versions of national independence will yet emerge in the Dominican Republic and Haiti. New cookbooks do continue to be published. In the Dominican Republic, Silvia Henríquez de Pou's *Mujer 2000* series extends the work of Cordero Infante, Ornes Perelló, and Bornia, and historians and journalists are starting to write openly about the African contributions to Dominican cuisine.[43] In Haiti, the first cookbook written in Kreyòl by Kreyòl-speakers, *Ann nou fè konsèvasyon manje*, was published in 2001.[44] The next chapters on Dominican and Haitian creations of the twenty-first century remain to written.

6

National Culture Cook-Up and Food Independence in Jamaica and Barbados

J AMAICA AND TRINIDAD AND TOBAGO became the first of the British West Indian islands to gain independence in 1962; Guyana and Barbados followed, a few months apart, in 1966. By 1984, the political landscape of the former British West Indies looked much like it does now, with only Bermuda, Anguilla, the British Virgin Islands, Montserrat, the Cayman Islands, and Turks and Caicos remaining British overseas territories. Across the now former British West Indies, a new spate of cookbooks appeared in conjunction with independence movements: in Antigua Gwen Tonge's 1973 *Cooking Antigua's Foods*, followed by the 1977 *Favourite Antiguan Food and Drink Recipes*; in St. Vincent and the Grenadines, the 1970 *Tropical Pot Pourri*;[1] in Dominica, Jean Finucane's 1974 *Go On Man, Cook Dominican*.[2] Within a year of independence, Guyana saw the History and Arts Council's *Guyanese Food Recipes* (1967), Grenada the Grenada Homemaker's Association's *Grenada Independence 1974 Homemaker's Cookbook* (1974), and St. Kitts and Nevis Laddie Hamilton's *The St. Kitts and Nevis Independence Cookbook* (1983). The especially large number of independence-era cookbooks in Jamaica and Barbados offer, as I will demonstrate in this chapter, an intimate view of the slow and sputtering transitions of national culture from colonial domination to independence with variable doses of Black Power and transnational commercialism as formerly British colonies finally gained independence in the mid-late twentieth century.[3] In both Jamaica and Barbados, far from being either the beginning or end of decolonization, the official declarations of independence were steps in a dance (of political, economic, and social power) whose rhythms and moves traverse the cookbooks that participate in it. The cookbooks considered here do not tell how to serve up independence but rather how to stir the pot, revealing the ways that Jamaican and Barbadian women worked to negotiate tradition and innovation, preservation and change, in the long and awkward process of ending and following colonial rule.

Jamaican Transitions

In the first half of the twentieth century, led by an increasingly racially mixed upper-class Creole community, Jamaican cookbooks transitioned from hosting the projects of White Creole West Indian women—community building, self-fashioning and "defense of native style"—to offering recipes for an independent national culture that embraces and holds up the creole as the confluence of African, Indigenous, European, and Asian traditions and as the foundational flavor of independence. We can trace the shape and trajectory of this transition across four cookbooks published between Mrs. F. H. Watkins's 1908 *West India Recipes* (which I discuss in chapter 1) and the 1957 *Farmer's Food Manual*, whose publication marks a clear turn to recipes for an independent Jamaica.[4] These cookbooks demonstrate continuity from the work of White Creoles in the late nineteenth and early twentieth centuries. They trace the shifting definitions of the term *Creole* and notions of Creoleness as well as the grip of White Creole culture and power in Jamaica well past political independence. In the decade after the *Farmer's Food Manual*, the Black nationalist recipes that had been simmering finally rose to the top. This section examines how cookbooks configured and reconfigured Jamaican cuisine as the centerpiece of the long British Empire, the new nation on the world stage, and Black nationalism in the new world in conjunction with similar patterns in the political sphere.[5]

Food Independence in Jamaica and Barbados 303

6.1. Cover of *100 Jamaica Recipes*, 1926. Source: Schlesinger Library, Harvard University.

In 1926, Mrs. F. S. Edmonds published *100 Jamaica Recipes*, a collection of Jamaican creole dishes prepared by Jamaican cooks, collected from everyday life (see figure 6.1). Who exactly F. S. Edmonds was is unclear, and the cookbook's assertion of an independent culinary culture rests almost entirely on the provenance of the individual recipes, whose sole attribution is that they are Jamaican.[6] The cover features a Black woman holding out a plate of food (see figure 6.1). She is drawn in realist detail, turning toward the viewer but with her gaze down and away and her dish partly obscured by the title, so that her work, and her personhood, are simultaneously acknowledged and ignored. Between its covers, *100 Jamaica Recipes* inscribes the push and pull of change and

> ### Baked Ackees with Cheese
>
> Prepare the ackees in the ordinary way. Put in buttered pie dish with layers of grated cheese, sprinkle with breadcrumbs, bake and serve.
>
> —EDMONDS, *100 JAMAICA RECIPES*, 18

stability in Jamaican kitchens in the mid-late 1920s. It addresses a primarily Jamaican audience; the often untranslated and unexplained use of Jamaican Creole food language in the recipes and the directions assume that the reader or cook the text is instructing knows the "ordinary way" of talking about, measuring, and preparing such things as ackee.

Yet not all the recipes derive from everyday life in 1926 Jamaica. *100 Jamaica Recipes* exactly replicates several recipes from Caroline Sullivan's 1893 *Jamaica Cookery Book* and reprints several others minimally modified, without attribution. In so doing, the cookbook's assertion of an independent culinary culture re-inscribes and extends the power of elite Jamaican women whose work it supports. *100 Jamaica Recipes* embraces creole Jamaican cuisine in the same breath as it upholds the normative power of European cuisine, as when, for example, the recipe for "Jamaica Asparagus"—made from spinach stalks—names asparagus as the model that "Jamaica asparagus" can only approximate.

If *100 Jamaica Recipes* addresses a secondary audience beyond the elite Creoles whose image of Jamaica as a colonial nation it promotes, it is not the Black cooks and market women whose knowledge the cookbook collects and represents but the newcomers to Jamaica—the ongoing flow of British functionaries and fortune-seekers—who will benefit from information about the differences between "Plantain, Yam, Yampee, and Sweet Potatoes" and the explanation that "Salt fish—a most popular dish in Jamaica made into Fritters, patties, curried, etc. etc. is most delicious" (20).

The 1928 *Peter Pan Book of Recipes* is probably the first Jamaican cookbook written by a mixed-race Creole woman.[7] A fundraiser for the Jamaica Wesleyan Children's Home, the book's selection of recipes for breadfruit, cassava, coconut, and other Jamaican foods alongside those for macaroni, scones, and junket led B. W. Higman to describe it as "a general cookbook, unreflective of any local orientation" (82). A similar range of recipes appears in the 1939 *Sweets, Snacks, Savouries, Unusual Coctails*, compiled by Edith E. Brown and Margaret G. Worlledge, also a fundraising cookbook, this one for the Jamaica Branch of the British Sailors Society.[8] While it aligns itself with a British legacy and European traditions via a line from Shakespeare across the front cover and quotes from Cervantes to William Thackeray throughout, *Sweets, Snacks, Savouries, Unusual Coctails* also responds to the English colonialist disdain for White Creoles. Under the heading "A Jamaican Breakfast" and as an introduction to the section on "Hot Sweets," Brown and Worlledge quote Lady Nugent's 1802 description of Jamaican "late breakfast" that ends with the remark, "It was all as astonishing as it was disgusting." In juxtaposing Nugent's judgment to the taste of the recipe, *Sweets, Snacks, Savouries, Unusual Coctails* speaks back to Lady Nugent's disparagement of the White Creole.

Sweets, Snacks, Savouries, Unusual Coctails is part of the work of community of elite British, White, and mixed-race Creole Jamaicans forging relationships among themselves and with Jamaica.[9] Most of its recipes are attributed to specific women, from the wife of the prominent Jamaican writer and *Daily Gleaner* editor Herbert George de Lisser to several women descended from the old plantation-owning Farquharson family, who were also involved in the first Women's Conference of 1939 and in subsequent women's organizing. Despite pushing back against Lady Nugent's disparagement of island-born women and cuisine, *Sweets, Snacks, Savouries, Unusual Coctails* cannot hide the fact that Dalea Bean's observation that "war-specific social work continued to be the domain of Jamaica's white and near-white women" also extends to Creole nationalism (153). The recipe selection and organization in *Sweets, Snacks, Savouries, Unusual Coctails* show the cookbook's interest in

Banana Custard

bananas and strawberry jam as required

2 tablespoons sugar
4 eggs
1½ pints (about) scalded milk
pinch of salt

Break into a basin two whole eggs and the yolks of two more, reserving the whites to make a meringue top. Beat slightly, just enough to mix the eggs together, and then add two tablespoons of sugar and a good pinch of salt. Beat only enough to blend the eggs and sugar together. Over this pour gradually, stirring all the time, about 1 ½ pints scalded milk. Put one layer sliced bananas, and one layer strawberry jam into pudding, or soufflé dish. Repeat till dish is nearly full, then pour custard sauce, over same. Bake in moderate oven till firm, about twenty minutes to half an hour. Top with stiff white of egg and brown slightly in slow oven.

MRS. H. G. DE LISSER
—BROWN AND WORLLEDGE, *SWEETS, SNACKS, SAVOURIES, UNUSUAL COCTAILS*, 13

revalorizing those aspects of Jamaican creoleness that maintain the existing divisions of early twentieth-century Jamaican society. The Hot Sweets section, like the rest of *Sweets, Snacks, Savouries, Unusual Coctails*, embraces the profusion and volume Lady Nugent objected to but does not offer recipes with the combinations of "hot and cold meat, stew and fries, hot and cold fish pickled and plain, peppers, ginger sweet-meats, acid fruit, sweet jellies" that Lady Nugent worried about (cited on p. 12). As if following Lady Nugent's advice, *Sweets, Snacks, Savouries, Unusual Coctails* carefully separates sweets and savouries, hot and cold into distinct sections. Of the seventeen recipes in the Hot Sweets section, organized alphabetically from "Angel Pudding" to "Zambaglione," only five focus on distinctly Caribbean ingredients—and two of those also call for distinctly English ingredients—and none present distinctly Jamaican preparations or titles. The section on Hot Savouries, with a similar proportion of Jamaican-English ingredients and preparations, has no recipes for hot meats or stews, peppers, or ginger sweetmeats. The inclusion of a recipe from an English cookbook and, in the forward, of the old English rhyme "Pudding and Pie" suggests that in as much as the cookbook speaks to Lady Nugent's critique of Creole cuisine, it does so more by embracing a long English tradition of gluttony Lady Nugent had tried to dissociate from the properly British than by valorizing the foods that come onto elite tables in and through the encounters of Black and White women in Jamaica.[10]

With British and White Creole women leading the publication of prewar and wartime cookbooks in the West Indies, it is not surprising that as the war took its toll in the 1940s, no cookbooks were published in Jamaica. It wasn't until 1956 that the next, *Recipe Round-Up*, appeared. A fundraising cookbook like its predecessors, *Recipe Round-Up* reflects the interest of the pre- and post-independence elite in establishing the national continuity of pre- and post-independence Jamaica. Released in new editions in 1957, 1960, and 1968, *Recipe Round-Up* upholds and reiterates the continuity of the culinary taste and social affiliations of elite Jamaican women during the transition from colony to independent nation. The editions differ little in content, and each includes a preface by a governor's wife.[11] While *Recipe Round-Up* combines some noticeable Jamaican recipes, like pepperpot, with more British and Anglo-West Indian standards, it inscribes a new Jamaican culinary cosmopolitanism with Dutch, Russian, Hawaiian, Spanish, Portuguese, Brazilian, Cuban, French, "Javanese," South African, Indonesian, and German dishes. It also has several Indo- and Chinese-Caribbean recipes. The recipes are not organized in international or multicultural sections but by dish and food type. Though this organization may obscure the Indo- and Chinese-Jamaican dishes and may represent the reach of the British Empire as much as the recognition of Indo- and Chinese-Jamaican women's culinary work, at least two of the recipes are attributed to Chinese-Jamaican women.[12] The named contributors and by extension the audience of *Recipe Round-Up* are decidedly elite, but they

Chicken Chop Suey

4 lbs chicken, fresh and boneless
½ lb. shrimp
2 lbs. bean sprouts
½ lb. celery
1 lb. Chinese cabbage
1 lb. carrots
1 tin bamboo shoots
1 tin chestnut
½ lb. cabbage
2 large onions
4 roots scallion
1 ½ cups oil
½ teaspoonful Chinese powder (Ve-Tsin)
3 cloves garlic
1 teaspoonful rum
½ teaspoonful green ginger juice
1 teaspoonful cornstarch

Slice the chicken into thin pieces and add salt to taste with ½ teaspoonful Chinese sauce and 3 cloves of garlic. Mix together and add the rum, green ginger juice and the scallion. Heat 1 cup of oil and put it in the chicken and shrimps. Cook, stirring for 5 minutes and then remove the chicken and shrimps.

Slice the Chinese cabbage and the other cabbage about ½-inch thick. Add salt to taste and cook in hot oil (½ cup) for three minutes. Add the bean sprouts, sliced carrot, chicken and shrimps together with ½ cup hot water. Bring to a boil. Cook and stir for 3 minutes. Mix in the cornstarch and Chinese powder. Add the celery, onions, bamboo shoots and chestnuts. Serves 8.

MRS. IRIS LYN-KEE-CHOW
—*RECIPE ROUND-UP,* 33

represent a slightly more racially and ethnically diverse set of women than in previous Jamaican cookbooks.[13]

Published just a year later, in 1957, *The Farmer's Food Manual* marks a sharp turn in the genealogy of Jamaican cookbooks. First, it was prepared not by individual or charitable groups of ladies, but by the Jamaica Agricultural Society with the help of the Jamaica Social Welfare Commission, two groups whose work, and leadership, were prominent in Jamaican decolonization and the formulation of an independent Jamaica. The Jamaica Agricultural Society worked to ensure that small farmers—who were generally Black—saw a share of the profits of Jamaican farm produce sold locally and abroad.[14] Dora Ibberson, one of the contributors to the manual, describes the Jamaica Social Welfare Commission, which was founded by Norman Manley, as "operated by Jamaicans for Jamaicans" (176). *The Farmer's Food Manual* formulates the national conception of "our people" as "local," served by public agencies, and in need of political and culinary sustenance in its dedication "to the leaders in agricultural and health services who over the years have pointed to the close relationship between local agricultural production and the nutrition of our people." Penned by Manley, the soon-to-be first premier of Jamaica, and at the time chief minister and minister of agriculture and lands, the forward emphasizes *The Farmer's Food Manual*'s emergence from a concerted effort on the part of local government to attend to "the special circumstances of . . . Jamaica . . . in regard to the foods that we need to eat, with special reference to the foods that we produce for ourselves. It also tells us how to cook them, how to make them nice, and how to preserve their special qualities" (4). Given that Manley, who was himself of mixed race, heeded New York Jamaica Progressive League member Jamie O'Meally's warning to "avoid race issues" in his advocacy of Jamaican independence, Manley's attention to the "special"-ness that attend the nutritional needs of poor Jamaicans offered a mode of addressing the economic interests of the majority-Black poor without naming race.

While Jamaican men working in politics and agriculture provide the initial framing of *The Farmer's Food Manual*, the introduction attributes much of the work that went into the book to women in the field of home economics: Mrs. Doreen Kirkcaldy, secretary of home economics; Miss Dora Ibberson, Dr. Lydia Roberts, and Dr. Helen Abell (9–10). The biographies of these women, only two of whom were themselves Jamaican, reveal the complex alliances and allegiances among Jamaica's independence movement, the Black nationalism being articulated in Jamaica by Marcus Garvey, the social uplift programs of often conservative elite transnational Black women's organizing, and the "family values" projects of many Anglo and American social welfare groups, as well as the governmental home economics and agricultural extension programs like those in the U.S. Virgin Islands and Puerto Rico, whose work often involved treatment of non-White Caribbean families and individuals that was paternalistic at best. Doreen Kirkcaldy, a Black Jamaican educated at the Tuskegee Institute and Cornell University, would go on to work for over twenty years in various government ministries, running the culinary arts component of the Jamaica Festival,[15] managing Grace Kitchens, and leading the National Consumer's League, among other things.[16] Helen C. Abell, a Canadian with an advanced degree from Cornell, only briefly came to Jamaica as part of a career in international development work.[17] Dr. Lydia Roberts was a professor of Home Economics at the University of Puerto Rico, part of the group of American women that includes Grace Ferguson and Elsie Mae Willsey, which I discuss in chapter 3, and whose support of local food cultures often turns out to be predicated on a view of them as primitive, undeveloped, and ignorant.[18] Ibberson, who had served as the social welfare advisor for the British Colonial Office's West Indies Development and Welfare Organization, wrote in a 1957 article in *Civilisations* on "Social Development in the British West Indies" that "social development in the British West Indies works with practically no indigenous population. Children of Africa have lived with us and mingled their blood with ours for three-and-a-half centuries and their middle class is westernized" (173). As much as it is part of the work of independence, *The Farmer's Food Manual* also emerges out of projects like that of the West India Social Survey, the purpose of which Barbara Bush summarizes as being "to research aspects of African Caribbean culture that acted as a barrier to progress" and reflects what Nicole Bourbonnais calls "the class and racial tensions underlining ideas about illegitimacy" and "'irregular' family structures in Jamaica" ("Colonial Research" 451; 42–43). I insist on these biographical and ideological links to show how the projects of middle- and upper-class "propriety" and of Jamaican independence were, in the 1950s and 1960s, mutually supportive.

Its introduction links *The Farmer's Food Manual* to a Jamaican and a West Indian commitment to food independence: aligning local food production with local food consumption for the economic, political, and nutritional benefit of Jamaicans living and storing their profit, families, and futures in Jamaica, with an eye also trained on food tourism as a site of potential benefit to the local Jamaican economy (9). At first glance, the essays in the opening part of the *Farmer's Food Manual* concur in their diagnosis and prescription: there is a problem with nutrition in Jamaica, and Jamaicans can address it through their own food and government systems. However, as Dr. W. E. McCulloch's detailed nutritional and economic analyses of Jamaican food problems and their solutions paradigmatically show, the "fixes" the *Farmer's Food Manual* proposes involve bringing the poor Black Jamaican majority in line with middle-class and elite culinary and domestic norms as they push for Jamaican independence.

McCulloch, a Jamaican physician and a director of the Jamaica Welfare League, a vocal critic of colonial policies, an advocate of national sovereignty, and a social reformer, exposes what Bourbonnais calls "the social and cultural distance between these middle- and upper-class nationalists and the 'common mass' of the island," and the former's desire to develop a "truly national policy" based on their own values and interests (66). In his essay on "Our Food," McCulloch's culinary class bias and investment mark the argument that Jamaicans should eat more meat, more raw vegetables, and less ground provisions: "Here in Jamaica there is not enough food nor enough of the rights kinds of food. In fact, we can say that seasonally there is too much of the worst kinds of food, as for example yams" (71). The singling out of "root crops" and especially of yams evidences an elite disdain for the nutritional and culinary acumen of slaves and their descendants who survived on ground provisions not only because they were forced to, but also because they knew, from Afro-Indigenous culinary traditions, of their benefits and preparations.[19] Perhaps out of ignorance, McCulloch condemns one of the most nutritional and high-yield ground provisions, holding up instead Anglo-American and European foodstuffs introduced as part of the colonial project (beef, mutton, pork) that (we know today) turn out to be associated with far more medical and environmental problems than yams. McCulloch's economic argument, that "white flour at fivepence per lb supplies the same amount of energy as 1/3d. worth of yams at fourpence per lb" (73) and more generally that "the flesh-forming proteins supplied by these [root] crops cost about five times that supplied by flour" (77), without mentioning how the industrialization of wheat is a primary cause of this cost disparity, does not consider who benefits from the selling of root crops versus wheat, or most significantly, the fact that most rural Jamaicans can grow their own root crops while they must purchase white flour. McCulloch's bias is clear when he eschews data in making such claims as "I know no analysis of the cho-cho but it can be safely assumed that it is of poor dietetic value" (82).[20] Throughout "Our Food," McCulloch ignores the significant—and, Manley might say, "special"—farming, nutritional, and culinary knowledge on which the poor Black majority of Jamaica drew to "make do" in the midst of the massive poverty they continued to experience through the first half of the twentieth century. Going a step further than McCulloch, his colleagues Drs. G. B. Jelliffe, D. Bras, and K. L. Stuart, in *The West Indian Medical Journal* article "Diets of Poorer Class Children," reprinted in *The Farmer's Food Manual*, are openly contemptuous of the beliefs and practices of families that "came from the poorer classes and were of predominantly African extraction." According to their explanation: "Large families are common amongst these groups and, despite the obvious economic impossibility of looking after them adequately, much desired. Numerous superstitions foster this attitude—as, for example, the belief that a woman must have as many babies as 'knots' in the umbilical cord of her first born, as otherwise she will sicken and die" (101).

The positions of McCulloch, Jelliffe, Bras, and Stuart exemplify a contradiction astutely noted by Bourbonnais: that while middle- and upper-class nationalists insisted that "the interests of the masses 'must predominate over all others', they also seemed deeply skeptical of the ability of the working classes (stereotyped as ignorant and sexually/ socially immoral) to define interests and act in ways for the construction of a stable independent nation" (66). As with the contributions of McCulloch and his colleagues, most of *The Farmer's Food Manual* holds out an ideal of new Jamaican domestic health that draws less on the culinary and domestic traditions of the Jamaican majority than on the normative exemplarity of the United States and Canada. Even when a distinct food-wheel graphic of "Protective Foods for Jamaica" precedes the American and Canadian food guides in *The Farmer's Food Manual*, underlining Manley's mantra that dietary recommendations should reflect local conditions, the recommendations for Jamaica reproduce the imported divisions, separating out four distinct groups of "other foods that we should eat"—"milk; meat, fish, fowl, eggs; yellows and greens (vegetables); fresh fruits"—and setting them over and above the lump of "foods we all eat," consisting of "tea, cocoa, sugar, ground provisions, coconut oil, flour, margarine, peas, rice" (124). The command accompanying the graphic, "for good health eat one from each group every day," belittles current practice and casts Jamaican staples as an inchoate unordered mass of things (see figure 6.2).

Yet despite the *Manual*'s dismissal of Afro-Indigenous-centric visions of Jamaican food, Afro-Indigenous and "poor" culinary knowledge occupy a central place in *The Farmer's Food Manual*. As in other cookbooks, this happens mainly in the recipes themselves, collected in Part Two of the book, but even in the preface and introduction to that section there is a shift to praising the ingenuity of those cooks who know "the secret of . . . making the most of whatever foods are at hand. Whether it be yam, breadfruit, carrots, mutton, fish, or salad, it is possible to turn out a good product or a very poor one—depending on the

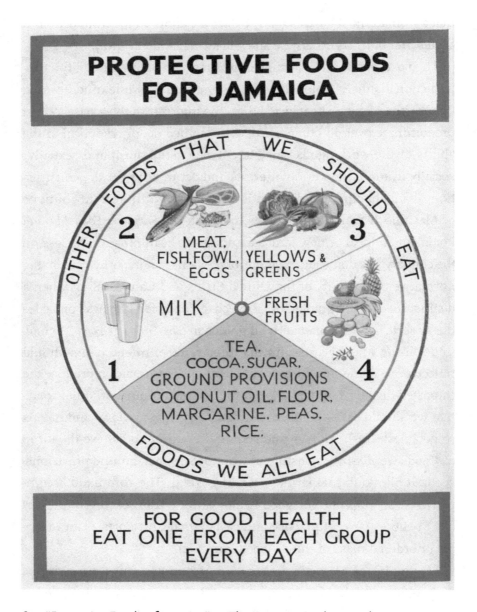

6.2. "Protective Foods of Jamaica" in *The Farmer's Food Manual*, 1957. Source: University of Miami, Richter Library.

cook" (121).[21] That Jamaican women dominate the narrative in Part Two also reminds us that even as class divisions and interests certainly separate women, the kitchen is one of the primary places where women of different classes meet, mix, and have the opportunity to recognize one another's skills and knowledge, and even to share values and practices.[22]

The recipes in *The Farmer's Food Manual*, ignoring McCulloch's dicta, rely heavily on provisions[23] and represent a multiethnic and multiracial rural Jamaican cuisine consisting not only of Afro-Indigenous dishes like "Calaloo and Rice," "Pigeon Pea Stew," and "Pepper Pot Soup" but also Indo- and Chinese-Caribbean dishes like "Kedgeree or Nice Rice," "Metagee," and "Chinese Stew." These, as the title of the next chapter of *The Farmer's Food Manual* asserts, are the foundation on which "Jamaican Recipes" rest.

The order of the first several chapters in part 2, along with the order of recipes within "Jamaican Recipes," corresponds not to the standard European cookbook organization that follows the order of a formal European lunch or dinner (appetizers, soups, fish and meats, vegetables, desserts, drinks) but rather to the Afro-Indigenous organization of one-dish meals that are eaten at a variety of different times of day. "Jamaican Recipes" starts with an image followed by the all-caps A BREAKFAST TRAY that at once describes the image and suggests a section heading. The two recipes on the page, "Grilled Mullet and Oranges à la fourchette" and "Salt Fish and Ackees," are indeed classic Jamaican breakfast dishes. The recipes that follow in "Jamaican Recipes"—from "Escoveitched Fish," to another "Pepper Pot Soup" to "Corn Porridge"—and the next section, One Pot Meals, insist on a Jamaican organization where meals and dishes represent the coming together of indigenous, African, European, Indian, and Chinese. The recipes and their organization in *The Farmer's Food Manual* are not Afrocentric, but neither are they are not Eurocentric. The presence of chapters focused on "Milk and Cheese," "Eggs," "Cereals," "Honey in Dietary," and "Peanuts" reminds the reader that, sponsored by the still-colonial government, *The Farmer's Food Manual* is a production of nutritionists, home economists,

Calaloo and Rice

The use of one pot is the common way of cooking for many rural families in Jamaica. Here is a case where you can cook such a thing as callaloo and rice together to make a rather nourishing cheap dish.

2 cups rice
1½ lbs. callaloo leaves
1½ tablespoons margarine or cooking fat
1 lime
2 tomatoes (small)
1 peg garlic
½ cup water
½ lb. salt pork (or crabs when in season)
1 whole green pepper
12 okhraes
1 onion
½ teaspoon black pepper
Escallion

Method. Pick and cut up leaves. Cut up and scald pork, cut up okhraes, seasoning, garlic, onion, tomatoes and escallion. All ingredients together including salt, butter and whole green pepper and water. Put to boil for about 30 minutes or until leaves are soft. Remove whole pepper and stir with fork or spoon until leaves become fine and smooth. Serve.

—FARMER'S FOOD MANUAL, 142

agriculturalists, and politicians eager to reshape Jamaica's food picture in profound and often contradictory ways, on the one hand promoting the colonialist and neocolonialist overvaluation of dairy products and, on the other, counteracting the colonial overvaluation of sugar-cane products and embracing a continuing connection to Afro-Indigenous foods such as peanuts and honey.[24]

The first Jamaican cookbook published after 1962 celebrates Jamaica's newly gained independence and positions Jamaican cuisine on the world stage as cosmopolitan, multicultural, and marketable. The cover of Leila Brandon's 1963 *A Merry-Go-Round of Recipes from Independent Jamaica* features the new Jamaican coat of arms on which the colonial motto "Indus Uterque Seruiet Uni," referring to the servitude of all Indigenous Jamaicans to the British Crown, was replaced by the motto of independent Jamaica: "Out of Many, One People." Brandon, born in Kingston and married to the prominent Kingston solicitor and sportsman Alphonse Brandon, belonged to the Jamaican elite. It is to and for this elite that Brandon speaks in her cookbook. In her preface, Brandon indicates the source of the recipes as "Jamaican women" who "have a natural flair for good cookery"—notably herself and her friends. *Merry-Go-Round* calls on these women, and their daughters, to embrace the "economic changes [that] more and more demand that young people should be able to acquit themselves in this field [of cookery]," offering them instruction and casting cooking as a cause for celebration and as an opportunity for personal as well as national development.[25] Brandon's address to "Jamaicans living away from home who have a nostalgic longing for dishes peculiarly Jamaican, and also to visitors to Jamaica who have a flair for cooking and would like to try their hands at dishes they have enjoyed here" links the ability to cook to the ability to participate in cosmopolitan exchanges. On behalf of elite Jamaican women and in support their political and economic interests, Brandon's cookbook asserts Jamaican cuisine's place at the international table and Jamaican products' place in the world market.

In an article in the *Daily Gleaner* published upon the cookbook's release, the writer, identified only as B. G., tells the story of *Merry-Go-Round*'s conception at a dinner party at Brandon's home, when "conversation turned to the need for a book of recipes introducing foreign housewives to the use of our canned fruit, vegetables and liquors which are exported. The sale of them would be more, it was believed, if the people abroad who purchased them know how to use the items" (14). The economic interests that direct Brandon's pitching of Jamaican products to North American audiences through *Merry-Go-Round* support the ideological ones, and vice versa. Interweaving economic and political independence, and in good capitalist tradition, Brandon's recipes with their frequent clarion calls for Jamaican products move Jamaica from a producer of raw materials and a consumer of processed goods and recast it as a producer of processed goods whose sale would benefit the Jamaican nation both culturally and economically.

A month later, in December 1963, the *Sunday Gleaner* noted that Brandon's cookbook was "now in use in the embassy in Washington," cementing its placement of Jamaican cuisine at the world table ("Message to Jamaican Women," 28). In translating Jamaican independence for the world, *Merry-Go-Round* also instructed elite Jamaicans in raising the profile of Jamaican cuisine, at home and abroad. In "Cookbooks and Caribbean Cultural Identity," Higman mentions that Brandon presents a particularly "high" and international vision of Jamaican cuisine. Brandon does intersperse recipes for Euro-American dishes such as "Duck in Red Wine Sauce" with those for Jamaican innovations like "Lobster Soufflé with Mushroom Sauce," "A De-Luxe Stew," and her own Jamaican adaptation of "Arroz con Pollo." But while Brandon's construction of Jamaican "high cuisine" exhibits a certain Francophilia in its *souflées* and *à las*, it also works to include and elevate more common Jamaican dishes and culinary practices. Her recipes for "A Lenten Fish Recipe (Jamaica Red Snapper)" and "Jamaica Red Peas Soup" with croutons exemplify how she conjoins "low" and "high" Jamaican cuisine both by reminding the reader that dishes that may seem "high" are actually Jamaican staples and by offering twists on Jamaican staples that give them cosmopolitan "flare" (39; 85).[26] The cookbook as a whole also achieves this combination, for *Merry-Go-Round* includes large numbers of Jamaican "low" cuisine staples from "Codfish Fritters: Jamaica 'Stamp & Go'" to "Curried Goat," concentrated in, but not confined to, the section on "miscellaneous luncheon and supper recipes."

The delicate balance between Europhilia, kitschy commodification of Jamaican tradition, elitism, and assertion of Jamaican specificity plays out not only in the recipes but also in the "Jamaican Proverbs" that Brandon regularly includes at the bottom of a page. These proverbs, and the

Jamaica Red Peas Soup

1 pint red peas
4 quarts water
1 ½ lbs soup meat
¾ lb pig tails
Salt
½ lb coco
3 stalk escallion
1 onion
1 sprig thyme
1 whole unbroken green hot pepper

METHOD

Place soup meat, pigs tails, and peas in a large soup kettle with about 4 quarts water. Boil until peas are nearly cooked, then add seasoning, coco, and whole unbroken hot pepper. Boil until peas are cooked; remove pepper and discard. Remove meat and place in a separate dish. Pass soup through a colander and rub out peas, discarding the skins. Taste for flavour and at this stage add salt if necessary, and more boiling water if necessary. This soup should be moderately thick. Serve with croutons.

Croutons

Cut day-old bread in ½"-¾" slices, then into strips ½" wide, and then into cubes. Arrange on a cookie sheet, and bake in a slow oven of 300 degrees F. until golden brown, turning occasionally, or fry in melted fat or salad oil in a skillet, turning until all sides are golden brown.

—BRANDON, *MERRY-GO-ROUND*, 85

translations that follow most of them, make an authenticating gesture that asserts the book's connection to Jamaican folk tradition and inscribes Jamaican patois and Jamaican national culture in the international exchange of words and ideas but at the same time risks reducing Jamaican folk tradition to a poor, folkloric past from which independent Jamaican is emerging. The translations are meant to convey the meaning of the proverbs to an international audience, but the strangeness of some translations—"Greedy choke puppy./*Enough is as good as a feast*" (42)—and the absence or partialness others—"Behind dark it is "Darg'; before dag it is 'Mr. Darg'./Rock 'tone (stone) in riber bottom neber know sun hot" (46)—might demonstrate authentic sonic flavor but hardly communicates with a non-Jamaica audience. Of course, Brandon's international audience is in large part Jamaican, and the work of translation to carry Jamaican domestic traditions over into the elite and international spaces of the cosmopolitan cookbook addresses Jamaicans—at home and abroad—as much anyone else. Nonetheless, the translations make explicit what might otherwise pass unnoticed: that *Merry-Go-Round* is a work of translation and that most readers are themselves translators. Like the recipes for well-known favorite dishes, the proverbs don't as much instruct in a new Jamaican tradition as they do forge a new relationship to it. As independent Jamaica takes its place as an equal on a world stage, Brandon insists, there is pride and profit in the international exchange of local specificity, as well as in the business of elite women taking up such "low" interests as proverbs and cooking.

While the recipes and the proverbs inscribe Afro-indigenous Jamaicans in the elite space of Brandon's the new national imagination, the section on "Two famous Chinese dishes" marks the inclusion in the "many" out of which the motto of independent Jamaica promises to make "one" not only of people of African, Indigenous, and European descent, but those of Asian descent. Brandon's is the first Jamaican cookbook to have a designated section on Chinese dishes. The moniker "famous" indicates the established place of Chinese dishes in Jamaica. The two dishes, "Chinese Chop Suey" and "Chinese Sweet and Sour Pork," are classics of Chinese diaspora cuisine. The recipes themselves are as connected to Jamaica as to China, calling for a combination of Jamaican and Chinese, local and imported ingredients.[27] The section on "famous Chinese dishes" shows Brandon's work to depict Jamaican cuisine as both multiethnic and native. At the same time, Brandon avoids confronting the racial and cultural tensions that are still

Chinese Chop Suey

3 lbs chicken (diced after bones have been removed)
2 lbs lean pork diced
2 lbs shrimp cut to size of a finger joint
2 lbs bean sprouts (fresh)
black pepper
salt
4 chochos—med. size
cornstarch
salad oil
2½ lbs cabbage
1 lb carrots
1½ lbs onions coarsely chopped
20 stalks escallion coarsely chopped
2 cloves garlic, chopped fine
Chinese soy sauce
Chinese Ve-Tsin powder
½ lb celery
2½ lbs Chinese celery (Khun Choy) optional.

METHOD

Hours before preparation time, chop all vegetables in long, slender pieces. Set aside in refrigerator.

To diced meat add 1 tablespoon sugar, 1 teaspoon salt, small amount of cornstarch, say 1 tablespoon, 1 teaspoon Ve-Tsin powder, black pepper to taste, 2 tablespoons cold water, and 2 tablespoons soy sauce. Mix all thoroughly by hand. Set aside.

Heat a large saucepan with about ¼ cup salad oil and over high heat add the vegetables with 1 tablespoon salt. Steam for about 7 minutes or just until vegetables begin to show signs of being cooked, *but not limp*. Add the bean sprouts and cook for 1 minute longer, then remove from fire.

(continued next page)

> *(continued from previous page)*
>
> In a very large saucepan, heat 2 cups oil to boiling point and add the meat and shrimps, turn a little. Cook for about 5 minutes, then add vegetables. Make a pit in the centre of the vegetables and add the onions, scallion and beaten chopped garlic. Let the meat remain at the bottom of the saucepan. Steam for a minute or two until vegetables and meat are cooked. If necessary add a little cornstarch to thicken sauce. *Do not overcook.* Serve at once. This recipe will serve 12 people.
>
> —BRANDON, *MERRY-GO-ROUND*, 18

very much in play in the new nation by not directly naming the African, Indigenous, or European heritages of Jamaican cuisine—"Jamaican" is the only other location Brandon associates with any dish.

While Brandon's book remained in print through at least four different editions into the late 1980s,[28] a spate of new Jamaican cookbooks, with more insistent inward gazes, took a central position. The first two of these, *Jamaican Cuisine* (1964) and *Banana Recipes* (1966) were published by independent Jamaica's new public relations and media agency, the Jamaica Information Service.[29] *Jamaican Cuisine* and *Banana Recipes* represent the apotheosis of the elite Jamaican early independence efforts to formulate a new Jamaican national culture that both builds on and distances itself from its Afro-Indigenous heritage and often ignores its majority Black and poor population.[30] The Jamaica Information Service cookbooks' glossy pages, full of color pictures, include recipes for such Jamaican staples as pepperpot, curried goat, and banana and fish tea, but their narrative focus on the new—new foods, new appliances— turns starkly away from the culinary histories on which they draw. The introduction to *Jamaican Cuisine* makes this quite explicit:

> Two years ago [in 1962] we reached a great and significant point in our chequered history. We gained our independence. Since then . . . we have determined to make the most of what we have, to promote

our own culture and to make others conscious that we are an autonomous, integrated people with something good to offer the world. And that brings us to the purpose of this presentation. This is mainly a review of Jamaican cooking, ignoring the most obvious and unimpressive dishes and bringing the better ones back to mind. But it is also more than that. It is an attempt—if not the first, then certainly one of the first—to suggest how to use our old, familiar Jamaican ingredients in new, interesting and delicious ways. (n.p.)

Jamaican Cuisine, in "ignoring the most obvious and unimpressive dishes," all but explicitly ignores the bases of Afro-Jamaican peasant survival and sustenance, the "boiled yams, cocos and sweet potatoes" and "rather heavy puddings" whose preparation *Jamaican Cuisine* appears to attribute to a lack of imagination rather than a lack of resources. At the same time, the claim to be "bringing the better [Jamaican dishes] back to mind" erases people and places who have continued preparing such dishes as pepperpot, goat curry, stamp and go, and salt fish and ackee. If they exist only in a distant past from which they can be recovered, then so do the Afro-Jamaican peasant, poor, and working classes for whom they have consistently remained both staple foods and sources of income.

Jamaican Cuisine's "innovation" involves eschewing categories like one-pot dishes and instead ordering its sections following the Euro-American model of meals from appetizers and soups through fish and meat to alcoholic and nonalcoholic beverages. In individual recipes, this move manifests in dishes that combine Afro-Indigenous Jamaican ingredients, though not acknowledged as such, with imported and Jamaican prepared ingredients—such as tomato sauce and Pickapeppa sauce—and cheese, especially the iconically American cream cheese,[31] with names that highlight Euro-American culinary favorites of the day—from the Francophile "Cassava-Cheese Bouche" to "Breadfruit Chips with Avocado Cream Cheese Dip" and "Shrimp Loaf with Yampie."[32]

1966's *Banana Recipes*, composed of a selection of recipes from the 1965 Jamaica Festival's Culinary Arts Competition, whose highlight food

> ### Curried Goat
>
> 2 lbs. mutton
> 2 tbs. cooking fat
> 1 tbs. curry powder
> ½ lb. diced potatoes
> 1 tsp. salt
> 1 onion
> 2 peppers
> 1 tsp. black pepper
> 1½ cups water
>
> Trim, wipe and cut meat into 1" pieces. Season well with salt, pepper and onions. Rub in curry well and allow to stand for about an hour. Heat fat in skillet. Add meat and saute. Add water. Cover tightly and allow to cook on low flame until meat is tender. Add potatoes and cook until very soft and gravy is somewhat thickened. Serve piping hot in a ring of fluffy rice. Garnish with chutney.
>
> —*JAMAICAN CUISINE*, N.P.

was the banana, continues *Jamaican Cuisine*'s project of publicizing and promoting Jamaican culinary innovation while ignoring its Afro-Indigenous legacy. *Banana Recipes* simply passes over and elides slavery in its origin story of the banana: "The banana had its origin in the East, and mention of it is made in ancient Hindu, Chinese, Greek, and Roman literature. It was first brought to the Western Hemisphere in 1516 by the Portuguese and reached Jamaica from Martinique in 1835." The Portuguese did transport bananas to the Americas, but from Africa, to where the banana had spread widely by at the latest the first century AD, and in conjunction with the slave trade.[33] By the late sixteenth century, bananas grew throughout the Caribbean, and their importance in Jamaican slave diets is well documented by the eighteenth century.[34]

The myth that banana production only started in Jamaica in the late nineteenth century and then only for export prevents *Banana Recipes*

> ### Shrimp Loaf with Yampie
>
> 1 lb. raw shrimps
> ¼ lb. butter
> 1 lb. yampie
> 4 tsp. tomato sauce
> 1 gill milk
> 1 tsp. dry mustard
> 1 tsp. brown Pickapeppa sauce
> 2 tbs. vinegar
> 2 large chopped onions
> 1 clove garlic, minced
>
> Put shrimps in rapidly boiling water for about three minutes. Shell and remove black veins. Cook onions with half the butter, turning often, until golden brown. Add shrimps, sauces, mustard, garlic and vinegar. Mix well and saute about three minutes. Remove from heat. Peel and boil the yampies. When soft, mash them quickly with remainder of butter and milk. Beat until light and fluffy. In a greased loaf tin put alternate layers of yampie and shrimp mixture ending with a layer of yampie. Brush top with milk. Bake in moderate oven until delicately browned, about 20 minutes. Serves 6.
>
> —*JAMAICAN CUISINE*, N.P.

from attributing the ways that "Jamaicans themselves thought very little of this valuable fruit" to the class-biases of elite Jamaicans who in general "thought very little of" slave and peasant cuisine. Instead, *Banana Recipes* casts both the consumption of bananas in Jamaica and the low regard they were held in as side-effects of the export economy: "The 'rejects'—fruit considered unsuitable for export—were cooked green or casually put aside to ripen." The proposed solution, tellingly, is not to revalue peasant creations like hard food or the many stews and curries made with green bananas and plantains, but to instead elevate bananas in the Jamaican market and on the Jamaican table through reference to their popularity on the world market. Thus, for example, in the nine

> ### "Scratch-Me-Back" Cocktail
>
> 1 ripe banana
> ½ slice pineapple
> ½ slice pawpaw
> ½ slice watermelon
> 3 oz. sweetened condensed milk
> 3 oz. evaporated milk
> 3 oz. rum
> Ice
> Nutmeg
>
> Peel banana, pawpaw and pineapple. Slice them and blend together in blender. Add milk and rum, then add ice and blend again. Serve sprinkled with grated nutmeg.
>
> Serves 2.
>
> —*BANANA RECIPES*, N.P.

recipes in the "Bananas as appetisers" section, only one title is distinctly Jamaican. "'Scratch-Me-Back' Cocktail" is also the only recipe in the section to include a Jamaican food name, pawpaw, in the ingredients, though the two kinds of canned milk and the cocktail itself are generally recognized as U.S. imports. In the same section, cream cheese is the core ingredient of two of the recipes—"Banana Cheese Dip" and "Banana Balls"—and three recipe titles refer to Euro-American terms or icons—"Playboy Banana Canapes," "Banana Nova," and "Banana Pizza." To make these dishes part of the new Jamaican cuisine cooked by elite housewives and in fancy hotels, they had to be rid of their history as local dishes passed through the work of slaves and peasants and repositioned as creations of the new transnational Jamaican economy that was bringing new things to and from Europe and the United States.

The Jamaican economy did not fare well in the 1960s, internationally or domestically. Economic and racial disparities continued to mark post-independence Jamaica, and the refusal of those in the Jamaican social elite and ruling political parties (generally the same people) to address them led in the late 1960s and early 1970s to the resurgence of Black nationalism in Jamaica, now called Black Power and embodied by Walter Rodney and by Afrocentric Jamaican cookbooks.[35] *Festivals and Recipes*, produced by the United Nations Women's Group in Jamaica around 1970 as a fundraiser for the Save the Children's Fund Schools,[36] is the first cookbook to render the Afro-Jamaican central. It does so by situating the Jamaica Festival as a celebration not only of independence but also of the emancipation from slavery: "Early August not only symbolizes Jamaica's attainment of political independence in 1962, but it is reminiscent of August 1, 1838, which has been celebrated as Emancipation Day" (46). This linkage of Jamaican independence with emancipation was central to Jamaica's Black Power movement.

With the mass protests following the ruling Jamaican Labor Party's ban and expulsion of Walter Rodney in 1968[37] and Norman Manley's retirement speech saluting Black Power, calling "to those who know how much is wrong in this country and to those who suffer from those wrongs, join together to use political black power to make the black man free in his own country to live a decent, a civilized and happy life," the time for an Afrocentric Jamaican national culture had come.[38] Teresa E. Cleary's 1970 *A Cook-Book with Jamaica Run-Dung* (*Jamaica Run-Dung* in later editions) evokes a space in which Jamaican housewives give pride of place to the culinary culture that had elsewhere been relegated to the poor and undesirable underside of Jamaica's new national self-conception. *Jamaica Run-Dung* exhibits what Afrocentrism looks like for race-conscious Afro-Jamaican women, and its reception and circulation show just how far its call resonated, and continues to resonate, in Jamaica.

Jamaica Run-Dung is the first Jamaican cookbook to feature Jamaican patois in the title and to claim it as the language of Jamaican kitchens. Run-Dung, also written run dun (as in the recipe title in *Jamaica Run-Dung*) rundún, and rundown, appears to originate in Jamaica.[39] Generally, run-dung is a coconut water- or coconut milk-based sauce or

Run Dun

1 clove garlic
Black Pepper and
Vinegar to Taste
1 stalk Skellion
1 sprig of Thyme
1 lb Shad or Mackerel
4 Cups Coconut Milk
1 large Onion
1 Country Pepper (Jamaican)
⅔ Tomatoes

METHOD:

1. Soak fish for about ½ hour, then wash thoroughly and remove bones
2. Boil coconut milk for about ½ hour, or until oil is almost formed.
3. Add fish and allow to cook for about 10 minutes.
4. Season and allow to simmer for another 5 minutes.

—CLEARY, *JAMAICA RUN-DUNG*, 29

soup that can be used over or with a variety of fish, meats, and vegetables. The title's patois grammar—in which "Jamaica" functions as an adjective to "run-dung"—signals the book's stance. The native, vernacular, local, and nonelite cuisine is not just the object of Cleary's book but moreover its constitutive force.

Part of the Brainbuster series published by Cleary's husband that also features *Cleary's Street Guide of Jamaican Capitals, Jamaica Proverbs,* and *Jamaica Brukin's, Jamaica Run-Dung* is part of a larger project coming from and working to highlight Afro-Jamaican culture. In reviews of Cleary's book, Alex D. Hawkes writes, "My friends in the book shops hereabouts have long lamented the fact that no Jamaica cook-book was available. There are several Caribbean or West Indian volumes, but often they afford supposedly indigenous recipes, hence Mrs. Cleary's work is a welcome addition in the field" (29); and J. A. announces: "And now a cook-book for Jamaicans by a Jamaican" (37). While claims of firstness mark most early to mid-twentieth-century Caribbean cookbooks and reflect, among other things, the limited circulation of many of these, Cleary's introductory remark that her cookbook fulfills "the need for a truly Jamaican cookbook" suggests that previous cookbooks published on the island were not "truly" Jamaican; that her cookbook offers an indigeneity that none of them possessed. This newly truly Jamaican cuisine stands out for its elevation of cuisine, and culinary language, linked to poverty, peasantry, and Blackness.

Cleary positions herself as, "like a good many of us Jamaican women," an "ardent cook and collector of recipes, most of which came to me by word of mouth, and trial and error" and which she has stored in a scrapbook.[40] Her description of "a good many of us Jamaican women" as both the inheritors of oral recipe transmission and the transcribers and collectors of copies of those recipes locates Jamaican women in the interstices of oral culinary tradition and cookbook publication. Cleary's address to the "accomplished cook" she hopes "will find a recipe or two which is new to you" in *Jamaica Run-Dung* anticipates a readership who turns to the book not in order to replace oral or practical instruction, but rather because the cookbook serves as a gathering space for women who share culinary knowledge acquired through oral and physical transmission and know how to make use of the powers of written publications. Of course, that literacy rates in Jamaica in 1970 were around 50 percent reminds that *Jamaica Run-Dung* is not addressed to, or likely to have been read by, poor, predominantly Black, Jamaicans. *Jamaica Run-Dung* does, however, address the literate Jamaicans who have devalued their poor, Black compatriots and excluded them from the national imagination, and the women emerging from poverty and illiteracy.[41] By offering written versions of information and language likely to be familiar to illiterate women, *Jamaica Run-Dung* might even help women acquire literacy.[42]

Cleary also addresses young women who, as Brandon explained, grew up in homes that employed cooks and expected to do so themselves, but who in the economic downturn of the 1960s and 1970s found themselves having to forgo a cook and perform the duty themselves: "But if you have just acquired a husband and know nothing of kitchen mechanics—oh, pardon me, culinary arts—grab a copy of this book for the way to his heart is through his stomach" (3). Cleary's aside about "culinary arts" speaks to women of a new or aspirant middle class who know how to cook but are eager to elevate their culinary repertoire and for whom the simple possession of a cookbook signals an upwardly mobile class position; that the cookbook details recipes they already know and love is a bonus that confirms the social value of those very dishes.

The local-to-local, nonelite address of *Jamaica Run-Dung* is evident in everything from the assumption that most coconut products are made in one's own kitchen from various parts of coconuts to the specification of both "fresh" and "salt" beef (reminding that there is no default to fresh meat) and to the regular use of Jamaican patois. Cleary's recipe for "Cow Kin Soup" is exemplary in these regards, using Jamaican patois in the title, Jamaican English in the ingredients and instructions, and representing a dish more common to the Jamaican rural poor than to the elite. "Cow Kin Soup" also alludes to the Jamaican proverbs about cow skin—"beg watta cyann bwile cow kin"; "yuh cyann siddung pahn cow bak cuss cow kin"—that remind the reader of the importance of self-sufficiency and of recognizing the value of the often-overlooked elements that sustain us.[43] In giving pride of place to locally grown ingredients and locally developed dishes that have been devalued as the food of the poor, Cleary holds up Jamaican cuisine as Afro-Indigenous cuisine, and vice versa. The recipe for "Curried Goat," for example, subtly repositions even the local recipes that have long made it into Jamaican cookbooks. Cleary's "Curried Goat" recipe is nearly identical to the one in *Jamaican Cuisine* (see above)[44] except for the serving suggestion: while *Jamaican Cuisine*'s recommendation for "Curry Goat" is to "Serve piping hot in a ring of fluffy rice. Garnish with chutney," *Jamaica Run-Dung* counsels, "This can be served either with rice or green bananas or both" (32). The shift in tone—from instruction to recommendation and the discarding of phrases and words that draw on the ennobling language

> ### Cow Kin Soup
>
> Black Pepper and
> Salt to taste
> 1 stalk Skellion
> 1 tablespoon Ketchup
> 1 small Onion
> 1 lbs Cow Skin
> 2 cups Peas
> ¼ lb Pig's Tail
> ¼ lb Salt Beef
> 3 pegs Breadfruit
>
> METHOD:
> 1. Cut cow skin into small squares after washing
> 2. Put to boil with peas, and about 30 minutes later put in pig's tail and salt beef.
> 3. When peas is properly cooked add breadfruit then season and allow to simmer for another 30 minutes or until cooked.
>
> N. B. Any known variety of peas may be used for this soup.
>
> —CLEARY, *JAMAICA RUN-DUNG*, 23

of haute cuisine ("piping hot," "fluffy," and "garnish")—matches the shift in content, most notably the suggestion to use green bananas instead of or alongside rice. That *Jamaica Run-Dung* remained on Sangster's list of the top ten best-selling cookbooks in 2003 attests to the fact that Cleary's recipes for an Afrocentric Jamaica inclusive of the peasant, poor, and middle-class traditions that make up its national table continues to be foundational to contemporary Jamaica's culinary self-understanding.[45]

Following Michael Manley and the People's National Party's landslide victory in Jamaica's 1972 elections, Jamaica's Ministry of Agriculture embraced the shift to the Afrocentric conception of Jamaican cuisine that *Jamaica Run-Dung* represented, throwing its support behind cookbooks like Novelette C. Jones's 1977 *Cook Up Jamaican Style: Eating What We Grow*, "dedicated to that most wonderful of persons, The Jamaican Housewife" and aiming to fill what the minister of agriculture, in his forward to the same book, identifies as the problem that "as Jamaicans, we do not produce enough literature of a practical nature for the use of our own people in their native surroundings" (1).[46] Though the narrative portions on the cookbook are in Standard Jamaican English, "cook up" is Jamaican patois, which is also regularly used for ingredient names.[47] Neville Gayle's introduction acknowledges that *Cook Up Jamaican Style* responds to Jamaica's economic struggle:

> Any keen observer who strolls through our ships, markets or supermarkets these days can hardly fail to take note of the looks of disappointment and anxiety on the faces of just about all the hopeful buyers. The disappointment is caused mainly by the limited choice which they have and by their failing to find some of the things they want. Anxiety is there because of the lagging doubts as to whether the family budget will stretch as far as it should. (3)

However, Gayle quickly adds, "This is the kind of problem which they share, perhaps unknowingly, with shoppers all over the world, even in some developed countries" (3). *Cook Up Jamaican Style*'s solution is that Jamaican housewives help themselves and their nation by taking up the challenge "to use, in tasty and attractive ways, the products of our land" (3). Indeed, with the help of the cookbook, the housewife can "show that, by her skill and thoughtful efforts, she has lifted the humble green banana or sweet potato or yam to a place of honor on the dining table" (3).

Cook Up Jamaican Style includes the revised Jamaican nutrition image that foregrounds local foods like bananas, breadfruit, and paw paw, tying the work of Jamaican housewives to that of governmental agencies concerned with agriculture and nutrition (see figure 6.3).[48] Here, Jamaican housewives and the Jamaican government support one another. *Cook*

6.3. "Jamaican Nutrition" in *Cook Up Jamaican Style*, 1977. Source: University of Florida, George A. Smathers Library, Special Collections and Area Studies.

Up Jamaican Style calls on Jamaican housewives, especially the urban poor, to return to local produce, to revalue ground provisions and cornmeal, but also to be creative, presenting recipes as suggestions and inspirations, as in the introduction to the section on beverages: "It is hoped that the recipes included here will stir your imagination to use local fruits and vegetables, in the effort to keep the family cool, and maintain good health" (19). Like most agriculture department and home economics collaboration cookbooks, *Cook Up Jamaican Style* has ample didactic sections on nutrition, health, and kitchen basics, some taken directly from the *Food Guide for Jamaica*. It is distinguished by its acknowledgment of prior knowledge and creativity of Jamaican housewives[49] and its inclusion of a contributor's name next to most recipes. These features ensure that *Cook Up Jamaican Style* represents less the voice of a government agency or teacher removed from and speaking down to the readers than a community effort: the mutual aid and support of Jamaican housewives for one another. In its pages, Jamaican women appear not as the needy and passive recipients of government aid and basic instruction in how to cook but as the sources of—and as the support for how to value, focus, and renew—Afro-Indigenous Jamaican cuisine in order to attain food independence for themselves and for the nation.

The recipes for "African Bread" and "African Cake" indicate the book's Afrocentrism: *Cook Up Jamaican Style* is the first Jamaican cookbook to name dishes as "African." While terms like "Guinea" appear in recipe titles in earlier cookbooks, Jones's use of "African" in her recipe titles reclaims a general affiliation with the continent through the history of slavery and plantation society and positions Jamaica as part of a pan-African diasporic reorientation to and through Black Power. The recipes for "African Bread" and "African Cake" represent, like most Jamaican dishes, the legacies of Indigenous, African, Asian, and European cuisines as they met through the Columbian Exchange and developed throughout the colonial period. The main difference between *Cook Up Jamaican Style*'s "African Bread" and "African Cake" and similar recipes in other cookbooks (whose names do not make reference to Africa), are the mashed peas.[50] Peas (also known as beans) are indigenous, in different varieties, to both the Caribbean and Africa and have remained common in both cuisines, so that their inclusion is unlikely to account for the titling. The use of "African" in recipe titles represents a titular affiliative gesture while the significant use of mashed peas as well as of peas and other legumes, provisions, and vegetables demonstrates a concerted effort to elevate and even extend the long slave, peasant, and poor practice of featuring them in all dishes and meals. Jones's accomplishment is to present the economic exigence that explicitly contributes to *Cook Up Jamaican Style*'s embrace of "eating what we grow," as an opportunity for Jamaicans to value and uphold the Afro-Jamaican

African Cake

4 cups peas (boiled and mashed)
2 cups sugar
2 cups butter or margarine
2 cups flour
6 eggs
1 ¼ cups raisins
1 ½ teaspoons mixed spice
3 teaspoons baking powder
1 ½ teaspoons vanilla
¼ teaspoon almond essence
1 ½ teaspoons nutmeg
½ cup milk or orange juice
½ teaspoon salt (omit if margarine is used)
½ teaspoon grated orange rind

PREPARATION
1. Clean and chop fruits.
2. Grease and line 2 9" tins.
3. Preheat oven at 350° F.

METHOD
1. Cream margarine and sugar.
2. Separate egg whites from yolks. Add yolks gradually to the creamed mixture and blend well.
3. Add fruits and peas and mix well.
4. Sieve flour and add to it all other dry ingredients.
5. Fold in flour mixture alternately with liquid.
6. Add vanilla and almond essence and mix well.
7. Fold in stiffly beaten egg whites.
8. Pour batter into cake tins and bake at 350° F for 1 hour.

Servings: 12

JENNIFER WILLIAMS
—JONES, *COOK UP JAMAICAN STYLE*, 26

culinary savvy and ingenuity that has produced such Jamaican domestic delights as "Mackerel and Banana Cook-Up" and laid the ground for innovations like "Yam Hill."

Cleary and Jones's cookbooks represent the height of synergy between home cooks and government food programs across class boundaries in the Afro-centering of Jamaican culinary culture. The collaboration never developed into the type of full-fledged food independence movement that emerged at a similar time in Barbados, and that I will explore in the next section. In the late 1970s as Jamaica's economic difficulties grew, support for Manley and for Black Power in Jamaica plummeted, and in 1980 the Jamaica Labour Party (JLP) won the elections and Edward Seaga became prime minister. Nonetheless, the Afrocentrism of the Jamaican national imagination and of Jamaican cookbooks was so well established that it remained largely in place even as Seaga's conservative capitalism changed the Jamaican economy and its focus turned away from food independence programs.

Elsa Miller's cookbooks illustrate a culinary trajectory, over the course of the 1970s and 1980s, from the nationalist food independence project that flourished under Michael Manley to a focus on commercial culinary enterprise.[51] Miller, a professional chef, self-published her first cookbook, *Cook It My Way*, in 1975.[52] Many of those recipes reappear in her *Caribbean Cookbook: Using the Foods We Grow* (1979), published by Kingston Publishers Ltd. and prefaced by "the editors," most likely Mike Henry who was chairman of Kingston Publishers Ltd. and about to be elected to the Jamaican Parliament. *Caribbean Cookbook* balances on the fine line between using tourism to bolster local economies and showcase the achievements of an independent, Afrocentric Jamaica and succumbing to a tourism that is the latest version of rendering Caribbean raw material the stuff of European and U.S. profit and pleasure. A majority of Miller's dishes are what have come to be the standards of post-independence Jamaican cookbooks. She specifies the "Jamaican" in many recipes titles such as "Jamaica Fish Tea" (12) and "Baked Spicy Snook (found in Jamaican Rivers)" (21), asserting the national qualities of those dishes. Miller also locates Jamaican cuisine in a broader

Caribbean context, referencing other Caribbean locations in recipe titles like "Conch Soup (Bahamian)" (11) and "Souse (from Barbados)" (25). And she affirms the African heritage and affiliation of Jamaican food when she designates as Nigerian a green papaya dish "Paw Paw (Papaya)-Nigeria" (13), calls Foo Foo "a well known African dumpling," (40) and includes recipes like "Guinea Hen African Style" (24). At the same time, Miller's credentials, touted on the back cover of *Caribbean Cookbook*, rest on her European training—"Mrs. Miller took cooking lessons in France and in England chiefly to learn to make the dishes she enjoyed to eat!"—and her work in the tourism industry—"She has also managed several small hotels—both here in Jamaica, and abroad and worked in the Catering Departments of larger Hotels." The editor's forward reiterates this marketing of the cookbook first to "our foreign visitors" and then to "those of us who live here," as if making clear that the subtitular project of "using the foods we grow" aims as much at the international tourist market, and a transnational Jamaican economy, as at food sovereignty.

In 1982, at the same time that Kingston Publishers released a second printing of *Caribbean Cookbook*, still with Miller's authorship front and center on the cover, it issued a new edition, titled *Caribbean Cooking and Menus with Barbecues and Special Sauces*, that identifies it as a "companion book to *Caribbean Cocktails* by Mike Henry."[53] Miller's authorship no longer appears on the front cover, though it remains clearly indicated on the inside title page that also lists "Barbecue Recipes by Grace Kitchens Ltd. and Sonny Henry. Menus by Sonny Henry."[54] The *Daily Gleaner* article on the publication of the cookbook, however, omits mention of Miller, reporting only that *Caribbean Cooking and Menus with Barbecues and Special Sauces* was compiled by Sonny Henry, "with the help of Grace Kitchens, Ltd." ("Kingston Publisher Ltd. Launches Five Books"). Aside from the new barbecue section, the only other differences between Miller's *Caribbean Cookbook* and the new *Caribbean Cooking and Menus* inside the pages of the cookbook are that the drink recipes have been moved into a designated section, five recipes have been removed, and one has been retitled.[55]

Caribbean Cooking and Menus is, however, fully reframed as part of the Jamaican commercial culinary powerhouse Grace Kitchens and as part of the shared work of Grace Kitchens and Mike Henry to focus, with the JLP, on Jamaica's commercial growth.

Grace Kitchens, established in 1969 under the direction of Doreen Kirkcaldy "to develop recipes which emphasise [sic] economic and innovative use of locally-grown foods and, of course, products from Grace Brand,"[56] represents the expansion of its parent company, Grace-Kennedy, from manufacturing and marketing of food products into recipe production and marketing that extended in the early 1970s first to a radio show, "Recipes from Grace Kitchens," and then to a Grace Kitchens television show. GraceKennedy itself was by the 1960s a powerful force in the Jamaican economy and deeply invested in the economic success of the newly independent government. However, in the mid-1970s GraceKennedy determined that after "the [People's National Party] leadership had clearly indicated a shift of interest and approval from the 'imperialist' United States to 'socialist' Cuba, there began a flight from Jamaica of those at the professional, managerial and entrepreneurial levels, together with their capital" and shifted support from the PNP to the JLP ("Internal and External Grace").[57] At the same time, Grace Kitchens expanded the community and charitable work of its nutrition programs, relaunched its television program as *Creative Cooking*, and collaborated with Mike Henry in the republication of Miller's work—with ever less credit to her—under the "Creative Cooking series."[58]

In 1989, another "revised edition" of Miller's *Caribbean Cookbook* was released under the title *Creative Jamaican Cooking and Menus*, with authorship attributed to Elsa Miller and Leonard "Sonny" Henry.[59] Yet another revised edition appeared in 1991 as *Creative Bahamian Cooking and Menus with Barbecues, Special Sauces, and Menus*, with a few new Bahamian recipes, again with authorship attributed to Elsa Miller and Leonard "Sonny" Henry and the barbecue section attributed to Grace Kitchens Ltd. Then, in 1999 LMH Publishers issued a third edition, *Creative Caribbean Cooking and Menus*. The copyright for *Creative Caribbean Cooking and Menus* is attributed to Mike Henry and the authorship to "Master Chef Leonard 'Sonny' Henry and Mike Henry," although the vast majority of recipes in *Creative Caribbean Cooking and Menus* are the same as those in Miller's *Caribbean Cookbook* and *Caribbean Cooking and Menus*. A 2006 edition, titled *Caribbean Cooking and Menus, new edition*, is attributed to "Late master chef Leonard 'Sonny' Henry, Mike and Dawn Henry."

In the giving way of Black nationalist cookbooks written by Jamaican women to male-dominated Jamaican commercial cookbooks, we might see the closing of a circle that starts with culinary colonialism and eventually ends with commercial cookbooks published by White Jamaicans who reconstitute their power through capitalism and the food production market. *Busha Browne's Indispensable Compendium of Jamaican Cookery* (1993), positioning itself as the legate of antislavery colonialists-turned-culinary entrepreneurs, certainly uses a label and marketing strategy, for the products and the book, that harken back to the colonial era with bemused nostalgia. But by the 1990s, the enormous volume of Jamaican cookbooks in Jamaica and around the world demonstrated that there were big pots of Jamaican cookery in other hands—from Enid Donaldson's *The Real Taste of Jamaica* (1993) to Ayesha Williams's *Vegetarian Cooking: Jamaican Style* (2013) to the Rastafari-cum-global capitalism of Levi Roots to the diasporic and transnational Jamaican home cooking of Craig and Shaun McAnuff and Nekisha Roachè.

Food Independence in Barbados

The contentions of power, knowledge, and pleasure, of dominion, servitude, and independence that mark Barbados over the past four hundred years have long played out in cookbooks, as I discuss in chapter 2. But while the culinary colonialism of Barbadian cookbooks before the 1960s may have rendered them useless and perhaps even harmful to most Barbadian women, since the mid-1960s, I find a thriving tradition of Barbadian cookbooks that position Austin Clarke's "woman (who does most of the cooking)" not only as the repository of domestic traditions worth preserving in writing but also as a key player in the creation of national culture where Barbadian food and Barbadian cooks are dynamic natural and national resources. Similarly to the developmental arc I have traced in Jamaica, but with significant regional differences, Barbadian cookbooks after the mid-1960s enlist and insert women in the construction of national culture first within the space of the new nation, using and being natural resources for domestic growth and security, and then in the transnational projects of developing food tourism as a national resource and maintaining the national identity of a Barbadian diaspora.

In 1964, two years before independence, the *Bajan Cookbook* appeared, the first cookbook published in Barbados since the 1942 *War Time Recipes for Use in the West Indies*.[60] Its foreword positions *Bajan Cookbook* as a second edition of *War Time Recipes for Use in the West Indies*, but several key features set it apart from its predecessor and place it at the cusp of a renewed culinary tradition. As Beatrice Stow, wife of then governor of the colony of Barbados, writes in the foreword:

> Many of us in Barbados are still using the *West Indies wartime Cookery Book* [sic] compiled from recipes used by well-known housewives and cooks. This edition is now out of print but there has been an increasing demand from hotels and visitors for a Cook Book containing recipes of well-known West Indian dishes using ingredients obtained locally. It is hoped that this new and up-to-date edition will be useful in both hotels and private houses. (n.p.)

Although Stow addresses a tourist and foreign audience, she explains that she does so to offer them a "new edition" of a book already well known and used by Barbadian "housewives and cooks." Furthermore, the titular shift from a West Indian cookery book to a Bajan cookbook that denotes this new "edition" locates the updated book in a Creole rather than an English Barbados. Indeed, Stow renamed not only the new "edition" but also the one that she claims as her original. The paraphrase Stow uses in place of the title, the "*West Indies wartime cookery* book," imagines a cookbook coming from the West Indies, whereas the actual title, *War Time Recipes for Use in the West Indies*, names a book produced not by but for the West Indies, and indeed not for West Indians but for visitors who would use it while temporarily in the West Indies. Finally, the recipes included in the two cookbooks are so significantly different that *Bajan Cookbook* appears more as a distinct cookbook that to some degree draws on and claims the place of the earlier one than as its second edition.[61]

Bajan Cookbook casts itself as a fundraising cookbook ostensibly addressed to non-Barbadians. The first paragraph of the foreword to *Bajan Cookbook* proposes to help hotels and visitors in private homes in Barbados; the second paragraph introduces its goal of raising funds for a cause, something a number of Barbadian cookbooks in the next several decades would emulate. "Our thanks are due . . . not least of all to those who purchase copies [of this edition], the profits from which will be given to Child Care in Barbados."[62] Fundraising cookbooks, as noted in chapter 2, work as much to create community through the sharing of recipes as to instruct locals or tourists in how to make dishes. Indeed, the paucity of explanations, in *Bajan Cookbook's* recipes, of how to do such things as prepare salt fish along with the absence of descriptions of ingredients common in Barbados but not in many northern locations, such as ochra, suggest that, in spite of the introductory gesture, the cookbook is not primarily addressing "visitors" who are new to the Caribbean. Instead, *Bajan Cookbook* shares how particular Barbadians make particular versions of dishes, and buying or owning the book signals a token of membership in community of people who support Barbadian causes. The figuration of *Bajan Cookbook* as written by and for "housewives and cooks" itself groups domestic and professional cooks, mobilizing the movement of women and their work between private and public spheres and perhaps even holding up the cooks who work in private homes as professionals. Furthermore, the selection and organization of recipes in *Bajan Cookbook* shows the Barbadian "housewives and cooks" to be a dynamic group who invent and reinvent recipes as much as they preserve and pass them on. *Bajan Cookbook* offers the only recipes I have seen for such dishes as "Rolled Flying Fish and Melts," "Fillets of Flying Fish à la Ritz," and "Iced Curry Soup." *Bajan Cookbook*'s last section, entitled "Recipes from Old Barbados (which modern cooks may find of interest),"[63] also speaks to Barbadian "housewives and cooks" who unabashedly forget and rediscover some recipes. This section includes a recipe for "Roast Kid" that involves such things as hanging the meat, and is rare in subsequent cookbooks, but also a recipe for Johnny Cakes, which feature in many subsequent cookbooks as both traditional and common.[64] Whether or not Johnny Cakes actually were in danger of disappearing for a while in Barbados, their inclusion in the section asserts the evolving, dynamic nature of interest in and knowledge about Barbadian national (food) culture.

Bajan Cookbook inaugurated the figuration of food as a Barbadian domestic national product, a rhetorical move that Carmeta Fraser would use to propel her push for food independence a decade later. For a decade after independence, as Barbados struggled to maintain the balance of power between its largely Black and progressive political leadership and its largely White and conservative economic power brokers, *Bajan Cookbook* remained the only explicitly Barbadian cookbook.[65] Barbadians who wrote cookbooks in the late 1960s and early 1970s published them as regional rather than national works. Some were written from England, like Rita Springer's 1968 *Caribbean Cookbook*, while others, like Yvonne Collymore's 1972 *Cooking Our Way*, emerged from regional nutrition programs.[66] In 1976, Carmeta Fraser, in conjunction with a first unsuccessful bid to enter Barbadian politics, launched the first in a series of nationalist cookbooks advocating for the political and nutritional importance of using Barbadian raw and processed products. As her career progressed—she succeeded in gaining a seat in the Barbados Senate, became a renowned culinary entrepreneur, and led Barbados's National Organization of Women—Fraser's slogans, "Food comes first" and "Eat what we grow, grow what we eat!," became as iconic as she did.

As a collection of recipes one might use in the kitchen, Fraser's first cookbook, the 1976 *National Recipe Directory*, is a curiosity. While it looks like a standard cookbook made up of various well-ordered recipes, it offers little instruction about food preparation, and its organization follows a semi-alphabetical format that makes locating dishes difficult.[67] It also does not offer the comprehensiveness that the title suggests, as the recipe selection omits many dishes easily recognized as Barbadians' "national dishes," such as pudding and souse, flying fish, jug jug, or mauby.[68] *National Recipe Directory* does little to help the Barbadian woman who has, in Clarke's words, not "retained what her mother taught her" (3). Instead, it aims to place Barbadian women cooks at the forefront of a set of cultural and economic innovations designed to support independent Barbados's emergence from the remains of colonial control. As the editors' introduction announces, *National Recipe Directory* "contains information which has been carefully formulated with you ... the housewives in mind," and the role that it imagines for these housewives is both domestic and national, for "the dishes which you shall produce by employing [the Carmeta Fraser way], will bring pleasure and happiness to your entire family" and "as the Barbadian housewife uses these recipes, she will also be promoting national development by making maximum use of the food which the Government is providing through the Agricultural Development Corporation" (n.p.).

Fraser's work to center Barbadian women in the national project stands in contrast to Edward Cumberbatch's long piece on "Food Development" that operates as a second framing narrative in *National Recipe Directory*. Cumberbatch was general manager of the Agricultural Development Corporation, which had been launched by the independent government in 1966 and charged with "the task of taking the new crops and techniques developed by research and translating them into viable projects conducted on a plantation scale on the 8 plantations which are under its control" (Pilgrim, 59). His primary address is to "the food advisor," a personage who should in turn speak to the Barbadian housewife, whom Cumberbatch characterizes as conservative and concerned primarily with the family budget and the meals and tempers "of her husband and children" (3). Presenting the argument that preparing Barbadian foods "has to do with national culture," Cumberbatch laments in order to exhort:

> So many Caribbean housewives give the impression in the presence of [others] that they are apologising for local cuisine. The menu we use to impress others (especially locals like ourselves) must reflect a foreign flavor. And so often, what the guest really would like to try is cou-cou, pudding and souse, jug-jug, peas and rice-stew or bakes. If we are to project a Caribbean culture we MUST show pride in our own dishes. This will call for experiment in the kitchen by homemakers and home economists; it will mean that the average housewife must become more adventurous, trying well known foods in different ways. (5)

As Cumberbatch conflates "local cuisine" and "traditional favorites" (especially those guests want to try), he makes the "guest" (presumable White and wealthy) the arbiter of authentic culture (to be determined and consumed by guests, of course) and ignores entirely the long history of women's experimentation, adventure, and pride in local ingredients and dishes that made "our own dishes," passed on the knowledge of how to prepare them, and enabled women like Fraser to center women's food work in the economic, political, and cultural foundation of a truly postcolonial Barbados.

Much as Cumberbatch's words arrogate the power to men in government and position women as lynchpins in a strategy conceived and executed by men in charge of larger domestic configurations, Fraser's name on the cover of the book comes above Cumberbatch's and is followed by a series of credentials that underwrite her position in governmental power. The front cover attribution reads: "recipes by Mrs. Carmeta Fraser, J.P., M.C.F.A." and then in a second line "ADC General Manager Speaks!" Fraser's post-nominals confer institutional authority and legitimacy, asserting her position not only over that of the ADC general manager but also situating her recipes as emanating as much from her institutional status as from her position as a housewife.[69] And recipes like that for "Avocado Barbadienne" show, in place of the false dichotomy that Cumberbatch offers, the ease of composing an unapologetically local, inventive, and Francophile dish.

Avocado Barbadienne

1 shell sea egg
1 medium sized onion
1 teaspoon olive or vegetable oil
1 piece hot red pepper
1 large avocado
1 lime
1 tablespoon margarine

For decoration:
1 piece red sweet pepper
1 bunch lettuce
2 sprigs parsley
2 slices of lime

Pick the sea egg well, remove all prickles. Add the chopped onion, hot pepper, and other seasonings. Fry sea egg mixture in the hot margarine lightly. Wash the lettuce leaves and place on a platter. Cut the Avocado in half, pour a little oil over it. Using a stainless steel knife, cut the Avocado in half, pour a little lime juice and vegetable oil over it. Using a stainless steel knife, cut out the flesh from the Avocado in dices.

Mix the sea egg mixture with the Avocado and place in the Avocado shells. Decorate with red sweet pepper and parsley. Serve on lettuce leaves. Use as a supper dish or for a quick lunch.

—FRASER, *NATIONAL RECIPE DIRECTORY*, N.P.

Fraser's few narrative sections in *The National Recipe Directory* tout the nutritional value of Barbadian products and the economic value of growing and preserving your own food or of buying local. Section titles like "Remember, Housewives!" make clear that this information is not new to housewives, though they certainly can be encouraged to "preserve your fruits and vegetables when they are in season and cheap" (50). Fraser's recipes speak to housewives who already have a strong sense of the ingredients and methods, such as that for the bottling syrup: "use 8 oz. of sugar to 1 pint of water. This will vary according to the sweetness of the fruit" (51). She includes well-known favorites like "Fish Tea," "Green Banana Cou Cou," and "Conkies," and new inventions from "Avocado Barbadienne" to "Tomato Pancakes," but what is most novel in *The National Recipe Directory* are Fraser's many recipes using Barbadian value-added products, such as "mellokreem" and "Instant Yam," manufactured by the Agricultural Development Corporation. Fraser shows how to make everything from favorites like "Yam Pone" to her own creations like "Sunny Yam" using the Instant Yam that is advertised alongside them. The many advertisements in *National Recipe Directory* feature a number of local entrepreneurs not directly linked to ADC who also offer Barbadian prepared foods, such as Roberts Manufacturing Company's VelvoKris, ECAF products' "packed" condiments and spices, and Catelli Food Products' "macaroni products," brands like Spitfire and Queen's that make syrups and sauces, as well as Bim's soft drinks from Barbados Beverages Ltd., "the only soft drink plant owned and controlled by the public of Barbados," and Wibix, from the West Indian Biscuit Company. While many of the older and larger companies like Roberts Manufacturing reflect the hold White Barbadians maintained on economic power through Barbados's independence,[70] the development of public manufacturing by ADC and Barbados Beverages, coupled with the mutual support of *The National Recipe Directory* and many smaller companies owned by Black women such as E. Alkins and Son that made the Spitfire pepper sauce[71] bespeak a project of food independence that brings Black women into focus both as middle-class housewives who purchase and serve local foods and as entrepreneurs who create Barbadian value-added products and the dishes made with them. Barbadian women, Fraser's cookbook seems to say, in spite of Cumberbatch's words, are at the intersection where national domestic food business happens.

Fraser's next cookbook, the 1981 *Come Cook with Us the Bajan Way: Let's Eat What We Grow, Grow What We Eat*, embeds the exhortation to cook national food as part of the national project her title invokes. Her byline emphasizes Fraser's continued combination of political and economic service to the nation and documents her rise in both: "By Senator Carmeta Fraser, B.S.S., J.P., M.C.F.A., Food Promotion Director, Barbados Marketing Corporation." In the wake of what Hilary Beckles describes as the inability of Earl Barrow, the first Barbadian prime minister, and his Democratic Labour Party, in the first decade of independent Barbados's existence, "to implement structural changes in the ownership of productive resources" that could check the enduring power of Barbados's White corporate elite, who continued to control the bases of Barbados's economy which themselves remained in sugar and expanding tourism (535), Fraser offers and advocates for a remarkable bridge between political and economic self-control for an Afrocentric Barbados. By focusing, in *Come Cook with Us,* even more than in *The National Recipe Directory,* not on the farm and the factory but on the home where local food is made from their products, Fraser enlists Barbadian housewives in the project of food independence and so enters sideways into the debate about how, and how much, to shift Barbadian agriculture and manufacturing from export-focused sugar and sugar by-products to local food production.

The brief introduction to *Come Cook with Us the Bajan Way* connects preserving traditional foods with developing local innovation through a celebration of culinary work: "This Booklet is but a sample of what can be done with our local foods. We encourage you to serve up your old Barbadian delights and have fun in your kitchens as you experiment with new and exciting dishes using up your local foods" (2). Fraser's encouragement invokes knowledgeable readers, well aware of "what can be done with our local foods," for whom the booklet's "sample" models how a mutual dependence of food independence and domestic skills supports and elevates women's work. The first section title, "Some Old Bajan Favourites," indicates a sampling from a larger group well known to readers, reiterating the status of *Come Cook with Us* as invitational rather than instructional. "Some Old Bajan Favourites" and the next section, "Traditional Xmas Dishes," include many recipes omitted from *The National Recipe Directory,* such as souse, mauby, flying fish,

> ## Cou Cou
>
> 8 medium sized okras
> 8 ozs. Cornmeal
> 1½ pints water
> 2 tablespoons butter or margarine
> 2 teaspoons salt
>
> METHOD:
> Wash and slice okras and drop into boiled salted water. Cook until okras are tender. Pour off and reserve about ¾ of the water leaving the remainder in with the okras. Stir in cornmeal with coucou stick, pressing against the sides of the pot to remove any lumps. Gradually stir in remaining liquid a little at a time, stirring until mixture is thick and smooth. Turn into a well buttered bowl and serve with steamed flying fish.

cornmeal cou cou, and jug jug, as well as some nearly direct repetitions (as with "Cassava Bakes," "Cassava Pone," and "Guinea Corn Porridge"). Fraser balances these "old" and "traditional" sections with ones devoted to fish, vegetables, and salads that offer Fraser's unique creations like "Fish En Nuts," delivering on the promise that cooking what we grow is both a return to well-known favorites and an opportunity for invention. The recipes themselves address a skilled reader who already knows the details of many steps and ingredients that are only alluded to in recipes, like those for preparing flying fish in lime and salt.[72]

The impact of Fraser's project to ensure that Bajan cuisine is prepared by women presiding over domestic production in which feeding the family and feeding the nation coincide was significant. When Barbadian cookbook writers later turned to writing for the tourist market, they often insisted, like Jill Hamilton in *Taste of Barbados* (198?), "I have a strong sense of nationalism in my eating habits" (i). The reach of Fraser's project to involve Barbadian women in the production and use of

> ### Steamed Flying Fish or Buckled Flying Fish
>
> 4 flying fish (well cleaned and boned and put into a mixture of lime and salt)
> 1 tablespoon Bajan Seasoning
> Eschalot, thyme, marjoram, parsley, hot pepper
> 2 onions sliced
> 2 medium tomatoes sliced
> ½ teaspoon lemon or lime juice
> 1 teaspoon mustard
> 1 tablespoon melted butter or margarine
> Salt and pepper to taste
> Lemon or lime slices
>
> METHOD:
>
> Remove the flying fish from the lime and salt mixture and wash thoroughly. Season well with Bajan seasoning, then fold each fish over, putting the tail through the mouth. Arrange in a well greased enamel plate, add a little boiling water, top with onion, tomato slices, a teaspoon mustard and a teaspoon pepper sauce, sprinkle with lime or lemon juice, then pour over the melted margarine. Cover with another enamel plate. Steam until fish is tender. Serve with lemon slices.
>
> NOTE: This method of steaming fish is easy and can be done by placing the cover enamel plates on the top of the cooking pot or in the top of a double boiler. Greaseproof paper may also be placed on top of the fish before covering with the plate.
>
> —FRASER, *COME COOK WITH US THE BAJAN WAY*, 4

local produce and locally manufactured products makes it to the twenty-first century with BADMC's Carmeta's line, most recently producing gluten-free flours from Barbadian ground provisions. The ease with which that project can be co-opted by plain commercialism, however, are clear in the Barbados Red Cross Society's 1983 *What's Cooking*, which includes an advertisement for Wibisco products featuring a Fraser recipe, but also manifests the attachment of upper-class Barbadian women for Euro-American dishes that rely on cream cheese and canned soups and fish that are most likely to be imports. Fraser's success as a Black businesswoman and politician in expanding public agriculture and manufacturing programs and the interest of Barbadian women in "eating what we grow" continued to run up against the sustained economic opposition and power of the private agricultural and corporate sector, dominated by White elites, which held in place an economy that relied on the private production and exportation of plantation products and the importation of foods (Beckles 536–537). Yet, in 1986, public support went with Fraser and the Democratic Labour Party in an election that returned Errol Barrow as prime minister with a mandate to enact radical changes in Barbados.

Barrow's death in 1987 left his economic reforms unfinished and a cookbook on its way to publication. *Privilege*, co-authored with Trinidadian Kendal A Lee, is in many ways a remarkable exception to standard Caribbean cookbook fare. It is one of the few Barbadian cookbooks penned by male authors and the only one that explicitly addresses a primary male audience—the subtitle specifies: "Cooking in the Caribbean for men only (and for women who care)."[73] The short sections such as "Cooking Rice in Bed" (77) and detailed instructions playfully address an audience unfamiliar or uncomfortable with quotidian cooking. Barrow and Lee's explanation, for example in the instructions for coo-coo, of how to cut ochroes and how long to boil them, contrasts with Fraser's assumption that readers already know such things. But like Fraser's cookbooks, Barrow and Lee offer no explanatory remarks about such ingredients as pigtail that one would expect to find in tourist-focused cookbooks. Indeed, they explain in the introduction that *Privilege* is "basically for men like us" (xii).

As they bring upper-class men from across the Caribbean into the world of home cooking, Barrow and Lee insist on the importance of using "ordinary" domestic products, as for example in the recipe for pudding that directs the reader to "peel two or three pounds of ordinary sweet potatoes—not the American yam variety or the yellow caroline leaf type" (90). Their appeal to local culinary culture tied to food independence

Coo-Coo (Barbadian)

Ochroes (okras): 6
Corn meal (maize): 1 cup
Cold water: 3 cups
Butter or margarine: 1 tablespoon
Salt: 1 teaspoon

1. Place corn meal in a bowl and pour 1 cup of cold water over it. This is called "wetting." In some islands, the corn meal is poured directly into the boiling okra stock.
2. Wash and cut ochroes across, discarding tips and stems. Place in two cups boiling water and salt, and cook for about 5 minutes. Pour off half water, and set aside.
3. Add wetted meal to ochro mixture gradually, stirring with flat wooden stick (coo-coo stick) to ensure there are no lumps. After the meal has been added, keep heat low and add some of the ochro water which you set aside at stage 2. Keep stirring until smooth and meal is thoroughly cooked and stiff. Add butter. Turn off heat and serve when ready with boiled fish or beef stew or curry. Boiled sweet potato is also a great compliment. Best when served hot.

A coo-coo stick is shaped like a miniature cricket bat. It is about 14" long, made from wood, and is obtainable in Barbados.

—BARROW AND LEE, *PRIVILEGE*, 86

may be less explicit, and more regional, than Fraser's, but Barrow's name recognition as prime minister of Barbados also renders his work inextricably nationalist. Lee's name recognition as Chinese-Caribbean also merits remark. Both in the authorship and in the recipes, from "Stir-Fry Spicy Pork" to "Privilege," Barrow and Lee present a multiethnic regional and national affiliation grounded in "agricultural areas" and local productions (81). Their stories of learning and sharing cooking, with and from each other and the women in their lives, also offer a rare vision of gender as well as racial equality in the care of the home, the community, the nation, and the region.

With Barrow's death in 1987 and Fraser's in 1993, the intense focus they maintained on food independence and agricultural reform as central to decolonized Barbadian economic and cultural independence gave way to an increasing focus, starting in the early 1980s, on a tourism-based economy. Local food tourism, and purchase of Barbadian cookbooks by tourists, might be more sustainable and more likely to benefit the majority of Barbadians than cruise tourism and the purchase of golf packages and jet-ski tours by tourists,[74] but it is incredibly difficult to separate the different forms of tourism, and the tourist-facing cookbooks show how even sustainable food tourism often relies on the perpetuation of the old colonialist tropes of exoticizing and tropicalizing Barbadian food in the descriptions and supplementary material. Jill Walker's and Jill Hamilton's many respective cookbooks, for example, surround recipes with explanations of "unusual local ingredients which often puzzle our visitors" (Walker, *Jill Walker's Cooking in Barbados*, 3), descriptions of "the sunny cuisine of the Caribbean," and nostalgic evocations of "when all the mouth-watering dishes were prepared in a buck pot" (Hamilton, *Little Caribbean*, 4). In the twenty-first century, however, cookbook writers like Sally Miller are using the tourist cookbook format—Miller's *Bajan Cooking in a Nutshell* is the same three-inch-square size as Hamilton's *Little Caribbean*, with a similar blue background and a similar image of Barbadian food in ocean-themed dishware—to address a tripartite audience of "people in the Caribbean . . . West Indians living abroad and all friends of the Caribbean" (4). The designation of the third audience not as "visitors" but as "friends of the Caribbean" repositions the Caribbean from a tourist destination to be enjoyed, reaped, and left, to a site of interactive equal exchange. Sally Miller's foreword may not advocate for cooking what we grow, but it does focus on local foods when it asserts "People in the Caribbean will rejoice in a cookbook featuring ingredients that are readily available throughout the region" (4), and hints at the value of West Indian food exports with the remark that "the vast majority of the ingredients required can now be purchased in most major supermarkets" (4).[75] Miller and also LaurelAnn Morley in her *Caribbean Recipes Old and New* (2005) also include some of the less tourist-directed traditional dishes like pudding and souse. As they do so, they create new recipes that simplify and speed the preparation of the dish so that it fits with the time and complexity of other recipes in the book.

Whereas the "Pudding and Souse" recipe in *Bajan Cookbook*, for example, starts with instructions to "wash and clean thoroughly with lime juice and salt the intestines of a pig and leave to soak in lime juice and salt until required for the stuffing" (16), Morley follows Barrows and Lee in the inclusion of a mechanical sausage stuffer option and, following the instructions for how to stuff and steam the pudding in the casings, suggests, "Pudding may also be steamed without the pig casings over a double boiler" (49). Sally Miller's *Contemporary Caribbean Cooking* goes even a step further in adapting the recipe, not only instructing to cook the pudding without casings but also offering a substitution of pork chops for pig's head and trotters.

As the pudding and souse recipes are simplified, new dishes appear. Building on the storied traditions of Barbadian culinary creativity such as turning haggis into jug jug and developing falernum, Morley and Miller claim as their own some dishes that were once seen as patently European, likes Sally Miller's Basil Pesto (*Contemporary Caribbean Cooking*, 6). They develop unique creations at once "worldly" and "local" like "Rum Chicken Liver Paté," (*Contemporary Caribbean Cooking*, 24) and "Barry's Orange Fish" (Morley, 92) that can and will be cooked around the world by "West Indians living abroad and friends of the Caribbean" who become a base for national economies, and by Barbadian women who read and write cookbooks. The BADMC's renewed attention to Carmeta's, with new products, lines, and stores launched in 2016,[76] demonstrates the enduring value of Carmeta Fraser's project and the enduring power of the personality she cultivated and shared through her cookbooks. For if I may conclude by reworking Clarke's claim cited in the introduction to this book, "in every self-respecting Barbadian household the woman (who does most of the cooking, whether she is wife, daughter, or maid) [can] be caught... with a cookbook. To read a cookbook would suggest that she had ... retained

Pudding and souse

Pudding, made with sweet potato, is generally stuffed into pig's intestine and steamed as black or white pudding, but it is quite nice steamed in a pudding bowl. It is served with souse (following page).

Pudding:
2–3 lbs/1–1.5kg sweet potato
2–3 green topped spring onions, finely chopped
2 tablespoons fresh thyme leaves
2 tablespoons fresh marjoram
4 tablespoons butter
1 tablespoon light brown sugar
½ teaspoon powdered cloves
1 very hot bonnet or chilli pepper
1–2 tablespoons flour (optional)

1. Peel and grate sweet potato on the very fine, but bumpy side of the grater that gives the finest texture.
2. Mix the grated sweet potato with the herbs, butter, sugar, cloves, and minced hot pepper. Add enough hot water to make a soft but not runny texture. Add 1 or 2 tablespoons flour if the sweet potatoes are not very starchy and the mixture is too runny.
3. Pour into a pyrex or metal steaming bowl and steam over boiling water for an hour or until an inserted scewer comes out clean.

Steeped in tradition, souse in Barbados is usually made with pig's head and trotters. However pork chops, with the skin on, are easier to find and cook and make an excellent, less fatty, very tasty souse. Conch also makes a delicious souse. Pudding and souse is made and sold throughout Barbados every Saturday. Although generally eaten as a main course dish with pudding and pickled breadfruit, soused pork chops make an excellent canapé or appetizer.

Souse:

½ pig's head
3 cups 24floz/725ml water
1 onion
Bunch of herbs
Pepper sauce, black pepper and salt to taste
1 chicken stock cube (optional)
2 cups/3–6 peeled cucumbers, finely chopped—choose cucumbers with as few seeds as possible
½ cup/2 medium onions, finely chopped
⅓ cup lime juice (juice of 2 or 3 limes, enough to give the pickle a good twang)
1 teaspoon salt
Small bunch parsley, finely chopped
1 teaspoon hot pepper, very finely chopped or ½ teaspoon red pepper sauce—adjust to taste

To garnish:
Sweet pepper rings and parsley

1. Wash and clean the pig's head and place in a saucepan with water, onion, herbs, pepper sauce, pepper, salt and stock cube if using. It is said, 'de sweeter de souse water, de sweeter de souse'. Bring to the boil and simmer for about ½ hour or until the pork is tender.
2. Meanwhile, prepare the pickle of cucumber, onion, lime juice, salt, parsley and hot pepper and refrigerate.
3. When pig's head is cooked, strain off the liquid, reserving a little and allow to cool. Remove meat from the bone and cut into strips crossways (each slice should have skin, fat and meat and be about 1" thick).
4. Add the sliced pork to the pickle and mix well. Souse should be eaten within 6 or 8 hours of being made, as the pickle tends to deteriorate after that.
5. Serve garnished with parsley and sweet pepper rings.

—SALLY MILLER, *BAJAN COOKING IN A NUTSHELL*, 50–51

what her mother taught her; that she . . . know[s] how to cook; that she . . . know[s] how to take care of her man; that her mother had [succeeded] to teach her how to 'handle herself' in the kitchen," in government buildings, and in the transnational marketplace where she can boil and bake Barbadian natural resources into Barbadian national resources (3–4).

Conclusion

I STARTED WITH THIS QUESTION: What do Caribbean cookbooks do other than instruct in how to make the dishes they list? The answers are so many and so intertwined that I resist simply presenting a concluding summary. If the opening question was *what*, then the investigation actually delves into *how*: how Caribbean cookbooks do things other than instruct in the dishes that they list and how to read Caribbean cookbooks for all of their instruction in the lives of women, the interactions—across and within differences of race, class, and education—between cooks and mistresses, market women and housekeepers, mothers and daughters, teachers and students, and the work of formulating new and distinct local, regional, and national food identities, of collecting, selecting, and inscribing material for a culinary archive, of articulating and encouraging food independence.[1] Cookbooks are but one slice of foodways and foodwork, they are the slice on which oral and practical knowledge and instruction gets written down. The work done by colonial women of collecting recipes from cooks, companions, market women, and acquaintances as well as from favorite cookbooks or memories of European classics and favorites is at once the work of colonial appropriation—on an intimate and domestic scale; of preservation, even if the most colonialist; and of creation, the creative work of selection, combination, and inscription, which not only carries traces of the unacknowledged voices but also marks the voices, views, and tastes of the acknowledged. These must all come together, in awkward and messy ways, to accomplish the colonialist destructive creation of the Caribbean as we know it and to set up the independence era's creative recuperation of national sovereignty.

Pumpkin Soup

When I first started this project, I knew I wanted to identify one dish to single out for broad comparison—one dish that would crystalize the sameness in difference of Caribbean, Jamaican, Cuban, Haitian, etc., cuisine. As it turned out, this one dish, a dish I almost didn't consider at all because it is so rarely held up by critics and gourmands alike, is pumpkin soup. Like the ubiquitous rice and beans, the subject of Richard Wilk and Livia Barbosa's *Rice and Beans: A Unique Dish in a Hundred Places*, pumpkin soup/soupe joumou/soupe de giraumon/soupe de potiron/caldo de calabaza/sopa de auyama appears in the majority of Caribbean cookbooks as well as in those from across the Americas, from the 1850s through the late twentieth century. Like callaloo, which has gained wide recognition through its titular use by the preeminent journal in Caribbean studies, the central ingredient of pumpkin soup is indigenous to the Caribbean while its method of preparation is indigenous across the globe. Unlike callaloo and several other common dishes discussed throughout the main argument of this book, pumpkin soup is marked by how unremarkable and innocuous it is in the very many cookbooks that include it.

Amy Wolff's American missionary cookbook *Mountain Maid Best Made* is the first cookbook to list "Soup Joumou (Pumpkin Soup)" as holding a special status, with an explanation that states, "Traditionally in Haiti, this soup is the first food to be eaten on New Years Day—to bring you good luck" (21).[2]

Only in Haiti does soup joumou rise to the level of a "national dish," prized in the celebration of Haitian independence on January 1. Soup joumou's status as the dish of January 1 originated on January 1, 1804 when Marie Claire Heureuse Félicité Bonheur Dessalines served it to

Potage crème de potiron
(Cream of Pumpkin Soup)

Potiron: 375 grammes;
Beurre: 30 gr.;
Lait: 0 lit. 375;
Eau: ¾ de litre;
1 oignon;
Sel gris;
Croûtons frits.

Avoir une belle tranche de potiron dont on enlèvera la peau et les pépins. La couper en morceaux. Faire revenir, dans une casserole, 20 grammes de beurre et un oignon haché fin. Lorsqu'il sera doré ajouter ¾ de litre d'eau chaude, puis les morceaux du potiron, assaisonner de sel et faire cuire une demi-heure. Lorsque le potiron tombera en purée, le passer au tamis, puis remettre sur le feu, et incorporer à ce potage trop épais la quantité de lait chaud nécessaire pour obtenir une crème un peu épaisse. Tourner toujours de façon que rien n'attache à la casserole et servir sur des croûtons frits au beurre en ajoutant une noix de beurre frais.

Pumpkin: 375 grams;
Butter: 30 gr.;
Milk: 0 lit. 375;
Water: ¾ of a liter;
1 onion
Grey salt;
Fried croutons

Have a nice slice of pumpkin from which to remove the skin and seeds. Cut it into pieces. Sauté, in a casserole, 20 grams of butter and a finely minced onion. When it is browned, add ¾ of a liter of hot water, then the pumpkin pieces, season with salt and cook for a half hour. When the pumpkin is falling apart, pass it through a strainer, then put it back on the fire, and add to this too thick soup the amount of warm milk needed for a thin cream. Stir continuously so that nothing sticks to the pot and serve over croutons fried in butter, adding a dollop of cold butter.

—MAYARD, *CUISINE DES PAYS CHAUDS*, 92

> ### Soup Joumou (Pumpkin Soup)
>
> Traditionally in Haiti, this soup is the first food to be eaten on New Years Day—to bring you good luck.
>
> 1 lb. beef stew meat
> 1 lb. chicken
> 1 lb. cabbage
> 1 onion
> 3 cloves
> 3 medium size turnips
> ¼ lb vermicelli
> 1 tablespoon lemon juice or vinegar
> 1 lb. joumou (pumpkin)
> Celery leaves
> 3 big carrots
> 1 hot pimento, whole with stem
> 6 medium-sized potatoes
> ¼ qt. water
>
> Use a 9 qt. kettle to boil the beef and the chicken. Remove scum. When the meat begins to get tender (about 2 hours or 1 hour in pressure cooker) add all vegetables. Continue boiling until meat is tender and vegetables are cooked (½ hour). Turn off the heat and let cool. Cube the meat and strain the vegetables through a fine sieve. Return cubed meat and liquid to kettle and bring to boil. Add the pimiento, being careful not to break or puncture it. (It is added more for aroma than flavor) Simmer until vermicelli is cooked.
>
> —WOLFF, *MOUNTAIN MAID BEST MADE*, 21

her husband, Jean Jacque Dessalines, a symbolic reclamation of a food said to be prized by French colonizers but denied to slaves.[3] The symbolism is powerful, although the historical record leaves unclear whether this status applies to the fresh-meat-laden quality of contemporary recipes for Haitian soup joumou—which was often called soupe grasse in early Haitian cookbooks—or to soups made with simply pumpkin and other vegetables also detailed in those same cookbooks. This exception of Haitian soup joumou symbolizes one of the central findings of this book: Caribbean "specialities" and national dishes are as much the inventions of independence and nationalist movements or particular interests as they are preservations or recuperations of precolonial or African origins and distinctions. Likewise, the absence of soup joumou in early Haitian cookbooks reflects as much the elite positioning of Caribbean cookbook writers—like Gaillard and Magloire-Prophète—and the evolving status of standardized dish names and ingredients as it does the absence of a generalized acceptance of the dish as symbolizing Haitian freedom and the return/creation of gourmet cuisine to/for the formerly colonized.

By concluding with pumpkin soup, I want to draw attention to the way that this book engages with the unremarked and unremarkable that are nonetheless central, persistent, important, and emblematic. Caribbean cookbooks themselves have heretofore been largely unremarked, as has the work of undistinguished women who wrote them in colonial endeavors and national independence movements and that of cooks, market women, and kitchen help who left traces of their lives and histories in the recipes collected and curated by the women whose names do appear on the cookbook covers. So I bring out the pumpkin soup.

The central ingredient in pumpkin soup, viz. pumpkin, calabaza, giraumon, or joumou, and in Linnaean taxonomy cucurbita, is indigenous to the Americas.[4] It was among the first foods to be brought from the Americas to Europe, where it quickly indigenized (HS Paris et al.). It was one of the staples of provision grounds kept by slaves for their own nourishment during the plantation era. It was grown across the Caribbean in gardens and small plots and sold at markets for free Afro-Indigenous families to prepare for themselves and for cooks to use in preparing meals for colonial functionaries, planation great houses, and everywhere else. And, of course, soups made with boiled, mashed, or pureed fleshy vegetables, be they pumpkins, yams, or parsnips, are indigenous throughout the world. Pumpkin, and thus pumpkin soup,

La spécialité haïtienne est la "soupe-grasse"
(The Haitian Specialty Is « Fat Soup »)

Soupe grasse. Mettre dans une marmite profonde, un bon morceau de poitrine, de jarret, de culotte, des os. La remplir d'eau froide, ajouter un peu de sel, pas trop. Sans couvrir, donner une ébullition lente. Ecumer dès la montée de l'écume, ajouter un demi verre d'eau pour provoquer une nouvelle montée de l'écume. Ecumer à nouveau, réajouter la même quantité d'eau. Refaire la même opération, jusqu'à ce que le bouillon devienne clair. A ce moment-là, mettre 2 carottes, 2 poireaux, ½ navet, 2 ou 3 feuilles de choux, une dizaine de feuilles d'oseille attachées à un cordon, une branche de céleri, une gousse d'ail, 2 ou 3 pommes de terre, 2 ou 3 malangas. Puis le complément, un bon morceau de "jouroumou" de couleur bien jaune, et facultatif, un morceau de boeuf ou de porc salé. Faire reprendre lentement ébullition. Couvrir pour éviter évaporation et continuer la cuisson sur feu modéré 2 à 3 heures en petits bouillotements. A point, enlever les feuilles d'oseille, écraser au tamis-pilon le jouroumou, les délayer dans la soupe. Saler. Poivrer. Mettre de la vermicelle, un rien d'eau s'il en manque, laisser cuiller la vermicelle. Hors du feu, ajouter une bonne cuillerée de beurre. Servir chaud avec du pain grillé. La soupe grasse tamisée en passoire fine est un agréable potage, et les viandes bouillies sont mangées à la vinaigrette.

Fat Soup. Put into a deep pot, a good piece of brisket, hocks, skirt, bones. Fill it with cold water, add a little salt, not too much. Uncovered, bring it to a simmer. Skim as soon as the scum rises, add a half cup of water to provoke a new rising of scum. Skim again, add again the same amount of water. Repeat the same operation until the broth becomes clear. At that moment, add 2 carrots, 2 leeks, ½ turnip, 2 or 3 cabbage leaves, about ten sorrel leaves tied with kitchen string, a celery branch, a clove of garlic, 2 or 3 potatoes, 2 or 3 malangas. Then the compliment, a good piece of nice yellow pumpkin, and optional, a piece of salt beef or pork. Slowly return to a boil. Cover to avoid evaporation and continue to cook over medium heat 2 to 3 hours at a simmer. When it is done, remove the sorrel leaves, crush the pumpkin with a pestle, incorporate them into the soup. Salt. Pepper. Add some vermicelli, a very little water if needed, let the vermicelli cook. Remove from the stove and add a good spoonful of butter. Serve hot with toasted bread. Strained fat soup is an agreeable potage, and the boiled meats are eaten with a vinaigrette.

—GAILLARD, *RECETTES SIMPLES DE CUISINE HAÏTIENNE*, 329

is not unique in this way, which is exactly why it is so significant: it is representative of the ways that so many foods and dishes spread, overlapped, fed multiple communities, and served multiple purposes. It emblematizes the ways that, thanks to creolization, the same food appears under a great variety of different names, with a great number of different ideas about where it "comes from" and who it "belongs to," all submerged in a coinciding understanding of its being Caribbean.

The variety of names for this nourishing, if not remarkable soup, all stemming from the variety of names for its central ingredient, reflect the circuitous paths of belonging, claiming, appropriating, tracing, and resurging that characterize Caribbean recipes and the Caribbean generally. The Arawakan term, auyama, is still used in the Dominican Republic and the Tupi (indigenous Brazilian language) jirimu is recognizable in the Kreyòl joumou or jouroumou and the French giraumon. The French potiron, of unknown origin, slipped around the seventeenth century from referring to large mushrooms to also designating pumpkins. Meanwhile, the English pumpkin derives from the Greek and Latin terms used for melons. Calabaza, most common in Spanish, derives from the Persian term for melon, xarboze. Melons are indigenous to Africa and tropical Asia and entered Europe probably in the twelfth century, along with the terms that eventually became pumpkin and calabaza; pumpkin and calabaza were transferred to cucurbita in the fifteenth century and became commonly used for them in Europe in the sixteenth century.

The Columbian Exchange of the fifteenth and sixteenth centuries brought pumpkins to Europe, where they were quickly domesticated, along with so many other Caribbean plants, so that when Europeans settled in the Caribbean in the seventeenth, eighteenth, and nineteenth centuries, they "discovered" what they already knew. Europeans could arrive in the Caribbean and find themselves at home, because they had already taken the Caribbean "home" with them. At the same time, Europeans could "find" pumpkin soup in the Caribbean because Indigenous Caribbean cooks, European settlers, and African slaves and their descendants continued to make it in the Caribbean. Thus, when the

European and White Creole Caribbean cookbook writers "found" pumpkin soup recipes, they included them less frequently as a noteworthy "new" discovery than as a regular food to be included in the soup sections of colonial cookbooks. And then in the independence era, Creole and Afro-Indigenous Caribbeans reclaiming and establishing their status as sovereign natives of the Caribbean could take up pumpkin soup as their own; it is grounded in the Caribbean in the same way that they are, rhizomatically, not attached to a single root but connecting and separating, expansively.

Distinguishing Caribbean Recipes

Since the Columbian Exchange, hybrid agricultural novelties and edible heirloom treasures have grown together in the Caribbean, ready to be harvested and preserved, chopped, boiled, and served in myriad manners that remain linked through base elements, growing conditions, modes of mixture, and preparation techniques. Caribbean cuisines and their recipes are grounded in specific islands and nations, each one local and creole, locally creole, moored to an imagined land that is not a territory but a home, a domestic center for a national identification. Sameness in difference, difference in sameness, is an inherent quality of any set of recipes for the same dish. Recipes exemplify how any category of things exists because of both the fact that they are recognizably "the same" and that they are recognizably different from one another. (Of course, sometimes, as I have found in some cookbooks, it turns out that a new title or author or order masks a relatively flat-out copy of recipes previously published in another cookbook.) The details of the differences and similarities can, of course, matter, and repetition is its own kind of meaning-making device.

This book has delved into close readings of individual recipes combined with deep historical, agricultural, and culinary contextualization to explore how lexicons and word choice, specificity of instruction, tone, and the presence or absence of specific ingredients, assert political and cultural affiliations, recognitions, expectations, and so on. Taken together, the recipes for pumpkin soup, as my final exemplar, show a similarity in the central ingredient, pumpkin, and the basic technique: peeling and seeding it and cooking it in a liquid with a few other vegetables, minimal spices, and sometimes various kinds of meat. The main differences relate to the title, the type of liquid, and the presence or absence of various kind of meat. These differences do not correlate to any lines of demarcation by island, colonial occupier, or time period, with the exception of the Haitian cookbooks' soupe grasse/soup joumou, which almost always includes a significant array of salt and fresh meats as well as vermicelli noodles. It is for this reason that pumpkin soup ultimately performs so well as a final emblem of the continuity and similarity of Caribbean foods and recipes that bring them together and of the distinctions among cuisines developed under different geographies, colonial occupiers, colonial economies, demographics, dates and modes of independence, and the interests and attachments of cookbook writers.

The first cookbook to inscribe a recipe for pumpkin soup, Juan Cabrisas's *Nuevo manual de la cocinera catalana y cubana* (1858), calls it "potage de calabaza." It specifies to peel the pumpkin and remove the seeds and includes the very Spanish almonds as well as a concluding note that melon can be substituted for pumpkin (56). Here we see the deep ties to European cuisine of early Caribbean cookbooks, especially involving the need to use imported ingredients like almonds and the sometimes strange treatment of ingredients—like the suggestion to substitute melon for pumpkin, which indicates either a limited knowledge of the specific ingredients or else a limited knowledge of cooking on the part of the Europeans and White Criollos who wrote the first cookbooks (56).

The specification at the end of Caroline Sullivan's pumpkin soup recipe, in her 1893 *Jamaica Cookery Book*, that "this soup is particularly palatable" (9), similarly indicates a certain unfamiliarity of herself or her audience with the general Caribbean palate, in which pumpkin soup clearly figures (Sullivan did promise to refrain from "giving any European cookery") and also the ease with which pumpkin soup enters

> ### *Potage de calabaza* (Pumpkin Soup)
>
> *Se hace tajadas de la calabaza, quitando la corteza y las pepitas, se hace cocer en poca agua y luego de cocida se pasa por un molinillo y se colará por un cedazo claro; se pican las almendras y el arroz, si quiere hacerse con arroz, con agua ó leche, se añade sal y se pone al fuego, despues de algunos hervores, se saca del fuego y se sirve; si se quiere en lugar de calabaza, se puede poner melon.*
>
> Slice the pumpkin, removing the skin and seeds, cook in a little water and once cooked run through a food mill and strain through a fine sieve; finely chop the almonds and the rice, if you want rice, with water or milk, add salt and put on the fire, after a brief boil, remove from the heat and serve; if desired, instead of pumpkin you can use melon.
>
> —CABRISAS, *NUEVO MANUAL DE LA COCINERA CATALANA Y CUBANA*, 56

the English palate. Because neither Cabrisas nor Sullivan stops to explain what pumpkin is like or to detail its special properties, they allow it to sit at the edge of the familiar and exotic, the old possession and the new acquisition. That Sullivan's recipe also calls for curry powder highlights how British and White Creole cultures in the British colonies were linked to the global British colonial project, which was in part responsible for both the circulation of British colonial wives between India and the Caribbean and the import of Indian indentured laborers to British-controlled islands after the end of slavery there.

By the time "Sopa de calabaza" appears in Sisi Colmina's 1991 edition of Nitza Villapol's *Cocina al minuto*, it is simply a variation on the "basic recipe for creamed vegetable soups [receta básica para sopas de vegetales a la crema]" in which the "cooked vegetables" consist of "1 cup of cooked calabaza, cubed or pureed" (92). This reflects how the audience for Caribbean cookbooks has extended from housekeepers and others who instruct their cooks to Caribbean women who know how to cook and appreciate reminders and suggestions and variations, while

> ### Pumpkin Soup
>
> One large slice of pumpkin or half a small pumpkin
> Three pints of water
> Some soup meat or a little salt pork or salt beef
> Black Pepper
> Thyme
> Curry-powder
>
> Cut up the pumpkin, add it to the water putting with it the soup meat (if fresh meat) and a little thyme and black pepper. Bring to the boil. In about half an hour add a small bit of salt pork or salt beef, or else salt to taste. In about another half-hour strain the soup through a colander and serve curried: this soup is particularly palatable
>
> —SULLIVAN, *JAMAICA COOKERY BOOK*, 9

the authorship of Caribbean cookbooks has extended from the elite to the middle and working class. The work of composing collections of recipes that depict those relations is what this book, in turn, has laid bare. Cookbooks, like recipes do not exist in isolation. They both operate in relation to personal and national narratives, and in relation to one another.

How to Do Things with Cookbooks

Cookbooks show and do. Throughout this book I play with words that convey both: for example, represent, contain, manage. A book that simply shows is an inactive repository. Still interesting, but inert. Its author is the unknowing bearer of situations that she lives in and through but that she does not shape. Hence, I keep insisting on what cookbooks do, how they instruct readers not only in things like how much or what kind of flour to use but also in how to relatively value wheat, yuca, and corn flour, and either directly or indirectly how to recognize and relatively

Receta básica para sopas de vegetales a la crema
(Basic Recipe for Creamed Vegetable Soups)

3 cucharadas de mantequilla
4 cucharadas de harina
2 tazas de leche
1 cucharadita de sal
1 taza de vegetales cocinadas

Derrita la mantequilla sin dejar que se queme. Bata la harina con la leche y la sal. Añádala a la mantequilla y cocínela a fuego lento o baño de María* hasta que hierva y espese ligeramente. Añádale el vegetal cocinado y déjela a fuego lento, aproximadamente 2 o 3 minutos más. Si desea conservarla caliente por más tiempo, déjela a baño de María. Da 4 raciones.

3 tablespoons of butter
4 tablespoons of flour
2 cups of milk
1 teaspoon of salt
1 cup of cooked vegetables

Melt the butter without letting it burn. Beat the flour with the milk and the salt. Add it to the butter and cook it over low heat or in a double boiler until it boils and thickens slightly. Add the cooked vegetable to it and leave it over low heat, about 2 or 3 minutes more. If you want to keep it hot for longer, leave it in the double boiler. Makes 4 portions.

Variaciones (Variations)

. . .

Sopa de calabaza (Pumpkin Soup)

Use 1 taza de calabaza cocinada, en cuadritos o puré

Use one cup of cooked pumpkin, in cubes or pureed.

—VILLAPOL, *COCINA AL MINUTO*, 1992, 91–92

Pumpkin Soup

3 lbs Pumpkin
1 lb Soup Meat
½ lb Pig's Tail
1 Onion
2 stalks Skellion
1 lb Cocoa [sic]
1 sprig Thyme
1 clove Garlic
1 country Pepper

METHOD:
1. Set soup meat and pig's tail to boil in about 4 quarts of water.
2. When meat is almost cooked add pumpkin, cocoa [sic] and seasoning.
3. Boil until pumpkin and cocoa [sic] are soft.

—CLEARY, *JAMAICA RUN-DUNG*, 25

value specific Indigenous, African, or European histories or the general idea of those and of their mixing in the Caribbean.

Cookbooks bring into print and public circulation domestic concerns that are often relegated to the private sphere. In the nineteenth and early twentieth centuries, they were often one of the few places that women were authorized, even trained, to share their expertise. At the same time, they serve to keep women in their place. And they, like so much else, were open in the Caribbean first to White women, then to elite women of an array of races, and then to the middle- and working-class women who actually did the cooking. So they are an intermediary space, one where power is negotiated, wielded, taken. Likewise, as in much writing, women, like food, have been objects, metaphors, figures used in the service of ideas that passed through them but did not include them as subjects. As women (and some few men) began writing about women as subjects, they still carried

> ### Sopa de calabaza a la crema
> ### (Cream of Pumpkin Soup)
>
> 1½ tazas de calabaza majada
> 3 tazas de salsa blanca
> 1 cebolla rallada
>
> Añada a la calabaza majada, la cebolla y la salsa blanca. Deje hervir y sazone a gusto. Cuele y si queda espesa añada del agua en que hirvió la calabaza. Sirva caliente con galletas saladas o tostadas de pan.
>
> 1½ cups of mashed pumpkin
> 3 cups of white sauce
> 1 grated onion
>
> Add the onion and the white sauce to the mashed pumpkin. Let it boil and season to taste. Strain and if it is too thick add some of the water that the pumpkin boiled in. Serve hot with crackers or toasted bread.
>
> —CABANILLAS, *COCINE A GUSTO*, 109

symbolic weight, but they became themselves substantive, the creators as much as the bearers of messages. And since cooking and cookbook writing is so often a domestic practice, a practice done primarily by women, I am not simply making a comparison; I am demonstrating a critical convergence. In cookbook writing, women and food are not pass-throughs, they *are* substance—whether free or constrained or some place in between. By extension, cookbooks must do more than convey how to make the recipes that they include. What stands out, then, is exactly the simultaneity I continue to emphasize: the both-and quality of cookbooks. They record and instruct how to make dishes and they convey ideas about domestic production, organization, order, and value, about taste and quality that are also ideas about gender roles, racial divisions, class boundaries, political affiliations, and national imaginations.

As sites of domestic instruction and production, cookbooks both tie women to the space of the home and show the many diverse, even powerful, ways that they use it. Through cooking, women participate in non-heterosexual reproduction, though often at the heart of a heteronormative family structure. Women who write cookbooks for other women refuse, sidestep, or do something other than repeat the model of one mother to her biological children through embodied instructions. As much as White women who author cookbooks made up of the recipes of their cooks, their friends' cooks, and the market ladies they buy from reproduce the racial hierarchy in which they get credit for and exert control over Afro-Indigenous women, they also trace their intimate interactions with those women, and the knowledge and skill those women share with them. And as much as Afro-Indigenous women who authored

---

Pumpkin Soup

6 people
2 onions
1 lb. pumpkin
2 dessertspoons split peas
2 teasp. parsley
Pepper and salt
Bones from joint or piece of ox-tail
Stock and outside leaves of cabbage
¼ teasp. thyme
1 stalk celery or celery leaves
2 tbls. butter

Fry onion till golden brown. Drain fat. Peel and cut pumpkin. Add rest of ingredients and cover with water. Simmer for an hour. Rub through sieve before serving.

—THE CHILD CARE COMMITTEE, *BAJAN COOKBOOK*, 4

cookbooks in the early to mid-twentieth century used them to assert their places in "the master's house," they also used them as tools for experimentation, substitution, and increasing control of "the master's tools." When they did that, they recuperated ownership of the tools of their ancestors that—by force—built and fed "the master's house" in the first place.

Reading Cookbooks for Pleasure

This book came out of my own enjoyment of cookbooks. I read cookbooks for pleasure. I like to be told what to do, even though I often don't do what I am told. Cookbooks often make space for just that: add salt to taste, they instruct; or they say to add spinners to a soup at the very end, but I put in yuca twenty minutes before I'm ready to serve and it comes out delicious because I followed the directions, sort of.

In the midst of studying the impacts of colonialism and the struggles for national independence, it is a treat to get to read about what tastes good, what nourishes, what looks nice, what goes well together. Cookbooks, even as they intervene in colonial orders and decolonial movements, are about pleasure as well as survival. They make, and they tell how to make. They carry traces, where, in Glissant's words, "the trace was lived as one of the places of survival. For example, for the descendants of the Africans transported into slavery into what would soon be called the New World, it was usually the only possible form of action" (*Treatise*, 9). And when the struggle against colonial domination has reached a point where innovation is possible, cookbooks contain new recipes that, as Fanon writes of the literature of independence, "brings an urgent breath of excitement, arouses forgotten muscular tensions and develops the imagination" (*Wretched*, 174). Cookbooks are among the arts through which "the colonized subject restructures his own perception" and "the world no longer seems doomed" (*Wretched*, 176). Of course, making can be destructive, but it is always also creative. Just as culinary colonialism instructs in the ways that colonialism both

Anna's Curried Pumpkin Soup
ST. THOMAS, U.S. VIRGIN ISLANDS

YIELD: 6 SERVINGS

Anna was my husband's grandmother; a lovely, intelligent lady, and wonderful cook.

1 large yellow onion, minced
2 cloves garlic, minced
1 small habanero pepper, seeded and minced
1 stalk celery, minced
1 large carrot, sliced
2 cups chicken stock
1 cup vegetable stock
1 cup dry white wine
2 pounds pumpkin or dark yellow, meaty squash, peeled, seeded and diced
2 tbs. butter
½ cup heavy cream
2 tbs. curry powder, toasted in a dry skillet for 2 minutes
Salt and freshly ground black pepper
Cinnamon and nutmeg

1. Sauté onion, garlic, celery, habanero pepper, celery and carrot until onion is soft. Add chicken and vegetable stock, along with wine, bringing to a simmer. Add pumpkin and cook until vegetables are tender. Remove from heat and cool 20 minutes. Purée in blender until smooth. Return to stockpot, slowly reheat, folding in butter, cream and curry powder. Season to taste with salt and pepper. Dust with cinnamon and nutmeg.

—SPENCELEY, *A TASTE OF THE VIRGIN ISLANDS, TOO!*, 9

destroyed and created the Caribbean as we know it, recipes for independent national culture reveal how independent nationhood created the "native" cultures whose autonomy it putatively restored. With these two concept-metaphors, we can read how Caribbean cookbooks represent cuisines of creolization that, in the words of Jamaica Kincaid, "take—period. Take anything. . . . Just anything that makes sense. Just take it" from every possible source ("A Lot of Memory," 168).

Full and Ready for More

As my patterns of demonstration throughout this book reveal, much of the work of nineteenth- and twentieth-century Caribbean cookbooks involves establishing Caribbean native, national culinary cultures at the confluence of a particular combination of people, plants, and practices, primarily from other origins, on a particular island. These cookbooks work for a coincidence of the domestic and the national even as they offer divergent depictions of the state of the home and the home of the state. Their formation of national cuisines in the wake of culinary colonialism has been the subject of this book, examined through a comprehensive collection of cookbooks from select islands and periods. In the twenty-first century, political independence has largely disappeared as the horizon for freedom in places where it was never achieved. Likewise, a growing recognition that nation-state status has not resolved Euro-American domination is addressed through cookbooks that increasingly posit diasporic and transnational culinary cultures. Even as increasing numbers of national cookbooks thrive in places like Cuba, Jamaica, and the Dominican Republic, diaspora and transnational cookbooks process and produce new imaginary homelands subtended with new forms of allegiance and recipes for new nationalisms. These works outline—in a variety of ways and to different degrees—the double movement of deterritorialization and reterritorialization Glissant describes as a gesture of Relation of the *Tout-Monde* (*Treatise*) that keeps Caribbean cookbooks on the move.

As this book comes to a close, I reflect on just how packed it is with information about cookbooks, food histories, and colonial and national politics, but also how very few of the cookbooks that I have encountered, and how very little even of those, I have been able to write about. The archive is vast, and as much as I try to constitute it as *an* archive by gathering it here in this study, I am painfully aware of how hard future

> ### *Soupe (au giromon)* ([Pumpkin] Soup)
>
> *Eplucher et couper en petits morceaux une belle tranche de giromon que vous mettez à bouillir dans de l'eau légèrement salée.*
>
> *Quand la cuisson est suffisante, passer au presse-purée, ajouter un quart de litre de lait et quelques cuillerées de riz bien lavé.*
>
> *Servir quand le riz sera cuit, en ajoutant un morceau de beurre.*
>
> Peel and cut into small pieces a nice slice of pumpkin that you boil in lightly salted water.
>
> When it is cooked enough, put it through a food mill, add a quarter of a liter of milk and a few spoonfuls of well-washed rice.
>
> Serve when the rice is cooked, adding a pat of butter.
>
> —JULIEN LUNG-FOU, *LES RECETTES MARTINIQUAISES DE DA ELODIE*, PP. 59–60

researchers and I will have to work to see, hold, read, and ensure the future of many Caribbean cookbooks mentioned here and the many more not included.

One of the questioning threads that reappeared again and again as I wrote this book is: are cookbooks and nations things of a bygone era? Are we in a transnational digital age that has left them behind, perhaps even revealed their irrelevance? There are certainly, as I write about elsewhere, formulations of home and home cooking that do not rely on the independent nation-state,[5] and, as I hope others will write about, a wonderful array of blogs and vlogs and YouTube channels and TikToks and more that show what digital modes can do for Caribbean food instruction and vice versa. But cookbooks continue to be published as well, and nations persist. And it seems to me that pausing to consider the moments when they coincide, when cookbooks participate in colonial expansion reforming the national worldscape and in decolonizing and national independence, this opens a new door to understanding both

Crema de auyama (Cream of Pumpkin Soup)

Ingredientes

2 cucharada mantequilla
1 cebolla blanca grande rebanada
2 libra de auyama [0.9 kg] pelada y cortada en trozos pequeños
1½ cucharadita sal (o más, al gusto—cantidad dividida)
1 cucharada perejil picado
4 tazas caldo de vegetales
1 tasa leche evaporada
¼ taza crema agria (opcional)
1 cucharadita nuez moscada recién molida

Elaboración paso a paso

1. *Saltear vegetales: Calentar la mantequilla a fuego bajo en una olla. Añade la cebolla, la auyama y una cucharadita de sal, y cuece removiendo hasta que la cebolla se torne translúcida.*
2. *Hervir: Vierte el caldo y agrega el perejil. Cuece tapado hasta que la auyama esté blanda (unos 7 minutos). Retira del fuego y deja enfriar a temperatura ambiente.*
3. *Licuar: Pon la mezcla de auyama y la leche en una licuadora y licúa hasta que se quede sin ningún grumo.*
4. *Recalentar. Vierte en una olla y calienta a fuego medio, remueve regularmente para evitar que se pegue al fondo. Cuando haya adquirido una consistencia un poco cremosa, prueba y sazona con sal al gusto si es necesario, retira del fuego.*
5. *Servir: Una vez servida, agrega un poco de crema agria y espolvorea con nuez moscada*

Notas

Creme de auyama vegana (vegetariano estricto)

Se eres vegetariano estricto, evita todos los ingredientes con leche y sustituye la mantequilla por aceite de tu preferencia. Agrega una taza extra de caldo para sustituir la leche.

Ingredients

2 tablespoon butter
1 large sliced white onion
2 pound of pumpkin [0.9 kg] peeled and cut into small pieces
1½ teaspoon salt (or more, to taste—divided)
1 tablespoon minced parsley
4 cups vegetable broth
1 cup evaporated milk
¼ cup sour cream (optional)
1 teaspoon freshly grated nutmeg

Step by step instructions

1. Sauté vegetables: heat the butter over low heat in a pan. Add the onion, the pumpkin and a teaspoon of salt, and cook, stirring, until the onion becomes translucent.
2. Boil: Pour in the broth and add the parsley. Cook covered until the pumpkin is soft (about 7 minutes). Remove from heat and let cool to room temperature.
3. Blend: Put the pumpkin mix and the milk in a blender and blend until there are no chunks left.
4. Reheat: Put the mixture in a hot pot over medium heat, stir regularly to avoid it sticking to the bottom. When it reaches a slightly creamy consistency, taste and season with salt to taste if necessary, remove from heat.
5. Serve: Once served, add a little sour cream and sprinkle with grated nutmeg.

Notes

Vegan (Strict Vegetarian) Cream of Pumpkin Soup

If you are a strict vegetarian, avoid all the ingredients with milk and substitute your favorite oil for the butter. Add an extra cup of broth to substitute for the milk.

—GONZÁLEZ, [RECETA + VIDEO] CREMA DE AUYAMA RICA Y FÁCIL (COCINADOMINICANA.COM) past and present. The foundation of this book, by examining two of the first major waves of Caribbean cookbooks, offers a lookout point from which the present moment can be viewed; it gathers a body of cookbooks and analyses that can serve as points of comparison and contrast to what follows; and it lays out models and modes for reading Caribbean cookbooks in new times and doing new things.

Acknowledgments

THIS BOOK TOOK SHAPE through the delicious conversations with wonderful interlocutors and friends at the Islands in Between, West Indian Literature, Caribbean Studies Association, and Digital Caribbean Conferences: Emily Taylor, Alison Donnell, Elsa Luciano Feal and Edgardo Pérez, Lisa Outar, Antonia MacDonald, Evelyn O'Callaghan, Leah Rosenberg, Larry Breiner, and many more. Kimberly Guinta, your support for this book as an idea allowed it to become a reality. Thank you to the Digital Caribbean NEH Seminar and the organizers at the University of Florida and the Digital Library of the Caribbean (DLOC) for so much material and immaterial, physical, and virtual support. And thank you to my students in Topics in Digital Humanities: Caribbean Cookbooks that emerged from that seminar and fed this book. To all of the librarians who helped me to access manuscripts in the midst of the pandemic, cross-check undated volumes, and track down partial references, thank you so very much. Thank you to Salem State University and especially the Center for Research and Creative Activities for the support of sabbaticals, research grants, writing groups, and editorial assistance. Thank you to Janelle Schwarz for the developmental editing that got me through the last round of revisions. To my dear colleague and provider of the most delicious oil downs Jude Nixon, more please. Thank you to all my departmental colleagues and friends, especially Roopika Risam, J. D. Scrimgeour, Jan

Lindholm, Julie Whitlow, Stephenie Young, Jessica Cook, Al DeCiccio, and Bill Coyle. To Renée and Dave and Liz and Blanca and Jaci and Fleur and Avi and Jason and Meghan and MaryLauran and Mike and Matt and Odette and Brian and Regula and all of my support in cooking and eating and otherwise being well-nourished, thank you. Thank you Amy and Tom for life from the first seed and kitchen and book through everything and always. Matthias, gentleman friend and partner in all the delight and the work, including countless readings and editing of so many drafts of this book, thank you. Lucca, for running and kicking and hugging and laughing all through the writing of this book, and growing into a wonderful, beloved, young man.

Notes

Introduction

1. See, for example, Anne L. Bower, Sherrie A. Innes, and Janet Theophano.
2. See, for example, Keith Stavely and Kathleen Fitzgerald.
3. See, for example, Kelley Fanto Deetz, Toni Tipton-Martin.
4. See, for example, Efraín Barradas, Beatriz Calvo Peña, Christine Folch, B. W. Higman, Hannah Garth, Sarah Lawson Welsh.
5. I follow scholars like Kimberly Palmer in using "Afro-Indigenous" to bring attention to ways that while Indigenous or Amerindian race was rarely identified or considered in nineteenth and early twentieth century Caribbean racial classifications, many Caribbeans categorized as non-White also had Indigenous background, and Maroons and other groups who existed at or beyond the borders of plantation life drew together people of African and Indigenous heritage.
6. This association of the "Indians" with the "monstrous" practice of eating one another seems to be responsible for the linguistic conflation of Caribal (Carib, Caribee, Caribbean) and Canibal (cannibal).
7. For a detailed analysis of "new world food and coloniality," see Zilkia Janer.
8. From early colonial food writing along with recent historical, agricultural, and botanical investigations, a picture of the basic origins and contours of Caribbean foods becomes clear. Yuca, peppers (ají), tubers like malanga and sweet potato (batata or boniato), calabaza (auyama, joumou), chayote, corn, tomato, tropical fruits, greens, and many spices were cultivated in the Caribbean before the arrival of Spaniards. Indigenous to Africa (or, if we go back another two thousand years or so, to Asia, or if we go all the way back to around 3000 BC, to New Guinea) and naturalized in the Caribbean in the early sixteenth century, are plantains and yams. Similarly, while the naturalization of pigs in the Caribbean in the early seventeenth century

seems to have led to their perception as "American" by the nineteenth century, pork was introduced to the Americas from Europe in the early colonial period. Europeans also brought many vegetables that quickly naturalized. From Asia and Polynesia but brought by the explorers and colonists: sugar cane, breadfruit, and more fruits.

9. I take the phrase "colonial/modern . . . system" from María Lugones. Lugones has argued that "a systemic understanding of gender constituted by colonial/modernity in terms of multiple relations of power" emerged as colonialism "imposed a new gender system" that introduced "gender itself as a colonial concept and mode of organizing relations of production, property relations, of cosmologies and ways of knowing" (186).

10. I discuss Linnaean taxonomy at greater length in "Caribbean Ecopoetics." See also Elizabeth DeLoughrey on Linnaeus's impact on the Caribbean.

11. Sloane also gives recipes for "cool drink," cane drink, banana drink, and China drink (lxxi). Père Labat records similar drinks, as well as Maby, Grappe, fermented fruit juices, eau de vie, Sang-gris, Limonde à l'Anglaise, Ponche, and a "savage" banana drink (Vol. I, ch. XVII, pp. 411–423).

12. The term "Mulatto," like so many racial terms common in the colonial Caribbean, originated in the racist work of classifying racial castes. "Mulatto" was widely used in the nineteenth-century West Indies as a self-identificatory and descriptive term, with no special offensive weight, for individuals of mixed White European and Black African ancestry. Mary Seacole, in *The Wonderful Adventures of Mrs. Seacole in Many Lands*, refers to herself as Mulatto.

13. See http://petryknorberto.blogspot.com/2011/12/manual-del-cocinero-cubano.html.

14. Of course, as Norberto Petryk's blog suggests, access to Cuban archives has been uniquely fraught for anyone living in the United States, where it is still not possible to purchase a copy of the 2017 edition of the *Manual del cocinero cubano*, and the refusal of many Cubans outside of Cuba to recognize the legitimacy of the current government contribute to a particularly rampant practice of reproduction without permission, even, as I detail in chapter 4, of more recent cookbooks. However, this is not a mark of Cuban exceptionalism. Following up on Higman's "hors d'oeuvre" piece, I found the Jamaican archival material in a similar situation. A search for Caroline Sullivan's 1893 *Jamaica Cookery Book* turned up copies held at the National Library of Jamaica, the British Library of St. Pancras, and the U.S. Library of Congress; copies of the 1897 edition at the British Library and Harvard's Schlessinger Library; copies of the 1908 edition at the New York Public Library, the University of Chicago Library, and the University of Miami Library; *A Collection of 19th Century Jamaican Cookery and Herbal Recipes* published in England in 1990, listing Marjorie Pringle Campbell as the author and containing the same material as Sullivan's book, available for purchase and at libraries; and 1996 and 2003 editions, published

in London, of *Classic Jamaican Cooking* by Caroline Sullivan with a note on the copyright page reading "originally published, in slightly different form ... as *The Jamaica Cookery* Book by Aston W. Gardner & Co., Kingston, in 1893," also on the market and in libraries.
15. See https://www.facebook.com/Cocina-Criolla-de-Amanda-Ornes-vda-Perell%C3%B3-1409437159355697/.
16. Lawson Welsh's reading of the "race, class and gender" of Mrs. Yearwood's *West Indian and Other Recipes* lays the groundwork for my own understanding of cookbook organization.
17. Few of the cookbooks treated in this book have been previously translated. All translations are my own, unless otherwise indicated.
18. Gilman Ostrander, who wrote in the 1970s that "every schoolboy knows that the triangular trade was the one in rum, slaves, and molasses between colonial New England, Africa, and the West Indies," traced the terms Triangular Trade and Triangle Trade to New England historians from the eighteenth century, though "it was only the last third of the nineteenth century that historians discovered the triangular trade." While Ostrander argued that the term was more mythological than descriptive, it continues to be widely used, perhaps most influentially for this book by Sidney Mintz in his work on *Sweetness and Power*.
19. Also key to the larger theoretical and conceptual discussions of the creole and creolization are Kamau Brathwaite's *The Development of Creole Society in Jamaica, 1770–1820* and Antonio Benítez-Rojo's *La Isla que se repite*.
20. Creole has similar uses and meanings, with distinct valences, in Brazil, the Reunion Islands and Mauritius, and the Southern United States.
21. Aisha Khan cautions that "creole" has been extended so far as to render it largely vapid and even when the Caribbean is held up as the creole par excellence, "creolization is not explored in terms of events or processes; rather, it is envisioned as an abstractly cultural phenomenon" (273). My attention in this book to the very material manifestations of creole as an adjective printed in specific cookbooks in specific contexts heeds Khan's warning.

Chapter 1   Nineteenth-Century Cocineros of Cuba and Puerto Rico

1. Although there had been pro-independence movements in both Cuba and Puerto Rico since at least the early nineteenth century, 1868 was the year of the first major revolts on both islands.
2. The term "Mulatto," like so many racial terms common in the Spanish colonies, originated in the racist work of classifying racial castes. "Mulatto" was widely used in nineteenth-century Cuba and Puerto Rico as a

self-identificatory and descriptive term, with no special offensive weight, for individuals of mixed White European and Black African ancestry.
3. For a discussion of "Race and Black Mobilization in Colonial and Early Independent Cuba," see Aline Helg.
4. For a study of siterios and independence in Cuba, see Shannon Dawdy; for a study of jíbaros and independence in Puerto Rico, see Francisco Scarano.
5. Toni Tipton-Martin points out that White American cookbook authors did the same thing with enslaved and employed Black cooks in their homes.
6. Fernando Ortiz introduces his concept and use of transculturation in *Cuban Counterpoint*, especially pages 97–103.
7. Their titles and subtitles echo those of at least two others: the 1831 Mexican cookbook *El cocinero mexicano* and the 1828 Spanish cookbook *Manual del cocinero, cocinera y repostero, con un tratado de confiteria y botilleria, y un método para trinchar y servir toda clase de viandas, y la cortesanía y urbanidad que se sebe usar en la mesa*, itself a translation from the fifth edition of a French cookbook (presumably Joseph Saugrin's *Le cuisinier bourgeois et royal*), "augmented with a few items" by D. Mariano de la Rementería y Fica. These echoes reinforce the genre of the cookbook to which they all belong as well as the use of cookbook titling to announce national independence (Mexico won independence from Spain in 1821). A number of the recipes in Coloma y Garcés's books appear clearly derived from the Spanish *Manual del cocinero*, with, for example, the recipe for "Olla de cocido a la vigilia" in *El cocinero puertorriqueño* repeating exactly the instructions of that for "Caldo de vigilia" in the *Manual de cocinero*, but replacing a few ingredients and instrument names; for example, rather than "a cabbage [berza], a parsnip, and a celery root" (34), the Puerto Rican calls for "two yellow plantains [plátanos pintones], a cabbage [col], a celery root, a lettuce and some chard" (28). *El cocinero mexicano* has its own version of "Caldo magro para vigilia" whose instructions and ingredients are quite similar but do not have the verbatim repetitions of the Spanish as do Coloma y Garcés's cookbooks.
8. A fourth edition, published in 1971 by Editorial Coquí and edited by Emilio M. Colón, and a fifth edition, published by Ediciones Puerto in 2004 and edited by José Carvajal, similarly do not name the author of *El cocinero puertorriqueño*.
9. In 1857 Coloma y Garcés published a second domestic manual, the *Manual Recreating the easy, neat, useful, and necessary secrets for home economics, or, the all-knowingness of Cuban mothers to whom this work is dedicated* [*Manual recreativo de secretos fáciles, curiosos, útiles y necesarios para la economía doméstica ó sea el sabelo todo de las madres de familias cubanas a quienes dedica esta obra*]. In the 1860s he turned to agriculture, publishing five agricultural manuals including a "catechism" of agricultural lessons to be taught in rural schools, a manual of agricultural accounting, and an almanac. His last book appears to be the 1872 *Manual del jardinero cubano*.

10. Furthermore, of the twenty-five recipes simply dropped from the *Manual del cocinero cubano* in the Puerto Rican edition, nine have Cuban place names in the title, another three are ajiacos, and another two are dishes featuring ajíes dulces.
11. The recipe in *El cocinero puertorriqueño* more closely resembles a cross between Cuban "mangú" and what is now called "caldo con mofongo" than the "mofongo" made of mashed fried pork skin plantains of contemporary Puerto Rico.
12. Cruz Miguel Ortíz Cuadra in *Eating Puerto Rico* traces "mofongo" to the Angolan Kikongo "mfwenge-mfwenge," meaning "a great amount," or "mfwongo" meaning "plate" (149). "Mofongo" also has phonetic resonances with other African-derived dishes that have retained names similar to their African ones, like fufú, mangú, and quimbombó.
13. The Cuban includes atoles later and has no overarching paragraph but does offer four distinct atole recipes.
14. The entry for "atole" in *El cocinero mexicano*, first published in 1831, confirms its status as a drink. *El cocinero puertorriqueño* specifies that "atoles" "are always made from starches, water or milk, and very little salt," and describes the general recipe as the following: "Take as many small spoonfulls of flour as cups to be made, dissolve it in a little water: put over the fire as much water or milk as cups to be made.... When the water thus prepared boils, add the dissolved flour little by little, stirring continuously with a white, dry and clean, wooden paddle. It can be quickly cooked and thickened, without being allowed to ball up" (11). The recipes in the *Manual del cocinero cubano* are quite similar, though that volume distinguishes porridges [papillas] as a subset of atoles.
15. If the change to the first pages of *El cocinero puertorriqueño* also results from an editorial desire to change the very beginning of the book in order to stake a claim on Puerto Rican culinary territory and ensure sales of this "new" cookbook, what that change is nonetheless matters.
16. In *Manual del cocinero cubano*, the recipe for "Cafiroleta" calls for "panetela" while *El cocinero puertorriqueño* calls for "bizcocho." Both words translate to "biscuit" but are regionally specific.
17. The first recipe for tembleque that I have been able to find in a cookbook is in Berta Cabanillas et al.'s 1950 *Cocine a gusto*, though as I discuss in chapter 13, between *El cocinero puertorriqueño* and *Cocine a gusto*, no Spanish-language, Puerto-Rican authored cookbook was published, and the bulletins of the University of Puerto Rico's Department of Home Economics did not include dessert recipes.
18. For studies of the trajectory of Puerto Rican sugar industry, see Sidney Mintz, "Labor and Sugar in Puerto Rico and Jamaica, 1800–1850," and Francisco Scarano, *Sugar and Slavery in Puerto Rico*.
19. I examine the reemergence of Puerto Rican national cuisine in the 1950s in "A Little Puerto Rican Food Culture."

20. The only copy of the 1857 edition that I have been able to locate is held by the University of Miami. While the University of Miami library catalog lists the publication date as 1857, that date is not present in the book itself. The earliest version that I have found that lists a publication date is clearly a later edition (made clear by the new store listed as selling the book), dated 1864.
21. Louis A. Pérez Jr. and Christine Folch attribute authorship of this to Enrique Langarika, but it is clear from the cover, publication information, and Eusebio Leal's prologue that Langarika is the editor of the 1996 edition and that the 1862 edition was published under the "Imprenta y Librería La Cubana" of Havana, without listing an author.
22. Dúnyer Pérez Roque suggests the recipes in the *Novísimo manual* are entirely new and cites details of the recipe for "*Tocineta de monte a lo pinero*" that support his claim. However, the recipe for *Tocineta de monte a lo pinero* and the two recipes that Pérez Roque cites in detail are among the small portion of fully new recipes in the *Novísimo manual*. Pérez Roque's analysis of those additions offers a strong case that the mark that Noviatur put on his edition is one of Francophilia.
23. For detailed studies of nineteenth-century Cuban immigration and demographics, see Sarmiento Ramírez, "Cuba," and Pérez Roque.
24. No records of the Inn in Havana remain. There was also a famous nineteenth-century Buenos Aires inn by the same name. Records of that inn do not list a J. P. Legran as a chef.
25. Rand and Avery only appear to have published one other Spanish-language book, the 1891 *El método moderno para aprender inglés: dedicado a los hispanoamericanos*, by Sydenham Phillips Cohen Henriques, although they did publish other titles related to Latin America in English, including Francis Jewett Parker's 1865 *The Mexican Empire and the American Union*. Rand and Avery went through a series of dramatic financial and ownership problems in the 1880s that culminated in the entire business, from typefonts to books, being sold at auction (Fayant).
26. José Florencio Turbiano y Paula's 1877 *El propagador de conocimientos útiles* focuses on the cultivation of plants supposed to fight yellow fever; the three-volume *El agricultor, horticultor, jardinero, e higienista agrícola cubano* (1878–1879) is his most important work of agricultural reform. He also published the 1878 a *Tratado sobre las gallinas, palomas, canarios y ruiseñores* and in 1893 the exercise in environmentalism and nomenclature, *Arboricultura y floricultura cubana con una descripción de los árboles, arbustos, bejucos, plantas aromáticas y de jardinería, indígenas y exóticas, sus nombres comunes y botánicos*. He also was apparently involved in the popular hypnotism movement, publishing in 1881 *Manual de magnetismo animal y sonambulismo magnético, sus procederes, fenómenos y aplicación puestos al alcance de todos*.
27. In this, I follow B. W. Higman's argument in *Jamaican Food* and *How Food Made History* (182).

28. While the impersonal *se* can look like the passive voice, it is differentiated by not referring to a direct object.
29. For a linguistic explanation of the impersonal *se*, see Suñer.
30. When the first Cuban woman to author a cookbook, in 1923, takes over the impersonal *se*, she prefaces her work with an overarching imperative: *"Lo que me he propuesto y espero haber conseguido es que el ama de casa pueda darle el libro a su cocinera y decirle: Haga este plato y que aquélla lo pueda hacer"* (6).
31. It is not uncommon for recipes for plain boiled plantains to instruct to cook the plantains with the skins on and then remove them after. While plantain peels are edible, they are not tasty.
32. All three recipes call for distinctly Cuban ingredients, though the "Cuban" and "Creole" both call for plantains while the "Andaluz" does not.
33. Though "vaca marina" does suggest some idea of the mammalian quality of the manati, it too makes an incorrect association of manatee with cow (the manatee is related to the elephant). The Taíno etymology of *manati* relates to a large (*ma*) thing (*na*) and to a great spirit (*ti*).
34. In *El cocinero puertorriqueño*, the fufú recipes are retitled funche. In other cookbooks, funche is not the same as fufú but is rather a corn-based preparation that seems to draw both on indigenous corn porridges and breads and on fufú. Sokolov's analysis of coocoo comes to a similar conclusion.
35. The omission of any fufú from Legran's *Nuevo manual del cocinero cubano y español* and Winslow's selection single them out, among the early cookbooks, as diminishing Afro-Caribbean foods (though Winslow's much smaller overall selection makes the omission less pointed).
36. Usually called okra, ochro, or gumbo in English, quimbombó is also called "gombo" or "molondrón" in the Dominican Republic. "Gombo" derives from "quimbombó" but stands out less in English and Spanish.
37. Ortíz Cuadra examines the connotations associated with plantain across its history (140–147).
38. The names for these vary not only in English and French but also across the Spanish-speaking islands. For example, in the Dominican Republic malanga is called yautía, and boniato is called batata. The differences, as well as the variety within each vegetable (malanga/yautía, for example, comes in at least four different "colors"), lead to confusions about the differences among the plants. Yam, mapuey (probably an entirely different Indigenous rhizome but called ñame mapuey in Cuba), and boniato are, for example, regularly described with the characteristics of one another.
39. "Viandas" are called "víveres" in the Dominican Republic, and "ground provisions," "provisions," "hard food," and "food" in the Anglophone Caribbean.
40. What is included in *El cocinero puertorriqueño* is not only unacknowledged but already deeply marked by the violence that makes it so hard to know what were, for example, Carib and what were Taíno preparations and words,

or where more specifically than "Africa" anything from that continent originated.

Chapter 2   Domestic Control in West Indian Women's Cookbooks at the Turn of the Twentieth Century

1. Given the importance of naming and identifying as colonial and decolonial practice and the evolving nature of language, especially in the multilingual colonial Caribbean, I must note the contours of some of the key terms in this chapter. "The West Indies" is a British formulation to designate the entire Caribbean in distinction from the East Indies (on and around the Asian subcontinent) that has more recently come to specify the British colonies and post-colonies as a subset of the Caribbean. As detailed in the introduction, "Creole" when used for people in turn-of-the-century West Indies designated alternatively those of European ancestry born in the Caribbean, those of African ancestry born in the Caribbean, and those of mixed European, African, and perhaps also Indigenous or Indian ancestry born in the Caribbean. And when used for food, "creole" referred to dishes of mixed origin marked by their Afro-Indigenous elements. "Native" in the West Indian context similarly refers to people, plants, and dishes born in the Caribbean; unlike "creole," however, and also unlike "Native" in the North American context, it makes no claims about ancestry, rendering it both more mobile and more vacuous than "creole." What collectors and contributors call themselves as well as their cookbooks and recipes—Jamaican, West Indian, Creole/creole, native, and so on—evoke and invoke the state of domestic affairs, the lingering effects of earlier power plays, and the stirrings of new nationalisms. How those nominal affiliations relate to the personal and community histories that they convey betrays the ways that the gender, race, and colonial status of English, Creole, and "Native" women are not only intersecting but mutually constitutive and reveals the work of cookbooks to maintain heterocolonial order and manage challenges to it. While Jamaica, Trinidad, and British Guiana feature in the titles and some of the narrative sections of the cookbooks that I examine in this chapter, because they are used interchangeably with West Indian and creole and do not appear in recipe titles, and because the other features of the cookbooks engage in culinary colonialism, I do not focus on these cookbooks as asserting national characters or cuisines, but rather as making island-based regional claims to colonial distinction and belonging.

2. Racial terminology is the source of much controversy both because of the implications of specific terms in specific places and times and because of significant fluctuation in the terms and their meanings. In the British West

Indies in the nineteenth century, "White" and "Negro" were two poles of racial differentiation between which were at least seven other terms. "Coloured" was used as a catchall for non-White. I use "White" and "Black" to refer to the general racial division between those designated "White" and those designated with any variation of non-White. I specify "mixed race" where the spectrum, and the space between poles of White and Black, is important. I use "Creole" to designate mixing more generally, with attention to all of the nuances of that term that I discuss in the introduction and chapter 1. For a detailed account of racial categories in nineteenth-century Jamaica and Barbados, see Arnold Sio.

3. Keith Stavely and Kathleen Fitzgerald examine Amelia Simmons's work in *United Tastes: The Making of the First American Cookbook.*

4. Toni Tipton-Martin analyzes the work of Black American women cookbook writers in *The Jemima Code.*

5. Even in the digitized *Gleaner* archives, parts of this text are unclear. I have indicated the words that I have had to guess with brackets containing a question mark.

6. The second edition introduced forty-six new recipes (although the first edition announces three hundred and twelve recipes, several recipes are also numbered a, b, and c in the 1893 edition and assigned full numbers in the 1897 edition) and the subtitle changed from "three hundred and twelve simple receipts and household hints" to "three hundred and sixty-four simple receipts and household hints." There are only very minor revisions to the text that is repeated.

7. Each edition was listed in advertisements by Gardner's booksellers and advertised individually in Jamaica's largest newspaper, the *Daily Gleaner.*

8. An Emilia Caroline Sullivan, born to John Augustus Sullivan's second wife, Jane (Tyler) Sullivan, in Wales in 1830, appears to have lived her life in Wales. John August Sullivan and his third wife, Eliza (Williams) Sullivan, had many children baptized in Jamaica but none recorded with a first name Caroline.

9. The Musgraves left Jamaica in 1883 when Anthony Musgrave was assigned to Queensland, Australia, where they stayed until 1888, when Anthony Musgrave died and Jeanne Lucinda Musgrave returned to England. For more on Jeanne Lucinda Musgrave, see Marcia Thomas. While it is certainly possible that Caroline Sullivan was a beneficiary of the Women's Self-Help Society, it is more likely that she knew Lady Musgrave in other ways.

10. Clearly based on extensive historical and contemporary research, *Life and Food in the Caribbean* is a memoir and cookbook more than a scholarly work.

11. The 1908 edition of *The Jamaica Cookery Book* lists two publishers: Aston W. Gardner Co. of Kingston, Jamaica, and The Gamage Building, Holborn, E. C. of London. An 1899 announcement in the *Daily Gleaner* that *The Jamaica Cookery Book* had been added to the Institute of Jamaica

library as well as the Library of Congress and Schlessinger Library's acquisition histories do suggest that Sullivan's book was in circulation through the early twentieth century.

12. Rubin's argument about the "traffic in women" emerges from her feminist analysis of Claude Levi-Strauss's "exchange of women."
13. It is possible that among these "newcomers" could also be English (or Irish or Scottish) women coming to Jamaica not as colonial wives but at intermediary levels such as those of housekeeper, or the kind of "upper servant" advertised in the February 18, 1893, *Daily Gleaner* as "wanted immediately," with the qualification, "Must have a good knowledge of cookery (although not required to cook as a cook is kept) as well as nursing if necessary."
14. Higman similarly posits that "no doubt, West Indian planters and merchants, and their wives, possessed copies of such cookbooks [as Hannah Glasse's *The Art of Cookery*] but they did not reprint them or produce works defining a particular 'West Indian' cuisine" until Sullivan's ("Cookbooks," 79). Advertisements in the April and May 1890 *Daily Gleaner* for Mrs. Breeton's *Book of Household Management*, sold by Justin McCarthy at 8 & 10 King Street in Kingston, and in several issues of the 1895 *Daily Gleaner* for *Everybody's Cookery and Household Guide*, distributed by Gardner's, confirm this assertion.
15. Lawson Welsh examines how nineteenth-century European travelers wrote about "creole" and foods in overwhelmingly negative terms (*Food, Text, and Culture in the Anglophone Caribbean*, 43–75).
16. Ingredients and preparations indigenous to Asia, especially India and China, that are now recognized as part of the West Indian creole and with distinct histories in the Caribbean, appear in Sullivan's cookbook only in forms brought to the West Indies via colonial trade: cloves, cinnamon, and nutmeg appear in the soups section, and elsewhere a large number of recipes call for rice and a few call for curry. Most of these were naturalized in Caribbean cuisine in the early colonial period. Curry arrived a little later, via English colonial families that had previously served in India. Curry also arrived again in the West Indies with Indian indentured servants who were first brought to Jamaica in 1845. That Sullivan's three "curried" recipes call for curry powder but are not in any other way linked to Indian culinary traditions and are not accompanied by any other Indian or Indo-Caribbean dished indicates that she only includes Indian elements of West Indian cuisine that entered via English colonial wives.
17. Although education expanded greatly in Jamaica after 1867, in 1890 only 28 percent of school-age children attended school of any level. For more on colonial education in Jamaica, see Brian Moore and Michelle Johnson. Mary Seacole, who published her *Wonderful Adventures of Mary Seacole in Many Lands* in 1857, represents the importance of the small population of literate middle-class mixed-race Creole women who could have read and

written back to Sullivan. Seacole's account of her own work as a cook in inns and as a small businesswoman in Jamaica describes a world in which she and someone like Sullivan could certainly have crossed paths, literally or literarily, and in which their communities were deeply divided by race, class, and access to colonial power. Seacole settled in Britain in 1870 and died in 1881, so she herself is unlikely to have literally crossed paths with Sullivan and could not have read *The Jamaica Cookery Book*.

18. The recipe appeared in the *Daily Gleaner* in a letter to the editor on Saturday, May 18, 1895. The name of the sender is illegible.
19. The title of the recipe for "Orange Biscuits or Little Cakes, from Receipt of 1809" gestures toward an attribution, but the recipe contains no further information about where Sullivan encountered the 1809 receipt.
20. Established in 1834 by the Jamaican Jewish DeCordova brothers, the *Daily Gleaner* was the major and centrist newspaper of Jamaica. Since 1992 titled simple the *Gleaner*, it has had many iterations including the *Weekly Gleaner*, the *Weekend Gleaner*, and the *Sunday Gleaner* and is also frequently referred to as the *Jamaica Gleaner* or the *Kingston Gleaner*. The pan-Africanist *Jamaican Advocate*, founded in 1894, opened a decidedly Black publication, and the *Jamaica Times*, starting in 1898, offered a space for feminism and nationalism through its focus on women teachers.
21. The "Meals for a Small Family" section confirms that all "Breakfasts" include substantial savory components among their several dishes (115). In a similar vein, the inclusion of "Pepper Pot" in the "soups" section betrays the "native" tradition of one-pot meals that resists the English multi-course meal order.
22. The same image appeared, in color, on a postcard published, like *The Jamaica Cookery Book*, by Aston W. Gardner in a series that also included "Our House-Cleaner," "Our Housemaid," and "Market Women." For more on the postcards, see the Cousins Hereward postcard collection at UWI-Mona.
23. Kelley Fanto Deetz's study of cooks on Virginia plantations offers much that also applies to Caribbean plantations, especially those under British rule and especially during the period when both Virginia and much of the Caribbean were British colonies.
24. The same sentence appears in *West Indian Yams* with "Yams" in the place of "Sweet Potatoes."
25. For a detailed biography of John Redman Bovell in the context of his work, see Galloway.
26. The similarity of the recipes suggests that she also prepared the ones in *Sweet Potatos*.
27. Danielle Delon in the preface to her 2016 edition of the *Handbook of Trinidad Cookery* writes that Mrs. Edward Lycott Bovell, "a Yearwood from Barbados," who moved to Trinidad and was friends with Mrs. Lickfold, is the contributor of the recipes in *Cooking West Indian Yams*. Delon's

information, from archival research including the private collection of the Bovell family, either confuses two Bovell brothers and their wives, or else points to an exchange of recipes among sisters-in-law who then end up variously credited. John Redman Bovell, born in Barbados in 1855 or 1856, married Elizabeth Jemmott in 1880, and they remained in Barbados. His brother Edward Lycott Bovell, born in Barbados in 1861, married Blanche Yearwood and migrated to Trinidad where he partnered with George F. Higgins to buy and manage the Cocal estate in Manzanilla.

28. The two banana recipes appear in the dessert section.
29. Higman offers an "hors d'oeuvre" for these cookbooks and touches on them in *Food in Jamaica*, and the introduction to the 2016 edition of Lickfold's *Handbook of Trinidad Cookery* contextualizes that work, but Lawson Welsh's examination of Yearwood's *West Indian and Other Recipes* is the only in-depth study of one of these cookbooks (203–215).
30. Their grandson, John Spriggs, drawing on journals that Hilary kept and notes that other family members added to them, explains that "Jack being the youngest son had to make his own way in life so on February 28, 1884 he left England and went [to] Trinidad where he worked on cocoa estates there. How they kept in touch is unclear but it was usual for workers like Jack to be given home leave every three years and it was on one of these that on 24 November 1894 that Hilary and Jack were engaged. Jack returned to Trinidad early January 1895."
31. Thanks to John Spriggs and other descendants of Hilary Hodd Lickfold for sharing this information, which fills in and corrects that given by Angelo Bisserssarsingh in his foreword to the 2016 edition.
32. The prevalence of families like Yearwood across the West Indies, the frequent movement of individuals from one island to another, and Lickfold, Watkins, and Yearwood's identification of most contributors by last name, husband's initials and last name, or simply initials make it difficult to trace the biographies of the contributors precisely. Bissessarsingh's foreword to the 2016 edition of *A Handbook of Trinidad Cookery* details the backgrounds of many of the contributors to that volume and notes that "a mutual feature of almost all the ladies who contributed recipes to the tome is that they were white and Anglican. They also belonged to a loosely formed organization which would, 14 years later, blossom into the local chapter of the Mothers' Union, founded in England in 1876" (n.p.). For further discussion of White colonial women's circles, see Gartrell, Brownfoot, Strobel, and Wilson.
33. It does carve out space for women who are not mothers, even for women who are not legally attached to those who depend on them, in the traditional work of women in the home.
34. Personal communication from John Sprigg, grandson of Lickfold: "There was a reason my Grandmother went to the trouble of putting together a cookbook of Trinidadian recipes. She was a very devout member of the

Church of England and living in Sangre Grande there was no church. She thus became a driving force in the push to have a church built. One of the ways to generate money was a cookbook, and so she took it upon herself to publish one. In time the Church of St. James the Just was built in Sangre Grande. She and Jack Lickfold are buried in the churchyard there. I believe the church has now been replaced but it has a stained glass window dedicated to her."

35. See Lawson Welsh, 443. Juliet Edmonds and Cherita Girvan write that "the Bessie Yearwood Home was set up in 1876 as the result of the efforts of the charitable and well-to-do Mrs. Yearwood. The home was meant for destitute and ill-treated children, of any race or creed and from any parish. The home is housed in a relatively small house and therefore take[s] only a few children. . . . It could house seven" (240).

36. Founded in Jamaica in 1865, the Lady Musgrave Self-Help Society "aimed to provide income-earning possibilities for 'gentlewomen who had fallen on reduced circumstances' . . . by providing a market for upper class women's crafts and preserves and training working class young women in housewifery skills" (Reddock, "The Early Women's Movement" 102).

37. Steeve Buckridge's analysis that the Lady Musgrave Society "was a leisure activity for white women to teach freed women Victorian needlework, decorum, and dressmaking skills" reminds that helping "the natives" and "freed women and men" fits neatly into colonial projects (100).

38. In all of the cookbooks, about 20 to 30 percent of the recipes have titles that specify recognizably Afro-Indigenous or Creole ingredients or methods, and about 3 to 5 percent Indo-Caribbean. The distinctions are minor but worth noting: about 20 percent of Yearwood's and Psaila's recipes are distinctly Afro-Indigenous or Creole, and about 4 percent are Indo-Caribbean; 27 percent of Lickfold's recipes are distinctly Afro-Indigenous or Creole, and about 3 percent are Indo-Caribbean; and about 34 percent of Watkins's recipes are Creole, and about 5 percent are Indo-Caribbean.

39. Yearwood, for example, does give numerous recipes that call for eddoes, yam, breadfruit, and okra and includes one recipe for roasted (green) plantains but includes recipes for plantain and banana primarily in sweets.

40. "Melangène" is used commonly in the Caribbean and occasionally in France for what is also known as eggplant in English, aubergine in French, berenjana in Spanish, and melanzana in Italian. The plant arrived in the Caribbean with Europeans (it had earlier arrived in Europe from North Africa or the Middle East).

41. For more on the history of pepper pot, see Candice Goucher, Theresa Altieri Taplin, Gibron Rahim, Gillian Richards-Greaves, and Austin Clarke.

42. While tamales represent a similar Indigenous wrapped and steamed preparation, the term "Conky," probably derived from the Ga "Kenkey" (and the Jamaican term "duckunoo," from the Asante Twi word for the same dish), indicates the West African origins of the preparation.

43. Rose water, like curry, made its way to the Caribbean both through England (via colonialists from India) and with Indian indentured laborers (rose water originated in Iran, making its way to India during the Mughal empire).

Chapter 3 Colonial and Neocolonial Fortification in the French Antilles, Puerto Rico, and the U.S. Virgin Islands

1. Just like "West Indies" in English designates the British holdings in the Caribbean and is extended to refer to the Caribbean as a whole, "les Antilles" in French designates France's Caribbean holdings and refers to the Caribbean as a whole.
2. I have written on these in "A Little Puerto Rican Food Culture..." and "Recipes for National Culture in Guadeloupe and Martinique."
3. See, for example, my "Home Cooking: Transnational and Diasporic Caribbean Cookbooks."
4. The *Larousse* dictionary's entry on "outre" explains the particular case of uses like *outre-mer* thus: "outre, used in a composite meaning 'located beyond [*situé au-delà-de*]', is linked by a dash to the element that it precedes." For analyses of the political history and alignments of the *départments d'outre-mer*, see Kristen Stromberg Childers. That, in 2015, Martinique and French Guiana shifted again to each become a "unique territorial collectivity" of France involves, among other things, a refusal of the "outre-mer" terminology.
5. For a full discussion of Carême, see Priscilla Parkhurst Ferguson.
6. Earlier Universal Expositions in Paris had colonial sections, and there were two prior colonial expositions in Marseille in 1906 and 1922, but 1931 was the first Colonial Exposition in Paris.
7. Querillac led a seminar on "Preparation of the European woman for colonial life" at the 1931 Colonial Exposition, probably part of feminist sessions focused on expanding women's roles in the colonies. For a full discussion of French colonial women, see Marie-Paule Ha and Clotilde Chivas-Baron.
8. De Noter was a French horticulturalist and linguist. His many other works range from early publications like the 1890 *Étude synpotique sur l'horticulture en Algérie* and the 1901 *Dictionnaire français-argot* through numerous works on home and industrial food production, occasionally including attention to Algeria and "les cinq parties du monde," to his last two books, *Le jardin potager colonial* (1930) and the 1931 cookbook. Dedicated to former French prime minister Aristide Briand and prefaced by the French writer Paul Reboux, de Noter's book is a celebration of French colonialism as it benefits the "good French bourgeois" of the 1930s, who can build on the work of "our great explorers" to give the greatest of dinner parties (xii). Rabette was a journalist and novelist, whose other cookbooks are *Almanac-manuel*

de la cuisinière (1890?), focused on compending French menus, and *Les conseils des Catherines: 920 recettes pratiques pour la maîtresse de maison* (1929). Anne Querillac, née Chasseriaud, was a French journalist. She was widowed young when her husband, Jean Querillac, a captain in the French colonial infantry, died during World War I. Her other publications include articles in *L'art vivant* (1926), *La femme au travail* (1937), and *La Legion*'s 1941 volume dedicated to "La France d'Outre Mer."

9. Though France also possesses St. Martin, it is not referred to in any of the cookbooks.
10. "Câpresse" is a term used in the French Antilles to describe a light-skinned Black woman. In French colonial racial taxonomy, a câparesse was the child of a White and a Mulatto.
11. Eliza Dooley's 1948 *Puerto Rican Cookbook* is another example, as is Marie Thérèse Julien Lung-Fou's 1950 *Les recettes de cuisine martiniquaise de Da Elodie*.
12. Édouard Glissant includes an entry for "Da" in the glossary of *Le discours antillais*: "The black nurse-maid. Has her equivalent all over the Caribbean region and the Southern United States. Ideal (victimized) fictional character. Black, slave, and nonetheless loving and heroic" (826). She appears to offer her services in French food advertising of the early twentieth century such as the Comptoir des Colonie's coffee posters and P. Bardinet's 1920s Rhum Negrita posters.
13. Throughout the preface, Querillac repeats this structure of praising Chloé's culinary knowledge and then immediately diminishing her as a child, a sex object, a primitive, or a representative of times gone by (x, xi).
14. Callaloo (calalou) leaves go by many different names and furthermore come from a variety of different plants in what Linnaean taxonomy names the Araceae or arum family, also known as aroids; taro, eddo, tannia, and cocoyam are in that same family. Aralia ("araliée" in French; Araliaceae in the Linnaean binomial) is a different family of plants (including, most famously, ginseng). "Araliée" is the French name for a Malgash or Malaysian tribe in whose flora French colonialists were particularly interested, as evidenced by Emmanuel Drake del Castillo's "Notes sur les 'araliées' des îles d'Afrique orientale," published in the 1897 issue of *Journal des botaniques*.
15. Querillac uses the word "épluché," which specifically means to remove the skin or to peel. "Lavé" or "frotté" are the terms to designate okra that has undergone the correct processing.
16. Querillac is identified in *Cuisine coloniale* only by her first initial, allowing a certain gender mobility, although her public presence at the Colonial Exposition was clearly as a woman. Querillac is also co-author, with Pierre de Trévières, of the 1927 *Manuel nouveau des usages mondains en France et à l'étranger: la tradition, la vie modern*, whose primary focus on French men's manners helps to explain her attention to men's social positions,

though it also raises questions about her place in discourses that seem to primarily be between men.

17. Manioc (yuca) is native to the Antilles, but thanks to the Columbian exchange, by the first half of the seventeenth century (when Querillac's story is set), it had become, as Querillac asserts, "common to all tropical countries" (25).
18. It appears that this story was first published in French in Auguste Le Hérissé's 1911 *L'Ancien Royaume du Dahomey* (266–270). A version quite similar to Querillac's was published in April 1964 in the fourth issue of *AWA: La revue du femme noire*, "according to a Dahomian story collected by SIM." (SIM is the Salon International des Mines de Sénégal formed in 1964 by the Senegalese director of mines and geography).
19. Although in Querillac's version, the connection between the manioc and the penis is not explicit, in Le Hérissé's version Death quite clearly transforms the boy's penis into a manioc and gives it to her. Also, in Le Hérissé's version, the first wife, Alouba, is not put to death but rather is given to a hyena to be carried out to the bush.
20. That the proverb in this recipe, along with most of the others that Querillac includes, also appears in Lafcadio Hearn's 1885 *"Gombo Zhèbes": Little Dictionary of Creole Proverbs* both confirms it as a proverb and places Hearn's work alongside the accounts of African folktales collected by French colonialists as a possible source for Querillac's work.
21. In "Recipes for National Culture in Guadeloupe and Martinique," I consider how cookbooks like Marie-Magdelaine Carbet's 1978 *Cuisine des îles ou le bon manger antillais* may offer instructions for an autochthonous Antilles without an independent nation-state.
22. Ary Ebroïn, author of the 1972 *La cuisine créole*, and André Veille, who wrote the introduction to the 1975 *Da Mathilde, 325 recettes de cuisine créole*, belonged, with Nègre, to Rôtisseur clubs. Nègre's book contains several pages of advertisements for Veille's restaurants and hotels and lists Ebroïn's book in its bibliography.
23. *Les recettes martiniquaises de Da Elodie* appears to be Julien Lung-Fou's first publication (although the absence of a date in the first edition makes the 1950 dating approximate). Her subsequent publications include *Fables créoles* (1958), *Trois bonnes fortunes: Trois comédies en un acte* (1969), *Les piments doux: 25 fantaisies* (1976), *Contes créoles* (1979), *Le carnaval aux antilles* (1979), and *Contes animuax* (1980). She also illustrated Marie-Magdelaine Carbet's poetry collection *Musique noire* (1958).
24. Julien Lung-Fou is said to have selected the last name Lung-Fou in order to honor her Cantonese-immigrant grandfather. Patrick Chamoiseau, at the dedication of the Martinican library named in her honor, described her as a foremother of Créolité, citing her vocal embrace of mixed African, Chinese, and European ancestry as central to her Martinican identity (Montray Kréyol).

25. Ellen Walsh explains that "The perception that, despite statutory separation of church and state, the new United States regime favored Protestantism and that missionaries had ready access to the colonial state and other agents of Americanization" is based in associations of church and state left over from Spanish imperialism (89). She notes that "Missionaries and the colonial state had many, varied interactions, both public and private. Insular governors publicly supported the missionary project by giving welcoming speeches at the annual denominational conventions and occasionally intervening in bureaucratic matters or giving advice. Many colonial officials belonged to, and were quite active in, Protestant churches, particularly in San Juan, the bureaucracy's center" (89).
26. For detailed discussions of the Puerto Rican women's movements at the turn of the twentieth century, see Ivette Romero-Cesareo; Maria del Carmen Baerga; Linda C. Delgado and Felix Matos; and Maria de Fátima Barceló Miller.
27. Winifred Connerton makes a similar argument in regard to U.S. nurses in Puerto Rico in the first decades of the twentieth century.
28. *The Barton Cookbook*'s section on meat, for example, starts with a list of accompaniments for different roasts and "General Directions for Boiling or Roasting Meat."
29. For an examination of White images of African American women, the mammy figure, and African American cookbooks, see Toni Tipton-Martin.
30. The two possible exceptions, Johnny cakes and cod fish balls, were "claimed" in the early twentieth century by both New England and the West Indies.
31. By comparison, the two recipes for pilau in the *Housekeeper's Guide to British Guiana* are: "Pilau, (1). 1 fowl, a few slices of bacon, rice, 2 eggs, tomato and parsley. Boil a fowl, take it from the water and cut in pieces, then fry some bacon with it. Boil some rice in a little of the water the fowl was boiled in and take the rest of the water and make a nice gravy. Boil two eggs hard. Bank the rice in the middle of a dish, then put alternately pieces of fowl and bacon. Garnish with slices of hard-boiled egg, tomato and sprigs of parsley" (35); "Pilau. (2). 1 chicken, ½ lb rice, a little salt, 1 gill of cream, a little nutmeg, ½ lb. raisins (seeded), ½ oz butter. Parboil the rice in salted water, add to it the chicken (whole) and enough water to cover well. Allow to simmer gently for ¾ of an hour. When nearly done add the raisins. After the chicken is cooked remove it to a hot dish, add the cream, a little grated nutmeg and the butter to the rice and raisins, pack into small moulds of even size and turn out on to the dish round the chicken" (35).
32. Bailey K. Ashford was a U.S. Army physician who helped to found and then taught at the San Juan School of Tropical Medicine. For more on Ashford's life, see his autobiography, *A Soldier in Science*.
33. See Solsiree del Moral and Elisa González for further discussions of education policies and practices in Puerto Rico.

34. This lacuna seems to have been rectified, however, in some editions as Ortíz Cuadra cites Ferguson acknowledging that "it was in hotel kitchens, in small pueblos, or in the kitchens of families kind enough to bid me welcome that I learned the art of preparing Puerto Rican dishes" (323, n. 95).
35. Willsey's publications in this group include the 1925 *Tropical Foods*, Bulletin of the Puerto Rico Department of Education no. 3, whole number 62 (re-issued, it appears, by the Department of Education of Porto Rico in 1927 as *Tropical Foods: Chayote, Yautia, Plantain, Banana*); the 1927 *Vegetables: Rice and the Legumes*, Tropical Foods Bulletin no. 3, Bulletin University of Puerto Rico Department of Home Economics vol. 1, no. 2; and what appear to be translations of *Tropical Foods*, the 1931 *Vegetales tropicales: yautía* by Willsey and Carmen Janer Vilá, Publication of the University of Puerto Rico College of Education no. 11, Bulletin University of Puerto Rico Department of Home Economics vol. 3, no. 8, the 1931 *Vegetales tropicales: chayote* by Willsey and Clara Aurora Ruiz, Publication of the University of Puerto Rico College of Education no. 9, Bulletin University of Puerto Rico Department of Home Economics vol. 1, no. 6, and *Vegetales tropicales: batata* with no co-author, University of Puerto Rico College of Education no. 10, Bulletin University of Puerto Rico Department of Home Economics no. 2, no. 7; and a series of "circular de extensión"s in Spanish for the UPR Agricultural Extension Service in the 1930s: the 1937 *El Panapén: modos de prepararlo para la mesa* by Willsey and Rosa M. Ordoñez and *La yuca: modos de prepararla para la mesa* by Willsey and Estrella Moll Schwarzkopf, the 1938 *La berenjena: modos de prepararla para la mesa* by Willsey and Angela Pastrana, and the 1939 *El plátano: modos de prepararlo para la mesa* by Willsey and Angelina Mercader.
36. For further consideration of home economics, albeit with a U.S. focus, see Laura Shapiro.
37. See, for example, Victor S. Clark; Bailey Diffie and Justine Diffie; Arthur D. Gayer, Paul T. Homan, and Earle K. James. This analysis persisted throughout the twentieth century, as exemplified by James Dietz and Emilio Pantojas-Garcia, and continues to be used by scholars such as Romero-Cesareo (782). However, Cesar J. Ayala and Laird W. Bergad's argument for a different development pattern has been followed by scholars such as José Solá to show that in the first three decades of the twentieth century, Puerto Rican farms did continue to produce a strong volume of subsistence crops for the local market.
38. The exceptions are "Scalloped Chayote," "Sweet Pickled Chayote," "Riced Yautia," "Scalloped Yautia," "Cream-of-Yautia Soup," "Ripe Plantain Souffle," and "Scalloped Ripe Plantain," given only in English, and "Albornia de chayote," "Tostones de platano," "Pasteles de Platano," "Empanadas de platano," "Pastelillos de platano," "Alcapurrias," and "Guanimes de platano," given only in Spanish, in quotation marks.

39. Given the scarce number of previous Puerto Rican cookbooks, along with the nature of recipe evolution, it is difficult to give exact origin points for most recipes or to pinpoint most culinary innovations, but only the U.S.-style dishes with Puerto Rican vegetables do not have a wide dispersion in other Puerto Rican or Caribbean cookbooks (earlier and later).
40. Vol. 1, no. 6, *Vegetales tropicales: chayote* by Willsey and Clara Aurora Ruíz; vol. 2, no. 7, *Vegetales tropicales: batata* by Willsey; vol. 3, no. 8, *Vegetales tropicales: yautía* by Carmen Janer Vilá and Willsey.
41. Because many of these were published first as Agricultural Extension Service circulars and bulletins in the mid-1930s, and then reissued, in a different order, as titled booklets between 1937 and 1939, publication dates can be confusing. Extension Circular No. 1, listing Estrella Moll Schwartzkopf and Willsey as authors, takes on *La yuca*. Circular No. 2, *El plátano*, by Angelina Mercador and Willsey, combines the English plantain and banana from *Tropical Fruits*. Rosa M. Ordoñez and Willsey's Circular 4 is *El panapén*. Angela Pastrana and Willsey's *La berenjena* is No. 6. Mary E Keown, auxiliary director of the Agricultural Extension Service in charge of the Work of Home Demonstrations from 1934–1935, is the sole compiler of Bulletin No. 7, *La conservación de frutas y vegetales en Puerto Rico*. This last shifts from an authorial attribution "by [por]" used in the circulars. It appears that the circulars and the bulletins were separate series and appeared alongside one another, both published by the Agricultural Extension Service. I have only been able to locate a limited number of each.
42. Orcasitas is also author of circular No. 14, *Conservación de carnes en el hogar*, and No. 15, *Como preparar los productos enlatados en su despensa para servirlos en mesa*, which acknowledges building off Keown's work.
43. In 1931, when the first Spanish-language bulletins were published, Spanish was the language of instruction in Puerto Rico only through grade four, followed by a transitional period in both Spanish and English in grades five to seven, and English only after that.
44. Grains are more important in Europe and perhaps also on a worldwide scale, but tubers and roots have historically been of equal if not greater import in the Americas (where corn and wild rice were the only grains regularly used before conquest). I have not been able to find a copy of the English-language precedent to *La yuca* but I believe that it is one of the 1925 bulletins that Willsey wrote, perhaps *Vegetables: Rice and the Legumes*.
45. Nearly all of the circulars repeat *Tropical Food*'s introductory insistence on *standard* (always italicized and in English) measures.
46. In spite of the efforts of commissioners of education to enforce English-language instruction in Puerto Rico, the shift to Spanish in the circulars reflects how the successes of the U.S.-run school system in raising literacy rates in Puerto Rico over the first half of the twentieth century (from 20 percent in 1899 to 55 percent in 1930, to 68 percent in 1940, and

73.3 percent in 1950) rested on the ability of teachers like Willsey and those she trained to work in Spanish.

47. I examine Cabanillas's work in "A Little Puerto Rican Food Culture . . ."
48. Henry Dooley was a member of the San Juan Municipal Council and several-time mayoral candidate and a partner in the import-and-export business Dooley, Smith & Co. with offices in San Juan, Ponce, and Havana. He died in 1932.
49. That she paints an image of a figure rather than tells a story of a person is evident in the ways that Dooley's claim of Isabel's twenty-eight-year dedication to her kitchen conflicts with her previous claim that as soon as she brought her daughter back from the United States, Isabel "took the wee one into her arms, I found a new cooked installed in the kitchen, and from that time to the day of her death Isabel trailed her beloved Mary" (viii).
50. "Illustrations from paintings by Mrs. Henry W. Dooley" appear in *Seven Sonnets on Puerto Rico*, published in New York in 1938. That collection ends with Sonnet 7, "L'envoi," whose passing acknowledgment of Puerto Rican history is subsumed under a paen to American liberation: "The savage, and the slave, the Don from Spain,/Who now, a people free and bound and proud,/Grope in confusion that the soul would fain/O'ercome. May Freedom's flag disperse this could/Of dark discord, and give them the joy/And peace that man can nevermore destroy."
51. As with the case of Willsey, Ruíz, Janer Vilá, Schwartzkopf, Mercador, Ordoñez, Pastrana, Keown, and Orcasitas, the distinction between colonizer and colonized is not always so complete. Puerto Rican home economics and Extension Service publications, as much as Ferguson's textbook and the Ladies Aid Society's *Porto Rican Cookbook*, facilitated Dooley's work, but they also were decolonial training grounds for the authors of *Cocine a gusto*. The differences between, as much as those within, the cookbooks written by U.S.-born women colonialist defenders of native style for U.S.-based "newcomers" and the circulars written with and for Puerto Rican women laid the ground for a Spanish-language cookbook's recipes for national culture that I examine in "A Little Puerto Rican Food Culture . . ."
52. See Valens, "A Little Puerto Rican Food Culture" and "Home Cooking."
53. In 1933, President Franklin Roosevelt launched the Good Neighbor policy that, in the words of the State Department, "emphasized cooperation and trade rather than military force to maintain stability in the hemisphere" (Office of the Historian).
54. I must keep insisting on the complication of using racial terms across space and time. Part of what the U.S. rule in the Virgin Islands does is to install U.S. racial categorization in which anyone who has "one drop" of African ancestry is Black. So while I use that terminology, I am painfully aware of its role in translating Virgin Islands culture into U.S. terms.
55. The 1936 Organic Act gives the governor full power of veto and the responsibility for appointing all government employees. It also establishes a

judicial branch under the control of a district court judge and a district attorney appointed by the president of the United States.
56. The act has been revised and amended several times. Most significantly, the 1956 revision provides for the possibility of the establishment of a constitution of the Virgin Islands and the 1968 amendment provides for an elected governor. For the details of the revisions and amendments, see the U.S. Code 48 Territories and Possessions, ch. 12, U.S. Virgin Islands, https://uscode.house.gov/view.xhtml?path=/prelim@title48/chapter12&edition=prelim.
57. For a description of Virgin Islands indigenous and native foods, see Lee Newsom and Elizabeth Wing. For a discussion of agriculture and food production in the Virgin Islands during the colonial period, see William Chapman, 136.
58. School lunches in the Virgin Islands were free until January 1954. For a discussion of the passage of the bill authorizing the collection of money for school lunches, see the *Daily News*, "The School Lunch."
59. The inside cover describes the booklet as representing "a cooperative effort of the V.I. Extension Service, College of the Virgin Islands; the Virgin Islands Department of Agriculture; and the Virgin Islands Department of Health" and is signed by "Nutrition Education Committee, 'Food in Every Yard' Project sponsored by the Virgin Islands Department of Agriculture in cooperation with the St. Croix Nutrition Committee." I have not been able to determine who was on the "Nutrition Education Committee" or who participated in "Food in Every Yard."
60. The 1978 edition, also listed as Bulletin 1 of the Virgin Islands Cooperative Extension Service, is sometimes listed as a revised edition; I have been unable to locate any previous edition. It was published in a revised edition in 1985.
61. Many of these were originally published, similar to the Puerto Rican circulars, as Extension Program Bulletins: Native Recipes is No. 1, Holiday Cooking is No. 7, Breads is No. 8.
62. Tinsley is referring here to the Dutch West Indies, which are, as Chapman points out, closely tied architecturally and culturally to the Virgin Islands through at least the early nineteenth century. The yard is the space of traditional Virgin Islands cooking not only because much cooking was done in coal pots over open fires located in yards, but also because through the early twentieth century, rather than a kitchen most wealthy Virgin Islands residences had a separate cook house with an entrance onto the yard, which was also surrounded by slave or servant dwellings (Chapman, 149).
63. As listed in the USDA Food Composition Databases.
64. "Mammaee Apple" "is not unlike the quince" (28) and to cook the tanier the reader is instructed to "follow any recipe as for potatoes" (51).
65. While the nutrition science has certainly evolved, the USDA has been calculating the nutritional value of foods in the U.S. food supply—which

includes the food supply of its territories—since 1909. According to the 2020 USDA Food Composition Database, a cup of West Indian cherry has more than four times the amount of vitamin C of a cup of guava.

66. The second edition of *Native Recipes* was published in 1978. I have not been able to find a copy of the first edition or its exact date of publication.
67. Olivia H. Henry closes her prefatory remarks with, "We sincerely hope you will enjoy using the booklet as well as we have enjoyed putting it together."
68. Olivia H. Henry also uses Creole in the titles of two of her contributions to the 2004 *Glory Days of Frederiksted*, "De Style of De Day" and "Ms. Francis's Conversation with 'De Bwoy.'"
69. Wayne James's August 8, 2018, post on his *Manlymanners* blog on "The History of the Cuisine of St. Croix" lists "the last three editions of *Native Recipes*, published by the University of the Virgin Islands Cooperative Extension Services under the informed guidance of Mrs. Olivia Hinds Henry, widow of Oscar E. Henry" as comprising, with Amy Mackay's *Le Awe Cook* and Laura Moorhead's *Kruzan Nynyam from Mampoo Kitchen*, "the most notable . . . books on Crucian cuisine." It also notes (in 2018) that "those cookbooks, written back in the '70s, 80s, and 90s are today not as widely known or read as they were when first published. And no comprehensive cookbook on Crucian foods has been published in the 21st century. As such, there are cooks, especially non-native ones, who are cooking pseudo-Crucian dishes, their creations oftentimes the result of eyeballing, blind-tasting, and outside influences."
70. These include "cream of mushroom soup" (31), canned tomato products (48, 49, 55), and canned beans (44, 46, 49, 55).
71. Arona Petersen's 1990 *The Food and Folklore of the Virgin Islands* might continue this mode, but it seems more like its last hurrah. The book is a collection of Petersen's *Daily News* columns written over the previous decades. That *Daily News* executive editor Elizabeth Rahe praised Petersen as "the best of the Old-Time Virgin Islands" signals that end rather than the continuation of what she represents, confirmed in the fact that *The Food and Folklore of the Virgin Islands* is, at the time of this writing, out of print.

Chapter 4   Cuban Independence, to Taste

1. An unmarked group or identity is the one that is the same as the dominant norm, the one that is assumed when nothing is specified, while a marked identity or group is one that is singled out at the other (against which the "sameness" of the "same" is visible).
2. See, for example, Beatriz Calvo Peña. Christine Folch lays out the grouping that I follow.
3. Perhaps coincidentally, Dr. Gonzalo Aróstegui y Castillo's name also invokes—via the shared Aróstegui—the revolutionary Gonzalo de Quesada

y Aróstegui who was, with José Martí, one of the architects of Cuban independence, a member of the Cuban Constitutional Convention, and editor of Martí's *Obras literarias*.

4. Aróstegui reports that the *Manual del cocinero cubano* is out of print. He makes no mention of the other nineteenth-century Cuban cookbooks.

5. Martí's vision of "our mestiza America [nuestra America mestiza]" focuses on a rethinking of the place of the Indigenous in our understanding of Cuba and the Americas with little explicit attention to African heritage, but many of his fellow revolutionaries, such as Juan Gualberto Gómez, addressed the racial violence of colonialism and formulated the revolution as one that united Afrocubans and White Criollos. For discussion of the debates over the independence movement and race and racism in the late nineteenth century, see Luis Álvarez Álvarez and Olga García Yero.

6. A *"parilla"* is a flat grill that can be placed over any kind of low heat, charcoal, electric, or gas. An old-style *"asador"* consists of two large metal or wooden grills to which the meat, often an entire animal, is attached, set upright in a triangle over an open fire or charcoal pit.

7. Oviedo records the use of the term "barbacoa" (Book VII ch. I). Citing Oviedo, Cayetano Coll y Toste identifies "barbacoa" as "Indo-Antillian" (208). For a discussion of "Indo-Antillian" Arawak and Carib languages see Alexandra Aikhenvald.

8. While these electric ovens were most likely imported from the United States, Triay's silence on their origin fits with the cookbook's refusal to embrace U.S. goods and products.

9. Female literacy in Cuba rose from 38 percent in 1899 to 61 percent in 1919 and 73.7 percent in 1937 (McGuire and Frankel, 101). I have not been able to find statistics that break down female literacy by race, class, or occupation, but as no special efforts were made to expand the literacy of poor Black women, the rapid rise in female literacy was most likely concentrated among the wealthier and Whiter.

10. The subtitular claim of the 1923 *La sagüera* to be a "most useful expanded collection of tested recipes" suggests that it is a second edition, though I have found no other.

11. The 1937 *La cocina y el hogar* is a second edition, "aumentada y corregida." I have not been able to locate a copy of the first edition or to ascertain its date of publication. It was issued in an updated edition in 1977 by Minerva Books.

12. My examination of these works builds on Folch's wonderful study of "race in prerevolution Cuban cookbooks." Testimony to the evolving richness of this field is that I was able to locate books that were unavailable to Folch; thus I modify her claim that Crespo was the first Cuban woman to author a cookbook with the information about Reyes Gavilán.

13. Folch explains that the pseudonym Marquesa de Sevigne is borrowed from the Marquise de Sevigne, "itself a pseudonym for Marie de

Rabutin-Chantal, a seventeenth-century French writer best known for her letters and witty sayings," and notes that "the anonymous (but presumably female) author of *Buena mesa* thus invokes a tradition of female scholarship merely by using the name" (212).

14. For more on women's organizing in Cuba, see Stoner, Pérez Jr., and Martha Gómez Ferrals.
15. I have not found direct evidence of women cookbook writers who were also organizers, but I have not been able to search all of the records of women's organizations in early twentieth-century Cuba.
16. Dawdy surveys the shifts in agriculture and nutrition in "*La Comida Mambisa.*"
17. Birth, marriage, migration, census, and ship and airplane records and Florida International University Library's incredible *Enrique Hurtado de Mendoza Collection of Cuban Genealogy* sometimes identify race but not always, and the basis on which race is determined as well as the categories and terms have changed over time and especially outside of government records are inconsistent and unreliable. Furthermore, details about women are especially difficult to find in these records.
18. Contemporary Cuban chef, cookbook writer, and radio personality Néstor Salazar, for example, refers to it along with the work of Nitza Villapol and Gilbert Smith Duquesne as the classic Cuban cookbooks that have influenced him (José Abreu Cardet).
19. A small Moenck family tree and a brief mention of one member of the de los Reyes Gavilán family appear in the *Enrique Hurtado de Mendoza Collection of Cuban Genealogy*, but Maria Antonieta de los Reyes Gavilán y Moenck does not.
20. Pérez Miró was himself a medical doctor and does not appear to have worked on or published anything else related to food.
21. As with Maria Antonia de los Reyes Gavilán y Moenck, I can find records of both Crespo and Setién families but not of Berta Crespo y Setién.
22. For a full discussion of the Cuban school systems in the 1930s and 40s, see Severin Turosienski.
23. Reyes Gavilán does have one recipe, for Fricassé de pollo con petits pois, that starts "the chicken should be killed in the evening" (181).
24. Although "ama de casa" translates as "housewife," it literally means "mistress of the house." The Spanish term, in other words, does not refer to a marital status but to one of ownership and leadership. Of course, it is also assumed that an "ama de casa" is married to the "amo" (master) and follows his ruling order.
25. For a discussion of the U.S. presence in Cuba in the first half of the twentieth century, see Louis A. Pérez Jr.
26. Cited in translation in Pérez's *On Becoming Cuban*.
27. Alfonso is the only one to write "Sandwiches."

28. Similarly, the British Ladies Committee in Aid of War Relief's 1941 *Cookery Book* in its section on "Platos Cubanos" lists both arroz con pollo and ajiaco, but in that order.
29. The first of *El arte de la cocina*'s four arroz con pollo recipes does not call for peas at all and calls for olives but does not explain if they are canned or not (132).
30. For a developed discussion of Afrocubanismo see Emily Maguire. In "La cocina afrocubana," Fernando Ortiz writes that "the keen Cuban folklorist Lydia Cabrera is preparing a recipe collection of the cuisine that the Blacks brought us or created," but the book was never completed and there is no evidence of notes toward it in her papers (*¿Gusta usted?*, 671).
31. After citing, for example, arguments for the Arabic, African, and Indigenous roots of "ají," he determines that the African is correct (407–408). Recent confirmations of the Indigenous origins of ají include studies in botany (Kraig H. Kraft et al.) and Arawakan language (Granberry and Vescelius).
32. For more on Villapol's biography, see Melissa Fuster, Hanna Garth, Marcos López González, and Sisi Colmina González.
33. For detailed consideration of *¿Gusta usted?* see Folch.
34. Cotta's cookbook does the same and merits more detailed analysis that I can give it here. And Villapol's entry in *¿Gusta usted?*, "Como cocinar al minuto," directly addresses working women (584).
35. Though the Cuban "basic foods" appears to be a government production, Villapol and Martínez embrace it as their own, making no mention of a source.
36. Martínez left Cuba for the United States shortly after the Cuban Revolution.
37. For a discussion of the agrarian reforms, see Dawdy.
38. It is unclear what nutritional components Villapol is considering and what data she is drawing on as she holds up rice and wheat over viandas. Recent studies show that yuca has comparatively less carbohydrates, sugars, and protein than wheat flour, rice, and corn (Montagnac, Davis, and Tanumihardjo). In the 1980 edition, Villapol expresses concern about both too much carbohydrates and too few proteins in the Cuban diet.

Chapter 5   Dominican and Haitian (Re)Emergence

1. For a detailed discussion of the place of agriculture in Dominican political and economic life from the end of Spanish rule through the Trujillo dictatorship, see Richard Lee Turits.
2. For detailed discussions of women under the Trujillo regime, see Virginia Mota and Lauren Derby.

3. For detailed studies of women's movements under Trujillo, see Mota. For a study of women's support for Trujillo, see Derby. Anti-Trujillist feminists were also active, though primarily in exile in the United States and Puerto Rico. For documentation of their work, see the section on "Feminismo anti-trujillista en el país y en el exilio" in Ginetta Candelario, April Mayes, and Elizabeth Manley.
4. The exact publication date is unknown. Maritza Olivier in *Cinco siglos de la mujer dominicana* lists it as 1890, which is the year of Cordero Infante's birth. Cordero Infante's introduction refers to Trujillo as el Generalísimo, a title he took on between 1931 and 1934, suggesting a publication date around or shortly after then.
5. Maritza Olivier's 1975 *Cinco siglos con la mujer dominicana* lists one other cookbook: Irma Marion Landais's 1942 *Receta de artes culinario* (Imprenta Roldán). I have not been able to locate any copy of that book.
6. In the early 1970s, President Bosch contended that only ten thousand households in the Dominican Republic were able to afford domestic help; the vast majority of those were urban and employed more than one servant, generally from the urban poor (Tancer 215).
7. We can see here Cordero Infante's belief in Trujillo's agrarian reforms not only supporting the Dominican economy but also responding to (her own) popular advocacy for further development to also support Dominican nutrition.
8. The poem is Gastón Figueira's "El maíz"; she gives a version of the Guaraní myth of Panambí and Abatí and refers briefly to the Aztecs (40–41).
9. "Auyama" is probably linked to the Cumanogoto "huahuayama." Cumanogoto people and language are indigenous to what is now eastern Venezuela.
10. Although locrio closely resembles paella or various Caribbean rice and meat dishes, the word "locrio" derives from the Andean locro, a grain- or potato-and-meat stew whose name comes from the Quecha *rocro* or *ruqru*. "Locrio" may come from a conjunction of *locro* and the adjective *criollo* (locro criollo becoming locrio).
11. See, for example, Mark Sundaram.
12. For an overview of the conflicting data and numbers about the number of Haitians killed in the Parsley Massacre, see Michele Wucker (50–51).
13. For detailed studies of Trujillo see Bernard Diederich; Derby; Turits.
14. Given the proximity of their social circles, it is likely that the three women at least knew of one another, though in the "presentación" of the ninth edition of Bornia's *Cocina dominicana*, her daughter Eunice Bornia writes that "her work is the first and most voluminous book of Dominican cuisine."
15. For a history of Chinese Dominicans, see Edith Wen-Chu Chen. For a study of Asian Dominicans, see Roger Sanjek.
16. "Chinese sauce [salsa china]" is a sweet soy sauce that appears to have already been produced by Dominican companies in the 1950s.

17. The several Indigenous languages that were spoken on the island now known as Hispaniola belong to the Arawakan and Cariban language groups.
18. Espinosa Orozco's most famous piece during his time in the Dominican Republic is probably his 1956 pamphlet denouncing Jesús Galíndez as both a communist and "the prototype of the overlapping hypocrite, capable of the lowest actions under the mantle of an apocryphal Christianity" (3). The pamphlet was published shortly after Galíndez was disappeared by the Trujillo regime for writing a dissertation on Dominican history at Columbia with a perspective that Trujillo did not appreciate.
19. For a detailed discussion of how and why this occurred, as well as how it carries into late twentieth-century Haiti, see Robert Fatton.
20. It was only in the late nineteenth century that a few Catholic girls' primary schools opened and public secondary education was organized for Haitian women. The first vocational school for girls in Haiti opened in 1902, with a course of study that included cooking. For a detailed study of Haitian education in the nineteenth century, see Job Clement.
21. New editions of Gaillard's cookbook appeared in 1959, 1966, 1971, 1975, 1981, 1985, 1997, and 2009. Only one new Haitian cookbook was published under François (Papa Doc) Duvalier's regime, Mme. Arthur Rampy's 1965 *Cuisine et patisserie*, and under Jean-Claude (Baby Doc) Duvalier's dictatorship (1971–1986), only one more, Mariette Jean's 1974 *Cuisine et savoir vivre*, along with the first of religious aid organization fundraiser cookbook, the 1980 Mountain Maid Self-Help Project's *Mountain Maid Best Made Cookbook*.
22. Where Haitian place, food, and other names have both French and Kreyòl spellings, I use the Kreyòl.
23. For a full study of Constantin Mayard, see Gérard Lehmann's introduction to *Pages retrouvées de Constantin Mayard*.
24. The LFAS was instrumental in the 1944 law granting Haitian women the right to dispose of their own salary and in 1946 in bringing to the Constituent Assembly a vote on women's suffrage. The assembly denied women the right to vote based on arguments that combined misogyny and concern over Haitian women activists' affiliations with White and international-dominated Christian groups (Madeleine Sylvain-Bouchereau). LFAS continued to fight for women's suffrage until 1950, when it was finally granted, albeit with a lengthy wait period imposed between the granting and the ability to exercise, and in 1956 the LFAS was part of the suit that forced the government to ratify the women's vote after President Magloire attempted to avoid doing so.
25. In the 1930s Suzanne Comhaire-Sylvain made regular contributions to *La voix des femmes* describing the lives of Haiti's peasant women that regularly included comments on their misguided beliefs and un-Christian behavior and that offered such recommendations as, "The peasant needs

to know how to read, to have a few principles of hygiene, to know her true personality in order to be able to defend herself" ("Notre Paysanne un aspect de sa vie," 3) that depict peasant women as not only illiterate but also unclean and un-self-aware.

26. Mayard, Gaillard, and Magloire-Prophète were not prominent members of LFAS, but Mayard did publish an article on "La Maison" in the January 1936 issue of the LFAS journal *La voix des femmes*, and *La voix des femmes* published a review of and excerpt from *Cuisine de pays chauds* in 1941 ("Notre bibliothèque à reçu").

27. Bellegarde-Smith criticizes all Haitian movements that do not account significantly for the peasant majority. However, his first book, on Dantès Bellegarde, shows the importance of offering, as Robert Lacerte puts it, "appreciative and critical" studies of the Haitian elite of the mid-twentieth century (502). In the introduction to *Haiti: The Breached Citadel*, Bellegarde-Smith writes that "a true picture of Haitian society cannot be realized . . . without a special effort to consider the role, status, and concerns of Haitian women in all areas of national life" (8), though he does not develop this point with any consideration of the role of LFAS or elite women in his discussion of twentieth-century Haiti.

28. In Linaean taxonomy, the distinction is made with the designations *Musa sapientum* and *Musa paradisiaca* in English banana and plantain.

29. Mayard attributes the recipe for "Beignets de Bananes" to the French chef and cookbook writer Édouard de Pomiane, under whom she appears to have studied in Paris; several rice recipes to Blanchard de La Brosse, the colonial governor of French Indochina in the 1920s; and the recipe for "Mais on soso aux abbatis de poulet" to "A Martinican Woman [Une Martiniquaise]."

30. The meal starts with classic combinations born out of the Columbian Exchange in "Potage Rosa—Maria" and "Tomates au gingembre" that both rest on Indigenous tomatoes and Indian spices. The next dish, "Achards de legumes varilava," is based on "achards"—pickled vegetables common in Mauritius and the Reunion Islands—that "are sold in cans," and "varilava"—Malagasy pickled herring. The main course, "Cochon de lait roti à la Hova," refers to a Malagasy cooking technique, while the side, "Coeurs de Palmier à la crème" comes from French Indochina, and the dessert, "Gateau St.-Denis Glace" is French.

31. While walnuts, almonds, and apricots are originally from Persia, Asia, and Armenia, respectively, by the sixteenth century they were well established throughout Western Europe and recognized as key ingredients in French desserts.

32. For an overview of Chinese-Haitians, see Kreyolicious's entry "Chinwa: The Untold Story of Chinese Haitians." (Since Kreyolicious's death, the blog has been taken down; it can still be accessed via Wayback machine, web.archive.org.)

33. For a detailed discussion of Haitian politics in the 1940s and 1950s, see Matthew Smith's *Red and Black in Haiti*.
34. *Larousse gastronomique* was first published in Paris in 1937 and was in its fourth edition by 1949.
35. "Diondion" or "djondjon" is the Haitian Creole word for a black mushroom indigenous to Haiti, and "jouroumou" or "joumou" is the Haitian Creole for pumpkin.
36. In *Tricinquantenaire*, her last name is listed as Prophète. In *Cuisine sélectionnée*, it is listed as Magloire-Prophète.
37. Magloire-Prophète includes one dish labeled "Pie Chinois," but nothing beyond the title connects it to China or to Chinese-Haitian cuisine. She also includes one chicken dish with curry, one "Riz à l'Indienne" and another, "Riz pilaf ou pilaw," with no mention in either case of a connection to India or to Indo-Caribbean cooking beyond what can be gleaned from the cooking method itself (the Indian rice is cooked using a combination of boiling and steaming whereas the "Creole rice" is simply boiled; the "Riz pilaf ou pilaw" is cooked with onion).
38. The only cookbook to which Rolande Valme Thevenin and Paule St. Eloi Alexis refer is Diane Spivey's *The Peppers Cracklings and Knots of Wool Cookbook—The Global Migrations of African Cuisine*. That they are themselves amateur historians conducting research from the United States both helps to explain the lacunae and underlines the paucity of research into Haitian culinary history of all kinds.
39. The other books on the list are Union School PTA's 1981 *What's Cooking in Haiti* (Union School was founded in 1919 for the children of U.S. Marines during the occupation; by the 1960s it had become one of Haiti's elite, private, U.S.-accredited schools); Winnie Weaver's self-published *Haitian How-To's*; Linda Wolfe's 1970 Time/Life Books *Recipes: The Cooking of the Caribbean Islands*; and Doris Longacre's 1976 *More-with-Less*, a classic Mennonite cookbook used by protestant missionaries throughout the world.
40. Stéphanie Renauld Armand moved to Haiti in 1996, where she helped to establish the Public Relations and Event group Wellcom' Haïti (wellcom-haiti.com).
41. The earliest print edition of *Goût d'Haïti* that I can locate was published in 2001 in Haiti under Éditions SRA, Stéphanie Renauld Armand's own imprint. It is possible that she self-published a version in 2000 prior to founding SRA, though I have not been able to locate any such version.
42. The illustrations for *Goût d'Haïti* were commissioned for the book. According to Rosny Ladouceur, the artist, credited as Benjamin and signing his work as LBM, died of AIDS before the book was published.
43. See, for example, Carlos Esteban Deive, Bernardo Vega, Emilia Pereyra.
44. The book is a collaborative production of the Canadian NGO Partenariat Acadie-Haiti, the Canadian Université de Moncton, Jzale Remay of

Gwoupman fanm Apladem, Jacmel, and scholars from the Haitian Université de Quisqueya.

Chapter 6 National Culture Cook-Up and Food Independence in Jamaica and Barbados

1. No author is listed in *Tropical Pot Pourri*.
2. The Bahamas are an outlier, with ten cookbooks between 1949 and independence (1973) published for tourist audiences, often by chefs at major hotels, or by interest groups such as the Methodist Church of Freeport and the Freeport Hebrew Congregation.
3. An important parallel project of regional food planning and cookbooks also thrived through the independence period, with both private works by individual authors like Rita Springer and public projects like the Caribbean Food and Nutrition Institute. A study of those works and projects would complement my focus on national cookbooks.
4. In the lead-up to the publication of the *Farmer's Food Manual*, *Caribbean Home Library* published several government-sponsored cooking pamphlets that became the basis of the recipes in the book. Kirkcaldy writes in the introduction to the *Farmer's Food Manual*, "part II of the Manual has been based largely on the publications of the Jamaica Social Welfare Commission" (10).
5. Deborah Weeks offers a concise overview of how in Jamaican political parties an initial shift away from purely White power, begun in 1930s, congealed into a "colored" elite power that lasted through independence, then was challenged by Black Power in the late 1960s. Black Power took hold in the early 1970s as Michael Manley took the mantle of the PNP from his father and won the 1972 elections on a Black Power platform.
6. Biographical information on Mrs. F. S. Edmonds is scant. In the 1930s, Mrs. F. S. Edmonds was active in the Kingston Charity Organization Society and served as secretary of the Montego Bay Self Help Home. According to the 1937 *Handbook of Jamaica* the Montego Bay Self Help Home, started in 1906, has "the object of helping the women and girls of the town and parish. There are a limited number of girls in residence. Some of these girls, on leaving the Home, have taken situations as servants. The incomes of those who are in the Home are supplemented by taking orders for mattress making, upholstering, chair caning, laundry work, preserves, needlework, etc. There is a sales room where native curiosities, baskets, plain and fancy needlework can be purchased" (508). An F. S. Edmonds was on the 1914 and 1915 Jamaica College football (soccer) team; an F. S. Edmonds (perhaps the same) died in the First World War. An F. A. and an E. A. Edmonds are listed on the 1916 Jamaica College cricket and football teams,

respectively. These may have been brothers of F. S. or they may be misidentified (and actually be F. S.).

7. The few libraries that hold the book list the author as Mrs. William Walderston Baillie. I believe she is Olga Mabel Kathleen Leyden (Mandeville, 1898–1978), who was married to Frederick William Watson Baillie (Mandeville, 1893–1964). Her grandmother, Ete or Ada, was Black, born in Ghana or Ethiopia or Jamaica.

8. J. L. Worlledge, most likely Margaret's husband, who contributed the recipe for "Golden Delight (Specially for children)," was part of the British Colonial military forces. He served in Kenya in the 1920s, was the commandant appointed in 1940 by the British Colonial Office to run the camp established in Mona for refugees from Gibraltar, and left Jamaica for England in 1941. By 1949 he was the director general of the Colonial Audit.

9. Of the other contributors I have been able to identify, Mrs. Otto Crowden was the wife of Otto Crowden, a justice in Kingston in 1919, and Lady Noelle Richards was the wife of Sir Arthur Richards (governor of Jamaica, 1938–1943); Lady Cuffe is referred to as the wife of the governor of Jamaica in 1938 ("In the Beginning"), although there has been no Cuffe governor of Jamaica and of course Cuffe recalls the famous slave rebellion leader, Paul Cuffee; Emma Edith (Tucker) Watson, whose parents were English, was the wife of Edgar Watson, a Scott born in England who resided for some time in Jamaica; Elizabeth Craig was born in Jamaica in 1914 to a Jamaica-born mother and an England-born father.

10. The recipe for "Zambaglione" is from Francis and Vera Meynell's *The Week-end Book*, first published in London in 1924.

11. The prefaces of the first and second editions of *Recipe Round-Up* are by Lady Sylvie Foot, the third by Lady Bridget Blackbourne, and the fourth by Lady Alice Campbell. During Blackbourne's tenure, Jamaica's executive went from "governor," appointed as the representative of the monarch, to "governor general," still appointed as the representative of the monarch but now on the advice of the prime minister of independent Jamaica.

12. Chicken Chop Suey to Mrs. Iris Lyn-Kee-Chow and Hop Po Gai Ding to Mrs. Moo-Pen. Both Lyn-Kee-Chow and Moo Pen are common Chinese-Jamaican surnames, dating to at least the turn of the twentieth century. According to the May 18, 2005, *SunSentinal* obituary for Jamaica-born Egbert "Tenny" Cha-Fong, he married Iris Lyn-Kee-Chow in 1957.

13. The difficulty of finding biographical information on these women, increased by the fact that many of them are identified by their husband's names, makes it impossible for me to offer more details or more certainty.

14. The Honorable Rudolph Burke, president of the Jamaican Agricultural Society in 1957, was a Black Jamaican and a founding member of the People's National Party who would go on to be a member of the independence constitution committee in 1962 (Michael Burke, "Rudolph Burke in Black History").

15. The Jamaica Festival is the national celebration of independent Jamaican art and culture. The Culinary Arts Division published an annual compendium of winning recipes; I have been able to locate only the *Daily Gleaner* articles about the compendia.
16. Kirkcaldy is the author of the 1958 *Meal Planning* published by the Jamaica Agricultural Society. She also worked with the Jamaica Tourist Board to attract American tourists to Jamaica by "demonstrating our exotic recipes" (Leon, 2) and contributed to the 1970 United Nations Women's Group in Jamaica's cookbook, *Festivals and Recipes*. For a full account of Doreen Kirkcaldy's life, see Crescencia Leon's "Dorreen Kirkcaldy Adding Spice to Jamaican Food."
17. Dr. Helen C. Abell earned her undergraduate degrees in Guelph and Toronto in home economics and her MA and PhD in rural sociology at Cornell University in Ithaca, New York. Between 1952 and 1962, she was the head of the Rural Sociology Research Unit for the Economic Division of Canada's Department of Agriculture. During that time, she completed projects for the Canadian International Development Agency, UNESCO, and FAO in Columbia, Ghana, Indonesia, Jamaica, and Nigeria. For more details on Abell's life, see the University of Guelph's "Helen C. Abell Collection."
18. Jordynn Jack describes Roberts's work in Puerto Rico as offering a model for collaborative work that makes clear that "the most persuasive knowledge about nutrition in Puerto Rico is knowledge generated collaboratively, in consultation with multiple stakeholders," (123) which results in such things as devising nutrition plans around such things as "'A whole dinner in one dish,' in line with the typical native custom among low-income rural families" (Roberts, 303, cited in Jack, 123), although of course the food guide that she developed for Puerto Rico, even if it was in addition to rather than in place of the earlier one, did "promote the consumption of fruits, vegetables, milk and proteins that were not normally eaten by Puerto Ricans" (Jack, 123).
19. In *The Farmer's Food Manual*'s first appendix, "Historical Notes on the Food Plants of Jamaican," Clinton V. Black does cite John Parry's "Salt Fish and Ackee" but only Parry's argument that "the most striking fact about the food plants of Jamaica is that—like the people and the domestic animals—they are nearly all exotics" (29), which Parry uses to build an argument for Jamaican plants and foods as necessarily creole. Black does not refer to Parry's conclusion, that "without the institution of slave provision grounds, without the constant search for crops to stock those grounds, emancipation, in the form which it took in Jamaica, would have been economically and socially very difficult, perhaps impossible. It was the presence of a great variety of products and easily cultivated food plants which enabled unskilled praedial slaves to become the sturdy independent peasantry who inhabit the hills of Jamaica today" (35). However ignored

by Black, Parry's work singles out provision grounds and slave work in cultivating (and, I would add, cooking) provisions as foundational of emancipation and independence in Jamaica.

20. In fact, cho-cho or chayote has protein content similar to that of many fruits that McCullogh praises along with significant amounts of fiber, folate, and zinc, which he does not seem to consider in any foods.

21. Although the piece is signed by Helen C. Abell, a note at the beginning attributes much of the work to Doris Morant, senior education officer in the Department of Education and assistant director to the 1955 West Indies Home Economics Training Course.

22. After the forward, listing Abell as author but with a note crediting Morant, the introduction is credited to Mrs. Sybil Wint-Williams. For more details on Doris Morant's biography, see the *Daily Gleaner* article "Jamaican Wins Medal." Sybil Claire Wint was born in 1926 in Jamaica.

23. Of the over three hundred recipes in *The Farmer's Food Manual*, over fifty have provisions in the title and many more feature provisions as central ingredients, including seven of the eighteen "One-Pot Meals" that make up the first recipe chapter.

24. Similarly, the last chapters in Part Two follow a more standard European organization: "Soups," "Fish Including Shellfish," "Meat," "Green and Yellow Vegetables," "Dessert," "Sauces," "Fruits," "Preserves," "Beverages Hot and Cold," "Baking." *Farmer's Food Manual* is a mixed bag, a starting point, one that shifts among multiple positions.

25. Anthony Gambrill in his 2014 *Gleaner* article "Read, cook, nyam" confirms, "Mrs. Brandon's cookbook . . . probably saved our marriage. I undertook marriage with one recipe in my repertoire. . . . My wife Linda had to ask me the first morning, 'How can you tell when water is boiling?' This didn't' seem as ridiculous 40 years ago as it sounds today. She was brought up in a household where the cook, Madge, was master of her domain and only the mistress of the house could enter the kitchen safely" (F8).

26. Brandon's recipe for "Read Peas Soup" uses croutons in place of the peasant staple boiled dumplings, but it does not call for straining the soup, a practice that "H. G. D." (H. G. DeLisser) identifies, in a 1939 column in the *Daily Gleaner*, as what is done to the soup when it is "served at an aristocratic table" ("Random Jottings: As I See the World," 12).

27. The origin stories for both dishes are many. "Sweet and Sour" is not a designation used for a particular dish in China, but sugar-and-vinegar sauces are common in many different Chinese regional cuisines. "Chop Suey" probably comes from the Cantonese "tsap seui," meaning mixed leftovers. Most Chinese-Jamaicans are of Hakka, not Cantonese, origin, but by the twentieth century, both "Chop Suey" and "Sweet and Sour Pork" were staples of Chinese cuisine throughout the Americas.

28. The second edition of *A Merry-Go-Round of Recipes from Independent Jamaica* came out shortly after the first with only very minor changes.

Starting with the third edition, in 1967, the word "independent" disappeared from the title. In the third edition along with changing the title, Brandon removes a few recipes and adds a few others. Most notably, in the Cakes section, she removes the "Jamaica Independence Fruit Cake" and adds "Dundee Cake (à la Jamaique)," in Chinese Dishes she adds a note "about Chinese cooking" and two new recipes—"Mr. J. Wong's Chicken Escallion" and "Cha-Hui-Ssu"—in the Chicken section she adds five new recipes, including one Indo-Caribbean ("Curry Flavoured Baked Chicken"), and throughout she adds a smattering of Jamaican classics ("Run Down," "Turned Cornmeal") and other Indo-Caribbean and Caribbean dishes (mango chutney, curried ackee sauce). In the revised fourth edition, in 1970, the front cover changes completely, sporting a woman, against the backdrop of a full yellow sun, with sharp features and light skin but with half of her face and a quarter of her chest black, as if shadowed, wearing a traditional creole headscarf and hoop earrings and carrying on her head a basket of tropical fruit. The fourth edition, "with additional recipes," adds more recipes throughout and also a new section, More Miscellaneous Luncheon and Supper Recipes, made up primarily of dishes of Euro-American heritage—the "Braised Ginger Pork" and "Shish Kabob" being the only exceptions. These shifts make more apparent the focus of the first editions on Jamaican-ness, on asserting and establishing Jamaican national (culinary) culture both at home and abroad. That Brandon moved away from this project could signal its success: independent Jamaican culinary culture and export food economy were so well established that there was no longer a need to focus so insistently on them. Though it could also indicate a split in Jamaican culinary culture as the elite increasingly turned to the Euro-American (Brandon eventually moved permanently to the United States) and the next generation of Jamaican (culinary) nationalism turned to Black nationalism and to Afro-Caribbean foodways.

29. The Jamaica Information Service focused primarily on "writing and distributing press releases and photographs, writing publications, mounting public education campaigns, and producing stories for radio, film and television" (Jamaica Information Service, "History of the JIS").

30. Weeks, drawing on the work of Colin Palmer and Rex Nettleford, summarizes this phenomenon: "When Jamaica became independent from the British in 1962, the national motto —Out of many, one people—was fashioned to proclaim to the world that Jamaica was proof that racial harmony could be achieved. Not only did the middle and upper class Jamaican population embrace this ideal, the general population also broadly supported the notion. Despite such sentiments, many black Jamaicans continued to be torn between their nationalist identity and the reality that the poor, general population in Jamaica was nearly always black, and the middle and upper class population was nearly always white or colored" (47).

31. Cream cheese was first sold under that name around 1873 by the American dairyman William Lawrence. By the end of the nineteenth century "cream cheese" was being mass produced by several U.S. companies.
32. For a discussion of the popularity of the loaf in the United States over the course of the twentieth century, see Frank Bruni and Jennifer Steinhauer; for a discussion of the popularity of French culinary terminology in twentieth-century American cuisine, see Dan Jurafsky; for history of chips in the United States, see April White. While British fish and chips also uses the term "chip" to refer to a fried starchy food, the chips in Jamaican cuisine are made from thin-cut starchy foods and resemble the American potato chip far more than the British "chips."
33. For an archaeological study of bananas in Africa that dates their presence there to about 2000 BC, see Michael Balter. For a historical study of the movement of the banana and plantain from Asia to the New World, see Higman, *How Food Made History*, 49–50.
34. See, for example, Parry's "Plantation and Provision Ground." Because *Banana Recipes* does not mention the plantain once, it is not clear whether it subsumes plantains under bananas or whether it separates them out so fully that it excludes even their mention from this cookbook. Plantains and bananas are related, and their history is shared. In the Latin binomial system, they are both classified in the family Musacae and genus Musa and separated as distinct cultivars within that genus. In culinary terms, plantains are sometimes separated by their need to be cooked, and bananas are sometimes distinguished as "dessert." In market terms, they are often separated by the higher export potential (to Europe and North America) of bananas.
35. For detailed analyses of the rise of Black Power in Jamaica, see Walter Rodney, Selwyn Ryan, and Weeks. Higman's analysis of Jamaican callaloo shows a parallel revaluation of foods associated with poor and Black Jamaicans in the food columns and sections in the *Daily Gleaner* during the same period ("Jamaican Versions of Callaloo," 361–362).
36. Members of the Book Committee were Mrs. A. Benitez, Mrs. H. Bruchmann, Mrs. C. Coates, Mrs. R. Cook, Mrs. A. Cser, Mrs. J. Dosne, Mrs. Fuge, Mrs. K. Gray, Mrs. W. Howells, Mrs. J. Johnston, Mrs. E. Kramer, Mrs. F. Lunt, Mrs. P. O'Sullivan, Mrs. W. Paterson, Mrs. R. Prince, Mrs. T. Rees, Mrs. M. Tinker, Mrs. G. Viner, Mrs. W. Voeth, Mrs. V. Williams, and Mrs. D. Wozab.
37. Rodney was Guyanese. He moved to Jamaica with his wife and child when he accepted a teaching position at the University of the West Indies, Mona. While he was in Canada for the 1968 Black Writers Conference, the Jamaican government declared him persona non grata, banning him from his post and from returning to Jamaica.
38. For Manley's full speech, see "Text of Manley's Speech," *Daily Gleaner*, 11 Nov. 1968. By returning to Norman Manley here, after showing his role in

The Farmer's Food Manual, I am indeed suggesting that over the course of his political career, Manley realized the weakness of the original project of elite Jamaican rule in the service of "One People" that did not expressly focus on centering Black Jamaicans and the concerns of the poor, primarily Black, Jamaican majority, and as he stepped down made way for the turn to Black Power that his son, Michael Manley, championed for the PNP and for Jamaica.

39. The etymology has not yet been well traced.
40. Cleary was born in Kingston. She attended St. Joseph's Girls School and was subsequently employed at a King Street store. It appears that she later served as principal of a school associated with St. Francis Xavier Church.
41. Sam Pragg offers an overview of Jamaica's literacy programs from the 1970s to the 1990s.
42. I discuss the role of cookbooks in the promotion of literacy in more depth in previous chapters. Wendy Wall also writes about "kitchen literacy" in early modern English domestic guides.
43. "Beg watta cyann bwile cow kin" literally translates as "Begged water cannot boil cow skin," that is, that it is not possible or practical to beg enough water to boil cow skin, implying that if you want to boil cow skin, or to get something difficult done, you had best rely on yourself rather than begging for others' help. "Yuh cyann siddung pahn cow bak cuss cow kin" literally translates as "You cannot cuss the cow's skin while you are sitting upon the cow's back," cautioning that the cow's skin, lowly as it may be, is an integral part of the cow and that while we are sitting on the cow we are benefiting from the cow and its skin, or more generally conveying that it is important to be grateful for assistance and not disparage what or who helps us. "No dribe fly from odder man cow'kin" is another example.
44. Cleary calls for a little more water, and her instructions differ in a few words.
45. The most recent edition of *Jamaica Run-Dung* was published in 2003 in Kingston by Alston Cleary. Sangster's is one of the largest bookstores in Kingston. For an article on the listing, see "What's Cooking on the Local Scene?" (E3).
46. Jones also worked, under the Scientific Research Council, on the 1966 *Food Guide for Jamaica*, which is not a cookbook but a nutrition guide, and with the Ministry of Agriculture authored the recipe pamphlets *Variety with Vegetables*, *Chickens for the Table*, *Meat that Satisfies*, and *Let's Eat Bananas* (1981), and with Herbert M. Knight *Make and Use Your Own Home Made Hams* (1983). In 1984 Jones became the president of the Jamaica Home Economics Association, supported by GraceKennedy, whose head, Carlton Alexander, was also the honorary president of the association.
47. For a twenty-first-century Jamaican recipe for Jamaican callaloo cook-up with a defense of Jamaican patois, see Debbie Debs.

48. This is a simplified version of the chart published in the *Food Guide for Jamaica* (p. 4).
49. For example, in U.S.-based Agricultural Extension Service cookbooks in the U.S. Virgin Islands, the sections on canning call for specialized equipment and give detailed instructions in how to process the cans. In *Cook Up Jamaican Style*, by contrast, most recipes for canned and preserved foods have instructions like those for Lorna Little's "Guava Jam," "Pour into sterilized jars and seal" (p. 102), that assume that the cook knows how to sterilize and seal.
50. *Cook Up Jamaican Style* is the first cookbook to record Jamaican breads and cakes made with mashed peas. The only other recipe for a similar cake made with mashed peas is Chefmeow's "Pretty Black Eyed Pea Cake," which comes from a Texas estate. A 1975 *Daily Gleaner* article on the work of the Agricultural Extension Service, describing its recipe for "Peasy Cake," also made using mashed peas, as "an interesting mixture of ordinary cake ingredients and red peas" ("Consumer Week," 19), suggests that it is a new practice. Subsequent Jamaican food writing demonstrates that cakes made with mashed peas did become Jamaican specialties. Juliet Holmes's "Year-Round Jamaican Fruit Cake, Plain Cakes & Island Puddings" post on Wellesley Gayle's www.my-island-jamaica.com, for example, lists "peasy cake" as among the "distinctive offerings" of her business, Year-Round Jamaican Fruit Cake, Plain Cakes & Island Puddings, https://www.my-island-jamaica.com/yearround-jamaican-fruit-cake-plain-cakes-island-puddings.html.
51. More standard hotel-tourism cookbooks like Lady Mitchell's 1981 *The Prospect Great House Cookbook* were also published in the 1980s. A few Jamaican cookbook writers of the 1970s and 1980s sidestepped this commercialism. Norma Benghiat published commercial-tourist food writing like the 1988 "Chinese Cooking in Jamaica" for Air Jamaica's *Skywritings* in parallel with cookbooks like the 1985 *Traditional Jamaican Cookery* that combine nostalgia for a bygone Jamaica with a revaluation of peasant foods and a clear turn to a Jamaican diaspora readership. Irene Harvey's 1982 *The Jamaica Family Cookbook*, produced by Harvey's son, the Jamaican trumpet player Alphonse Reece, appeals to home cooking through the adoration of a famous son for his mother. Peggy Rankine published *Simply Delicious* around 1986 amid a series of fictional works on Jamaican entrepreneurship and entertaining. That most of these were published outside of Jamaica suggests that they belonging as much to the transnational and diaspora cookbooks that I examine in "Home Cooking" as to the national cookbooks that I focus on here.
52. Elsa Miller ran the kitchen at St. Anne's Bay's Windsor Hotel in 1955 (Kitty Kingston). In 1969 she ran a guest house at Spur Tree "for a big bauxite company" ("The Native"). Her first column as well as her first recipes were published in the *Daily Gleaner* in October 1977 (Miller, "Some Things Just

Aren't 'in' Anymore"; Miller, "Make Good Use of Cassava"). After that, her recipes and columns appeared regularly in the food sections of the *Gleaner* through 1995.

53. Mike Henry's *Caribbean Cocktails* was published in 1980 by Kingston Publishers Ltd. That same year, Mike Henry was elected member of Parliament, where at the time of writing he continues to serve, most recently reelected in September 2020. Mike Henry had already been active in Jamaican publishing for many years, including playing a key role in William Collins and Sons' 1966 publication of Louise Bennet's *Jamaica Labrish* ("Laughter and Speeches Launch 'Jamaica Labrish'") and working for Collins-Sangsters. He was with Kingston Publishers Ltd. by 1973 and later was chairman of LMH Publishing. Through Kingston Publishers Ltd. And LMH Publishing, Mike Henry, his brother Leonard "Sonny" Henry, and later Mike Henry's wife, Dawn, published a number of other cockbooks in the *Creative Cooking* series that also included recipes from Elsa Miller's *Caribbean Cookbook*. These cookbooks are increasingly pan-Caribbean and also trace the Henrys' move from Jamaica to Florida.

54. This may well be the cookbook announced in Crescencia Leon's March 1982 *Daily Gleaner* article on Doreen Kirkcaldy as forthcoming from Grace Kitchens. Sonny Henry worked as a chef at Sandals Resorts.

55. "Sweet and Sour Dolphin" and two Greek dishes and recipes for peacock and peahen appear in Miller's *Caribbean Cookbook* but not in *Caribbean Cooking and Menus*, and *Caribbean Cookbook*'s "Chicken Pago" is retitled, in *Caribbean Cooking and Menus*, as "Tropical Chicken."

56. Cited in Higman, *Jamaican Food*, p. 50. Although Grace Kitchens was first mentioned in the *Daily Gleaner* in a 1962 Grace advertisement that says "look out for special Recipes from Grace Kitchens" ("Cook with Taste Cook with Grace Foods"), a December 14, 1969, *Daily Gleaner* article reported the official opening of Grace Kitchens as having occurred on December 10, 1969 ("'Grace Kitchens' Opened"). In that article, Carlton Alexander, then director of GraceKennedy, is reported as saying that "the aim of the kitchens was mainly to establish better communications between Grace and the consumer and its motto was 'Service dedicated to helping families live fuller, happier lives,'" while the minister of trade and industry, Robert Lightbourne, is reported as saying "that he particularly welcomed the idea of Grace Kitchens which will be of help to present and future generations as this was the age of emancipation and the world over was increasing in cost of living" (78). In 1972 Grace Kitchens also launched a school nutrition program. Kirkcaldy was director of Grace Kitchens until at least 1982.

57. GraceKennedy was founded in 1922 when the American John Grace and the Jamaican Fred W. Kennedy (descended from Scots who came to Jamaica in the late eighteenth century), of the New York-based W. R. Grace and Co., realized that the Jamaica subsidiary, Grace Limited, for which they both

worked, was thriving while the U.S. company was struggling. Grace and Kennedy joined forces, along with the Jamaican accountant James Moss-Solomon (who would have been classified at the time as coloured), then of United Fruit Company, to separate fully from W. R. Grace and Co. As the Jamaican independence movement grew, Grace left the company and returned to New York. Kennedy remained at the helm until the early 1970s, when Carlton Alexander took over leadership. Under Alexander, in 1976, GraceKennedy helped to form the Private Sector Organization of Jamaica to "help guarantee the preservation of personal liberty, democracy and continued social and economic development" in Jamaica ("Internal and External Grace").

58. Grace Kitchens had been publishing recipes as part of its advertisements in the *Gleaner* since at least the mid-1960s, and Grace Kitchens recipes were regularly featured in the *Gleaner*'s food columns. *Creative Cooking* was launched by Heather Little-White, who was Grace's nutrition promotion manager and took over from Kirkcaldy as manager of Grace Kitchens in 1984. That year, Grace Kitchens expanded its school nutrition program to include children's homes ("Grace Kennedy to Contribute $100,000 towards Child's Month"). It was also reconfigured as Grace Kitchens and Consumer Center, which allowed it to work closely with the National Consumers' League, of which Kirkcaldy was president. The popularity and power of Grace Kitchens continues into the twenty-first century, with the 2019 cookbook *50 Not Out: Grace Kitchens' Greatest Hits* celebrating its fiftieth anniversary and a new online cooking series launched on its YouTube channel in September 2020. Higman details the connections between the Creative Cooking series cookbooks and Grace Kitchens' *Creative Cooking* (*Jamaican Food*, 50).

59. Jamaican author Kellie Magnus writes of Mike Henry telling her that "Henry himself, co-wrote *Jamaican Cooking and Menus* with his now deceased brother Leonard (Sonny) and his wife Dawn."

60. In 1960 CL Pitt and Company published *Barbados, West Indies: Barbadian Recipes*, a Barbados guidebook with one short recipe section.

61. For example, *War Time Recipes* includes eight dishes in its "Fish" section. *Bajan Cookbook*'s "Fish" section adds twenty-three new recipes.

62. Other Barbadian fundraising cookbooks include the multi-edition (1983, 1985, 1987) *What's Cooking? Favourite Recipes of Cooks in Barbados*, "compiled for the benefit of the Red Cross' Meals-on-Wheels Programme," and *Home Style Recipes: From Cooks in Barbados* (n.d.), "a presentation of recipes in aid of funds for support of substance-abuse rescue and rehabiliation programmes in Barbados." Jill Hamilton's early cookbook, the 1983 *The Barbados Cookbook*, was published as a fundraising effort for the Barbados Military Cemetery.

63. There is no such section in the *War Time Recipes*.

64. *War Time Recipes for Use in the West Indies* does not list roast kid or any kind of Johnny cakes or bakes, but it does have both "Breadfruit Cou Cou" and "Cornmeal Cou Cou."
65. For a detailed history and analysis of Barbadian politics and economics after independence, see Hilary Beckles, "Independence and the Social Crisis of Nationalism in Barbados."
66. Other cookbooks to come out of such programs include Trinidadian Winifred Grey's 1965 *Caribbean Cookery*.
67. The alphabetization shifts between of individual ingredients or recipes (starting with Avocado) and of dish types (after the Avocado section comes Breads Cakes Pone), but Cassava Pone, for example, appears in the next section, Cocktail Savouries, and the section after that, Recipes Presentation and Service of Tropical Drinks, is out of alphabetical order.
68. A partial explanation for the omission of many recipes may be the plan, which appears not to have been completed, for the *National Recipe Directory* to be an annual publication.
69. JP stands for justice of the peace. Fraser uses it throughout her publications. I have not been able to determine what MCFA stands for. Fraser does not use it in subsequent publications.
70. For a discussion of the racial politics of ownership and control at Roberts, see Sandra Sealey.
71. Alma Eileen Alkins, who went by Eileen, was the maker of Spitfire Pepper Sauce.
72. In contrast, Rita Springer offers a detailed explanation of how to bone flying fish and specifies amounts of lime juice and salt for the rub (49).
73. It is also one of the first Barbadian cookbooks published not in Barbados but in England, in 1988 by Macmillan Caribbean.
74. In 1981 Jeanne V. Beekhuis laid out the potential beneficial and harmful "impacts on the economic, social, and natural environments" of the new turn to "tourism in the Caribbean" and proposed a plan to mitigate the harm. In 2019 Daphne Ewing-Chow summarized the overwhelmingly harmful long-term consequences of the ways that tourism in the Caribbean has played out.
75. Miller's full-length and standard-sized *Contemporary Caribbean Cookbook* and LaurelAnn Morley's several cookbooks offer similar examples.
76. For reporting on the new investments in and successes of Carmeta's that also note the enduring power of Carmeta Fraser's work, see "BADMC Making Strides," Kerri Gooding.

Conclusion

1. I am eternally grateful to Toni Morrison for pointing out, in *The Bluest Eye*, that when it is too much to figure out "why," we can turn to "how."

2. While *Recettes simples de cuisine haïtienne* has a recipe for "the Haitian specialty," "Soupe Grasse" that singles out "jouroumou," listed in quotation marks, as "le complement" to be added along with many kinds of meat and vegetables (327), it does not mention any historical or national significance to the dish. Herzulie Magloire-Prophète does not mention soupe grasse or soup joumou at all in her article on Haitian food in the *Tricinquantenaire*, and while a recipe for "Soupe au Giraumon" appears in *Cuisine sélectionnée*, no mention is made of any special status (14). It would not be until Mariette Jean's 1974 *Cuisine et savoir vivre* that a cookbook gives "Soupe Nationale" as a title for "Soupe Grasse" and this following a recipe of "Giromaunade," a simple pureed pumpkin soup, that ends with the comment "giromaunade is an ancient Haitian culinary preparation. It is very nutritious and very healthy and could be used more today" (67).
3. See, for example, Nadège Green, Priya Krishna, Visit Haiti, Jenny Delacruz. For a discussion that considers the different claims about the original meaning of the tradition and which version(s) of the soup it refers to, see Jacquelyne Germain.
4. In Linnaean taxonomy, the family cucurbitacea is divided into three genera, one, cucurbita, to which pumpkin and calabaza belong, indigenous to the Americas, another to Africa and another to Southeast Asia (Welbaum, 10). Cucurbita is one of the first, perhaps the first, plant cultivated for food in the Americas (Welbaum, 39; Enrique Vela).
5. See, for example, Keja Valens, "Recipes for National Culture in Guadeloupe and Martinique," "A Little Puerto Rican Food Culture," and "Home Cooking."

Works Cited

Cookbooks

Alfonso y Rodríguez, Dolores. *La cocina y el hogar*. Habana: Cultural, S.A., 1937.

Armand, Stéphanie. *Goût d'Haïti*. Editions SRA, 2001.

———. *A Taste for Haiti*. Translated by Genevieve Douyon. Editions SRA, 2004.

Baillie, Mrs. William Walderston [?]. *Peter Pan Book of Recipes*. Kingston: Gleanor Co., 1928.

Baralt, Blanca Zacharie de. *Cuban Cookery: Gastronomic Secrets of the Tropics*. Havana: Editorial Hermes, 1931.

Barbados Child Care Committee. *Bajan Cookbook*. Barbados: The Committee, 1964.

Barbados Red Cross Society. *What's Cooking?* Barbados: n.p., 1983.

Barrow, Errol, and Kendal A. Lee. *Privilege: Cooking in the Caribbean*. London: MacMillan Caribbean, 1988.

Benghiat, Norma. "Chinese Cooking in Jamaica." *Skywritings* no. 56, 1988, n.p.

———. *Traditional Jamaican Cookery*. London: Penguin Books, 1985.

Betances de Pujadas, Estrella. *Recipes of Santo Domingo/Recetas Dominicanas*. Santo Domingo: Editora Amigo del Hogar, 1973.

Bolivar Aróstegui, Natalia, and Carmen González Díaz de Villegas. *La comida afrocubana: mitos y leyendas*. La Habana: Editorial José Martí, 2015.

Bornia, Ligia de. *La cocina dominicana*. Santo Domingo: Editora Taller, 1982 [1957].

———. *Cocina Ligia*. Santo Domingo: Editora Taller, 1972.

———. *La cocina Ligia en microondas*. Santo Domingo: Editora Taller, 1992.

———. *La cocina de Ligia en olla de presión*. Santo Domingo: Editora Taller, 1977.

———. *Comidas típicas dominicanas/Typical Dominican Meals*. Santo Domingo: Editora Taller, 1965.

Boulon, Erva. *My Island Kitchen*. St. Thomas: Virgin Islands Printing Corp., c. 1960.

Brandon, Leila. *A Merry-Go-Round of Recipes from Independent Jamaica*. Jamaica: Colour Graphic Printers, 1963.

British Ladies Committee in Aid of War Relief. *Cookery Book*. Havana, 1941.

Brown, Busha. *Busha Browne's Indispensable Compendium of Traditional Jamaican Cookery*. Kingston: Mill Press, 1993.

Brown, Edith E., and Margaret G. Worlledge. *Sweets, Snacks, Savouries, Unusual Coctails*. Kingston: Gleanor Co., 1939.

Browne, Marva Sprauve, and Vernon McDonald Browne. *A Catta Full of West Indian Dishes*. Cruz Bay, St. John: n.p., 1973.

Browne, Rosalind, Clarice C. Clarke, and the University of the Virgin Islands Cooperative Extension Service. *Breads*. St. Croix: College of the Virgin Islands Cooperative Extension Service, 1985.

Cabanillas, Berta, Carmen Ginorio, and Carmen Q Mercado. *Cocine a gusto*. Editorial de la Universidad de Puerto Rico, 1972 [1950].

Cabrisas, Juan. *Nuevo manual de la cocinera catalana y cubana*. N.p: Imprenta y Libreria de D Andres Graupera, 1858.

Campbell, Marjorie Pringle (attr.). *A Collection of 19th Century Jamaican Cookery and Herbal Recipes*. Kingston: Mill Press, 1990.

Carbet, Marie-Magdelaine *Cuisine des îles ou le bon manger antillais*. Verviers: Marabout, 1978.

Cardelli, M. *Manuel du cuisinier et de la cuisinière. Collection de manuels formant une encyclopédie des sciences et arts*. Paris: Roret, [1800?].

Clarke, Clarice C., Alice V. Henry, and the University of the Virgin Islands Cooperative Extension Service. *The World Food Day Cookbook*. St. Croix: Cooperative Extension Services, University of the Virgin Islands, 2000.

Clarke, Clarice C., and the University of the Virgin Islands Cooperative Extension Service. *Mango: Bits and Bites*. St. Croix: Cooperative Extension Services, University of the Virgin Islands, 1999.

Cleary, Teresa E. *A Cook-Book with Jamaica Run-Dung*. Kingston: Brainbuster Publications, 1970.

Collymore, Yvonne. *Cooking Our Way*. Kingston: Caribbean Universities Press, 1972.

Coloma y Garcés, Eugenio. *Manual del cocinero cubano*. La Habana: n.p., 1856.

Combie, Valerie Knowles, Clarice C. Clarke, and the University of the Virgin Islands Cooperative Extension Service. *Virgin Islands Holiday Cooking*. St. Croix: Cooperative Extension Services, University of the Virgin Islands, 1987.

Cordero Infante, Eulalia. *La cocina dominicana: recetas practicas culinarias y consejos de economía doméstica*. Santiago, República Dominica: Editorial El Diario, [193_?].

Cotta de Cal, Maria Teresa. *Comidas criollas en ollas de presión*. Havana: Talleres de Goldaraz y Cia, 1951

Crespo y Setien, Berta. *El arte de bien guisar o La cocina practica en Cuba*. Habana: Librería Cervantes, 1926.
Cunninghame, Judy. *Some Fruits & Recipes of Jamaica*. U.S. Virgin Islands: Caribbean Natural Colour Ltd., 1971.
Da Mathilde. *Da Mathilde, 325 recettes de cuisine créole*. Paris: Éditions de la pensée moderne, 1975.
Debs, Debbie. "Debbie Dung a Yaad Jamaican Callaloo Cookup." *The Jamaican Cooking Journey*, https://www.youtube.com/watch?v=gokyJUJ-NpA, 19 Jan. 2019.
De Jesús, Maria Dolores. *El burén de Lula*. San Juan: Instituto de Cultural Puertorriqueña, 2017 [2010].
Delon, Danielle, ed. *A Handbook of Trinidad Cookery: The First Cookbook of Trinidad and Tobago with Rare Glimpses of Trinidad in 1907*. Trinidad and Tobago: Classique Publications, 2016.
de Noter, Raphaël. *La bonne cuisine aux colonies: Asie-Afrique-Amérique*. Paris: L'Art culinaire, 1931.
Díaz de Mujica, Blanca. *Manual de cocina y directorio doméstico*. La Habana: Ucar García y Cia., [1945?].
Donaldson, Enid, and Ray Chen. *The Real Taste of Jamaica*. Kingston: Ian Randle Publishers, 1993.
Dooley, Eliza K. *Puerto Rican Cookbook*. Richmond, VA: Dietz Press, 1948.
Ebroïn, Ary. *La cuisine créole*. Paris: Editions Emile Desormeaux, 1972.
Edmonds, Mrs. F. H. *100 Jamaica Recipes*. Kingston: Gleanor Co., 1926.
El arte de cocinar eléctricamente en las cocinas eléctricas. Compañía cubana de electricidad, 1929.
El cocinero de enfermos convalecientes y desganados. Habana: Imprenta y Libreria La Cubana, 1862.
El cocinero mexicano. Mexico: Consejo Nacional para la Cultura y las Artes, Culturas Populares, 2000 [1831].
El cocinero puertorriqueño. Ediciones Puerto, 2004 [1859].
Favourite Antiguan Food and Drink Recipes. St. Johns, Antigua: Southwell Publishing Co., 1977.
Ferguson, Grace J., and Puerto Rico Dept. of Education. *Home Making and Home Keeping: A Text Book for the First Two Years' Work in Home Economics in the Public Schools of Porto Rico*. San Juan: Bureau of Supplies, Printing, and Transportation, 1915. https://catalog.hathitrust.org/Record/101766505/Home.
Fernández Monte, Eddy, and Miriam Rubiel Díaz. *Cocinando a lo cubano*. La Habana: Editorial La Mujer, 2017 [2015].
Finucane, Jeane. *Go on Man, Cook Dominican*. Roseau, Dominica: The Social League, 1974.
Fleurimond, Nadege. *Haïti Uncovered: a regional adventure into the art of Haïtian cuisine*. Gaithersburg, MD: Signature Book Printing, 2014.
Fraser, Carmeta. *Come Cook with Us the Bajan Way: Let's Eat What We Grow, Grow What We Eat*. Bridgetown, Barbados: FAO, 1981.

———. *National Recipe Directory*. Bridgetown, Barbados: Dalton Enterprises, 1976.

Gaillard, Niniche Viard. *Recettes simples de la cuisine haitienne*. Port-au-Prince: Les Presses Libres, 1950.

Gómez, Ana Dolores, and Nitza Villapol. *¡Como celebrar unas pascuas Cubanas! exposición de mesas por provincias servidas con platos típicos por las populares expertas Ana Dolores Gómez y Nitza Villapol*. N.p: n.p, [195_?].

González, Clara. *Cocina Dominicana*. www.cocinadominicana.com.

González de Valle, Ambrosio. *La comida diaria*. Habana: Cultural, S.A., 1933.

González Pérez, Carmen. *Encanto del hogar: manual de la buena mesa*. Santiago de Cuba: Ros, 1940.

Goodhue, Isabel. *Good Things and Graces*. San Francisco: P. Elder and Co., c. 1911.

Grace Kitchens. *50 Not Out: Grace Kitchens' Greatest Hits*. N.p.: Grace Kitchens, 2019. https://fliphtml5.com/eqsh/jlcq/basic.

Grenada Homemaker's Association. *Grenada Independence 1974 Homemaker's Cookbook*. St. George's: Grenada Independence Secretariat History and Literature Division, 1974.

Grenadian. *Cookery in the West Indies Made Easy*. Grenada: n.p., 1910.

Hamilton, Jill. *A Little Caribbean Cookbook*. San Francisco: Chronicle Books, 1990.

———. *Taste of Barbados: The Handbook of Local Food and Drink*. Barbados: J. Hamilton, [198_?]

Hamilton, Laddie. *The St. Kitts and Nevis Independence Cookbook*. Basseterre, St. Kitts: Creole Graphics, 1983.

Harvey, Irene. *The Jamaica Family Cookbook*. New York: Lore Publishing, 1982.

Henríquez de Pou, Siliva. *Mujer 2000: Recetas de cocina*. Santo Domingo: Editora Amigo del Hogar, 1988.

Henry, Alice V., Clarice C. Clarke, and the University of the Virgin Islands Cooperative Extension Service. *The World Food Day Cookbook*. St. Croix: University of the Virgin Islands Cooperative Extension Service, 2000.

Henry, Leonard, and Mike Henry. *Creative Caribbean Cooking & Menus*. Kingston: LMH Publishing, 1985.

Henry, Oliva H., and the College of the Virgin Islands Cooperative Extension Service. *Native Recipes*. St. Croix: College of the Virgin Islands Cooperative Extension Service, 1978.

History and Arts Council, Ministry of Education. *Guyanese Food Recipes*. Georgetown: National Government Publication, 1967.

Hodson, K. E. *War Time Recipes for Use in the West Indies*. Bridgetown, Barbados: n.p., 1942.

Imperial Department of Agriculture for the West Indies. *Recipes for Cooking Sweet Potatoes from the West Indies*. Bridgetown, Barbados: V. Gale, Printers to the Government of Barbados, 1901.

———. *Recipes for Cooking West Indian Yams*. Bridgetown, Barbados: V. Gale, Printer to the Government of Barbados, 1902.

Jadan, Doris and Ivan. *St. John Cookpot Calypso*. N.p., [195_?]

———. *V.I. Cuisine with Ivan and Christine: A Holiday/ Every Day Cookbook for Virgin Islands Children and Their Friends from 9–99*. Virgin Islands: Doris Jadan, 1975.

———. *A Virgin Island Cookpot Calypso*. St. Thomas: n.p., 1965.

———. *The Virgin Islands Cookhouse Cookbook*. Cruz Bay, Virgin Islands: Doris Jadan, 1973.

Jamaica Agricultural Society. *The Farmer's Food Manual*. Glasgow: University Press, 1957.

Jamaica Information Service. *Banana Recipes*. Kingston: Jamaica Information Service, 1966.

———. *Jamaican Cuisine*. Kingston: Jamaica Information Service, 1964.

Jamaica Society for the Blind. *Recipe Round-Up*. Mandeville, Jamaica: n.p., 1956.

Jean, Mariette. *Cuisine et savoir vivre*. Port au Prince: Imp. Seminaire Adventiste, 1974.

Jones, Novelette C. *Cook Up Jamaican Style: Eating What We Grow*. Kingston: Extension Division, Ministry of Agriculture, 1977.

Jones, Novelette C., Eric H. Back, Evadne Ford, and the Scientific Research Council. *Food Guide for Jamaica*. Kingston: n.p., [1966?].

Julien Lung-Fou, Marie Thérèse. *Les recettes de cuisine martiniquaise de Da Elodie*. Fort de France, Martinique: Imp. Antillaise Saint-Paul, [1950?].

Keown, Mary E. *La conservación de frutas y vegetales en Puerto Rico*. Boletín de Extensión Núm. 7, Servicio de Extensión Agrícola, Colegio de Agricultura y Artes Mecánicas, Universidad de Puerto Rico, en Cooperación con del Departamento de Agricultura de Estados Unidos, Reimpreso, 1938.

Kirkcaldy, Doreen. *Meal Planning*. Jamaica: Central Information and Publicity Services in J.A.S. under the auspices of the Co-ordinated Extension Services, 1958.

Ladies Aid Society of the First Methodist Church of San Juan. *Porto Rican Cookbook*. San Juan: M. Burillo & Co., 1915.

Ladies Guild of Santo Domingo. *Recetas dominicanas: Dominican Recipes*. Santo Domingo: Ladies Guild of Santo Domingo, 1977.

Lamy, Fendy. *Food for the Body, Food for the Soul: A Family Treasury of Recipes*. N.p.: TotalRecall Publications, 2018.

Lickfold, Barbara Hilary Hodd. *The Handbook of Trinidad Cookery*. Ross, Hartfordshire: Richard Powle, 1907.

Legran, J. P. *Nuevo manual del cocinero cubano y español*. Havana, 1864 [1857].

Lenhart, Nan M. *The Heart of the Pumpkin: Healthy Cooking with Caribbean Fruits and Vegetables*. Edited by Carol B. Flemming and Clarice C. Clarke. St. Croix: University of the Virgin Islands Cooperative Extension Service, 1989.

Lindgren, Glenn, Raul Musibay, and Jorge Castillo. *Three Guys from Miami Cook Cuban*. Layton, UT: Gibbs Smith, 2004.

Longacre, Doris. *More-with-Less*. Harrisonburg, VA: Herald Press, 1976.

López Lay, Aurora. *El moderno cocinero criollo*. Habana: Edicuba, 1943.

Lugo McAllister, Aida. *Aida's Kitchen a lo Boricua*. North Mankato, MN: Corporate Graphics, 2013.

Mackay, Amy. *"Let Us Cook" = Le Awe Cook: A Collection of Authentic Cruzan Recipes*. St. Croix, Virgin Islands: Antilles Graphic Arts, 1980.

Madrinas de las Salas "Costales" y "San Martín" del Hospital Universitario "General Calixto García." *¿Gusta, usted? Prontuario culinario y . . . necesario*. Imprenta Úcar, García, S.A., 1956.

Magloire-Prophète, Herzulie. "Cuisine Haïtienne." *Tricinquantenaire de l'indépendence d'Haïti*. Lausanne: Formes et Couleurs, 1954.

———. *Cuisine sélectionnée*. Port-au-Prince: Henri Deschamps, 1955.

Mayard, Louise. *Cuisine des pays chauds*. Santiago de Chile: Impr. Molina Lackington y cia, 1940.

McAnuff, Craig, and Shaun McAnuff. *Original Flava*. London: Bloomsbury Publishing, 2019.

Mercador, Angelina, and Elsie Mae Willsey. *El plátano: modos de prepararlo para la mesa*. Circular de Extensión, Núm. 2, Servicio de Extensión Agrícola, Colegio de Agricultura y Artes Mecánicas, Universidad de Puerto Rico, en Cooperación con del Departamento de Agricultura de Estados Unidos, Reimpreso, 1939.

Meynell, Francis, and Vera Meynell. *The Week-end Book*. London: Nonesuch Press, 1924.

Miller, Elsa. *Caribbean Cookbook: Using the Foods We Grow*. Kingston: Kingston Publishers, 1979.

———. *Caribbean Cooking and Menus*. Kingston: TEP Bahamas, 1982.

Miller, Sally. *Bajan Cooking in a Nutshell*. St. Thomas, Barbados: Miller Publishing, 2010.

———. *Contemporary Caribbean Cooking*. St. Thomas, Barbados: Wordsmith International, 2002.

Mitchell, Lady. *The Prospect Great House Cookbook*. Bermuda: Island Press, 1981.

Moorehead, Laura L. *Kruzan Nynyam from Mampoo Kitchen*. St. Thomas: Pacific Printing Service, 1977.

Morley, LaurelAnn. *Caribbean Recipes Old and New*. St. Joseph, Barbados: LaurelAnn Morley, 2005.

Mountain Maid Self-Help Project. *Best Made Cookbook*. Port-au-Prince: Mountain Maid Self-Help Project, 1980.

Murray, Dea. *Cooking with Rum, Caribbean Style*. St. Thomas: Rolfe Associates, Division of Alcar Corp., 1982.

———. *Famous Native Recipes of the Virgin Islands*. St. Thomas: Dearon Publishing, 1969.

Nègre, André. *Les Antilles et la Guyane: à travers leur cuisine.* Caen, France: Impr. Ozanne, 1967.

Nodal, Blanca R. *Cocina internacional.* Camagüey, Cuba: Imprenta Ramentol, 1932.

Noviatur, J. F. [pseud.]. *Novísimo manual del cocinero pastelero dulcero y licorista cubano.* Havana: Imprenta La Idea, 1891.

Orcasitas, María T. *Como preparar los productos enlatados de su despensa para servirlos en la mesa.* Circular de Extensión Núm. 15, Servicio de Extensión Agrícola, Colegio de Agricultura y Artes Mecánicas, Universidad de Puerto Rico, en Cooperación con del Departamento de Agricultura de Estados Unidos, 1937.

———. *El conejo: modos de preparar la carne para la mesa.* Circular de Extensión Núm. 17, Servicio de Extensión Agrícola, Colegio de Agricultura y Artes Mecánicas, Universidad de Puerto Rico, en Cooperación con del Departamento de Agricultura de Estados Unidos, Reimpreso, 1938.

———. *Conservación de carnes en el hogar.* Circular de Extensión Núm. 14, Servicio de Extensión Agrícola, Colegio de Agricultura y Artes Mecánicas, Universidad de Puerto Rico, en Cooperación con del Departamento de Agricultura de Estados Unidos, Reimpreso, 1939.

———. *Harina de maíz: modos de prepararla para la mesa.* Circular de Extensión Núm. 10. Servicio de Extensión Agrícola, Colegio de Agricultura y Artes Mecánicas, Universidad de Puerto Rico, en Cooperación con del Departamento de Agricultura de Estados Unidos, Reimpreso, 1938.

Ordoñez, Rosa M., and Elsie Mae Willsey. *El panapén: modos de prepararlo para la mesa.* Circular de Extensión Núm. 4, Servicio de Extensión Agrícola, Colegio de Agricultura y Artes Mecánicas, Universidad de Puerto Rico, en Cooperación con del Departamento de Agricultura de Estados Unidos, Reimpreso 1937.

Ornes Perelló, Amanda. *Cocina criolla.* Editora del Caribe, 1962 [1955].

———. *Manual de economía doméstica.* Santiago, Rep. Dominicana: Imp. La Información, 1938.

Ovide, Stéphanie. *French Caribbean Cuisine.* New York: Hippocrene Books, 2002.

Paris, Robel. *Haitian Recipes.* Port-au-Prince: Imprimerie Henri Deschamps, 1955.

Pastrana, Angelina, and Elsie Mae Willsey. *La berenjena: modos de prepararla para la mesa.* Circular de Extensión Núm. 6, Servicio de Extensión Agrícola, Colegio de Agricultura y Artes Mecánicas, Universidad de Puerto Rico, en Cooperación con del Departamento de Agricultura de Estados Unidos, Reimpreso, 1938.

Peláez, Ana Sofía, and Ellen Silverman. *The Cuban Table: A Celebration of Food, Flavors, and History.* New York: St. Martin's Press, 2014.

Perez, Jacinia. *Puerto Rican Vegan Cookbook.* Jacinia Perez, 2019.

Petersen, Arona. *The Food and Folklore of the Virgin Islands*. Ft. Lauderdale: Romik, 1990.
Platt Stockelberg, Alicia. *Mrs Platt's Recipes Cakes and Confections*. Havana, 1947.
P.O.P. *The Nabob's Cookery Book*. London: Frederick Warne & Co., 1870.
Prieto Dávila, Blanca. *Folleto de recetas de cocina y repostería cubana*. Habana: Secretaría de Agricultura, Negociado de Economía Doméstica, Servicio de Publicidad y Divulgación, 1932.
Psaila, Marie. *Housekeeper's Guide for British Guiana and the West Indies*. Demerara, Guyana: Argosy Co. Ltd., 1912.
Querillac, Anne. *Cuisine coloniale: les bonnes recettes de Chloé Mondésir*. Paris: Société d'éditions géographiques maritimes et coloniales, 1931.
Rabette, Charlotte. *Almanach-manuel de la cuisinière*. Paris: Delarue, [1890?].
———. *Les conseils des Catherines: 920 recettes pratiques pour la maîtresse de maison*. Paris: Payot, 1929.
———. *La cuisine exotique chez soi*. Paris: Éditions de portiques, 1931.
Rampy, Mme. Arthur. *Cuisine et patisserie*. Port-au-Prince: Impr. de l'État, 1965.
Rankine, Peggy. *Simply Delicious*. Jamaica: n.p., [1986?].
Remay, Uzale, Université de Moncton Centre de recherche sur les aliments, and Partenariat Acadie-Haïti. *Ann nou fè konsèvasyon manje*. Montréal: Éditions du Remue-Ménage, 2001.
Rementería y Fica, Mariano de, translator. *Manual del cocinero, cocinera y repostero, con un tratado de confiteria y botilleria, y un método para trinchar y servir toda clase de viandas, y la cortesanía y urbanidad que se sebe usar en la mesa*. Madrid: Librería de Cuesta, 1828.
Reyes Gavilán y Moenck, Maria Antonieta. *Delicias de la mesa*. Havana: Avisador Comercial, 1923.
Richards-Greaves, Gillian. *Rediasporization: African-Guyanese Kweh-Kweh*. University Press of Mississippi, 2020.
Roachè, Nekisha. *From My Mudda's Kitchen*. N.p.: Nekisha Roachè, 2014.
Roots, Levi. *Caribbean Food: Made Easy with Levi Roots*. London: Mitchell Beazley, 2013.
———. *Food for Friends*. London: Mitchell Beazley, 2010.
———. *Levi Roots' Reggae Reggae Cookbook*. London: Collins, 2011.
La sagüera, utilísima colección ampliada de recetas probadas. Havana: Montalvo, Cardenas & Co., 1923.
Schwartzkopf, Estrella Moll, and Elsie Mae Willsey. *La yuca: modos de prepararla para la mesa*. Circular de Extensión Núm. 1, Servicio de Extensión Agrícola, Colegio de Agricultura y Artes Mecánicas, Universidad de Puerto Rico, en Cooperación con del Departamento de Agricultura de Estados Unidos, Reimpreso, 1937.
Sevigne, Marquesa de [pseud.]. *El arte de la buena mesa*, segunda edición. La Habana: Cardenas y cia, 1939.

La Sociedad de Dependientes de Restaurantes, Hoteles y Fondas de la Provincia de La Habana. *Auxiliar gastronómico pro turismo*. La Habana: Cultural, 1937.

Spenceley, Angela. *Just Add Rum!: A Caribbean Cookbook: Starters & Light Fare, Tropical Drinks*. St. Thomas: Virgin Islands Cards, 1999.

———. *A Taste of the Virgin Islands*. St. Thomas: Virgin Island Card, 1998.

———. *A Taste of the Virgin Islands Too! Cookbook: Everything You Need to Know about Virgin Islands Cooking*. St. Thomas: Coconut Press, 2000.

Springer, Rita. *Caribbean Cookbook*. N.p: Evans Bros., 1968.

Steel, Flora Annie. *The Complete Indian Housekeeper and Cook*. London: W. Heinemann, 1898 [1888].

Sullivan, Caroline. *Classic Jamaican Cooking: Traditional Recipes and Herbal Remedies*. London: Serif, 1995.

———. *The Jamaica Cookery Book*. Kingston: A. W. Gardner & Co., 1893.

Tonge, Gwen. *Cooking Antigua's Foods*. St. Johns, Antigua: G. Tonge, 1973.

Tree, L. M., ed. *The Handbook of Trinidad Cookery*, 2nd ed. Port-of-Spain: Muir Marshall, 1910.

Triay, José. *Nuevo manual del cocinero criollo*. Havana: Imprenta y papelaría la moderna poesía, 1914 [1903].

Tropical Pot Pourri. Kingstown, St. Vincent and the Grenadines: n.p., 1970.

Village Improvement Society of Barton, Vermont. *The Barton Cookbook*. Barton, VT.: Monitor Press, 1913.

Union School PTA. *What's Cooking in Haiti?* N.p., 1981.

United Nations Women's Group in Jamaica. *Festivals and Recipes*. Kingston: Instant Print, [1970?].

Valldejuli, Carmen Aboy. *Cocina criolla*. N.p, 1954

Varona de Mora, Ernestina. *Manual de la cocina moderna*. Habana: Montalvo y Cardenas, 1932.

Villapol, Nitza. *Cocina al minuto*. Havana: Editorial Orbe, 1981.

———. *Cocina al minuto I*. Compilación Sisi Colmina González. Miami: Nitza Villapol, 2016 [2005].

———. *Cocina al minuto II*. Compilacón Sisi Colmina González. Miami: Nitza Villapol, 2016 [2005].

———. *Cocina al minuto: con sabor a Cuba*. N.p.: Createspace Independent, 2017 [2016].

———. *Cocina al minuto, recetas fáciles y rápidas de hacer con sabor a Cuba*. Compilación Sisi Colmina. Miami: Penguin Random House Grupo Editorial, 2019.

———. *Cocina al minuto, selecciones de recetas favoritas*. Ediciones Cubamerica, 1997 [1968].

———. *Cocina criolla*. Mexico, D.F.: Ediciones Zocalo, [1970?].

———. *Cocina cubana*. Mexico, D.F.: Compañía de Publicacions, [1975?].

———. *Cocina cubana, alegre sus mesas con recetas tradicionales de la mejor de las Antillas*. Habana: Editorial Científica-Técnica, 1992 [1973?].

———. *Cocina cubana, cocina al minuto*. Compilación Sisi Colmina. N.p.: Ediciones Nitza Villapol, 2005.

———. *Cuban Flavor: Typical Creole Cuisine Recipes*. Translated by Fernando Nápoles Tapia. Havana: Editorial José Martí, 1999.

———*Desde su cocina: más de 350 recetas de la obra de Nitza Villapol*. Habana: Editorial Científica-Técnica, 1999.

———. *Los dulces de Cuba*. Habana: Editorial Científica-Técnica, 1996.

———. *Elegantes, originales, prácticas ideas en nuestra exposición anual de mesas servidas con platos preparados expresamente por la distinguida experta Nitza Villapol*. N.p, [195_?]

Virgin Islands Extension Service. *Virgin Islands Fruits and Vegetables: Recipes*. St. Croix: Virgin Islands Cooperative Extension Service, College of the Virgin Islands, 1969.

Walker, Jill. *Jill Walker's Cooking in Barbados*. Welches St. Thomas, Barbados: Best of Barbados, 1983.

Watkins, Mrs. F. H. *West India Recipes*. Kingston: Lady Musgrave's Women's Self Help Society, 1908.

Weaver, Winnie. *Haitian How-To's*. Winnie Weaver, n.d.

Williams, Ayesha. *Vegetarian Cooking: Jamaican Style*. Kingston: LMH Publishing, 2013.

Willsey, Elsie Mae. *Tropical Foods: Bulletin no. 1—Vegetables, Chayote, Yautia, Plantain, Banana*. Government of Porto Rico, Department of Education, Bulletin no. 3, 1925.

———. *Vegetables: Rice and the Legumes. Tropical Foods: Bulletin no. 3*, Bulletin University of Puerto Rico Department of Home Economics, vol. 1, no. 2, 1927.

———. *Vegetales tropicales: batata*. University of Puerto Rico College of Education no. 10, Bulletin University of Puerto Rico Department of Home Economics no. 2, no. 7, 1931.

Willsey, Elsie Mae, and Carmen Janer Vilá. *Vegetales tropicales: yautía*. Publication of the University of Puerto Rico College of Education no. 11, Bulletin of the University of Puerto Rico Department of Home Economics vol. 3, no. 8, 1931.

Willsey, Elsie Mae, and Clara Aurora Ruíz. *Vegetales tropicales: chayote*. Publication of the University of Puerto Rico College of Education no. 9, Bulletin University of Puerto Rico Department of Home Economics vol. 1, no. 6, 1931.

Winslow, la Señora. *Cocinera económica de la Señora Winslow o sean instrucciones de la manera de preparar diversos platos al estitulo [sic] español*. Boston: George C. Rand and Avery printers, n.d. [186_?].

Wolfe, Linda. *Recipes: The Cooking of the Caribbean Islands*. Amsterdam: Time-Life International, 1970.

Wolff, Amy. *Mountain Maid Best Made Cookbook*. Mountain Maid Self Help Projects, n.d.

Women's League of St. Thomas. *Virgin Islands Native Recipes*. Charlotte Amelie, St. Thomas: Carib Graphic Arts, 1954.

General Works

Abbad y Lasierra, Iñigo, and José A. Acosta. *Historia geográfica, civil y natural de la isla de San Juan Bautista de Puerto Rico.* Puerto Rico: Impr. y librería de Acosta, 1866. Pdf retrieved from the Library of Congress, www.loc.gov /item03006061/.

Abreu Cardet, José. "Néstor Salazar: Señor de la cocina." *Radio Angulo,* 4 April 2017, https://www.radioangulo.icrt.cu/memoria-holguinera/16518 -nestor-salazar-senor-de-la-cocina.

Ahulwalai, Deepi, and Steff Ferrari. *A Woman's Place: The Inventors, Rumrunners, Lawbreakers, Scientists, and Single Moms Who Changed the World with Food.* Boston: Little, Brown, 2019.

Aikhenvald, Alexandra. "Arawak Languages." *Encyclopedia of Language and Linguistics,* 2nd ed. Amsterdam: Elsevier, 2006, pp. 446–449. doi: 10.1016/ B0-08-044854-2/02292-6.

Allen, Carolyn. "Creole Then and Now: The Problem of Definition." *Caribbean Quarterly,* vol. 44, no. 1/2, 1998, pp. 33–49. JSTOR, www.jstor.org/stable /40654020. Accessed 19 Feb. 2021.

Allen, Robert N. "Foreign Service Dispatch No. 314" from Ciudad Trujillo, D.R., 13 Dec. 1956. http://www.latinamericanstudies.org/embassy/R24-314-12-13 -1956.pdf.

Altieri Taplin, Theresa. "Philadelphia Pepper Pot." *The Encyclopedia of Greater Philadelphia,* https://philadelphiaencyclopedia.org/archive/philadelphia -pepper-pot/.

Álvarez Álvarez, Luis, and Olga García Yero. *El Pensamiento cultural en el siglo XIX cubano.* Havana: Editorial de Ciencias Sociales, 2013.

Anderson, Benedict. *Imagined Communities.* New York: Verso, 1983.

Appadurai, Arjun. "How to Make a National Cuisine: Cookbooks in Contemporary India." *Comparative Studies in Society and History,* vol. 30, no. 1, 1988, pp. 3–24.

———. *Modernity at Large.* Minneapolis: University of Minnesota Press, 1996.

Arnau, Gemma, et al. "Understanding the Genetic Diversity and Population Structure of Yam (Dioscorea alata L.) Using Microsatellite Markers." *PLoS One,* vol. 12, no. 3, 2017, doi:10.1371/journal.pone.0174150.

Ashford, Bailey K. *A Soldier in Science: The Autobiography of Bailey K. Ashford.* San Juan: Editorial de la Universidad de Puerto Rico, 1998 [1934].

Austin, Elisabeth. "Reading and Writing Juana Manuela Gorriti's 'Cocina ecléctica': Modeling Multiplicity in Nineteenth-Century Domestic Narrative." *Arizona Journal of Hispanic Cultural Studies,* vol. 12 (2008), pp. 31–44. JSTOR, www.jstor.org/stable/20641895.

"BADMC Making Strides." *Barbados Advocate,* 22 May 2016, https://www .barbadosadvocate.com/business-news/badmc-making-strides.

Baerga, Maria del Carmen, ed.. *Género y trabajo: La industria de la aguja en Puerto Rico y el Caribe hispano*. Río Piedras: Editorial de la Universidad de Puerto Rico, 1993.

Balfour, Sharifa. "Celebration of Jamaica's Heritage." *Gleaner*, 25 May 2018, http://jamaica-gleaner.com/article/art-leisure/20180527/celebration-jamaicas-heritage.

Balter, Michael. "Early Africans Went Bananas." *Science*, 5 Jan. 2006, https://www.sciencemag.org/news/2006/01/early-africans-went-bananas.

Balutansky, Kathleen M. "A Conversation at the Haitian Studies Association Meeting October 15, 1994." *Callaloo*, vol. 18, no. 2, 1995, pp. 439–450. JSTOR, www.jstor.org/stable/3299092.

Baralt, Blanca Zacharie de. *El Martí que yo conocí*. Havana: Editorial Trópico, 1945.

Barceló Miller, Maria de Fátima. *La lucha por el sufragio femenino en Puerto Rico, 1896–1935*. Rio Piedras, P.R.: Huracán, 1997.

Barradas, Efraín. "*El cocinero puertorriqueño, El manual del cocinero cubano* y la formación del nacionalismo en el Caribe." *Saberes y sabores en Mexico y el Caribe*, edited by Kym Hyge, Patrick Hollard, and Rita de Maeseneer. Leiden: Brill Rodopi, 2010, pp. 267–179.

Barrow, Errol. "What Kind of Mirror Image Do You Have of Yourself?" Text of Speech delivered 13 May 1986, www.caribbeanelections.com.

Bean, Dalia. *Jamaican Women and the World Wars: On the Front Lines of Change*. London: Palgrave Macmillan, 2018.

Beckles, Hilary. "Independence and the Social Crisis of Nationalism in Barbados." *Caribbean Freedom: Economy and Society from Emancipation to the Present*, edited by Hilary Beckles and Verene Shepherd, Princeton, NJ: Markus Wiener Publishers, 1996, pp. 528–539.

Beekhuis, Jeanne V. "Tourism in the Caribbean: Impacts on the Economic, Social and Natural Environments." *Ambio*, vol. 10, no. 6, 1981, pp. 325–331. JSTOR, www.jstor.org/stable/4312729.

Beetham Margaret. "Of Recipe Books and Reading in the Nineteenth Century: Mrs. Beeton and Her Cultural Consequences." *The Recipe Reader*, edited by Janet Floyd and Laurel Forster. Lincoln: University of Nebraska Press, 2003, pp. 2–30.

Bellegarde-Smith, Patrick. *Haiti: The Breached Citadel*. Toronto: Canadian Scholars' Press, 2004.

———. *In the Shadow of Powers: Dantès Bellegarde in Haitian Social Thought*. Atlantic Highlands, NJ: Humanities Press International, 1985.

Benítez-Rojo, Antonio. *La isla que se repite*. Barcelona: Editorial Casiopea, 1998.

Bernabé, Jean, Patrick Chamoiseau, and Raphaël Confiant. *Éloge de la créolite*. Paris: Gallimard, 1993.

Berti, Ilaria. "Curiosity, Appreciation, and Old Habits: Creolization of Colonizers' Food Consumption Patterns in Three English Travelogues on the

Caribbean." *Caribbean Food Cultures: Culinary Practices and Consumption in the Caribbean and its Diasporas*, edited by Wiebke Beushausn, Anne Brüske, Ana-Sofia Commicheau, Patrick Helber, and Sinah Kloß. Bielfeld: Verlag, 2014, pp. 115–132.

B. G. "Jamaican Cooking Coming into Its Own." *Sunday Gleaner*, 3 Nov. 1963, p. 14.

B. G. D. "Review of *Barrières* by Roger Dorsinville." *Books Abroad*, vol. 23, no. 1, 1949, pp. 55–55. JSTOR, www.jstor.org/stable/40088002.

"Black History Spotlight: Laura Moorhead White." Stcroixsource.com, 16 Feb. 2006, https://stcroixsource.com/2006/02/16/black-history-spotlight-laura-moorhead-white/.

Bourbonnais, Nicole. "'Dangerously Large': The 1938 Labor Rebellion and the Debate over Birth Control in Jamaica." *NWIG: New West Indian Guide/Nieuwe West-Indische Gids*, vol. 83, no. 1/2, 2009, pp. 39–69. JSTOR, www.jstor.org/stable/43390766.

Bower, Anne L. *Recipes for Reading: Community Cookbooks, Stories, Histories*. Amherst: University of Massachusetts Press, 1997.

Brandon, Leila. "Jamaican Corned Beef," "Patriotic Pudding," and "Ackee Served as a First Course." *Daily Gleaner*, 24 Jan. 1980, p. 17.

Brathwaite, Kamau. *The Development of Creole Society in Jamaica, 1770–1820*. Oxford: Oxford University Press, 1971.

———. *History of the Voice*. London: New Beacon Books, 1984.

———. *Middle Passages*. New York: New Directions, 1992.

Briggs, Laura. *Reproducing Empire: Race, Sex, Science, and U.S. Imperialism in Puerto Rico*. Berkeley: University of California Press, 2002.

Brillat-Savarin, Anselme. *Physiologie du goût*. Paris: Librairie de la Bibliothèque nationale, 1876.

Brownfoot, Janice N. "Memsahibs in Colonial Malays: A Study of European Wives in a British Colony and Protectorate, 1900–1940." *The Incorporated Wife*, edited by Hilary Callan and Shirley Ardener. London: Croom Helm, 1984, pp. 186–210.

Bruni, Frank, and Jennifer Steinhauer. "A History of Meatloaf, Long May It Reign." *Bon Appetit*, 6 March 2017, https://www.bonappetit.com/story/history-of-meatloaf.

Buckridge, Steeve O. *African Lace-Bark in the Caribbean: The Construction of Race, Class, and Gender*. London: Bloomsbury Academic, 2016.

Burke, Michael. "Rudolph Burke in Black History." *Jamaica Observer*, 2 Feb. 2012, http://www.jamaicaobserver.com/columns/Rudolph-Burke-in-Black-History_10680691.

Burnet, Ian. *Spice Islands*. Kenthurst, Australia: Rosenburg Publishing, 2013.

Bush, Barbara. "Colonial Research and the Social Sciences at the End of Empire: The West Indian Social Survey, 1944–57." *Journal of Imperial & Commonwealth History*, vol. 41, no. 3, 2013, pp. 451–474. EBSCOhost, doi:10.1089/03086534.2013.816072.

———. *Slave Women in Caribbean Society, 1650–1838*. Bloomington: Indiana University Press, 1990.

Byrd, Brandon. "The Transnational Word of Moral Elevation: African American Women and the Reformation of Haiti, 1847–1950." *Palimpsest: A Journal of Women, Gender, and the Black International*, vol. 5, no. 2, 2016, pp. 128–150.

Cabanillas, Berta. "Orígenes de los hábitos alimenticios del pueblo de Puerto Rico." *Revista española de antropología americana*. vol. 1, no. 6, 1955, pp. 199–215.

Calvo Peña, Beatriz. "Cocina criolla." *Catauro: revista cubana de antropología*, vol. 7, no. 12, 2005, pp. 76–84.

Candelario, Ginetta E. B., April Mayes, and Elizabeth S. Manley, *Cien años de feminismos dominicanos: una colección de documentos y escrituras clave en la formación y evolución del pensamiento y el movimiento feminista en la República*, 2 vols. Santo Domingo: Editora Centenario, 2016.

Candlin, Kit, and Cassandra Pybus. *Enterprising Women: Gender, Race, and Power in the Revolutionary Atlantic World, 1700–1900*. Athens: University of Georgia Press, 2015.

Carbet, Marie-Magdelaine. *Musique noire*. Fort-de-France, Martinique: Éditions Dialogue, 1958.

Carmichael, Mrs. *Domestic Manners and Social Conditions of the White, Coloured, and Negro Population of the West Indies*. London: Whittaker, Treacher, and Co., 1833. https://babel.hathitrust.org/cgi/pt?id=mdp.39015005551794;view=1up;seq=5.

Carney, Judith. *Black Rice: The African Origins of Rice Cultivation in the Americas*. Cambridge, MA: Harvard University Press, 2002.

Casas, Bartolomé de las. *Brevísima relación de la destrucción de las Indias*. Edited by José Miguel Martínez-Torrejón. Publicaciones de la Universidad de Alicante, Digitalia, 2006 [1552].

Castellanos, María Bianet, Lourdes Gutiérrez Nájera, and Arturo J. Aldama, eds. *Comparative Indigeneities of the Américas: Towards a Hemispheric Approach*. Tucson: University of Arizona Press, 2012.

"Celebrating the Heritage of Jamaica." *Gleaner*, 27 Aug. 2017, http://jamaica-gleaner.com/article/art-leisure/20170827/celebrating-heritage-jamaica.

"Centennial." *Virgin Islands Daily News*, 20 Sept. 2016, pp. A10–A11.

Chanca, Diego Alvarez. "Letter of Dr. Chanca on the Second Voyage of Columbus." *The Northmen, Columbus and Cabot, 985–1503: The Voyages of the Northmen; The Voyages of Columbus and of John Cabot*, edited Julius E. Olson and Edward G. Bourne, New York: Charles Scribner's Sons, 1906, pp. 281–313.

Chandrasekara, Anoma, and Thamilini Joseph Kumar. "Roots and Tuber Crops as Functional Foods: A Review on Phytochemical Constituents and Their Potential Health Benefits." *Journal of Food Science*, 2016. doi: 10.1155/2016/3631647.

Chapman, William. "Slave Villages in the Danish West Indies." *Bondmen and Freedmen in the Danish West Indies: Scholarly Perspectives*, edited by George F. Tyson. St. Thomas: Virgin Islands Humanities Council, 1996.

Chefmeow. "Pretty Black Eyed Pea Cake." Grouprecipes.com, http://www.group recipes.com/43480/pretty-black-eyed-pea-cake.html. Accessed 13 Nov. 2020.

Chen, Edith Wen-Chu. "'You Are Like Us, You Eat Plátanos': Chinese Dominicans, Race, Ethnicity, and Identity." *Afro-Hispanic Review*, vol. 27, no. 1, 2008, pp. 23–40. JSTOR, www.jstor.org/stable/23055221.

Chevalier, Auguste. "Contribution à l'histoire de l'introduction des bananes en France et à l'historique de la culture bananière dans les colonies françaises." *Journal d'agriculture traditionnelle et de botanique appliquée*, 1944, no. 272–274, pp. 116–127. https://www.persee.fr/doc/jatba_0370-3681_1944_num_24 _272_1796.

Childers, Kristen Stromberg. *Seeking Imperialism's Embrace: National Identity, Decolonization, and Assimilation in the French Caribbean*. Oxford: Oxford University Press, 2016.

Chivas-Baron, Clotilde. *La femme française aux colonies*. Edited by Mari-Paule Ha. Paris: L'Harmattan, 2009.

Clark, Victor S., et al. *Porto Rico and Its Problems*. Washington, DC: Brookings Institution, 1930.

Clarke, Austin. *Pig Tails 'n Breadfruit: A Culinary Memoir*. New York: New Press, 1999.

Cleary, Al. *Cleary's Street Guide of Jamaican Capitals*. Kingston: Brainbuster Publications, 1970.

———. *Jamaica Brukin's*. Kingston: Brainbuster Publications, 1972.

Cleary, Al, and Keith Reece. *Jamaican Proverbs*. Kingston: Brainbuster Publications, [1970?].

Clement, Job B. "History of Education in Haiti: 1804–1915." *Revista De Historia De América*, no. 88, 1979, pp. 33–74. JSTOR, www.jstor.org/stable/20139335.

Cohen, Cathy J. "Punks, Bulldaggers, and Welfare Queens." *The Routledge Queer Studies Reader*, edited by Donald E. Hall and Annamarie Jagose. London: Routledge, 2013, pp. 74–95.

Coll y Toste, Cayetano. *Prehistoria de Puerto Rico*. San Juan: Tip. Boletín mercantil, 1907.

Colmina González, Sisi. "Prólogo" and "Nitza Villapol breves apuntes para una semblanza." *Cocina al minuto I* by Nitza Villapol, edited by Sisi Colmina González. Miami: Nitza Villapol Inc., 2005.

Coloma y Garcés, Eugenio. *Apendice necesario e indispensable para la práctica pedánea, que contiene el modo de actuar en una causa complicada en desembarco de negros bozales . . . [etc.]*. Habana: Imprenta La Cubana, 1860.

———. *Catecismo de agricultura cubana*. Havana: Imprenta "La Antilla," 1863.

———. *Manual del jardinero cubano*. Habana: Imprenta Militar de la Vinda de Soler, 1872.

———. *Manual de práctica pedánea*. Habana: Imprenta La Cubana, 1853.

———. *Manual recreativo de secretos fáciles, curiosos, útiles y necesarios para la economía doméstica ó sea el sabelo todo de las madres de familias cubanas a quienes dedica esta obra*. Havana: Spencer y Companía, 1857.

Colonial Secretary, compiler. *The Grenada Handbook, Directory, and Almanac for the Years 1901–1902.* London: Sampson Low, Marston & Co., 1901.

Columbus, Christopher. *The Voyages of Christopher Columbus, Being the Journals of His First and Third, and the Letters Concerning His First and Last Voyages, to Which Is Added the Account of His Second Voyage Written by Andres Bernaldez. Now Newly Translated and Edited, with an Introduction and Notes, by Cecil Jane.* London: Argonaut Press, 1930.

Columbus, Christopher, and Lionel Cecil Jane. *Selected Documents Illustrating the Four Voyages of Columbus.* London: Routledge, 2010 [The Hakluyt Society, 1929]. https://play.google.com/books/reader?id=9_s6AAAAIAAJ&hl=en&pg=GBS.PP9.

Comhaire-Sylvain, Suzanne. "Notre paysanne un aspect de sa vie," *La voix des femmes,* vol. 1 no. 3, 1935, p. 3.

Condé, Maryse. *La parole des femmes.* Paris: L'Harmattan, 1989.

Connerton, Winifred C. "Working towards Health, Christianity and Democracy: American Colonial and Missionary Nurses in Puerto Rico, 1900–30." *Colonial Caring: A History of Colonial and Post-Colonial Nursing,* edited by Helen Sweet and Sue Hawkins. Manchester: Manchester University Press, 2015, pp. 126–144. JSTOR, www.jstor.org/stable/j.ctt18dzrdn.12.

"Consumer Week." *Daily Gleaner,* 16 Oct. 1975, pp. 19 and 24.

"Cook with Taste, Cook with Grace Foods." *Daily Gleaner,* 8 Nov. 1962, p. 17.

Cooper, Carolyn. "Who Is Jamaica?" *New York Times,* 5 Aug. 2012, www.nytimes.com/2012/08/06/opinion/who-is-jamaica.html.

Craige, John Houston. *Cannibal Cousins.* New York: Minton, Balch and Co., 1934.

"Criollo." *Diccionario etimológico Castellano en línea,* 2018. http://etimologias.dechile.net/?criollo.

"Criollo." *Diccionario de la lengua Española, edición tricentenaria.* Real Academia Española, 2020. https://dle.rae.es/criollo?m=form#otras.

Crosby, Alfred W., Jr. *The Columbian Exchange: Biological and Cultural Consequences of 1492.* Westport, CT: Greenwood Press, 1972.

Cubeancuentro. "El primer libro de cocina de cuba." Cubaencuentro.com, 26 Feb. 2021, https://www.cubaencuentro.com/cuba/noticias/el-primer-libro-de-cocina-de-cuba-339269.

"Daily Thoughts" (n.a.). *Oxford Magazine: A Weekly Newspaper and Review,* vol. 26, 24 June 1908, pp. 11–12.

Dash, J. Michael. "Engagement, Exile and Errance: Some Trends in Haitian Poetry 1946–1986." *Callaloo,* vol. 15, no. 3, 1992, pp. 747–760. JSTOR, www.jstor.org/stable/2932017.

———. "*Jean Price-Mars and Haiti* by Jacques C. Antoine; *Monsieur Toussaint* by Edouard Glissant; *Heremakhonon* by Maryse Condé." *Caribbean Quarterly,* vol. 27, no. 4, 1981, pp. 50–52. JSTOR, www.jstor.org/stable/40653432.

Dawdy, Shannon Lee. "*La Comida Mambisa*: Food, Farming, and Cuban Identity, 1839–1999." *New West India Guide,* vol. 76, no.1–2, 2002, pp. 47–80.

Deive, Carlos Esteban. *El indio, el negro y la vida tradicional dominicana*. Santo Domingo: Museo del Hombre Dominicano, 1978.

———. *Las culturas afrocaribeñas*. Santo Domingo: Sección Nacional de República Dominicana IPGH, 2015.

Delacruz, Jenny. "Soup Joumou: A Haitian New Year Tradition!" 31 Dec. 2021, www.cobbscreekpublishing.com/post/soup-joumou-a-haitian-new-year-tradition.

Delgado, Linda C., and Felix Matos, eds. *Puerto Rican Women's History: New Perspectives*. Armonk, NY: M. E. Sharpe, 1998.

DeLisser, H. G. "Random Jottings: As I See the World." *Daily Gleaner*, 20 Dec. 1939, p. 12.

DeLoughrey, Elizabeth. "Island Ecologies and Caribbean Literatures." *Tijdschrift voor Economische en Sociale Geografie*, vol. 95, no. 3, 2004, pp. 298–310.

———. "The Politics of Place." *The Routledge Companion to Anglophone Caribbean Literature*, edited by Michael Bucknor and Alison Donnell. London: Routledge, 2011, pp. 265–275.

———. "Postcolonialism." *The Oxford Companion to Ecocriticism*, edited by R. Gerrard, Oxford: Oxford University Press, 2014, pp. 320–340.

De Maeseneer, Rita. "Celebrar, tragar, amamantar lo cubano: los contextos culinarios en 'Cecilia Valdés' de Cirilo Villaverde." *Iberoamericana*, vol. 9, no. 36, 2009, pp. 27–46. JSTOR, www.jstor.org/stable/41676965.

de Noter, Raphaël. *Dictionnaire français-argot*. Paris: A. Merciant, 1901.

———. *Étude synoptique sur l'horticulture en Algérie*. Algiers: Impr. De P. Fontana, 1890.

———. *Le Jardin potager colonial*. Paris: Société d'éditions géographiques, maritimes et colonials, 1930.

Derby, Lauren. "The Dictator's Seduction: Gender and State Spectacle during the Trujillo Regime." *Callaloo*, vol. 23, no. 3, 2000, pp. 1112–1146. JSTOR, www.jstor.org/stable/3299727.

———. *The Dictator's Seduction: Politics and the Popular Imagination in the Era of Trujillo*. Durham, NC: Duke University Press, 2009.

Deutsch, Monroe E. "E Pluribus Unum." *Classical Journal*, vol. 18, no. 7, 1923, pp. 387–407. http://penelope.uchicago.edu/Thayer/E/Journals/CJ/18/7/E_Pluribus_Unum*.html.

Diederich, Bernard. *Trujillo: The Death of the Goat*. London: Bodley Head, 1978.

Dietz, James. *Economic History of Puerto Rico: Institutional Change and Capitalist Development*. Princeton, NJ: Princeton University Press, 1986.

Diffie, Bailey, and Justine Diffie. *Porto Rico: A Broken Pledge*. New York: Vanguard, 1931.

Dorsinville, Roger. "Roger Dorsinville." Interview translated by Mohamed B. Taleb-Khyar. *Callaloo*, vol. 15, no. 2, 1992, pp. 542–545.

Drake del Castillo, Emmanuel. "Notes sur les 'araliées' des îles d'Afrique orientale." *Journal de botanique* 1897, pp. xi, 1–5, 57–66, 124–125.

Dubois, Laurent. "Haitian Sovereignty: A Brief History." *Who Owns Haiti? People, Power, and Sovereignty*, edited by Scott Freeman et al. Gainesville: University Press of Florida, 2017, pp. 16–28.

Duck, Leigh Anne. "'Rebirth of a Nation': Hurston in Haiti." *Journal of American Folklore*, vol. 117, no. 464, 2004, pp. 127–146. JSTOR, www.jstor.org/stable/4137818.

Dufour, Dana L. "Cassava." *Encyclopedia of Food and Culture*, edited by Solomon H. Katz and William Woys Weaver. New York: Charles Scribner and Sons, 2002.

"Economical Dishes Needn't Be Unattractive." *Gleaner* Food Supplement, 8 Feb. 1968, pp. 11, 17, 19.

Edmonds, Juliet, and Cherita Girvan. "Child Care and Family Services in Barbados." *Social and Economic Studies*, vol. 22, no. 2, 1973, pp. 229–248.

Espinosa Orozco, Sixto. "La verdad sobre Galíndez." *Galíndez el comunista: su labor de corrupción política*, by Sixto Espinosa Orozco and José Angel Saviñon, n.p., 1956. http://www.eusko-ikaskuntza.eus/PDFFondo/irujo/12864.pdf.

"Eugenio Coloma y Garcés." Real Academia de la Historia, http://dbe.rah.es/biografias/63992/eugenio-de-coloma-y-garces.

Everington, E. "Cassava Starch and Its Uses." *West Indies Agricultural Bulletin*, vol. 12 (1912), pp. 527–530.

Ewing-Chow, Daphne. "The Environmental Impact of Caribbean Tourism Undermines Its Economic Benefit." *Forbes*, 26 Nov. 2019, https://www.forbes.com/sites/daphneewingchow/2019/11/26/the-carbon-footprint-of-caribbean-tourism-undermines-its-economic-benefit/#49c302c53cb5.

Falcomer, Ana Luisa, et al. "Health Benefits of Green Banana Consumption: A Systematic Review." *Nutrients*, vol. 11, no. 6, 29 May 2019, p. 1222. doi:10.3390/nu11061222.

Fanon, Frantz. *The Wretched of the Earth*. Translated by Constance Farrington. New York: Grove Press, 1963.

Fanto Deetz, Kelley. *Bound to Fire: How Virginia's Enslaved Cooks Helped Invent American Cuisine*. Lexington: University Press of Kentucky, 2017.

"The Fashion Show at 'Le Perchoir" Opening." *Haiti Sun* 2, no. 12, 9 Dec. 1951, https://ufdc.ufl.edu/AA00015023/00064.

Fatton, Robert. *The Roots of Haitian Despotism*. Boulder, CO: Lynne Rienner Publishers, 2007.

Fawcett, William. "Jamaica Plum or Tree Tomato." *Bulletin of the Botanical Department, Jamaica*, no. 40, Feb. 1893, p. 4.

———, ed. "Yams." *Bulletin of the Jamaica Department of Agriculture* vol. 4, 1906, pp. 3–6.

Fayant, Frank. "The Real Lawson." *Success Magazine*, Oct. 1907, pp. 663–703.

Faye, Patricia E. "Coalpot and Canawi: Traditional Creole Pottery in the Contemporary Commonwealth Caribbean." *Interpreting Ceramics*, no. 10, 2008, http://www.interpretingceramics.com/issue010/articles/05.htm.

Fernández de Oviedo, Gonzalo, Francisco Guerra, José Amador de los Ríos, and Real Academia de la Historia (España). *Historia general y natural de las indias, islas y tierra-firme del mar oceano*. Madrid: Imprenta de la Real Academia de la Historia, 1851.

Fernández Prieto, Leida. *Espacio de poder, ciencia y agricultura en Cuba: el círucla de hacendados, 1878–1917*. Madrid: Consejo Superior de Inestigacaiones Científicas, 2008.

Folch, Christine. "Fine Dining: Race in Prerevolution Cuban Cookbooks." *Latin American Research Review*, vol. 43, no. 2, 2008, pp. 205–223.

Forster, Nancy, and Howard Handelman. "Government Policy and Nutrition in Revolutionary Cuba: Rationing and Redistribution." *Universities Field Staff International Reports*, no. 19, South America, 1982.

Fouchard, Jean. "Jean Fouchard." Interview by Dr. Rowell. Translated by Mohamed Tayeb-Khyar. *Callaloo*, vol. 15, no. 2, 1992, pp. 321–326.

———. *Plaisirs de Saint-Domingue: notes sur la vie sociale, littéraire et artistique*. Port-au Prince: Imprimerie de l'État, 1955.

Fox-Genovese, Elizabeth. *Within the Plantation Household: Black and White Women of the Old South*. Chapel Hill: University of North Carolina Press, 1988.

Franey, Pierre. "Gourmet Cooking in your Kitchen." *Daily Gleaner*, 24 Jan. 1980, p. 17.

Fraunhar, Alison. *Mulata Nation: Vizualizing Race and Gender in Cuba*. Jackson: University Press of Mississippi, 2018.

"Frederic Tudor—Ice King." *Bulletin of the Business Historical Society*, vol. 6, no. 4, 1932, pp. 1–8. JSTOR, www.jstor.org/stable/3110755.

Fuentes, Marisa J. *Dispossessed Lives: Enslaved Women, Violence, and the Archive*. Philadelphia: University of Pennsylvania Press, 2016.

Fuster, Melissa. "Writing Cuisine in the Spanish Caribbean: A Comparative Analysis of Iconic Puerto Rican and Cuban cookbooks." *Food, Culture & Society*, vol. 18, no. 4, 2015, pp. 659–680. doi: 10.1080/15528014.2015.1088195.

Galloway, J. H. "Botany in the Service of Empire: The Barbados Cane-Breeding Program and the Revival of the Caribbean Sugar Industry, 1880s–1930s." *Annals of the Association of American Geographers*, vol. 86, no. 4, 1996, pp. 682–706.

Gambrill, Anthony. "Read, Cook, Nyam." *Sunday Gleaner*, 27 April 2014, p. F8.

Garth, Hannah. "They Started to Make Variants." *Food, Culture & Society*, vol. 17, no. 3, 2014), 359–376. doi: 10.2752/175174414X13948130847981.

Gartrell, Beverley. "Colonial Wives: Villains or Victims?" *The Incorporated Wife*, edited by Hilary Callan and Shirley Ardener. London: Croom Helm, 1984, pp. 165–185.

Gayer, Arthur D., Paul T. Homan, and Earle K. James. *The Sugar Economy of Puerto Rico*. New York: Columbia University Press, 1938.

Germain, Jacquelyne. "Haiti's Beloved Soup Joumou Serves Up 'Freedom in Every Bowl.'" *Smithsonian Magazine*, 30 Dec. 2022. https://www

.smithsonianmag.com/travel/haitis-beloved-soup-joumou-serves-up-freedom-in-every-bowl-180981378/

Gibson, Carrie. *Empire's Crossroads: A History of the Caribbean from Columbus to the Present Day*. New York: Grove Press, 2014.

Gilles, Alain. "Essai sur les clivages et le formations politiques haïtiennes." *Canadian Journal of Latin American and Caribbean Studies/Revue Canadienne des études latino-américaines et caraïbes*, vol. 9, no. 17, 1984, pp. 13–31.

"The Girl Who Is Liked." *Daily Gleaner*, 5 July 1893.

Girod, François. *La vie quotidienne de la société créole*. Paris: Hachette, 1972.

Glissant, Édouard. *Caribbean Discourse: Selected Essays*. Translated by J. Michael Dash. Richmond: University of Virginia Press, 1989.

———. *Le discours antillais*. Paris: Gallimard, 1997 [1981].

———. *Treatise on the Whole-World*. Translated by Celia Britton. Liverpool: Liverpool University Press, 2020.

Gómez Ferrals, Martha. "Sufragio Femenino: un triunfo sobre espinas y azahares." *La Demajagua*, 10 Jan. 2020, http://lademajagua.cu/sufragio-femenino-triunfo-espinas-azahares/.

González, Clara. "Crema de auyama." Cocinadominicana.com, [Receta Video] Crema de Auyama Rica y Fácil.

González, Elisa M. "Food for Every Mouth: Nutrition, Agriculture, and Public Health in Puerto Rico, 1920s–1960s." PhD diss., Columbia University, 2016.

Goucher, Candice. *Congotay! Congotay! A Global History of Caribbean Food*. London: Routledge, 2014.

Goutalier, Régine. "Les États généraux du féminisme à l'Exposition coloniale, 30–31 mai 1931." *Revue d'histoire moderne et contemporaine* vol. 36, no. 2, April-June 1989. pp. 266–286. doi: 10.3406/rhmc.1989.1493.

Gooding, Kerri. "Sales Up as BADMC Carmeta's Pushes Local First to Lower Imports." *Loop News*, 20 Dec. 2018, http://www.loopnewsbarbados.com/content/sales-badmc-carmetas-pushes-local-first-lower-imports.

Gordon, Lewis. *What Fanon Said: A Philosophical Introduction to His Life and Thought*. New York: Fordham University Press, 2015.

"Grace Kennedy to Contribute $100,000 towards Child's Month." *Daily Gleaner*, 12 May 1984, p. 17.

"'Grace Kitchens' Opened." *Daily Gleaner*, 14 Dec. 1969, p. 78.

Granberry, Julian, and Gary Vescelius. *Languages of the Pre-Columbian Antilles*. Tuscaloosa: University of Alabama Press, 2004.

Green, Nadège. "Soup Joumou: A Haitian New Year Tradition, a Reminder of Slave-Led Revolution." WLRN Radio, wlrn.org, 29 Dec. 2016.

Green, William A. "The Creolization of Caribbean History: The Emancipation Era and a Critique of Dialectical Analysis." *Caribbean Freedom: Economy and Society from Emancipation to the Present*, edited by Hilary Beckles and Verene Shepherd. Princeton, NJ: Markus Wiener Publishers; Melton, UK: James Curry Publishers; and Kingston: Ian Randle Publishers, 1996 [1993], pp. 28–40.

Groute, Alice, "Lettre ouverte aux Président, Vice-Président et aux Membres de l'Assemblée Constituante et aux femmes haïtiennes." *La femme haïtienne répond aux attaque formulées contre elle à l'assemblée constituante*, Port-au-Prince: Société d'Editions et de Librairie, 1946, pp. 20–24.

Guridy, Frank A. "'Enemies of the White Race': The Machadista State and the UNIA in Cuba." *Caribbean Studies*, vol. 31, no. 1, 2003, pp. 107–137. JSTOR, www.jstor.org/stable/25613392.

Ha, Marie-Paule. "Introduction." *La femme française aux colonies*. By Clotilde Chivas-Baron, edited by Mari-Paule Ha. Paris: L'Harmattan, 2009, p. vii–xxvi.

Hakluyt, Richard. *The Principle Navigations, Voyages, Traffiques, and Discoveries of the English Nation, collected by Richard Hakluyt and edited by Edmund Goldsmid, Vol. XII. America Part I*. http://www.gutenberg.org/cache/epub/13605/pg13605-images.html.

———. *The Principle Navigations, Voyages, Traffiques, and Discoveries of the English Nation, collected by Richard Hakluyt and edited by Edmund Goldsmid, Vol. XIII America Part II*. https://www.gutenberg.org/files/25645/25645-h/25645-h.html#toc71.

Handbook of Jamaica. N.p.: Jamaica Information Service, 1937.

Hardy, Georges. *Ergaste ou la vocation coloniale*. Paris: Armand Colin, 1929.

Hawkes, Alex D. "Jamaica Cook-Book Has 'Wide Array of Goodies.'" *Daily Gleaner*, 14 Jan. 1971, p. 29.

Hearn, Lafcadio. "Gombo Zhèbe." *Little Dictionary of Creole Proverbs, selected from six creole dialects. Translated into French and into English, with notes, complete index to subjects and some brief remarks upon the creole idioms of Louisiana*. New York: Will H. Coleman, 1885.

Helg, Aline. "Race and Black Mobilization in Colonial and Early Independent Cuba: A Comparative Perspective." *Ethnohistory*, vol. 44, no. 1, 1997, pp. 53–74. JSTOR, www.jstor.org/stable/482901.

Henry, Olivia H. "De Style of De Day." *Glory Days of Frederiksted*, edited by Marvin E. William. St. Croix, V.I.: Our Town Frederiksted, 2004.

———. "Ms. Francis's Conversation with 'De Bwoy.'" *Glory Days of Frederiksted*, edited by Marvin E. William. St. Croix, V.I.: Our Town Frederiksted, 2004.

Higman, B. W. "Cookbooks and Caribbean Cultural Identity: An English-Language Hors-d'Oeuvre." *New West Indian Guide/Nieuwe West-Indische Gids*, vol. 72, no. 1-2, 1998, pp. 77–95.

———. "Domestic Service in Jamaica since 1750." *Muchachas No More: Household Workers in Latin America and the Caribbean*, edited by Elsa M. Chaney and Mary Garcia Castro. Philadelphia: Temple University Press, 1989, pp. 37–66.

———. *How Food Made History*. Hoboken, NJ: Wiley-Blackwell, 2011.

———. "Jamaica Coat of Arms: Rice and Peas." *Rice and Beans: A Unique Dish in a Hundred Places*, edited by Richard Wilk and Livia Barbosa. London: Bloomsbury, 2012, pp. 61–80.

———. *Jamaican Food: History, Biology, Culture*. Mona, Jamaica: University of the West Indies Press, 2008.

Holleman, L. W. J., and A. Aten. *Processing of Cassava and Cassava Products in Rural Industries*. Rome: FAO, 1956.

Hubert, Paul, and Emile Dupré. *Le manioc*. Bibliothèque Pratique du Colon, 1910.

Hurston, Zora Neale. *Tell My Horse*. New York: J. B. Lippincott, 1938.

Ibberson, Dora. "Social Development in the British West Indies/Relevement social dans les Indes Occidentales Britanniques." *Civilisations*, vol. 7, no. 2, 1957, pp. 173–186. JSTOR, www.jstor.org/stable/41231298.

"In the Beginning." *Gleaner*, 27 May 2018, https://www.pressreader.com/jamaica/jamaica-gleaner/20180527/282553018910239.

Innes, Sherrie A. *Cooking Lessons: The Politics of Gender and Food*. Washington, DC: Rowman & Littlefield, 2001.

"Institute of Jamaica Additions to the Library." *Daily Gleaner*, 20 Sept. 1899.

J. A. "*Jamaica Run-dung*—(a Cook-Book with over 100 Recipes)." *Sunday Gleaner*, 31 Jan. 1971.

Jack, Jordynn. "Lydia J. Roberts's Nutrition Research and the Rhetoric of 'Democratic' Science." *College Composition and Communication*, vol. 61, no. 1, 2009, pp. 109–129. JSTOR, www.jstor.org/stable/40593517.

Jacomé, D. "Cuba en la memoria—la cocina cubana." https://m.facebook.com/CubaEnLaMemoria/photos/a.504268366251872/4333238130021524/?type=3&source=57&__tn__=EH-R.

"The Jamaica Cookery Book." *Daily Gleaner*, 18 Dec. 1893.

Jamaica Information Service. "History of JIS." https://jis.gov.jm/corporate/, accessed 25 Sept. 2020.

"Jamaican Wins Medal." *Daily Gleaner*, 26 Jan. 1943, p. 3.

James, Lauren. *Colonial Food in Interwar Paris: The Taste of Empire*. New York: Bloomsbury, 2016.

James, Wayne. "The History of the Cuisine of St. Croix—from the Middle Passage to Present-Day." Manlymanners, 8 Aug. 2018. https://manlymanners.wordpress.com/2018/08/08/the-history-of-the-cuisine-of-st-croix-from-the-middle-passage-to-present-day/.

Janer, Zilkia. "(In)Edible Nature: New World Food and Coloniality." *Cultural Studies*, vol. 21, no. 2–3, 2007, pp. 385–405. doi:10.1080/09502380601162597.

Julien Lung-Fou, Marie-Thérèse. *Le carnaval aux Antilles*. Fort-de-France: Désormeaux, 1979.

———. *Contes animaux, proverbes, titimes our devinettes*. Fort-de-France: Désormeaux, 1980.

———. *Contes créoles: contes, légendes, proverbes, devinettes et autres histoires fantastiques: Textes en français et en créole*. Fort-de-France: Désormeaux, 1979.

———. *Fables créoles*. Fort-de-France: Dialogue, 1958.

———. *Les piments doux: 25 fantaisies*. Fort-de-France: n.p., 1976.

———. *Trois bonnes fortunes: Trois comédies en un acte*. N.p: n.p, 1969.

"June Bell Barlas, 80, Passes Away." *St. John Tradewinds*, 4–10 Nov. 2013, pp. 16–17.

Jurafsky, Dan. *The Language of Food: A Linguist Reads the Menu*. New York: W. W. Norton, 2014.

Keay, John. *The Spice Route: A History*. Berkeley: University of California Press, 2006.

Keown, Mary E. *La conservación de frutas y vegetales en Puerto Rico*. Boletín de Extensión Núm. 7, Reimpreso Noviembre 1938.

Khan, Aisha. "Journey to the Center of the Earth: The Caribbean as Master Symbol." *Cultural Anthropology*, Vol. 16, No. 3 (Aug., 2001), pages 271–302.

Kingston, Kitty. "Personal Mention." *Daily Gleaner*, 4 Jan. 1955, p. 12.

"Kingston Publishers Ltd. Launches Five Books." *Daily Gleaner*, 2 Dec. 1983, p. 18.

Kincaid, Jamaica. "A Lot of Memory: An Interview with Jamaica Kincaid," by Moira Ferguson. *Kenyon Review*, vol. 16, no. 1, 1994, pp. 163–188.

———. *My (Garden) Book*. New York: Farrar, Straus & Giroux, 1999.

Kirkwood, Deborah. "Settler Wives in Southern Rhodesia: A Case Study." *The Incorporated Wife*, edited by Hilary Callan and Shirley Ardener. London: Croom Helm, 1984, pp. 143–164.

Kraft, Kraig H., et al. "Origin of Domesticated Chili Pepper in Mexico." *Proceedings of the National Academy of Sciences*, vol. 111, no. 17, 21 Apr. 2014, pp. 6165–6170.doi: 10.1073/pnas.1308933111

Kreyolicious. "Chinwa: The Untold Story of Chinese Haitians." Kreyolicious.com, http://kreyolicious.com/chinwa-story-haitian-chinese/6924.

Krishna, Priya. "Soup Joumou Recipe from Cindy Similien." *New York Times Cooking*, www.cooking.nytimes.com/recipes/1021716-soup-joumou.

Labat, Jean-Baptiste (Père). *Nouveau voyage aux isles de l'Amérique. Tome 1*. La Haye, 1724. https://gallica.bnf.fr/ark:/12148/bpt6k5545370j.texteImage.

Lacerte, Robert K. "Review of *In the Shadow of Powers: Dantès Bellegarde in Haitian Social Thought* by Patrick Bellegarde-Smith." *The Americas*, vol. 43, no. 4, 1987, pp. 501–502. JSTOR, www.jstor.org/stable/1007198.

Ladouceur, Rosny. "Un palais pour le goût d'Haïti." *Le nouvelliste* 9 Oct. 2014. https://lenouvelliste.com/article/136783/un-palais-pour-le-gout-dhaiti

Lawson Welsh, Sarah. *Food, Text, and Culture in the Anglophone Caribbean*. Washington, DC: Rowman & Littlefield, 2019.

———. "'If I Could Mix Drinks Like My Grandfather I Would Be Worth Marrying': Reading Race, Class and Gender in Mrs. H. Graham Yearwood's *West Indian and Other Recipes* (1911 and 1932)." *Journal of Postcolonial Writing*, vol. 54, no. 4, 2018, pp. 442–455.

Layne, Anthony. "Race, Class, and Development in Barbados." *Caribbean Quarterly*, vol. 25, no. 1/2, 1979, pp. 40–51. JSTOR, http://www.jstor.org/stable/40653372.

Le Hérissé, Auguste. *L'Ancien Royaume du Dahomey*. Paris: Larousse, 1911.

Leon, Crescencia. "Doreen Kirkcaldy Adding Spice to Jamaican food." *Sunday Gleaner Magazine*, 14 March 1982, p. 2. https://gleaner.newspaperarchive.com/kingston-gleaner/1982-03-14/ p.-30/.

"Les recettes de cuisine de Niniche Viard Gaillard." *Le nouvelliste*, 8 June 2011.

Lewis, Gordon K. "British Colonialism in the West Indies: The Political Legacy." *Caribbean Studies*, vol. 7, no. 1, 1967, pp. 3–22. JSTOR, www.jstor.org/stable/25611989.

López González, Marcos E. *Nitza Villapol: breve historia de su vida*. Miami: Nitza Villapol Inc., 2005.

Lucas, Sir Charles Prestwood. *A Historical Geography of the British Colonies, Vol. 2: The West Indies*. Oxford: Clarendon Press, 1890.

Ludmer, Josefina. "Las tretas del débil." *La sartén por el mango*, edited by Patricia Elena González and Eliana Ortega. Puerto Rico: Ediciones Huracán, 1985, pp. 47–54.

Lugones, María. "Heterosexualism and the Colonial/Modern Gender System." *Hypatia*, vol. 22, no. 1, 2009, pp. 186–209.

Lundahl, Mats. *Peasants and Poverty: A Study of Haiti*. London: Routledge, 2015 [1979].

Mackie, Christine. *Life and Food in the Caribbean*. Amsterdam: New Amsterdam Books, 1991.

Magnus, Kellie. "Cooking by the Book." Moonstoneblue.com, 2 Aug. 2016, http://moonstoneblue.com/jamaicacatalogue/cooking-by-the-book/.

Maguire, Emily. *Racial Experiments in Cuban Literature and Ethnography*. Gainesville: University Press of Florida, 2011.

Manley, Norman. "Text of Manley's Speech." *Daily Gleaner*, 11 Nov. 1968, p. 8.

Martí, José. "Our America." Translated by Esther Allen. Portal José Martí. http://www.josemarti.cu/publicacion/nuestra-america-version-ingles/.

Martindale, Carol. "Rita Springer Laid to Rest." NationNews, 2 Feb. 2013, https://www.nationnews.com/nationnews/news/9723/rita-springer-laid-rest.

Martinez-Echazabal, Lourdes. "Mestizaje and the Discourse of National/Cultural Identity in Latin America, 1845–1959." *Latin American Perspectives*, vol. 25, no. 3, 1998, pp. 21–42. JSTOR, www.jstor.org/stable/2634165.

Martyr of Algeria, Peter. *De Orbe Novo*. Translated by Frances Augusts MacNutt. 1912. Project Gutenberg. https://www.gutenberr.org/ebooks/12425.

Masiello, Francine. "Between Civilization and Barbarism: Women, Family and Literary Culture in Mid-Nineteenth Century Argentina." *Cultural and Historical Grounding for Hispanic and Luso-Brazilian Feminist Literary Criticism*, edited by Hernán Vidal. Minneapolis: Institute for the Study of Ideologies and Literature, 1989, pp. 517–566.

Mayard, Constantin, and Gérard Lehmann. *Pages retrouvées de Constantin Mayard*. Saint-Malo: Coëtquen Editions, 2005.

Mayard, Luoise. "La maison." *La voix des femmes*, vol. 1, no. 4, 1936, pp. 10–11.

McGuire, James W., and Laura B. Frankel. "Mortality Decline in Cuba, 1900–1959: Patterns, Comparisons, and Causes." *Latin American Research Review*, vol. 40, no. 2, 2005, pp. 83–116. JSTOR, www.jstor.org/stable/3662802.

McLeod Bothune, Mary. Letter to Mrs. Robert McGuire, 21 April 1950. In "Insularidad y gusto habanero (I Parte)," by Jorge Méndez Rodríguez-Arencibia. *Revista excelencias gourmet*, no. 63, https://www.excelenciasgourmet.com/es/recetas/insularidad-y-gusto-habanero-i-parte.

Merritt, Brittany J. "Developing Little England: Public Health, Popular Protest, and Colonial Policy in Barbados, 1918–1940." PhD diss., University of South Florida, 2016, https://scholarcommons.usf.edu/cgi/viewcontent.cgi?article=7313&context=etd.

"Message to Jamaican Women." *Daily Gleaner*, 16 Dec. 1963, p. 28.

Miller, Elsa. "Make Good Use of Cassava." *Daily Gleaner*, 6 Oct. 1977, p. 18.

———. "Some Things Just Aren't 'in' Anymore." *Daily Gleaner*, 3 Oct. 1977, p. 5.

Miller, Francesca. *Latin American Women and the Search for Social Justice*. UPNE, 1991. EBSCOhost, search.ebscohost.com/login.aspx?direct=true&AuthType=cookie,ip,cpid&custid=ssc&db=nlebk&AN=34505&site=ehost-live&scope=site.

Miller, Tom. *Trading with the Enemy: A Yankee Travels through Castro's Cuba*. New York: Macmillan, 1992.

Mintz, Sidney. "Black Women, Economic Roles and Cultural Traditions." *Caribbean Freedom: Economy and Society from Emancipation to the Present*, edited by Hilary Beckles and Verene Shepherd. Princeton, NJ: Markus Wiener Publishers; Melton, UK: James Curry Publishers; and Kingston Ian Randle Publishers, 1996 [1993], pp. 238–244.

———. "Labor and Sugar in Puerto Rico and Jamaica, 1800–1850." *Comparative Studies in Society and History*, vol. 1, no. 3, 1959, pp. 273–281. JSTOR, https://www.jstor.org/stable/177876.

———. *Tasting Food, Tasting Freedom: Excursions into Eating, Culture, and the Past*. Boston: Beacon Press, 1996.

Montagnac, July, Christopher Davis, and Sherry Tanumihardjo. "Nutritional Value of Cassava for Use as a Staple Food and Recent Advances for Improvement." *Comprehensive Reviews in Food Science and Food Safety*, vol. 8, no. 3, 2009, pp. 181–194.

Moore, Brian, and Michelle Johnson. *Neither Led nor Driven: Contesting British Cultural Imperialism in Jamaica, 1865–1920*. Mona, Jamaica: University of West Indies Press, 2004.

Moral, Solsiree del. *Negotiating Empire: the Cultural Politics of Schools in Puerto Rico, 1898–1952*. Madison: University of Wisconsin Press, 2013.

Mota, Virginia. "El feminismo y la política en la República Dominicana 1931–1945 y 1966–1974." *La mujer en América Latina*, vol. 2. Mexico: Sep/Setentas, 1975, pp. 60–85.

Moya Pons, Frank, ed. *Historia de la República Dominicana*. Madrid: Ediciones Doce Calles, 2010.

"Mrs. Mary E. Watkins." *West India Committee Circular*, 27 July 1939, p. 334.

Munro, Martin. "Can't Stand up for Falling down: Haiti, Its Revolutions, and Twentieth-Century Negritudes." *Research in African Literatures*, vol. 35, no. 2, 2004, pp. 1–17. JSTOR, www.jstor.org/stable/3821341.

"The Native." "Jottings." *Daily Gleaner*, 12 July 1969, p. 3.

"NCNW Reception for Mrs. Magloire Brilliant." *Defender*, 12 Feb. 1955.

Nettleford, Rex. *Identity, Race and Protest in Jamaica*. New York: William Morrow, 1972.

Newlyn, Andrea K. "Redefining 'Rudimentary' Narrative: Women's Nineteenth-Century Manuscript Cookbooks." *The Recipe Reader*, edited by Janet Floyd and Laurel Forster. Lincoln: University of Nebraska Press, 2003, pp. 31–51.

Newsom, Lee A., and Elizabeth S. Wing. *On Land and Sea: Native American Uses of Biological Resources in the West Indies*. Tuscaloosa: University of Alabama Press, 2004.

Nicholls, David. "Ideology and Political Protest in Haiti, 1930–46." *Journal of Contemporary History*, vol. 9, no. 4, 1974), pp. 3–26.

North, Elizabeth. "Book Review: A Collection of 19th c. Cookery and Herbal Recipes." *Daily Gleaner*, 22 Nov. 1990, p. 31.

"Notre Bibliothèque a reçu: Louise Mayard: *Cuisine des pays chauds*, 1ère édition Imprenta Molina Lackington y Cia, Santiago, Chile, 1940." *La voix des femmes*, vol. 6, no. 55, 1941, p. 9.

Nugent, Maria Lady. *Lady Nugent's Journal: Jamaica One Hundred Years Ago: reprinted from a journal kept by Maria, Lady Nugent, from 1801 to 1805, issued for private circulation in 1839*. Edited by Frank Cundall., London: Published for the Institute of Jamaica by A & C Black, 1907.

Nuñez Torres, Violeta Esperanza. "Historia de la alimentación humana." PhD diss., Universidad Autónoma de Santo Domingo, Facultad de Farmacia y Ciencias Químicas, 1955.

O'Callaghan, Evelynn. *Women Writing in the West Indies, 1804–1939: "A Hot Place, Belonging to Us."* London: Routledge, 2004.

Ocasio, Rafael. *Afro-Cuban Costumbrismo: From Plantations to the Slums*. Gainesville: University of Florida Press, 2012.

Office of the Historian, U.S. Department of State. "Good Neighbor Policy, 1933," https://history.state.gov/milestones/1921–1936/good-neighbor#:~:text=President%20Franklin%20Delano%20Roosevelt%20took,maintain%20stability%20in%20the%20hemisphere.

Olivier, Maritza. *Cinco siglos con la mujer dominicana*. N.p., 1975.

Ortiz, Fernando. "La comida afrocubana." *Revista bimestre cubana*, vol. 18, no. 6, 1923, pp. 401–423; vol. 19, no. 5, 1924, pp. 329–336; and vol. 20, no. 1-2, 1925, pp. 94–112.

———. "La comida afrocubana." *¿Gusta usted?* by Las Madrinas de las Salas (Costales) y (San Martín) del Hospital Universitario (General Calixto García), 1999 [1956].

———. *Cuban Counterpoint: Tobacco and Sugar*. Translated by Harriet de Onís. Durham, NC: Duke University Press, 1995.

———. "The Human Factors of Cubanidad." Translated by Joao Felipe Goncalves and Gregory Duff Morton. *HAU: Journal of Ethnographic Theory*, vol. 4, no. 3, 2014, pp. 445–480.

Ortíz Cuadra, Cruz Miguel. *Eating Puerto Rico: A History of Food, Culture, and Identity*. Translated by Russ Davidson., Chapel Hill: University of North Carolina Press, 2013.

Ostrander, Gilman M. "The Making of the Triangular Trade Myth." *William and Mary Quarterly*, vol. 3, no. 4, 1973, pp. 635–644.

Osuna, John Joseph. "Education in Puerto Rico." *Teachers College, Columbia University Contributions to Education*, no. 133, 1923.

"Outre." *Larousse*. https://www.larousse.fr/dictionnaires/francais/outre/56950?q=outre#56620.

Oviedo, Gonzalo Fernández de. *Historia general y natural de las Indias, I*. Madrid: La Real Academia de la Historia, 1851 [1535]. https://babel.hathitrust.org/cgi/pt?id=gri.ark:/13960/t4bp3sz9f;view=1up;seq=85.

———. *Natural History of the West Indies*. Translated and edited by Sterling A. Stoudemire. Chapel Hill: University of North Carolina Press, 1959.

———. *Sumario de historia natural de las Indias*. Toledo, 1526. https://www.wdl.org/en/item/7331/view/1/1/.

Owens, June. "Koves Returns with Tropical Dishes for Sulgrave's New Sidewalk Café." *New York Times*, reprinted as "Food: Chef in Haiti," *Haiti Sun*, 26 Aug. 1956, p. 8.

Palmer, Colin A. "Identity, Race, and Black Power in Independent Jamaica." *The Modern Caribbean*, edited by Franklin W. Knight and Colin A. Palmer. University of North Carolina Press, 1989, pp. 111–128.

Palmer, Kimberly J. "Performing Resistance: Memory and Mobilisation of Afro-Indigenous Identity for Social Change in Saint Vincent." *Caribbean Quarterly*, vol. 16, no. 2, 2014, pp. 76–87.

Palmié, Stephan, and Francisco Scarano, eds. *The Caribbean: A History of the Region and Its Peoples*. Chicago: University of Chicago Press, 2011.

Pantojas-Garcia, Emilio. *Development Strategies as Ideology: Puerto Rico's Export-Led Industrialization Experience*. Boulder, CO: Lynne Rienner Publishers, 1990.

Paris, H. S., M. C. Daunay, M. Pitrat, and J. Janick. "First Known Image of Cucurbita in Europe, 1503–1508." *Annals of Botany*, vol. 98, no. 1, 2006, pp. 41–47. doi: 10.1093/aob/mcl082.

Parkhurst Ferguson, Priscilla. "Writing Out of the Kitchen: Carême and the Invention of French Cuisine." *Gastronomica*, vol. 3, no. 3, 2003, pp. 40–51. JSTOR, www.jstor.org/stable/10.1525/gfc.2003.3.3.40.

Parry, John H. "Plantation and Provision Ground: An Historical Sketch of the Introduction of Food Crops into Jamaica." *Revista de historia de América*, no. 39, 1955, pp. 1–20. JSTOR, www.jstor.org/stable/20136915.

———. "Salt Fish and Ackee." *Caribbean Quarterly*, vol. 2, no. 4, 1951, pp. 29–35. JSTOR, www.jstor.org/stable/40652550.

Pereyra, Emilia. "La gastronomía dominicana, alquimia de tres culturas." Diario Libre, 28 Sept. 2017, https://www.diariolibre.com/gastroclub/la-gastronomia-dominicana-alquimia-de-tres-culturas-GX8257558.

Pérez, Louis A., Jr. *On Becoming Cuban: Identity, Nationality, and Culture*. Chapel Hill: University of North Carolina Press, 1999.

Pérez Roque, Dúnyer Jesús. "Sabores franceses en la cocina cubana." N.p., 2014, https://www.academia.edu/40219120/Sabores_franceses_en_la_cocina_cubana.

Peraza Sarausa, Fermin. *Bibliografía cubana 1957*. La Habana: Editorial Lex, 1958.

Perkins, Blake. "Outlaw Elements and Culinary Adaptation: Some Peculiarities of Jamaican History and Its Food." *British Food in America*, no. 62, 2019, https://www.britishfoodinamerica.com/Another-Caribbean-Number-featuring-Jamaica/the-lyrical/Outlaw-elements-and-culinary-adaptation/#.XerOwehKi1t.

Philips, Grace Spencer. *Seven Sonnets on Puerto Rico*. New York: Avon House Publishers, 1938.

Pilcher, Jeffrey. "Eating à la Criolla: Global and Local Foods in Argentina, Cuba, and Mexico." *IdeAs* 3, 2012, pp. 2–16.

Pilgrim, E. C. *The Role and Structure of Agriculture in Barbados and the Agricultural Development Programme*. Barbados: Ministry of Agriculture, 1969.

Ponte, Antonio José. "No temenos recetas para los alimentos del futuro." *Emisférica*, vol. 12, no. 1-2, 2015. https://hemisphericinstitute.org/en/emisferica-121-caribbean-rasanblaj/12-1-essays/e-121-essay-ponte-no-tenemos-recetas.html.

Poyo, Gerald E. "The Cuban Experience in the United States, 1865–1940: Migration, Community, and Identity." *Cuban Studies*, vol. 21, 1991, pp. 19–36.

Pragg, Sam. "Jamaica-Education: The Long Road to a Literate Population." Inter Press Service News Agency, ipsnews.net, 28 Jan. 1997, http://www.ipsnews.net/1997/01/jamaica-education-the-long-road-to-a-literate-population/.

Price, Richard, and Sally Price. "Turning Coo-Coo." *NWIG: New West Indian Guide/Nieuwe West-Indishce Gids*, vol. 70, no. 1-2, 1996, pp. 113–131. JSTOR, https://www.jstor.org/stable/41849745.

Prince, Mary. *The History of Mary Prince, a West Indian Slave*. London: Westley & Davis, 1833.

Querillac, Anne. "Les arts de la femme: Abat-jour et boules de verre." *L'art vivant*, no. 31, 1926.

———. N.t. *La femme au travail*, 1937.

———. N.t. *La legion*, no. 3, 1941.

Querillac, Anne, and Pierre de Trévières. *Manuel nouveau des usages mondains en France et à l'étranger: la tradition, la vie moderne*. Paris: Delamain et Boutelleau, 1927.

Rahe, Elizabeth. "Native Touch Arona Petersen Has Been Called a Symbol of the Best of the Old-Time Virgin Islands, with Their Patchwork History and Common-Sense Values." *South Florida Sun Sentinel*, 5 July 1990, https://www.sun-sentinel.com/news/fl-xpm-1990-07-05-9002020505-story.html.

Rahim, Gibron. "A Guyanese Christmas Tradition." *Guyana Chronicle*, 24 Dec. 2017, https://guyanachronicle.com/2017/12/24/our-pepperpot/.

Rea, Patrick Michael and City University of New York Liberal Studies *The Historic Inability of the Haitian Education System to Create Human Development and Its Consequences*. Dissertation City University of New York. City University of New York, 2015.

Reddock, Rhoda. "The Early Women's Movement in Trinidad and Tobago, 1900–1937." *Subversive Women: Historical Experiences of Gender and Resistance*, edited by Saskia Wieringa. London: Zed Books, 1995, pp. 101–120.

———. "Feminism and Feminist Thought: An Historical overview." *Gender in Caribbean Development*, 2nd ed., edited by Patricia Mohammed and Catherine Shepherd, Jamaica: Canoe Press University of the West Indies, 1999, pp. 53–73.

Reese, Ashanté M. "Tarry with Me: Reclaiming Sweetness in an Anti-Black World." *Oxford American*, no. 112, 2021, https://oxfordamerican.org/magazine/issue-112-spring-2021/tarry-with-me.

Regan, Gaz. "Cocktail: What Is It and Where Did the Word Come From?," gazregan.com, 22 March 2012, http://www.gazregan.com/cocktail-what-is-it-and-where-did-the-word-come-from/.

Rifkin, Mark. "Romancing Kinship: A Queer Reading of Indian Education and Zitkala-Ša's *American Indian Stories*." *The Routledge Queer Studies Reader*, edited by Donald E. Hall and Annamarie Jagose. London: Routledge, 2013, pp. 333–354.

"Rita Springer." Totally Barbados. https://www.totallybarbados.com/articles/about-barbados/people/meet-a-bajan/rita-springer/#.XfpbtGRKi1s. Originally published in the Barbados Tourist Center's *Ins and Outs of Barbados*, 2005.

Robinson, Nancy. "Women's Political Participation in the Dominican Republic: The Case of the Mirabal Sisters." *Caribbean Quarterly*, vol. 52, no. 2/3, 2006, pp. 172–183. JSTOR, www.jstor.org/stable/40654568.

Rodney, Walter. *The Groundings with My Brothers*. London: The Bogle L'Ouverture Publications, 1969.

Rodriguez, Roberto Cintli. *Our Sacred Maíz Is Our Mother: Indigeneity and Belonging in the Americas*. Tucson: University of Arizona Press, 2014.

Romero-Cesareo, Ivette. "Whose Legacy?: Voicing Women's Rights from the 1870s to the 1930s." *Callaloo*, vol. 17, no. 3, 1994, pp. 770–789. JSTOR, www.jstor.org/stable/2931854.

Rosenberg, Leah. "The New Woman and 'the Dusky Strand': The Place of Feminism and Women's Literature in Early Jamaican Nationalism." *Feminist Review*, no. 95, 2010, pp. 45–63. JSTOR, www.jstor.org/stable/40928109.

Rubin, Gayle. "The Traffic in Women: Notes on the Political Economy of Sex." *Toward an Anthropology of Women*, by Gayle Rubin, New York: Monthly Review Press, 1975, pp. 157–210.

Ryan, Selwyn. "The Struggle for Black Power in the Caribbean." *The Black Power Revolution 1970: A Retrospective*, edited by Selwyn Ryan and Taimoon Stewart. St. Augustine, Trinidad: I.S.E.R., The University of the West Indies, 1995, pp. 25–57.

Salon International des Mines de Sénégal (SIM). "Comment Alouba fut transformée en homme." *AWA: la revue de la femme noire*, no. 4, 1964, p. 28.

Sánchez, Kathleen. *Chinese Cubans: A Transnational History*. New Brunswick, NJ: Rutgers University Press, 2013.

Sanders, Grace Louise. "La voix des femmes: Haitian Women's Rights, National Politics and Black Activism in Port-au-Prince and Montreal, 1934–1986." PhD diss. University of Michigan, 2013.

Sanjek, Roger, ed. *Caribbean Asians: Chinese, Indian, and Japanese Experiences in Trinidad and the Dominican Republic*. New York: Asian/American Center at Queens College, CUNY, 1990.

Sarmiento Ramírez, Ismael. "Alimentación y relaciones sociales en la cuba colonial." *Anales del Museo de America*, no. 11, 2003 pp. 197–226.

———. "Cuba: una sociedad formada por retazos: composición y crecimiento de la población en los primeros 68 años del siglo XIX." *Caravelle*, no. 81, 2003, pp. 111–146.

Scarano, Francisco A. "The Jíbaro Masquerade and the Subaltern Politics of Creole Identity Formation in Puerto Rico, 1745–1823." *American Historical Review* 101, no. 5, 1996, pp. 1398–1431.

———. *Sugar and Slavery in Puerto Rico: The Plantation Economy of Ponce, 1800–1850*. Madison: University of Wisconsin Press, 1984.

Schiebinger, Londa. "Prospecting for Drugs: European Naturalists in the West Indies." *Colonial Botany: Science, Commerce, and Politics in the Early Modern World*, by Londa Schiebinger and Claudia Swan. Philadelphia: University of Pennsylvania Press, 2005, pp. 119–133.

Schiebinger, Londa, and Claudia Swan. *Colonial Botany: Science, Commerce, and Politics in the Early Modern World*. Philadelphia: University of Pennsylvania Press, 2005.

"The School Lunch." *Daily News*, 4 Jan. 1954, n.p.

Schuller, Mark. "Haiti's 200-Year Ménage-à-trois. Globalization, the State, and Civil Society." *Caribbean Studies*, vol. 35, no. 1, 2007, pp. 141–179. JSTOR, https://www.jstor.org/stable/25613094.

Scott, Nina M. "Juana Manuela Gorriti's Cocina ecléctica" Recipes as Feminine Discourse." *Hispania*, vol. 75, no. 2, 1992, pp. 310–314. JSTOR, www.jstor.org/stable/344026. doi:10.2307/344026.

Scott, Rebecca. "Former Slaves: Responses to Emancipation in Cuba." *Caribbean Freedom: Economy and Society from Emancipation to the Present*, edited by Hilary Beckles and Verene Shepherd. Princeton, NJ: Markus Wiener

Publishers; Melton, UK: James Curry Publishers; and Kingston, and Ian Randle Publishers, 1996 [1993], pp. 21–27.

Seacole, Mary. *Wonderful Adventures of Mrs. Seacole in Many Lands*. London: James Blackwood, 1857. https://www.gutenberg.org/files/23031/23031-h/23031-h.htm.

Sealey, Sandra. "Black History Month: Roberts Rose from Humble Beginnings." *Nation News*, 21 Feb. 2017, https://www.nationnews.com/2017/02/21/black-history-month-roberts-rose-from-humble-beginnings/

Shapiro, Laura. *Perfection Salad: Women and Cooking at the Turn of the Century*. New York: Modern Library, 2001 [1986].

Shepherd, Verene. "Emancipation through Servitude: Aspects of the Condition of Indian Women in Jamaica, 1845–1945." *Caribbean Freedom: Economy and Society from Emancipation to the Present*, edited by Hilary Beckles and Verene Shepherd,. Princeton, NJ: Markus Wiener Publishers; Melton, UK: James Curry Publishers; and Kingston and Ian Randle Publishers, 1996 [1993], pp. 245–250.

———. *Women in Caribbean History*. Kingston: Ian Randle Publishers, 2012.

Singh, Ranjit, Clement Sankat, and Saheeda Mujaffar. "The Nutmeg and Spice Industry in Grenada: Innovations and Competitiveness, A Case Study." Presented at the Workshop on the Role of Science, Technology, and Innovation in Increasing Competitiveness in the Productive Sector. University of the West Indies Saint Augustine, Trinidad, Nov. 2003.

Sio, Arnold A. "Race, Colour, and Miscegenation: the Free Coloured of Jamaica and Barbados." *Caribbean Studies*, vol. 16, no. 1, 1976, pp. 5–21.

Sloane, Hans. *A Voyage to the Islands of Madera, Barbados, Nieves, S. Christophers, and Jamaica, with the Natural History of the Herbs and Trees, Four-Footed Beasts, Fishes, Birds, Insects, Reptiles, &c. of the last of those Islands*. London: Printed by B. M. for the author, 1707. https://ia800501.us.archive.org/0/items/mobot31753000820123/mobot31753000820123.pdf.

Smith, Matthew J. "Vive 1804!: The Haitian Revolution and the Revolutionary Generation of 1946." *Caribbean Quarterly*, vol. 50, no. 4, 2004, pp. 25–41.

———. *Red and Black in Haiti: Radicalism, Conflict, and Political Change, 1943–1957*. Chapel Hill: University of North Carolina Press, 2009.

Sokolov, Raymond. *Why We Eat What We Eat: How the Encounter between the New World and the Old Changed the Way Everyone on the Planet Eats*. New York: Simon & Schuster, 1991.

Solá, José O. "Colonialism, Planters, Sugarcane, and the Agrarian Economy of Caguas, Puerto Rico, between the 1890s and 1930." *Agricultural History*, vol. 85, no. 3, 2011, pp. 349–372. JSTOR, www.jstor.org/stable/10.3098/ah.2011.85.3.349.

Sourieau, Marie-Agnès. "Suzanne Césaire et *Tropiques*: de la poésie cannibale à une poétique créole." *French Review*, vol. 68, no. 1, 1994, pp. 69–78. JSTOR, www.jstor.org/stable/396640.

Stavely, Keith, and Kathleen Fitzgerald. *United Tastes: The Making of the First American Cookbook*. Amherst: University of Massachusetts Press, 2017.

Stoler, Ann Laura. *Carnal Knowledge and Imperial Power: Race and the Intimate in Colonial Rule*. Berkeley: University of California Press, 2010 [2002].

Stoner, Kathryn Lynn. *From the House to the Streets: The Cuban Woman's Movement for Legal Reform, 1898–1940*. Durham, NC: Duke University Press, 1991.

Strobel, Margaret. "Gender and Race in the Nineteenth- and Twentieth-Century British Empire." *Becoming Visible Women in European History*, 2nd ed., edited by Renate Bridenthal, Claudia Koonz, and Susan Stuard. Boston: Houghton Mifflin, 1987, pp. 375–398.

Sundaram, Mark. "Cocktail." *The Endless Knot*. http://www.alliterative.net/cocktail-transcript1.

Suñer, Margarita. "Demythologizing the Impersonal 'Se' in Spanish." *Hispania*, vol. 59, no. 2, 1976, pp. 268–275. JSTOR, www.jstor.org/stable/339502.

Sweeney, Megan, and Susan McCouch. "The Complex History of the Domestication of Rice." *Annals of Botany* vol. 100, no. 5, 2007, pp. 951–957. doi:10.1093/aob/mcm128.

Sylvain-Bouchereau, Madeleine. "Les droits des femmes et la nouvelle constitution." *La femme haïtienne répond aux attaque formulées contre elle à l'assemblée constituante*. Port-au-Prince: Société d'Editions et de Librairie, 1946, pp. 3–14.

Tancer, Shoshana B. "La Quisqueyana: The Dominican Woman, 1940–1970." *Female and Male in Latin America*, edited by Ann Pescatello. Pittsburgh: University of Pittsburgh Press, 1973, pp. 209–230.

Taylor, Rupert. "The Blood-Soaked History of Nutmeg." 12 Oct. 2016, https://owlcation.com/humanities/The-Blood-Soaked-History-of-Nutmeg.

Theophano, Janet. *Eat My Words: Reading Women's Lives through the Cookbooks They Wrote*. London: Palgrave, 2002.

Thomas, Marcia. "Racist or Women's Advocate? The Case of Lady Musgrave, 1833–1920." *Jamaica Observer*, 23 June 2020, https://301-joweb.newscyclecloud.com/opinion/racist-or-women-s-advocate-the-case-of-lady-musgrave-1833-1920_196919.

Tillman, Ellen D. *Dollar Diplomacy by Force: Nation-Building and Resistance in the Dominican Republic*. Chapel Hill: University of North Carolina Press, 2016.

Tinsley, Omise'eke Natasha. *Thiefing Sugar: Eroticism between Women in Caribbean Literature*. Durham, NC: Duke University Press, 2010.

Tipton-Martin, Toni. *The Jemima Code: Two Centuries of African American Cookbooks*. Austin: University of Texas Press, 2015.

Torre, José María de la, and Vidal Morales y Morales. *Lo que fuimos y lo que somos, o, La Habana antigua y moderna: 1857*. Habana: Librería "Cervantes," 1913.

Torres Saillant, Silvio. "The Tribulations of Blackness: Stages in Dominican Racial Identity." *Callaloo*, vol. 23, no. 3, 2000, pp. 1086–1111. JSTOR, www.jstor.org/stable/3299726.

Turbiano y Paula, José Florencio. *El agricultor, horticultor, jardinero, e higienista agrícola cubano*. Habana: Impr. De R. Espina, 1878–1879.

———. *Arboricultura y floricultura cubana con una descripción de los árboles, arbustos, bejucos, plantas aromáticas y de jardinería, indígenas y exóticas, sus nombres comunes y botánicos*. N.p.: Imp. "La Universal" de Ruiz y Hermano, 1893.

———. *Manual de magnetismo animal y sonambulismo magnético, sus procederes, fenómenos y aplicación puestos as alcance de todos*. Habana: Imprenta El Fénix, 1881.

———. *El propagador de conocimientos útiles*. Habana, n.p., 1877.

———. *Tratado sobre las gallinas, palomas, canarios y ruiseñores*. [Habana]: Impr. Viuda de Barcina, 1878.

Turits, Richard Lee. *Foundations of Despotism: Peasants, the Trujillo Regime and Modernity in Dominican History*. Stanford, CA: Stanford University Press, 2003.

Turosienski, Severin. *Education in Cuba*. Washington, DC: U.S. Office of Education, Bulletin 1943, no. 1.

University of Guelph. "Helen C. Abell Collection." Archival and Special Collections of the Library of the University of Guelph. https://www.lib.uoguelph.ca/find/find-type-resource/archival-special-collections/agriculture-and-rural-heritage/helen-c-abell.

U.S. Congress. "An Act to Provide a Civil Government for the Virgin Islands of the United States." United States Statutes at Large, 74th Congress, Session II, ch. 699, pp. 1807–1818, 22 June 1936, https://www.loc.gov/law/help/statutes-at-large/74th-congress/session-2/c74s2ch699.pdf.

U.S. Department of the Interior, Office of Education. *Public Education in the Virgin Islands*, 1934.

Valens, Keja. "Home Cooking: Diaspora and Transnational Caribbean Cookbooks." *Becoming Home: Diaspora and the Anglophone Transnational*, edited by Jude V. Nixon and Mariaconcetta Costantini. Wilmington, DE: Vernon Press, 2021, pp. 109–134.

———. "A Little Puerto Rican Food Culture . . ." *Sargasso*, 2016–2017, I and II, pp. 3–22.

———. "Recipes for National Culture in Guadeloupe and Martinique." *Transcultural Roots Uprising: The Rhizomatic Languages, Literatures and Cultures of the Caribbean*, edited by N. Faraclas, R. Severing, C. Weijer, E. Echteld, and M. Hinds-Layne. Willemstad: University of Curaçao and Fundashon pa Planifikashon di Idioma, 2013, pp. 297–304.

Valme Thevenin, Rolande, and Paule St. Eloi Alexis. *L'odyssée de la cuisine haïtienne*. Coconut Creek, FL: Educa Vision, 2006.

Vega, Bernardo. *Dominican Cultures: The Making of Caribbean Society*. Princeton, NJ: Markus Wiener, 2008.

Vega Pérez de Arlucea, Ana. "El primer libro de cocina cubana lo escribió un español." *El diario vasco*, 20 Feb. 2021, https://www.diariovasco.com/gastronomia/primer-libro-cocina-20210220101357-ntrc.html.

Vela, Enrique. "La calabaza, el tomate, y el frijol." *Arqueología mexicana*, Edición Especial 36, Oct. 2010.
Veloz, Livia. *Historia de feminismo en la República Dominicana*. N.p., 1977.
Verna, Chantalle. "The Ligue Féminine d'Action Sociale: An Interview with Paulette Poujol Orioli." *Journal of Haitian Studies*, vol. 17, no. 1, 2011, pp. 246–257.
Villapol, Nitza. "Introducción." *Bohemia*, 3 March 1967, pp. 40–41.
———. "Hábitos alimentarios africanos en América Latina." *África en América Latina*, edited by Manuel Moreno Fraginals. Mexico: siglo ventiuno editores, 1977, pp. 325–336.
Visit Haiti. "Soup Joumou." www.visithaiti.com/food-drink/soup-joumou.
Wall, Wendy. "Literacy and the Domestic Arts." *Huntington Library Quarterly*, vol. 73, no. 3, 2010, pp. 383–412. JSTOR, www.jstor.org/stable/10.1525/hlq.2010.73.3.383.
Walsh, Ellen. "'Advancing the Kingdom': Missionaries and Americanization in Puerto Rico, 1898–1930s." PhD diss. University of Pittsburgh, 2008. http://d-scholarship.pitt.edu/7641/1/EWalsh_ETD_2008.pdf.
Welbaum, Gregory E. *Vegetable Production and Practices*. Wallingford, Oxfordshire, UK; CABI, 2015 [2014].
Wucker, Michele. *Why the Cocks Fight: Dominicans, Haitians, and the Struggle for Hispaniola*. New York: Farrar, Straus& Giroux, 2014.
War Office. *A Guide to Families Going to the Caribbean*. The War Office (PP.9), June 1959. http://www.archhistory.co.uk/taca/postings.html.
Weeks, Deborah G. *Movement of the People: The Relationship between Black Consciousness Movements, Race, and Class in the Caribbean*. Master's thesis, University of South Florida, 2008.
"What's Cooking on the Local Scene?" *Gleaner*, 18 Dec. 2003, p. E3.
White, April. "The Story of the Invention of the Potato Chip Is a Myth." *JSTOR Daily*, 4 May 2017, https://daily.jstor.org/story-invention-potato-chip-myth/.
Wiedorn, Michael. *Think Like an Archipelago: Paradox in the Work of Édouard Glissant*. Albany, NY: SUNY Press, 2017.
Wilk, Richard. "Nationalizing the Ordinary Dish: Rice and Beans in Belize." *Rice and Beans: A Unique Dish in a Hundred Places*, edited by Richard Wilk and Livia Barbosa. London: Bloomsbury, 2012, pp. 203–218.
Wilk, Richard, and Livia Barbosa, eds. *Rice and Beans: A Unique Dish in a Hundred Places*. London: Bloomsbury, 2012.
Williams, Marion. "Aspects of Public Policy in Barbados 1964–1976." *Social and Economic Studies*, vol. 26, no. 4, 1977, pp. 432–445. JSTOR, http://www.jston.org/stable/27861679.
Wilson, Kathleen. *The Island Race: Englishness, Empire and Gender in the Eighteenth Century*. London: Routledge, 2003.
Winslow, Mrs. *Mrs. Winslow's Domestic Receipt Book for 1876*. New York: Jeremiah Curtis & Sons, 1875. https://babel.hathitrust.org/cgi/pt?id=uc1.31822031019060;view=1up;seq=1.

Wondrich, David. "Ancient Mystery Revealed! The Real History (Maybe) of How the Cocktail Got Its Name." *Saveur*, Jan. 2016, https://www.saveur.com/how-the-cocktail-got-its-name.

Wynter, Sylvia. "Beyond the Word of Man: Glissant and the New Discourse of the Antilles." *World Literature Today*, vol. 63, no. 2, 1989, pp. 637–648.

Zlotnick, Susan. "Domesticating Imperialism: Curry and Cookbooks in Victorian England." *The Recipe Reader*, edited by Janet Floyd and Laurel Forster. Lincoln: University of Nebraska Press, 2003, pp. 72–87.

Index

Page numbers for full recipes in text boxes appear in *italics*.

Abell, Helen C., 310, 412n17, 413nn21–22
abundance and edibleness, trope of, 9, 14, 16, 18
Acassan [Acassan] (recipe), 280, *281*
Acción Feminista Dominicana, 242, 243
accra, 8, 19, 292
African and Afro-Caribbean people, 4, 12; Afro-Cubans, 198; Afro-Dominican cuisine, 247; creolization and, 5; women, 29, 34
African Cake (recipe), 334, *335*
"African Food Habits in Latin America" (Villapol, 1977), 229–230
African languages, 19
Afrocentrism, 8, 119, 315, 327, 331–332, 347
Afrocubanidad (Afro-Cuban movement), 210–211, 405n30
Afro-Indigenous people, 12, 26, 381n5; Afro-Indigenous roots in Cuba, 208–217; cuisine, 17, 35, 63, 113, 261–262; heritage embraced in Cuban cookbooks, 52; incorporated into technological progress and class mobility, 194; knowledge of, 48; origins relegated to distant past, 134; recipes subsumed under English culinary history, 98–99; women, 5, 6, 29, 111, 371–372
Agricultor, horticultor, jardinero, e higienista agrícola cubano, El (Turbiano y Paula, 1878–1879), 386n26
Aida's Kitchen a lo Boricua (Lugo McAllister, 2013), 161
ají, 43, 60, 62–64, 109, 191, 200, 202, 215, 227, 236–237, 247, 275, 381n8, 405n31
ajiaco, 3, 19, 46, 57, 68, 188, 191, 199–200, 206, 208, 211, 215, 226, 385n10, 405n28; "ajiaco broth," 63; ajiaco criollo, 203; as Cuban national dish, 206; multiple types of creolization embodied in, 60; with plantain, 57; recipes from *Cocina al minuto*, 227–232; recipes from *Nuevo manual de la cocinera catalana y cubana*, 64; recipes from *Nuevo manual del cocinero criollo*, 188; recipes from *Nuevo manual del cocinero cubano y español*, 58, 64; Taíno-based name of, 63

459

"Ajiaco a la criolla," 206
Ajiaco criollo [Creole Ajiaco] (recipe), 226, 227–229
Ajiaco de monte [Mountain Ajiaco] (recipe), 64
Ajiaco de Puerto Principe [Puerto Principe ajiaco] (recipe), *189*
Ajiaco de tierra-dentro [Inland Ajiaco] (recipe), 64
ajíes dulces, 385n10
alcapurrias, 152, 398n38
Aldabó, D. Enrique, 184
"Alegría de Maní," 67
Alexander, Carlton, 416n46, 418n56, 419n57
Alfonso y Rodriguez, Dolores, 194, 198, 199, 205–206
Alkins, Alma Eileen, 420n71
Almanac manuel de la cuisinière (Rabette, 1890?), 394–395n8
Alva Ixtlilxochitl, Fernando de, 254
Alvarez, Julia, 243
Ancien Royaume du Dahomey, L' (Le Hérisse, 1911), 396nn18–19
Anderson, Benedict, 3
Anduze, Mildred V., 17, 168
Angola peas, 137
Anguilla, 301
Anna's Curried Pumpkin Soup (recipe), *373*
Ann nou fè konsèvasyon manje (2001), 300
Antigua, 20
Antilles, 20, 21
Antilles et la Guyane, Les: à travers leur cuisine (Nègre, 1967), 134, 138
Appadurai, Arjun, 3, 28, 243
Arawakan language, 259, 363, 407n17
Arboricultura y floricultura cubana (Turbiano y Paula, 1893), 386n26
Armand, Stéphanie Renauld, 297, 298, 409nn40–41
Aróstegui y Castillo, Gonzalo, 185–86, 402n3, 403n4

Arroz con pescado a la oriental [Oriental Rice with Rice] (recipe), 224–225, 226
arroz con pollo, 146, 188, 200, 405n28; emergence as Cuban national dish, 206; Jamaican adaptation of, 318; modernization and, 206, 208
Arroz con pollo [Rice with Chicken] (recipe), 207–208
Art de la cuisine française au dix-neuvième siècle, L' (Carême, 1828), 125
Arte de bien guisar o La Cocina práctica en Cuba, El (Crespo y Setien, 1926), 194, 195–196, 200
Arte de cocinar eléctricamente en las cocinas eléctricas, El (Compañía Cubana de Electricidad, 1929), 194
Arte de la buena mesa, El (Sevigne, 1939), 195, 196, 404n13, 405n29
Art of Cookery, The (Glasse), 390n14
Aruba, 20
Ashford, Bailey K., 144, 153, 397n32
Asian-Cuban cuisine, 229
asopado, 261
assimilation, 169
"atole," 44, 385n14
Austin, Elisabeth, 90
authenticity, 48, 49, 183, 243; containment of, 117; figure of Chloé Mondésir and, 126; of Haitian food, 268–269, 297, 298
authorship, 13, 16, 26, 49, 154; by elite women, 26, 241; extended from elite to middle class, 367; male, 36; Puerto Rican women and, 152–153, 155
Auxiliar gastronómico pro turismo (Sociedad de Dependientes de Restaurantes, Hoteles y Fondas, 1937), 194, 205
Avena para "estirar" la carne [Oats to "Stretch" Meat] (recipe), *234*

Avocado Barbadienne (recipe), 344, *345*, 346
avocados, 170, 203, 250, 420n68; in recipes, *133, 286, 345*
Ayala, Cesar J., 398n37

bacalao, 188, 191, 202, 215, 231, 232; in recipes, *191, 262*. *See also* salt fish
Bacalao a la cubana [Cuban Salt Cod] (recipe), *191*
"Bacalao a la vizcaina (Typical Spanish recipe)," 215
BADMC Carmeta line, 349, 353
Bahamas/Bahamian recipes, 337, 338, 410n2
Baillie, Olga Mabel Kathleen Leyden, 411n7
Bajan Cookbook (Child Care Committee, 1964), 340, 341–342, 371, 419n61
Bajan Cooking in a Nutshell (Miller, 2010), 352, 353, *354–355*
Baked Ackees with Cheese (recipe), *304*
Bacallao, Margot, 218
banana: in Linnaean taxonomy, 408n28, 415n34; in Magloire-Prophète's recipes, 292, 293–94, *293*; in Mayard's *Cuisine des pays chauds*, 271, *272–273*, 286; origins and history of, 324; in slave diets, 324; in *Virgin Islands Fruits and Vegetables*, 170–71, 173; in Willsey's *Tropical Foods Bulletin*, 152
Banana Cake with Cream Cheese Icing (recipe), *172*
Banana Custard (recipe), *306*
Banana Recipes (Jamaica Information Service, 1966), 322, 323–326, *326*, 415n34
«Bananes vertes mures» au gratin ["Ripe Green Banana" Gratin] (recipe), *272–273*
Bananes vertes pesées [Weighted Green Bananas] (recipe), *286*

Baralt, Blanca (Blanche) Zacharie de, 194, 198, 200, 202, 213
Barbados, 17, 20, 27, 95, 106, 339–356; Agricultural Development Corporation (ADC), 343, 344, 346; Black and progressive political leadership of, 342; food independence movement, 336, 339–56; independence from Britain (1966), 301; national culinary culture, 119; White economic power brokers in, 342, 346, 350
Barbados Cookbook, The (Hamilton, 1983), 419n62
Barbados cookbooks, 56, 339–356
Barbados Red Cross Society, 349
Barbosa, Livia, 358
Barradas, Efraín, 15, 35, 37
Barrow, Errol, 347, 350, 351, 352, 353
Barton Cookbook, The (1913), 142, 397n28
Batata (boniato, sweet potato), 46, 251, 381n8, 387n38
Batista, Fulgencio, 182, 217, 218
Bean, Dalea, 305
Beckles, Hilary, 3, 347
Beekhuis, Jeanne V., 420n74
Beetham, Margaret, 72
Bellegarde-Smith, Patrick, 268, 279, 287, 408n27
Benghiat, Norma, 417n51
Benítez-Rojo, Antonio, 383n19
Bennet, Louise, 418n53
Berenjena, La: modos de prepaparla para la mesa (Willsey and Pastrana, 1938), 154–55, 398n35, 399n41
Bergad, Laird W., 398n37
Bermuda, 301
Bernabé, Jean, 23
Berti, Ilaria, 77, 82
Best Made Cookbook (Wolff, 1980), 297, 298
Betances, Ramón Emeterio, 33
bija (achiote), 250

Black, Clinton V., 412n19
Black Creoles, 108, 137
Black Criollos, 35, 59
Black Nationalism, 279, 290, 302, 310, 327, 414n28
Blackness, 7, 30, 241; "Creole" designation and, 23–24, 108; excluded from Trujillist "criollo," 241, 244, 249, 254–255; Haitian, 266, 278, 290; Jamaican, 331; revaluation of, 8
Black women, 3, 5, 72, 116; "Jemima Code" and, 73; literacy of poor Black women in Cuba, 403n9; stereotypes about, 141, 142; womanist liberation, 119
blogs, food instruction, 375
Bobory [Bobory] (recipe), 282, 283
bobotee, 112
bocadito, 204, 223
Boiled Pumpkin (recipe), 93, 93
Bonaire, 20
boniato (batata, sweet potato), 46, 66, 211, 387n38
Bonne cuisine aux colonies, La: Asie-Afrique-Amérique (Noter, 1931), 125
Bornia, Ligia de, 243, 255, 256–257, 262–64, 300
botany, 12
Boulon, Evra, 168
Bourbonnais, Nicole, 311, 313
Bovell, Blanche Yearwood, 391–392n27
Bovell, Edward Lycott, 392n27
Bovell, Elizabeth Jemmott, 99, 392n27
Bovell, John Redman, 96, 98, 99, 392n27
braises, 22
Brandon, Alphonse, 317
Brandon, Leila, 17, 317, 318–320, 414n28
Bras, D., 312, 313
Brathwaite, Kamau, 6, 383n19
bread, absence of, 10
breadfruit (panapen, buen pan, labapen), 11, 22, 31, 94, 305, 313,
332, 381n8, 393n39, 420n64; in recipes, 250, 331, 354
Breads (Virgin Islands Extension Service, 1985), 168
Briggs, Laura, 148
Brillat-Savarin, Anselme, 59
British Ladies Committee in Aid of War Relief, 195, 405n28
Brown, Edith E., 305
Browne, Marva Sprauve, 178
Buckridge, Steeve, 393n37
Bulletin of the Botanical Department, 85–87
Buñuelos de yuca [Yuca Fritters] (recipe), 210
Burke, Rudolph, 411n14
Bush, Barbara, 310–11
Busha Browne's Indispensable Compendium of Jamaican Cookery (Brown, 1993), 339

Cabanillas, Berta, 3, 13, 157, 385n17
Cabrera, Lydia, 405n30
Cabrisas, Juan, 48, 49, 50, 57, 58, 365
caçabi, 19, 276. *See also* casabe, catibía
Cafiroleta [Cafiroleta] (recipe), 45
cakes, 10, 22, 112
calabaza (auyama, joumou, potiron), 66, 215, 232, 381n8; roots of Carib auyama, 250, 406n9; variety of names for, 363. *See also* pumpkin
Calaloo and Rice (recipe), 315, 316
Calalou au Maigre [Thin Calalou] (recipe), 130
"Caldo Magro Para Vigilia," 384n7
callaloo, 3, 27, 100, 358, 415n35, 416n47; calalou of French Antilles, 128, 129, 130, 395n14; calalú, 211; kalliloo, 177; as "native" staple, 112, 132
callilu (Indian kale), 83
Calvo Peña, Beatriz, 50, 60
Campbell, Marjorie Pringle, 76, 382n14
Candlin, Kit, 13
cannibalism, accounts of, 9–10, 381n6

capitalism, 220, 318, 336, 339
Carbet, Marie-Magdeleine, 396n21
Carême, Marie-Antoine, 125
Cargill, S. R., 76
Cariban language, 259, 407n17
Caribbean Cocktails (Henry, 1980), 337, 418n53
Caribbean Cookbook (Springer, 1968), 342
Caribbean Cookbook: Using the Foods We Grow (Miller, 1979), 336, 337, 418n53
Caribbean Cookery (Grey, 1965), 420n66
Caribbean Cooking and Menus with Barbecues and Special Sauces (Henry, 1982), 337, 418n55
Caribbean Discourse (Glissant), 1
Caribbean Food and Nutrition Institute, 410n3
Carib dishes, 34, 44
Carib Indians, 10, 26
Carmichael, Mrs., 13
Carvajal, José, 384n8
casabe, 19, 62, 67, 68. See also caçabi, catibía
cassareep/cassaripe, 31, 114
cassava, 10, 12, 19, 112, 115, 154, 259, 282, 283, 305, 348, 420n68. See also yuca, manioc
Cassava Conkies [Mrs. E. T. Cox] (recipe), 116, *117*
Cassava Pone (recipe), *116*
Castro, Fidel, 182
Catecismo de agricultura cubana (Coloma y Garcés, 1863), 54
Catell Food Products (Barbados), 346
catibía, 211. See also caçabi, casabe
Catta Full of West Indian Dishes, A (Browne, 1973), 178
Cayman Islands, 301
Central America, 211, 212
Céspedes, Carlos Manuel, 33
Césaire, Suzanne and Aimé, 275–276

Chamoiseau, Patrick, 23, 138, 396n24
Chanca, Diego Alvarez, 10, 11
Chapman, Frank, 104, 401n62
chayote, 19, 31, 58, 146, 151, 189, 276, 381n8; cho-cho, 94, 312, 413n20; Haitian cuisine and, 276; tallote, 146; tayote, 46; in Willsey's *Tropical Foods Bulletin*, 152
"Chayote Stew (*chayote guisado*)," 151
Cherry Jam (recipe), *171*
Chicken Chop Suey (recipe), *308*, 411n12
Chickens for the Table (Jones, 1981), 416n46
Chinese-Caribbean cuisine, 21, 135; in Barbados, 351; in Dominican Republic, 258–59, *258*; in Haiti, 276, 278, 282, 409n37; in Jamaica, 307, 315, 320, *321–322*, 411n12, 413n27, 417n51
Chinese Chop Suey (recipe), 320, *321–322*, 413n27
chips, Jamaican, 323, 415n32
cho-cho, 94, 312, 413n20
chocolate, 250
Chop Suey (chino) [Chop Suey (Chinese)] (recipe), *258*
chutneys, 101, 113
Cinco siglos con la mujer dominicana (Olivier, 1975), 406n5
Clarke, Austin, 1, 14, 28, 243, 339, 343, 353
class, 29, 239, 249, 264, 299, 357, 370; colonial hierarchies of, 182; negotiated in domestic spaces, 2; racial coding of, 265; tensions around family structures and, 311, 312–313
Classic Jamaica Cooking: Traditional Recipes and Herbal Remedies (Sullivan, 1995), 77
Cleary, Teresa E., 327, 328–331, 416n40

Cocina al minuto (Villapol and Martínez), 17, 218; African and Indigenous food cultures emphasized in, 230–231, 232, 235; editions of, 218–220; recipes from, *224–225*, *226*, *227–229*, *234*, *366*, *368*; support for Cuban Revolution expressed in, 230–232, 233

Cocina criolla (Ornes Perelló, 1955), 17, 243, 256, 257–259; recipes from, *258*, *262*

Cocina criolla (Valldejuli, 1954), 17, 161

Cocina de Ligia en olla de presión, La (Bornia, 1977), 257

Cocina dominicana, La (Bornia, 1957), 243, 256, 257, 263–264, 406n14

Cocina dominicana, La (Cordero Infante, 1930s), 243, 406n4; recipes from, *247–248*, *250*, *251*, *252*, *254*

Cocina ecléctica (Gorriti, 1890), 90

Cocina internacional (Nodal), 194

Cocina Ligia (Bornia, 1972), 257

Cocina Ligia en microondas, La (Bornia, 1992), 257

Cocina y el hogar, La (Alfonso y Rodriguez, 1937), 194, 198, 205–206, 403n11; changing places for women and, 223; recipes from, *215*

Cocine a gusto (Cabanillas, 1950), 370, 385n17, 400n51

Cocinera económica de la Señora Winslow (1860s or 1870s), 48, 51–52, *51*, 53, 387n35

Cocinero de enfermes convalecientes y desganados, El (1862), 48, 53, 55, 65, 386n21

Cocinero mexicano, El (1831), 384n7, 385n14

Cocinero puertorriqueño, El, 33, 36, 40–47, 145, 161, 387n40; on color of sugar, 67; fufú (funche) recipes in, 387n34; male readers addressed by, 53; *Manual del cocinero cubano* as different edition of, 37, 348n7; as only Spanish-language cookbook in Puerto Rico, 139; published without named author, 38, 384n8; Puerto Rican differentiated from Cuban cuisine, 40–47, 385n10, 385nn14–16; recipes from, *42*, *43*, *45*; response to scarcity of foodstuffs, 233; White Criolla women addressed by, 54

cocktails, 204, 219, 326, 420n68; history of, 252–253, 254; recipes, *254*, *258*; rum-based, 101

Cocktail "Trujillo" ["Trujillo" Cocktail] (recipe), *254*

coconut, 250, 305

Cohen, Cathy J., 163

Collection of 19th Century Jamaican Cookery and Herbal Recipes, A (Campbell, 1990), 76, 382n14

Collymore, Yvonne, 342

Colmina González, Sisi, 218, 219, 366

Coloma Partearroyo, Pedro, 37

Coloma y Garcés, Eugenio de, 15, 33, 36, 48, 48–49, 57, 186; coincidence of Cuban and Puerto Rican cuisine, 36–40; interests and values of, 38–39, 384n9; men as readers addressed by, 53. See also *Manual del cocinero cubano*

Colombia, 23

Colón, Emilio M., 384n8

Colonial Exposition (Paris, 1931), 125, 126, 134, 394nn6–7

colonialism: Caribbean created and destroyed by, 4, 24–25, 179, 237–238, 372–373; Caribbean culture claimed for Europeans, 40; "collectors" appropriating Afro-Indigenous material, 78–79; creolization and, 5; defense of native style, 27, 103, 109, 119, 146, 158, 161; "development" and, 160; gender system imposed by, 382n9; heterocolonial

order, 72, 80, 114, 122, 130, 131, 388n11; neocolonialism, 119, 121, 158, 179, 181; paradisiac trope of, 42, 138; paradoxes of, 4, 5, 9, 179; proto-feminism coinciding with, 140; settler colonialism, 2, 4, 24, 34, 79, 163; shift from appropriation to assimilation, 124, 140, 144
colonial/modern system, 11–12, 382n9
"Columbian Exchange," 11, 277, 334, 363, 364, 396n17, 408n30
Columbus, Christopher, 4, 10, 249–50
Come Cook with Us the Bajan Way (Fraser, 1981), 346–48, *348*, *349*
Comhaire-Sylvain, Suzanne, 407n25
Comida diaria, La (González, 1933), 194
Comidas criollas en ollas de presión (Cotta de Cal, 1951), 219, 405n34
Comidas típicas dominicanas / Typical Dominican Meals (Bornia, 1965), 257
communism, in Cuba, 218, 220
Como preparar los productos enlatados en su despensa para servirlos en mesa (Orcasitas), 399n42
Compañía Cubana de Electricidad, 194
Complete Indian Housekeeper, The (Gardiner and Steel, 1888), 80
Condé, Maryse, 14, 268, 277
Conejo, modos de preparar la carne para la mesa (Willsey), 157, 399n42
Confiant, Raphaël, 23
congrí, 235
conkies, 115–116, 393n42
Connerton, Winifred, 140
Conseils des Catherines, Les (Rabette, 1929), 395n8
Conservación de carnes en el hogar (Orcasitas), 399n42
Conservación de frutas y vegetales en Puerto Rico (Keown), 155, 399n41
Contemporary Caribbean Cooking (Miller), 353, 420n75

coocoo, 387n34; coucou, 112
Coo-Coo [Barbadian] (recipe), *351*
cookbooks: Afrocentric, 119; ambivalent politics of, 264; as and in the archives, 14–24; archives and, 14–24; authorial identity obscured, 78; class interests and, 28; colonial, 13; creolization and, 5; Cuban and Puerto Rican, 33; diaspora and transnational, 374; from elite to middle- and working-class authors and readers, 366–367, 369; French colonial (1930s), 119; functions beyond cooking instruction, 357; gender/race/class encoded and challenged by, 3; national culture and, 6; national independence and, 123; ordered relation between components of, 18–19; read for pleasure, 372–374; recipes copied from other cookbooks, 364; role in Caribbean culture, 1; as tools of power, 29; tourism, 178; U.S. Virgin Islands, 167–168; women's creativity and expertise expressed in, 369–370; written by descendants of colonizers, 8–9; written by men, 34, 339, 350; written predominantly by women, 2, 5
Cookery Book (British Ladies Committee in Aid of War Relief, 1941), 195, 405n28
Cooking Antigua's Foods (Tonge, 1973), 301
Cookery in the West Indies Made Easy (1910), 96, 99–102; recipes from, *101*, *102*
Cooking Our Way (Collymore, 1972), 342
Cook It My Way (Miller, 1975), 336
cooks, 4, 17, 304; Afro-Indigenous, 7, 63, 111; Black and mixed-race women in elite homes, 114; Creole, 23; Cuban, 50; Da Elodie, 136–139,

cooks (cont.)
158; Haitian, 272; illiterate and semiliterate, 14; Indigenous, 63; Isabel (Dooley's cook), 158–159, 400n49; knowledge of, 56; literacy of, 201; Mestizo, 63; near-mythical, 127; Puerto Rican, 41; stereotype of servant/mammy and, 158–159; substitution and improvisation by, 29, 182, 238; White colonial women's dependence on, 88, 391n23. *See also* Mondésir, Chloé, as colonial fiction

Cook Up Jamaican Style: Eating What We Grow (Jones, 1977), 332–334, 336, 417nn49–50; Afrocentrism of, 334; "Jamaican Nutrition" chart, *333*; recipes from, *334, 335*

Cordero Infante, Eulalia, 243, 244, 257, 300, 406n4; absence of references to African origins of any food, 251–252, 262; biography of, 244; influence on other cookbook writers, 259; on sancocho as symbol of Dominican people, 245–48, 251; as Trujillo supporter, 244, 406n7. *See also Cocina dominicana, La*

corn, 22, 115, 155, 213, 215, 381n8; corn imports to Cuba, 233; tied to Indigenous past, 250

cornmeal, 94

Cornmeal Duckoonoo (recipe), 82, *83*

cosmopolitan: in Cuba, 181; in Jamaica, 307

Cotta de Cal, Maria Teresa, 219, 405n34

coucou, 112; coocoo, 387n34

Cou Cou (recipe), *348*

Cow Kin Soup (recipe), 330, *331*, 416n43

Craig, Elizabeth, 411n9

cream cheese, American, 323, 415n31

Cream Cheese Icing (recipe), *172*

Creative Caribbean Cooking and Menus (Henry and Henry), 338–339

Creative Cooking series, 418n53

Crema de auyama [Cream of Pumpkin Soup] (recipe), *376–377*

Crema de auyama rica y facil (González, cocinadominicana.com), *376–377*

"Creole" (criollo/a, créole, kreyòl) designation, 22–24, 383n20; in British West Indies, 388n1, 389n2; in Cuba and Puerto Rico, 26; in Jamaica, 305

creole cuisine, 13, 18, 65, 187, 238, 292; in British West Indies, 388n1; cocina criolla, 24; Cuban, 67, 387n34; Dominican, 255; erasure of Afro-Indigenous culinary work, 111–112; European travelers' negative reactions to, 80, 390n15; Haitian, 269–285; local grounding of, 364; of New Orleans and Louisiana, 22–23; (re)establishment of, 27; White women's appropriation of, 110

Creole language, in Virgin Islands, 175, 178, 402n68

Creoleness (créolité), 23, 30, 138, 240–241; Dominican, 259; Glissant and, 181–182, 276; Haitian, 240, 275, 278, 284; Jamaican, 302, 306; Kreyòl language and, 284; as pan-Caribbean construct, 240; White and Black, 108, 302

Creole Savoury [Melangene] (recipe), 110, *110*

creolization, 3, 6, 9, 47, 79, 113, 373–374; as abstract cultural phenomenon, 383n21; blurring of distinctions and, 116–117, 178–179; contrast with appropriation and assimilation, 153; cultures of hybridity and, 69; definition of, 23; Glissant's definition of, 83–84; hopeful promise of, 299; interracial collaboration in domestic spaces and, 114; invisible downtrodden supports of, 16; kitchen as site of, 82; new national culture and, 36; paradoxes of colonial rule and, 5; recognition of Afro-Indigenous elements in, 122; stripped of intimate connection to Afro-Indigenous traces, 174; as togetherness-in-difference, 25; tropicalism and, 269; White women's defense of native style and, 109

Crespo y Setien, Berta, 194, 195–196, 198–199, 403n12; Afro-Indigenous recipes and, 213; cosmopolitan turn and, 203

Criollo identity, 58–61, 186; anticolonial criollismo, 181; constructed as White, 184; constructed in line with Mestizo, 252, 255; criollo cuisine, 216; Dominican, 243, 252, 254–255; racially unmarked Whiteness of, 183, 402n1; shift in meaning of, 190–191; Trujillo regime and, 241

Crosby Alfred, 11

Crowden, Mrs. Otto, 411n9

Cruz, Lourdes, 264

Cuba, 20, 26, 27, 33–40, 48–69, 181–230, 374; Afro-Indigenous culinary history in, 206; changing places for women in, 197–201; creole cuisine in, 24; Cuban food company brands, 223; exile community, 218, 235, 236; French colonial elites' flight from Haitian Revolution to, 49; independence from Spain (1898), 29, 122, 181; as "land of sugar," 67, 68; national culinary culture, 119; perpetual revolution, 29; proliferation of cookbooks in late 19th century, 47; racial dynamics of, 191, 192, 198, 208–217, 404n17; revitalized "native" national culture, 216; siterios (mixed-race peasants), 35; slavery on sugar plantations, 34; U.S. intervention and economic interests in independent Cuba, 182, 202–203, 206; yellow fever in Havana, 52

Cuban cookbooks, 15, 72, 238; Afro-Indigenous foodstuffs in, 184; changes brought by independence expressed in, 182; dishes divided into "classic" and "country," 216; domestic modernization and cosmopolitanism in, 29, 181, 194–196; English-language, 205; grammar of instruction in, 55–56, 387n30; racialization in nineteenth-century cookbooks, 58–69; recipes for perpetual revolution, 217–238; unmarked traces of Indigenous and African elements, 69; White Criollo men as authors, 53–58; working-class women as audience, 217

Cuban Cookery: Gastronomic Secrets of the Tropics (Baralt, 1931), 194, 205; recipes from, 207–8, 214; stereotypical "African" sketch in, 213, 214

Cuban Revolution (1959), 182, 218, 230

Cuban women cookbook writers, 181, 387n30; changing places in independent Cuba, 197–201; cosmopolitan turn and, 201–208; domestic modernization and, 194–196; in era since Cuban Revolution, 217–238; position between domination and dominated, 217

Cuffee, Lady, 411n9

Cuisine coloniale: Les bonnes recettes de Chloé Mondésir (Querillac), 125, 126–134, 138, 395n16; recipes from, 129, 130, 131–134, 132, 133; "story of Dahomey" in, 130–131, 396nn18–19

Cuisine des îles ou le bon manger antillais (Carbet, 1978), 396n21

Cuisine des pays chauds (Mayard, 1940), 266, 267, 269–278, 280; "La cuisine des îles," 275; English translation of, 297; recipes from, 271, 272–273, 274, 278, 359, 408n29; reviewed in *La voix des femmes*, 270
Cuisine et patisserie (Rampy, 1965), 407n21
Cuisine et savoir vivre (Jean, 1974), 407n21; 421n2
Cuisine exotique chez soi, La (Rabette), 125
Cuisine sélectionnée (Magloire-Prophète, 1955), 17, 266, 287, 289, 421n2; cover, 291; Francophilia of, 290–91, 292; recipes from, 293–294, 293
Cuisinier bourgeois et royal, Le (Saugrin), 384n7
culantro, 31, 259
culinary colonialism, 7, 8, 9, 339; Afro-Indigenous foods subsumed under White Criollo order, 36; appropriation and expropriation, 95, 103; of English-language cookbooks in Puerto Rico, 140; extension into twentieth century, 122; formation of national cuisines in wake of, 374; recipes for national independence continuous with, 180; in West Indies, 71, 95–103, 388n1
culinary cultures, 24, 72; African and Indigenous, 7, 8; Cuban, 186; Cuban and Puerto Rican, 35; diasporic, 30; hybrid, 47; national, 3, 18, 27; national identity and, 180
Cumberbatch, Edward, 343–344, 346
Curaçao, 20
Curried Goat (recipe), 324, 330
curry, 112, 258, 277, 323, 366, 390n16, 409n37, 414n28; in recipes, 225, 324, 351, 367, 373,
Curtis, Jeremiah, 50, 51–52
cusubé, 46, 211

Daily Gleaner (Jamaica newspaper), 75, 76, 85, 305, 389n5, 389n7, 390n13; advertisements for *The Jamaica Cookery Book* (1895), 88, 89; foods associated with poor and Black Jamaicans in, 415n35; on Grace Kitchens, 418n56; history of, 391n20; on Jamaica Festival, 412n15; on *A Merry-Go-Round of Recipes from Independent Jamaica*, 317, 413n26; Miller column and recipes in, 417n52; on "Peasy Cake" recipe, 417n50; White elite of Jamaica and, 85
dairy products, overvaluation of, 316
danger and scarcity, trope of, 9, 14, 16, 18
Dash, J. Michael, 290
decolonization, 3, 4, 15, 47, 108, 309
Deetz, Kelley Fanto, 391n23
Delicias de la mesa (Reyes Gavilán y Moenck, 1923?), 194, 195, 211, 213; recipes from, 204, 212
de Lisser, Herbert George, 305
de Lisser, Mrs. H. G., 306
Delon, Danielle, 391n27
DeLoughry, Elizabeth, 3
De Maeseneer, Rita, 49, 50
Democratic Labour Party (Barbados), 347
Depestre, René, 290
Dessalines, Jean Jacques, 360
Dessalines, Marie Claire Heureuse Félicité Bonheur, 358, 360
desserts, 209–210, 216, 230; in British West Indies, 110, 113; in Cuban and Puerto Rican cookbooks, 45, 46
deterritorialization, 374
"development" discourse, 163
Development of Creole Society in Jamaica, 1770–1820, The (Brathwaite), 383n19
Díaz, Junot, 243
Díaz de Mujica, Blanca, 195

Dirtz, James, 398n37
Discours antillais, Le (Glissant), 395n12
"distant reading," 18
djondjon (diondion), 284, 287, 289, 291, 409n35
Domestic Manners and Social Condition of the White, Coloured and Negro Population of the West Indies (Mrs. Carmichael, 1833), 13
Dominica, 301
Dominican (Republic) cookbooks, 238, 240–241, 255–264
Dominican Republic, 20, 23, 27, 119, 239–264, 374, 387n36; acknowledgment of African contributions to cuisine of, 300; dictatorial regimes and U.S. occupation, 29–30, 239; independence from Spain (1821), 122, 239, 249; national culinary culture and dictatorship in, 242–255; period of unification with Haiti, 249; women's rights in, 299
Donaldson, Enid, 339
Donnell, Alison, 3
Dooley, Eliza K., 140, 157–161, 395n11, 400n49
Dooley, Henry W., 158, 400n48
Dorsinville, Roger, 290
doukounou, 277; duckunoo, 393n42
drinks, 230, 254, 346, 382n11, 385n14. See also cocktails
duckunoo, 393n42; doukounou, 277
dumplings, 91, 92, 115
Duquesne, Gilbert Smith, 404n18
Duvalier, François (Papa Doc), 239, 266, 407n21
Duvalier, Jean-Claude (Baby Doc), 407n21

E. Alkins and Son company (Barbados), 346
Eating Puerto Rico (Ortíz Cuadra), 385n12
Ebroin, Ary, 396n22

Edmonds, Mrs. F. S., 303, 410n6
eggplant (aubergine, berenjena, melangene), 58, 110, 132, 154, 271, 393n40
Éloge de la créolité (Chamoiseau, Bernabé, and Confiant), 23
"Éloge du café" (Saint-John Perse), 292
Encanto del hogar: manual de la buena mesa (González Pérez, 1940), 195
Espinosa Orozco, Sixto, 263, 407n18
Estimé, Dumaris, 279
Étude synpotique sur l'horticulture en Algérie (Noter, 1890), 394n8
Eurocentrism, 109
Europeans, 4, 7; classificatory systems of, 11–12; creolization and, 5; early explorers and chroniclers, 11, 17; myth of "discovery," 66. See also White Creole women; White Criollos
Ewing-Chow, Daphne, 420n74

Facebook, 17
Fanon, Frantz, 3, 6, 7, 15, 74, 79; on colonial delegitimization of local culture, 143; on colonialist "defense of native style," 27, 103, 109, 119, 146; on development of national culture, 167; on emergence of national consciousness, 27–28, 119; on literature of national independence, 372; on native intellectuals embracing colonial culture, 34, 174; resuscitation of precolonial native culture and, 46; on revitalized "native" national culture, 216; warnings about nationalism, 240
Farmer's Food Manual (Jamaica Agricultural Society, 1957), 302, 309–313, 315–316, 413n24, 416n38; contradictory views on colonialist food culture, 315–316; "Historical Notes on the Food Plants of Jamaica" (appendix), 412n19; "Protective Foods of Jamaica," 313, 314; recipes from, 313, 315, *316*, 413n23

Favourite Antiguan Food and Drink Recipes (Tonge, 1977), 301
Fawcett, William, 85
feminism, 16, 24; in Cuba, 197; in Dominican Republic, 242; eugenics and, 148; in Haiti, 268, 407nn24–25; nonwhite middle class in Jamaica and, 84; proto-feminism, 79, 140; Puerto Rican nationalism and, 153
Ferguson, Grace, 139, 144, 145–146, 154, 310, 398n34
Fernández Prieto, Leida, 52
Féroce de Morue [Ferocious Cod] (recipe), 133, 134
Festivals and Recipes (United Nations Women's Group in Jamaica, 1970), 412n16
"Fillets of Flying Fish à la Ritz" (recipe), 342
Finucane, Jean, 301
Fish à la Zingara [Jacks] (recipe), 100, 101
Fleurimond, Nadege, 277
Florida, 23
flour, U.S.-produced, 173
flying fish, 347, 349
Foäche, Stanislas, 12
Folch, Christine, 49, 184, 213, 215, 386n21
Folleto de recetas de cocina y repostería cubana (Prieto Dávila), 194
Food and Folklore of the Virgin Islands, The (Petersen, 1990), 402n71
Food Guide for Jamaica (Scientific Research Council, 1966), 333, 416n46
food sovereignty, 337
France, 27, 179, 276
Francophilia, 52, 276, 292, 318, 323, 344, 386n22
Fraser, Carmeta, 17, 342, 343, 351, 352, 420n69
free Blacks, 14, 35, 361

French Antilles, 121, 122, 123, 124–139, 178, 394n1; Antillean products presented as exotic objects, 124–39; cuisine as France's exotic Other, 139; preservation of "native style" in, 127. *See also* Guadeloupe; Martinique
French cuisine, 125, 135, 241
French language, 20, 22, 137, 279
Freud, Sigmund, 59
Fried Raise Johnny Cakes (recipe), 175, *176*
fritters, 101, 112
fruits, tropical, 22, 60, 113, 381n8, 414n28
fufu (foofoo, fufú, foufou), 19, 91, 191, 211, 213, 235; as "native" staple, 112; tonmtonm, 290; West African origins of, 65
Fufú de malanga y plátano / Fufú de malanga ó plátano [Malanga and Plantain Fufú / Malanga or Plantain Fufú] (recipe), 65
Fufú de malanga y plátano [Malanga and Plantain Fufú] (recipe), 212
funche, 146, 261, 387n34; African origins of, 155; funche cubano, 213
Funche de Coco [Coconut Funche] (recipe), 156
funche recipes, 147, 156, 262

Gaillard, Niniche Viard, 266, 292, 298, 407n21, 408n26; cuisine built on Mayard's work, 278; elite positioning of, 361; standardization and, 281; upper-class women as audience of, 279–280
Galette de Gari [Gari Cake] (recipe), 278
Gallina encebollada a la matancera [Onion Chicken a la Matancera] (recipe), 190, *190*
Gambrill, Anthony, 413n25
Garcés y Muñoz, María de la Paz, 37
García Yero, Olga, 15
Gardener, Aston W., 76

Gardiner, Grace, 80
Garth, Hannah, 3, 234
Garvey, Marcus, 310
Gaveau, Marie. *See* Mayard, Louise
Gayle, Neville, 332
gender, 72, 119, 168, 238, 351, 370, 388n11
genocide, 2, 69
Glasse, Hannah, 390n14
Glissant, Édouard, 1, 3, 6, 374; on black nurse-maid, 395n12; créolité concept, 181–182, 276; "creolization" concept, 23, 83, 117, 138, 249; on elites and "collective consciousness," 240; on "fragile knowledge" of slaves, 114; on "hybrid cultures," 34, 47; on interplay of word- and world-making, 6–7; on national identity, 243; on the trace as place of survival, 13, 47, 94, 114, 372
goat mutton, 80, 81
"gombo." *See* okra; quimbombó
Gombo Zhèbes (Hearn, 1885), 396n20
Gómez, Juan Alberto, 403n5
Gómez, Máximo, 184
Gómez de Avellaneda, Gertrudis, 39
González del Valle, Ambrosio, 194
González Pérez, Carmen, 195
Goodhue, Isabel, 141
Good Things and Graces (Goodhue, 1911), 141
Go on Man, Cook Dominican (Finucane, 1974), 301
Gorriti, Juana Manuela, 90
Goutalier, Régine, 125
Goût d'Haïti / A Taste for Haiti (Armand, 2001), 297, 298, 409nn41–42
Grace, John, 418–19n57
GraceKennedy, 338, 416n46, 418n56, 418–419n57
Grace Kitchens Ltd., 310, 337, 338, 418n56, 419n58
grains and grain flours, 22, 154, 289, 399n44

"Grajea Menuda" recipes, 67
Grenada, 20, 21, 56, 99–103, 301
Grenada Independence 1974 Homemaker's Cookbook (Grenada Homemaker's Association, 1974), 301
Grey, Winifred, 420n66
grill (*parilla*), in Cuban cooking, 192, 403n6
Grillots [Grillots] (recipe), 286
Guadeloupe, 20, 27, 122, 124–136, 135, 292; as "département d'outre mer," 124; French culinary control in, 179
guanime, 152, 398n38
guava, 173
Guiana, French, 122, 124, 126, 135, 179, 394n4
guisados, 152
Guiso de quimbombó [Okra Stew] (recipe), 236–237
guisos, 215
¿Gusta usted? (Madrinas de las Salas Costales y San Martín, 1956), 219, 405n34
Guyana (British Guiana), 20, 21, 56, 103–119, 301, 388n11
Guyanese Food Recipes (History and Arts Council, 1967), 301

"Hágalo así" (Laredo, radio cooking program), 195
Haiti, 12, 20, 23, 27, 239–242, 265–300; "authenticity" of Haitian cuisine, 294–298; Black nationalism in, 279, 290; Bouqui and Malice (Creole tale), 298; dictatorial regimes and U.S. occupation, 29–30, 239, 265–269; independence from France (1804), 122, 239, 358; mulâtrisme (promotion of Mulatto heritage), 241, 266–267, 290, 294; national culinary culture, 119; noiriste ideology, 266, 267, 269, 285, 290, 294; period of

Haiti (cont.)
unification with Dominican Republic, 249; soup joumou (pumpkin soup) as national dish, 358; status as "Black Republic," 249; vodou religion, 268, 279, 285, 295; women's rights in, 299
Haitian cookbooks, 17, 238, 239, 365; French cuisine embraced by, 241; in Kreyòl, 300; political regimes leading to dictatorship and, 266–269; pumpkin soup absent from early cookbooks, 361
Haitian How-To's (Weaver), 409n39
Haitian Recipes (Paris, 1955), 295, 296, 297, 298
Haitian Revolution (1804), 4, 49, 69, 265–269
Haitian women, 238, 266, 272; access to education and the vote, 266; Creoleness and, 278; elite, 29, 240, 275; feminist movement and, 267–268; national unification and, 279; standardized measures and, 271; upper-class women with servants, 279–280
Hamilton, Jill, 348, 352, 419n62
Hamilton, Laddie, 301
Handbook of Trinidad Cookery (Lickfold, 1907), 103, 105, 107, 391n27, 392n29, 392n32; recipes from, 110, 112, 113
Harina de maíz: modos de prepaparla para la mesa (Orcasitas), 153, 155, 156
Harvey, Irene, 417n51
Havana Home Economic School (Escuela del Hogar de la Habana), 198
Hawkes, Alex D., 328–329
Hearn, Lafcadio, 16, 396n20
Heart of the Pumpkin, The (Virgin Islands Extension Service, 1989), 162, 168, 177–718
Henríquez de Pou, Silvia, 300

Henry, Dawn, 339, 418n53, 419n59
Henry, Leonard "Sonny," 337, 338, 339, 418nn53–54, 419n59
Henry, Mike, 336, 337–339, 418n53, 419n59
Henry, Olivia H., 173, 177, 402nn67–69
heteronormativity, 146, 371
Higgins, George F., 392n27
Higman, B. W., 3, 21, 77, 110, 305, 382n14, 390n14
Hispaniola, 20, 299
History of Mary Prince, a West Indian Slave, Written by Herself, The (Prince, 1831), 13
home cooking, diasporic constructions of, 123
Home Economics Department, University of Puerto Rico, 139–140
Home Making and Home Keeping (Ferguson, 1915), 139, 144, 144, 147
Home Style Recipes: From Cooks in Barbados (n.d.), 419n62
Hominy for Cake, Pudding, Biscuits, or Pap (recipe), 91
hot peppers (ajíes). *See* pepper (ají)
Housekeeper's Guide for British Guiana and the West Indies, The (Psaila, 1912), 103; recipes from, 110, 111, 116, 397n31
How Food Made History (Higman), 21
Hurston, Zora Neale, 265
hybridity, 34, 47, 69, 79, 170
Hygenie Práctica (Ashford), 144

Ibberson, Dora, 309, 310
"Iced Curry Soup" (recipe), 342
Imperial Department of Agriculture for the West Indies, recipe pamphlets of, 95–96, 97
indentured labor, 4, 16, 112, 390n16; Chinese-Caribbean, 4; Indo-Caribbean, 4, 100, 112, 366, 394n43; plantation monoculture and, 231

Indian Ocean islands, cuisine of, 275, 276, 408n30
Indigeneity, 7, 8, 44, 63, 192
Indigenous languages, 19
Indigenous people: creolization and, 4; foodways, 17, 47, 211, 259; women, 5, 34
Indispensable and Necessary Appendix [Apendice necesario e indispensable] (Coloma y Garcés, 1854), 37–38
Indo-Caribbean cuisine, 21, 112, 113, 283, 390n16; in Dominican Republic, 259; in Haiti, 278, 283, 409n37; in Jamaica, 307, 315, 413–414n28
ingredients, 19; Afro-Indigenous, 68, 323; creole mixing of, 62; Europeanized, 101, 282; from French colonies, 125; Jamaican mixed with English ingredients, 82; naming of, 11, 18, 19; "native," 10; presence or absence in recipes, 364
Isla que se repite, La (Benítez-Rojo), 383n19

Jack, Jordynn, 412n18
jackfish, 100
Jacobs, Leopold, 167
Jacomé, D., 49
Jadan, Doris, 167
Jadan, Ivan, 167
Jamaica, 12, 20, 26, 27, 73–95, 302–339, 374, 388n1; Afrocentric conception of cuisine, 327, 331–332, 334, 336; Black Power movement, 301, 327, 334, 336, 410n5; Brandon's promotion of Jamaican products, 317–318; British and White Creole elite of, 76; economic and political upheaval of 1960s, 326–327; independence from Britain (1962), 301; national culinary culture, 119; race and class divisions in, 322, 414n30
Jamaica Agricultural Society, 309, 411n14, 412n16
"Jamaica Asparagus" (recipe), 304
Jamaica Cookery Book, The (Sullivan, 1893), 26, 71, 73, 304, 382–383n14; community formation and, 74, 78–95; first and second editions of, 75, 84–85, 389n6; organization of sections, 87, 391n21; publishers of, 389–90n11; recipes from, 82–87, 82, 83, 87, 91–93, 91–93, 367, 390n16; reviewed in the *Daily Gleaner*, 75, 389n5; title page, 74
Jamaica Family Cookbook, The (Harvey, 1982), 417n51
Jamaica Festival, 310, 323, 327, 412n15
Jamaica Information Service, 322, 414n29
Jamaica Labour Party (JLP), 336, 338
Jamaica Labrish (Bennet, 1966), 418n53
Jamaican Cuisine (Jamaica Information Service, 1964), 322–323; recipes from, 322, 324, 325, 330
Jamaica Plum [jocote] (*Spondias purpura*), 86
Jamaica Red Peas Soup (recipe), *319*, 413n26
Jamaica Run-Dung [A Cook-Book with Jamaica Run-Dung] (Cleary, 1970), 327–331, 416n45; recipes from, *328*, *330*, *331*, *369*; reviews of, 328–329
Jamaica Social Welfare Commission, 309, 410n4
Jamaica Welfare League, 311
James, Lauren, 125
James, Wayne, 402n69
Janer, Zilkia, 125
Janer Vilá, Carmen, 160, 398n35, 400n51
Jardin potager colonial, Le (de Noter, 1930), 394n8
Jean, Mariette, 407n21, 421n2
Jelliffe, G. B., 312, 313
Johnny Cakes, 175, 176, 342, 397n30, 420n64
Jones, Novelette C., 332

Julien Lung-Fou, Marie Thérèse, 136–139, 158, 375, 395n11, 396nn23–24
Jurafsky, Daniel, 19

kedgerees, 112, 277, 315
Kennedy, Fred W., 418–19n57
Keown, Mary E., 155, 160, 399nn41–42, 400n51
Khan, Aisha, 383n21
Kincaid, Jamaica, 12, 373–374
Kirkcaldy, Doreen, 310, 338, 412n16, 418n54
kitchen, as womb of the house, 27, 122
knowledge, culinary, 14, 87, 96, 146, 170; Afro-Indigenous, 313; "native" as extinct origin and, 175–176; readers' assumed lack of, 174, 177
Kreyòl (Haitian Creole) language, 19, 22, 279, 284, 291, 300, 363
Kruzan Nynyam from Mampoo Kitchen (Moorehead, 1977), 165–166, 178, 402n69

Labat, Père, 9, 382n11
La Brosse, Blanchard de, 408n29
Lacerte, Robert, 408n27
Ladies Aid Society, First Methodist Church of San Juan, 139, 140, 144, 154, 400n51
Ladouceur, Rosny, 297, 409n42
Lady Musgrave Self-Help Society, 75, 107, 393nn36–37
Landais, Irma Marion, 406n5
Langarika, Enrique, 386n21
Language of Food, The (Jurafsky), 19
Laredo, Adriana, 195
Larousse gastronomique, 281, 409n34
Latin America, 22, 125, 143, 250, 278; Cabrisas in, 50; criollo cuisine and, 145, 243, 254; gendered history of, 90; Haitian culinary culture and, 276; "mestizo" identity in, 249, 252, 255; Monroe Doctrine and, 265

La Villa, Sergio, 202, 203
Lawson Welsh, Sarah, 3, 77, 108, 383n16, 390n15, 392n29
Leal, Eusebio, 386n21
Lechón asado [Roast Suckling Pig] (recipe), *214*
Lechón relleno [Stuffed Suckling Pig] (recipe), 192, *193*
Lee, Kendal A., 350–351, 353
Lee, Muna, 159
Leeward Islands, 20, 104
Leger, Alexis (Saint-John Perse), 292
Legran, J. P., 15, 48, 49–50, 55, 386n24
Le Hérisse, Auguste, 396nn18–19
lengua (tongue) recipes, 60, *61*
Leroy, F. Morisseau, 275
Let's Eat Bananas (Jones, 1981), 416n46
Let Us Cook = Le Awe Cook: A Collection of Authentic Cruzan Recipes (Mackay, 1980), 178, 402n69
Levantine people, 4, 5
Levi-Strauss, Claude, 390n12
Lickfold, Barbara Hilary Hodd, 103, 105, *105*, 107, 382n30, 392–393n34; as collector, 108; Indo-Caribbean contributors named by, 112; "native" recipes inscribed by, 109, 118, 393n38; racialized domestic management and, 117; as White Creole collector, 111
Lickfold, John Edmund, 104, 105
Life and Food in the Caribbean (MacKie, 1991), 77, 389n10
Ligue Féminine d'Action Sociale (LFAS), 268, 279, 407n24, 408nn26–27
Linnaean taxonomy (Latin binomial system), 12, 86, 98, 135, 395n14, 415n34; distinction between banana and plantain, 408n28; pumpkin and, 361, 421n4; in *Virgin Islands Fruits and Vegetables*, 174
Linnaeus, Carolus, 12
literacy, 2, 14, 84, 329, 416nn41–42

Little Caribbean Cookbook, A (Hamilton, 1990), 352
locrio (rice with meat), 250, 406n10
Locrio de buen pan [Breadfruit Locrio] (recipe), 250
Longacre, Doris, 409n39
López González, Marcos E., 218
López Lay, Aurora, 195
Ludmer, Josefina, 150
Lugo McAllister, Aida, 161
Lugones, María, 382n9
Lyn-Kee-Chow, Iris, 308, 411n12

Machado, Gerardo, 182, 218
Mackay, Amy, 178, 402n69
MacKie, Cristine, 77
Madagascar and Malagasy cuisine, 128, 277, 408n30
Madrinas de las Salas Costales y San Martín, 219
Magloire, Paul, 267, 279, 290
Magloire-Prophète, Herzulie, 17, 266, 287–294, 298, 361, 408n26, 421n2
Magnus, Kellie, 419n59
Make and Use Your Own Home Made Hams (Jones and Knight, 1983), 416n46
malanga, 66, 211, 381n8, 387n38
Malanga á la Criolla [Creole Malanga] (recipe), 56, 57
Mala rabia [Mala Rabia] (recipe), 251
"Mala-Rabia" recipes, 67
malarrabia, 260
mamey apple, 170, 401n64
"Manatí o vaca marina a lo pinero" ["Manatee or Sea Cow à lo pinero"] (recipe), 62–63, 387n33
Mango: Bits and Bites (Virgin Islands Extension Service, 1999), 168
"Mangoes Pickled in Mustard Oil [Anchar]" (recipe), 112
mangú, 385nn11–12
Mangú [Mangu] (recipe), 252

"Manjar blanco criollo" (recipe), 67
Manley, Michael, 331, 336, 410n5
Manley, Norman, 309, 327, 415–416n38
Manual de cocina y directorio doméstico (Díaz de Mujica, 1945), 195
Manual de economía doméstica (Ornes Perelló, 1938–1940), 256, 258, 262
Manual de la cocina moderna (Varona de Mora, 1932), 194
Manual del cocinero, cocinera, y repostero (1828), 384n7
Manual del cocinero cubano (Coloma y Garcés, 1856), 15–16, 33–40, 186, 199, 235; access to Cuban archives and, 382n14; ajiaco recipes in, 63; *El cocinero puertorriqueño* as different edition of, 37, 384n7; *El cocinero puertorriqueño* differentiated from, 40–47, 385n10, 385nn14–16; cookbooks published after, 48; fufú recipe in, 65; plantain recipes in, 66; recipes from, 45, 60, 61, 62–63, 192, 385n16; selections republished as separate titles, 48–49, 51
Manual del jardinero cubano (Coloma y Garcés, 1872), 384n9
Manual de práctica pedánea (Coloma y Garcés, 1853), 37
Manual Recreating the easy, neat, useful secrets for home economics (Coloma y Garcés, 1857), 384n9
margarine, U.S.-produced, 173
Maroons, 179, 381n5
Martí, José, 184, 185, 186, 403n3; racial equality goal of, 208, 235; vision of "mestiza America," 403n5
Martínez, Martha, 218, 220, 223, 405nn35–36
Martinique, 20, 27, 122, 124–126, 135, 138–138, 276; as "département d'outre mer," 124, 394n4; French culinary control in, 179; paradisiac trope and, 138. See also *Recettes de cuisine martiniquaise de Da Elodie*

Massaguer, Conrado W., 213
matahambre, 211, 226, 232
mauby, 347
Mauritius, 408n30
Mayard, Constantin, 267
Mayard, Louise, 266, 267, 291, 292, 298, 408n26; assumption of shared knowledge with readers, 272; Creole tropicalism of, 269, 275, 278; creolization and, 270. See also *Cuisine des pays chauds*
McAnuff, Craig and Shaun, 339
McCulloch, W. E., 311, 312, 313
Meal Planning (Kirkcaldy, 1958), 412n16
measurement, conventions of, 31, 151, 174, 399n45
Meat that Satisfies (Jones, 1981), 416n46
melangene (aubergine, eggplant, berenjena), *58, 110, 132,* 154, 271, 393n40
melcocha, 211
"Melcocha" recipes, 67
Menéndez, Irene, 152
"Menú de la Semana, El" (Laredo, food column, 1946–1959), 195
Mercador, Angelina, 154, 160, 398n35, 399n41, 400n51
Merritt, Brittany, 104
Merry-Go-Round of Recipes from Independent Jamaica, A (Brandon, 1963), 17, 317–320; editions of, 413–14n28; recipes from, *319, 321–322,* 413n26, 414n28
mestizaje, 213, 240
Mestizo identity, 58, 186, 249, 403n5
Mexico, independence from Spain (1821), 44, 384n7
middle classes, 28, 29, 116, 299, 346; aspirant, 255, 330; Black and mixed-race, 71, 390n17; British West Indies, 71, 108; "Coloured," 108; domestic management and, 197; in Jamaica, 88, 311, 331; kitchen technology and, 192; nonwhite, 84; "propriety" projects of, 311; Villapol and middle-class women, 219, 223, 234, 235; westernized, 310
Miller, Elsa, 336–337, 338, 417n52
Miller, Sally, 352
Mintz, Sidney, 3, 209, 383n18
Mirabal, Maria Teresa, 264
Mitchell, Lady, 417n51
Moderno cocinero criollo, El (López Lay, 1943), 195
mofongo, 152, 385n12
Mofongo criollo [Creole Mofongo] (recipe), *42–43*
"mojo criollo," 186, 189
Mondésir, Chloé, as colonial fiction, 126–134, 137, 395n13
monoculture, agricultural, 150, 197, 217, 231, 265
Montego Bay Self Help Home, 410n6
Montserrat, 301
Moo-Pen, Mrs., 411n12
Moore, Hannah, 107
Moorehead, Laura, 165–66, 178
Morant, Doris, 413nn21–22
Moravia, Adelina, 268, 277
Moravia, Charles, 267
More-with-Less (Longacre, 1976), 409n39
Morley, LaurelAnn, 352–353, 420n75
Morris, Daniel, 96, 98
Moss-Solomon, James, 419n57
Mota, Virginia, 242
Mountain Maid Self-Help Project, 297, 358, 360
Mrs Platt's Recipes Cakes and Confections (Stockelberg, 1947), 195
Mujer 2000 series (Henríquez de Pou), 300
Mulattoes, 14, 35, 382n12, 383–384n2; with fully White paternal line, 59; in Haiti, 239, 265, 266, 278
Munro, Marin, 23
Murray, Dea, 178
Musgrave, Anthony, 75, 389n9

Musgrave, Lady Jeanne Lucinda, 75
My Island Kitchen (Boulon, ca. 1960), 168

"Natilla criolla," 45
national culture, 6, 7, 30, 69, 160; "authentic," 28; Barbadian, 340; food as central component of, 8; Jamaican, 319; women's roles in shaping, 264
nationalism: in Barbados, 348; in Haiti, 275, 287; in Jamaica, 84
National Organization of Women (Barbados), 342
National Recipe Directory (Fraser, 1976), 17, 342–346, 347, 420n68; recipes from, 344, 345, 346
nation-building, 3, 15, 18, 197
nationhood, independent: creolization and, 5; paradoxes of, 4, 5, 9; supported by descendants of colonizers, 4; women's participation in, 29
"native" cuisine, 30, 94, 117
"native culture," 3, 46, 112, 140, 163, 174; in British West Indies, 388n1; independent nationhood and, 4, 373; reconfigured and invented, 28; White Creoleness and, 108
"natives," 72, 84, 92–94; assimilation of, 124; erasure of, 95, 111–112, 118; "native" informant, 90; "native" staples, 112
Native Recipes (Virgin Islands Extension Service, 1978), 168, 176, 401n60
Nègre, André, 134, 135–136, 138, 139, 396n22
"Negro" designation, 389n2
Nen Flo (Florence Connor), 166–168
neocolonialism, 119, 121, 158, 181
Nicholls, David, 269
Nodal, Blanca R., 194
Noter, Raphaël de, 125, 126, 136, 394n8

Noviatur, J. F. (José Florencio Turbiano y Paula), 49, 52, 386n22, 386n26
Novísimo manual del cocinero pastelero dulcero y licorista cubano (Noviatur, 1891), 49, 53, 386n22
Nuevo manual de la cocinera catalana y cubana (Cabrisas, 1858), 48, 50, 53, 62; ajiaco recipes in, 63, 64; products of European colonialism as reference points for Cuban cuisine, 68; pumpkin soup ("potage de calabaza"), 365, 366; White Criolla women addressed by, 54–55
Nuevo manual del cocinero criollo (Triay, 1903), 183–194; front cover, 184, 185; preface by Aróstegui, 185–86; recipes from, 189, 190, 191, 193
Nuevo manual del cocinero cubano y español (Legran, 1864 [1857]), 16, 48, 50, 52–53, 386n20; ajiaco recipe in, 63, 64; fufú recipes omitted from, 387n35; male readers addressed by, 53; recipes from, 56, 57, 58, 68
Nugent, Lady, 13, 305, 306, 307
nutrition, 2, 3, 7, 311, 333; basic food group charts, 220, 221–222, 313, 314, 333, 405n35; "civilized eating" and, 165; malnutrition, 165, 232; monoculture and reduction in, 197; nutritional knowledge, 110, 167; nutritional versus commodity value, 173; USDA calculation of nutritional value, 401–402n65

O'Callaghan, Evelyn, 3, 73, 84, 88
Ochro Soup (recipe), 82–83, 83
Odysée de la cuisine haïtienne, L' (Valme Thevenin and St. Eloi Alexis, 2006), 294
oildown, 100

okra ("gombo"), 112, 114, 128, 213, 395n15; African origins of, 155, 277; molondrones (Dominican Republic), 261, 387n36; recipes with, 236–237, 348. *See also* quimbombó
Olivier, Maritza, 406n5
Olla cubana o ajiaco [Cuban Pot or Ajiaco] (recipe), 58
"Olla de cocido a la vigilia," 384n7
O'Meally, Jamie, 309
100 Jamaica Recipes (Edmonds, 1926), 303–304
oral traditions, 2, 13, 28
Orcasitas, María T., 153, 154, 155, 158, 160, 399n42, 400n51
Ordoñez, Rosa M., 160, 398n35, 399n41, 400n51
Ornes Perelló, Amanda, 17, 243, 255, 256, 257, 300
Ortiz, Fernando, 153, 188, 226, 235; Afrocubanidad vision of, 181, 183, 210–211, 217–237, 405n30; transculturation concept, 6, 36, 216
Ortíz Cuadra, Cruz Miguel, 3, 67, 206, 385n12, 398n34
Ostrander, Gilman, 383n18
ovens, electric ("automatic tropical kitchens"), 192, 193, 403n8
Oviedo y Valdés, Gonzalo Fernández de, 9

Padda, Darshan S., 173
Padin, José, 144
Page, Lillian Hope, 76
"Palanqueta" recipes, 67
Palanqueta criolla [Creole Palanqueta] (recipe), 68
Palmer, Kimberly, 381n5
Panama, 23
Panapén, El: modos de prepaparlo para la mesa (Willsey and Ordoñez, 1937), 398n35
Panatela Ada [Ada's Sponge Cake] (recipe), 209

"Pancakes and Hot Cakes," 224–225
Panecicos de catibía [Catibía Breads] (recipe), 259–260, 260–261
Pantojas-Garcia, Emilio, 398n37
Paris, Robel, 266, 295
Parry, John, 412n19
Partido Dominicano, 243
Pastrana, Angela, 154, 160, 398n35, 399n41, 400n51
Pastrana, Pura, 152
Pâté de veau à la banane mûre [Veal Pâté with Ripe Banana] (recipe), 293–294
pâtés, 292
patriarchy, 35, 40, 95, 124; female voice of authority in imitation of, 90; heterocolonial, 131; heteropatriarchy, 79, 130, 150, 201; White patriarchal domination, 119
pawpaw, 326, 332, 337
peas, 112, 334, 417n50
pepper (ají), 43, 60, 62–64, 109, 191, 200, 202, 215, 227, 236–237, 247, 276, 381n8, 405n31
People's National Party [PNP] (Jamaica), 331, 338, 411n14, 416n38
Pepper Pot (recipe), 115
Pepper Pot [Mrs. B's cook] (recipe), 115
Pepper-Pot [Mrs. E. L. Bovell] (recipe), 113
Pepper-Pot [R. Braithwaite] (recipe), 113
pepperpots, 3, 27, 315; Afro-Indigenous culture and, 114; as "native" staple, 112; new ingredients added after servings, 30–31
Peppers Cracklings and Knots of Wool Cookbook, The (Spivey), 409n38
Perez, Jacinia, 161
Pérez, Louis A., Jr., 206, 386n21
Pérez Miró, Abraham, 198, 404n20
Pérez Roque, Dúnyer, 386n22
"Perino" recipe, 12
Perkins, Benjamin A., 50, 51–52

Peter Martyr, 11
Peter Pan Book of Recipes (Baillie, 1928), 305
Petersen, Arona, 402n71
Petryk, Norberto, 15–16, 382n14
Phillips, Grace Spencer, 159
Philosophia Botanica (Linnaeus, 1751), 12
pigeon peas, 177
pigs, naturalized in Caribbean, 11, 381n8
Pig Tails 'n Breadfruit (Clarke, 1999), 1
Pilau of Green Peppers (recipe), 143, *143*
pilau recipes, *143*, 397n31
Pilau recipes, of Psaila, 110, *111*
pimentón, 146
Pinterest, 17
piononos, 152
plantains, 22, 27, 141, 393n39; adapted to Euro-American culinary norms, 173; African origins of, 190; Afro-cubanidad and, 211; as complex carbohydrate, 177; in Cordero Infante's *Cocina dominicana*, 252; grown by slaves, 94; instructions on preparation of, 57, 387n31; in Linnaean taxonomy, 408n28, 415n34; plantain wine, 213; in slave and peasant diets, 66, 67; in soups, 66, 215, 226; tostones de plátano, 146; as "viandas," 66; in Willsey's *Tropical Foods Bulletin*, 152
Plátano, El: modos de prepaparlo para la mesa (Willsey and Mercader, 1939), 154, 398n35, 399n41
Plat national haïtien [Haitian National Dish] (recipe), 272, *274*
Polynesia, 22
Pomiane, Édouard de, 408n29
"Popular-Style Roast Pig" [*Lechón asado al gusto general*] (recipe), 192
Porto Rican Cookbook (Ladies Aid Society, 1915), 139, 140–142, 157, 400n51; cover, 142; recipes from, 142–44, *143*, 397n30
Potage crème de potiron [Cream of Pumpkin Soup] (recipe), *359*
Potage de calabaza [Pumpkin Soup] (recipe), *365*, *366*
potato soup, 165, 167
Poulet en Piläo [Chicken in Pilau] (recipe), 101, *102*
Poulet en sauce [Chicken in Sauce] (recipe), *288*
prepared foods, 346
Price-Mars, Jean, 266
Prieto Dávila, Blanca, 194
Prince, Mary, 13
Pringle family, 77
Privilege (Barrow and Lee, 1988), 350–351, *351*
Propagador de conocimientos útiles, El (Turbiano y Paula, 1877), 386n26
Prospect Great House Cookbook, The (Mitchell, 1981), 417n51
"provisions," 20, 94, 100, 112, 165, 289, 311, 312, 313, 315, 333, 334, 349, 387n39, 413n19, 413n23. *See also* "viandas" ("víveres")
Prybus, Cassandra, 13
Psaila, Luigi, 106
Psaila, Marie, 103, 104, 106–107; as collector, 108; "native" recipes inscribed by, 109, 118, 393n38; racialized domestic management and, 117; as White Creole collector, 111
Public Education in the Virgin Islands (U.S. Interior Dep't., 1934), 163–165, 167, 169
"Pudín cubano," 45
"Pueblo del interior, Un" (La Villa), 203
Puerto Rican Cookbook (Dooley, 1948), 140, 157–161, 395n11
Puerto Rican cookbooks, 15, 69, 72
Puerto Rican Vegan Cookbook (Perez, 2019), 161

Puerto Rico, under Spanish control, 20, 26, 27; jíbaros, 35; Puerto Rican cuisine differentiated from Cuban, 40–47; slavery on sugar plantations, 34

Puerto Rico, under U.S. control, 47, 121, 170; agricultural extension programs, 121, 155, 310, 400n51; Americanization agenda, 139, 148, 152, 397n25; brief independence before, 139; "commonwealth" status, 122; eugenics movement and, 148; failure of independence movements, 179–180; home economics, 119, 145–146, 148–149, 153, 310, 400n51; installation of English as language of good nutrition, 124, 145; local culinary knowledge captured by U.S.-born women, 123–124; "Porto Rico" designation (1898–1931), 140, 143–145, 148, 150, 153; standardization in, 150–152; subsistence farming and, 398n37

pulque (Mexican alcoholic drink), 254

pumpkin, 22, 93, 166, 177, 409n35; in Linnaean taxonomy, 361, 421n4; as "native" staple, 112. *See also* calabaza (auyama, joumou, potiron)

Pumpkin and Rice (recipe), 93

pumpkin soup, 361–164, 421n2; Cabanillas recipe, 370; Cabrisas recipe, 365, 366; as emblem of continuity of Caribbean foods/recipes, 365; Gaillard recipe, 362; González recipe, 376–377; Julien Lung-Fou recipe, 375; Mayard recipe, 359; Spenceley recipe, 373; Wolff recipe, 358, 360. *See also* soup(e) grasse/joumou/au giraumon, sopa de calabaza; crema de auyama; potage de calabaza/crème de potiron

Pumpkin Soup (Child Care Committee recipe), 371

Pumpkin Soup (Cleary recipe), 369

Pumpkin Soup (Sullivan recipe), 365, 366, 367

Pumpkin Soup [Mrs.B's Cook] (recipe), 111, *112*

"Puré de maíz tierno," 216

purées, 292

Quaker Oats Co., 205, 206

Querillac, Anne Chasseriaud, 125, 126–134, 136, 138, 394n7; culinary colonialism of, 139; dependence on cook Chloé, 158

quimbombó (okra, ochro, gumbo), 155, 232, 261, 385n12; Afrocubanidad and, 211; in Cuban "criollo" cuisine, 191; West African origins of, 65, 387n36

Quimbombó guisado [Dressed Okra] (recipe), 212

Rabette, Charlotte, 125, 126, 136, 394–395n8

race, 5, 40, 72, 238, 239, 299, 357, 370; "câpresse" in racial taxonomy of French Antilles, 127, 395n10; colonial hierarchies of, 182; management of, 119; negotiated in domestic spaces, 2; racial categories in West Indies, 389n2; racial dynamics of Cuba, 191; racial mixing of Martinique, 136–137, 396n24; U.S. "one drop" categorization, 400n54; White women and racial hierarchy, 371. *See also* Mulattoes

racism, 79, 141, 160; Cuban Revolution aim of ending, 225; obscured by maternalism, 162; U.S. occupation of Haiti and, 265

Rahe, Elizabeth, 402n71

Ramos, Luz María, 152

Rampy, Mme. Arthur, 407n21

Rand and Avery publishing house, 51, 52, 386n25
Rankine, Peggy, 417n51
Real Taste of Jamaica, The (Donaldson, 1993), 339
Receta básica para sopas de vegetales à la crema [Basic recipe for Creamed Vegetable Soup], (recipe), 366, 368
Receta de artes culinario (Landais, 1942), 366, 406n5
Recettes de cuisine martiniquaise de Da Elodie (Julien Lung-Fou, 1950), 136–139, 375, 395n11, 396n23
Recettes simples de la cuisine haïtienne (Gaillard, 1950), 266, 278–285; pumpkin soup recipe, 362, 421n2; recipes from, 280, 281, 282, 283, 284–285, 285, 286
Recipe Round-Up (1956), 307, 308, 411n11
Recipes for Cooking Sweet Potatoes from the West Indies (Imperial Dept. of Agriculture, 1901), 96, 98–99, 391n26
Recipes for Cooking West Indian Yams (Imperial Dept. of Agriculture, 1902), 96, 97, 98, 99
Recipes for Independent Jamaica, 8
recipes for national independence, 7–8, 9, 13, 24, 136; autonomy of "native" cultures and, 373; Creole communities and, 117; in Cuba, 182; emergence in twentieth century, 27
Recipes: The Cooking of the Caribbean Islands (Wolfe, 1970), 409n39
Red Peas Soup (recipe), 91–92, 92
Reese, Ashanté, 31
Rementería y Fica, D. Mariano de la, 384n7
Reproducing Empire (Briggs), 148
reterritorialization, 374
Réunion Islands, 275, 277, 383n20, 408n30

Reyes Gavilán y Moenck, Maria Antonieta, 194, 195, 198, 201, 210, 403n12, 404n19, 404n23; Afro-Cuban and Afro-Indigenous culinary histories upheld by, 211; transnational recipes and, 202; U.S, products put to Cuban use, 203, 204
rice, 22, 141, 213
rice and beans, 27, 358
Rice and Beans: A Unique Dish in a Hundred Places (Wilk and Barbosa), 358
Richards, Lady Noelle, 411n9
Rifkin, Mark, 163, 164
Roachè, Nekisha, 339
Roberts, Lydia, 310, 412n18
Roberts Manufacturing Company (Barbados), 346
Rodney, Walter, 327, 415n37
Rodríguez, Luis Felipe, 202
Rodríguez-Arencibia, Jorge Méndez, 49
"Rolled Flying Fish and Melts" (recipe), 342
roots, 113, 399n44
Roots, Levi, 339
Ropa vieja a la habanera [Havana Ropa Vieja] (recipe), 200, 200
Ropa vieja cubana [Cuban Ropa Vieja] (recipe), 61, 62
"ropa vieja" recipes, 61–62, 62, 188, 211, 387n32
Rosenberg, Leah, 84
rose water, 116, 394n43
Rubin, Gayle, 79, 390n12
Ruíz, Clara Aurora, 160, 398n35, 400n51
Run Dun (recipe), 328

Sagüera, La (dessert cookbook, 1923), 194, 403n10; recipes from, 209–210, 209, 210
Saint Lucia, 20
Saint Martin, 20, 122, 135, 395n9

St. Eloi Alexis, Paule, 294, 409n38
St. John Cookpot Calypso (Jadan and Jadan, 195?), 167
St. Kitts and Nevis Independence Cookbook, The (Hamilton, 1983), 301
St. Vincent and the Grenadines, 301
Salazar, Néstor, 404n18
salt beef, 146, 199; as European food, 82; "fresh" beef and, 330; in recipes, *64, 83, 228, 331, 362, 367*
salt fish, 22, 80–81, 87, 92–94, 304, 315, 341; European travelers' negative reactions to, 80; as "native" staple, 112; salt cod in Martinique, 137
"Salt Fish and Ackee" (Parry), 412n19
"Salt Fish and Ackees," 315
"Salt fish and Akees" (Jamaica breakfast dish), 87
Salt Fish and Rice (recipe), 87
Salt Fish Fritters (recipe), 87
Sam, Jean Vilbrun Guillaume, 265
San Antonio, Condesa de (Antonia María Micaela Dominguez Borrell), 39
sancocho, 3, 245–248
Sancocho [Sancocho] (recipe), *247*
Sancocho de gallina [Chicken Sancocho] (recipe), *248*
Sándwich con Chutney [Chutney Sandwich] (recipe), 204, *204*
sandwiches, American, 203–204, 223
sauce créole, 24
Sauce Ti-Malice (recipe), 284, *285*
Saugrin, Joseph, 384n7
"Scalloped Yautía," 152, 398n38
Scarron, Paul, 290–291
Schlessinger Library (Harvard), 16
Schwartzkopf, Estrella Moll, 154, 160, 398n35, 399n41, 400n51
"Scratch-Me-Back" Cocktail (recipe), 326, *326*
Seacole, Mary, 13, 390–391n17
Seaga, Edward, 336

Seven Sonnets on Puerto Rico (Phillips), 159
Sevigne, Marquesa de, 196, 198, 199, 201, 403–404n13; cosmopolitan turn and, 203, 204, 206; on Cuban sweets, 209; distancing from the Afro-Indigenous, 215
Shepherd, Verene, 3
Shrimp Loaf with Yampie (recipe), *325*
Shuller, Mark, 265
Siboney people, 219
Siglo, El (Cuban agriculturalist newspaper), 59
Simmons, Amelia, 73
Simply Delicious (Rankine, 1986), 417n51
Singh, Banni, 112
skellion, 83; in recipes, *82, 83, 93, 328, 331, 369*
slavery, 2, 16, 47, 69, 98, 159, 179; bananas and slave trade, 324; in Danish West Indies, 173; end of slavery in Cuba, 38; foods associated with slave and peasant diets, 188, 191, 251, 294, 325, 363; foods grown by slaves, 20, 94; in Haiti, 241, 277, 360; indentured labor as replacement for, 4, 100–101, 366; ingredients prevalent in slave diets, 20, 83, 94; malnutrition of slaves, 232; plantation monoculture and, 231; plants brought from Africa by slaves, 22; salt fish as food of slaves, 137; slave contribution to Dominican foods, 260; slave cuisine, 13; slave rations, 112, 114; in Spanish Caribbean, 34–35; subsistence farming and, 12
Sloane, Hans, 12, 382n11
Sociedad de Dependientes de Restaurantes, Hoteles y Fondas de la Provincia de La Habana, La, 194, 205
Sokolov, Raymond, 387n34
Solá, José, 398n37

Sopa de calabaza [Pumpkin Soup] (recipe), 366, 368
Sopa de calabaza à la crema [Cream of Pumpkin Soup] (recipe), 370
"Sopa de plátano," 226
Sopa de plátano [Plantain Soup] (recipe), 215
Sopa de plátanos verdes ó criolla [Green Plantain or Creole Soup] (recipe), 66
"Sopa de tortuga o de la Isla de Mona," 42
Sopa puertorriqueña or puré paradisiaco [Puerto Rican Soup, or Paradisiac Puree] (recipe), 42
"Soufflé de boniatos," 216
soufflés, 292, 318
Soupe (au giromon) [(Pumpkin) Soup] (recipe), 375
Soupe à Congo [Congo Soup] (recipe), 131, 132
soup grasse/joumou, 360–61, 362, 365, 421n2. See also pumpkin soup
Soup Joumou [Pumpkin Soup] (recipe), 358, 360
soups, 42–43, 66, 215, 235, 331, 386n26
souse, 100, 347
Spain, 34–35, 44, 50
Spanish language, 20, 22, 124, 259, 363; as language of instruction in U.S.-controlled Puerto Rico, 152, 154, 399n43
La spécialité haïtienne est la «soupe-grasse» [The Haitian Specialty Is "Fat Soup"] (recipe), 362
Spenceley, Angela, 178
spices, 56, 381n8
Spitfire Pepper Sauce, 346, 420n71
Spivey, Diane, 409n38
Sprauve, Elaine Ione, 166–167
Spriggs, John, 392n30
Springer, Rita, 342, 410n3, 420n72
starches, 10, 11, 235

Steamed Flying Fish or Buckled Flying Fish (recipe), 349
Steel, Flora Annie, 80
stereotypes, 137–138, 141
Stewed Kid or Goat Mutton (recipe), 82
Stewed Tree-Tomato (recipe), 85, 86, 86
stews, 22, 165, 206; in British West Indies, 100, 112, 114; in Cuban and Puerto Rican cookbooks, 43, 57, 68
Stockelberg, Alicia Platt, 195
Stoler, Ann Laura, 103, 107
Stoner, Kathryn Lynn, 197
Stow, Beatrice, 340–341
Stuart, K. L., 312, 313
sugar, 12, 22, 46, 95, 113; Barbados sugar industry, 347; Cuban Revolution as final resistance to sugar economy, 230; Cuban sugar production, 45; forced Black labor in Cuban sugar industry, 208; melado (cane syrup), 251, 261; "new sugar," 94; plantations in Dominican Republic, 242; refined and unrefined, 67; sugar cane, 11, 190, 316; U.S.-owned companies in Cuba, 202
Sullivan, Caroline, 26, 71, 103, 108, 109, 304, 382n14; biography of, 73–78, 118; as a "collector" or "compiler," 78–79, 111; community of White Creole women and, 78–95; as intermediary dependent on "native" knowledge, 91–94, 111; positioned as bridge between English and "native" cultures, 81; pumpkin soup recipe of, 365, 366, 367. See also *Jamaica Cookery Book, The*
Sullivan, Charles Frederick, 75–76
Sullivan, John Augustus, 75, 389n8
Sweetness and Power (Mintz), 383n18
"Sweet Pickled Chayote," 152, 398n38

sweet potato (batata, boniato), 22, 112–113, 381n8; Imperial Department of Agriculture recipe pamphlet for, 96, 98–99
sweets, 46, 67, 113
Sweets, Snacks, Savouries, Unusual Coctails (Brown and Worlledge, 1939), 305–7
Sylvain, Georges, 279
Sylvain-Bouchereau, Madeleine, 279, 407n24

Taíno dishes, 34, 44
Taíno Indians, 10, 26, 63
tallote, 143, 146. *See also* tayote, chayote
tapioca, 10, 130
tasajo, 188, 191, 211, 215, 261
tassau de dinde, 292
Taste of Barbados (Hamilton, 1980s), 348
Taste of the Virgin Islands, Too! A (Spenceley, 2000), 373
tayote, 46. *See also* tallote, chayote
tembleque, 45, 46, 385n17
terra nullis doctrine, 9
Thomas, Mildred, 167
TikToks, food instruction, 375
Ti-Malice sauce, 284, 285, 298
Tinsley, Omise'ke Natasha, 169, 401n62
Tipton-Martin, Toni, 384n5
"Tocineta de monte a lo pinero," 386n22
Tonge, Antigua Gwen, 301
Torre, José María de la, 37, 62
Torres Saillant, Silvio, 249
"Tortilla de plátanos maduros," 216
tourism, 98, 135, 168, 178, 420n74; in Barbados, 341, 347, 352; in Cuba, 202, 205, 208–209; in Haiti, 298; in Jamaica, 337, 412n16
Traditional Jamaican Cookery (Benghiat, 1985), 417n51
transculturation, 6, 36, 69, 153, 216

Tratado sobre las gallinas, palomas, canarios y ruiseñores (Turbiano y Paula, 1878), 386n26
Treatise of the Whole-World (Glissant, 2020), 7, 13, 47, 84, 94, 114, 117, 153, 372, 374
Tres Reyes Inn (Havana), 50, 386n24
Triangle Trade, 22, 277, 383n18
Triay, José E., 183–194, 206, 211
Tricinquantenaire de l'independence d'Haïti (Haiti Tourist Information Bureau, 1954), 287, 288, 289, 291, 421n2
Trinidad and Tobago, 20, 21, 56, 103–119, 301, 388n11, 420n66
Tropical Foods (Willsey, 1925), 152, 154, 398n35
Tropical Foods Bulletin, 149, 151–153
tropicalism, 269–278, 279
Tropical Pot Pourri (1970), 301
Trujillo, Rafael Leonidas, 23, 239, 244; controlled progress of elite women and, 255–264; dissidents and critics eliminated by, 407n18; Dominican feminists and, 242–243; elite women supporters of, 244, 262–264, 406n7; Haitians massacred under, 256; immigration from Asia encouraged by, 259; Mulatto heritage of, 255; rise to power, 242; women ill treated by, 242, 247, 256
tubers, 154, 220, 381n8, 399n44
Turks and Caicos, 104, 301
turtle soup, 112

Union School PTA, 409n39
United Fruit Company, 171, 202, 419n57
United Nations Women's Group in Jamaica, 327
United States, 27, 258, 414n30; culinary products imported into Jamaica, 323, 415n31; "Good Neighbor" policy, 162, 400n53;

import-export economy of Cuba and, 231; military occupation of Haiti, 265; Monroe Doctrine, 265; neocolonialism of, 181, 188; U.S. imports and cosmopolitan turn in Cuba, 201–208, 223; U.S.-owned agricultural industries in Puerto Rico, 140
Universal Negro Improvement Association, 208
University of the West Indies, libraries of, 16
Ureña de Henríquez, Salomé, 256
Urgell, Providencia, 152
USDA (U.S. Department of Agriculture), 170, 401–402n65; basic food group chart, 220, *221*

Valentin, María Adela, 152
Valldejuli, Carmen Aboy, 17, 161
Valme Thevenin, Rolande, 294, 409n38
Variety with Vegetables (Jones, 1981), 416n46
Varona de Mora, Ernestina, 194
Vegetales tropicales series (Willsey and coauthors), 398n35, 399n40,
Vegetarian Cooking: Jamaican Style (Williams, 2013), 339
"viandas" (provisions), 20, 59, 66, 211, 232, 387n39
Viard, Marie Anne Rosita Eugénie (Niniche), 267
Vidal Marmolejos, Ligia Oneoda. *See* Bornia, Ligia de
Village Improvement Society of Barton, Vermont, 141–142
Villanueva, D. Gerardo, 193–194
Villapol, Nitza, 17, 181, 183, 366, 404n18; on African food habits in Latin America, 229–230; "basic foods" for nutrition and, 220, 223; biography of, 218; embrace of Cuban Revolution, 218, 219, 230; reformulation of tradition and, 226, 229, 234–237; working-class women addressed as audience, 217, 235, 405n34
Virgin Island Cookpot Calypso (Jadan and Jadan, 1965), 167–168
Virgin Islands, British, 301
Virgin Islands, U.S., 20, 27, 119, 121, 123, 162–180; agricultural extension programs and cookbooks, 124, 162, 164, 168, 177, 178, 310, 417n49; Americanization in, 165, 166; commodification of cooking, 178; Creole culture of, 169; failure of independence movements, 180; Organic Act (1936), 162–163, 400–401n55, 401n56; public education and "development discourse" in, 163–165; school lunches in, 164–165, 166, 167, 401n58; U.S. purchase from Denmark (1916), 122, 162
Virgin Islands Fruits and Vegetables: Recipes (Virgin Islands Extension Service, 1969), 168, 169–171, 173, 402n66; ambivalence toward Virgin Islanders, 173–174; emphasis on recipes designed for single-family kitchens, 171, 173; reassertion of Virgin Islands culture in, 175; recipes from, *171, 172,* 175, *176*; U.S.-imported foods/ingredients promoted in, 177, 402n69
Virgin Islands Holiday Cooking (Virgin Islands Extension Service, 1987), 168, 177
Virgin Islands Native Recipes (Anduze, 1954), 17, 167, 168, 401n59
"víveres," 20, 259, 387n39
vlogs, food instruction, 375
Voix des femmes, La (Haitian feminist publication), 268, 270, 275, 408n26

Walker, Jill, 352
Walker, Mary Georgina, 106
Wall, Wendy, 416n42
Walsh, Ellen, 397n25
War Time Recipes for Use in the West Indies (Hodson, 1942), 340–341, 419n61, 420n64
Watkins, Edith Haynes Cobbett, 106, 107, 108, 302; "native" recipes inscribed by, 109, 118, 393n38; racialized domestic management and, 117; as White Creole collector, 111
Watkins, Frederick Henry, 103, 104, 106
Watson, Emma Edith Tucker, 411n9
Weaver, Winnie, 409n39
Weeks, Deborah, 410n15, 414n30
"West India Cherry" (acerola, Barbados cherry), 170, 173, 402n65
West Indian and Other Recipes (Yearwood, 1911), 103, 107, 383n16, 392n29; recipes from, 115, 116, 117
West Indian Biscuit Company, 346
West Indian cookbooks, 72, 95–119
West Indian Recipes (Watkins, 1908), 103, 106, 107, 112, 115, 302
West India Social Survey, 310–311
West Indies, British, 26, 57; Asian ingredients and preparations brought by colonial trade, 390n16; independence movements, 301; White women cookbook writers, 103–108
West Indies, Danish, 173
West Indies, Dutch, 21, 401n62
What's Cooking? Favourite Recipes of Cooks in Barbados (Barbados Red Cross Society, 1983), 349–350, 419n62
What's Cooking in Haiti (Union School PTA, 1981), 409n39
White category, in Cuba, 58–59
White Creoles, 3, 7, 292, 364, 366; in British West Indies, 71; English colonialist disdain for, 305

White Creole women, 29, 57, 72, 90; Afro-Indigenous and Indo-Caribbean recipes included in cookbooks of, 113; in Jamaica and Barbados, 30, 302, 307; married to men serving in colonial government, 99, 104; relation to colonial power, 119
White Criollos, 33, 40, 47, 50, 69, 238; Cuban authenticity and, 48, 49; limited knowledge of cooking, 365; male readers addressed in cookbooks authored by, 54; pro-independence, 38; "ropa vieja" claimed by, 62; self-image as both native and superior, 34; shared concern with Spaniards, 44; social order of Cuba and, 53; sugar plantations/industry run by, 35, 41; White Criolla women, 54
Whiteness, 68, 259
White women, 13, 71–72; community of, in Jamaica, 78; cookbook writers between colonial control and black domestic labor, 103–108; culinary colonialism of, 114; defense of native style, 108–119; "newcomers" to Jamaica, 79, 80, 84, 390n13; power in the domestic economy, 73; racialized domestic management and, 95; Sullivan, Caroline, 73–74
Wilk, Richard, 358
Williams, Ayesha, 339
Willsey, Elsie Mae, 139–140, 148–154, 160, 310, 400n51. See also *Tropical Foods*
Wilson, Kathleen, 114
Winslow, Charlotte N., 49, 50–52
Wolfe, Linda, 409n39
Wolff, Amy, 297, 358
women, 7, 16; Afro-Indigenous, 5, 6, 29, 111, 371–372; Barbadian, 302, 339, 343, 346, 348–349, 350, 353;

Chinese-Caribbean, 29; cookbooks as intermediary space for, 369; in Cuba, 38–39; diversity of Caribbean women, 29; domestic formation of proto-national tastes and, 57; domestic work entering into public sphere, 5; Dominican elite women and Trujillo regime, 241, 243, 255–264; Indo-Caribbean, 29; literacy of, 2, 14, 84, 329, 390n17, 403n9; majority of cooking done by, 1–2; "native," 26; participation in both colonial and decolonial nation-building, 18; shifting place within colonial societies, 122; stereotypes about, 1; trope of New World land as woman, 27, 122; U.S. assimilationist project in Puerto Rico and, 140, 143–45; White Criolla, 54–55; working-class, 217, 235. *See also* Black women; Cuban women cookbook writers; White Creole women

Women's Christian Temperance Union, 140

Women's League of St. Thomas, 167

Women's Self-Help Society (Jamaica), 75, 389n9

Wonderful Adventures of Mrs. Seacole in Many Lands, The (Seacole, 1857), 13, 390n17

World Food Day Cookbook, The (Virgin Islands Extension Service, 2000), 168

Worlledge, J. L., 411n8

Worlledge, Margaret G., 305, 411n8

Yam Pudding (recipe), 99

yams (ñame mapuey), 22, 66, 112, 173, 215, 387n38; Afrocubanidad and, 211; Imperial Department of Agriculture recipe pamphlet for, 96, 97, 98, 99; Sullivan on, 94

yautía, 146, 152, 387n38

"Yautía Custard," 151

Yearwood, Elizabeth Ann Clarey Manning, 103, 104, 106, 107, 383n16; as collector, 108; "native" recipes inscribed by, 109, 118, 393n38; racialized domestic management and, 117; as White Creole collector, 111

Yearwood, Henry Graham, 104

YouTube channels, food instruction, 375

yuca (manioc, cassava), 10–11, 19, 112, 186, 211, 215, 381n8; canucos (plots of yuca), 11; cassaripe and, 114; "Columbian Exchange" and, 396n17; as complex carbohydrate, 177; in cusubé, 46; Dominican cuisine and, 250; grown by slaves, 94; Haitian cuisine and, 276, 277; palanqueta and, 67; racialized affiliation and, 62; as "viandas," 66

Yuca, La: modos de prepaparlo para la mesa (Willsey and Schwarzkopf, 1937), 151, 154, 398n35, 399n41, 399n44

"Zambaglione" (recipe), 306, 411n10

"Zambumbia," 67

Zlotnik, Susan, 73

About the Author

KEJA L. VALENS is professor of English at Salem State University, where she teaches and writes on Caribbean literatures, literatures of the Americas, queer theory, and foodways. She is author of *Desire between Women in Caribbean Literature* and coeditor of *Passing Lines: Sexuality and Immigration*, *The Barbara Johnson Reader*, and *Querying Consent: Beyond Permission and Refusal*. Her recent essays appear in *Becoming Home: Diaspora and the Anglophone Transnational*; *Teaching Race in Perilous Times*; *Caribbean Literature in Transition, 1970–2020*; and *Trans Studies: The Challenge to Hetero/Homo Normativities*.

AVAILABLE TITLES IN THE CRITICAL CARIBBEAN STUDIES SERIES:

Giselle Anatol, *The Things That Fly in the Night: Female Vampires in Literature of the Circum-Caribbean and African Diaspora*

Alaí Reyes-Santos, *Our Caribbean Kin: Race and Nation in the Neoliberal Antilles*

Milagros Ricourt, *The Dominican Racial Imaginary: Surveying the Landscape of Race and Nation in Hispaniola*

Katherine A. Zien, *Sovereign Acts: Performing Race, Space, and Belonging in Panama and the Canal Zone*

Frances R. Botkin, *Thieving Three-Fingered Jack: Transatlantic Tales of a Jamaican Outlaw, 1780–2015*

Melissa A. Johnson, *Becoming Creole: Nature and Race in Belize*

Carlos Garrido Castellano, *Beyond Representation in Contemporary Caribbean Art: Space, Politics, and the Public Sphere*

Njelle W. Hamilton, *Phonographic Memories: Popular Music and the Contemporary Caribbean Novel*

Lia T. Bascomb, *In Plenty and in Time of Need: Popular Culture and the Remapping of Barbadian Identity*

Aliyah Khan, *Far from Mecca: Globalizing the Muslim Caribbean*

Rafael Ocasio, *Race and Nation in Puerto Rican Folklore: Franz Boas and John Alden Mason in Porto Rico*

Ana-Maurine Lara, *Streetwalking: LGBTQ Lives and Protest in the Dominican Republic*

Anke Birkenmaier, ed., *Caribbean Migrations: The Legacies of Colonialism*

Sherina Feliciano-Santos, *A Contested Caribbean Indigeneity: Language, Social Practice, and Identity within Puerto Rican Taíno Activism*

H. Adlai Murdoch, ed., *The Struggle of Non-Sovereign Caribbean Territories: Neoliberalism since the French Antillean Uprisings of 2009*

Robert Fatton Jr., *The Guise of Exceptionalism: Unmasking the National Narratives of Haiti and the United States*

Rafael Ocasio, *Folk Stories from the Hills of Puerto Rico/Cuentos folklóricos de las montañas de Puerto Rico*

Yveline Alexis, *Haiti Fights Back: The Life and Legacy of Charlemagne Péralte*

Katerina Gonzalez Seligmann, *Writing the Caribbean in Magazine Time*

Jocelyn Fenton Stitt, *Dreams of Archives Unfolded: Absence and Caribbean Life Writing*

Alison Donnell, *Creolized Sexualities: Undoing Heteronormativity in the Literary Imagination of the Anglo-Caribbean*

Vincent Joos, *Urban Dwellings, Haitian Citizenships: Housing, Memory, and Daily Life in Haiti*

Krystal Nandini Ghisyawan, *Erotic Cartographies: Decolonization and the Queer Caribbean Imagination*

Yvon van der Pijl and Francio Guadeloupe, eds., *Equaliberty in the Dutch Caribbean: Ways of Being Non/Sovereign*

Patricia Joan Saunders, *Buyers Beware: Insurgency and Consumption in Caribbean Popular Culture*

Atreyee Phukan, *Contradictory Indianness: Indenture, Creolization, and Literary Imaginary*

Nikoli A. Attai, *Defiant Bodies: Making Queer Community in the Anglophone Caribbean*

Samuel Ginsburg, *The Cyborg Caribbean: Techno-Dominance in Twenty-First-Century Cuban, Dominican, and Puerto Rican Science Fiction*

Linden F. Lewis, *Forbes Burnham: The Life and Times of the Comrade Leader*

Keja L. Valens, *Culinary Colonialism, Caribbean Cookbooks, and Recipes for National Independence*